Leisure and Recreation Management

Fifth edition

This revised edition reflects the changes that have taken place in sport, leisure and recreation management in recent years. Issues such as health promotion, cultural strategy and social inclusion have risen to the top of the policy agenda. Commercial pressures, changes to the voluntary and public sector, and the emergence of sport development professionals have all profoundly influenced the landscape.

Leisure and Recreation Management is a comprehensive, informative and accessible guide for students and contains all you need to know about:

- **Leisure Management** – principles and practice for leadership, staffing, training, programming, event management, leisure marketing and more
- **Leisure Products** – exploring key areas in tourism, arts and sport
- **Leisure Planning and Provision** – in the public, voluntary and private sectors
- **Key Themes in Leisure, Recreation and Play** – understanding leisure as a social issue
- **Leisure and Cultural Heritage** – the social and historic factors shaping current leisure

Exploring every important concept and innovation, and full of textbook features to assist learning and understanding, *Leisure and Recreation Management* is essential reading for students and professionals interested in the theory and practice of managing sport, leisure and recreation.

Dr George Torkildsen is a pioneer of leisure management theory. His career has spanned teaching, lecturing, management and management consultancy all over the world. He is former Chairman of World Leisure and is an honorary life member of ILAM and ISRM.

Leisure and Recreation Management

Fifth edition

George Torkildsen

Routledge
Taylor & Francis Group

LONDON AND NEW YORK

First published 2005
by Routledge
2 Park Square, Milton Park, Abingdon, Oxon OX14 4RN

Simultaneously published in the USA and Canada
by Routledge
270 Madison Avenue, New York, NY 10016

Routledge is an imprint of the Taylor and Francis Group

© 2005 George Torkildsen

Typeset in Goudy and Quay Sans by Bookcraft Ltd, Stroud, Gloucestershire
Printed and bound in Great Britain by Bell & Bain Ltd, Glasgow

British Library Cataloguing in Publication Data
A catalogue record for this book is available from the British Library

Library of Congress Cataloging in Publication Data
Torkildsen, George.
   Leisure and recreation management / George Torkildsen. – 5th ed.
      p. cm.
   Includes bibliographical references and index.
   1. Leisure. 2. Leisure – Management. 3. Recreation. 4, Recreation – Management.
   I. Title.
   GV181.5.T67 2004
   790'.06'9–dc22   2004051173

ISBN 0-415-30995-6 (hbk)
ISBN 0-415-30996-4 (pbk)

Contents

Figures

Tables

Dedication and acknowledgements

I dedicate this fifth and final edition of *Leisure and Recreation Management* collectively to many people: my wife Margaret, family, friends, colleagues and all who have contributed over a period of nearly twenty years to the editions of the book. Their names are listed for posterity in previous editions.

For this fifth edition I acknowledge with thanks the outstanding contribution of Sue Tarling who handled the administrative and secretarial work with skill and much patience.

I also acknowledge and thank readers of draft chapters who provided valuable critiques:

Jim Lynch and Sally-Anne Maidment, Chapter 9 and Chapter 10
Ian Barclay, Chapter 11
Don Earley and Ray Cole, Chapter 12
Colin Tilley, Chapter 18 and Chapter 19.

Of the four photographs accompanying the Part opening pages, those to Parts 1 and 2 are reproduced courtesy of Corel, Parts 3 and 4 courtesy of Webshots.

The Institute of Leisure and Amenity Management afforded me the use of its excellent Information Centre and Bookshop (Information Centre Manager: Lucy Roper).

To those mentioned and the many others who provided encouragement and support, my heartfelt thanks.

Preface

The terms 'leisure' and 'recreation' mean different things to different people. So while this book is built on available evidence and research, it is written from a perspective of my own background, experience and career as teacher, manager, consultant, observer and 'lifetime' student of leisure and recreation management.

The leisure and recreation, or re-creation, I write about is universal – it needs to be experienced, felt, rather than inadequately described. Yet the purpose of the book is to attempt to describe, to try to explain and to bridge gaps between theory and practical management. I do so with humility, acknowledging the inadequacies, but in the belief that, in the words of Ted Blake, 'if it's no good in theory, it certainly is no good in practice'.

When we hear the words 'leisure' and 'recreation', all of us have images in our minds. These will be different person to person, but they might include, for example: holidaying, bucket and spade in hand making sandcastles with the grandchildren; sitting by the pool sipping cold Chablis; picnicking in the park or out in the country-side; reading a newspaper or a novel, feet up, domestic chores completed, cosy and warm; or just meditating or day dreaming. These are images of freedom from constraints and obligations, away from unrelenting pressures of parenting or caring for elderly parents, away from the rat race, the pressures of work. We can be ourselves. We might choose to be entertained at a concert or a rock festival or just meet up with friends at the pub or in the coffee bar. The images could be extended to 'working' at our leisure: absorbed in our hobbies, DIY and gardening; playing sports; coaching the youth team; line dancing; singing in the choir; doing voluntary work; and raising money for charity.

Now, to have 'leisure', to live the life we want to live, to do the things we want to do, freed from undue constraints, and to be all that we want to be, is a dream few achieve and some might not even want because with such freedom comes the responsibility to make good choices. Yet we have more knowledge, more resources and more opportunity than before, in which to have a fullness of living, undreamed of in time past. The question is: has leisure a central role in a way of life that harnesses opportunities for self-fulfilment, at harmony with oneself and the world? Without an understanding of such leisure, albeit as an ideal – the 'good life' for one and all – we cannot have sound principles on which to formulate policies for leisure planning, provision and management.

The philosophy – love of wisdom – of which I speak is nothing new. The Ancient Greek philosopher Aristotle described a philosophy, of which leisure was a corner-stone, as being about free and exalted souls. It is a far cry from trying to acquire happi-ness by buying more and more material possessions, consuming more and more leisure goods and seeking endless, fleeting pleasurable experiences. Many children today are quickly bored when not being entertained.

Yet philosophy, like theory, is not just thinking, for it is concerned with reality. It is practical. Our philosophy of life and leisure must be born out of the reality of our culture and our circumstances. Ancient Greek philosophy was shaped by a political system based on an aristocracy of a privileged élite and an economic system based on slavery. This is not for us. Our philosophy of leisure must be based on our culture, social and economic systems, human rights, equal opportunities, personal dignity and a belief that what is good and elevating for the individual is also good and elevating for the community.

A poem written after the Second World War captures something about the quality of life and it fits well with the slogan 'Leisure is Life Worthwhile', and the 'pleasure principle', a term I coined in the third edition and which is explained in Chapter 8.

The Wealth of the World

There is a new wealth.
There is a new world culture developing. The new wealth is not gold to be buried in Kentucky.
This new wealth cannot be stolen.
This new wealth can be passed on to one's children without any estate taxes.
This new wealth can be exported and imported without tariffs.
This new wealth is general enjoyment of living − is abundant living itself.
It is living in the beautiful, in music and drama and sport. It is comradeship in joyous
   human activity.
It is sharing of the cultures of people.
This kind of wealth is largely inside the individual.
This kind of wealth is the soul of a people working and playing together.
Once it is established in the individual, in the home, in the community, all is changed.
People are alive. The community itself lives. The nation finds all values greatly increased.
Exchange this kind of wealth of living between peoples, between nations, and the whole world
   becomes a different place.
A place of joy and strength. A place of comradeship.
A place where people will to live because life is so worthwhile.

Howard Braucher from *A Treasury of Living*, May 1947

Part 1

1

Introduction

Setting the scene

What leisure is and what it means to people are probably more important now than ever before and the influence of government and its agencies has never been more evident. In this fifth edition, while much of the text is new or re-written, the philosophy and fundamental principles on which to plan and manage leisure survive and through further investigation are strengthened. In particular, leisure in historical and cultural perspectives have been covered in much fuller detail than in previous editions to enhance scholarship and provide foundations for strategic thinking. Additional chapters covering each of the main leisure 'products' are also included.

Leisure can be perceived in many contexts: individual, community, national and international. Its delivery is both local and global. Moreover, global conditions affect each country far more now than in the past; the world economic climate, for example, has an impact on every nation. The terrorist tragedy inflicted on the United States of America on 11 September, 2001 had, and will continue to have, profound effects, not only in the military, political and economic arenas, but also in our ways of life, including leisure. The international tourist market declined and visitor attractions and activities such as theatre-going were affected, not only in New York, but also in London and many major cities throughout the world. The SARS epidemic in 2003 had an enormous impact on events in China, the Far East and elsewhere. In the United Kingdom, domestic and international tourism were negatively affected by the 'foot-and-mouth' crisis, particularly in countryside recreation. Northern Ireland has suffered a generation of visitor difficulties because of 'The Troubles', and, at the time of writing, stability in the Middle East is precarious.

In spite of international and national tensions, however, leisure and recreation in the United Kingdom continue to flourish and spending on leisure is projected to grow. Today, people of all ages demand choice and have higher expectations for healthier lifestyles, quality services, more facilities and better customer service and management.

This book carries the title 'Leisure and Recreation Management', which at first glance appears straightforward and understandable. However, straightforward it is not; it can convey a number of different images and meanings. To leisure professionals, it is likely to encompass an appreciation of leisure in its widest sense from ballroom dancing and bowls to bungee jumping, the management of services and facilities and the practical outcomes in the forms of participation in play, recreation, sport, art, entertainment, travel and tourism. Increasingly, leisure is perceived as cultural expression to the extent that the British government expects local authorities to prepare 'cultural strategies', going beyond former boundaries of 'leisure' strategies. Culture itself, however, is a complex concept. This book is intended to explore and throw light on the subjects, to increase knowledge and understanding in some small measure, and show how our quality of life can be enhanced by opportunity and effective management.

The first questions to be raised are fundamental: What are leisure and recreation? Is there any need to manage people's leisure, or are we creating false needs? In the public sector, are we providing costly services and facilities for no overwhelmingly good reason? Why the concern?

Nature provides us, in the natural environment, with abundant resources for leisure and recreation. One could argue that there is no need for expensive additional facilities, for services, programmes and management. Nature has provided fields, woods, rivers, beaches and sunshine. We have the challenge of the mountains, winter snow, the seas and the sky. There is beauty to behold, solitude in the country and peace away from the crowds.

It could be said that we should be quite capable of providing for all our recreational needs and for those of our children, or those unable to care for themselves, without additional facilities, services, programmes and management. Nature has provided us with the means to survive, to seek and explore, to find, to grow and to multiply. Nature has provided us not only with the desire to play and to find recreation, but also with the human capacity and resourcefulness so to do.

Yet the demand for man-made additional resources for leisure and recreation is greater now than it has ever been. Access to the countryside is increasingly limited; footpaths are being destroyed; playing fields are sold for development. Opportunities often have to be provided simply for children to learn how to play with other children. Indeed, it has needed a United Nations Convention to spell out that children have the rights to play, recreation, leisure, health and safety.

When the energies of some young people are channelled into acts of violence or vandalism, we see evidence of unsatisfied needs. Leisure opportunities could surely provide for the experiences that youth seeks and help meet some of those needs. One could also suggest that opportunities are needed for adults, for families, for the lonely, the old, the disabled and the disadvantaged to experience the satisfactions that leisure holds. Leisure Managers believe that such experience can enhance their quality of life.

The assumption is made in this book that leisure and recreation must be concerned, first, with people. Leisure planning and management are not just about buildings and facilities, but the question of human rights, the dignity and the uniqueness of the individual. It is from this standpoint that planning and management are debated and this thread, however tenuous, links discussion on principles, planning and management.

The book deals with approaches towards better management and performance. It is not, however, a technical textbook dealing with leisure 'hardware': buildings, facilities, design, maintenance, catering, bars, accounting, nor with many specialisms and technical matters. These aspects are covered elsewhere. Instead, this book is concerned with the leisure 'software': namely, the quality of the experience, the principles underlying provision and the 'people approach' to leadership and quality management.

Leisure and recreation are made possible by means of a range of services and facilities, both indoor and outdoor, in and around the home, in the urban environment, in rural areas and in the countryside. A range of services and programmes are provided by the public, institutional, voluntary and commercial sectors to meet the diverse needs and demands of individuals, families, groups, clubs, societies, and businesses.

Leisure and recreation demands and facilities

In the home

Resources and equipment for social recreation, entertainment, hobbies and pastimes.

Outdoor facilities

Gardens and open spaces, allotments, play areas and sports grounds.

Facilities for entertainment, art, music, drama, literary activities, education, sport and physical recreation.

General and specialist facilities

Halls and meeting rooms, libraries, theatres, museums, sports and leisure centres, swimming pools, community centres, entertainment centres, pubs, clubs, cinemas, concert halls, studios and art and craft workshops.

Recreation in the countryside

Good road networks, maps and signposting, stopping-off points, scenic viewing points, picnic sites, car parking, camping and caravan sites, clean beaches and lakes, water recreation areas, walkways, footpaths, nature reserves and many others.

Tourism

Tourist Information Centres, travel agents, visitor attractions, cheap rail and air fares, hotels and hospitality.

Demands are met, however, not just by providing facilities, but in attracting people to use and enjoy them, through services, management policy and efficient and effective management action. The reverse is also true. A strike or staff dispute at airports or on the railways can cause immense hardship for business and leisure passengers, sometimes stranded at locations around the world. A greater number of resources are available for leisure today than before. With them come greater opportunities and greater problems – opportunities which should be seized and problems which leisure professionals must help to solve.

Significance of the book

In terms of leisure and recreation management, the purpose of this book is to explore, describe, inform, challenge, improve and enhance. Leisure planners, providers and managers are in key positions for using resources and creating opportunities, which can help to enhance the quality of life for many people. However, there has been little research into people's needs in the context of leisure and their implications upon the planning, development and operation of facilities. Significant in this field of interest is the fast-emerging business of Leisure Management, giving rise to new education courses and attracting thousands of people into careers in leisure.

Structure of the book

The book is structured broadly in four parts.

- The first part considers leisure and culture in historical context, the variety of meanings of leisure, recreation and play and their roles in helping to meet some of the needs of individual people and in society as a whole.
- The second part is focused on the providers of leisure services, facilities and activities in the public, voluntary and commercial sectors, the trends in leisure and on the planning process.
- The third part is a new addition to the book and describes the range of leisure products to be found in tourism, countryside, open space, the arts and sport.
- The fourth part bridges the gap between theory and practice and deals with management, marketing, programming, events, staffing and training.

After I have set the scene in the first chapter, Chapter 2 deals with leisure in a historical perspective. Chapter 3, Cultural heritage and leisure, considers the cultural history of leisure, particularly in Britain; it is written in light of recent interest by government and its direction to local authorities to prepare Local Cultural Strategies. Chapter 4 explores the different meanings and interpretations of leisure. Chapter 5 focuses on children's play: the play world has developed its own playwork career structure, distinct from leisure and recreation.

Chapter 6 explores in depth the concept of human needs. Leisure services are said to be based on the needs of people; yet policy makers, researchers, planners and managers have insufficient insights into them. Yet, the satisfying of people's needs through leisure opportunity is one of the principles behind providing services. The questions are raised: what are the factors which attract people to leisure activity and, importantly, what circumstances constrain or detract them?

Chapters 7 and 8 are relatively short. Many people today are searching for satisfying or even 'ultimate' experiences. Chapter 7, Leisure and the experience society, considers whether we are becoming an 'experience society'. Chapter 8 is an integrating part of the book in theoretical terms, pulling together the concepts of play, leisure and recreation and the needs of people, into what I term and explain as the 'pleisure principle'. It also presents a theoretical model to illustrate the essential relationship between leisure, people's needs and management.

Having explored leisure in a personal sense, what it is and what it means to people, the rest of the book deals with the provision, planning, products and management of leisure. Chapters 9 to 11 focus on the major providers of leisure services and facilities: namely the public, voluntary and commercial sectors. Chapter 9 deals with central and local government and the immense influence that they have on providing for leisure and recreation. Government legislation in particular enables and also constrains what local government and other providers may do and may not do. The lead role taken by the Department of Culture, Media and Sport, its agencies and the effect of the National Lottery on provision of facilities and services is described.

Chapter 10 deals with the voluntary sector. The opportunities offered to people through the vast range of thousands of voluntary clubs, associations and organizations represent collectively a massive contribution to leisure and recreation. In many cases, voluntary organizations are inextricably linked to public providers and public money. This is exemplified in the movement towards more 'not for profit organizations', and the renaissance of charitable trusts established to offer community leisure services and facilities. The chapter also considers the importance of volunteerism.

The commercial sector is covered in Chapter 11. This sector provides much of the popular leisure activities, for example package holidays, media in the home, gardening and DIY and on household pets. Leisure outside the home is examined by looking into specific market sectors. These include visiting a pub and eating out, going to a cinema or theatre, playing tenpin bowling and bingo, and visiting family and friends, entertainment centres, leisure parks, theme parks and destination attractions. These are growth areas of leisure.

Chapter 12 is concerned with the planning process. It looks into the role of the government, planning policy guidance, development plans, and the ways in which demand can be assessed. The chapter also describes planning 'models' such as the Six Acre Standard, the Playing Pitch Strategy, the Facilities Planning Model and the preparation of a Local Cultural Strategy.

Leisure is a changing, volatile industry and is affected by changes in legislation, demography, in the economy and the trends in people's leisure behaviour. Chapter 13 is a brief résumé of the importance of trend analysis in the planning and provision for leisure and describes some of the trends that have occurred in recent years.

Chapters 14 to 17 provide a picture of leisure products, agencies, services and participation in the 'products' of leisure. Chapter 14 deals with tourism, probably the largest and fastest expanding sector in the United Kingdom and globally. Covered in this chapter are tourist visit profiles, promoting tourism, destination attractions and tourism and heritage worldwide and in the United Kingdom.

Chapter 15 considers issues about leisure and the environment. It includes leisure use of the countryside within the context of protecting heritage, wildlife and habitats and leisure use of the national parks, forests and woodlands, the urban fringe and urban green spaces.

Chapter 16 is concerned with the arts, museums and libraries sectors and includes national policy on the arts, the Arts Council, the new government agency, Resource, responsible for museums, galleries and libraries, and the effects of new technology and the Internet.

Sport, physical recreation and physical activity are prominent areas in leisure provision and leisure management. Chapter 17 covers a broad span of issues, including sport and cultural identity, sports policy and the government's national strategic plan for sport, provision at national and local levels, the work of sports councils, sports coaching and development and health and fitness.

Having considered leisure and the needs of people, leisure policy and planning and the range of leisure products and services, we move to management. The management, marketing and programming of leisure and recreation facilities is the key part of leisure management which delivers the products to individuals, groups and to the general public.

Chapter 18 describes the principles and foundations of management and core management factors which apply to all managers. Good management is the means by which an organization can meet its aims and objectives, in a style that encourages good relationships within the organization and with clients and customers. Lessons are learned from the management gurus and their implications for management today. Leadership and decision making can be considered to be the two most important aspects of good management. Chapter 19 covers a number of issues, including leadership versus management, leadership styles, team building, group behaviour, the process of decision making, communication, delegation, coaching and mentoring.

The marketing of leisure and recreation is covered in Chapter 20. It explains the marketing approach, the concept of social marketing and the influence that marketing has on potential customer behaviour. The chapter explores the possibilities for improved marketing of services and products, particularly in the public sector. In the commercial world, marketing leisure products has proved to be an effective means of making greater profits. The question is raised: should public service marketing be processed in a different way? The discipline of marketing has become somewhat academic. Core concepts of marketing are explained: mission, market analysism, market positioning, segmentation and the use of the elements in the marketing mix to meet marketing strategies. The chapter concludes with the process of writing a marketing plan.

Chapter 21 examines one of the most important leisure management skills, that of programming of leisure services and facilities. Managers must have sufficient knowledge of programming because it is the means by which leisure and recreation are delivered to clients and customers and organizational objectives can be met. The chapter explains what programming consists of, directional programming strategies, programming methods for general and target markets. The chapter concludes with ways to prepare a programme plan.

Chapter 22 deals with one of the most improved, and written about, areas of leisure management – the planning and management of special events. Events are an important part of any comprehensive leisure programme. Well organized, they can be a boon; badly organized, they can spell disaster and deter people from coming to such events in future. Leisure Managers must be capable of leading or controlling the planning and staging of events. This chapter sees major events as landmarks of history and describes these as mega, hallmark and major events. The main focus of the chapter is on special local events and covers the event planning process and organization and provides a suggested seven-stage event planner as an example of how events might be managed from beginning to end.

Leisure managers and staff are the most important asset available to organizations. Chapter 23 looks into staffing and organizational structures. The chapter covers some of the discrete staff and organizational issues: the principles of management which affect staffing, creating organization and staffing structures, employment of staff and legislation, and staff selection, recruitment and appraisal. The chapter also includes the preparation of a staff handbook and guidelines for managers on staffing and structures.

Chapter 24 provides a broad overview of the education and training scene in the leisure sector, an essential area which has expanded substantially and improved considerably in the recent past. This chapter also covers education for leisure, a much overlooked area from which young people in particular can learn and obtain leisure interests and skills for life incorporating a lifestyle involving both serious and casual leisure interests. This chapter also includes a description of the range of training courses, initiatives emanating from the government and standardization. The chapter concludes with an acknowledgement of the contribution to leisure management of the professional institutes and the question is posed, is Leisure Management still an emerging profession or has it now emerged? Chapter 24 provides some brief conclusions and points for discussion.

Many employers equate management with administration and thus appoint administrators. While the good manager should be able to administer, organize and learn, administration is only one of the many functions of management.

The profession of leisure management is accumulating many good administrators. This book is written in the hope that it will also accumulate many good leisure academics, professionals and managers.

Finally, in Chapter 25, all the strands of the book – leisure philosophy, planning, provision and management – are drawn together into a theoretical framework for community leisure services and facility management which provides the linkages and bridges the gap between theory and practice.

2

Leisure in historical perspective

Introduction

The first thing to be said about leisure is that it is not new. 'That is the principal point', said Aristotle, 'with what kind of activity is man to occupy his leisure?'

This chapter places leisure and recreation in historical context. It is not, however, the history of leisure, *per se*, rather leisure viewed in different historical settings.

Why do we need to consider leisure in historical context? We could answer by asserting that history and scholarship are important to our understanding of how we have arrived at where we are, and why. More, we are what our history has made us; we live our history. As people, we do much of what humans have always done; in many ways we behave like our ancestors. While today's adults and parents are alarmed at young people's fashions and lifestyle, anthropologists remind us that there is nothing new. Body painting? The earliest humans in Africa used red ochre for body painting in preparation for ritual dances. Tourism today has origins in ancient pilgrimage, exploration and invention.

Our culture and leisure behaviour, in part, are rooted in the past. They are founded on a history of what people in the past have done, and on customs and traditions handed down over the centuries. This chapter gives a flavour of the history and Chapter 3 gives greater focus to cultural heritage, and they need to be read in tandem.

Leisure: an ancient heritage

Leisure has been identified with élitism and class privilege since the earliest civilizations. However, leisure probably began with primitive cultures once the pressures for sustenance, security and basic needs were removed, or in celebration after the hunt or during inclement weather. In simpler societies, the line between work and leisure is not indelibly drawn. In times past, and even in many parts of the world today, there are people who work so hard and long to sustain themselves and their families that their lives are devoid of what we might term 'leisure'. Peasant life often means working to survive, and playing when opportunity permits. In simple social systems leisure is part of the rhythms of life: night and day, the climate, the seasons, the harvest. Margaret Mead's vivid descriptions of life in Samoa (Mead, 1928) illustrate the ebb and flow of life, as distinct from a separation of life into work and leisure. Opportunity for leisure came with the obligations towards festivals, celebrations, feasts, weddings, special days and with the sacred mythology of early cultures. Godbey (1978) points out that there was no deliberate leisure, nothing that was the result of the exercise of individual choice. In such societies, leisure is structured around the life cycle of necessary daily tasks; it is integrated into the daily or seasonal life pattern rather than being separate from it. Cutten (1929) states:

> It was from these days or hours of primitive leisure, when crude but very real beginnings were made, that the arts, the sciences, the games and all the products of civilization date. In fact, civilizations were the products of leisure, and yet they have not always admitted their origin.

In many parts of the world, the development of agriculture widened the gap between the ruling classes and the rest of the population. Early advanced cultures, with clearly differentiated work roles, developed élite classes and leisure became associated with 'high culture', social standing and political status. For example, the Egyptian, Assyrian and Babylonian cultures included many 'leisure' activities but these were primarily activities of the upper strata in society: the nobility, the military and religious leaders. Drinking and gambling were common. In ancient Assyria and Babylon there were royal estates and parks, zoological and botanical gardens and large formal gardens of geometric designs. The terraced Hanging Gardens of Babylon became one of the seven wonders of the world. Developments also occurred in the Indian subcontinent and in China, famous for its gardens.

> Egyptians, Assyrians and Babylonians enjoyed horseracing, wrestling, boxing, archery, arts, dance, music, drama, hunting, warfare and lavish entertainment.

In *Retail, Leisure and Tourism* (Wootton, 1989), under the subheading 'Nothing new under the sun', we read:

> The Sumerian and Mesopotamian caravanners of 4,000 years ago originated the concept of combining retail with leisure. They knew well the importance of creating just the right atmosphere for selling. No unit would depart from Damascus on its journey to Jeddah without the support of a full complement of magicians, snakecharmers, story-tellers, dancers, sword swallowers and craftsmen who theatrically fashioned goods *in situ* and offered them for sale to the public. Showmanship and retailing read as one. The act of a simple purchase a̶s̶s̶u̶r̶e̶d̶ ̶t̶h̶e̶ importance of an event. Advance men travelled from village to village to draw th̶ the caravanner made sure that his customers were placed in the mood to purchase

them with a good time in the process. It is clear, we cannot understand present leisure without understanding something of the past. None appear to have thought more about leisure than the Ancient Greek philosophers, so that is where we start.

In ancient Egypt, hieroglyphs, 'sacred' writing in stone, were used for royal and religious writing. Children played with balls, spinning tops, dolls and model animals and games of leap-frog and hopscotch. Board games, such as *senet* or 'passing' were played; pieces were moved from square to square, different coloured squares denoting good and bad luck. Ancient Egyptians also liked fashion. Most people had short hair and wore wigs; children's heads were shaved, except for a lock of hair, called 'the sidelock of youth', which grew over one ear. Both sexes wore colourful jewellery; wide collars were made of jewels or beads; both outlined their eyes with kohl and women used henna to stain their nails orange, cheeks and lips were coloured with red ochre.

Egypt, first part of the Assyrian and then Persian empires, was conquered by Alexander the Great in about 300 BC and became part of the Roman Empire.

Leisure and the Ancient Greeks

The early Greek civilization has influenced current leisure thinking and this is primarily as a result of the writings of Plato and Aristotle (see Further reading). At the height of Greek civilization, the growing professionalization of sport, public entertainment and competitions, saw in contrast the birth of the 'leisure ethic': the intelligent use of free time was the purpose of life. The natural life of man was collective, life in the community. The ideal was the perfection of civil life and political life. The 'proper life' was good citizenship and good citizens were created out of leisure and education.

Greek philosopher and writer, Plato (429–347 BC) was an Athenian nobleman. He saw no hope for 'man' unless rulers became philosophers or philosophers became rulers. He was a devoted follower of Socrates. After Socrates' death, he founded his Academy in Athens in 387 BC.

Aristotle (384–322 BC), a Greek philosopher and scientist, joined the Academy in Athens; he failed to become head of the Academy at Plato's death. However, he went on to found the library and museum, the Lyceum. Aristotle was said to have written 400 books on a very wide range of subjects, including logic, ethics, politics, metaphysics, biology, physics and poetry.

Plato expressed a low regard for manual labour and a high regard for well-employed leisure, with the capable citizen performing music, drama, sport, citizenship and education during leisure time. Much of Plato's writings include reconstructions of the thoughts and dialogues of Socrates, his mentor. Time for thought, contemplation, philosophy and self-development are required for happiness. That time, for Plato, is leisure. A study of Ancient Greek words illustrates the philosophical juxtaposition of culture, education and leisure. The word *paideia* meant 'culture' and *paidos*, 'boy' or 'child'; *peod* forms the root of our word 'pedagogy', the art and science of teaching. *Paideia* also referred to education and self-improvement.

Now the Greek word *schole* denoted both schooling and leisure; it led to the Latin *scola* and English 'school' and 'scholar'. Aristotle, in Book 1 of the *Politics*, defines leisure as time free from the necessity to work. Leisure is different from work (*ascholia*) and from children's play (*paideia*). Leisure leads to aesthetic, spiritual or intellectual enlightenment through a search for understanding. Manual workers were believed to be incapable of leisure. This was not simply a case of discriminating against those earning a living by the sweat of their brows; it was rather a belief that kinds of work performed in manual occupations made workers unfit for the duties of citizenship. Development of the concept of the natural slave was a solution to the problem of getting the necessary work done, so that the rest of the city could be free for the more worthwhile pursuits.

Two aspects of that Greek civilization have endured until today: the distinction between work and leisure, and the Greek leisure ethic. The purpose of knowledge was to enable a person to make the right choices. Central to Aristotle's philosophy was how to attain happiness. According to him, moderation in all things was in keeping with natural justice. Happiness, he said, is continuous: leisure is not a brief period but a life-time (Goodale and Godbey, 1988). The work–leisure distinction may well have begun with the Greek philosophers. Work was associated with the toil of manual labour and with providing the necessities of life, while leisure was valued as those moments of life in which one contemplated the eternal truths and participated in music and drama. Aristotle placed business and war on one side and leisure and peace on the other; this view held that no occupation could be regarded as leisure. 'We are unleisurely in order to have leisure', he claimed, 'facts, as well as arguments, prove that the legislator should direct all his military and other measures to the provision of leisure and the establishment of peace.'

However, not all members of society could pursue the ideal leisure. Leisure was not only an individual pleasurable pursuit, but for a public good. The leisured man was required to contribute to improve public life. He would also strive for perfection in arts, music, sport; the Greek gymnasium was the centre for leisure schooling. Not only was this leisure life for men, it was only for some men. Daily work was carried out by slaves, craftsmen and women: those with far less social status within a well-defined class struc-ture. What distinguishes the leisure of Ancient Greece from that found anywhere in the history of leisure is the strong connection between leisure and state government.

Plato did not share this understanding of the work–leisure divide. In the Republic, Plato employs the word *schole* with different meanings, such as spare time, freedom from other activities and self-possession or freedom. There is a further concept of leisure as idleness. When Plato referred to this, he used the word *agria*, that is, a degen-erate condition and not to be thought of as leisure. Hence leisure becomes the *quality* of the activity.

The Greek conception of leisure was central to a much wider view of the life and nature of a free man. However, the range of activities that qualified as leisure was severely restricted. To Plato, music, poetry and philosophy lead to beauty and eternal truths. To Aristotle, only music and contemplation were worthy of the name leisure. Moreover, as Godbey (1978) points out, the style of life and leisure was for the privileged élite; the Greek ideal, even if it existed as set out in the writings, was for only a very small proportion of the population. The Greek ideal is therefore something of a myth. Indeed, it is not consistent with what actually occurred, in practice, in Ancient Greece. The early Olympic Games, the stadia, gymnasia, extensive gardens and the open-air amphitheatres for festivals all illustrate the range of leisure pursuits and the range of public provision of facilities. In addition, while in the early days all citizens were

Among the Ancient Greek words which survive in the English language are: pedagogy, gymnasium, stadium, lyceum and academy.

encouraged to participate and compete, this spirit of amateurism gave way to specialist performers, commercialization and mass spectatorship and led from the amateur to the professional.

Although founded on slave labour and élitism, the Greek leisure ethic shows that leisure can be an essential opportunity for the development of man and woman and the unity of body and mind. Moreover, whether myth or fact, the spirit of the Greek ideal is still a goal to which many subscribe and there exist, even today, small enclaves of esoteric minority pursuits devoted to the enlightenment of mankind. Moreover, our inheritance from the Ancient Greek philosophers is immense in philosophy, education, government, science, art, drama and poetry – and the search for the good life in which wisdom, virtue and leisure were pursued. As Goodale and Godbey (1988) remind us, a symposium is a gathering of learned people to share ideas: 'to them it was a drinking party. The Greek *schole* became not only school but also *skole*, a drinking song. Ancient philosophers were full of life.' Alas, the leisure ideal died with the Ancient Greeks and little evidence of its resurrection is found until the birth in Europe of the university and the Renaissance.

Leisure and the Ancient Romans

The empire of the Ancient Romans established in 27 BC continued until AD 395, when it divided into Eastern and Western empires. Roman culture spread across the known world. In ancient Rome military conquest led to affluence, a powerful nation and a move from agricultural democracy to urban populations with a class structure. Masses of the new urban population had considerable free time and as many as two hundred holidays a year by AD 354. Leisure was important for the Romans, but its importance was different from that of the Greek leisure ethic. Sports were practised for maintaining physical fitness and for war. Leisure was utilitarian rather than aesthetic. Baths, amphitheatres and arenas were constructed for the benefit of the mass of the population.

> In Rome itself there were over 800 public baths provided at little or no cost to the public.

Free time, however, became a problem. Emperors attempted to keep people content by providing free food and entertainment: 'bread and circuses'. Slaves not only toiled, but were also used for entertainment, which at first included music, drama and sports, but later included contests, simulated land and sea battles, chariot races and exhibitions of violence. Violent spectacles included animals and then humans; professional gladiators fought to the death. The Colosseum, built about AD 80, became the hub of life in Rome and large arenas, gymnasia, parks and baths were built in most large towns. The Circus Maximus could hold 385,000 spectators. As Rome became more decadent it declined. Historians have suggested that the inability to cope with leisure was one cause of the fall of the empire (Miller and Robinson, 1963). Economically, and perhaps in other ways, the spectacles contributed to the financial ruin of the empire, as the aristocracy competed to outdo each other, often to the point of bankruptcy.

Britain became a province of the Roman Empire for 300 years when it was conquered in AD 43. Although a late acquisition of the Romans and a relatively small and 'far-flung' province, the interest of tourists today in Roman Britain is substantial, compared with many other parts of the ancient Roman Empire. Julius Caesar landed in

Kent in 55/54 BC, spent a short time in England and returned to Rome. A hundred years later, Emperor Claudius conquered the south of England. Camulodunum (Colchester) became the first capital, Londinium the second. Not all tribes surrendered; Caractacus and Boudicca resisted, unsuccessfully. Emperor Hadrian (AD 117–138) shored up the Empire's defences, building Hadrian's wall to keep out the warlike Scottish tribes.

And what of leisure? The Romans left a lasting legacy and this is described in the next chapter, which traces our cultural heritage back to those ancient times. Ancient Rome shows that mass leisure is no new phenomenon. It illustrates leisure in a social context of urbanization and the political use of leisure to quieten the masses. It also shows the massive investment in public recreation facilities and services and, above all, the growth of leisure consumption rather than participation.

> Famous for road-building, the Romans laid 8,000 km of roads in Britain alone.

The social structure of the Roman society is exemplified in the word 'plebeians'. This was the name given to all people who were not the privileged 'patricians'. At first, they had no civil rights and were forbidden to marry patricians. In 493–492 BC the plebeians forced the Senate to appoint their own tribunes and an assembly and they gradually gained admission to all Roman offices. Thus, from later Republican times, the term plebeian implied low social class.

Although, like the Greeks, the Romans built and planned for leisure, the stress for them was upon law and custom and consumption, a political instrument, as distinct from learning, discovering and enlightenment. Later cultures used the example of Rome to show the consequences of uncontrolled misuse of leisure.

Leisure constraints of the Middle Ages

The fall of the Roman Empire and the spread of Christianity had profound and lasting effects on leisure and recreation. The Catholic Church taught that the purpose of life was to prepare for the next life. The early part of the Middle Ages, from about 400 to 1000 is often called, aptly, the Dark Ages. For centuries it was for most people a time of relative drabness. The first of the monasteries was founded by St Augustine in North Africa. The monasteries represented lives segmented into discrete parts; the Benedictines preached, 'Work, do not despair'. Work became a virtue, as it is today, a far cry from its role according to Ancient Greek philosophy.

The monasteries expanded, preaching hard labour, good works and self-deprivation. As a reaction to the extremes and debased activities of the Romans, the Church prohibited most kinds of leisure activity except those relating to worship and religious observance. Work was glorified; idleness was evil. However, while music and morality plays flourished, social drinking, gambling and secular music were practised by the public often on 'holy'-day celebrations, and the aristocracy continued their leisure activities of hunting, falconry and holding tournaments. But life in the Dark Ages was harsh to the common man. Civil rights were unheard of, their beginnings probably not starting until the Magna Carta, the Great Charter that was sealed at Runnymede in 1215 by King John of England in response to baronial unrest. The charter defined the barons' feudal obligations to the monarch, opposed his arbitrary justice and confirmed the liberties of the English Church. With changes over the years, the charter was subsequently upheld by parliamentarians in the seventeenth century as a statement of fundamental civil rights.

During the late Middle Ages, up to approximately 1500, there were some relaxations from the strictures of the Dark Ages, but life for the masses remained much the same with religious festivals coming as breaks in the round of toil. However, there continued throughout the Middle Ages the phenomenon of leisure élitism, a modified Greek ideal for the landed gentry and political leaders. Leisure activities included hunting, hawking, music and dance. Sports and jousting were a means of entertainment, but were primarily preparation for feuding noblemen and for war, which was a constant threat.

> The Great Fairs attracted entertainers: singers, dancers, jugglers, magicians, fortune tellers, dancing bears and sports such as wrestling, archery, jousting, dog and cock fighting and gambling followed.

For the masses, leisure came through the church's 'holy'-days and from the trading markets: medieval leisure shopping. In the thirteenth and fourteenth centuries royal charters set up boundaries for the Great Fairs, attracting merchants from Europe and Asia. Religious festivals and wakes, likewise, attracted entertainers and made for revelry. Gradually, the power of the Church declined, but Europe was still controlled by powerful monarchs.

The Renaissance and awakening to leisure

The two movements of the Renaissance and the Reformation developed in historical parallel. One was a cultural revolution and the other a religious one, influencing the work ethic and a moral way of life. Over the centuries the power of the Catholic Church declined, permitting a reawakening in humanity and the arts. The fifteenth century marks the transition from the medieval world to modern Western civilization.

The Renaissance, 're-birth' in French, was an intellectual and cultural movement that began in Italy, spread to northern Europe and flourished until the middle of the sixteenth century. During this time, there was a revival of classical learning, art, architecture, the philosophy of 'humanism' and the dignity of 'man' advocated by the fourteenth-century poet and scholar, Petrarch. The High Renaissance denotes a period around 1500–1520 during which flourished artists such as Leonardo da Vinci, Raphael and Michelangelo. In the sixteenth century, the Renaissance spread to northern Europe and was seen in the art of Dürer, the scholarship of Erasmus, and in Britain, the plays of Shakespeare and in the court of Elizabeth I. The spread of knowledge and liberalism – the liberal arts liberated from ignorance – broke through religious dogma. Liberal thought, however, opened up opportunity for both enlightenment and extravagance and a breakdown in order and discipline. The Italian Renaissance collapsed through greed and excess. Upon its decline came other philosophies such as that of Niccolò Machiavelli, who advocated gaining power by whatever means, fair or foul.

It was not until the time of the Renaissance that leisure ideals became more generalized and more opportunities were available to the masses. The populace continued to enjoy both religious and secular festivals. The development of printing enabled literature to become available to a wider public, since it had previously only been available to those who studied in monasteries, universities and aristocratic homes. Music, drama and dance were performed professionally in theatres, and education became more readily available. Later, educators such as Rousseau and Locke extolled the benefits of play in the education of children.

Jean Jacques Rousseau (1712–78) was a French philosopher and writer. His novel *Emile*, on education, expanded his views on human nature and the need for society to provide children with opportunities for free expression of mind, body and spirit. His work inspired later pioneers in the fields of adventure play and physical education. His style and romantic outlook inspired poets such as Shelley, Byron and Wordsworth.

During these times, the nobility became the patrons of the arts and the works of many of the great artists of that time hang in galleries all over the world today.

During the Renaissance, the Protestant Reformation took hold in many parts of Europe and later moved on to America. The liberalism brought about by the Renaissance had also encouraged a pleasure-seeking aristocracy, a public more prone to drinking, gambling and practising cruel sports and a worldly, often corrupt, Church; these and other factors led to the Reformation.

The Reformation and the work ethic

The Reformation was a religious movement in sixteenth-century Europe and began as an attempt to reform the Roman Catholic Church and ended with the establishment of independent Protestant Churches. The critical examination of the Bible, the need for translation into language understood by the population, the development of printing and the growth of nationalism, collectively weakened papal jurisdiction within the states of western Europe. In 1517, Martin Luther began a revolt against the established church in Germany, where marriages and divorces could be purchased and indulgences (monetary penance) were believed to wipe clean the slate of sin, given sufficient payment. Calvin and Knox began similar reformed churches.

Luther's attack on the sale of indulgences and, subsequently, on papal authority, was condemned by the pope and the Holy Roman Emperor, but gained the support of several German princes. The consequent conflict was not resolved until 1555. In Switzerland, the Reformation was initiated by Zwingli in Zurich in 1520, spread to Basle, Berne, and to Geneva, where it was led by John Calvin. Calvinism was adopted in France, the Low Countries, England, Scotland, and subsequently in North America. In France, where Protestants were called Huguenots, the Reformation became involved in a political struggle for control of the crown, giving rise to the Wars of Religion. A time of austerity followed, with emphasis on religious matters and a diminishing of many leisure activities. In some communities, even children's play was discouraged as it was said to foster 'idleness'.

A turning point in English history came with Henry VIII's divorce from Catherine of Aragon and marriage to Anne Boleyn. The Act of Appeals (1533) abolished the pope's rights and the Act of Supremacy declared that the King of England was supreme head of the Church of England. The sale or destruction of all the religious houses and monasteries of the Catholic Church has had major implications, including that of tourism in Britain today. By the turn of the century, England had rejected the authority of the papacy in Rome and the Anglican Church was established during the reign of Elizabeth I but, as now, rifts between warring religious factions continued.

The Counter-Reformation of Ignatius Loyola, with the creation of the Jesuits, had a lasting legacy in Europe. The Tudor dynasty of monarchs Henry VII, Henry VIII, Edward VI, Mary I and Elizabeth I (1485–1603) ended with the death of Elizabeth. The Stuarts were one of England's least successful dynasties, though James I's reign brought some growth in political stability and a lessening of religious dogma. To counteract the growing religious opposition to active leisure pursuits, James I of England issued the Book of Sports in 1618, making it legal for working people to play certain games outside church hours.

The Puritans, drawn from the poor and middle classes, were dissidents who sought to purify the church along the lines of Luther and Calvin and as a protest against the pleasures of the rich. They became entangled in the political struggle between parliament and king, which was to lead to civil war.

The Civil War (1642–51) was between Charles I and parliament. The Parliamentarians were also called Roundheads, referring to the short haircuts of apprentices who demonstrated against the king at Westminster. Their drab appearance contrasted to the flamboyant Cavaliers of the king. The formation of Oliver Cromwell's New Model Army brought about the decisive defeat of Charles at Naseby in 1645. The second Civil War ensued in 1648. Charles was tried and executed in 1649 and a Commonwealth established.

The Restoration of the monarchy came in 1660 with the return from exile and reign of Charles II.

Post-Renaissance and Reformation

Early philosophy was based on subjective thought, ideas and religious precepts. The Renaissance brought in its wake great discoveries in world exploration, science, medicine, astronomy, mathematics and philosophy. The greatest 'explosion' was in art and painting in northern Italy, with the works of Botticelli, Leonardo da Vinci, Michelangelo, and hundreds of others. As the movement spread across northern Europe, there came also philosophers such as Bacon, Hobbes, Locke and Spinoza; poets such as Spenser, Dryden and later Voltaire, the French dramatist and historian; and also there came great writers, Shakespeare and Molière, painters including Rembrandt, and landscape architects such as André le Nôtre who designed gardens for Louis XIV at the Palace of Versailles, and later Capability Brown.

René Descartes (1596–1650) embodied the notion of the philosopher-scientist, as Leonardo da Vinci had done a century before. The world was becoming a smaller place, as a result of the adventures of explorers like the Spaniard Mendoza, the colonizer of South America; Sir Francis Drake's voyage around the world; and the growth of world trade with trading companies such as the East India Company. There was non-stop activity in the scientific world as well. Not surprisingly, there was reaction against such rationality, for example, with the 'Romantic movement' of Rousseau.

Despite being heavily suppressed by the Reformation, the cultural revolution of the Renaissance continued. In the seventeenth and eighteenth centuries, parks and gardens were developed for the nobility, who went hunting and fishing and enjoyed the beauty of the gardens. Commons and plazas were developed for the public. Holidays were declared by the kings and lords. The Tuileries and Versailles gardens in Paris, the Tiergarten in Berlin, and Kensington Gardens in London were gradually opened to the public.

In the seventeenth century, scholars such as Newton, Locke, Pascal and Descartes had questioned accepted beliefs. In France, philosophers such as Voltaire attacked established religion. Individual liberty and equality were embodied in the work of

Rousseau and others. The period in eighteenth-century history called the Enlightenment or Age of Reason was a philosophical movement that sought to replace authoritarian beliefs with rational scientific inquiry.

The humanism of the Renaissance sought the creativity and development of people through education and greater freedom. Although the Renaissance brought about more freedom for leisure, the Reformation has been shown to have had an even greater effect on Western attitudes. The Reformation was a period which idealized work and distrusted the evils of leisure, and the work ethic has persisted into the twenty-first century. The Protestant ethic sought to condition leisure to behaviour which made men and women fit for devotion and work.

It was another revolution, the Industrial Revolution, which was to suppress still further the opportunities for leisure development for the mass of the people in the short term, but which in fact led to 'mass leisure' in the longer term.

Effects of the Industrial Revolution

The Industrial Revolution of the eighteenth and nineteenth centuries led to profound social changes. Factories brought about the growth of cities. Populations were uprooted from the land, and from small towns and villages, to the cities. The consequent rise in urban population, overcrowding, poor housing, poverty, crime and the increase in working hours and child labour, all militated against leisure. British industrial history records examples of the hardship caused by the Industrial Revolution and the exploitation of the workers, poor wages and conditions of the miners, the cotton-mill workers and many others.

From the villages where people lived amid nature, where children could play in the fields and families could walk in the countryside, people came to live in cramped conditions with little room to play and little time to enjoy leisure. Recreation areas were not planned. For children, often viewed as cheap labour, the consequences were devasting and many forms of play were condemned as evil.

From the mid-1800s to well into the 1900s a reform movement took shape. Reformers were deeply concerned about welfare, especially the welfare of children. They were deeply troubled by the conditions of an urban life bereft of opportunities for healthy exercise and play. The urban churches, in many cases, gradually began to recognize such problems and to come to terms with a new role in regard to recreation.

The reformers dealt more with the concept of recreation than leisure; they sought 'wholesome' opportunities for activity after work which refreshed and renewed the worker for more work. The central element of the leisure philosophy of social reformers was that recreation served socially useful ends, a theme which has continued ever since.

It was in response to appalling social conditions that the organized recreation movement began. At the turn of the last century, an interest in leisure as it relates to industrial society was awakened. It was during this period also that several of the writings and theories of play and recreation began to emerge as reactions to social conditions. The Great Depression of the 1930s and world wars were to bring still further social emergencies.

Also re-emerging at this time was what Thorsten Veblen described as 'the leisure class'. Capitalism, urbanization and industrialization had brought about yet another division in society. In America, Veblen (1953) began to identify weaknesses in the industrial system. He criticized the 'leisure class' and its 'conspicuous consumption'. With industrialism, the arbitrary division of labour and class continued to exist and to perpetuate itself. Status becomes symbolized by purchasing power and accumulation of wealth. To Veblen, writing at the turn of the last century, leisure was perpetuated for the leisure classes.

It was during times of hardship and social injustice that social pioneers persuaded governments to act. In Britain, public health and physical recreation, baths and parks and open spaces were gradually made available to the public. But leisure was never the right of the masses until it was recognized as a part of life separate from the excessively long working hours. The Saturday half-day was a significant turning point in Britain towards an acceptance of leisure for the mass of the people.

Into the twenty-first century

Gradually the working class began to demand leisure, not for any idealism or enlightenment, but for time off, because workers (and unions) were now selling their time. The demand for work and free time led to the organization of modern work and the world of public, voluntary and industrial recreation.

The twentieth century saw the growth of recreation, but equally as important, the need for children's play as a process of learning for the young, and leisure for the sake of enjoyment rather than just for social welfare. In the first half of that century, a vast number of amenities for people to enjoy in their free time were provided: public parks, 'baths', public houses in their thousands and music halls. After the First World War, there came cinemas and spectator sports. Then, after the Second World War, came the greatest leisure attraction of all time – the television – and in its wake, immense advancement in technology, easing work and domestic chores and providing more time and resources for leisure.

Today there are over 3,000 public sports centres and 600 commercial health and fitness clubs.

In 1965, Michael Dower (1965) wrote for the Civic Trust a watershed publication *Fourth Wave – The Challenge of Leisure*. He wrote:

> Three great waves have broken across the face of Britain since 1800. First, the sudden growth of dark industrial towns. Second, the thrusting movement along far-flung railways. Third, the sprawl of car-based suburbs. Now we see, under the guise of a modest word, the surge of a fourth wave which could be more powerful than all the others. The modest word is leisure.

Yet, 40 years on, for the working population, including those caring for homes and families, the patterns and rhythms of life are determined by work and its demands, and spare time, the residual, is labelled as leisure.

The leisure industry in 2003 employed an estimated 2.5 million people, accounting for one in every five new jobs.

The 1960s also witnessed the start of leisure and recreation management as we know it today in the United Kingdom. An explosion of leisure facilities began with the birth of the community multi-sport centre at Harlow. National centres followed the opening of the Crystal Palace National Sports Centre; and then came community arts and recreation centres. The creative arts, music, fashion, festivals and exhibitions, have flourished and tourism and visitor attractions have burgeoned.

The growth in facilities is captured in the use of new names and descriptions. From parks, pitches and pools, sports and arts has evolved a wider, new leisure vocabulary which includes: leisure centre, leisure pool, leisure ice, health and fitness club, GP Referral, themed bar and restaurant, multi-screen cinema, clubbing and – of huge impact on additional facilities and projects – the National Lottery.

Conclusion

Leisure and recreation, as we have seen from their history, have had profound effects on our ways of life. Leisure is as much a part of life as work, and it plays an equally important part in our development and the quality of our lives. The House of Lords Select Committee in 1973 described leisure as 'almost as important to the well-being of the community as good housing, hospitals and schools'.

After 30 years, we are not there yet, but we are a number of steps forward.

Leisure and recreation influence, and play a significant part in re-enforcing and re-shaping, our culture, a subject we turn to in Chapter 3.

Discussion points

1 It is said that history repeats itself, that we live our history; it has made us what we are and how we behave. Defend or reject these statements in the context of leisure and recreation.

2 The concept of leisure has changed over time since the eras of the Ancient Greeks, Romans, Middle Ages, Renaissance, Reformation, Industrial Revolution and Victorian times and into the twenty-first century. In your opinion, which era has had the greatest influence on current perceptions and practices in leisure and recreation? Explain why.

Further reading

For a detailed history of leisure see:

Chubb, M. and Chubb, H. (1981), *One Third of Our Time*, Wiley, Chichester.

For more about early Greek philosophy see:

Plato (1952), Complete Works, *Encyclopaedia Britannica*, Chicago, IL.

Aristotle (1952) Aristotle 2. Great Books of the Western World, *Encyclopaedia Britannica*, Chicago, IL.

For a fuller discussion on leisure and the Ancient Greeks see:

Kelly, J. (1982), *Leisure*, Prentice-Hall, Englewood Cliffs, NJ.

Goodale, T. and Godbey, G. (1988), *The Evolution of Leisure*, Venture Publishing, State College, PA.

3

Cultural heritage and leisure

Introduction

Leisure is an important ingredient of culture, possibly more so than work and other aspects of life. Local authorities are directed by government to plan strategically and write forward-looking 'cultural strategies'. The role of Leisure Managers is to deliver broad-based services that serve to build upon their district heritage and culture, traditional and new. However, in England and Wales only libraries and allotments are statutory services; leisure, recreation, sports, arts and play are not: they remain 'permissive' services which may, or may not, be provided. Yet a local authority still needs to prepare a Cultural Strategy, leisure being a prominent feature.

Leisure directors and managers tend to take lead roles in preparing Local Cultural Strategies, and the mechanics of these are discussed in Local Cultural Strategies, p. 234, Chapter 12. The first question they face is: what is the culture of our area? And on a wider scale, how does our culture fit within the regional and national culture and how is it unique? There will be no short definitive answers. The essence of a local culture would not be captured in snapshots of the present time, but in a very large album of pictures, depicting the lives of past and present generations.

In the United Kingdom, cultural and leisure influences go back many centuries, to the Celts, Anglo-Saxons, to Roman, Viking and Norman invaders and to all our rulers and monarchs. Religion, and particularly Christianity, also has had profound effect on culture, tradition and leisure.

Different religions are now increasingly being practised in Britain so that the Established Church no longer represents the nation as a whole. Social life is also influenced by other nations' cultures. Most people who 'eat out' will be eating Indian, Chinese or Italian food rather than traditionally British meals. Britain's culture is a tapestry of many shapes and colours and today embraces hundreds of different languages and dialects. It is a cosmopolitan culture, though local cultures are often highly distinct: they are unique to their area, even within the same city. In the same borough an inner-city area may be decidedly different culturally from a leafy suburb.

Foundations of culture in the United Kingdom

The foundations of our leisure culture, of our play, recreation, arts, sport, festivals, health and fitness and travel and tourism, have been laid over two thousand years.

Theatre owes much to Greek tragedy, medieval plays and the plays of Shakespeare. The word 'theatre' originates from the Greek *theatron*, and from it we get the words theatrical, being histrionic, melodramatic and stagy. Ancient Greek theatre adjoined religious centres in Athens, Epidaurus and Delphi. Secularized theatres were a feature of most Roman towns and Renaissance court theatres imitated Roman models. The open-air Elizabethan theatre represented a more popular tradition.

The arts world also has some roots in the past. Classical art of the 'old masters' can sell for millions of pounds. Much classical music was composed hundreds of years ago. Opera originated in Florence in the early seventeenth century as the result of attempts to revive Greek tragedy and to reproduce its musical elements. Ballet originated in the formal dances of the French court, notably under Louis XIV. Churchgoers sing hymns of Charles Wesley, composed in the eighteenth century.

In 2002, the Duke of Northumberland sold the small painting, *Madonna of the Pinks* to the Getty Museum for £35 million.

What of sport? Team games using a football were played in China around 200 BC, in Ancient Greece and Rome, and from the twelfth century in England, where the violence and lawlessness of the game then resulted in considerable injury. The greatest sports event in the world today, the Olympic Games, is derived from the ancient Greek athletic festival at Olympia.

Ancient Celtic heritage

An ancient people, the Celts spread across Europe, splitting into different tribal groups. They had been in Britain since at least the sixth century BC. First recorded around 600 BC as Ierne (Ireland) and Albion (Britain), a voyager of 325 BC called the islands 'Pretanic', which became the Roman 'Britannia'. 'The "civilized" Romans feared the 'barbarian' Celts, although fascinated by their strange customs, savage energy and tactical skill in battle. Bravery, pride, hospitality, boastfulness, unpredictability and a readiness to take offence were other Celtic attributes. They were also renowned drinkers' (Williams, 2003). At international rugby and football matches, we still witness the joyous celebrations whenever the Scots, Welsh or Irish win against 'the old enemy', the English. And, in Scotland, a famous football team is called Glasgow Celtic. But Celtic names abound most in Wales and Cornwall, though Kent is Celtic.

Celtic craftsmen, musicians and poets were highly ranked in the tribal hierarchy. They produced not only tools and weapons, decorated metalwork that constituted much of the tribe's wealth, they also enjoyed music and language, the 'weaving of words', which are traits as obvious today as in times past. Quick to absorb new ideas, they also learned farming and building skills to suit the lands they settled in. In Gaul, for example, they grew olives and planted vines to make their own wine. 'A Greek of Caesar's time, describing a Celtic tribal feast, recorded that "among them are also to be found lyric poets whom they call bards. These men sing to the accompaniment of instruments which are like lyres, and their songs may be either of praise or of obloquy". No bardic poetry was written down, but, locked in folk memory, echoes of the ancient songs passed down into the legends of Ireland and Wales' (Williams, 2003).

Celts are famous for using geometric forms to create decorative circles, spirals, whorls and ellipses. Many motifs are familiar today, such as the three-legged *triskele*, the emblem of the Isle of Man. Celtic art and intricate design can be seen in museums worldwide. The Celts loved adornments, wearing glass beads and bangles in vivid colours, and their fashions are still captured in a number of today's 'alternative' life-styles, music and folklore. Ritual and magic linked the Celts to their gods. Ritual was guarded by druids, the tribal priests. Focal to religious rites were trees and water sources that received offerings to the sacred spirit of the place. Most modern Europeans have Celts among their ancestors, but only in Britain and Ireland have Celtic peoples survived within a culture that stretches back to the dawn of European history.

The Roman legacy

The Romans left a legacy for public leisure and recreation. In the towns, public amenities for relaxation were provided either from taxation or by individuals who were expected to be generous because of the office they held. Large bathing establishments were considered essential for cleanliness and as a means of social contact where business deals could be made. Silchester and Leicester had large establishments; Bath and Wroxeter provided public swimming baths and the word 'baths' is still used by older people in common language for swimming pools.

Public entertainment was provided at the theatre, amphitheatre and the circus. Theatres in Colchester and Verulamium had a temple close by. Having a theatre and temple on the same site made it easier to celebrate festivals dedicated to certain deities. Festivals attracted fringe groups who entertained and sold food and goods to the crowds. These events would then be a mixture of a fair, pilgrimage and market. In Leisure Management today, we pride ourselves on being good event managers; the Roman events attracted thousands of people to open-air facilities who needed feeding and entertaining: an equally daunting task for the authorities then:

The Romans preferred knockabout farce to more serious dramas. All parts, even women's, were played by men. The business of keeping 5,000 people entertained would be a constant headache to the public authorities. This was one reason why the entertainments became increasingly cruel and degraded as taste became debased and the public demanded increasingly sensational experiences.

Clayton, 1980

The circus was popular in Rome. Although no evidence is found of an actual circus construction in Britain, walled enclosures could have been suitable for horseraces and horseracing could be held anywhere. The modern circus takes its name from the large arenas – round or oval race tracks surrounded by tiers of seats – with their chariot races in ancient Rome, but there is no similarity in content. Modern circus was invented chiefly around London during the late eighteenth century by skilled horsemen with gymnastic ability, techniques often learned as British army cavalrymen during the Seven Years War (1756–63) (Clayton, 1980). They turned their skills performing stunts on horseback at fairgrounds and pleasure gardens; bestriding three horses at a canter was a particular crowd favourite. To the equestrian artistry was added tumbling and clowning. However, the circus took some time to be accepted as family entertainment, given the jealousies of theatre managers and government actions to redress disorder, crime and cruelty to animals that had long attended gatherings of large, pleasure-seeking crowds.

Well-off Britons began to take on Roman customs, live like Romans and speak Latin. They became Romano-Britons. The Romans worshipped thousands of gods and spirits and the Emperor was also thought of as a god. Like the Romans, Britons, also pagan, adopted many of the Roman gods to worship. St Patrick, patron saint of Ireland, was probably born in the fourth century to a Romano-British family. Captured and taken to Ireland as a slave, he later escaped, became a priest and returned to Ireland as a missionary. St Patrick's legacy, for example, is deep-rooted in Irish culture, legend and folklore.

> The Romans left a lasting heritage, not just of roads, cities, mosaics, wall-paintings, carvings, jewellery, glassware, coins and toys, but also cultural traits.

As the Roman Empire began to lose its power and dominance, Britain increasingly came under attack from other countries. By 410 the Romans had left the country, which was then defenceless under repeated attacks from the Anglo-Saxon and Viking invaders.

The Anglo-Saxon and Viking invaders

The Angles were from Angein in northern Germany; the Saxons from central Germany; and the Jutes probably from Jutland in Denmark. The Vikings or Norsemen came mostly from Norway, Sweden and Denmark. In 793 they attacked Lindisfarne, stealing precious gold and silver and setting fire to the church. In 865 the 'Great Army' of Vikings swept across northern and eastern England. Jorvik (York) became their centre of power. Many excavations have been made in the city with finds of jewels, combs, coins and even ice skates. Today, York is a tourist destination, with Jorvik the name of a major themed attraction.

The Vikings loved eating, drinking, music and playing games; they told stories about their god, Odin, and warriors called the Valkyries. They believed that warriors who died in battle would go to live with Odin in Valhalla.

The Anglo-Saxons made beautiful jewellery, ornaments and utensils out of gold, silver and bronze, decorated with pictures of animals and birds. They were skilful potters and glassmakers. Important Saxons were buried in ships which were thought to sail off to the

The days Tuesday, Wednesday, Thursday and Friday are named after Viking gods: Thor was the god of thunder and lightning and Frigg, Odin's wife, the earth goddess.

home of their gods. In 1939, the remains of a king's ship, of about 650, were dug up at Sutton Hoo in Suffolk, full of gold cups, jewellery and armour.

The first king to call himself King of England was Offa of Mercia (757–796). He built a huge defence called Offa's Dyke along the length of the Welsh border, probably, as with Hadrian's Wall, to stop invasion. Alfred the Great became King of England in 871 at the age of 22. He gave the invading Danes 'Danegeld' to leave Britain, but to no avail. However, eventually Alfred defeated the Danes at the Battle of Edington. The Danish leader Guthrum agreed to be baptized, took the name Aethelstan, and then promised to stay in the north and east of England, where Danish roots can be traced.

Culture, rulers and nobility

In 1066, the prosperous England of Anglo-Saxons was conquered by Duke William of Normandy. The Norman Conquest introduced feudalism, with landlords holding vast estates. The mass of the population were peasants and worked on their lords' estates; as serfs, or villeins, they were thought to be incapable of owning property. Lords became rich and powerful. French language and culture was adopted at the king's court and among educated people generally. English developed into a varied collection of dialects, often unintelligible to one another. The English language and strong national identity in England did not exert itself until patriotic feelings were generated by the Hundred Years War against the French and with Henry V's victory at Agincourt in 1415 (Willoughby, 1997).

Next in rank to the king in medieval society were the barons and some earls. Prominent baronial families came from both France and England and some are still represented in the House of Lords which began in the Middle Ages as the Great Council, or Parliament of the king, which it was the right of all barons to attend. Below the barons in rank were members of the knightly class or gentry, whose representatives in the Commons were described as 'knights of the shire'.

Britain was a Catholic nation and religion and power went hand in hand. Great monasteries were built. The spectacular ruins visited by tourists today show the immense wealth and prestige of the medieval monasteries. In their time, they were the venues for colourful rituals, extravagant feasts, pageantry, religious gatherings and spectacular tournaments: contests re-enacted today in battledress, to entertain and also to enrich our understanding of the past. The romance still survives, happily without real bloodshed, and without the background of feudalism and cruelty which made serfs of the 'peasants' and provided abundant riches for the few.

Many of the houses and castles of the rich and powerful also survive from the Middle Ages, including those of bishops, barons and merchants. Depicted in many paintings, they were the venues for feasts and festivals, involving elaborate preparation by large numbers of servants. In today's world of film stars, pop stars and footballing heroes, we see on our television screens extravagant weddings, celebrations and parties. So it has been with the rich and famous for hundreds of years. The lords and ladies of the Middle Ages were also great travellers, constantly on the move, in wagons, between their own scattered estates or in the train of the monarch.

Music, entertainment and 'merrymaking' were features of the life of royal households; noblemen and the gentry employed minstrels, servants, and trumpeters, drummers and fifers for household events. The minstrels were poets, singers and story-tellers, as well as musicians. On great feast days and ceremonies, travelling performers were enlisted, including acrobats, jugglers, conjurors and tumblers. Entertainment in fancy dress was popular. Even at tournaments, the knights might dress up as characters from Arthurian legend. Chess was a game enjoyed by the nobility. Complicated chess problems were sometimes set by the minstrels and the whole household might be involved in a game, with large stakes placed on the outcome. Gambling has always been with us.

Hunting and falconry were pastimes, particularly of the rich. Falconry was regarded as a noble art. 'It was a sign of high rank to be seen with a hawk on one's wrist, even in church' (Willoughby, 1997). Stretches of primeval forest and wilderness were still the haunt of wild boar and wolves. The Norman kings subjected much of the countryside to a 'forest law' in order to protect the game and reserving the best 'sport' for themselves. The forest law made life very difficult for residents in the area. Medieval forests that still survive include the New Forest, Sherwood Forest and Epping Forest, the remnant of a great royal forest that once included the whole of Essex. The hated forest laws were often flouted, as colourfully depicted in the stories of Robin Hood, part true, part myth, first set in the reign of Edward I, not the later Richard I of film and legend (Willoughby, 1997). Deer, foxes and wild boar would generally be pursued on horseback with hounds; bows and arrows would be used. Noble ladies participated as fully as the men. Hunting was central to their lives for both food and sport. In the United Kingdom today, protests are made outside and inside Parliament for people's rights to hunt. The difference, however, is that in medieval times protests were from the peasants, hunting mainly for food.

'Manners maketh man'

The knights, although the élite, were expected to prove their worth, which is why many of them went to fight in the Crusades. Another important virtue was *courtoisie*, a grasp of manners appropriate in court circles. An ideal knight was 'immaculately turned out, graceful in his movements, and highly cultured. His was an intellectual as much as a physical calling, in which a ready wit, eloquence in speech, and even musical accomplishments were highly prized. The chivalrous knight should also take care of the poor and defenceless, and, to all comers, show open-handed largesse or generosity. It was often, if not always, the recognition of fair ladies that he sought in his quests.' (Willoughby, 1997).

The world of private and commercial leisure today is influenced by ideas from medieval times. Wealthy businesspeople are attracted to the traditions of hunting, fishing and shooting. Branding, thought of as new, is centuries old. The original Coats of Arms were part of the costume of knights; they were military insignia, a distinction of those knights in active service. Then they were used by the families of the knights, on their seals or in manuscripts as marks of identity. Later, Coats of Arms were also used by the gentry and by clerics, as well as by towns and corporations, such as the 'livery companies' and trade guilds of London. Heraldry is one of the enduring medieval inventions; and Coats of Arms (or their equivalents) are used throughout the world as symbols of family and corporate identity.

The Tudors and Stuarts

National culture is invariably associated with its rulers. The Tudors were the ruling dynasty of England from 1485 to 1603. The name originates from Owen Tudor, a Welshman in the service of Henry V who married his widow, Catherine of Valois. The Stuarts, who originated in Brittany, were the ruling dynasty of Scotland from 1371 to 1714 and of England from 1603 to 1714. During the reign of the Tudors, substantial country houses began to be built, right up to the Edwardian era and First World War. They were to become the stately homes, many of which are now tourist destinations. These were the times of gifted painters and sculptors, master craftsmen, carvers, furniture makers and decorators, outstanding contributors including Thomas Chippendale, William Morris and Edwin Lutyens and by creative artists like Sir Christopher Wren, John Constable and Lancelot 'Capability' Brown (Brimacombe, 2003). Centuries after their time, they are remembered: Wren for architecture, particularly St Paul's Cathedral, the first building in England with a dome; East Anglia is referred to as 'Constable country'; and the French admirers of Brown's landscaped parks call them *le jardin anglais*.

> The Tudor monarchs were Henry VII, Henry VIII, Edward VI, Mary I and Elizabeth I.

Henry VIII, Elizabeth I, Charles I and Charles II had a significant impact. Henry had grand palaces and brought Hans Holbein to England; Charles I introduced Anthony Van Dyck. These painters greatly influenced English portrait painting. Charles II appointed Wren as his Surveyor General.

Despite his Dissolution of the Monasteries, and the break with Rome which may have delayed the arrival of the Renaissance in Britain, Henry VIII had a major influence on culture and style. Great houses such as Burghley, Hatfield, Longleat (the site today of a Center Parc) and Woburn (the home of a visitor safari park) were built and Tudor and Jacobean furnishing and interior design flourished in stately houses (Brimacombe, 2003).

Elizabeth I reigned for nearly 45 years between 1558 and 1603. In the UK in 2003, she was voted as one of the top ten 'Greatest Britons', remembered as the Virgin Queen who repelled the Spanish Armada in 1588 and presided over a 'Golden Age' of English culture. Elizabethan England, firmly Protestant, became home to artists fleeing religious persecution.

Tudors played games such as 'hoodman blind', club kayles (skittles), real or royal tennis, board games, dominoes, dice, chess and cards. Their sports included archery, bowls, football and wrestling, their entertainment watching bear-baiting and cock-fighting; they also enjoyed music and dancing. Wealthy families played instruments such as the virginals (a small harpsichord) and the lute, and sang madrigals, Elizabethan songs still sung today. Folk dance, including maypole, 'ring' dancing and sword dancing were popular and court dances – the galliard, pavan and courante – were developed from folk dances and performed by the nobility. The well-to-do Tudors dressed in embroidered brocades and velvets, decorated with jewels and gold thread. Drama and poetry flourished; religious plays gave way to popular plays and poetry.

> Marcus Gheeraerts introduced painting on canvas and became a leading portrait painter. His classic *Rainbow Portrait of Elizabeth* hangs in Hatfield House.

The art-loving aristocracy indulged in the Grand Tour, described as:

... an intellectual odyssey around the cultural sites of Europe – Paris, then Florence, Venice, Naples and, most particularly, Rome. Sometimes they took with them aspiring architects – the young Inigo Jones, for example, discovered Palladianism courtesy of the Earl of Arundel, while both William Kent and Robert Adam were taken to Italy by wealthy aristocrats ...Upon their return, the enlightened nobility wished to recreate their classical experiences at home, employing the best English and Continental stylists.

Brimacombe, 2003

Religion and cultural heritage

Religions and their traditions play a large part in the formation of a nation's culture, whether or not people are adherents. For those who are, attendance for worship and activities can take up a considerable amount of 'free' time, indeed, it can be viewed as 'leisure'.

Christianity came to Britain at the time of the Roman invasion. For the first few hundred years of its life, Christianity shared its history with the Continental Church. Pope Gregory the Great sent St Augustine in around 604 to convert the English. About a hundred years later, the gospel ('good news') was proclaimed in Ireland by St Patrick. In the sixth century, Christianity was re-established in Scotland with St Columba, who founded the island monastery of Iona. St Aidan (651) went from Iona to establish a monastery on Lindisfarne, also known as Holy Island. The 'Golden Age' of Northumbria ended with the sacking of Lindisfarne in 793 and in 875 by the Vikings of Scandinavia, probably the last pagans of old Europe.

It was during the reign of Alfred the Great (849–99) that the foundations of a nation were built on the Christian faith. Alfred's work came to fruition in St Dunstan, Abbot of Glastonbury, who was later to be made Archbishop of Canterbury. The last Anglo-Saxon king of England was Edward the Confessor (1003–66), who had the Abbey at Westminster built. The Anglo-Saxon era ended when Duke William conquered England.

Norman barons used English stonemasons to build castles, cathedrals, parish churches and monasteries. By 1150, there were around 500 monasteries, a large number in the north of England (Proud, 2001). Part of a feudal society, these monastic foundations grew rich on tithes and on the acquisition of land. Wherever the Normans settled, they imposed a system of land distribution (fiefs); feudalism divided society into lords and vassals and introduced the notions of 'free' and 'unfree'.

The scriptures were in Latin, unfamiliar to the mass of the population. Translators of the Bible into English, for all to read – particularly John Wycliffe (c. 1330–84) – were branded heretics and risked trial and imprisonment. A century later, William Tyndale (c. 1494–1536) and Miles Coverdale followed Wycliffe with a translation into English.

In 1534, Henry VIII established himself as the head of the Anglican Church. The reformed Church flourished during the brief reign of Henry's heir Edward VI, but Mary I (1516–58) restored the Church of Rome, putting to death the Reformers who were caught, earning her nickname 'Bloody Mary'. However, Mary's sister, Elizabeth, revived the Anglican Church. By the Elizabethan Act of Supremacy and Act of Uniformity, the Church of England was established.

After the warring of Catholic and Protestant monarchs, James I brought comparative peace. A new translation of the Bible, known as the Authorized Version or King James Bible, had a lasting effect on English language and culture.

Between 1828 and 1832, laws were passed sweeping away restrictions imposed on Roman Catholics in the Catholic Emancipation Act of 1829.

The Industrial Revolution witnessed poverty, disease, child labour and factory-working, in appalling conditions. Masses of people were forced from the land into towns by land enclosures and agricultural reforms. In response to these social conditions, philanthropic organizations, friendly societies and workers' clubs were established. Funds were raised from the wealthy and distributed to worthy causes. Many of our voluntary and charitable organizations today stem from these times. Hannah More (1725–1833), a Quaker, started schools when education for working people was almost unheard of. She was helped by people like John Newton and William Wilberforce, most associated with the Slavery Abolition Act.

So what of today and the relevance of religious history? Clearly, a great deal has been done to counter hardship and poverty. Mistrust and strife continues, however, between different branches of the Christian Church and between followers of different faiths. Some terrorism is founded on religious bigotry and feuding which was started centuries ago. In Northern Ireland, religious and political differences meant that facilities such as leisure centres, were developed separately according to the religious divide, thereby duplicating costly provision. However, there are many examples of such facilities being carefully managed to bring communities together through sport and recreation. In other parts of the United Kingdom, the cultural divide still surfaces. The football clash in Scotland between Glasgow Celtic and Glasgow Rangers reflects a cultural rivalry with overtones of religious conflict. Within the context of leisure, opportunities can be opened up for people from divided communities to work together and have fun together. This is seen in sport participation, where people are equals, playing to the same rules, on a 'level playing field', or where mountain climbers rely on others for their safety, or in the fashion and pop culture of young people. Leisure management has much more to offer than managing services and facilities.

One positive legacy for people's leisure comes from many religions' holy days: Christianity's Christmas and Easter, the Jewish Passover, the Hindu festival Divali, and the Muslim Eid, marking the end of the fast of Ramadan.

Holy days, culture and leisure

Holidays, by definition, are non-working times, an extended period of anticipated recreation, especially away from home; they can also be days of festivity when no work is done. The problem, and opportunity, for the leisure profession, is that when other people are on holiday or at leisure, leisure staff are working; unsocial hours are a feature of work in the leisure industry.

'Holy' has the same roots as 'whole' and 'wholeness'.

Holidays are a chance of getting away from it all, re-charging the batteries and for some a change of gear or even a change of lifestyle. There is a huge industry surrounding the desire of holidaymakers to buy property abroad and to move there to live.

Salley Vickers, in *Mr Golightly's Holiday* (Vickers, 2003) sees signs that the holiday – the 'spiritual odyssey' – is returning for some, at least, to its original meaning:

Spiritual retreats, often in a place of particular natural beauty, are becoming more popular. Monasteries across Europe are opening their doors to seekers of silence and Gregorian chants, which are not found in holiday resorts.

Vickers suggests that the reason for the rise in 'holy' holidays is the recognition that happiness and hedonism are not synonymous. In other words, pleasure-seeking in itself does not bring lasting happiness.

Art, music and literature and cultural heritage

Cultural history is recorded in many ways. Painting and other arts such as sculpture were in the earliest centuries not perceived as leisure pursuits, but as means to a practical end, or else they were commissioned by the wealthy for their prestige. Formal artistic cultural heritage draws upon a range of styles such as Gothic, Baroque, Georgian and Regency.

The Gothic movement, from around 1150 to 1500, is the architectural style of the great cathedrals of Europe with their elaborate altarpieces, paintings and sculptures. Gothic also pertains to a literary style and survives to this day in a style of print and handwriting. The Gothic cathedral St Paul's was destroyed in the Great Fire of London in 1666, and was re-built by Sir Christopher Wren.

The Baroque style of art, music and architecture from about 1550 continued throughout Europe until the eighteenth century. It was typified by elaborate and ornate scrolls and curves. The name stems from the Italian *barocco*, meaning bizarre, after the founder of the style, Federigo Barocci. Religious paintings would show, for example, the Madonna or the saints, fleecy clouds and cherubs. Ancient mythology was also popular.

Georgian style architecture was prevalent during the reigns of George I to George IV (1714–1830). Of several different influences, it was dominated by Palladianism, an architectural style developed in the sixteenth century by Palladio and based on classical Roman public architecture: well proportioned, elegant, symmetrical. It was first introduced into Britain by Inigo Jones. The Georgian period was also the time of Gainsborough, the Royal Crescent in Bath, Hepplewhite and Chippendale, elevating English furniture design, and Capability Brown's landscaped parks.

Architect Robert Adam employed more than 2,000 craftsmen: joiners, cabinet makers, upholsterers, carpet weavers and a variety of tradesmen, artists still appreciated today internationally.

The highly decorative Regency style with heavy furniture, exotic woods and veneers such as rosewood, was fashionable for a relatively short period, 1800 to 1830, and influenced by French Empire style. The Regency era is epitomized by the architect John Nash and landscape painters Joseph Turner and John Constable. Despite a troubled life, Nash created one of the most talked-about buildings – the Brighton Pavilion – and rebuilt much of central London. The careers of Turner and Constable ran in tandem. Constable, best known for paintings such as *Flatford Mill*, gave the world a perception of the English countryside. In contrast, Turner's impressionistic style, like the dramatic *Snowstorm*, took time to be accepted and survived with the support of art critic, John Ruskin.

English Romanticism is usually dated from the publication of *Lyrical Ballards* by Wordsworth and Coleridge in 1798 and is associated with the poetry of Keats, Shelley and Byron and the novels of Walter Scott. In Germany, Goethe and Schiller were renowned, and in France, inspired by Rousseau, were writers such as Chateaubriand and Victor Hugo.

The Arts and Crafts movement derived from William Morris and his Pre-Raphaelite associates. The movement revived the principles of medieval craftsmanship and promoted the ideal of the artist as craftsman-designer. This movement had an influence on the emerging Art Nouveau style. In due course emerged the style called Art Deco in the 1920s and 1930s following the 1925 Exposition Internationale des Arts Décoratifs et Industriels Modernes in Paris. William Morris (1834–96) was a poet, artist, craftsman, design genius and 'utopian' socialist. His work included painting, distinctive tapestry, stained glass, hand-painted tiles and wallpaper.

> Raphael (1483–1520) was an Italian Renaissance painter and architect. Artists before him painted subjects of a moral or religious character.

In terms of art today as a means of, and for, leisure, not only do we have galleries, museums, theatres, libraries and exhibitions, we also have Public Art, Street Art and Environmental Art to enhance our quality of living. The relevance of these art forms and facilities for Leisure Managers is that they have to be planned, designed, paid for and managed, taking into account the aims of the providers and perceptions of the public.

Works of art and crafts are also brought to the notice of the public via the television; antiques fairs and road shows have become popular. Most Leisure Managers in the United Kingdom will include antiques fairs and craft sales in their programmes, and sports halls have been put to 'arts' use for three good reasons:

- increasing demand
- added revenue and
- drawing in a wider market of leisure participants.

A heritage of great musicians

Music in all its forms is a huge part of the entertainment and leisure industry and contributes greatly to the economy. The pleasure of making music is part of our culture, past and present. What of our musical heritage, though? Much of the everyday music of the past centuries is not known generally, though specialist groups still sing and play, and period dramas on the television and in films are accompanied by appropriate music of the time. The popular music of Victorian times, however, such as the light operas of Gilbert and Sullivan, is well known and traditional hymns are sung in churches and some schools. Popular songs of the World War period, redolent of national pride and determination, are part of the culture of today's older generation.

Much of Britain's classical traditions, however, derive from Continental Europe, particularly from Germany. Ever-popular for classical music lovers are the works of Bach, Beethoven, and Mozart, among many others.

Johann Sebastian Bach (1685–1750), in his lifetime, achieved greater recognition as an organist than as a composer. Ludwig van Beethoven (1770–1827) won a considerable following for his piano playing and compositions in Vienna. At the age of 30, he began to go deaf, an experience that increased his loneliness and eccentricity, but this did not stop his prolific composing and indeed, about 600 of Beethoven's works survive.

Wolfgang Amadeus Mozart (1756–91) showed extraordinary musical talent at the age of four, and toured in Germany, Paris and London. In the last years of his life, Mozart achieved some of his finest works including operas *Cosi fan tutte* and *The Magic Flute*.

Britain's musical heritage is, of course, built on a great deal more than classical traditions. Popular ballads, folk music and rhymes have been handed down. Today's popular music is built on traditions from the music halls, brass bands, big bands, jazz, folk music, rock and roll, and pop music.

A heritage of language, writers and poets

Nowhere is culture demonstrated more than in the language spoken by its people. In Norman England, only those who spoke Latin or Norman French were awarded state office. But after the devastation of the Black Death in 1348–49 in Europe, English poetry was being written, and at Agincourt, Henry V roused his troops in English. Much literature stems from translations of the Bible into English. Another is the legacy of William Shakespeare.

Shakespeare, the greatest English dramatist, has been revered for hundreds of years. No other single person has made such a significant contribution to the English language. His plays are to this day enormously popular and the re-construction of the famous Globe Theatre is one of the most important cultural venues and tourist attractions in London.

Jane Austen (1775–1817), the daughter of a clergyman, settled in Chawton in Hampshire in 1809. Her six major novels were published between 1811 and 1818. Their heroines are drawn from the rural landed gentry and her novels are distinguished by her insight into the development of relationships and personal and social tensions. Much of her work has been dramatized for film and television.

Three British novelists, the sisters Charlotte, Emily and Anne Brontë, provided some of the best-known 'period' novels. Daughters of the rector of Haworth, an isolated village in Yorkshire, their popularity has made 'Brontë country' a busy tourist destination.

Charles Dickens (1812–70), was the son of a naval clerk. He worked in a factory when his father was imprisoned for debt and later as a solicitor's clerk and court reporter. He achieved immediate fame with his first book, *The Pickwick Papers* in 1837. His novels depict the destructive power of money, greed and ambition and showed his radical views on society. His legacy to culture is immense, in Britain and other parts of the world.

As well as authors, Britain has produced great poets and it is the poets of times past that are most known today. Robert (Robbie) Burns (1759–96) was a Scottish poet, son of a poor farmer in Ayrshire. His poems range from sentimental love lyrics to broad humour. Burns' Night is celebrated all over the world, re-affirming nationhood and Scottish culture. William Wordsworth (1770–1850) was a British poet: an enthusiastic republican, and one of the founders of socialism. Wordsworth settled in the Lake District and his poems described his feelings of mystical union with nature. His masterpiece is said to be *The Prelude*, but he is more fondly remembered for his poem 'Daffodils'. Samuel Coleridge (1772–1834) is well known for his poems 'Kubla Khan' and *The Rime of the Ancient Mariner*. In Britain today, poetry is a minority interest, but the national position of Poet Laureate still exists, with the poet being obliged to write for special state and royal occasions.

A good deal of people's leisure time, however, is spent on reading novels for pleasure. Holiday reading, for example, is big business. The Booker Prize and other awards are annual landmarks, like the Academy Awards for films. Biographies of celebrities from the worlds of sport, entertainment and politics are popular, and bestsellers are often from the genre of children's fiction. World record levels of sales were made by J.K. Rowling's Harry Potter books.

> The most popular novelists include Maeve Binchy, Catherine Cookson, Sebastian Faulks, Ken Follet, John Grisham, James Patterson and Ruth Rendell, many of whom are household names.

Characters in children's fiction remain bedded in our culture in rhymes, songs, poems, comics and books. Their fascination, even when we are haunted with them, stays with us, and some children's books are avidly read by adults.

Communication in writing has changed dramatically with technological advances. First there was the printing press, then typing, speeded up with the invention of the computer and word processing. Then followed emailing for quicker sending and receiving of messages and now the versatile mobile phone enabling voice communication on the move. Text-messaging, with pictures, brings instant communication in 'writing': and maybe a new cultural form of literature?

Legacies of the Victorian Age

The strongest influence of history, in terms of mass leisure and popular culture, in the United Kingdom and in many parts of the world, comes from the Victorian heritage.

Queen Victoria, crowned when she was only 20, reigned from 1837 to 1901. Her sense of duty and strict moral code came to symbolize the ethos of the middle and late nineteenth century: the Victorian Age. Prime Minister Disraeli made her Empress of India in 1876 and this was the 'jewel in her crown'. Victoria married her cousin Prince Albert, who was active in his patronage of the arts and is remembered for his organization of the Great Exhibition in 1851. That event inspired and influenced other great national exhibitions, such as the 1951 Festival of Britain which, coming after the Second World War, looked forward to economic, social and cultural prosperity, in which leisure, sports and arts would play important roles.

> By 1901 the British Empire covered a quarter of the world's surface, including Canada, India, Australia, New Zealand, large areas of Africa, parts of the Far East and Guyana in South America.

The English of Victorian times reinforced the class structure: the 'upper class' of the aristocrats and landed gentry, living in country estates, the 'middle class' of bankers, mill owners and lawyers, living in detached villas and large terraced houses, and the 'lower class', typified by labourers, mine workers and mill workers. It was the lower classes who lived in filthy overcrowded slums and worked in nearby mills and factories during the Industrial Revolution. Charles Dickens' novels exposed the dreadful working and living conditions of the poor.

In 1842, the Miners Act outlawed employment in the mines of all women and girls and all boys under the age of ten. In the mills, women and children were employed to look after machines because they were cheaper than men to employ. Moreover, children were small enough to crawl under machines and clean them. In 1864, the Climbing Boys Act banned using boys under the age of ten for cleaning chimneys.

The Education Act, 1870, made it compulsory that every child have a school place, and Board Schools must be built in areas where there were not enough education places. 12,000 churches were built during the Victorian era and most people except the very poor attended church at least once on Sundays. In rural areas, the church was the centre of local life.

Invention and mass production

At the beginning of Queen Victoria's reign, most travel was by horse-drawn coach. Heavy goods went by canal. This era then witnessed the growth of the railway system designed by engineers Thomas Telford, Robert Stephenson and Isambard Brunel. Brunel was a formidable engineer whose work included the Great Western Railway, viaducts, tunnels, stations and bridges. In 1845, the *Great Britain*, built by Brunel, was the first propeller-driven ship to cross the Atlantic.

Brunel's Royal Albert Bridge transports Great Western Railway trains across the River Tamar from Devon into Cornwall; a major attraction is Brunel's suspension bridge over the Avon Gorge.

In 1840, Sir Rowland Hill invented the Penny Black postage stamp and launched the Penny Post. Florence Nightingale founded a nursing school in London in 1860 thereby pioneering the age of modern nursing.

The Victorian age saw the mass production of goods in vast quantities from mills and factories. Yet it also witnessed the Gothic Revival, with the formation of the Pre-Raphaelite Brotherhood and the Arts and Crafts Movement rejecting mass production in favour of hand-crafted work such as furniture, household goods, ornaments and even toys. Some toys of the Victorian era are now selling for large sums of money at toy auctions.

During the Victorian period, great buildings were designed, such as the new Houses of Parliament, the Albert Hall and the Albert Memorial. Symbolizing the Victorian era are works linked to the queen herself: Osborne House, her home on the Isle of Wight, and the Royal Mausoleum at Frogmore, where Queen Victoria is buried alongside Prince Albert.

The Great Exhibition and beyond

Prince Albert was the patron, but Henry Cole (1808–82) was the genius behind the 1851 'Great Exhibition of the Industry of All Nations' and the complex of museums and universities at South Kensington in London (Bonython and Burton, 2003).

The Great Exhibition of 1851 was held over 140 days; six million people came and Queen Victoria visited 30 times. The Exhibition was housed in Joseph Paxton's huge glasshouse in Kensington Gardens. Cole's controversial conviction was that the design of ordinary things is at least as important as 'fine art'. He later developed the Science Museum and the Victoria & Albert Museum which were separated in the early twentieth century to accommodate 'things that worked' and 'things that did not'. The Exhibition was seen as a symbol of national identity, industry and creativity and was adopted by other countries.

In 1893, the Columbian Exhibition put Chicago on the international map; the giant Ferris wheel made its first appearance there.

Exhibitions, especially those of national importance, leave a legacy for leisure and culture:

- In Britain, the 1851 Exhibition led to the Science and Victoria & Albert Museums, two great tourist and educational attractions.

35

- The British Empire Exhibition of 1924 left the Wembley stadium.
- The Paris Expo of 1925 produced Art Deco.
- The Columbian Exhibition in Chicago led indirectly to the vast Disney theme parks: Walt Disney's father had worked at the Columbian Exhibition of 1893.

Historical beginnings of the tourism and leisure industry

All the inventions which involve transport contribute to cultural heritage and leisure. The horse and cart, horse-drawn carriages, barges, boats, yachts, and ships, trains, balloons, planes and helicopters, bicycles, cars and buses – all roads, rail, canals, seas and the air – all these have in themselves enabled us to enjoy leisure and sport, and helped us to travel to leisure facilities and destinations, thereby creating the massive domestic and international tourism industry. Travel by land and sea developed alongside human ingenuity, but travelling in the sky was an invention beyond the comprehension of most people and continues to baffle most.

Ptolemy, a second-century Egyptian mathematician, astronomer and geographer, was probably the first person to conceive of mapping the planets and the world, though the sun and planets were thought to move around the earth.

The tourism and leisure industry owes much to the invention of maps and atlases. Travel into the unknown, even from town to town, let alone across countries, would be exceedingly difficult without them. When Gerard Mercator was born in 1512, the geography of the globe was little known, though attempts to map the world had been tried many centuries before. He was also the first person to conceive of mapping the entire surface of the planet and also present multiple maps in a book: the atlases we are all familiar with today.

In the Victorian and Edwardian era, travel was no longer an exclusive prerogative of the rich and upper classes. With better roads, railways and sea ferries, travel became more widespread. Mass travel could be said to be a major legacy of the age; with this increase in travel, the travel guidebook became another Victorian invention. In particular, two authors cornered the market of the more discerning travellers, John Murray and Karl Baedeker (Palmowski, 2002). Early guidebooks focused on travel to Switzerland.

Mass travel and leisure

The Industrial Revolution made it possible for more people to participate in leisure time pursuits and to travel. Engineering and innovation brought about industrial change; it also ushered in a new age of leisure and pleasure. Victorian inventions included the weekend, the seaside holiday, popular sports and a revolution in entertainment. For the first time, for the masses, there was free time and spare cash. Before the Victorian era, most people worked seven days a week on the land. Booming industry attracted people to the cities. They worked long hours and earned 'real cash', instead of being paid in products from the land. The Lancashire cotton mills closed on Sundays to clean the machinery. Leisure time, in addition to holy days and church attendance, had arrived. Indeed, in Britain, the shape of leisure was dramatically changed with the advent of the half-day closing on Saturdays.

After Saturday half-day closing came in, more people than ever before or since went to English Football League matches; cinema attendances were also at their highest.

The coming of the railways ushered more change. By 1841, business people could travel from London to Bristol and back on the same day. The railways

In 1841, Thomas Cook took 570 people from Leicester to Loughborough for a temperance picnic, which is believed to the first 'package trip'.

then took people to seasides like Blackpool, which has since become the most visited seaside resort in Europe.

The British seasides, generally, are now in decline: Blackpool being one of the exceptions. For a hundred years or so, they were the holiday magnets – a popular culture of their day. They were the butt of comedians' jokes, especially about landladies, yet fondly remembered for 'bracing fresh air', 'walking over the water along the pier', 'kiss-me-quick' hats, buying 'penny licks', penny slot machines and saucy postcards.

Many Leisure Managers today are involved in creating new images, services and facilities in coastal towns, to win back domestic tourists and compete with the modern brands of 'sand, sea, and sangria' of Mediterranean resorts and America's theme parks.

Many sports played today in the UK and worldwide owe their origin or their rules to the Victorian era. Before then, for example, there was 'mob football', with no rules. But the railways enabled the sport to be played against teams in other cities. Rules were needed to ensure that they were playing the same game. The rules came in the 1850s following the first Football Association meeting in a London pub.

Health resorts and spas

Spas, steam rooms and saunas are part of modern health and leisure centres in both the private and public sector. 'Spa' is an acronym for the Latin *sanitas per aqua* (health through water). One of the most famous in England is the Bath spa. The spa tradition, however, is much stronger in Continental Europe, particularly in Germany and France with great spas such as in Baden-Baden, Carlsbad, Evian and Eugenie-les-Bains, with an emphasis on health as well as on relaxation, beauty and luxury.

With the spread of Christianity, springs revered by pagans for their healing qualities were renamed after saints, something not approved of after the Reformation. Eliza-

The best spas had 'masters of ceremony': the most famous was Bath's Beau Nash, whose rules of proper conduct and behaviour became legendary and were followed by others.

beth I revived the idea of the spa, but as a secular activity. Spa towns became England's first 'resorts' and places where the ambitious up-and-coming people of the eighteenth century could mix with the wealthy for contacts, business and to learn how to behave 'in society'. The spa towns bustled with inns, milliners, shoemakers, but also with petty thieves and prostitutes.

With the arrival of rail travel in the nineteenth century, the grand spas of Europe were within reach of the 'upper class'; English spas remained for the 'middle class'. However, the spas could not compete with the new-found leisure craze of 'the seaside'. Today, our sport and leisure centres are increasingly being linked with medical and health provision. In 1948, the British Spa Federation persuaded Aneurin Bevan to make eight of the great spas part of the new National Health Service, but they died of underfunding.

A culture of playing games

Johan Huizinga in *Homo Ludens* ('man the player') believed that 'genuine pure play is one of the main bases of civilization' (see Chapter 5). In *Games of the World*, written for UNICEF (Grunfeld, 1982), the editors provide documentary and pictorial evidence that seems to bear Huizinga out. They focus on traditional games that have stood the test of time, 'games that reflect the accumulated wisdom and ingenuity of mankind'.

They take as their starting point the writings of the King of Castile, Alfonso X, who compiled the first *Book of Games* in 1283, some 700 years ago.

The origins of games make fascinating reading. In the British Museum is a solid stone game board and rudimentary chequers from the Egypt of 1320–1085 BC. On display is archeological evidence of a number of elaborately inlaid game boards among the treasures of Ur in Ancient Sumeria. The 'royal game' of Ur was played with two sets of seven counters, black and white; the 'men' found with this board were either of shell with lapis lazuli dots or black shale with shell dots.

> In this, as in other areas, the Sumerians made vital beginnings that have had significant consequences. It was they who invented cuneiform writing, and their method of keeping time – 24 hours, 60 minutes – is with us yet. Dividing a circle into 360 degrees was also a Sumerian invention.
>
> Grunfeld, 1982, p. 57

By far the most popular and important of many board games of ancient Egypt was *senet*, played by all levels of society, evidenced by diagrams scratched into tombs and temples by priests and builders. The pharaohs played on magnificent boards made of rare woods and ivory, by master craftsmen, such as one board found in the tomb of Tutankhamen. Egyptian religious writings mention games of *senet*, played by the spirits of the departed in the underworld. Morris is the name of another board game mentioned in Alfonso's *Book of Games* and also in the Talmud, in Shakespeare's *A Midsummer Night's Dream* and in medieval writings of France, Germany and Britain. Chess, King Alfonso's personal passion, had been developed in India centuries earlier; its elephants, maharajas and chariots replaced by castles, kings and bishops. Backgammon, one of the entertainments of the thirteenth-century nobility, evolved from the Roman game *tabula*.

According to Grunfeld, the 'games-impulse' is a universal one that has not known cultural or language boundaries:

> Just as the ancient and primitive religions of the world show profound similarities in their fertility rites and their sun and moon worship, many games appear to be common property to human beings everywhere. Indeed, the comparison is not at all farfetched; many games now thought to be mere children's pastimes are, in fact, relics of religious rituals, often dating back to the dawn of mankind. Tug of war, for example, is a dramatized struggle between natural forces; knucklebones were once part of the fortune-teller's equipment; even hopscotch was related to ancient myths about labyrinths and mazes, later adapted to represent the Christian soul's journey from earth to heaven ... Casting lots, such as dice or knucklebones, gave human beings an opportunity to consult the gods in making difficult decisions, while the results of games played by champions were interpreted by priests and others skilled in reading the future.
>
> Grunfeld, 1982, p. 57

Certain games originated as training for the young or for acquiring skills such as races, darts and hoops, and chess was used as an imaginative reconstruction of a battlefield. Some primitive games are known across the world, with variations which tell us about the particular cultures. Cat's cradle is known in Asia, Africa, Europe and the United States.

The Eskimos have several favourite games; one of them is cat's cradle. The player narrates a story at each stage, and in this fashion, the legends of the Innuit (Eskimo) have been handed down unaltered from generation to generation. The individual string figures are a way of helping the storyteller remember his tales – a mnemonic device. The figures represent birds, kayaks, sledges, bears, foxes, and other features of Arctic life. Farther south, the Navaho Indians of the south-western United States make string figures representing tents, coyotes, rabbits, and constellations of stars. In New Guinea, they symbolise spears, drums, palm trees, fishes, and crabs. Each people has its own figures, taken from its own environment. Each has its own set of values and traditions associated with the game. Some Eskimos believe in a 'spirit of cat's cradle', and over indulgence in the game may put a player in the spirit's power. Hence, moderation in all things!

Grunfeld, 1982, p. 57

Some of the games embedded in British culture are shuttlecock, spinning tops, hopscotch and conkers and some of these games have been played all over the world for centuries.

Shuttlecock is a game with a small feather ball or disc which is kicked from player to player, and has been played in China, Japan and Korea for 2,000 years. A version of the game is played with decorative wooden paddles called battledores. Drawings from classical Greece show a version of the game, which was also part of new year celebrations in Tudor England. Today, versions of the game are played in back gardens and on beaches at the seaside. Spinning tops is universal. The old Roman game was called *turbo* (Latin for 'top'). Yo-yo is believed to have originated in ancient China and is pictured on classical Greek pottery. Hopscotch is not Scottish, but from Old English, meaning to mark or score lightly; it was played in Russia, India and China and possibly the oldest evidence is the game inscribed into the floor of the Forum in Rome.

Conkers appears to be a very British game. 'Conkers' is a corruption of 'conquerors'. String is threaded through a hole in the horse chestnut conker and contests are held between two conker players; the object is to win the fight by breaking the opponent's conker. Popular belief is that the best – the hardest – are to be found at the top of horse chestnut trees. Sticks and stones are pitched at the highest branches to dislodge the chestnuts. Various recipes exist for preparing a proper conker: baking, soaking in vinegar; and there is a language of 'conkering', with the yell of 'strings' when they are tangled.

Culture, sport and the Olympic movement

The ethos and values enshrined in the 'Corinthian spirit' and the Olympic movement have stood the test of time and have had a significant influence on our culture for fair play, sportsmanship and international relationships, despite fierce competition.

Since their renaissance in 1896, the Olympic Games have become the greatest sporting event in the world. In Ancient Greece, a peace was declared during the long period of the Games. The modern Olympic Games have also survived two world wars. The 2000 Games were held in Sydney, Australia, and attracted 10,200 athletes from 200 countries who competed in 28 sports, performing in around 300 events. The event enhanced, greatly, the reputation of the city and Australia. The 2004 Olympic Games in Athens was equally spectacular.

On the 6 April, 1896 at Athens, King George I of Greece opened the first Olympic Games of modern times; the second was held in Paris in 1900.

The Olympics have had long-lasting effects on the host nations: social, economic and cultural. Barcelona in 1992 helped to regenerate the city and attract many more people to the city and to Spain long after the event. In terms of the economy, Montreal in 1976 suffered huge losses, while in Los Angeles, possibly for the first time, the Games were financially profitable as they were later in Atlanta in 1996. Munich in 1972 suffered from a devastating terrorist attack. Moscow in 1980 was boycotted by some nations. Seoul in South Korea overcame the potential problems of a divided country. Hence, despite wars, tragedies, political and economic difficulties, the Olympic Games have survived and prospered.

International showcase sport produces personalities who can enrich culture and enliven our leisure, whether that is active or passive, in the form of spectating, television viewing, radio listening or reading the newspapers. Sport also provides a ready topic of conversation and communication between its followers. However, sport can also make for social divisions and is sometimes seen as a cauldron for spectator violence. A popular perception is that some international sport is a substitute for conflict and war.

World stars from other parts of the world are also revered. New champions come and go, yet sports are often associated with the past; our sports heritage is made up of instantly-recognized names.

Culture, pastimes, customs and traditions

Case Study: the Olympic Games

The Games have also been a great cultural festival and commemoration of nationhood, though Berlin in 1936 could have been a stain on the movement, with Hitler's twisted belief in 'Aryan supremacy'. However, the black athlete, Jesse Owens, confirmed that he was the fastest man in the world and won four gold medals. Hitler refused to congratulate him. In America, it was forty years after his triumph that Owens was awarded the Presidential Medal of Freedom in 1976. Symbolism is powerful.

Muhammad Ali had come to our attention as Cassius Clay winning the Olympic heavyweight boxing gold medal, later to become the world champion. In 1996, despite his suffering from Parkinson's disease, Atlanta chose Muhammad Ali to light the Olympic flame. In Sydney, Cathy Freeman of aboriginal origin, lit the flame and also met the highest expectations put upon her by the Australians by winning the 400 metres in record time. These moments are some of the most powerful symbols of our time in uniting people through the medium of sport.

After language, the customs and traditions of a nation, district or town give strong indications of their cultural identity. The customs and traditions of Britain range from great state occasions to annual village fêtes. These traditions have associations with rites of passage, the turning of the seasons, traditional holidays and celebrations to mark events, real or imagined, built up on legends and myths of the past like spirits of the woodlands. We still tell stories of elves, goblins, and fairies, of giants depicted in chalk at Cerne Abbas in Dorset and Wilmington in Sussex, water monsters and mermaids, dragons, witches and wizards. Customs that have lasted and which are celebrated regularly give an insight into the cultural history of a country.

The English monarchy dates back a thousand years and with it rituals of pageantry, patronage, state and government. One of the most famous of these is the Trooping of the Colour at Horse Guards Parade, London, which has celebrated the sovereign's official birthday since 1805. Another ceremony occurs before every state opening of parliament, when the yeomen of the guard, in their scarlet and gold uniforms, assemble in the Prince's Chamber of the House of Lords and then search the cellars beneath the Palace of Westminster, a routine that survives despite the fact that the building is heavily policed night and day.

Other traditions are the Changing of the Guard, the Ceremony of the Keys at the Tower of London, Swan-Upping and the Royal Maundy, when purses of money are distributed (Kightly, 1986).

Bonfires are very much part of the country's celebrations of past events. Since 1605, when Parliament declared 5 November a public holiday to celebrate the foiling of the Gunpowder Plot, the burning of effigies of Guy Fawkes has become widespread, particularly in England.

Thought to be the oldest civic custom in Britain, the nightly sounding of the City Horn at Ripon probably dates from Anglo-Saxon times. Until the first mayor was elected in 1604, law and order and protection of citizens was the responsibility of the wakeman. Today the horn is sounded every night from 9 o'clock four times in the market square and once outside the Mayor's house.

Closer to leisure time activities and the work of Leisure Managers are the local customs at holiday times: festivals, fairs, fêtes and flower shows. The now world-famous, colourful Notting Hill Carnival is a major event requiring full time organization and many hundreds of volunteers.

May Day celebrations have their origins in the Roman festival of Flora, goddess of flowers, which marked the beginning of summer. People would decorate their houses in the belief that the vegetation spirits would bring good fortune. The original maypoles were freshly felled trees, stripped of branches and adorned with garlands and ribbons. The Puritans tried unsuccessfully to stamp out this pagan custom. The crowning of a May Queen and ribbon-plaiting dances were not introduced until Victorian times. May Day in Oxford is brought in at sunrise by the choristers of Magdalen College singing hymns and May carols from the top of Magdalen Tower.

In the 1300s, Edward III banned the game of quoits, possibly developed from the Greek sport of discus throwing, in favour of archery, though quoits is still played today in many forms.

Wishing wells and well-dressing can be found in the villages of the Derbyshire Peak District, an area rich in wells and springs. This pagan custom of adorning wells with flowers and greenery was absorbed into the early Church, giving thanks rather than appeasing any water spirit.

Morris Dances, of obscure origins, are ritual dances traditionally only performed by men, though today there are male, female and mixed 'morris sides'. The most well-known morris events are held in the Cotswolds, Borders and the North-West. Sword dances and mumming plays – folk plays performed around Christmas, Easter and All Souls' Night – are associated with 'the morris'.

Popular culture and mass leisure

Within the framework of mass leisure has emerged the concept of 'popular culture'. It is important because it continually reaffirms common cultural values and identity of people in that culture. It also appears to embody or express the social and cultural change brought about in large measure through 'the new leisure'. Lewis (1978) states:

> Popular culture, then, is all culture not considered élite culture or serious art, or exclusively defined as the property of a minority subculture, and that is usually, but not necessarily, disseminated through some form of the mass media. It is culture consumed nearly entirely during the leisure time of the majority of members of a social system. Thus, my definition includes popular music, films, sports events, comic books, and even fast food dispensers such as McDonald's or Kentucky Fried Chicken.

Put simply, Gans (1974) points out that some culture is popular because people want it. It encompasses the kinds of pursuits and behaviour that most people do in their leisure time and the marketing and communications market makes the ideas of popular culture available. However, there is more to popular culture than just its popularity. It is popular not just because of its availability, but because it represents and is part of social development. The growth of a youth culture with its fashion, tastes, music and ways of life is symbolic of its identity. If culture is the way of life of a people, then popular culture is part of developing new types and new styles of culture: a new or different culture in the making. Some popular movements, however, will come and go: the Mods and Rockers of the 1950s and the flower people of the 1960s are far removed from today's youth culture.

Some new cultures will reject traditional cultures and mores, and some people may well experience little of their traditional culture and heritage. There will also be counter-culture movements, such as between a more liberalized and a less liberalized society. Counter-culture movements have been traced by Kando (1975) in *Leisure and Popular Culture in Transition*.

Lewis (1978) fears there is a real danger of 'cultural unemployment', as well as destruction of tradition. Kato's studies in Thailand (Kato, 1975) show that the popular heroes are mostly Japanese television stars rather than local heroes. Thai children see and hear very little about their 'national' popular heroes in the culture they consume. The fastest-growing restaurant chain is McDonald's. Thailand is now faced with diseases of the rich such as hypertension, heart disease and diabetes as well as diseases of the poor like malnutrition.

Western popular culture is being imported to populations worldwide. Television programmes, mostly American, Japanese, British or French, are beamed across the world. Billions are exposed to it and they may judge their own lives by what they see.

Lewis (1978) sees a threefold outcome of popular Western culture beamed across the world:

> ... first, it will bring out feelings of personal inadequacy; second, a turning outward to forms of political unrest and dissensions; and third, developing countries will accept such popular culture as the goal towards which they should strive, at exactly the same point in history when the

major economically developed countries are beginning to realize that the world does not have the energy, nor the resources, to support such life-styles of leisure.

Popular culture, however, has brought to the mass of people television, radio, popular music, fashion, sport and new life horizons. Mass leisure and popular culture are part of most civilizations today. It should be fashioned to improve the quality of life for the great mass of people, but, at the same time, prevent the destruction of a nation's culture and heritage.

Summary

This chapter has taken a broad look at the evolution of Britain's cultural heritage and the part that leisure and recreation have played in it. It has evolved from its Celtic, Roman, Anglo-Saxon and Viking past, from connections with France, other European countries and from the Commonwealth. It has been greatly influenced by the monarchy, parliament, religion, the effects of the Industrial Revolution, the legacy of the Victorian era, and the historical beginnings of the tourism and leisure industries.

Today's tourist attractions include the country's historic cathedrals, churches, castles, and stately homes built over a period of four hundred years with gifted designers, builders, landscape gardeners, painters, sculptors, and furniture makers.

Britain has a long and rich history of playing games and inventing sports. Today, over one hundred different sports are played by millions of people. Many traditions have died out, but some have lasted over centuries. The UK, however, does not have one national culture, it has several. There are different cultures in England, Scotland, Wales, and Northern Ireland, different regional customs, and local variations, which differ from town to town. Moreover, the cultures of different generations, between old and young, will differ. Fashion, for example, is an ingredient in culture and social status. Fashion, dominated by adult tastes in times past, shifted dramatically with the birth of a 'youth culture' in Britain around the 1960s and which today includes children's culture, taste and fashions. Group identity is shown in wearing a team's expensive football shirt, a pair of Nike trainers, or carrying a Vuitton bag. However, fashions of today, in historical terms, are likely to be short-lived. Cultural strategies need firmer foundation, though leisure professionals must be aware of tastes and fashions, which can weave their way into local cultural identities; some will linger and some will change with time.

Culture can be greatly influenced by the highly gifted artists, craftsmen and women, musicians, and those who excel and participate in the arts and sports, and thereby enhance a cultural identity.

Culture is no longer a concept identified as belonging to the few. Today, there is mass leisure and popular culture which has much to commend, yet some elements that need to be promoted with care and caution.

Leisure Managers need to focus on the cultures in their own areas, but also take account of regional and national trends, traditions and values.

Discussion points

1 The Olympic Games in Athens in 2004 illustrated how national cultural heritage can influence the staging of an international event. How might your local cultural heritage feature as an inspiration for special leisure events?

2 'Most people now accept that you cannot breathe new life into cities, towns and communities without culture. Sometimes the cultural element alone becomes the driving force for regeneration' (Tessa Jowell, Secretary of State for Culture, Media and Sport, 2004). Examine and discuss this statement in light of what you perceive as 'culture'.

3 Cultural activities are being increasingly used as part of strategies to tackle key government priorities such as crime, education, health, employment and in the creative design of buildings and public spaces. From a different perspective, culture matters for its own sake and is important in defining and preserving the identity of the individual and the community. Discuss the issues from both perspectives and describe the common ground.

Further reading

DCMS (Department for Culture, Media and Sport) (2004), *Culture at the Heart of Regeneration*, DCMS, London.

Evans, G.L., Shaw, P. and Allen, K. (2004), *The Contribution of Culture to Regeneration in the UK. A Review of Evidence*, DCMS, London.

4
Leisure and recreation: a variety of meanings

In this chapter

- Leisure as time
- Leisure as activity
- Leisure as a state of being or an end in itself
- Leisure as an all-embracing holistic concept
- Leisure as recreation
- Leisure and its relationship to work
- Leisure as a way of life

Introduction

The United Nations Universal Declaration of Human Rights states:

'Everyone has the right to rest and leisure, including reasonable limitation of working hours and periodic holidays with pay' (Article 24) and

'Everyone has the right freely to participate in the cultural life of the community, to enjoy the arts and to share in scientific advancement and its benefits' (Article 27).

What is leisure? This question has been discussed for a long time by philosophers, researchers, lecturers, sociologists and leisure directors, managers and students.

Whatever leisure is, it is important to people's quality of living. It is incumbent on leisure professionals, therefore, to understand what leisure is and what it does. As de Grazia (1962) says, leisure cannot exist where people don't know what it is. However, leisure can mean different things to different people; and leisure can mean different things in different cultures.

Given the importance of leisure to human existence, a nation's culture is made richer or poorer by the way its people use their leisure. Thomas Hobbes, the seventeenth century philosopher, said that leisure is the mother of philosophy. British prime minister Benjamin Disraeli believed that increased means and increased leisure are the two civilizers of man. Bertrand Russell, English pacifist, philosopher and mathematician, was of the opinion that to be able to fill leisure intelligently is the best product of civilization. Julian Huxley, British biologist, in similar vein said: 'The leisure problem is fundamental. Having to decide what we shall do with our leisure is inevitably forcing us to re-examine the purpose of human existence, and to ask what fulfilment means' (Gray and Pelegrino, 1973).

The words 'leisure' and 'recreation' appear on the surface to be self-explanatory concepts and most people will have little difficulty describing what they mean to them. Yet scholars have been unable to agree with clarity a description of leisure and recreation, let alone defining what the words mean. Indeed, the concept of leisure has been debated for well over two thousand years. In 2003, Edginton, Coles and McClelland, in *Leisure Basic Concepts*, provide over 200 definitions of leisure and recreation (Edginton *et al.*, 2003):

> Often, definitions are reflections of the social, cultural, economic, and political milieu. Definitions also reflect the period of time in which they are offered and the conditions surrounding that particular point in history. Numerous individuals have defined leisure, recreation, and play. Most definitions are culturally laden, reflecting the bias of an individual and the time in which he or she offered their perspective. It has been said that defining leisure, recreation, or play is difficult. We have found many, many definitions. The challenge comes in identifying the consistent elements found in each of the definitions.

A starting point to understanding is the derivation of key words. The Greek word *schole* was closely related to, or synonymous with, leisure, the implication being that leisure was non-work, but also was associated with learning and culture. The English word 'leisure' is derived from the Latin *licere*, 'to be permitted' or 'to be free'. Hence, the French word *loisir*, meaning free time, and the English 'licence': permission or freedom to act.

So here, at least, we should have common denominators which convey that in order to be 'in leisure' or 'at leisure', there must be an essential freedom to choose what we want to do and what we want to be. However, 'freedom' itself is open to different interpretation. Take, for example, de Grazia's view on the difference between free time and leisure.

> Work is the antonym of free time, but not leisure. Leisure and free time live in two different worlds. We have got in the habit of thinking them as the same. Anybody can have free time. Free time is a realizable idea of democracy. Leisure is not fully realizable, and hence, an ideal not alone an idea.
>
> de Grazia, 1962

Generally, leisure is defined in terms of freedom from constraint, freedom to choose, time left over after work or as free time after obligatory social duties have been met. However, according to the Parrys (1977), leisure as a social phenomenon itself 'involves social constraint and social obligation and can best be thought of as being embodied in a whole way of life. Such an idea immediately invokes the concept of culture'.

The concept of leisure permits widely varying responses. Leisure is commonly thought of as the opposite of work, but one person's work can be another person's leisure, and several activities combine both leisure and work characteristics. Freedom from obligation is often regarded as a key attraction of leisure, but many non-work activities – domestic, social, voluntary and community activities – involve considerable obligation. Some regard leisure as being an opportunity for relaxation and pleasure, but often people spend their leisure time in dedicated service, study, personal development, hard training, requiring discipline and involving stress. The problems of definition are considerable.

In this chapter, therefore, we consider first the variety of descriptions, definitions and meanings of 'leisure' and then of 'recreation' and draw out their core elements in order to gain a consensus of understanding. This is because Leisure Managers have to be able to explain what kind of programmes and activities fall within the scope of their 'leisure' and 'recreation' services.

Most theories have been developed in the twentieth century. Many arose out of the troubles of the Industrial Revolution; hundreds of theories and descriptions of leisure have been written from then until now. From the mass of literature, six discernible, though overlapping, approaches are evident. We now look at each in turn.

Leisure as time

Within the broad framework of leisure defined as time, there are many variations. Some make a very broad distinction, defining leisure as the time when someone is not working primarily for money. However, this leaves a large proportion of people's time which is filled in a multitude of ways. Such a definition of leisure is far too broad to be of use and is only perceived in the context of doing 'work'. The dictionary definition gives 'surplus time' to do with as we please. Several other writers refer to leisure as free time or unoccupied time.

> The Dictionary of Sociology *describes leisure as: 'free time after the practical necessities of life have been attended to'.*

Parker (1971) distinguishes between 'residual' definitions and others. Residual time is the time left after taking out of total time everything that is not regarded as leisure. To Brightbill (1964) and others, while leisure is concerned with time, it is only leisure if it falls into 'discretionary' time, that is, time beyond existence and subsistence, 'the time to be used according to our own judgement or choice'. Hence, three time-slots are identified: existence, subsistence and discretionary. Yet the matter is complicated further: what is necessary for some will be discretionary for others and many necessary activities such as eating and sleeping may be seen as discretionary activities. In general, however, the word 'leisure' is more likely to be correlated with positive or constructive behaviour compared to free time, which appears to have some negatively charged characteristics. Goodale and Godbey (1988) reason that 'we dislocate leisure by consigning it to particular periods during days, weeks and years'. Meyersohn appears to agree; leisure isn't just 'killing time', and it can't be measured by the hours one has off from work. 'It is a positive period in which people choose what they want to do' (Nash, 1965).

The American Association for Health, Physical Education and Recreation adopts a similar stance:

... we view leisure as time – time that is free for man to choose among alternatives ... [There exist] three basic functional aspects of leisure – relaxation, entertainment, and development ... Leisure is instinctively or knowingly selected as an antidote to the adverse effects of compulsory daily activities and the confusion and frustration arising from the densification of urbanization and population ... Leisure is the absence of pressure, the freedom from the obligation to work ... Leisure is the restorative, creative use of free time ...

Edginton *et al.,* 2003

At the two wings of the 'leisure as time' debate are the views of de Grazia and Shivers. Grazia (1962) denounces as a popular misconception the notion that free time is leisure. 'The mentality of "clock-watching" produces synchronization, impersonal tempo, conformity and unthoughtful action. The free time produced by industrialisation is typified by passivity, an uncritical spirit and craving for fun. We have not developed "true" leisure for the masses; it may well be beyond the capacity of most people'. In de Grazia's opinion – closer than most to Aristotle's view – leisure perfects man and woman and holds the key to the future. It needs to break the grip of the machine and release human energy for free expression and exploration of truth, beauty and knowledge. He casts doubt on whether there is indeed any freedom in the quantitative framework called 'free time'. Marcuse (1964), however, takes a totally opposing view, defining leisure as free time and questioning the freedom of leisure. Parker (1971) argues, setting the semantic problems aside, if free time and leisure are different conceptually, they cannot be measured by the same criteria. The distinction is not confined to the area of non-work: it applies also in the work sphere. Shivers (1981) in contrast to nearly all others, is unequivocal and straight to the point:

Leisure is free time and that is all. Whether it is used for personal indulgence, expressing creation, or indolence, is immaterial. Leisure remains incontrovertibly an element of discretionary time, not limited in any objective way except in terms of how it will be used or allowed to pass.

Leisure as activity

Another classical understanding of leisure is that it is made up of an activity or a 'cluster of activities'. The International Group of Social Sciences of Leisure (Dumazedier, 1960) states that:

Leisure consists of a number of occupations in which the individual may indulge of his own free will whether to rest, amuse himself, to add to this knowledge, or improve his skills disinterestedly or to increase his voluntary participation in the life of the community after discharging his professional, family and social duties.

Dumazedier (1967), the eminent French sociologist, also uses the word 'occupation' in a similar way: 'Leisure is activity – apart from the obligations of work, family and society – to which the individual turns at will, for relaxation, diversion, or broadening his individual and his spontaneous social participation, the free exercise of his creative capacity.'

Nash (1960) viewed the use of leisure for specific activities on four levels: passive, emotional, active and creative involvement. His leisure model illustrates use of leisure time with a progression of leisure activities in similar vein to Maslow's hierarchy of needs. Nash attaches a value to each level. Those at the apex of the pyramid are values to be regarded as worthy and those at the base are negative in value and undesirable. Many look at leisure as activities freely chosen. However, in reality, absolute freedom is rarely achieved. Dumazedier (1967) coined the term 'semi-leisure', to describe those activities which one was obliged to do, but that brought about satisfactions in the doing. Such activities as domestic chores, do-it-yourself, family obligations, and the like, could be pleasurable or diversionary and could function as 'semi-leisure'. Cooking while listening to music, or watching TV while doing the ironing, could come under Dumazedier's semi-leisure heading.

John Kelly in *Leisure* (1982) ranks, in order of importance, leisure activities of adults, relatively stable in socio-economic terms, in three communities in the United States. Leisure, for them, appeared to be informal, readily available and, largely, inexpensive. Of the most highly stressed, six out of ten families, in the absence of organized recreation, partake in the following activities:

1   marital affection and intimacy
2   reading for pleasure
3   family conversation
4   activity as a couple: walking, shopping, etc.
5   family outings
6   visiting family and friends
7   playing with children
8   watching television
9   outdoor sport
10 eating out
11 religious worship
12 short auto trips
13 gardening
14 home decorating
15 arts and crafts.

Leisure as a state of being or an end in itself

In the society of Ancient Greece – at least at the educated, privileged strata – the 'treasures of the mind' were the fruits of leisure which contained the joy and delight of life. Aristotle thought of leisure as a state of being, free from the necessity of work, and characterized by performance of activity for its own sake or its own end. The 'ideal man' would strive for perfection in arts, music, sport, school, and in military service. This ideal leisure made for an advanced society and for good governance. Neulinger (1974) in similar vein links leisure to engagement in activity.

> Leisure is a state of mind; it is a way of being, of being at peace with oneself and what one is doing ... Leisure has one and only one essential criterion, and that is the condition of perceived freedom. Any activity carried out freely without constraint or compulsion, may be considered to be leisure. To leisure implies being engaged in an activity as a free agent, and of one's own choice.

Bammel and Bammel (1966) move away from the notion of any connection between leisure as a state of being and activity. They claim: 'Leisure is a state of being, an attitude, a mental condition; it has nothing to do with time and little to do with space and activity'. What is described as the 'humanistic' model views leisure as an end in itself, a state of being. Pieper (1952) stressed the idea from a spiritual perspective: 'Leisure it must be understood, is a mental and spiritual attitude – it is not simply the result of external factors, it is not the inevitable result of spare time, a holiday, a weekend or a vacation. It is, in the first place, an attitude of the mind, a condition of the soul'.

Leisure, to Pieper, was not a means to an end, but rather an end in itself. This is also a concept similar to Huizinga's understanding of play; see Theories from the first half of the twentieth century, p. 74, Chapter 5).

Pieper, a theologian-philosopher, links leisure to culture through worship, festival and celebration: 'Culture depends for its very existence on leisure, and leisure, in its turn, is not possible unless it has durable and living link with the cultus, with divine worship'. Leisure, to Pieper, is a mental or spiritual attitude which is not the result of external factors, not the result of spare time and not idleness.

The ideal of leisure as a feeling or attitude of freedom and release from constraint appears to reflect an 'internal' experience, the result of emotional or psychological processes. Godbey (1994) continues this inner dimension:

> To have leisure is one of the oldest dreams of human beings – to be free from an endless round of labour, free to pursue what one wants, to spend time in voluntary, pleasurable ways, free to find and accept one's place in the world, free of the tyranny of nature and of other human beings, free to exist in a state of grace.

Kraus (2001) takes a more practical approach to the 'spiritual' dimension:

> Leisure implies freedom and choice and is customarily used in a variety of ways, but chiefly to meet one's personal needs for reflection, self-enrichment, relaxation, or pleasure. While it usually involves some form of participation in a voluntary chosen activity, it may be regarded as a holistic state of being or even a spiritual experience.

Leisure as an all-embracing holistic concept

Kraus uses the word 'holistic' to fuse together some of the meanings of leisure:

> The earlier views of leisure either as an end in itself (the classical view, which sees leisure as a celebration of life) or as the means to an end (leisure as recreation for renewed work or as a form of social control or therapy) are now being fused in a holistic concept of leisure.
>
> Kraus, 1982

While many authors define leisure as time, activity and a state of being, most of them incorporate all three aspects, giving greater weight in one direction. Indeed, many of the prominent writers use different definitions at different times, depending on the point which is being made at the time. This can be seen in several of the all-embracing descriptions of leisure. The three primary functions of leisure, according to Dumazedier (1967), are: relaxation, entertainment and personal development. Within these three aspects people find recovery from fatigue, deliverance from boredom and liberation from daily automatism: 'Leisure is the expression of a whole collection of man's aspirations on a search for a new happiness, related to a new duty, a new ethic, a new policy and a new culture. A humanistic mutation is beginning.'

Murphy (1975) believes that there has been erosion of the effectiveness of work to serve the need of self-identity. In contrast, there has been an increase in the value of leisure in establishing one's status and personal identity. He sees this as a major factor in the trend towards the fusion of work and leisure. The holistic view of leisure is seen in the context of the wholeness of the individual. A full range of possible forms of self-expression may occur during work or leisure. According to the holistic concept, 'the meaning of work and leisure are inextricably related to each other.'

However, work and leisure may not be as interrelated as Murphy suggests when people do not have the means to enjoy leisure, nor the positive attitude towards it, nor the perception of what it might mean in terms of life satisfaction. The more important questions are: what does leisure do for people; how do they perceive leisure and what does it mean to them? Neulinger (1974), a psychologist, takes an attitudinal approach. Leisure is concerned with people's attitudes and perceptions. Leisure has three dimensions in his paradigm: it includes perceived freedom, it is intrinsic and it is non-instrumental. Leisure is the perception of free choice for the sake of doing or experiencing. Neulinger and Crandall (1976) point out that we are no longer satisfied just to name the activities that people engage in; we now want to find out what they mean to people.

Leisure as recreation

Another meaning of leisure is that it is synonymous with recreation; it is just a question of semantics. So why concern ourselves with possible distinctions between the two concepts? The first thing to say is that we have these two words in the English language, they have different roots and, historically, they have been interpreted differently. Second, the answer 'they are whatever we think they are', is hardly an explanation on which to found a meaningful profession. Academics and practitioners need scholarship and understanding in order to act professionally. In historical terms, and even today in many societies, leisure conjures up pictures of sloth, idleness and decadence. The Victorian adage of the devil making work for idle hands is still alive. However, there were exceptions to the rule. Horatio Smith(1831), well ahead of his time, advocated recreation for 'strong minds and strong nations':

> None but a pompous blockhead or solemn prig will pretend that he never relaxes, never indulges in pastime, never wastes his breath in idle waggery and merriment ... Occasional playfulness, indeed, seems to be natural to all strong minds ... The more trivial our recreations, the more accurately will they often reveal the qualities of the mind, as the lightest feather we can toss up will best determine the direction of the wind. If this is true of an individual, it will be equally applicable to a nation whose familiar and domestic character we may much better ascertain from their sports, pastimes and amusements, than from those more prominent and important features to which historians have usually restricted themselves in their delineations.

'Recreation', like 'leisure', is a far from simple concept to grasp and to understand. Hundreds of writers have attempted so to do and the literature is filled with a plethora of theories as catalogued in *Definitions and Basic Concepts of Leisure, Recreation and Play* (Edginton *et al.*, 2003). They do not fall into any clear or logical categories and most of the theories overlap and appear to overstress values and 'wholesomeness'. The confusion is well illustrated in an editorial in *Parks and Recreation* (Gray and Greben, 1979) which listed approximately 200 words or phrases describing how 'recreation' was perceived by different people!

The word 'recreation' stems from Latin *recreatio*, restoration to health. Hence, the historic approach in defining recreation has been to consider it as an activity that renews people for work, an approach which has obvious limitations. While some definitions refer to recreation as restoration, most focus on it as a form of activity. Others, while corroborating the activity approach, apply the condition to it of social acceptance. Most view the activity as unobligated.

Recreation as leisure activities

The most widespread definition, and the one most acceptable to providers of leisure services, is that recreation is activities in which people participate during their leisure time; however, not just any activity will do. Recreation needs to provide satisfaction in some way. Typical activity definitions are provided by scores of writers including: Neumeyer and Neumeyer, Kraus and Bates, Butler, Jensen and Godbey and Parker.

The Dictionary of Sociology *defines recreation as: 'any activity pursued during leisure, either individual or collective, that is free and pleasureful, having its own immediate appeal, not impelled by a delayed reward beyond itself.'*

Kraus (2001) sees recreation as 'a fusion between play and leisure'. Neumeyer and Neumeyer (1958) suggest that recreation involves 'any activity pursued during leisure, either individual or collective, that is free and pleasureful, having its own immediate appeal, not impelled by a delayed reward beyond itself or by any immediate necessity.' Kraus and Bates (1957) add experiencing to the activity:

Recreation consists of activities or experiences which are carried on voluntarily in leisure time. They are chosen by the participants, either for pleasure or to satisfy certain personal needs. When provided as a part of organized community programs, recreation must be designed to achieve constructive goals.

Both Butler and Jensen follow similar themes: 'Recreation is any form of leisure time experience or activity in which an individual engages from choice because of the enjoyment and satisfaction which it brings directly to him' (Butler, 1976). 'Recreation is an act or experience, selected by the individual during his leisure time, to meet a personal want or desire, primarily for his own satisfaction' (Jensen, 1977).

Godbey and Parker (1976) add to recreation a re-creative function:

Recreation always indicates activity of some kind and, like leisure and play, it takes no single form. In its literal sense of re-creating, it may be seen as one of the functions of leisure: that of rewarding the self or of preparing for work.

The problem with the traditional activity dimension is that it is heavily slanted in certain preconceived directions, so much so that recreation to many people is synonymous with physical recreation and sport.

Recreation and wholesomeness

Jensen (1977) sees one of the characteristics of recreation as that 'it is wholesome to the individual and society'. Kelly (2000) believes that recreation:

> is intended to restore us to wholeness, to health, for whatever purposes we may have. We do not recreate only to work. We recreate to live ... Recreation is itself a part of living and has its own value to us ... That element of restoration for whatever we consider important, including ourselves, is one part of recreation ... Recreation has purposes and is organized for social ends. It is not just 'for its own sake'.

'Recreation' has been dogged by having to live up to a standard of moral and social value for the 'good' of individuals and the community. Miller and Robinson (1963) view recreation as the process of participation from a perceptive of leisure values. Meyer and Brightbill (1964) claim that recreation contains a wide range of characteristics such as purposefulness; it is also an 'attitude of mind' regarding leisure behaviour and has a direct influence on those factors which create personality. Recreation can produce 'feelings of well-being and satisfactions, pertaining to positive identity, growth, creativeness, balanced competition, character, mental capacity, dignity of the individual, physical conditioning, socialisation and a coping attitude'. Not surprisingly, Meyer and Brightbill view recreation as a social force. But such value orientations placed on recreation are questionable. Such descriptions may well overstress presumed recreational benefits, and resulting services based on such presumptions might repel people rather than attract them. However, there is no shortage of supporters for such an orientation. Butler takes a similar view; he sees recreation as a force influencing people's lives, and as a system of services which provide 'wholesome' experience, to counteract disruptive social influences.

It is logical to perceive that from this value orientation, 'wholesome' recreation will lead to recreation as an influence for social good. From this viewpoint, community recreation is a means for improving and maintaining societal cohesion and the quality of life; its development is dependent on social participation. Hence, community recreation is a system of services for wholesome, positively sanctioned activities.

The unity concept: recreation as re-creation

One could argue that recreation is for fun, relaxation and pleasure. Is it physiologically necessary? Is it needed to retain our equilibrium psychologically?

Shivers (1967), in contrast to other writers, tackles the concept of the 'experience that is re-creation'. Building on a theme of homeostasis (the process by which the body continues to produce the chemical balance necessary to maintain life; the process by which equilibrium is maintained), Shivers builds up to a definition of recreation based on the construct 'psychological homeostasis', that is, the satisfying of psychological needs, the process of mental balance. He reasons that if homeostasis is the condition that motivates behaviour, it must also serve as the motivational stimulus for recreation. When there is imbalance, we move towards re-balance in which harmony and accord between self and the environment are found. Shivers claims that this balance may be restored through recreation. Recreation is 'any consummatory experience, non-debilitating in character' (Shivers, 1967, p. 90). It produces unity and harmony within the individual. The unity of mind and body (psyche and soma) brought about at the time of 'consummation' is recreation. The distinguishing feature is its consuming and absorbing quality. It has the power to seize and hold one's attention to such an extent that the very meaning of subjective time and environment disappears from view. In this respect, it fulfils the need for psychological homeostasis. Hence, the individual experiences a balance or temporary harmony at the point of complete fulfilment from which stems a feeling of re-creation, or re-birth.

The basic difference between recreational value and recreation itself is in time rather than degree. Recreational value will be noted *after* the consuming experience has occurred, whereas recreation itself occurs at the time of the experience. This unity of mind and body Shivers describes as the 'unity concept' of recreation. However, even if such complete absorption is achieved (and that may be rare for most people), the theory raises the question of whether every satisfying, absorbing experience is recreation.

There have been some investigations into people's perceptions of recreation and the experiences they encounter, but the findings have limited scientific validity and further studies are needed. One piece of research elicited from college students, via self-reporting techniques, the most significant and memorable recreation experiences they had ever had. The results were reported by Gray (1980), and shown in Table 4.1. These personal 'recreation experiences' indicate that recreation is a highly significant component of total life experience. It also suggests that activities that do not generate some of these kinds of feeling may fail to produce a recreational result.

Gray and Pelegrino (1973) have adopted a similar definition, which is psychological in nature; recreation is defined in terms of a person's experiences:

> Recreation is an emotional condition within an individual human being that flows from a feeling of well-being and satisfaction; it is characterized by feelings of mastery, achievement, exhilaration, acceptance, success, personal worth and pleasure. It reinforces a positive self-image. Recreation is a response to aesthetic experience, achievement of person's goals, or positive feedback from others. It is independent of activity, leisure or social acceptance.

It is what happens within a person that determines whether or not recreation occurs. The unity within oneself, the mood and the situational elements themselves all go to make up the recreational experience. Hence, participating in an activity does not in and of itself provide recreation. The psychological response of the individual is what determines what is recreation for him or her.

Table 4.1 What is this thing called recreation?

- Heightened or reduced sensitivity to temperature, colour and smell
- Time distortion: 'time stood still', 'an hour seemed like a minute'
- Anticipation and expectation
- Escape: 'getting away from it all'
- Novelty; the sense of 'for the first time' brings freshness and uniqueness
- Relaxation, including release from social convention and personal demands
- Self-testing; challenge; and achievement, competence and self-worth
- Improved self-image: 'In the end we all experience only ourselves'
- Feeling a part of nature; beauty and awe
- Heightened appreciation and unusual perception
- Culmination; a turning point; reward for extended preparation; a watershed, life event
- Heightened insight; perspective clarity; illuminating experience; flashes of insight
- Order; regularity; clear and precise limits; rules
- Introspection; sorting out of life experience; release from sensory overload, contemplation; and communication with oneself
- Communion; love; friendship and identification with a group (perhaps the strongest single motivation for many recreation activities is the wish for social response)
- Personal development; learning; and extension of ability
- Refreshment; personal renewal; and recovery of powers
- Common experience; shared hardships; and teamwork
- Risk; apprehension; fear – being frightened is a part of the extraordinary experience
- Unity of mind and body; grace, co-ordination
- Feelings of excitement, freedom, control, power, creativity, inner peace, harmony, reward, competence; recreation experiences are a powerful stimulus to emotional response.

Source: Adapted from Gray, D. (1980)

Linking experience to activity

There is an apparent drawback to the school of thought that defines recreation as any experience at all: it loses any connection to either leisure or activity. Graham and Klar (1979) sum up the practical difficulties:

> Should all positive feelings be categorized as recreation? Is the scientist's moment of discovery recreation? Or the student's feeling of satisfaction with a term paper well done? If we assume that recreation is independent of either leisure or activity, virtually all satisfying experiences become labelled recreation, which seems too far reaching and presents barriers to communication since that is not the context in which most people view recreation.

Hence, recreation, by this definition, will not be easily applied since it incorporates so many types of experience. In their interim report (DoE, 1978), the Recreation Management Training Committee stated as their reference point: 'We take recreation to mean any life-enhancing experience which is the outcome of freely chosen activity.' Here, experience is allied to activity. Graham and Klar (1979) take the matter closer to 'recreation' activity. It is imperative, they believe, to put the experience into a recreation setting to achieve understanding: recreation experience occurs as a direct result of involvement in a recreation activity. It is an emotional condition providing inner satisfactions and feelings of well-being.

The principal point being made here is that the experience is not independent of recreation activity. It therefore avoids the broadness of definition that views all positive experiences as recreation, which is extremely difficult to put into any operational context.

> *Graham and Klar (1979) define a recreation experience as: positive emotional response to participation in a recreation activity, defined as such by the individual or by a sponsoring agency or organization.*

Recreation, well-being and leisure

Avedon (1974) and Gray and Greben (1974) look to recreation for providing well-being, a concept now permeating public and private leisure and health services. Yet the essence of 'well-being' is not new. Alexander Pope in his 'Ode to Solitude' nearly three centuries ago, in 1717, came even closer to recreation as an inner experience of well-being:

> Blest, who can unconcernedly
> Find hours, days and years slide
> Soft away, in health of body,
> Peace of mind, quiet by day,
> Sound sleep by night, study and
> Ease, together mixed, sweet
> Recreation.

The impact of recreation on well-being was studied by the Western Australian Government (MSR, 1995). 'Recreation', as defined by the community, included 'any activity that was undertaken in discretionary time and about which the participant had a choice'. It included active and passive elements. Indeed, involvement in passive recreational activities was the most widespread among the sample of people surveyed. All these activities could equally come under the banner of 'leisure'. Respondents found it difficult to define well-being, but an almost perfect correlation was found between 'satisfaction with one's life' and well-being. Contributing factors included health and self-esteem, interpersonal relationships and participation in recreational activities. Increasing satisfaction with recreation activities directly affected well-being and this held true for all ages.

The research demonstrated that recreational activities are far more diverse than competitive sport and non-competitive fitness activities. Recreational activities include a wide variety of both active and passive pursuits. Providers of recreational facilities and services, such as local government authorities, must meet this wider agenda.

Recreation and social cohesion

The question was raised earlier, are recreation and leisure the same things? That will depend on our own interpretation, but there are distinguishing features. In some ways, they share the same characteristics, but they play different roles in society. Searle and Bradley (1993) make the point that recreation is a part of the Western cultural system and is programmed to achieve certain purposes:

> Recreation is different from leisure. It is closely associated with the Industrial Revolution, it is somewhat culture-bound, it exists in parts to achieve broader social purposes (and, perhaps political purposes), it generates enjoyment, and it occurs as one form of expression during leisure.

Clearly, recreation provides benefits. Kelly (2000) clarifies succinctly: 'While some leisure may be destructive to the self or to society, recreation – by definition – is always beneficial in intent.'

The social cohesion theory is supported by Kraus (1999). Building on the theme of 'wholeness of mind, body and spirit', he defines recreation as, 'voluntary non-work activity that is organised for the attainment of personal and social benefits including restoration and social cohesion.'

In summary, recreation can be regarded as a means to an end, or as an end in itself. Looking at recreation experience, it follows that whatever activity or situation renews, revives, refreshes and re-creates for the individual, is a recreation for him or her at that time. This has far-reaching implications for leisure and recreation services. Any activity implies no right or wrong, no good or bad; no moral issues are at stake. But society will not allow just *any* activity. Although Western society is liberal, individuals are still constrained in what is and what is not acceptable behaviour. There is a belief in the right of the individual to self-expression and the expanding of experiences, but within society's social ethic.

Leisure and its relationship to work

As we have seen earlier in this book, in nomadic times and non-industrial agricultural times, work and leisure were intertwined and 'structured' around celebrations, seasons, rites of passage and the like. We also saw in the times of the ancient Greeks and Romans that, for 'the citizens', work other than the very essential, was anathema, a curse; the Greek word for work *ponos* meant sorrow. The philosophers agreed with the poets: the only solution, as most clearly expressed by Plato and Aristotle, was to have the vast majority, the slaves, provide the necessities and material goods for all, so that the minority – the citizens – could engage in leisure which produced the arts and sciences, politics, government and philosophy. A life of leisure, although it had obligations and responsibilities, could only be pursued by those who had been freed from the 'curse' of work. The blessing of leisure for some meant intensive work for many. The Greek citizens could not have pursued their leisure without widespread slavery; likewise, the English aristocracy could not have been the epitome of the cultured stock without serfs, peasants and a working class to provide for them.

Bertrand Russell (1935), in *In Praise of Idleness*, asserted that harm was caused by the belief that work was virtuous; the morality of work was the morality of slaves. Work was indeed slavery to the suppressed. The boys and girls, men and women who slaved in the coalmines and textile mills in England during the Industrial Revolution, had neither the time nor the energy to enjoy leisure.

The relationship between the concepts of 'work' and 'leisure' has been well debated and documented, though there are no satisfactory universally accepted theses. Most societies make a clear distinction between work and leisure. Indeed, leisure is seen as the antithesis of work. The dimensions of leisure include freedom to choose, intrinsic satisfaction and low relationship to paid work. Work, on the other hand, generally, is characterized by having constraints on personal choice, being highly structured and regulated, and lacking in freedom to choose.

The Industrial Revolution was probably the most significant influence on the separation between work and leisure and the distribution of leisure. It established an industrial (working) way of life; with the 'support' of the church, it strengthened the work ethic; and it encouraged recreation in non-work time to restore for the work ahead. Without 'work' time or 'obligated-to-duties' time, there would be no need to distinguish leisure time. The work ethic emerged from religious, political, and social conditions. Work was valued, not just for economic benefits, but for moral purposes also.

The word 'work' covers a multitude of things. It can mean:

- labour
- occupation
- employment
- effort and
- production.

Work, of course, may also be a time for personal development, creativity and other personal satisfactions. Marx's (1952) ideal model of work was 'a process in which man and nature participate, and in which man of his own accord starts, regulates, and controls the material recreations between himself and nature'. However, work in industry contradicts this ideal. Industry is typified by specialization, fragmentation, isolation, rigid time structuring, repetitiveness and depersonalization, all of which contribute to anonymity, a sense of helplessness and alienation for many workers. To the public at large, the question 'what is work?' is so obvious that definitions and attempts at understanding seem totally inappropriate.

To the public at large, work is paid employment. It is concerned with earning a wage, the money on which to live. In addition, work has been traditionally valued. It has been a means of self-identification.

In Western cultures today, however, many traditions no longer apply. In the United Kingdom, with the loss of a manufacturing base and growth in the service industries, there is more work available for females than males, though disparity in wage earnings, despite legislation, still applies in some occupations. Then there is the issue of unemployment causing for many people loss of esteem and dignity.

Those people who are made to retire early, are made redundant or who simply do not want to retire, can also find themselves feeling alienated, isolated and robbed of a purpose in life. Dependence on paid work as a means for organizing one's life and that of one's family is declining. This situation makes it a mistake to consider 'leisure' as 'time free from work'. Also, it is becoming less appropriate to consider 'work' only as a job for which one is paid. Half the population – home and family workers, the retired, the unemployed, students and many with disabilities – are not in paid employment and, therefore, are not included in the present conceptual boundaries of such a definition of leisure.

John Maynard Keynes (1963) revolutionized economic thought after the First World War. In 1930 he envisaged a future society whose needs could be satisfied with no more than fifteen hours of work per week, if it chose to devote its energies to non-economic purposes. He mused on a future when:

> We shall once more value ends above means and prefer the good to the useful. We shall honour those who can teach us how to pluck the hour and the day virtuously and well, the delightful people who are capable of taking direct enjoyment in things, the lilies of the field who toil not, neither do they spin.

Today, work is less like slavery for many and more like leisure for some. This is because of higher education levels among workers, a shift in jobs from manufacturing to the service sector, the rise of professionalism, and other factors. The leisure pattern of evenings, weekends and holidays is changing: the linear pattern is breaking up. Among the reasons are the changing roles of women, the changing age composition of our society, expanding continuing education, changes in attitudes toward work, and so on. Also, work is being removed from the workplace with computer links to home, laptop and palmtop computers, mobile and conference telephoning and text-messaging.

Changing times for work and leisure

The 1960s ushered in a new era for leisure in the United Kingdom: the first sport, leisure and arts centres, integrated local authority leisure services, corporate management, and joint use and dual provision in schools. In wider society there were the hippies and other alternative lifestyles, the creation of a youth culture with the growth in a new kind of popular music; young people had spending power. There was an upbeat spirit, and the age was described by Harold Macmillan as one in which 'you never had it so good'.

In 1965 Michael Dower (1965) wrote for the Civic Trust a watershed publication *Fourth Wave – The Challenge of Leisure*:

> Three great waves have broken across the face of Britain since 1800. First, the sudden growth of dark industrial towns. Second, the thrusting movement along far-flung railways. Third, the sprawl of car-based suburbs. Now we see, under the guise of a modest word, the surge of a fourth wave which could be more powerful than all the others. The modest word is leisure.

Equally important and equally significant are today's changes:

- an ever-increasing choice for consumers and increasing expectations
- demographic changes calling for improved programmes for growing market segments, such as the older age-groups.

Yet modern society still does not yet treat leisure seriously. The patterns and rhythms of life are determined by work and its demands, and spare time, the residual, is labelled as a leisure period. Blauner (1964) concluded in the mid-1960s that work remains the single most important activity for most people in terms of time and energy. Attitudes have changed since that time, but the premise still holds true for a large proportion of working people. This is so different from many forecasters' visions.

Recall Bertrand Russell who in 1932 suggested that if workers worked four hours a day, there would be enough for everybody; Clive Jenkins and Barrie Sherman who in 1979 wrote *The Collapse of Work* (Jenkins and Sherman, 1979). In *The Leisure Shock* (Jenkins and Sherman, 1981) they predicted:

> What is work? Will there be enough of it to go round? Must there or should there be enough of it to go round? Will many of us suffer withdrawal symptoms if we cannot have our share of it? ... Our approach is to have a reduced working week, month, year and lifetime, but with at least the same level of remuneration. This implies that some employers would have to take on extra labour, that both profits and returns to capital would fall – in other words a redistribution of monies towards labour.

However, 25 years later, a quite different picture has emerged. We still work long hours and come home exhausted. More than half of us suffer from stress. In Japan, thousands of people are thought to die each year from overwork. More people are more pressured about time, or lack of it. The patterns of work, shopping, leisure – the building blocks of life – are disappearing. We are moving to a world of the Internet, with home shopping, and home banking. Life's fixed timetables have given way to a post-industrial culture: the 24-hour society. We cram more and more into a reduced time slot, multi-skilling because time is a precious resource. We are time-conscious whether at work, shopping, cooking or at leisure: a contradiction of terms if ever there was one. We are in an age of technology which promises to increase personal autonomy and freedom, to cut waste and foster leisure. But we are in what Demos describes as 'the time squeeze' (Mulgan, 1995). (Demos is an independent think-tank whose aim is to create an open resource of knowledge and learning that operates beyond traditional political parties, identities and disciplines. Demos connects researchers and practitioners to an international network of people-changing politics.)

> Right across society, there is a sense of time being squeezed. And policy has lagged behind, as it always does, with a lengthening series of failures: the growing imbalance between overwork for some and zero work for others; poor management and public spaces and transport which has forced up the times taken to get to work, to care for (and transport) children, even to shop; and severe stress for millions – particularly women – trying to juggle competing responsibilities. This new post-industrial culture offers, perhaps for the first time in history, the promise of people using time for their own needs. But far from ushering in a leisured utopia, its most immediate effect has been a growing divide between those with too much work and those without any. In 'top' jobs, long hours have become a mark of status and success. In the 1930s the phrase

'banking hours' referred to a leisurely working day that began at ten and ended at four, with a generous lunch hour. By contrast today's bankers may be having to cope with 24-hour capital markets. One in eight British managers works more than 60 hours a week and more than half take work home during the week.

Guardian, 6 June 1995

These pressures are not confined to top executives. One in six households has no wage-earner; others fear redundancy; some are working all hours and at several different low-paid jobs just to pay the bills. So we have work overload on the one hand, with high stress and anxiety levels (for all levels of workers) and the dangers that these bring, and on the other hand no work for some. The job market demands that women with children return to work, yet most still have to care for the home and the family.

This raises the issue of the quality of the work. Many jobs do not add to the quality of life. As the French novelist Albert Camus commenting on work said: 'Without work, all life goes rotten. But when work is soulless, life stifles and dies.'

A problem exists in that large numbers of people cannot get any work and large numbers cannot get away from it. The answer, according to Natasha Walter, writing in *The Observer*, is not to see work as the ultimate good.

That ideal only widens the divide. It forces people in work to cling grimly on to their job – terrified of losing their grip on it, and uneasy about taking holidays and getting home in time for their children's bedtimes. And it encourages people out of work to believe that their lives are being wasted and that they will achieve nothing concrete until they have an employer and a pay packet. If we are really to see the beginning of a more equal society, the way forward must be to celebrate the other side of life, the delights of idleness.

Many people are searching for alternative lifestyles and a better balance between paid work and other aspects of life. Some fortunate academics and clergy are allowed sabbaticals to re-charge, to travel and to learn from beyond their own environment. Early in their lives, some students take a 'gap year' for the same reason.

In the past, leisure was seen as an escape from work. But this misses the point. Many of us enjoy work and find it fulfilling; and also many people work harder at their chosen leisure time occupations. Many people say that they would rather work at something worthwhile, for nothing, than to be unemployed. To be valued and to have self-worth is hugely motivating.

For many employees, the organization of work is changing, partly as a result of information and communication technology, and partly because new arrangements suit the lifestyles of workers, particularly women with dependent children. Human resources departments call it the work–life balance. The move away from standard hours for some, flexi-hours for others, part-time agency work, sub-contract work, even in the service and administration sectors, all go to make the traditional meanings of 'work' far more interwoven with other parts of life, including leisure. For example:

- working hours determine how much time is available for leisure
- paid work determines earnings and levels of disposable income

61

- work may determine one's level of energy, enthusiasm and motivation for leisure participation, and
- some work decisions, such as location or perks of the job, are made with lifestyle and leisure in mind – offices adjacent to a golf course or nursery have added value.

New technologies and patterns of work may well produce new-found free time, but it is as likely to result in trading leisure for extra income. However, it is not just the patterns of work that are changing, the types of job and work occupations we have are changing, and former work traditions no longer apply.

Is it work or leisure?

People's lives are segmented in a variety of ways, yet need to work in harmony as a whole. For example, a person may at one time be mother, grandmother, homemaker, part-time teacher, church leader, school governor, volunteer worker and recreation player. Which of these 'lives' is work, and which leisure? The difficulty with seeing leisure as time outside work is that many leisure activities are very hard work and some work situations are enjoyable, almost leisure-like. How many working people, just back from a family holiday, say they are glad to be back at work 'to recover', or that 'now I do need a holiday'? People whose work is associated with leisure pursuits – sports coaches, play workers, youth workers, artists, actors, musicians, art, craft and physical education teachers and Leisure Managers – are often asked when they are going to get a proper job!

Taking a quite different stance from previous writers and the claim that the work ethic is alive and well, Christina Odone (2002) suggests that there is an 'un-work ethic' and that leisure is taking the place of work. In an article for the *Observer*, 'Work? We're far too busy shopping and enjoying ourselves', she believes that our busyness is not about work, but about hedonism.

> Our busyness is not about work, but about hedonism (granted, Legoland is the children's idea of a hedonistic outing rather than yours). Never has a society spent more time in leisure activities or, for that matter, more money – leisure spending remains the healthiest sector of the economy, with £988 million spent each year on plays, concerts and shows and £572 million at the cinema. Middle-class families admit to spending two holidays a year abroad and studies reveal that many are now withdrawing equity from their homes to pay for these trips. (The national average is £780 a year.) And while talk of, and investment in, holidays takes up more of our time, work takes up less. An unprecedented number of people can afford to retire at fiftysomething to dedicate themselves to golf, watercolours or evening classes in Japanese. Compare this *dolce vita* with our ancestors' schedules. Then, the Protestant work ethic fuelled the machinery of everyday life.

In this brief section on work and leisure, we have seen that while leisure can be regarded as the opposite of work, this is by no means the full picture. Moreover, one person's recreation is another's work, and one person's leisure is another's drudgery. Furthermore, leisure, traditionally, is conceived as freedom from commitment, yet many leisure activities require considerable commitment. And those out of work, not by choice, do not count their enforced free time as leisure. Therefore, the two realms of work and leisure need to be considered not as dichotomized entities, but in far more fluid and complex dimensions. Koshar (2002) sees work and leisure for most adult people as intertwined, 'the one reciprocating the other's contradictions and tensions':

> The history of leisure has been inextricably intertwined with the history of work, and it is primarily the social history of the manual labouring classes that has directed attention to the way in which the advent of industrial capitalism created new conflicts over the control of time. New forms of work discipline demanded new apprehensions and disciplines of time ... If control over the length and quality of work time was one of the central conflicts in the history of leisure, control over the content of time spent away from work was equally significant.

Leisure as a way of life

Leisure has been defined in a variety of ways and as some kind of product, experience or process. Yet there remains another perspective or orientation mentioned earlier by the Parrys (Parry and Parry, 1977) and the essence of the findings of Goodale and Godbey (1988). It is idealistic and bears resemblance to the philosophy of Aristotle. Leisure is not a commodity of time or a state of mind, but a way of living:

> Leisure is living in relative freedom from the external compulsive forces on one's culture and physical environment so as to be able to act from internally compelling love in ways which are personally pleasing, intuitively worthwhile, and provide a basis of faith.
>
> Godbey, 1994

In noting that leisure is living, we avoid the notions of time and state of mind. We recognize that freedom is limited; we are not free to do anything we wish to do. So then, leisure as a way of living can offer opportunities or times with which we can choose what to do.

Aristotle, in Book 2 of the *Politics*, in describing the need for 'freedom from the necessity of labour', is concerned with how we use time. We need to be relatively free from those external compulsive forces so as to be able to act; it is a 'freedom to', rather than a 'freedom from' idea. And the motivation for those acts is intrinsic: not being motivated by some external force or pursuing some external reward. In life-enhancing terms, leisure appears to be the process of gaining freedom and finding meaning through self-understanding and self-improvement; it is a self-directed process. Idealistic, yes. But without ideals, values and goals, we have a shallow philosophy of life and leisure, and a lack of foundation on which to base a lasting profession of Leisure Management.

Summary

This chapter has explored some of the mundane and more colourful meanings of leisure. It means different things to different people. An understanding of the basic orientations provides leisure academics and practitioners the opportunity to sort through these and accept, reject or modify them. Parker (1971) considering the leisure meanings of time, activities and state of being, points out that they often overlap, but that the classification is useful in determining which aspect of the word has the greater emphasis with particular contexts. Godbey (1994) explained that leisure is not neatly confined to any one part of our lives or to any one social institution. Neulinger (1974) believed that leisure is a quality rather than a behaviour and the nature of that leisure will affect a person's quality of life.

Today we have more knowledge, more resources and more opportunity than ever before, in which to have a fullness of living, undreamed of in times past. The question is: has leisure a central role in a way of life that harnesses opportunities for harmony with oneself and the world? Without an understanding of such leisure, albeit as an ideal, we cannot have sound principles on which to formulate policies for planning, provision and management.

Discussion points

1 Leisure and recreation are often considered to be the same thing and used synonymously. Debate similarities and differences in order to explain to your organization what is meant by these concepts and to better communicate and manage services.

2 Can a case be made for defining recreation as re-creation, and if so, why, when and how? And if not, why not?

5
Children's play: foundation of leisure

Introduction

> The right to play is a child's first claim on the community. Play is nature's training for life. No community can infringe that right without doing deep and enduring harm to the minds and bodies of its citizens. Much that is unwholesome and dangerous to the nation, comes from the overcrowding and congestion of our towns and cities and, in particular, from the restrictions and frustrations to which they subject the lives of the boys and girls who grow up in them.
>
> Lloyd George, 1926, at the Inauguration of the National Playing Fields Association

> Play is not only important to the quality of life of children, it is of great importance for the country's future, to the creative industries and for the economy.
>
> Chris Smith, Secretary of State for Culture, Media and Sport, 1998

'Play' is a word much used in the English language. We most often think of children's play, going out to play, playtime, and playing games, but we use the word in far wider contexts and situations. We can go to see a play, play soccer, play the trumpet, play cards, play roulette. We can play the fool, play jokes, have tricks played on us, play truant, play the field or play around! We can play well or play badly, play into the hands of our opponents, play second fiddle, and let defeat play on our minds. Fair play is deeply rooted in our culture: 'come on guys, play the game'. Familiar in Western culture is the saying, 'all work and no play makes Jack a dull boy and makes Jill a dull girl'.

Play is the cornerstone of leisure and recreation. Through play:

- children acquire a range of skills

- children learn how to deal with new situations quickly by linking together things they have already learned
- children develop their physical, intellectual, emotional, creative and social ability, the difficult skill of give-and-take and to live in harmony with others.

Denied play opportunity, children suffer and so does the society in which they live. However, play in most countries is still under-valued and under-resourced.

Every opinion canvassed in the *Review of National Support for Children's Play and Recreation* (Torkildsen, 1993) believed unequivocally that play held substantial benefits for children. Wholesome development ('holistic' was a word often used), social education and learning were mentioned most often. Physical development, motor skills and creativity were also recognized. Many of those consulted spoke of the misunderstanding of the word 'play', often almost derided as being 'only child's play'. That play is not taken seriously and is under-funded was a theme which dominated most consultations. 'Children's play' gave the impression that its only function is fun, rather than enjoyment in doing many things, often very seriously.

Children are often referred to as the citizens of tomorrow. In fact, children and young people are citizens of today. The kind of adult citizens they will become, will depend on how citizenship for life is cultivated. Part of cultivating and enriching lives is through play. Play shapes human behaviour. Although theories of play, in the main, tend to be based on philosophical belief and observational experience, scientific evidence confirms that play has important functions for child development, learning and physical and social skills. Given these circumstances, it is surprising that play provision is an area of relatively low priority, particularly in terms of government funding in the United Kingdom. In some local authorities, the play service is the first to experience cuts in resources. This usually manifests itself with a reduction in the standards of maintenance of equipped playgrounds and a reduced number of playschemes, often considered simply as child-minding or as solutions to problems of nuisance. For example, increased charges, applied to some holiday playschemes, have resulted in the detriment of the service for the greater good of the greater number.

Children have little say in what we provide for them. Nationally, 20 per cent of the population are aged under 16 years and, in broad terms, about one-third of this group are under five, one-third of primary school age and one-third of secondary school age. Guided play, developmental play and recreation opportunity are needed for all children, but children have no voice in the decision-making processes. Children need to be observed, consulted and involved.

Children are growing up in a rapidly changing world of uncertainty, and parents, guardians, carers, teachers and playworkers have increasing concerns for them. There is general concern at the poor levels of health and fitness of children. Inactive children are likely to become inactive adults, increasing the risks of obesity and heart disease. Many spend hours every day in front of a television set or playing video games. The danger is in encouraging a generation of computer-game literate children, with finger dexterity, but who may be unable to throw and catch a ball or to interact socially and emotionally. Some children see their worth in what they own, wear and how they look. Creative play lifts children from being trapped at such a functional level and helps to give them confidence in their own worth.

Social anxieties exist with perceptions of inadequate parenting, latch-key children, child neglect and abuse, crime, drugs and a more hostile, unsafe environment, traffic problems and the lessening of play opportunity for many children in a culture of material competition. Child poverty is blamed, though this is only a risk factor, not a cause.

The understanding of play in the United Kingdom is encapsulated in key documents including:

- *Best Play* (NPFA/CPC/PLAYLINK, 2000)
- *The New Charter for Children's Play* (CPC, 1998) and
- *Getting Serious About Play – a Review of Children's Play* (DCMS, 2004).

Freedom, exploration, learning, fun and seriousness are some of play's characteristics.

Best Play: What play provision should do for children was produced as a result of a partnership between the National Playing Fields Association, PLAYLINK and the Children's Play Council and included consultation within the field of playwork. This important publication disseminates best practice and recognizes the value and quality of playworkers and providers. In the United Kingdom, its principles and values also act as foundations for the National Childcare Strategy, the Early Years Development and Childcare Partnerships. Best Play is about values and principles, about children and play, and how children benefit from play opportunities, services and spaces.

Best Play *defines play like this: 'Play is freely chosen, personally directed, intrinsically motivated behaviour that actively engages the child.'*

This chapter explores the concept of play and the relationship with leisure and recreation. It draws out the characteristics of play behaviour and attempts to understand what it is, why people play and what communities can do to provide for it.

An inborn propensity to play

Animals and humans have always played, it would seem. Dogs appear to be happiest (when not eating) at play: catching, fetching, teasing, playing games and having fun. The play of animals illustrates that play precedes culture and human civilization. Of all the animal kingdom, the latest species – human beings – play most of all.

The play of young children is experimental, exploratory. Objects stimulate curiosity and the imagination. We have all observed the infant who is far more interested in the paper or the box than in the present inside. Children need to experience and to delight in physical movement, to explore their environment and the objects within it, and to develop relationships with people. Playing with water, sand and pebbles, getting muddy, climbing trees, dressing up, imitating, make-believe, fantasy play, role playing, hiding and seeking, dancing, singing rhymes, listening to stories, sharing secrets, inventing, making things, and socializing are some of the characteristics of the world of children. Play, therefore, has the propensity to make learning irresistible.

Difficulties facing children's play

To play, children need opportunities, with time and space, free from constraints and dangers. What factors mitigate against play?

- When homes are cramped, noisy or overcrowded and without easy access to play spaces, and when neighbourhoods are dominated by traffic and polluted in other ways, children are exposed to risks and may be deprived of their independence to play.
- When children are anxious or fearful, subject to abuse, bullying and violence, their freedom to play is affected.
- When children and their parents are under pressure from negative social, educational and economic factors, play time is marginalized or ignored.

When children become inactive, they become less healthy, often obese; and when denied play, they take longer to recover from ill-health and trauma or are permanently damaged.

Children's natural propensity to play has been impaired by the loss of suitable public space, the impact of technology, such as television, the personal computer and the motor car, and the changing attitude of society towards children, reflected, for instance, in the increase in parental anxiety about child safety. Play provision should compensate for this loss. Ultimately, the aim of Best Play is to ensure that this compensation is adequate in the light of children's own needs, wishes, capacities and abilities.

Best Play, 2000

Play as an attitude of mind

Play is a mystery and an enigma. It is understood yet misunderstood; known yet unknown; individual yet universal and tangible, yet so internal that to someone 'outside' it is untouchable. The play of children is accepted, but the play of adults conjures up the image of muddy footballers on muddy pitches. However, play is not confined to the games of children, the sport of young people, the family outing or the birthday party. Play can pervade all aspects of life; not just physical play, but also the play of the mind, the play of words and the play of communications with people. To Sebastian de Grazia (1962):

The film *Oh, What a Lovely War!* carried the caption 'the ever popular war game with songs, battles and a few jokes'.

The world is divided into two classes. Not three or five or twenty. Just two. One is the great majority. The other is the leisure kind, not those of wealth or position or birth, but those who love ideas and the imagination. Of the great mass of mankind there are few persons who are blessed and tormented with this love. They may work, steal, flirt, fight, like all the others, but everything they do, is touched with the play of thought.

Play then can be evident in all walks of life, at home, at school, at work, in politics and unions, in religion, in business, in crime and vandalism, in international dealings and even in war.

The rules of play

One of the distinguishing signs of the play world is its strict adherence to invented rules, which suspend the ordinary rules of real life. The attitudes encompassed in play rules carry over from the play world into the 'real' world. Boxers play to Queensberry Rules, soldiers play to the rules of the Geneva Convention and even some criminals have a code of acceptable behaviour.

Parliamentary and local government rules are cloaked in the playful seriousness of obligatory procedures, the 'Chair', the 'points of order' and the adherence to the 'laws of the game'. Sometimes, as with children's games, it would appear that the procedures are more important than the business itself. 'Fair play' is often play acceptable to the rules. In this context, it is curious to find how much more lenient society is towards the 'loveable rogue' who cheats than it is towards the spoilsport. As Huizinga (1955) points out, the spoilsport shatters the play world and robs it of its illusion (*in lusio*, 'in play'); the game ends. The cheat, on the other hand, pretends to be playing the game and on the face of it acknowledges the rules, and the game continues. Play is a complex set of behaviours. Almost any situation or activity, it appears, can function for someone as a play activity if undertaken in the spirit of play.

Play, normally reserved for the playground and playing field, is indelibly printed upon the lives of boys and girls, men and women. It spans the frivolous and the utterly serious, the shallow and the deeply emotional. Play is in the very nature of human beings.

Play in historical perspective

From the earliest recorded times, human beings have played. Artifacts have been found, engravings and writings have been discovered and playthings have been unearthed from the distant past. In tracing human development, anthropologists have found not only implements for work and survival, but also playthings: toys, dolls, hoops, rattles, marbles and dice. Our ancestors were inventive and creative toy makers. Playing musical instruments, dressing up in ornate costume, pageantry and dancing may have resulted from, initially, just playing, or having fun. In later times, scientific discoveries and inventions may well have been the outcome of playing with a hobby, with intense and absorbing enthusiasm.

A good deal can be gleaned about the history of children's play by studying the playthings through the ages. In Ancient Greece, children played games using balls, tops and hoops. During the Sung Dynasty in China around a thousand years ago, children are seen in a painting riding hobby-horses, juggling and dressing up. Hobby-horses existed long before rocking horses. They are mentioned in writings from classical Greek and Roman times, appear on Chinese ceramics dating back centuries, and were popular from the Middle Ages in Europe (Lindon, 2001). While fun for children, the aim of adults was to help prepare boys for riding. A painting by the sixteenth-century Flemish artist, Pieter Brueghel, entitled *Children's Games*, shows children at a pretend wedding, rolling hoops, playing tug-of-war. The Bethnal Green Museum in London has many examples of toys from hundreds of years ago and the Victoria and Albert Picture Library has pictures of children playing at skipping, flying kites, with dolls and with kitchen equipment. Puppet plays have been used to tell morality and religious stories over the centuries in China, India and in Europe. Dressing up is a favourite play for children in most cultures, although it is thought to bring bad luck in some African communities.

Examples from all around the world show that children like to play, and need to play to learn and develop. And if it is fun in the doing, they learn even more quickly. Visit almost every country, observe children's behaviour and we will see them at play, often playing at the same things. However, perspectives on play do vary from culture to culture and playworkers in multi-cultural settings need to be aware of potential differences and use them to the benefit of all. In *Understanding Children's Play*, Lindon (2001) explores play with dolls in different cultures:

> A good example comes from the Kachina dolls. They are now made for tourists by Hopi Indians in Arizona and New Mexico. Yet, in the early 10th century, these carved and painted wooden figures of masked dancers were of spiritual significance. They represented Kachinas, the spirits who controlled nature and the weather. The figures were used with children, but with an instructional purpose to enable them to understand the religious beliefs of their society. Some doll-like figures seem to have had mainly a play purpose for children in a range of American Indian and Central American cultures. However, a dual purpose involving religious instruction also seems to have been quite common. Some toys in Mexico are still sold in connection with specific religious festivals and saints' days, although many are now more generally available. Traditional dolls in China and Japan usually seem to have had ceremonial and sometimes spiritual significance. They have been given to children, but not always with a play function in mind. In Japan, for instance, great emphasis has been placed on the value of dolls to help children to learn about Japanese history, cultural pursuits and human endeavour. The Girls' and Boys' Festival dolls are linked with two separate festivals, one for each sex. The dolls are designed to teach heroism and valour to the boys. The girls are instructed in the preservation of Japanese culture, including the importance of history and the royal family.

Today, discerning parents buy toys and playthings which are said to be educational, yet learning through play is not a new idea. Jigsaw puzzles date from the late eighteenth century when they were first known as 'dissected puzzles' and were made for instructional purposes.

A legacy from the Ancient Greek civilization

The roots of play philosophy and theory reach back to ancient times. In some respects, the classical era of Greece was one of the most enlightened. Although child labour was common, children had an important place in classical society. Play was given a valuable position in the life of children, according to both Plato (1900) and Aristotle (1926).

> That which is neither utility nor truth nor likeness, nor yet, in its effects harmful, can best be judged by the criterion of charm that is in it and the pleasure it affords. Such pleasure, entailing as it does no appreciable good or ill, is play.
>
> Plato, cited in Maclean *et al.*, 1963

Play and leisure gave an opportunity for children to develop. The primary force was education (*paideia*), inculcating qualities of responsibility, of honour, loyalty, pride and of beauty. The philosophical writings which remain indicate dedication to state and culture, the highest value being placed on productive citizenship. It is not surprising therefore to note that play (*paideia*, the same word as education) was considered an aspect of enculturation and cultural reinforcement.

Play to the Greeks was associated with childhood. Yet the citizenship of adult life and the appreciation of aesthetics, music, art, athletics, drama and poetry might be seen as the products of play. Today we tend to look at the opportunities for play as incorporating free choice, freedom from compulsion, often spontaneity. But the Greek citizen was bound to social commitment. There was a belief in universal personality or character which was held to be true of all noble persons. Hence life's activities were structured to fulfil this ideal. Play, then, was part of the means of integrating people into Greek culture as children. The Ancient Greeks laid a foundation of thought regarding play that has endured to influence leisure and recreation today. The perfectibility of human nature through play, its usefulness in mental, physical and social well-being and the necessity of social control were of great importance.

Later civilizations modified Greek attitudes towards play. The Roman culture exploited leisure and provoked a hedonistic philosophy, which abandoned the concepts of moderation and balance in play behaviour. The ensuing over-reaction to play left its mark on the cultures that followed. The church took strict moral control over play expression. There emerged a suspicion of 'play' as a social threat. The Middle Ages marked a period when there was no concept of childhood; children were viewed simply as small adults but with low status. Obedience to, and passive acceptance of, God's will characterized the ethos of these times; play, the active seeking of new experience, retained little place in the ideals of this world. The body was thought to detract from more spiritual activities, thus every effort was made to curb its impulses. The Reformation acted further to restrict play among those following its creeds. Work became all-important; consequently, play became separated from work behaviour, and was considered morally dangerous.

Philosophers and educators advocate play

Important contributions in the eighteenth and nineteenth centuries to counteract the decline in play philosophy came from Rousseau, Pestalozzi, Froebel, McMillan and Montessori. Rousseau, in his revolutionary text *Emile*, espoused the idea of the natural child, the child of nature; mankind should return to a state of nature marked by simplicity and freedom. Jean Jacques Rousseau (1712–78), concerned with social justice and an egalitarian society, promoted a dramatic change in the view of children and childhood. At that time, children were seen as 'born into sin'; they were thought to be evil and needed to be drawn towards goodness. He proposed the opposite view that children were naturally good and their positive nature could be harnessed through care and education. His was a Romantic view of childhood; he proposed letting children be themselves in their natural playfulness in safety away from the harsh realities of life. Early education should be focused on the learning needs of children and not on the strict authoritarian rote learning methods. Rousseau, and others with reformist and revolutionary ideas, forced society to accept two major changes: a distinction between children and adults, and the acceptance of play as an end in itself.

Johann Heinrich Pestalozzi (1746–1827) was a Swiss pioneer of mass education. In his day, he made several unsuccessful attempts to establish schools for poor children. Strongly influenced by Rousseau, his ideas on the intuitive method of education – moving in tune with children's development – were not recognized until much later. The first Pestalozzi International Children's Village was established in 1946 for war orphans at Trogen in Switzerland; a second was established in 1958 at Sedlescombe in Britain for the care and education of selected children from developing countries.

Friedrich Froebel (1782–1852) was a German pioneer of nursery education. Building on the ideas of Pestalozzi, he believed that play is the outward expression of an inner life and that young children should spend time together in creative play. 'Play is the purest, most spiritual activity of man … It holds the sources of all that is good. It gives, therefore, joy, freedom, contentment, inner and outer rest, peace with the world' (Froebel *et al.*, 1963).This led him to found the first kindergarten: the 'children's garden' at Blankenburg in 1837. Self-expression through play was his hallmark, with activities such as drawing, painting, weaving, sewing; Froebel's 'sixteen activities' were designed to interest children and support their learning. He also used what he called 'gifts', a precisely made series of wooden blocks in shapes such as ball, cylinder, cube, rectangle and square. Playing with these wooden blocks would teach children that everything around them was structured. Gifts were made and sold in sets and they still are today. Froebel's ideas were so radical at the time that he was accused of being subversive and the authorities in Prussia closed all the kindergartens. It was not until the 1930s that the philosophy developed towards allowing children more free expression in their art and craft work. Early childhood education in many countries was shaped significantly by his approach.

Maria Montessori (1870–1952), an Italian doctor, created a system of education for young children placing emphasis on development of the senses where a child learns for itself. She first worked with children with learning difficulties and those from impoverished backgrounds. Children she found preferred to work while at play and that this focus of activity was more challenging than frivolous activities. Montessori developed educational equipment designed by the French medical physiologist, Edouard Seguin, for children with learning difficulties. She extended these play materials into her system of 'didactic apparatus'. She opened her first *casa dei bambini* (children's house) in 1907 enabling children to manage the basic skills of life through self-education and exploration.

What is the influence on play today? Froebel and Montessori promoted play because of its potential for educational purposes.

> The new element of their approach was that children were believed to learn best through self directed activity, supported by intrinsic motivation. Both innovators broke away from the view that children needed to be driven by adult instructions and rote learning.
>
> Lindon, 2001, p. 122

Froebel, however, believed that children's spontaneous play was an integrating means of stimulating language and revealing children's feelings, thoughts and actions.

Margaret McMillan (1860–1931) was concerned with social inequalities and the well-being of children who lived in poverty. She promoted a nursery environment in which outdoor learning was as important as indoor. Also influenced by Seguin, she was concerned with diet, lack of fresh air and physical exercise. Her sister Rachel McMillan was experienced in visiting people in need in rural areas. Margaret McMillan set up the Open Air Nursery School in Deptford, London, in 1914, later to be named the Rachel McMillan Nursery School. Children chose their own activities including gardening, animals, dressing up and 'scientific' equipment.

Play theories: classical, recent and modern

A plethora of theories exists that define what play is and why people, especially children, play. Edginton *et al.* (2003) list around 70 definitions of play. To appreciate what the concept represents, a useful starting point is to examine the roots of the word. The word is used in the sense of amorous disport, dalliance, jest, fun, trifling, and with

> According to the Oxford English Dictionary, *'play'* derives from the Old English plega, meaning rapid movement, exercise, sport: free movement, brisk and vigorous action as in dancing, leaping, rejoicing, 'strutting as a cock bird before hens'.

games and gaming. It is also related to the Latin *plaga* meaning a blow, thrust or stroke, as when stroking an instrument or striking a ball. Play from earliest time, therefore, has had a connotation of action, pleasure, frolic and delight. More subtle uses such as the play of the mind, came later in its history. As there are so many theories, it is useful to categorize them in broad historical dates which give an indication of the thinking of the time and how ideas have changed.

Classical theories

Classical play theories are relatively well known, though some are better known than the rest and survive in the literature today. They include:

The Surplus Energy Theory (*c.* 1875), sometimes referred to as the Schiller-Spencer theory (Schiller, 1965), describes play as the expenditure of over-abundant energy which is unused in the normal processes of life sustenance.

The Instinct Theory suggests that play is caused by the inheritance of unlearned capacities to behave playfully. But this theory ignores the fact that children learn new responses that we classify as play.

The Preparation for Life Theory of Karl Groos (*c.* 1901)(Groos, 1901), based on Darwinian thinking, perceives play as nature's way of preparing the young of higher animals for the demands of life.

The Recapitulation Theory of G. Stanley-Hall (1904) is explained as an outcome of biological inheritance. It is another Darwin-influenced theory. Children are a link in the evolutionary chain, experiencing the history of the human race in play activities.

Stanley-Hall (1920) believed that play patterns were instinctive, generic expressions and re-enactments of early man's activities, that is, a recapitulation of racial development seen in water play, digging in the sand, climbing trees and in tribal gangs.

The Relaxation Theory of Patrick (1916) as described in *The Psychology of Relaxation* (Patrick, 1916), proposed that playful activity was caused by the need to find compensating outlets to allow relaxation and recuperation from the tension and stress of work.

Most of the early theories were based on instinct as motivation of human play and these theories now only survive when they are incorporated in other theories of play behaviour. Today play is considered to be much more complex than earlier theories suggested. All the older theories have some small merit, seeming to explain some aspects of behaviour, but they are over-optimistic in their simplicity. Each is relevant to different sets of problems. They take no account of individual differences. Ellis (1973) suggests: 'Old soldiers never die' and they linger on in the literature as 'armchair theories'. They seem to explain, albeit curiously, some aspects of human behaviour, but they have logical shortcomings and are not substantiated by empirical findings.

Theories from the first half of the twentieth century

In contrast to the classical theories, theories from the early twentieth century are concerned with attempting to explain the differences between the play of individuals. Luther Hasley Gulick (Gulick, 1975) writing in 1920 wrote:

> Play consists of that which people do when they have food, shelter, and clothing, when the physical compulsions of life are removed temporarily and the spirit is free to search for its own satisfactions. Then man is at his best ... Play has a greater shaping power over the character and nature of man than has any other one activity. A man shows what he really is when he is free to do what he chooses, and if a person can be influenced so that his greater aspirations – which are followed when he is free to pursue his ideals – are a gain, then character is being shaped profoundly ... Play is more than a name applied to a given list of activities; it is an attitude, which may pervade every activity. Play as a free expression of self, as the pursuit of the ideal, has direct bearing on the ultimate questions of reality and worth. The spirit of play has value as a philosophy of life ... A daily life in which there is no opportunity for recreation may be fraught with as much evil as leisure time given over to a futile frittering away of energy. Time for rest and recreation is an absolute necessity for personal development; it is necessary under modern industrial conditions.

The learning, developmental and psychoanalytic theories show that play contributes to the development of intelligence and a healthy personality. Children gain pleasure, overcome unpleasant experiences and develop mastery of their physical and social environment through play.

Some, like Huizinga (1955), claim that play is justification in and of itself without further rationalization, but animals play as well as humans and this seems to indicate that it performs some survival function. Ellis (1973) and others have identified a range of theories during the twentieth century.

Generalization and Compensation Theories rely on the belief that people's play choices are a result of the nature of their 'work'; presumably for children, this includes school work. People who perform work tasks well, and are satisfied by them, will tend to behave similarly during their leisure or play time. The Compensation Theory suggests that adults select their leisure activities to compensate for 'work' situations that do not satisfy their needs. These theories are over-simplistic, too general and take no account of non-work or pre-school play.

The Cathartic Theory dates from classical Greece, where dramatic tragedies and some music were believed to purge the audience of their emotions. The belief was that giving vent to feelings and emotions releases them. Feshbach (1956) questions whether the expression of aggression in a socially approved form will reduce the amount of socially disapproved aggressive behaviour. Aggression researchers are finding that frustration leads to heightened aggressive feelings, but that subsequent aggressive behaviour does not reduce aggression. Berkowitz and Green (1962) indicate that 'aggression begets aggression'.

The Psychoanalytic Theories stemmed from Sigmund Freud (1974), who observed that much play is motivated by pleasure. His ideas were later amended, formalized by Wälder (1933), and expanded by Erikson to show that play has multiple facets and cannot be explained by a single function. Erikson (1950) extended the ideas of infant development to stages of mastery and life development, taking into account effects of the environment. Play has a developmental progression in which a child adds new, more complex understandings about the world at each stage. He identified three stages: 'autocosmic' play concerns bodily play; the 'micro sphere' is playing with toys and objects; and the 'macro sphere' develops sharing. Play may be used to work through and master reality; the child finds identity through play. Infant play between mother and child is all-important; adult behaviour and attitude are also of great importance. He relates this interplay to ritualization; the ritual expression combines the elements of play and social tradition, providing individual identity in a structured and/or communal fashion.

The psychoanalytic theory, therefore, goes beyond the pleasure principle to explain the play of children that is related to experiences that are not pleasant. There are encounters that they cannot control which are often unpleasant. To Freud, the opposite to play is not what is serious, but what is real. Psychoanalytic theory suggests that children consciously add actual elements from their environment to their fantasies, mixing reality and unreality into their play. Adults are seen as more constrained by society, emphasizing their grasp of reality and hiding their tendency to deal with unreality in play. Thus adults are left with covert fantasies. Wälder suggests that 'fantasy woven about a real object is however nothing other than play'.

Play Therapy Theory followed on from psychoanalytic methods and were developed by researchers such as Melanie Klein (Klein, 1955). By playing out feelings, a child can bring them to the surface, get them out into the open, face them and learn to control or abandon them. When anxious, a child will prefer to play with items which are salient to the anxiety (hospitalized children like to play doctors and nurses). However, the psychoanalytic theories are another set of partial theories, explaining only some aspects of play behaviour. Play as a therapeutic process has long been recognized; children play out their distress and anxiety. Play can be a means of dealing with life's difficulties, fears and stressful conditions. Teachers of pre-school and school children and teachers in hospitals recognize the play patterns, attitudes and friendship divisions in settings such as in sectarian conflict, racial unrest and in war-torn countries. Psychoanalysts support these observations that play can help children deal with trauma and emotional healing. Daniel Goleman (1995) gives an example of a children's game called 'Purdy'. In 1989 in Stockton, California, Patrick Purdy fired bullets into a playground killing five children and wounding more before shooting himself. This had a long-term terrifying effect on the children. The game of Purdy was invented, and played in different ways. Some versions reflected the actual events, others pretended they had the guns and killed Purdy.

The Intellectual Development Theory of Swiss child psychologist Jean Piaget (1962) suggests that judgement, reasoning and logic learned during childhood have important consequences for children's education. The structure of intelligence is a function of two co-existing processes he called 'assimilation' and 'accommodation'. Assimilation is a process whereby the child imposes on reality his or her own knowledge and interpretations and thus often alters reality to fit what is known from previous experience. In accommodation, a child alters existing cognitive structures to meet the demands of reality. Hence, the child modifies feelings and thoughts when confronted with an object which appears novel: what he/she thinks is known must be altered to match what is encountered in the environment.

According to Piaget, the balance between assimilation and accommodation constitutes the basis of intelligence and all behaviour is the 'acting out' of this cognitive interplay. Play is characterized by the assimilation of elements in the real world without the balancing constraints of accepting the problems of accommodating them. The behaviour that occurs when assimilation predominates can be described as playful, and when accommodation predominates behaviour is viewed as imitative. So play is manipulative; children alter and restructure their environment to match experience and their existing knowledge: reality is altered; the child creates an imaginary play world.

Piaget described three main categories of children's play:

- practice play was the play behaviour typical of very young children
- symbolic play developed from two years onwards and became more varied up to six years of age – children's ideas were visible through their play
- games with rules developed from six or seven years of age, depending on their grasp of abstract ideas, including shared rules.

Hence, Piaget believed that play eventually becomes a game played with rules and structure. Following this theme, Corinne and John Hutt distinguished between two broad kinds of play (Hutt and Hutt, cited in Lindon, 2001). 'Epistemic play' focused on acquiring knowledge and information, dealing in problem solving and exploration. It was the more productive kind of play because it was more likely to promote learning. 'Ludic play' including symbolic and fantasy elements is the type of play which is repetitive, involves children's preferences, and is affected by mood states. Within Piaget's main grouping of games with rules, they categorized co-operative, competitive, games of skill or chance.

Sutton-Smith (1966), however, raised many objections to Piaget's thesis. He believes that play remains important, does not become more realistic or rationalistic as intelligence develops, but remains symbolic, ritualistic and playful, even into adulthood.

> Within that inner life, play is a mental process that builds upon and integrates many other processes in the developing child's mind – thinking, imagining, pretending, planning, wondering, doubting, remembering, guessing, hoping, experimenting, redoing, and working through. The child at play, using these varied mental processes, integrates past experiences and current feelings and desires.
>
> Sutton-Smith, 1997, p. 23

In essence, however, Piaget implies that play is the most effective aspect of early learning.

Stimulus–Response Theories of Thorndike, Hull, Skinner and others view play as learned behaviour, 'stimulus-response behaviour' (see Ellis, 1973, for discussion of these ideas). A response has an increased probability of occurring if it is accompanied by a pleasant or reinforcing event. If play behaviour is learned behaviour, then the learning will occur as a result of a whole variety of 'reinforcers' and reinforcing systems, for example, parents, other children and other adults sharing the same cultural and environmental influences.

Play, Games and Socialization Theory Empirical studies undertaken by Roberts and Sutton-Smith, an anthropologist and psychologist, show that individuals in different cultures perceive games differently, depending on the values and attitudes prevalent, and that such games serve to relieve social conflict and consequently enhance socialization (Roberts and Sutton-Smith, 1962). They put forward a theory of conflict enculturation. Conflicts induced by social learning (such as obedience, achievement, responsibility training) lead to an involvement in 'expressive models', such as games, through which these conflicts are moderated, lessened and assuaged. A learning process occurs which has cultural value both to the players and to their societies. They tested the hypothesis by studying the difference in rearing patterns and games played by the children in three societies. Clear evidence was found for an association between the predominance of one type of game and a particular emphasis in the rearing patterns.

Play as Self-Justification, an end in itself. Jan Huizinga, a Dutch historian, in his masterly book *Homo Ludens* (Huizinga, 1955) presents the cultural approach to play: 'Play is older than culture, for culture, however adequately defined, always presupposes human society, and animals have not waited for man to teach them their playing.' Huizinga showed play to exist in every aspect of culture. He defines play as follows:

> Summing up the formal characteristics of play we might call it a free activity standing quite consciously outside 'ordinary' life as being 'not serious', but at the same time absorbing the player

intensely and utterly. It is an activity connected with no material interest, and no profit can be gained by it. It proceeds within its own proper boundaries of time and space according to fixed rules and in an orderly manner. It promotes the formation of social groupings which tend to surround themselves with secrecy and to stress their difference from the common world by disguise or other means.

To Huizinga, play is self-justified. It can be present in all aspects of life: in work, business, leisure, sport, art, literature, music, religion and even in war. He believed most former theories to be only partial theories, which justified play as a means to an end: play was seen to serve something which it is not, leaving the primary quality of play untouched. Moreover, civilization had compartmentalized play, had grown more serious, had put play into second place. For the full unfolding of civilization we cannot neglect the play element: 'genuine pure play is one of the main bases of civilization.' Observation of the play rules were nowhere more important than in relations between nations. Once the rules were broken, society would be in chaos.

Huizinga believed that to play we must play like a child. When, for example, the play spirit is lost from sport, sport becomes divorced from 'culture'. He gives no explanation as to why people play, but he does describe play vividly. One can deduce from his description a number of interrelated characteristics.

1 Play is a free, voluntary activity. There is more freedom in the play world than in the real world. We cannot play to order; if the player is forced to 'play', it changes its nature; it is no longer play.
2 Play is indulged in for its own sake. It is unproductive and non-utilitarian.
3 Play is not 'ordinary' or 'real'. The player steps outside real life into a temporary sphere. The player knows it is only pretending, yet it is often utterly serious.
4 Play has boundaries of space and time. It has its own course and meaning.
5 Play is creative. Once played, it endures. It is repeated, alternated, transmitted; it becomes tradition.
6 Play is orderly and creates order. Into an imperfect world and the confusion of life it brings a temporary, limited perfection.
7 Play is regulated. It has rules and conventions; they determine what 'holds' in the temporary world. The new legislation counts; deviation spoils the play.
8 Play is 'uncertain'. The end result cannot be determined. When the result is a foregone conclusion, then the tension and excitement is lost.
9 Play is social. Play communities tend to become permanent social groupings even after the game is over (clubs, brotherhoods, gangs). Groups are often esoteric or secret: 'It is for us, not for others.' Inside the magic circle there are the laws and customs which suspend the ordinary rules of life.
10 Play, then, is symbolic.

Huizinga's theory is a philosophical one. Play exists, it has always existed; it is its own justification. But self-justification is something that cannot be measured. It gives insights but not explanations.

Socio-Cultural Theory The French sociologist, Roger Caillois, in *Man, Play and Games* (Caillois, 1961) presented a socio-culturally based theory of play building upon the theory of Huizinga. Caillois critically analysed the definition and redefined play as activity which is free, separate, uncertain, unproductive, and governed by rules or make-believe. Caillois developed a unique typology of the characteristic games of a society. Games are a clue to culture, helping to reveal the character, pattern and values of a society. The basic themes of a culture should be deducible from the study of play and games no less than from the study of economic, political, religious or family institutions. He claimed that the destinies of cultures can be read in their choice of games: 'Tell me what you play and I will tell you who you are.'

The choice of games will reflect the society. Caillois identified four general classifications of games:

- *agon* (competition): the desire to win by merit in regulated competition
- *alea* (chance): the submission of one's will to the luck of the draw
- mimicry (simulation): assuming a strange personality
- *ilinx* (vertigo): the confusion that giddiness provokes.

Games in each of the four categories were put on to a continuum representing an evolution from childlike play (*paidia*) to adult play (*ludus*). The first of these encompasses the spontaneous, frivolous, exuberant play, the frolic and the romping. The second is more concerned with man the thinker; the pleasure is in resolving difficulties. It represents those elements in play whose cultural importance seems to be the most striking. Rules are inseparable from play, once play acquires an institutional existence.

According to Caillois, while games reflect the functioning of a society, if corrupted, they indicate the weakness and potential dissolution of the culture. Although not completely explanatory, and often weak in accurate identifications of social expressions, Caillois's theory does illuminate another perspective for analysis of play.

Theories in the second half of the twentieth century

Studies of children's play behaviour are succinctly summarized in *Make Way for Children's Play* (Play Board, 1985) and general theories of play are described by Elizabeth Child (1985). Norbek (1979) puts forward the biological case: play is characteristic of biological immaturity; the young play much more than adults, but play is also a characteristic of adulthood.

> Through infantile play, members of a species acquire motor and other skills needed in adult life for survival. Young human beings, with a long period of immaturity, are aided in this process by provision of specific opportunities for play experiences.

An anthropological view suggests that the 'ultimate human being' is the person with varied behaviour. Play, in its multiple forms, appears to hold a position 'of prominence and vital importance'. Play fosters a wide range of adult behaviour. In *Looking at Play*, Hughes and Williams (1982) include 'a biological model'. They examine the ways human beings develop flexibility and how this development is necessary for survival and evolution:

In both instances, we suggest that PLAY is the mechanism by which flexibility is achieved. And by doing this, present an argument which states that play is a feature of human behaviour from birth to death, and is absolutely essential in forming the basis both for human survival and human development. Play, then, is concerned with two integral and related parts of the human learning process: It describes the way the body deliberately searches for, and locates stimuli – and in so doing, describes how it gains information concerning the nature of its world. It describes the means by which the brain assimilates and selects those stimuli which give it 'good' feelings (+ve effects), and how it pursues them. Without play as an interactive experience, learning would not take place and the human would not acquire the skills necessary for survival.

A similar line is taken by Brown (1990) in *A Playwork Training Pack*. Barnett (1979) believes children learn to be resourceful within the environment 'purely as a consequence of self-directed play'. Empirical support for this notion was found by Sylva (1977) and by Barnett (1976) herself, and free play was seen as necessary behaviour for survival. Play helps a child to explore the environment and thereby learn the procedures required to solve problems posed by the environment in later life. Play appears to be directly related to the divergent thought processes of the child and thus serves as the stimulus for normal cognitive development.

Play as arousal-seeking behaviour

Michael Ellis's book *Why People Play* (Ellis, 1973) is one of the most comprehensive and thorough studies of play. Ellis believes that there is no way of reaching any 'pure' definition and that the most satisfying explanation of play involves an integration of three theories:

- play as arousal-seeking behaviour
- play as learning and
- the developmentalist view of play; there is considerable evidence to support the view that play enhances learning and development.

Ellis defines play in this context as 'that behaviour that is motivated by the need to elevate the level of arousal towards the optimal'. Put another way, play is stimulus-seeking activity that can occur only when external consequences are eliminated: 'When primary drives are satisfied the animal continues to emit stimulus-seeking behaviour in response to the sensoristatic drive. The animal learns to maintain an optimal level of arousal.'

Researchers in arousal theory find that it is the stimuli that are complex, incongruous or novel that lead to arousal. In addition, the stimuli must have the ability to reduce uncertainty or to carry information to the individual. However, when situations are too complex, they have no arousal potential, and at the other end of the scale when the outcome is highly predictable, there is little uncertainty and the arousal potential diminishes. For example, the crossword in *The Times* will have no arousal potential for the easy-crossword dabbler; the gifted chess player will not be stimulated by the novice opponent. The play 'spirit' for many adults is often the play of the mind. Reading a thriller, following the fortunes of a favourite team in the newspaper, checking up on the Stock Exchange, doing crosswords, playing Trivial Pursuit, problem solving, are all activities actively sought by adults, in particular, who by virtue of their age have a richer store of experiences. However, stimulus-seeking behaviour means more than merely seeking exposure to any stimuli. The stimuli must have arousal potential. Knowledge seeking, for example, results in the reduction of conflicts, mismatches and uncertainties. Laughter, humour and smiling are created by situations such as novelty, surprise, incongruity, ambiguity, complexity – all of which possess arousal potential. Fun has arousal potential.

But not all stimulus seeking is play. The behaviour that seems to be clearly non-utilitarian is play. This may appear to lead to an artificial divide between work and play but clearly such stimulus-seeking behaviour can be found in both work and play. The theory appears to handle the question of work and play equally well. Indeed, it questions the validity of separating work from play. Thus Ellis provides an explanation for both special and individual motivation towards play, and also describes a researchable, physiological base for play. In terms of its value to people and society, play fosters individuality; it provides 'learnings' that reflect individual, unique requirements; and it prepares for the unknown. Play will not occur when the essential conditions necessary for play behaviour are absent. One of the most important aspects coming out of this work is the realization that people play when the content of their behaviour is largely under their control.

Playfulness

The psychologist J. Nina Lieberman has studied a concept which she identified as 'playfulness' and has observed and measured it in infants, adolescents, and adults (Lieberman, 1977). It is her thesis that playfulness is related to divergent thinking or creativity and that it has an important bearing on how we approach leisure. The three major components of playfulness are spontaneity, manifest joy and sense of humour.

Spontaneity shows itself in physical, social and learning dimensions and is a unitary trait in the young child. In the adolescent and adult, two separate clusters emerged in her studies which were labelled academic playfulness and social-emotional playfulness respectively.

The characteristics of academic playfulness

being alert	imaginative
bright	inquiring
enthusiastic	knowledgeable.

The outstanding characteristics of social-emotional playfulness

entertaining	witty
extroverted	making fun of himself/herself.
joking	The latter was also given the overall label of
light-hearted	'bubbling effervescence'.

At the infant level Lieberman found that the more playful child was also the more creative boy or girl. This was expressed in fluency, flexibility, and originality of thinking. In terms of intelligence, we know that two-thirds of the population fall within the middle range of intelligence quotients. In the case of creativity, the evidence appears to suggest different degrees of endowment and in different areas, for example, in specific talents such as science, music, writing and painting. Playfulness can therefore be part of any individual's make-up. Moreover, because of its importance in a person's general approach to work and play, playfulness should, in Lieberman's submission, be encouraged and developed throughout the lifespan of people.

Assuming this to be the case, we have to ask ourselves how playfulness can be developed. To develop spontaneity, Lieberman believes that there needs to be an emphasis on gathering and storing facts beginning as early as the pre-school level. Only if the child has a storehouse of knowledge is there a basis for parents and teachers to encourage playing with various permutations.

Manifest joy is the ability of showing pleasure, exuberance, friendliness and generally positive attitudes in everyday life. The joy that the adult shows at the child's growing competence will lead to the child's own sense of pleasure in his or her activities.

The ability of engaging in 'good-natured ribbing, gentle wit, creative punning, as well as poking fun at yourselves and others', Lieberman includes in her 'sense of humour' category. To develop this, a climate needs to be created which encourages 'psychological distancing'. Evidence was found that the cognitively more mature children preferred less hurtful expressions of humour. Humour is dependent on mastery of the situation; mastery can then lead to fun in learning.

Following Lieberman's argument, as we continue to learn throughout our lifespan, we therefore need to practise the psychological distancing which allows us to take seriously the task at hand, but not ourselves; we need to free ourselves from being preoccupied with ourselves and with our own problems, in order to cope, to be resourceful and for leisure to function as one of the means towards what Maslow terms 'self-actualization'. Maslow (1968) stressed the need for individuals to develop to their fullest degree of independence and creative potential.

The next logical step to ask is how playfulness can help in our approach to leisure. It seems self-evident that any individual whose approach to everyday living embraces spontaneity, manifest joy and sense of humour would be able to deal in a creative way with free time. It is apparent, though, that many individuals have these traits and are not aware of them, or do not realize the benefits of applying them to leisure. Other people will need actively to practise them in order to make them part of their everyday repertoire. To what extent we can discover ourselves, our skills and aptitudes and acquire the ability of stepping back and laughing at ourselves, is an area yet to be explored.

Play and the meaning of life?

Throughout history, philosophers and writers have suggested that play gives meaning to life. Huizinga, in particular, proposes play as the basis of culture and civilization, referring to people's 'natural' playfulness and anthropologists' view of play as a 'cultural universal'. Levy (1978) provides a late-twentieth-century philosophical viewpoint:

Play ... is necessary to affirm our lives ... It is through experiencing play that we answer the puzzle of our existence. Play is where our lives live ... Living in play means confirming our existence and celebrating life ... Play brings out the greatness, dignity, and sacredness of our existence, which in turn gives impetus and meaning to our lives ... Play offers us the opportunity to transcend the ordinary organic and ego levels of functioning and to experience the world of wonder, peace, love, and anguish at a very intuitive level; but these experiences must come from within, not from external pressures or influences as is often the case.

Play, therefore, can be defined not by the type of activity, but by the distinctive attitude and approach which the players take towards the activity.

Kraus (1971), in defining play, positions it as an important feature in most aspects of life. Play is:

- a form of behaviour, which is generally regarded as not being instrumental in purpose
- often carried out in the spirit of pleasure and creative expression
- often aimless, disorganized, and casual, or highly structured or complex
- commonly thought of as activity engaged in by children, but adults also play
- an instinctive drive, although much play behaviour is culturally learned
- regarded as voluntary, pleasurable, and non-serious, although it may involve risk and intense commitment
- apparently found in all cultures
- linked to important social functions such as law, religion, warfare, art, and commerce.

The development of adventure play

Serious consideration to providing for children's play in Britain came about through the pro-active ideas of the early educational philosophers and thinkers, and as a result of the reaction to social problems arising from the Industrial Revolution.

Mary Ward, in the 1860s, was one of the founders of the 'settlement movement' in Victorian Britain. This movement established the first play centres for working mothers, the first schools for children with disabilities and organized play provision for children in the school holidays.

In the early 1930s, the Danish architect, C. Th. Sorenson, conceived of children having the freedom to explore 'a sort of junk playground' in which they could 'make dreams and imagination a reality'. His first playground was opened in 1943 at the height of the Second World War on a new housing estate in the centre of Copenhagen.

Lady Allen of Hurtwood, a campaigner for children, following a visit to Copenhagen, established a campaign to build 'junk playgrounds' on waste grounds in England. Several projects, after the war, the first in Camberwell, South London, were championed by the National Playing Fields Association and the London County Council with grant aid and employed staff, but run by local volunteers.

Throughout the 1960s, 1970s and even into the early 1980s, adventure playgrounds continued to grow. The change of name to Adventure Playgrounds brought a certain respectability, but in some respects, may have lost some of the essential raw, down-to-earth quality. In the voluntary sector, the London Adventure Playground Association and the Handicapped Adventure Playground Association (now called

KidsActive) provided inspiration and support. It is only in recent years that the growth of play provision has shifted from the adventure play and open play to the playcare model.

Adventure play is important for children and young people. The adventure playground, although not enjoying the high profile of the 1960s and 1970s, provides opportunities for children to choose the ways in which they play. It is a place where children of all ages, under 'qualified', friendly, unobtrusive supervision, are free to do many things that they can no longer do in crowded urban developments, or at home. They can climb, dig, light fires, cook, camp, garden, play games, paint, dress up, or simply just talk and make friends. The adventure playground can be a place for learning and for making relationships.

Because adventure playgrounds provide space and materials for children to create their own play world, they try out many things and learn to develop confidence in their abilities. The lack of structure allows for variability, change and flexibility. But adventure playgrounds tend to end up looking like junk yards. In some areas they are acknowledged as good for the children, but no one wants one in their 'back yard'. However, the principle of the freedom to choose is fundamental to quality play experiences.

Today, the term 'adventure playground' is used more to represent a much sanitized version of its former self in public parks and is now even part of provision in commercial leisure, with indoor adventure centres (see Children's indoor play centres, p. 214, Chapter 11).

On a broader front, today all local authorities in the United Kingdom provide 'standard' outdoor playgrounds and play spaces, so there are many thousands that exist and have to be safe and well maintained. Playgrounds and safety issues are not covered in this book but planning for playspace is included in Chapter 12. In addition to these and other 'open' spaces and opportunities such as playschemes, the growth area in play has been in the 'closed' settings and in playcare. The emerging profession of play and playwork has spawned many hundreds of playworkers, paid and voluntary, and standardized training courses and qualifications. These are mentioned in Chapter 24.

Play in practice today

Theories are often academic and complex, as we have seen. Hughes (2002), drawing on his experience and others in the field, brings us down to earth with his taxonomy of fifteen types of play.

A taxonomy of play types

1 Symbolic play: Play which allows control, gradual exploration and increased understanding, without the risk of being out of one's depth. For example, a piece of string to symbolize a wedding ring.
2 Rough and tumble play: Close encounter play which is less to do with fighting and more to do with touching, tickling, gauging relative strength, discovering physical flexibility. For example, playful wrestling and chasing.
3 Socio-dramatic play: Acting out real and potential experiences of an intense

personal, social, domestic or relationship nature. For example, going to the shops, being mothers and fathers.

4 Social play: Where the 'rules' for social engagement and interaction can be explored and amended. For example, any social or interactive situation which contains an expectation on all parties such as games, or making something together.

5 Creative play: Play which allows new responses or new connections, with an element of surprise. For example, enjoying creation for its own sake, with materials and tools.

6 Communication play: Play using words or gestures. For example, mime or play acting.

7 Dramatic play: Dramatizing events. For example, presentation of a TV show or festive event.

8 Deep play: Play which allows the child to encounter risky experiences, to develop survival skills and conquer fear. For example, leaping, riding a bike on a parapet or balancing on a high beam.

9 Exploratory play: Play to access information such as handling, throwing. For example, engaging with an object by manipulation or movement, assessing its properties and possibilities such as stacking bricks.

10 Fantasy play: Play which rearranges the world in the child's way, a way which is unlikely to occur. For example, playing at being a pilot; or driving a fast car.

11 Imaginative play: Play where the conventional rules which govern the physical world, do not apply. For example, pretending to be a tree or ship.

12 Locomotor play: Movement in any and every direction for its own sake. For example, chase, hide and seek, tree climbing.

13 Mastery play: Control of the physical environment. For example, digging holes, changing the course of streams, constructing shelters, building fires.

14 Object play: Play which uses infinite and interesting sequences of hand–eye manipulations and movements. For example, novel use of any object such as paint-brush or cup.

15 Role play: Play exploring ways of being, although not normally of an intense nature. For example, dialling with a telephone, driving a car.

Adapted from A Playworkers Taxonomy of Play Types, PLAYLINK

Acting in the spirit of play defies specific definition. Analysing play by placing it into types and categories can help to deliver appropriate playwork, but does this have drawbacks in compartmentalizing play? With play therapy, for example, 'adults may be over-keen to group and interpret play because of their own interests'. Elizabeth Wood and Jane Attfield provide a warning:

> In the urge to explain and categorize play, we may be in danger of overlooking the fact that children define play themselves. They often establish mutual awareness of play and non-play situations. They create roles, use symbols, redefine objects and determine the action through negotiation and shared meanings. Often, their enactments of play themes and stories or their creation of play scripts reveal far more subtleties than academic definitions can capture.
>
> Wood and Attfield, 1996

Play themes and children's perceptions

While there is no definition of play which achieves universal agreement, in *Understanding Children's Play* (Lindon, 2001), the following themes are suggested by Lindon as encapsulating the broad range of literature on children's play.

Play is essentially a voluntary and pleasurable activity. It may be undertaken with great seriousness and attention and may give rise to significant learning. Children play because they want to and because it gives them enjoyment.

Lindon, 2001, p. 44–5

Play themes

- Children seem to play regardless of cultural background, although play is not identical across cultures.

- Circumstances can prevent or restrict play. Constraints may be placed by adults or the environment limits children's experience. Alternatively, developmental problems, disability or illness can shape play possibilities for children.

- Children play for play's sake. The activity is an end in itself and is not undertaken for an end product, although children do sometimes make something in play.

- Play is an activity involving children's own choices. It is motivated by children's feelings and internal thoughts and it can be hard sometimes for adults to fathom these motives.

- Play is often episodic, with emerging and shifting goals developed by children themselves. However, children return to favourite play themes and activities over time.

- Play supports children's social understanding and play is in turn fed by their experiences. The roles and themes acted out during play both use and help children to understand social rules and conventions.

- There is a subtle interplay between communication, social interaction and imagination in play. These features often become clear when you observe children who have difficulty in play, such as autistic children (see Useful websites).

- Play stems from children's own perception of the world and how it works. So it is a very personal creative activity. Within children's understanding, their play is meaningful in its connection to the non-play reality.

- Children mirror each other in play and so they reinforce, highlight and develop their own views and experiences. Play is usually rule governed, even when it looks thoroughly disorganized to adults. The rules may be understood by children, but not spoken out loud. Rules are voiced clearly by children if someone breaks them.

- Play provides a forum in which children can step back for a while, experiment and try out scenarios. Children can make their play represent reality in their own way, with an 'as if' or 'what if?' quality.

The importance of play for children today

The benefits of play

The benefits of play as experienced by children at the time that they are playing are summarized in *Best Play* (NPFA/CPC/PLAYLINK, 2000), which states that play:

- provides children with opportunities to enjoy freedom, and exercise choice and control over their actions
- offers children opportunities for testing boundaries and exploring risk
- offers a very wide range of physical, social and intellectual experiences for children.

There are also benefits for children from play that develop over time. *Best Play* states that play:

- fosters children's independence and self-esteem
- develops children's respect for others and offers opportunities for social interaction
- supports the child's well-being, healthy growth and development
- increases children's knowledge and understanding
- promotes children's creativity and capacity to learn.

One study of primary school children found that break-time 'maximised children's attention to school tasks when they returned to the classroom' (Smith, 1988).

Children deprived of play

The case for play provision does not rest only with its benefits, but also on the adverse consequences if children are deprived of play. Recent scientific research suggests: 'that a radically deprived environment could cause damage ... a brain can physically expand and contract and change depending on experience' (NPFA/CPC/PLAYLINK, 2000).

Hence, there is growing awareness of possible implications of play deprivation:

Depending on the types of play opportunity that are lacking, children could be affected in the following ways:

- poorer ability in motor tasks
- lower levels of physical activity
- poorer ability to deal with stressful or traumatic situations and events
- poorer ability to assess and manage risk
- poorer social skills, leading to difficulties in negotiating social situations such as dealing with conflict and cultural difference

More generally, without a good range of play opportunities, children may lose the chance to develop their emotional intelligence, independence, self-esteem and self-confidence, and to acquire self-management skills such as being able to see projects and tasks through to completion. In school and educational settings, a lack of play opportunities during playtime can impair concentration in the classroom ... it could be argued that children who never have the chance to try out a range of activities may have undiscovered or latent talents, abilities that might have developed if the right opportunities, encouragement and support had been available ... A lack of good play opportunities can also have adverse consequences on families and communities.

NPFA/CPC/PLAYLINK, 2000

Play is important to healthy personal development. It is self-evident that the physical activity involved in much play provides exercise which helps in co-ordination and develops skills for growing children. It is also clearly evident that play has a social dimension, promoting social and emotional skills to handle the ups and downs of life.

The Mental Health Foundation identified some children who are more resilient in the face of stressful life events than others. 'Those children who have good communication skills, a positive attitude, a problem solving approach and the capacity to reflect tend to be more resilient. The ability to plan, a belief in control, a sense of humour are all qualities that can lead to resilience' (Mental Health Foundation, 1999).

These findings echo much of Lieberman's characteristics of playfulness: spontaneity, manifest joy and a sense of humour.

Play and child development

We have seen that play is innate to the individual, yet occurs in all cultures. It is universal. Clearly, it is of significance in child development. It is a critically important feature of children's development of cognitive and emotional skills. In *Best Play*, the authors refer to the extensive research being carried out in the area of brain sciences and child development. 'Play now features as an important consideration in the current scientific studies on the development of the brain' (p. 9).

Citing work on brain imaging technology, Sutton-Smith (1997) states that in the first ten years of life, human children have at least twice the synaptic capacity as children over ten. Synapses are the links between nerve cells in the brain. Others link this 'plasticity' to the effects of 'enriched' environments. Goleman's identification has also prompted further studies with the hypothesis that play in young children may have a critical role in the enlargement of brain capacity. Clearly, the role of play in child development is under-explored, but it is now generally accepted the play has a vital contribution to make to learning, health and physical, social and mental well-being. As suggested earlier, play can make learning irresistible. Moreover, it is also suggested that in play settings, children learn how to learn.

What is acquired through play is not specific information, but a general (mind) set towards solving problems that includes both abstraction and combinatorial flexibility ... children string bits of behaviour together to form novel solutions to problems requiring the restructuring of thought or action.

Sylva, 1977

Play as empowerment

Yuen and Shaw (2003) provide a new perspective on play, arguing that through creativity and exploration children can be empowered to think for themselves and act accordingly. Researching play, where gender stereotypes may be reinforced and resisted, they considered the possible outcomes of structured and unstructured play:

> Research on play has indicated that this form of activity for children involves several different aspects or components. These include play as an empowering and transformative experience, play as a form of creativity, and play as an environment for learning. The emphasis placed on these components also differs between structured and unstructured play environments.

The transformative process means that children become confident in themselves, empowered in play to do things for themselves, feel in control and test out their skills. They create a world based on their own experiences, and through play children can 'transform themselves into others' roles', switching in and out of different situations. This experience is far more evident in unstructured activities compared to structured activities.

Within creativity, Yuen and Shaw include flexibility, originality and elaboration as well as curiosity, imagination and risk-taking. Creativity can involve 'convergent and/or divergent thinking'. Convergent thinking leads to experiences that form a single, convergent answer: there is one, right way. Divergent thinking on the other hand tends to result in many responses that promote exploration.

Structured play, because it is adult-organized, is likely to reinforce society's systems and hierarchies, competition, co-operation and democracy. Unstructured play is more likely to facilitate problem solving, improvisation and communication. As innovative ideas increase, children's abilities to think flexibly and produce original ideas also increase. Hence, while children are influenced by societal values and norms, they also have the ability themselves to influence these values based on how they respond to their own experiences – and these are more likely to be found in unstructured play. Moreover, although children's culture is not independent of adults or adult culture, children's peer groups create their own culture 'by selecting and rejecting various aspects of adult culture and making cultural innovations of their own' (Yuen and Shaw, 2003).

Protecting children at play and leisure

At the start of this chapter we noted that children are growing up in a rapidly changing world of uncertainty and that parents have increasing concerns for their safety. This level of unease has led in some cases to an over-protection of young children and some teenagers also.

Once-normal activities such as roaming about with friends, walking unescorted to and from school, and 'hanging out' are increasingly being restricted. The activities of children are monitored and constrained to ensure that they come to no harm. They also take less exercise, which has consequences for fitness and health.

It is important that children do not lose a sense of adventure and exploration which is very much part of play. Sue Townsend, author of the Adrian Mole diaries, wrote:

When I was a child, I was a member of a gang. Our territory consisted of a derelict manor house and its grounds, a large neglected orchard, mixed woodland and a spinney which had a clear water brook running through it. Each season had its own particular delights. In the winter, the gang would push old fashioned prams to the coal yards, load up and struggle back up the icy hill. In the summer, we picked apples and pears and blackberries; in the autumn, we roasted chestnuts over bonfires and brewed tea in old saucepans ... Playing was a serious business, without knowing it, we were preparing to join the adult world.

Townsend, 1993

The need for children's play environment is not confined to the urban population, but includes rural communities also. In some villages, there is no common or public land for children to play on, and the thin scatter of rural populations makes it difficult for children to meet others of similar ages and interests. Public transport tends to be infrequent or non-existent, and parents worry if their children go cycling (Collins and Melchen, 1992).

The term 'inner city' conjures up the idea of a set of problems which include poverty, unemployment, poor standards in health, education, transport and housing, decaying buildings, crime, drugs and lack of social and recreational facilities. However, those who live in inner cities are not the only people affected by such problems. In the Duke of Westminster's report (1992), crime, social unrest and tensions were said to threaten rural communities, but 'countryside' and 'rural' are not words which evoke the notion of problems.

As adults, we have the dual responsibility of allowing children the freedom to play, the freedom to take some risks and meet challenges, but at the same time to keep them safe from harm. Child Protection is an area of considerable research and debate, and is important in every area of a child's life: at home, at school, at play, at the leisure centre, at church, in clubs, at events and on the street.

Children at play are vulnerable, whether in open or closed settings, whether supervised or unsupervised. All people concerned with providing for children and children's play need to be vetted and, ideally, trained and qualified. So serious has been the problem that in September 2003 the Department for Education and Skills published a Green Paper called *Every Child Matters*. This consultation report set out a framework for improving outcomes for all children and their families, to protect them, to promote their well-being and to support all children to their full potential. This book does not cover this important area of concern, but all the main children's play organizations, some of whom are listed at the end of this chapter, provide guidance on these matters

Many of the issues arising from this chapter relate not just to play and children. Play has a significant part in leisure and recreation. Indeed, I contend it is the cornerstone of recreation and, as Paul Bonel (1993) reminds us, play is with us for life. Adults too need to play.

Play begins at birth and continues until we die. For adults, it's perhaps more comfortable to call it sport or recreation, art or leisure, but at some level and to some degree, we all play. For children, it is natural and necessary; they call it play and, for them, the fact that it's crucial to their healthy development is incidental.

Susan Millar (1968) would concur. As she suggests: 'Adults sometimes just play, but children just play far more.'

Discussion points

1 It is claimed that play shapes our behaviour, values, norms and the customs of all cultures. Play is a positive form of behaviour and has potential to enrich lives. To what extent can you defend these assumptions?

2 Play is generally viewed as child behaviour or childlike behaviour. Leisure is generally viewed in the context of adults. Is all play a form of leisure, but the reverse not the case? Debate play as 'a taste of leisure'.

3 Play is a way a child learns what no one else can teach. To what extent can this statement be supported?

Further reading

John, A. and Wheway, R. (2004), *Can Play, Will Play*, NPFA, London (The NPFA guide for playgrounds for disabled children).

Cole-Hamilton and Gill, T. for Children's Play Council (2002), *Making the Case for Play*, National Children's Bureau, London.

Children's Play Council (2002), *More than Swings and Roundabouts: Planning for Outdoor Play*, National Children's Bureau, London.

Useful websites

Children's Play Council (including the Play Safety Forum) at the National Children's Bureau: www.ncb.org/cpc

www.ncb.cpc/playsafety

Children's Play Information Centre at the National Children's Bureau: www.ncb.org.uk/library/cpis

The National Playing Fields Association: www.npfa.co.uk

Institute of Leisure and Amenity Management: www.ilam.co.uk

Play Wales: www.playwales.org.uk

Play Scotland: www.playscotland.org

Play Board Northern Ireland: www.playboard.org

KidsActive: www.kidsactive.org.uk

Autism Connect: www.autismconnect.org

National Children's Bureau: www.ncb.org.uk

6

People's needs and leisure

Introduction

In the preceding chapters we have looked at leisure, its variety of meanings and its relationship to recreation and play. An understanding of leisure, however, is of limited value unless it helps toward meeting some of the needs of individual people, groups of people and thereby is also of value to the wider community.

Leisure services are claimed by their providers to be based on the needs of the people they are intended to serve. Is this actually true, or is it wishful thinking? After all, do policy makers, planners, providers and managers of leisure services have sufficient insights into people's needs? Would it not be sufficient and far easier to quantify people's wants and demands? Should we be concerned with needs, which are difficult to understand, and even more difficult to measure? I believe that we should be. We are far more likely to provide appropriate facilities, services and programmes, if we have a better understanding of human needs. Indeed, we should know as much about the needs of people, the leisure 'experience' and what motivates people to leisure as we do about the activities we call leisure and recreation.

This chapter attempts to throw light on the concept of need, albeit briefly and in very small measure. I say in small measure because over a long time scientists have been challenged to understand human needs and the search for universal agreement continues. In this chapter we ask the simple questions: what are human needs, can leisure meet some of these needs and do leisure needs, as such, exist?

Do universal needs exist?

Before we can get near to debating the existence, or otherwise, of leisure needs, we need to understand something about human needs that apply to everyone: universal needs. It comes as a surprise to learn that some scientific researchers claim that universal human needs do not exist. Doyal and Gough (1991) report that 'wide consensus in modern thought agrees that universal and objective human needs do not exist or cannot be formulated coherently'. However, in *A Theory of Human Need*, they challenge this assertion and arrive at a different conclusion:

> It is at least plausible to assume that objective human needs exist in some sense. Yet there can be no doubt that our common-sense understanding of what sorts of things needs are is varied and often confused and ambiguous. This is due in part to the fact that the word 'need' is employed in everyday language in such diverse ways. One of the most common usages refers to needs as drives with which we have little choice but to conform. Another conceptualises needs as goals which for some reason or other it is believed that everyone either does or should try to achieve. It is this universality which supposedly differentiates needs from preferences or 'wants'.

Needs, drives and motivation

One simple view is that human need is something that is missing, a deficit. It has been defined as 'any lack or deficit within the individual either acquired or physiological' (Morgan and King, 1966, p. 776). Needs here are distinguished from drives and are seen as preceding them; they are the cause of motivation, rather than the motivation itself. Others equate need with the motivating force (Murray, 1938).

McDougal (1923) attempted to explain behaviour by reducing it to a series of innate, but modifiable, instincts. Instinct theory has now been generally discarded, but McDougal's theory was in many ways a watershed in motivational theory. It led to the further efforts of behavioural scientists to discover why we behave as we do. It also led many psychologists to look for more widely extended, diffusive concepts which explain human motivation. One of the central ideas to be salvaged from McDougal's theory was that of the purposeful, goal-directed nature of the greater part of human behaviour.

Drive is goal-directed; it releases energy. It is generally considered to be the motivating factor within human personality. There appear to be different sorts of drive such as the drive for food, the drive for sex, the exploratory drive, and so on. Summarizing the concept, Young (1961) says: 'Drive is a persisting motivation rather than brief stimulation. Drive is an activating energising process.'

Many psychologists who see the motivational aspect of human needs as drives do so in conjunction with the concept of homeostasis. People have a fundamental need to maintain a state of relative internal stability. Needs can therefore be perceived in terms of the elements that disturb homeostasis; drives are the forces which impel the individual to regain the equilibrium that has been lost. Homeostasis is easiest to understand in terms of physiological needs, for example, the relief of cold or hunger. Needs which are social in nature, such as the needs for achievement, self-fulfilment and acceptance, are less easily accounted for in terms of homeostasis. However, as indicated in the discussion on recreation in Chapter 4, the principle of 'psychological homeostasis' was used by Shivers as the basis of 're-creation'.

All human behaviour is motivated, according to Freudian theory. Nothing happens by chance, not even behaviour which appears to be 'accidental'. Thus we often remark on the 'Freudian slip': everyday errors and slips of the tongue, which far from being just 'accidental', are caused by underlying and unconscious wishes or intentions (Freud, 1974). In terms of motivation, Freud saw two fundamental driving forces in human beings: the sexual and the aggressive. The basic drives which motivate all behaviour operate unconsciously at a basic level of the psyche known as the id. They are not fixed patterns of behaviour, but function through 'external' demands and constraints, that is, the 'realities' of the outside world. The two psychic structures which channel and modify the basic drives are the ego and superego. They direct the basic drives into socially acceptable channels.

Freud placed great emphasis on the developmental stages of early childhood, but little on the later life cycle stages. Erikson (1959), however, viewed development as a process which continues throughout life: needs themselves are developmental, and change at different stages of the life cycle right up to old age.

It appears to be a reasonable conclusion that there is a relationship between need and motivation:

> In theories of motivation need is seen as a state or force within the individual. This can be either a deficit state leading to a search for satisfaction, or else a stage of psychological incompleteness leading to a movement towards completeness.
>
> IFER/DART, 1976, 2.46

In either case, need is a motivational concept referring to those processes – conscious or unconscious – involved in goal-orientated behaviour.

'Need' is often used to denote a drive or some inner state that initiates a drive, for example, 'humans need to sleep'. This is the approach taken by Maslow whose analysis of 'basic needs' is the most well-known worldwide. Maslow (1954, 1968) discerned five needs organized in a hierarchy. If humans are chronically hungry or thirsty the physiological motivation to secure food and water will be most powerful. After hunger and thirst needs have been met other higher needs emerge. Next, for adults (and even more for children) will be the needs for safety, orderliness and a predictable world. When these have been met, yet higher needs dominate until motivation for emotional and intellectual fulfilment take over.

Doyal and Gough, however, do not accept Maslow's hierarchy of needs; 'its strict temporal sequencing of motivations in question is simply false. Some people seem far more concerned with their self-actualisation than their safety – mountain climbers, for example' (Doyal and Gough, 1991, p. 36). Maslow's categories seem either to be combined or, at times to conflict. Doyal and Gough conclude that we should divorce the debate of needs as universal goals from that of motivations or drives. Thompson (1987) takes a similar stance; ' one can have a drive to consume something, like lots of alcohol, which one does not need and at the same time have a need for something, like exercise or diet, which one is in no way driven to seek'. In addition there are cultural differences in terms of needs and differences also within cultures.

The assertion made earlier that needs and wants could be separated and the latter could be recognized and more easily measured, now become more problematic. What are needs for some can be merely wants for others, and vice versa. Moreover, people have strong feelings about what they need and these feelings can vary between cultures, within cultures and change over time. Perceived need therefore may be a matter of culture or individual feeling. Subjective feeling however is not a reliable determination of human need. As Doyal and Gough (1991, p. 49) explain, we can strongly desire things which are seriously harmful and, in our ignorance, not desire things which we require to avoid such harm. The message should not go unheeded by Leisure Managers. We can provide excellent, accessible services and programmes which are good for our health, and charge nothing for them, yet people will buy alternatives which are expensive and inferior, but which they desire. The message is clear: you cannot even give away leisure activities and products if people do not want them.

What are intermediate needs?

> In *A Theory of Human Need* (Doyal and Gough, 1991), needs are defined as: those levels of health and autonomy which should be – to the extent that they can be – achieved for all peoples now, without compromising the foreseeable levels at which they will be achieved by future generations (p. 146).

Doyal and Gough reason that there are two main types of need, one concerned with survival, security and health (clearly, we need to survive and maintain good health in order to do so), and the second concerned with what they term 'autonomy' and learning. By autonomy, they believe that a basic personal need is to recognize ourselves as distinct and separate individual people; and through learning and education we grow and develop. Loss of health or autonomy entails disablement and an inability to create or to share in the 'good things' of life. Human beings are not capable of growing up and developing alone, therefore basic needs are provided for in a social context. Society has therefore created 'institutions' to provide for the realization of individual needs. The authors refer to these as societal needs and extend their thesis as to how they can be provided for, using the terms 'satisfiers' and 'intermediate needs'. They have called all objects, activities and relationships which satisfy our basic needs 'satisfiers'. Basic needs are always universal but their satisfiers are often relative.

> While the basic individual needs for physical health and autonomy are universal, many goods and services required to satisfy these needs are culturally variable. For example, the needs for food and shelter apply to all peoples, but we have seen that there is a potentially infinite variety of cuisines and forms of dwelling which can meet any given specification or nutrition and protection from the elements ... The existence of basic needs or capabilities which are universal to all people is quite consistent in theory with a rich variety of ways in which they can be met and a wide variation in the quantity of satisfiers required to meet them.
>
> Doyal and Gough, 1991, p. 155

Doyal and Gough identified eleven characteristics which they called 'intermediate needs'. Their eleven universal intermediate need 'universal satisfier characteristics' are summarized below.

Universal satisfier characteristics

1 Food and water: appropriate nutritional intake
2 Housing: adequate shelter, adequate basic services, adequate space per person
3 Work: non-hazardous work environment
4 Physical environment: non-hazardous environment
5 Health care: provision of appropriate care, access to appropriate care
6 Childhood needs: security in childhood, child development
7 Support groups: presence of significant others, primary support group
8 Economic security: economic security
9 Physical security: a safe citizenry, a safe state
10 Education: access to cultural skills
11 Birth control and child-bearing: safe birth control, safe child-bearing

adapted from Doyal and Gough, 1991

Do leisure needs exist?

We have seen that both 'leisure' and 'needs', which are easily understandable in common-sense language, are actually complex. More complexity arises when we link leisure to needs, and ask the question, do leisure needs exist? In most studies, not only of leisure management but of general management also, the most cited needs theory is that of Maslow's hierarchy. As suggested earlier, there are problems in the application of his theory because needs are not necessarily hierarchically ordered, nor divided into sectors, but often overlapping and occurring at the same time. However, the theory emphasizes the developmental needs of the individual. Need is not seen as the reduction of a state of tension or the return to homeostatic equilibrium. Instead people are seen as striving towards positive fulfilment and growth. Other authors with a humanistic approach to psychology also emphasize the human need for self-actualization and growth. If leisure has a place in such fulfilment and growth, then self-actualization could be perceived as one of the goals of leisure or, indeed, the ultimate goal.

One of the assumptions being made in this book is that what is fulfilling and meaningful and worthwhile for the individual, is likely to be worthwhile for the community also. Leisure, therefore, can be considered in a social and community context. Stokowski (1994) considered leisure in capitalism, modernity and post-modernity. She asked the question, is leisure an individual and societal need? Her findings suggested that leisure is a consistent feature of life in these 'human gatherings', but often for social control.

In other words they apparently indicate that leisure is something that human beings need just as they need food, shelter, warmth, security and protection. At the same time our discussion of leisure under capitalism and modernity suggests that leisure is seen as quite low down on the scale of essential social values. Under these cultures a donatory view of leisure is maintained. That is, leisure is regarded as something to be given as a reward to the individual and society or withheld as a punishment or as a way of controlling social behaviour.

Stokowski, 1994

Social needs

Bringing the debate closer to participation in leisure and recreation is the classical, much used concept of 'social needs' presented by Bradshaw (1972). Bradshaw classified social needs into four categories:

- normative needs
- felt needs
- expressed needs and
- comparative needs.

He explored a system by which the overlapping considerations of the four approaches to 'need' could be utilized to form a model to assist in making objective assessments of 'real' need.

Mercer (1973), and later McAvoy (1977) and Godbey (1976) applied Bradshaw's concepts to leisure and recreation. Godbey and others expanded the number of classifications with additional categories: 'created needs', 'changing needs' and 'false needs'. These seven needs are now described within a context of providing leisure and recreation services.

Normative needs and leisure These represent value judgements made by professionals in the recreation and leisure field (such as criteria for open space standards). They are usually expressed in quantitative terms. The use of normative needs as the major determinant of leisure provision can be challenged on a number of points, and may not be valid for the population as a whole. (For a full discussion of the problems and benefits of standards, see Assessment of demand, p. 238, Chapter 12.)

Felt needs and leisure These can be defined as the desires that an individual has, but has not yet actively expressed; they are based on what a person thinks he or she wants to do. According to Mercer (1973), felt needs are largely learned patterns; we generally want what we have become used to having. In many cases, felt needs are limited by the individual's knowledge and perception of available leisure opportunities. However, mass communication has expanded the individual's knowledge, ordinarily outside his or her realm of experience. Thus felt needs, on the one hand, are limited by an individual's perception of opportunities, but on the other hand they can be based on what a person imagines he or she would like to do. Individuals are likely to be happier participating in what they perceive they want to do during their leisure than if leisure options are simply dictated to them.

Expressed needs and leisure Those activities in which individuals actually participate are expressed needs. They provide the Leisure Manager with knowledge about current leisure preferences, tastes and interests. Expressed needs are felt needs put into action. However, if leisure resources, programmes and services are based solely on expressed needs (what people are doing), the practitioner may preclude the initiation of new services and programmes. Expressed need itself does not give a total picture of involvement potential, nor why people do or do not participate. Moreover, programming based on expressed needs may tend to favour those who are most demanding. New and novel provision may create its own demand, where none existed previously.

Comparative needs and leisure Often an individual or organization will compare itself with another individual or organization. This may be done purely out of interest, or it may serve to help to identify deficiencies. This approach can be applied to services, facilities, resources and programmes. Care must be practised when utilizing the comparative method in needs assessment. One cannot assume that what works well in one situation will automatically be effective in another.

Created needs and leisure Godbey (1976) has expanded on Bradshaw's taxonomy of social needs by adding a fifth level: created needs. The concept implies that policy makers and professionals can create leisure interests. Created needs refer to those activities which organizations have 'introduced to individuals and in which they will subsequently participate at the expense of some activity in which they previously participated' (p. 13). In other words, created needs refers to those programmes, services and activities solely determined by the organization and accepted by the participant without question, desire or prior knowledge.

According to Edginton *et al.* (1980) the created needs approach can be useful to the participant and to the organization as a method of defining needs:

> Many individuals are grateful to organizations for helping them identify an area of interest that previously they had not considered. In a sense, the approach is a form of leisure education that is an important component of the philosophy of recreation and leisure service organizations. The organization also benefits by serving as an agency that creates opportunities for stimulation and enrichment. As a result, individuals may look to the organization as a vehicle for providing innovative experience.
>
> Edginton *et al.*, 1980, p. 91

False needs and leisure Needs may be created which are inessential, and which are in fact false needs. Young (1961) points to the distinctions between what an individual is aware of needing and what others may think is needed. This raises the issue of the value which is placed on need by the individual and by outsiders. These values may differ.

Marcuse (1964) developed the concept that society encourages the individual to develop certain sorts of 'need', which serve the interests of society as a whole. Thus people acquire the 'need' for cars, washing machines, television, videos, computers, or mobile phones, which it is in the general interest of society to promote. Such needs Marcuse calls false needs for the reason that they are not strictly essential. However, they are hard to prove different from other sorts of need. People now 'need' computers and mobile phones.

Changing needs in leisure Rhona and Robert Rapoport in *Leisure and the Family Life Cycle* (1975) claim that although every person has needs, these needs change as one progresses from one phase of life to another. The key concepts which reflect the developmental nature of the changes in the life cycle are preoccupations: mental absorptions, interests and activities. Preoccupations arise at a deep level of motivation. Some preoccupations might be present throughout the life cycle but tend to become particularly salient at a given phase. The preoccupations attributed to each stage in the life cycle are worth considering since they are of fundamental importance if providers are to make the most appropriate provision for different segments of the population, such as: children, young people, young adults, middle agers, older people, and various sub-divisions within each segment.

The Rapoports believe that recreational activities arise out of interests, and interests arise out of preoccupations. There is no one-to-one relationship between preoccupations and interests, and particular interests can be satisfied through different activities. However, it appears that specific 'clusters' of interests are clearly related to each major life cycle phase. The Rapoports' thesis is that all people have a quest for personal identity. At the root of their search, people have fundamental preoccupations. Specific preoccupations can be experienced through a variety of interests, and expressions of interest may be facilitated through specific activities. Each person is seen as having a 'career' consisting of separate but interrelated strands. Three major strands relate to family, work and leisure. Each life strand therefore produces changes in preoccupations, interests and activities at life crises such as at marriage and at the birth of children.

Needs, demands and leisure

Leisure needs are often equated with demands, especially among policy makers, researchers, planners and managers. But there is a very real difference between the two. Researchers have generally been concerned with establishing recreation demand, rather than understanding people's needs. Large-scale surveys, for example, have identified certain demands, but have not discovered what motivates people to leisure and recreation and why people participate. 'Whereas a "need" appears to be conceptually "woolly" and operationally elusive, "demand" appears tangible, measurable, even predictable' (Kew and Rapoport, 1975).

In recent years, there has been a growing dissatisfaction with macro-social demand studies, and a feeling that if researchers are to provide information of real value to policy makers and planners, they must look for approaches that are also of relevance to the people being researched. Knetsch (1969) calls into question the concept of demand: 'The myth persists that somehow we are able to multiply population figures by recreation activity participation rates obtained from population surveys and call it demand.'

Effectiveness and efficiency are not the same thing. An effective leisure service could be described as one that ensures that the right opportunities are provided, at the right time and in the right place, based on the needs of the people it is intended to serve. This is, of course, impossible to achieve in the sense that any collective service cannot be all things to every person. Yet the approach which encourages ways for people to attain self-fulfilment can be stressed. If not, providers may provide an efficient service and ensure its smooth running but the service could be ineffective. Of the two, the provision of an effective service is the more important, as it is better to provide an effective service that meets needs, however inefficiently, than to provide a super efficient service that meets nobody's needs.

Although little direct research has been undertaken on the 'social' need of the individual being a prime motivating factor, Crandall (1977) found that the success of many leisure and recreation services may depend more on their ability to bring together compatible people, than on their programmes and facilities.

Tillman (1974) is one of many authors who have examined needs and identified those which are felt important in determining the 'leisure needs' of people. He listed needs for:

- new experiences such as adventure, relaxation, escape and fantasy
- recognition and identity
- security: being free from thirst, hunger or pain
- dominance: to direct others or control one's environment
- response and social interaction, to relate and react to others
- mental activity: to perceive and understand
- creativity
- service to others: the need to be needed, and
- physical activity and fitness.

However, the concept of 'leisure needs' is misleading. People have needs which can be satisfied in a variety of ways. One way of meeting some of them may be through leisure opportunity: leisure needs as such may not exist.

What factors influence leisure participation?

Many factors influence how people spend their time for leisure. They can be grouped as follows:

- individual factors: the stage of an individual's life, his or her interests, attitudes, abilities, upbringing and personality
- the circumstances and situations in which individuals find themselves: the social setting of which they are a part, the time at their disposal, their job and their income
- opportunities and support services available to the individual: resources, facilities, programmes and activities; their quality and attractiveness; and their management.

Recreation policy and planning are by no means simple. There is a complex mixture and interaction when thinking about the factors which affect participation. Table 6.1 outlines some of the discernible factors which individually, jointly or collectively affect participation. This listing is not comprehensive, but it illustrates the complexity and variety of influences which bear on an individual. In addition, even if people have identical circumstances and opportunities, one person may still choose one activity and another something entirely different. Nevertheless, by understanding some of the correlations between personal circumstances and participation, Leisure Managers can foresee some of the constraints and difficulties encountered by some people, and management approaches can be modified accordingly. Table 6.1 has three column headings which are the main influences affecting leisure and recreation participation:

1 Personal and family influences
2 Social and situational circumstances
3 Opportunities.

Table 6.1 Influences on leisure participation

PERSONAL	SOCIAL AND CIRCUMSTANTIAL	OPPORTUNITY FACTORS
• Age	• Occupation	• Resources available
• Stage in life cycle	• Income	• Facilities: type and quality
• Gender	• Disposable income	• Awareness
• Marital status	• Material wealth and goods	• Perception of opportunities
• Dependents and ages	• Car ownership and mobility	• Recreation services
• Will and purpose of life	• Time available	• Distribution of facilities
• Personal obligations	• Duties and obligations	• Access and location
• Resourcefulness	• Home and social environment	• Choice of activity
• Leisure perception	• Friends and peer groups	• Transport
• Attitudes and motivation	• Social roles and contacts	• Costs: before, during, after
• Interests and preoccupation	• Environment factors	• Management: policy and support
• Skills and ability – physical, social and intellectual	• Mass leisure factors	• Marketing
	• Education and attainment	• Programming
• Personality and confidence	• Population factors	• Organization and leadership
• Culture born into		• Social accessibility
• Upbringing and background		• Political policies

Personal and family influences

Choice and participation are influenced by the personality of an individual, his or her needs, interests, physical and social ability, the culture into which one is born, a person's will and purpose in life, and a whole range of other personal factors. Three factors are significant: age and stage in family life cycle, gender and education.

Age and stage in the family life cycle Age has an important influence, but its effect will vary depending on the person, the opportunities and the type of activity. For children, there is a rapid change in the space of a few years. For adults, participation in most active leisure pursuits declines as people grow older.

The availability of time also has an influence on recreational participation and the greatest amount of free time appears to be concentrated at the ends of the age continuum with the adolescent and the retired having considerably more time at their disposal than the middle age-group who live under a greater degree of time pressure.

Age should not be considered in isolation, however. Age may be less restrictive than life cycle changes, such as getting married and having children; for some, participation may increase with age as a result of the children leaving home or a person retiring from work. Although age may influence the level of fitness and energy, a reduction in family and work responsibilities may more than compensate for this.

Gender and leisure participation The leisure patterns of males and females show similarities and differences. However, obstacles have faced women in the form of family commitments, particularly looking after children; many go out to work yet maintain a home (Green *et al.*, 1987).

Women have had, and continue to have, greater constraints placed upon them than men. However, one of the misleading factors in looking for similarities and differences stems from the fact that most surveys have studied traditional recreation activities. Once a wider view of leisure is taken, encompassing the range of activities in and around the home, holidays, socializing, entertainment, excursions or walks in the park, a totally different picture starts to emerge. Looking at the broader spectrum, it would appear that overall participation rates do not differ substantially between men and women, though women take a greater part in 'cultural' activities, and men take part substantially more than women in active sport and sports spectatorship.

Education, educational attainment and leisure The type of education, the length of education and the educational attainment of people are closely related to upbringing, class, occupation, income and other factors. In general, the higher the qualification, the greater the degree of participation in leisure activities. This is evidenced in every General Household Survey over the past twenty years which has included lifestyle information.

Education influences to some extent the type of leisure choice. There is a sharp differential between members and non-members of the public library when related to educational institution and level of educational attainment. Possibly the best illustration is within the arts, where there is a high correlation between audiences for drama, opera and ballet and educational attainment, as recorded in the General Household Surveys.

Social and situational circumstances

The range of social and situational circumstances as they affect leisure participation include the home, school, work environment, income, mobility, time, social class, social roles and group belonging. Time availability is a major determinant of leisure behaviour. Working women have the least unobligated time of all groups, mainly because of home commitments. Retired people and unemployed men have the most time for leisure, but much of it may remain simply free time.

Income and leisure participation Income levels are closely linked to participation rates, and for almost all the leisure activities examined by the General Household Surveys, the proportion participating rose with income. In only three activities (bingo, needlework and going to clubs) did participation not increase with income. Even where little or no financial outlay is incurred, such as walking, participation rates were also higher. With betting, bingo and doing the pools, participation rates fell among those with higher-than-average incomes.

It is perhaps not surprising that since income correlates with both education and social class, the higher-income group has the higher participation rates in many recreational activities. If lower-income groups are to be attracted in larger numbers to community recreation, then greater social service approaches would need to be applied. Owning a large house with a garden, and driving a second car may immediately open the door to leisure activities which will be denied those living in a high-rise flat, without personal transport and on a low income.

Social class and leisure participation 'Social class' can be regarded as 'a grouping of people into categories on the basis of occupation' (Reid, 1977). Because of the inter-relationship between social class and income, education and mobility, it is generally considered that social class, as determined by occupation, is the most influential factor in determining recreational participation. Occupation is not therefore an independent characteristic, but is closely associated with other factors.

The General Household Surveys found that, generally, it was professional workers who tended to have the highest participation rates in leisure activities and unskilled workers who had the lowest rates. Moreover, the surveys conclude that the middle classes are not only more active culturally, socially and intellectually, but they also play more sport and travel more widely.

Social climate and leisure participation The concept of 'social climate' is a complex of factors in addition to those which relate to age, gender, income, occupation and education (IFER/DART, 1976). The attitudes and values of people in their social setting are seen as enabling or inhibiting factors concerned with leisure choice. Emmet (1971) argues that providers act both consciously and unconsciously as social filters, controlling who uses particular facilities and affecting the behaviour of those people. The social filters let through and channel different groups to different facilities. There appear to be both formal and informal social filters. The filters are influential in people's adopting of attitudes and behaviour appropriate to the situation. Behaviour patterns become habits. As Leigh (1971) points out, 'The habits of leisure are habits of mind as well as habits of behaviour' (p. 124).

Opportunity and leisure participation

It is no good providing opportunity unless good advantage is taken of it. Opportunity – making it possible for a person to participate or be involved – is essential to participation. Opportunity can come in a variety of forms: resources and services, political policies, management styles and systems, community leadership and support, and accessibility: physical, perceptual, financial and social.

Perception and leisure participation Perception refers to the world as it is experienced – as it is seen, heard, felt, smelt and tasted. Consequently, the way an individual perceives the world will largely determine his or her behaviour. The way people perceive leisure provision (facilities, activities and so on) may influence their participation more than the actual form of provision.

The perception of one's neighbourhood can have a significant effect on inhibiting recreation participation. If residents perceive their neighbourhood as being violent, the elderly (in particular) will be fearful of venturing out of the house at night. Consequently, how the public perceive their neighbourhood and its facilities can either encourage or inhibit participation.

Access and supply and leisure participation Recreation participation undertaken outside the home involves some travel, that is, walking, cycling, bus, taxi, car, train or plane. The method of travel can affect the level of satisfaction; it can determine time, distance and destination. Apart from walking, all other means of travel incur financial cost. The method of transportation will lessen or heighten the experience. However, though low mobility can act as a deterrent, higher mobility is not a prerequisite of greater participation: rather it can reduce some of the inconvenience associated with travel (Hillman and Whalley, 1977). The mobility conferred by the ownership of a car has revolutionized people's use of leisure time. For almost every activity, with the striking exception of bingo, the chances of participating in leisure activities were increased for car users by between 50 per cent and 100 per cent, according to the General Household Surveys.

Accessibility is influenced also by other important factors. Usage is affected by location and 'distance decay', whereby usage falls as the distance grows between the user's home and a facility. Moreover, those without transport who live near to public transport routes attend more frequently than those (within the same distance) who did not.

Awareness and leisure participation If people do not know that something exists, then obviously they will not go to visit it, unless they stumble upon it. Because leisure facilities are not sought in the same way as a shopping centre or place of work, knowledge about them derives from seeing them, hearing about them or reading about them. People passing a leisure facility *en route* to work or the shops will be more likely to use that facility than a comparable one because they have become more aware of it.

The influence of management on leisure participation

People's take-up of leisure opportunities and use of leisure facilities is determined, as we have seen, by some discrete factors and a number of interrelated factors. Effective management is no less important. The way a service or facility is managed can have a profound effect on the extent that they are used, and by whom they are used.

Management policy, marketing, attitude of staff, sensitive customer service, skilled programming reflecting the 'needs' of the community, all go towards creating a welcoming atmosphere and appealing image. For example, the pricing, administrative and booking systems at a leisure facility can consciously or unconsciously establish a type of social filter, deterring some people from attending.

People use leisure facilities for a variety of reasons. Sport centres, for example, can be places to go and socialize. With some mothers, the activity itself may be of quite secondary importance compared with getting out of the house, having the children happily occupied for an hour, and meeting and talking with people in the coffee bar. Management needs to be aware of these motivating factors in deciding management policy and delivery.

People's needs and leisure planning

Leisure planning and management exist, in large measure, to provide opportunities for individual people to participate actively or passively, seriously or casually in their time for leisure. This personal need can be met, in part, by effective leisure planning and management, but only if needs of different people are identified. Therefore, needs assessment should allow for a broad base of consultation and public involvement. It is suggested that such an approach will:

1   provide an increase in individual and community input and involvement in planning and decision making
2   provide the planner with a better understanding of the community and individuals within it
3   provide information as to the activities in which people are involved, the activities in which they would like to be involved and how these can be planned and provided for within an overall leisure delivery system
4   provide supportive facts and ideas on which to base decisions in the planning process.

The formal planning process is covered at some length in Chapter 12.

Two most important factors have emerged in this chapter, which need to be taken into account. First, people have diverse needs; therefore, levels of flexibility need to be written into planning and management systems. Second, these needs change or take on greater or lesser degrees of importance according to one's stage in the life cycle. Hence, standardization across the board will only be relevant in some circumstances as an individual will choose on the basis of certain personal and social elements current in his or her life.

Needs assessment should attempt an understanding of individual and group behaviour as it relates to recreation and leisure. It can accomplish several things. Through such assessment, planners and managers can become aware of people's underlying motivation, interests, opinions, habits, desires and knowledge regarding recreation and leisure. Practical ways of gathering such data include demographic characteristics, time use, leisure behaviour and opinions and attitudes. Hedges (1986), for example, sought to develop a technique for more accurate charting of people's leisure patterns through their lives, namely their 'leisure histories'. Clearly, methods must include both quantitative and qualitative assessments, though it is only qualitative methods that can reach below the surface.

Discussion and summary

No single theory and no clear consensus exist relating to people's needs, though all humans have the same basic, universal needs that have to be satisfied. In theories of motivation, need is seen as a force within the individual to gain satisfactions and completeness. There appear to be many levels and types of need, including the important needs of 'self-actualization' and psychological growth. There also appear to be many different ways in which needs can be satisfied. 'Leisure needs' as such may not exist, rather there are human needs which can find satisfaction through play, recreation and leisure.

The concept of social need incorporating normative, felt, expressed and comparative needs has been enlarged to include created, false and changing needs. Needs appear to change in relation to one's life stage, and one's preoccupations, interests and activities at that stage. It has been hypothesized that needs can be created but, in so doing, can result in some 'false' needs being brought about, with both positive and negative results for the individual and society.

Many discrete and complex, and often interrelated, factors condition people's choice and participation in leisure activities which meet their needs. Furthermore, there are the strongest links between leisure and other elements of life. A person's age and stage in the family life cycle, such as marriage, parenthood and retirement, affect opportunity and participation. Taking the widest view of leisure, the similarities in participation rates between men and women are more striking than the differences, though there are specific differences, and inequalities both within and between the sexes. The type and level of education people have undertaken has a profound effect on leisure participation. Education and recreation share in the same concern for the development of the 'whole' person – body, mind and spirit – through different approaches. The amount of income and property a person has influences leisure participation. Higher-income groups have higher participation rates in most active recreation activities.

Participation is closely and positively related to social status and the prestige of one's occupation. The 'middle classes' are not only more active culturally and intellectually, but also travel more and play more sport, compared with the 'working classes'. The way people perceive leisure provision influences participation. Preconceived ideas, too, can have important positive or negative effects. Car ownership has revolutionized people's leisure opportunities. The accessibility of facilities and their location, and an awareness of opportunities, are important considerations. People's use of facilities and services is affected, to a considerable degree, by management policy and management activity. Facilities must be both accessible and acceptable. The attitudes of providers and managers, and the quality of management, will help more people to find satisfying experiences through leisure and recreation opportunity.

While there are many constraints to leisure choices (and, in practice, few people are free agents to choose whatever they will), leisure can offer significant opportunity for individual action and for personal decision, should opportunity permit and the individual wish to exercise such choice. As choice has to do with the individual, two factors have to be stressed. First, there is a strong link between leisure and other elements of life, and second, because it 'matters' to the individual, the quality of the experience is of paramount importance.

People can still enjoy leisure even though they might have severe difficulties and constraints. From observation and working experience of people's use of leisure, it is clear that a great many people overcome the limitations of a poor education, family obligations and personal handicaps, and even overcome the obstacles of low income, insufficient facilities and resources, to find themselves preoccupying satisfying interests, self-fulfilling experiences and 'mountains to climb'. Leisure and recreation management, therefore, has much to offer in the way of enabling people to discover themselves, and to reach beyond their immediate grasp.

In terms of need, people appear to be three-dimensional:

- we are like everybody else, requiring the basic needs of security, belonging and shelter
- we are like some other people, sharing the same wants, the same groups and the same interests
- we are like no other person, a unique individual, the only one.

Leisure opportunity could enable us to be not only three-dimensional, but also to become all we think we are capable of becoming.

Discussion points

1 Leisure needs exist. Leisure needs do not exist. What arguments can be used to defend either of these statements?

2 Planning for leisure is claimed to be based on the needs of the people. From your experience, is this the case in your district? Show why or why not.

3 Some disadvantaged people have greater needs than most. The Disability Discrimination Act, 1995 which came into force in October 2004 goes some way in providing better access to opportunities for those with disabilities. However, there is also a wide range of people with social, educational and financial disadvantage. What can leisure and recreation management offer them when primary social and financial needs are not being met?

Useful websites

Disability Rights Commission: www.drc.gb.org

Disability Rights at Directgov: www.directgov.uk

Social Exclusion Unit: www.socialexclusion.gov.uk

www.cabinet-office.gov.uk/seu

Citizen's Advice Bureau (CAB): www.adviceguide.org.uk

Citizen's Advice Scotland (CAS): www.cas.org.uk

7

Leisure and the experience society

The concepts of leisure and human need have been difficult to understand and harder to try to explain. Bringing the word 'experience' into the debate muddies the waters still further. However, leisure must be experienced in order to exist, one might argue. This brief chapter focuses on people's search for experience as a key motivating factor for leisure participation.

A search for experiences

Experience can perhaps be explained scientifically in psycho-physiological terms, but to most people, experience is a word beyond description; wiser people might say it is about being and feeling: wordless. A case can be made to describe modern Western culture as, increasingly becoming an 'experience society' and that experience is taking precedence over traditional social processes and products. Jacobs (2002), following Pine and Gilmore's *The Experience Economy – Work is Theatre and Every Business a Stage* (Pine and Gilmore, 1999), suggests that we now find ourselves in an economy in which experience has become the most predominant commodity:

> Most money is earned nowadays by offering experiences, entertainment and dreams, whether or not linked to material products or services. The growth of the influence of experiences is a social phenomenon that overrides the economy; it penetrates all reaches of Western society. In the present day, social traditions have faded into the background and the positive experiences that give our lives shape and form have filled the vacated niches. Therefore, we can speak of the experience society. What is new is not that people experience things (people did that in the past too), but that experience is increasingly taking precedence over all kinds of social processes.

Castells (2000) in *The Information Age – Economy, Society and Culture*, states that: 'in contemporary culture, important social processes and functions shift from traditional institutions (nation state, religion, local culture, family) towards a diversity of "cultural communities" – networks of people from worldwide to local scale, organized around specific values'.

If it is experience that counts, this has profound implications for Leisure Managers and their leisure services: what people experience is more important than, for example, product and place or even price. Marketing gurus remind us that people want to buy dreams. Jensen (1999) in *The Dream Society* captures the same mood and trend; businesses have reached a new frontier of imagination, emotions and dreams. Consumption goods need what Wolfe (1999) describes as the 'E-Factor': the entertainment factor. Simply selling good products does not work any more, particularly in the leisure industry.

In Western cultures individualism has taken centre stage, whereas in tradition-based cultures, self-identity is determined to an extent by social rules and norms. Traditional social structures found in communities centred on coal mining and sea fishing, for example, ensured that sons followed their fathers into coal mining and fishing. Today, even if coal mines and fishing fleets still exist, young people, given the ability and opportunity, can take up careers that attract them rather than following tradition. However, the loss of social structures and traditions leaves voids that need to

The first twenty 'Things to do before you die'

1 Swim with dolphins
2 Scuba dive on Great Barrier Reef
3 Fly *Concorde* to New York
4 Go whale-watching
5 Dive with sharks
6 Skydiving
7 Fly in a hot air balloon
8 Fly in a fighter jet
9 Go on safari
10 See the Northern Lights
11 Walk the Inca trail to Machu Picchu
12 Climb Sydney Harbour Bridge
13 Escape to a paradise island
14 Drive a Formula 1 car
15 Go white-water rafting
16 Walk the Great Wall of China
17 Bungee jumping
18 Ride the Rocky Mountaineer train
19 Drive along Route 66
20 Fly in a helicopter over the Grand Canyon

BBC TV, September 2003

be filled positively if people's needs are to be met. The extent to which leisure can have an influence is under continuing debate. Sociologists in the 1960s talked optimistically of a Leisure Age. Will it ever come? And do people want it?

In September 2003, a BBC television programme called *50 Things To Do Before You Die* presented the findings of a survey about the things British people felt they must do in their lifetime. Adventure, exploration, exhilarating and risky activities, and visiting famous tourist destinations featured strongly. People's desires, of course, depend on what they have seen on television, heard on the radio, read about in the press, seen on the movies or found on the Internet. Of interest was that while seven destinations in the United States were listed, entertainment in the form of Disney attractions only managed to scrape into the top 50 list, despite being some of the most publicized destinations in the world. Experiencing action: swimming with dolphins, scuba diving on the Great Barrier Reef, diving with sharks, skydiving, going on safari and exploring the 'real' world held greatest attraction. Experiencing the wonders of nature were also sought after, for example the Northern Lights, waterfalls and the breathtaking place-experience of the Grand Canyon. The destination attracts more than five million visitors a year who travel there for one reason: to take in the landscape, to watch the landscape. Experiencing landscapes now attracts considerable attention and the number and area of protected heritage sites and nature conservation parks worldwide is growing fast. The increasing emphasis on destinations, heritage and the beauty of landscape are factors in the rise of the experience society.

Experience, imagination and meaning

T.S. Eliot, the poet and winner of a Nobel Prize for literature, wrote of the incompleteness of having the experience, but missing the meaning. Jacobs (2002) links experience to meanings and imagination and believes that imagination is a precondition of experience.

> What we experience is not the outer world *per se*, but the mental construction we build upon stimuli processed by the senses, and organized by meanings stored in the brain. Meanings are preconditions for experiences. The meanings in the brain of an individual are produced during the course of his life (Edelman, 1993). We can call this production of meanings either meaning-giving processes or *imagination*. Literally speaking, imagination is the production of images. In the sense used here, imagination is the production of mental images. Mental images are networks of meanings. Hence, imagination is the production of meanings. In the experience society, imagination is an important momentum, because meanings organize experiences.

Since meaning is a precondition of experience, what implications are there for the Leisure Manager? The destinations market provides good examples. The 'place experience' industry has to take control over the imagination of visitors, in order to design the experiences. Jacobs provides an example of how producers mark places with meanings in a materialistic way. He cites the example of resorts along the Mediterranean coast which are planted with palm trees to optimize the holiday experience of tourists, even though palm trees were not indigenous to the areas.

'Quality' experiences for leisure purposes can be decisive factors in determining visits and investments: people are willing to pay for the experience. In terms of business, producers are having to provide more spectacular or 'meaningful' experiences to maintain or capture market share. The growth in the tourism market for experiences is testimony to this assertion. People are experiencing landscapes of beauty, awe and wonder, or standing in places of history; or engaging in activities for adventure and even exposure to risk.

Extreme sports and experiences

One physical demonstration of the experience society is the growth in 'extreme sports' which provide adventure, risk, exhilaration, and near-ultimate, death-defying experiences. In *Extreme Sports*, Tomlinson (2001) describes over 40 air, land and water sports, growing numbers of new challenging extreme activities and growing numbers of adherents.

> Extreme sports are about individuality, higher and higher levels of achievement, redefining performance boundaries, and the personal satisfaction that comes from trying your best. Extreme sports deliver a sense of accomplishment, whether you establish a new level of ability or simply challenge yourself while having a great time. Extreme sports are about gravity, ingenuity, and technology. Gravity is the force that pulls climbers off rock faces, skiers down slopes and off cliffs, hang gliders toward the ground, and water downstream. Gravity makes warm air rise above cold, drives water to settle at the lowest available spot to create lakes and seas, creates the swirling mass of atmosphere that drives the winds.
>
> Tomlinson, 2001

Popular extreme sports

Barefoot waterskiing, ballooning, bungee jumping, caving through a labyrinth of tunnels underground, free-diving, swimming into the deepest reaches of the seas, in some cases to below 400 feet, mountain-boarding using a hybrid skateboard/snowboard, whitewater rafting, and wakeboarding, a relatively new extreme sport combining the skills used in waterskiing, surfing, windsurfing, skateboarding and snowboarding into one extreme boat-towed sport.

Enthusiasts of extreme sports are prepared to travel. Sports tourism caters, for example, for those training for triathlons or seeking out the strongest waves whether for surfing or kite surfing, or exploring new lands and the deepest caverns. It is widening the range of destinations and changing the face of some holiday resorts. These adventurers have also spawned an industry of new lifestyles, new sports clothing, which has burgeoned in the past few years and new foods and drinks for those aspiring to greater levels of fitness, endurance and health.

Worldwide, there are said to be 7 million snowboarders, 2.2 million surfers and body-boarders and 13 million skateboarders, and their market is estimated to total £5.8 billion. (Tomlinson, 2001).

Jules Verne wrote *Around the World in Eighty Days* in the late nineteenth century, relying on his imagination to tell of the exploits of his hero, Phileas Fogg. Phileas Fogg's adventures have been surpassed in real life. The Trophée Jules Verne is the prize given today for a crewed non-stop race around the world by sea.

Crossing the Arctic on foot and sledge, sailing around the world single-handed, diving to record levels in the deepest seas and other great feats of skill and courage, leave adventurers with the problem of what next to conquer.

The sky seems limitless: reaching the highest altitude, circling the world in a balloon, floating in the air, falling out of aircraft and opening parachutes at the last possible moment, jumping off high bridges attached to an 'elastic rope' and other hair-raising adventures continue to be invented. Take as an example Queenstown.

Case Study: Queenstown, Extreme Sports Capital

Queenstown, South Island, New Zealand, is known as the Extreme Sports Capital. Half a million tourists visit every year for death-defying thrills. A former gold-mining town on the banks of Lake Wakatipu in the Southern Alps, it was here that the first commercial bungee jumps were made, it is claimed, from the 150-foot Kawarau Bridge, and the 440-foot Nevis Highwire is said to be the second highest land-based bungee jump in the world.

World champions abound in Queenstown: sky surfers, base jumpers, paragliders, rock climbers and jet boaters. The ultra extreme sport is BASE jumping, described by most commentators as the most dangerous extreme sport in the world and illegal in America. Sky surfing – skydiving with a board attached to your feet and surfing through the air – is the second most dangerous. Quicker than free-falling, the danger is in being struck by the board when it is released, or getting the board tangled with your 'chute'. A Queenstown slogan reads 'Stare death in the face and you'll soon feel alive again!' (Factfile, Queenstown).

The term BASE is an acronym for Buildings, Antenna Tower, Span, Earth. BASE jumpers leap from objects which fall under the categories BASE represents. Generally, these objects are not high off the ground, and so parachutes must be deployed very quickly. *The Skydiver's Handbook* (Poynter and Turoff, 1998) suggests that this kind of jumping can be traced back 900 years, but modern BASE jumping is believed to have started in 1978, where daring parachutists first began jumping off El Capitan, a 3,000-foot cliff above Yosemite National Park.

Climb every mountain

The song with this title came from the film *The Sound of Music*, and exhorts us to press on until we find our dream. Conquering earth, sea and sky has driven men and women to the limits of skill and endurance in the face of the most treacherous oceans, freezing Arctic temperatures, the heat of the desert and inhospitable terrains to climb the highest peaks. Mountains, and the need to climb them 'because they are there' has always captured the dreams and imaginations of intrepid adventurers. Conquering Mount Everest was one of the extreme feats – extreme experiences – of all time.

Edmund Hillary and Sherpa Norgay Tenzing were the first to stand as the pinnacle of the world's highest mountain at 29,035 feet on 29 May, 1953. Attempts to conquer the mountain had claimed the lives of many people for more than a century. Although it has since been climbed by many mountaineers, there still remains a sense of awe and wonder surrounding Everest. Not surprisingly, the Nepalese consider these mountains sacred, known locally as Sagarmatha, Mother Goddess of the Sky. The romance of that first climb, coinciding with the coronation of Queen Elizabeth II, and the subsequent climbs by men and women to the top of the highest mountain, captures our imagination and spirit of adventuret. It hides the cruel, utterly exhausting reality of

There have been more than 1,700 ascents of K2 by more than 1,300 climbers, but only 188 have reached the summit; 22 of them (men and women) died.

mountaineers who must fight painfully, up five and a half vertical miles at freezing temperatures (at times plummeting to minus sixty degrees), and at oxygen levels lowered to dangerous levels.

K2, the second-highest mountain in the world, is said to be the deadliest, the most difficult to climb. 'K' stands for Karakoram and '2' for the second peak in this range of mountains. Climbing psychologist, Geoff Powter (2003) thinks that climbers have a 'repeating personality syndrome', a desire for constant change to create excitement. In the mountains, they yearn for home; at home they find life dull and routine.

Spiritual experiences and leisure

Religious 'searchings', revivals and pilgrimages have existed for thousands of years. Those well known today include pilgrimages to The Holy Land, to Mecca and to Lourdes. Almost every day there are tourists on a kind of pilgrimage to St Peter's Square and the outer Vatican in Rome. There are also sacred places throughout the world – places with powerful meanings that visitors and tourists want to visit. Often, the past and present merge with visitors' expectations of greater insights, 'new life' or healing of mind and body, to give life-enhancing experiences. To what extent can these destinations or places of pilgrimage equate with our understanding of leisure? Leisure can, after all, be what we want to do in our time for leisure. Just one of many examples which could fit into a leisure category of specialist holiday or 'spiritual tourism' and which links to the past, is founded on one of the beliefs of Ancient Greece.

Case study: The Asclepian temple at Epidauros

The Asclepian temple at Epidauros was a complex of sports and cultural facilities including a 14,000-seat amphitheatre which is still used for performances of Greek tragedies. It would have been like one of today's large sports and leisure centres, but with a difference. It was also a healing centre, one of the 'dream healing temples' of Ancient Greek medicine.

At such temples, patients would be put into 'incubation' for several nights until Asclepius (half mortal son of Apollo) appeared to them in a dream and diagnosed their complaint. Today, there are Dream Healing Pilgrimages, advertised as a panacea for mental and spiritual ills and an antidote to modern-day stress. The reasoning is that by dreaming and discussing our dreams, we can tap into our minds our own problem-solving techniques. The healing centres' concern is with total well-being, a holistic approach, with current programmes offering Reiki, Tai Chi, Pilates, yoga, nutrition, meditation and, importantly, a Retreat.

Heawood, 2003

In the United Kingdom and in most other countries today, there are hundreds of examples of health centres, anti-stress programmes, spiritual and religious retreats and clinics to help people to reconnect body, mind and spirit.

Leisure and a search for identity

Some fortunate people find life satisfaction in their work and are able to identify themselves in terms of their occupation, be it as an author, a secretary, a long-distance lorry driver, a lawyer, a doctor, a teacher or whatever. People, however, can also find life satisfaction in their leisure interests, activities and pastimes and they can become known for these pursuits rather than for what they do at work. They might be an actor in the pantomime, a singer in a band, a railway buff, a surfer, a playgroup leader, an artist exhibiting paintings or photographs in the library, captain of the cricket club at the top of the league, a fundraiser for charity or leader of the Adventure Scouts.

What is the connection between people's apparent search for identity and leisure? Clearly, leisure offers opportunities for self-development, creativity and adventure. Economists and sociologists may tell us that we have not reached the Age of Leisure, but leisure is seen, increasingly, not just as a time to be leisurely, nor as a soft option, but as offering opportunities for self-fulfilment and self-development. Take long-distance running, for example. Many of the same people who disliked compulsory runs at school now train most of the year in the hope of a place to run in The London Marathon. Olympic Games gold medallist in the steeplechase and former London Marathon Race organizer, Christopher Brasher, commented: 'Make no mistake, it is hard, desperately hard, to run 26 miles 385 yards and the only reward for the masses is that every single one of them is a winner.'

> The Great North Run attracted 47,000 runners in 2003, the largest field in the world.

There is an increasing body of distance runners, risk-taking extreme sports addicts, sky-divers, cavers, climbers, surfers, tri-athletes, artists, musicians, writers and explorers, pilgrims, spiritual searchers and seekers of stunning landscapes of beauty and wonder. They appear to be looking for worthwhile, fulfilling experiences: something beyond our current enslavement to routines of employment, possessions, television, mobile phones and the need to be entertained. What are all these people searching for, while giving their time and energy and sometimes risking their money, their loved ones and even their lives? There will be a variety of personal motivations: the drive for success, the need to overcome difficulties and hardships, the desire to 'be somebody'. Many people with severe physical handicaps strive to be as proficient as or better than the majority of us in many areas of life including some of the most gruelling sports.

Maslow described people's need and search for what he defined as 'peak experiences', brought about by 'affirmation of our identity and confirmation of our existence'. Peak experiences are some of those high moments in life when one is totally immersed in an experience or activity: at one with the world and with oneself. Top-class skiers say they have the sensation of blending into the mountain; runners, having gone through the pain barrier, have described a feeling of 'floating'; top gymnasts and dancers have achieved a moment of sheer 'perfection'. Archaeologists finding an ancient artifact or a tourist experiencing a stunning landscape or sunset, have their breath taken away: a heart-stopping moment. Although such experiences cannot be made to happen, some conditions can create an enabling environment. Most people who report having 'highs' in, say, music, drama, dance and sport, have usually achieved a high level of skill. The display of such skill is also the attractive magnet for those who watch. However, in many activities such as extreme sports and outdoor activities, it is in the doing that one experiences peaks. Spectators and supporters can share in moments of achievement but it is the doers who are most likely to achieve peak experiences or feelings of recreation or oneness. Yet, passive leisure can be moving also. Sitting in the audience at a moving symphony concert or standing in the pouring rain to hear a really great rock concert can also provide unforgettable experiences, some of which might match up with Maslow's definition of peak experience.

Many people seek self-fulfilment in a variety of ways and leisure allows them the freedom to be or to become all they believe they are capable of. The spirit is caught in the poem of Robert Browning: 'Ah, but a man's reach should exceed his grasp. Or what's a heaven for?' Such 'leisure', if it be leisure, is akin to the leisure ideal of the Ancient Greeks, but far more useful because it widens the scope of their extremely narrow choice: and it is open to all, or most, not just for the exclusive minority of privileged people.

The search for identity is important in understanding leisure behaviour. It is a search for the whole person, not a split person. The idea is exemplified in the growth of spiritual and meditative movements. Some Eastern disciplines and philosophies, for example, emphasize a unification of the body, mind and spirit, through movement, meditation and deep relaxation. They promise a unity with oneself and with the universe, and captured the imagination of the Western world during the last decades of the twentieth century. They filled the vacuum created by our artificial splitting of the body from the mind and spirit during the Age of Reason. With the rise of emotional distress and mental illness in the West, we have to ask the question whether, in addition to being an 'experience society', we are also a 'sick society'.

Are we a sick society?

There is a general perception in the medical profession that there are more illnesses of the mind than of the body in Western countries. People suffer from a range of ills that diminish their quality of life: depression, stress, loneliness, lack of self-esteem and, for a variety of reasons, an inability to cope with the pressures of modern-day lives. These conditions occur in all sections of the community, though some groups of people are more vulnerable and at greater risk, for example, the half a million homeless people in Britain.

According to a press report by Jo Revill (2003), Britain's 'Top 10' causes of stress are:

> Thirteen million working days were lost to stress in 2002, and in Britain we spend £670 million on massage, yoga and therapies to beat it.

- unemployment
- money problems
- single parenthood
- relationship problems and divorce
- having a baby and infertility; retirement
- family problems such as children in trouble and sick parents
- moving house
- death in the family and
- serious or terminal illness.

Estimates vary, but there is a general belief that one in five people in the United Kingdom will be affected by clinical depression at some point in their life. The risk of

In 2003, there were 2.8 million people receiving treatment for depression and an estimated further 8 million who have not been diagnosed or treated.

depression increases with age. Clearly, depression results in lowering a person's self- esteem and the full enjoyment of life enjoyed by a healthy person, such as love, friendship, adventure, creativity, sport and enjoying the richness the world has to offer. The result of all this is low self-esteem which undermines all our relationships and endeavours. Over the years, these negative propensities become established habits.

According to Anita Chaudhuri (2003), British women spent £300 million on headache tablets in 2002, and she suggested a few lifestyle changes that might help deal with the problem. A study published in the *British Medical Journal* (October 2002), quoted by Chaudhuri, found that there was a 'chronic overuse of headache drugs' which may account for as many as half the headaches suffered. In other words, headaches might be caused by taking too many headache tablets.

One of the causes of human distress is our vanity. Most of us want to look attractive, but some are driven to extreme lengths to achieve their goals. Weight loss is an example, but taken to extremes, it can lead to ill-health and to unattractiveness: quite the opposite of what was intended. A report by Datamonitor found that more than 34 million people went on a diet in 2002. Most of these millions do not include the poorer sections of society; the Consumers Association claim that it is the poor – in rich societies – that are the more obese and who need solutions, as it is the obese who are at the greatest risk of ill-health. We are alarmed at the soaring rate of child obesity in Britain. According to the Department of Health, one in every twelve 6-year-olds and one in seven 15-year-olds is obese and half a million children are more than 20 per cent over their 'ideal' weight. Seriously obese children are highly likely to be obese adults. Teenagers are now being diagnosed with Type II diabetes, triggered by being seriously overweight.

Britons spent an estimated £10.3 billion in 2002 trying to lose weight.

Some young people also suffer from depression and lack of self-esteem. Every year an estimated 160,000 people, 24,000 of whom are teenagers, are admitted to Accident and Emergency wards throughout Britain after acts of deliberate self harm (Johnstone, 2003). The situation is of such concern that 1 March, 2003, was designated Self-Injury Awareness Day, supported by The Samaritans, Mind and the National Self-Harm Network.

What is there about living in highly advanced, rich societies that drives people to self harm? Is it lack of self-fulfilment and low opinion of oneself? Some children, young people and even adults feel that they have to purchase material goods to keep up with their peers and so buy prestige, friendship and belonging. Expensive, brand-named goods can, seemingly, buy friendship and influence people. The need to conform to peer pressure is great. The mobile phone is another example. 'Britons are enslaved by the mobile telephone', was a headline in *The Times* (10 May, 2003). Nearly half of young adults 'have very strong feeling about their handset, describing its loss as similar to a bereavement'.

They were supposed to provide freedom, independence, control and fun. But instead it seems that mobile phones have enslaved us. We are emotionally dependent on them for our identity and feelings of self-worth and incapable even of going to the shops without whipping them out at regular intervals to call family and friends for advice ... Many younger users regard their phones as an extension of their physical being that they rely upon to forge and maintain their self-image. Even older, more sceptical, users rely on their phone for emotional fulfilment. The Henley Management Centre and the research company Teleconomy found that more than a quarter of all users regard their phone as 'essential', with a significant minority reporting that they feel strangely detached from life if they do not have it with them or are made to turn it off. Many say that their choice of phone is hugely important to their sense of identity, as it projects their self-image.

Frean, 2003

Texting and imaging have added to the allure of the mobile phone. It is early days in the life of the versatile mobile phone. While on the one hand it can empower and provide some control on our lives, on the other hand, its use for immediacy and location ('where are you?'), Frean suggests, is a form of control.

Many people only switch off the mobile to go to sleep and switch it on again the moment they wake up. Indeed, they wake up to the alarm on the mobile.

Many lives are being lived in an 'instant society': the demand is for instant attention and action. We can obtain anything we like, on credit, today.

Will Hutton, a journalist at *The Observer*, has written (2003) of the 'lust for instant gratification', that we live in a society which places a premium on instantaneity. We want results now; gratification now. 'We are becoming pseudo babies and long-established civilised codes by which we treat each other are fraying.' Individualism alone is not to blame.

The problem is when individualism degrades into self-obsession and narcissism, refusing to accept limits, or that the rewards of patient application over time cannot be reproduced in moments ... It is not individualism that is destructive, but individualism laced with instantaneity and with no acknowledgment of reciprocal obligations that corrodes.

Writing in the *Guardian*, Justin Cartwright (cited by Hutton, 2003) called this the new infantilism. 'Infantilism is no longer confined to youth'.

Summary

The discussion so far has illustrated that we are societies of people who strive for meaningful experiences, people who have needs for esteem and belonging. There is also a growing insistence on instant actions, and immediate responses to our demands. For a variety of reasons, many of us suffer illnesses of body and mind. But what does all this have to do with leisure and recreation, activities which seem far removed from hardships?

Case study: The Ellen MacArthur Trust

At the age of 23, Ellen MacArthur became the youngest and fastest woman to sail single-handed around the world. She launched her own charity, the Ellen MacArthur Trust, which gives children with cancer the chance to go sailing and experience some of the adventure that she has found in the sport. In a press interview (Hart-Davis, 2003) she said: 'Sometimes I hate it on the sea when the going gets tough – but it is my choice to be there. Yet the children have not chosen to suffer the traumas of illness. That's where you see real courage, in the way they can still manage to enjoy themselves ... To give them an experience like that can be a great form of medicine.'

To what extent can leisure play a part in alleviating lack of self-esteem, meet emotional, health and educational goals and make for more self-fulfilled people and a more 'wholesome' society? Clearly, the needs of some people are not being met. Anecdotal evidence exists to show how positive leisure can benefit, enormously, the well-being of people, but governments remain sceptical, calling for more substantive evidence. One of the thousands of heartening stories comes from young people with cancer and their adventure of sailing.

This chapter has moved away from perceiving leisure as services, physical products and activities, towards viewing leisure as something that has to be experienced. Such experiences can come from a wide range of stimuli, whether watching a sunset, looking at the landscape, being involved in risk-taking activities or quietly meditating or in the poet's words, 'to stand and stare'.

The question is now, how can we use this perception and arrive at a core of what it is to be 'at leisure'? In the next chapter, I introduce what I term the 'pleisure principle'.

Discussion points

1 People have always sought out different experiences – it is part of human nature. However, what is new is that the search for experience is taking precedence over all kinds of social processes; social traditions are giving way to the individual experiences that give our lives shape and form. Discuss this viewpoint and where leisure fits into the equation.

2 Some people, young people in particular, are seeking heightened experiences, 'ultimate' experiences. In some cases this can lead to binge drinking, drugs and anti-social behaviour. In a non-judgemental way, what role can be played by leisure professionals in channelling this drive for experiences into more worthwhile and positive experiences both for the individual and the community?

8
The 'pleisure principle'

Introduction

In the previous chapter, it was shown that people often go to great lengths to find or to buy satisfying experiences. Leisure can offer opportunities for such experiences.

This brief chapter, the smallest in the book, tries to get to the heart of the leisure product: the leisure experience. Leisure Managers need to create the environments and opportunities and deliver services and programmes for different people to experience leisure. Managers also have to manage resources – personnel, facilities and finances – to meet the business goals of their organizations. Operational management is dealt with in later chapters of this book. In this chapter my concern is in trying to get nearer to an understanding of the leisure experience.

In 1990, I coined the word 'pleisure' and have used it ever since. This chapter explains the term, and also directs leisure professionals to the implications of the 'pleisure principle'.

Core characteristics of play, recreation and leisure

Three of the concepts discussed in previous chapters and which I believe are the foundation stones for leisure and recreation management are 'play', 'recreation' and 'leisure'. In debating and dissecting each concept, a case can be made to treat each as distinct activities. In common language we can all distinguish children at *play*, young people and adults taking part in organized *recreation*, and being at *leisure*, lazing in a deck chair, drink in hand. And we can use all three words at once: 'playing recreational games in our leisure time'. Moreover, the feelings we might experience could be the same whatever words we care to use. Why, then, are we concerned with their differences? It is tempting to dismiss this line of enquiry as mere semantics which simply adds to the jargon. However, there is more to it than just words because we often provide for these three aspects of life in different ways. We provide *play* space, community *recreation* facilities or multi-use and

119

family *leisure* centres. My concern is in part academic: we need to get our terms straight or we work in a career of confusion and misunderstandings. It is also in part practical: leisure professionals must know what they are providing and to whom. By play, do we mean children's play or do we mean playing sport or playing cards? By recreation, do we mean taking part in organized recreation activities or could we be referring to the recreative experience of relaxing in the spa? By leisure are we engaged in recreation activity or simply day-dreaming, or reading a novel at our leisure? Let us summarize some of the key findings from the substantial discussion in the previous chapters.

Play *can be described as activity, freely chosen and indulged in for its own sake for the satisfaction it brings in the doing. Play exhibits childlike characteristics of joy, spontaneity, self-expression and a creation of its own special meaning in a play world.*

Recreation *is usually thought of as leisure time activities and pursuits and often tends to be more organized, whether in an informal game on the park or organized more formally by others. Recreation is more institutional in character than play or leisure. In its purest sense, however, recreation can be re-creation: an inner consuming experience that leads to revival. In this sense, recreation experience renews, restores and 'recharges the batteries'.*

Leisure *is perceived in a variety of ways – as time, activity, experience, or state of being. It can encompass play and recreation and can be casual or serious. In its idealistic sense, leisure can be perceived as experiencing activities, chosen in relative freedom, that are personally satisfying and innately worthwhile and that has the potential to lead an individual towards self-actualization and, ultimately, play a part in a self-fulfilling way of life.*

One can see readily that at the core of play, recreation and leisure, there exists a number of similarities and overlaps; after all, we can use each word to mean much the same thing. Collectively, they all mean freedom, absence of necessity, choice, self-initiating, self-expression, satisfaction in the doing, playfulness and, quite often, seriousness. There are, of course, differences between them too. Playfulness and spontaneity are found more in children's play and in the play of those elderly people who appear to have re-discovered the art of playing. Recreation carries a badge of respectability: doing things that are good for you. Leisure is a looser, more casual, less constrained term than recreation and encompasses a vast range of active and passive, casual and serious pursuits. Whether at play, recreation or leisure, people can experience a feeling of immense satisfaction in the doing, or of well-being, or a quality of experience that can lead to revitalization or an uplifting of the spirit. This can also occur at work and elsewhere, but it is when we are 'at leisure', free to make choices and be ourselves, that we are more likely to achieve a quality we might describe as 'wholeness' or an inner consuming experience. The experience goes beyond description afforded by words: but it needs a name.

As there is no word to describe this experience in the English language, I invented the word 'pleisure'. Figure 8.1 illustrates better than words the concept of the pleisure experience at the heart of play, recreation and leisure.

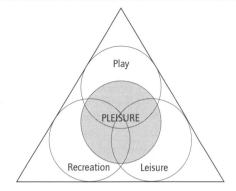

Figure 8.1 'Pleisure' at the heart of play, recreation and leisure

What implications does this have for the leisure professionals and managers? Put simply, the 'pleisure principle' implies that in terms of meeting the needs of individual people, clients and customers of leisure and recreation services, facilities and programmes, the quality of the experience is more important for them than the activities, programmes, numbers attending or the income generated. The activity itself may be quite secondary to what it does for a person, or what it means to him or her. Moreover, in terms of management, appreciating that Leisure Managers have business goals to fulfil, people are more likely to be attracted to and 'buy' activities that they perceive to be worthwhile or that bring satisfying experiences.

'Pleisure principles' into leisure management actions

Putting principles into practice is not an easy transition. Expediency is often the option we take and, understandably, management practices tend toward efficiency. If, as leisure professionals, we want to provide a choice of activities and opportunity for people to experience and develop leisure potential, then we must provide favourable environments: the right conditions, satisfactions and positive outcomes.

The right conditions Leisure programmes need to be designed with sufficient options for different people. There needs to be freedom of choice and also the opportunity for some self-initiation and spontaneity.

Satisfactions To be satisfying, there need to be levels of some of the following experiences: self-expression, challenge, novelty, stimulation, joy, playfulness, quality experiences (ideally, 'pleisure' experiences) and re-creative moments.

Positive outcomes To be effective, there should be some positive outcomes, for example, accomplishment, heightening of self-esteem and well-being, both physical, emotional, social and psychological.

Favourable experiences give satisfactions. Satisfactions lead to consuming interests. Consuming interests can lead to life-enhancing experiences, a goal of leisure. Providing for client and customer satisfactions can also lead to successful business outcomes.

Regrettably, it is not so simple. There are a number of individual and institutional barriers to providing services and programmes based on the needs of people. The reasons for this are complex. People, generally, are not free agents to do as they please and are limited in their response to leisure services and programmes. Some people have physical, mental and social limitations or their environments limit choice (such as the family, peer group, culture, resources). Leisure for others is eroded through obligations, lack of time or through enforced free time without the means or motivation to use it. Activities one might consider as leisure, such as sport, can be practised in such extremes that the spirit of play and fair play are submerged by the desire to win at all costs. And there are inequalities of opportunity, physical, social and economic. There still exist gender imbalances, for example, male-only golf clubs, even when skill levels are similar.

Do public sector providers adequately consider people's needs in planning services and facilities and formulating programmes? Successful private sector organizations, although concerned with financial profits, realize that providing for our wants can lead to greater profits. Public authorities sometimes provide fragmented services between tiers in the same authority and at times within the same department. People have to go from one local authority department to the next, to find a satisfactory solution to a problem. Organizations, professions, voluntary bodies and public departments can isolate themselves and operate independently. This leads to a lack of cohesion and mutual understanding which deprives people of their needs. An integrated approach to leisure service is certainly desirable, but there are also organizational and institutional barriers and increasing financial barriers to overcome. To provide as appropriately as possible for people, services and programmes should be founded on principles which enhance quality of life. Providers should recognize the obstacles and limitations to participation and make assumptions about which services and programmes can be developed to best meet people's needs. Aspects of good management and practice follow in later chapters in this book.

Discussion of issues

Providing for people's leisure is complex. Providing for their 'pleisure', even more so. Leisure implies freedom. Freedom implies choice. Choice enables people to be involved in activities which are either personally worthwhile and which lead to good citizenship or those which are of doubtful value, either to themselves or the community.

Consider, for example, the individual who flits from experience to experience, like an impulse buyer in a supermarket. Does he or she have the opportunity to gain an appreciation of the activity which will make it, in Godbey's words, 'intuitively worthwhile'? For most people, enjoyment and satisfaction in an activity increase as knowledge and skill increase. Whether gardening, playing drums, surfing or collecting old comics, all are enriched by an increase in knowledge and skill. 'Leisure involves sacrificing that which is potentially good for that which is potentially better. The lack of willingness to sacrifice one desirable activity in order to undertake another, however, suggests an inability to obtain leisure' (Goodale and Godbey, 1988, pp. 218–9).

As Jacob Bronowski (1965) pointed out, appreciation is essentially an act of recreation; a deep sense of appreciation envelops us and lifts us to a higher plane where we discover that there is peace, beauty and joy in this world. And that may carry over into increased appreciation of life itself. That is leisure's promise.

It seems hard for us to appreciate and accept the gift of leisure. Ideally, leisure can be a way of living the 'good life' for individuals and communities. But only we can determine for ourselves what that will be. However, education and knowledge will help to give the opportunity and ability to make good choices. Leisure education can help people to appreciate the opportunities that can be opened up and, importantly, how to make the right choices for their lifestyle. Education should not be limited to preparation for finding jobs. Schools and colleges are not simply employment agencies. Leisure education is much neglected. The more we learn about ourselves, about how to choose to find fulfilment, the better society we create.

Can we possibly achieve such a Utopia based on people's needs? People have diverse needs, and different people have different needs, which change according to their circumstances and stage in life. Old people have different needs from the young; disadvantaged people have different levels of need compared with those who are highly advantaged. People have a whole range of needs, some of which are basic to survival, some are essential to cope with living in an uncertain social world and some are at the apex of a complex human network bringing balance, harmony and self-worth to individual people. It is particularly in this latter category where leisure opportunity can help people to meet some of their needs. Leisure, therefore, is inextricably linked to other elements of life. For example, leisure for the vast majority of disadvantaged groups is likely to remain low while they are constrained by lack of income, poor housing and the unrelieved pressures of parenting.

If we want to provide leisure based on the needs of people, then local authorities (in particular) must make a number of assumptions on which to base principles, aims and objectives:

- that the services are open to all and meet individual needs, so that a person can choose activities, in relative freedom;
- that priorities should be balanced to serve the greatest number and those in greatest need, recognizing that those in greatest need may well be in the minority; and
- that services should not be pockets of competing interests.

The question is: with emphasis on freedom, can leisure actually be organized, planned and managed? The activity can be organized, but the experience cannot. What is the Manager's role? Normally considered as managing resources, services, facilities and programmes, leisure professionals have a wider remit. Their role is to:

- consult and involve people and then create environments and services to match the market profiles;
- extend the range of activities to offer a wide and varied choice; groups can be helped through supportive services and some can be enabled to create their own opportunities and manage themselves;
- assist employers in giving their employees recreation activities at workplaces and outside work;
- help provide leisure education for schools, colleges and organizations to inculcate leisure skills (physical, social, cultural and intellectual) which can help people, particularly young people, to make choices to realize their potential.

In these and other ways, Leisure Managers and other professionals can help to extend opportunities. The assumptions provide principles on which to force a reorientation towards an enhanced 'people approach' to leisure services. The reorientation stems from the belief that each individual has worth, has a need to express himself or herself, and that society will benefit from citizens who have the ability and resourcefulness not only to cope, but to be creative and find fulfilment in their lives, through leisure.

Leisure time can be, however, a two-edged sword without the opportunity, the means, the motivation and the ability to cope. Along with an increase in leisure participation, there has been an increase in anti-social behaviour, particularly in those areas where leisure opportunity is low. Free time has not solved the social problems of boredom, loneliness, and anti-social behaviour. Indeed, free time may have exacerbated those problems. Can leisure management help to solve some of them? Opportunity for leisure has no value to people, of course, unless advantage is taken of it. This is where Leisure Managers and professionals have a special role to play, that of enabling people to take up the opportunities by effective and sensitive marketing, education, leadership and service delivery.

The leisure management pyramid

To provide effective community leisure and recreation services, it is essential to consider the needs of people, the leisure products designed to meet the needs, and good management to deliver the services. A theoretical framework in the form of a conceptual model illustrates this essential linkage. The assumptions on which the model is based are fourfold:

- Leisure can provide satisfying and intrinsically worthwhile activities and experiences.
- People have needs and wants which Leisure Managers endeavour to meet through leisure programmes and activities.
- Management is the process of planning, providing, operating and delivering appropriate services and programmes to match the needs.
- Aims and objectives of an organization determine the results to be achieved.

How can these entirely different concepts be merged into effective leisure management? The pyramid model depicted in Figure 8.2 should be visualized as a transparent triangular pyramid, which has three sides, or planes, and a base:

1 Leisure plane
2 Needs of people plane
3 Management plane
4 Organizational aims: the base of the pyramid.

The pyramid therefore represents the uniting or binding of leisure, people's needs and management. For effectiveness, the three planes must function in accord, though balance points will vary depending on the objectives of the organization, the situation and the prevailing emphasis. For example, services directed at disadvantaged groups will give priority to the needs of people plane.

For efficiency and measurability, each of the three planes needs to contain levels of performance or target indicators. For simplicity and illustration only, these are shown in the model (Figures 8.3 and 8.4) at three levels: the lower tier or basic level; the middle tier or secondary level; and the upper tier or primary level.

Figure 8.2 Conceptual model for leisure management: leisure, policies, needs and management

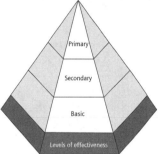

Figure 8.3 Conceptual model for leisure management: levels of performance

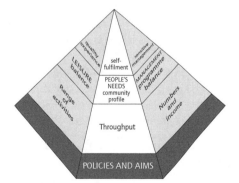

Figure 8.4 Conceptual model for leisure management: performance and effectiveness

Basic level At the lower, basic level, the Leisure Manager would seek to achieve a wide range of choice of activities, general service efficiency and customer service, high levels of throughput at attractive prices and a broad programme of casual, group, club and special programmes and events. The basic level, therefore, represents the numbers game, that is, an activities, head-counting and money-counting exercise. Many authorities and organizations measure success only at this point, an organization survival level. They stop at this point and, therefore, will fall short of providing an effective service.

Secondary level At the secondary level we could expect to see, in public services, a user profile reflecting broadly the catchment population and the target markets which the organization is aiming to attract. At this level, managers would seek to have a balanced programme to meet some of the needs of the different people and groups of like-minded people in the area. Greater emphasis will be given to the encouragement of community initiative, working with groups and organizations.

Primary or upper level At the top level, the manager will be concerned with individual client and customer needs, the quality of experience and the encouragement of long-lasting activities that are perceived by the individuals to be personally worthwhile and of importance.

The apex of the pyramid serves to illustrate the goal of leisure management, that is, personal self-actualization or self-fulfilment of individual people through leisure opportunity. It thus represents the highest quality of leisure experiences that people will want to 'buy' again and again, the satisfactions that can lead to an enhancing of the quality of life. It is to this goal of quality leisure and recreation that a manager must strive in order to give a service that can truly be called 'excellent leisure management'. However, *all* levels of service are important. Indeed, the greater number and those in greatest need are one of the priorities.

Why is such a model of use or relevance? It reminds managers that while they are dealing with leisure in its variety, they are providing for people and meeting organizational objectives. The model also illustrates that every individual is:

- like all people in having the same basic needs (the basic level of the pyramid);
- like some other like-minded people in sharing the same interests (the secondary level); and
- like no other person: a unique individual at the apex of the pyramid. At the top point of the pyramid there is no room for more than one.

The model allows for maximum flexibility, so that Leisure Managers can vary their responses to be appropriate to given situations, placing emphasis where needed. Good management needs to be flexible management, but the greater the flexibility, the greater the need for management excellence. Objectives are unlikely to be met without good management. Management is the essential process and delivery mechanism.

Discussion points

1 'Pleisure' is a word coined to describe a human inner experience that might be found whether in play, leisure or recreation. Is this simply semantics on the author's part or is there substance in this line of curiosity and enquiry? Discuss.

2 How do you perceive the difference, if any, between 'the pleasure principle' and the 'pleisure principle'? Explain your reasoning.

Part 2

9

Government, the public sector and leisure

Introduction

In previous chapters, the concept of leisure has been debated in terms of what it is, what it does and what it can do for individual people and for the community at large. Leisure service and facility managers were encouraged to provide programmes and activities which enable people to find satisfying leisure experiences. Providing satisfactions could achieve two main objectives: first, it could help to meet some of the needs of people, and second, it could help in meeting the business goals of an organization or a department by attracting more satisfied clients and customers. We now move from the conceptual and personal perspectives and start to deal with the leisure industry and the providers.

People's leisure and recreation is made possible through a wide range of providers, through powers and duties invested in government and through natural and man-made resources, services, facilities and management. Provision is needed in and around the home, in the urban environment, in rural areas, in the countryside, on dry land and on water. A range of services and programmes is required to meet the diverse needs and demands of individuals, families, groups, clubs, societies, agencies and organizations large and small.

There are many parties involved in the provision of leisure facilities:

- central government, primarily through its agencies

- unitary authorities
- county councils
- district councils
- parish councils
- institutions such as schools, colleges and universities
- private sector companies
- not-for-profit companies and charitable trusts
- a substantial number of voluntary organizations and
- national and local pressure groups.

In the past, there was a clear distinction between what was provided by the public, voluntary and commercial sectors, but today there are overlaps with some of the same sorts of facilities and programmes provided by each sector: health and fitness centres, bars and catering are examples. However, there are still distinct differences between different types of provider in philosophy and approach, though even these are gradually becoming blurred.

There have been huge changes in central government and local government in the last twenty years. Legislation over much of the 1980s and 1990s had the effect, on the one hand, of tightening councils' budgets, and, on the other hand, bringing flexibility into the ways in which services could be delivered and facilities managed. Although policy and decision making still came under the control of the local authorities, some councils perceived the measures as diminishing their management control. In particular, Compulsory Competitive Tendering (CCT), a Conservative Government initiative which lasted from 1992 to 1997, had a dramatic effect on the role of local government in relation to the management of services, including leisure. CCT also opened the door to a number of new leisure management contracting companies, not-for-profit companies and leisure trusts. The advantages in these alternative forms of operational management (as distinct from direct local authority management) included external investment and financial savings, particularly since trust bodies were entitled to substantial rate relief. When the Labour Government came to power in 1997 it abolished CCT and replaced it with Best Value, bringing with it a new language of 'stakeholders', 'joined-up government' and 'cross-cutting', dealing with major social issues across departments.

The last twenty years have also seen a changing terminology used to describe the growing profession and the burgeoning leisure industry. The first multi-use indoor centres of the 1960s, for example in Harlow, were called sport centres or sport and recreation centres, and new arts and 'cultural' facilities were called arts centres. Then new terms were adopted such as forum, indoor arena, magnum, dome and complex, until the more standardized term of 'leisure' took root, not only for facilities, but also for services. Leisure was now clearly identified as being a term encompassing sports, arts, play and recreation and was the word used most often to describe departmental services, the emerging profession, academic and management courses and a new career of Leisure Management. Local authorities sought to plan for leisure in the medium to long term and began to produce 'leisure strategies' in which leisure departments collaborated with planning and other departments and consulted with the community. No sooner had local authorities begun to move in the direction of broad-based leisure strategies when central government came forward with the word 'culture' and directed local authorities to prepare 'cultural strategies'. 'Culture', reflecting the government's Department of Culture, Media and Sport, was to be the umbrella concept and term to encompass not only the arts but sport, play and recreation and the widest range of leisure time activities. The problem for Leisure Managers is that it is difficult to convince the members of football, rugby and swimming clubs that they are now in the district's culture plan, when the government's own department is called 'Culture, Media *and* Sport'.

This chapter is concerned with central government in the United Kingdom and its agencies and with the powers of local governments and their provision of leisure services and facilities. The following two chapters deal with leisure provision in the voluntary and commercial sectors respectively.

The scope of public leisure services and facilities

In the United Kingdom, public services and facilities for leisure can be provided by a public authority, or by legislation for the general use of the public. Some facilities are provided by public funds for a restricted use, such as educational establishments, facilities for Her Majesty's Services and restricted forestry areas. While commercial operators have veered towards those facilities and activities that give a good return on their investment, the costs of land and construction have left the local authorities the task of providing more of the land-extensive facilities such as water recreation and parks, and more of the expensive buildings such as large public leisure complexes, public swimming pools, athletic tracks, theatres, sports centres and concert halls. Local authorities also provide indirectly through financial and other support, through planning decisions and generally by acting as an 'enabling authority'. Local authorities thus play a major role in the provision of facilities and opportunities for public leisure and recreation. Government agencies, such as new town corporations, regional water authorities and national park boards, also have major roles in recreation provision. All these bodies have powers or duties to assist in or to initiate provision.

The scope of recreation and leisure services within local authorities is very wide. However, there are a number of identifiable elements and spheres of influence; different authorities will have some or all of these elements depending on the location and the size of the authority, its policies and its responsibilities. These spheres and elements are shown in Figure 9.1. Many of the elements are combined or overlap; no two authorities are exactly alike either in provision or management. There are general similarities but specific differences.

Local authorities provide their range of facilities in a variety of ways. The public has access to a large number of facilities, for which no direct payment is made, such as urban parks, playgrounds, libraries, picnic areas, nature trails, beaches and country parks. While the public does not pay directly for these amenities, it does so indirectly through rates and taxes. Local authorities also provide facilities such as swimming pools, playing fields, golf courses, marinas, arts centres, theatres and sports centres, where there is a direct payment by the user, albeit often at highly subsidized charges.

While local authorities often look to voluntary and commercial sectors to provide for social activity and entertainment, they nevertheless do provide for entertainment, both directly and indirectly. They provide directly, for example, through village and community halls; community centres are particularly widespread in new town developments.

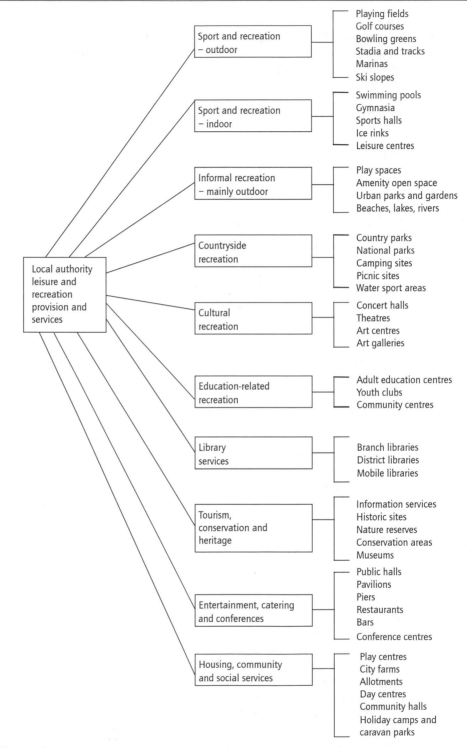

Figure 9.1 Examples of local authority leisure and recreation facilities and services

They also directly provide through the provision of civic halls which are used for entertainment, and urban parks with their bandstands and entertainment facilities. Many new leisure centres are also prime venues for public entertainment, in many cases being the largest public halls in the district. Most sports halls, for example, are the venues for antique and craft fairs, entertainment and large social events.

Despite the emergence of new facilities, such as indoor leisure and recreation centres and country parks, it is the staffing and management of traditional services which call for the largest part of local authority leisure and recreation services expenditure. When education-related services and libraries are included in the comprehensive coverage, then the picture becomes even clearer, with all the new areas of leisure expenditure taking up only a small proportion of the total.

Local authorities are not simply providers of facilities, they support organizations of all kinds (private institutions, voluntary organizations and even commercial bodies), when it is shown that greater service will be given to the public by so doing. The support given is basically of two kinds. The first is to make its own facilities and equipment available for use, with or without charge. The second is to make financial grants.

The local education authorities are usually involved in support to youth and community services and organizations, for example, by making schools available for youth and adult classes, and by making capital and annual grants to community associations and other social groups. They may pay the salaries of wardens, leaders, teachers and managers of community centres.

Local authorities have discretionary powers to assist in all manner of ways. For example they can:

- assist trust bodies to provide theatres and sports centres
- assist sports clubs to provide bowling greens and tennis courts
- assist community groups to provide facilities for children's play, community arts or facilities which help older citizens
- provide considerable support, indirectly, by sponsoring arts, sports and entertainment festivals and major events, by meeting deficits or by funding community events and activities
- give small services or small grants to organizations to help to provide for themselves, which can benefit the community enormously.

Planning and recreation

The redistribution of local authority funds for recreation based on individual, group and social need could enhance, particularly, recreation opportunity for the disadvantaged in the community.

The local authority planning function is crucial to recreation. As planning authorities, they can assist with the availability of land and resources. As housing authorities, they can assist with leisure in and around the home, in gardens and walkways, in neighbourhood play areas and play areas associated with high-rise dwellings. Local authorities give (and withhold) planning consent. They make decisions on development proposals and give consent for recreational facilities provided by other agencies. Planning authorities have to consider proposals in the context of broad overall and long-term policy. To consider leisure and recreation planning only in local terms would not take account of increased mobility, greater affluence and the movement across local authority boundaries. Local authorities are guided by government Planning Policy Guidance Notes (PPGs). PPG 17 applies to sport and recreation. Planning for leisure and recreation is covered in Chapter 12.

Countryside and regional facilities are particular areas of vulnerability for poor planning. Urban fringe leisure and recreation is gaining greater importance not only because of higher expectations, but also because of the cost of longer distance travel. Another aspect of movement into recreational areas is holidaymaking, tourism and sightseeing. Since local government reorganization, many local authorities have taken up their greater powers relating to the enhancement of tourism.

This brief résumé is sufficient to show that local authorities are major providers of leisure and recreation opportunities through planning, facilities, services, budgets and support. They have a duty to provide recreation opportunities through education and libraries. They have very wide discretionary powers in England and Wales (unlike those in Scotland and Northern Ireland, which have a duty to provide a wider range of services) to assist the arts, sports, informal recreation, countryside recreation, entertainment, conservation, tourism and youth and community services. In addition to these direct services, local authorities can assist leisure and recreation through many indirect ways, such as planning and housing and through social services that help the disadvantaged, who may need recreation services more than most, but who may make the least demand.

The origins and development of public recreation services

The development of public leisure and recreation services can be perceived in historical stages from:

- a long gestation period from the mid-nineteenth century to the mid-twentieth century
- post-Second World War initiatives
- an enlightened period of new ideas in the 1960s
- local government reorganization of the 1970s with a surge of new facilities and
- government interventions of the 1980s and 1990s in the shape of new legislations including Compulsory Competitive Tendering, Education Reform, the Children Act, and modernization introducing the concept of Best Value.

Leisure, like all other services, is subject to the laws of the land; while there is no comprehensive leisure or recreation Act, recreation is made possible and is guided and constrained by a whole variety of Acts, laws, statutes, government circulars and reports and regulations. Acts of Parliament impose duties or confer authority or powers to provide for recreation. Acts cover such diverse areas as allotments, swimming pools, parks, waterways, catering, clubs and associations, betting and gaming, public entertainment, libraries, licensing, countryside preservation, employment, institutions, charities and companies.

What is immediately evident in studying public provision for recreation is that it is historical, traditional, institutional and facility orientated. Progress is made within and through the system; changes, normally, will come about slowly. Despite the surge of new facilities in the 1960s and 1970s, the bulk of local government expenditure on recreation is still reserved for parks, pitches and pools, which is clearly a result of what is known, what exists, what is traditional and what local government is geared up to handle. So, how did it all start?

The first 100 years: mid-nineteenth century to mid-twentieth century

The origins of public leisure and recreation as we know them today go back to the nineteenth century. To understand the rationale behind early legislation, it is necessary to comprehend the poverty and the unhealthy and debilitating social conditions that prevailed for working class people – the vast majority of the population – at the time of the Industrial Revolution and the era of the puritanical work ethic, discussed in Chapter 2.

The Baths and Wash-Houses Act, 1846, from which many of our present-day recreation departments originated, was concerned primarily with personal cleansing and hygiene. However, swimming pools (called baths in those days) were built alongside these, mainly for instructional purposes, but also for recreation. Today the recreation role is paramount and the former 'baths' service in many cities embraces other indoor provision in the form of sports halls, squash courts, entertainment facilities and, of late, fitness centres.

Many parks departments also originated in the second half of the nineteenth century. The funding was partly philanthropic and partly provided by the local authorities. Many bequests of land were received and acquisitions made. Parks departments, like the baths departments, expanded their sphere of authority and took over areas for organized outdoor sports and facilities for tennis, athletics, golf, boating, bowls and the range of outdoor entertainments and festivals.

The Public Health Act, 1875 was the first major statutory provision enabling urban authorities to purchase, lease, lay out, plant, improve and maintain land for use as public walks or pleasure grounds. Later statutes had to be passed to empower local authorities to set aside parts of such lands for the playing of games. In the Public Health Act, 1936 authority was given to provide public baths and wash-houses, swimming baths and bathing places, open or covered, and the right to close them to the public for use by school or club and to charge admission. The Physical Training and Recreation Act, 1937 was introduced as a result of unrest in Europe. There was a need for a strong, fit nation. The Act was thus very much a movement towards national fitness, away from the Victorian idea of 'public walks and pleasure grounds'. Local authorities could acquire land for facilities and clubs, with or without charge for their use. The 1937 Act was the first major Act to use the word 'recreation', but support from government had come not because recreation was fun and enjoyable, but on the grounds of social and physical health and welfare, character training and improvement.

Post-Second World War initiatives

The recreation lobby continued promoting its arguments during and after the Second World War. Organizations such as the Central Council for Physical Recreation and the National Playing Fields Association played an effective, persuasive role.

The Town and Country Planning Act, 1947 made it possible for the development plans of local planning authorities to define the sites of proposed public buildings, parks, pleasure grounds, nature reserves and other open spaces or to allocate areas of land for such use. Powers were extended in the Town and Country Planning Acts of 1971 and 1974. The National Parks and Access to the Countryside Act, 1949 gave local planning authorities, whose areas include a national park, opportunity to provide accommodation and camping sites and to provide for recreation. The scope of countryside recreation was greatly enhanced with the passing of the Countryside Act, 1968. There has been great debate in recent years about the use and abuse of the countryside, balancing the preservation of heritage and the need for conservation on one hand, while on the other hand allowing for the growing interest in the countryside for people's recreation. Preserving open space for people's recreation is not a recent issue, however, but has been debated since the Industrial Revolution. However, facilities were needed in settings where people live and work.

Local authorities have considerable powers to provide for recreation through education facilities, personnel and services. The major Education Acts of 1918 and 1944, coming after two world wars, gave education authorities permissive powers (in 1918) to create facilities for social and physical training and then in 1944 made it mandatory for all education authorities to provide adequate facilities for 'recreation and social and physical training' for primary, secondary and further education. This resulted in the growth not only of the Youth Service, adult education and physical education (and hence sport), but also of facilities such as sports grounds, swimming pools, larger gymnasia and halls. However, it was not until many years later that larger, community-based facilities were made possible and that was only as a result of joint planning and provision between different tiers of authorities or between different departments.

> The Crystal Palace National Sports Centre was opened in 1964.

Up to this point, governments consistently viewed recreation as a beneficial means towards some other ends. The report of the Wolfenden Committee led to the eventual recognition by Parliament of recreation in its own right. The Committee was appointed in October 1957 by the Central Council for Physical Recreation (CCPR) and produced its report, *Sport and the Community*, in 1960 (CCPR, 1960), which examined the factors affecting the development of games, sports and outdoor activities in the United Kingdom. The committee recommended the establishment of a Sports Development Council. Although the Sports Council was to be formed many years later, the recommendations were never implemented. The report, however, was a watershed in the eventual acceptance of recreation by Parliament.

The 1960s: an age of leisure enlightenment

The Wolfenden Report, and the Albermarle Report on the Youth and Community Service (MoE, 1960), stressed the need for more and better facilities for indoor sport and recreation. Even before the Wolfenden Report was published, the first community sports centre, created by the Harlow and District Sports Trust, had opened its outdoor facilities in 1960 (its sports hall was opened in 1964). There followed one of the most significant developments in the history of leisure provision – the rapid growth of the multi-use, indoor leisure centre, which was then given greater impetus with the reorganization of local government in the 1970s.

In addition to this growth in indoor sport and recreation centres, youth and community services were developed by education authorities, country parks were promoted by the Countryside Commission, library services and the arts were also part of this leisure renaissance. The Plowden Report, *Children and their Primary Schools* (CACE, 1967), advocated the development of community schools to encourage interaction between home and school and proposed that a policy of 'positive discrimination' should favour schools in neighbourhoods of social and home disadvantage. The Public Libraries and Museums Act, 1964 repealed all other legislation, some going back to before the turn of the century. It placed a duty on every library authority to provide a comprehensive and efficient library service, and to promote and improve the services. The arts were subject of numerous reports, for example, the 1965 White Paper, *Support for the Arts: The First Steps* (DoES, 1965), and the Maud Report, sponsored by the Calouste Gulbenkian Foundation (see also Lord Redcliffe-Maud (1976), *Support for the Arts in England and Wales*, Calouste Gulbenkian Foundation, London). Redcliffe-Maud recommended that counties and districts should have a duty to ensure a 'reasonable range' of opportunity for arts enjoyment and that there should be a development plan for the arts with linkages to the education, libraries, museums and sport and recreation services. 'Joined-up' thinking is not new, even though often lacking in practice.

Despite the enabling Acts of Parliament, many of the major proposals for sport, the arts, and the youth and community service were never introduced. In addition, in practical terms, local authorities and other providers had still to operate through a maze of Acts or sections of old statutes. They also had to operate through a proliferation of departments and, as Molyneux pointed out (Molyneux, 1968), the system allowed and almost encouraged separate policies, separate budgets and different attitudes and changing policies towards recreation.

In 1968, with the establishment of a new county borough merging five former authorities, Teesside County Borough established a major committee and matching department for the arts and recreation. The new department, headed by a chief officer, spanned former services covering the arts, libraries, museums and art galleries, entertainments, sport and physical recreation, 'baths', parks and catering. Similar restructuring followed in a number of other authorities and in London boroughs. One of the major influences which led to these developments was the inquiry headed by the then John Redcliffe-Maud into the machinery of local government administration (MoHLG, 1967); it recommended the streamlining of committees and departments. Recreation services were ready to begin to rationalize the total sphere of leisure and recreation.

Dual use and joint provision and recreation

The 1960s and 1970s witnessed not only the advent of new purpose-built facilities and the restructuring of local government administration, but also the recognition that thousands of schools and education facilities were potential community leisure and recreation centres. The Department of Education and Science and the Ministry of Housing Local Government advanced a new policy guideline:

In assessing local needs and the resources to match them, it is appropriate to consider how far facilities for sport and physical education already provided or in the course of provision at schools and other educational establishments can be shared with other users or can be economically expanded to meet those needs. Consultation with other authorities will be necessary, not only because facilities in one area may serve neighbouring areas; but also there will normally be more than one authority with powers to provide them.

DES/MHLG, 1964

The Department of Education and Science's Circular, *The Chance to Share* (DES, 1970), gave more control to local authorities over their own local expenditure, free of government control, for locally determined schemes including almost all sport and recreation schemes. Local authorities could now go ahead in providing facilities, provided they stayed within their overall block allocation of capital investment.

Local government reorganization in 1974 and its effect on recreation

A Royal Commission under Lord Redcliffe-Maud was established in 1966 to consider the structure of local government in England, outside Greater London (Redcliffe-Maud, 1969). The commission proposed that the greater part of England should be divided into 58 unitary authorities. Public reaction to the unitary concept was, in general, unfavourable and three of the four local authority associations preferred a two-tier system. A government White Paper in 1970 (DoE, 1970) proposed a new structure based on 51 unitary areas and 5 metropolitan areas. In 1971 the new Conservative government's alternative proposals emerged with a compromise solution of a two-tier structure and a radical reorganization of boroughs and urban and rural districts; the Local Government Act, 1972 gave effect to the proposals contained in the 1971 White Paper. In 1974 six new metropolitan county councils were established and the 1,400 existing district councils were reduced to 333. As far as recreation services were concerned, the greatest impact was felt in the 296 non-metropolitan district councils. These councils were now larger and more powerful and had, in many cases, inherited a range of facilities. Reorganization also encouraged the creation of new facilities, particularly indoor leisure centres, before reorganization actually took place, leaving the incoming local authorities to 'pick up the tab'.

Prior to local government reorganization in 1974, most local authorities were structured on the basis of a number of departments operating under the control of committees. The committees competed for their share of the available financial resources. The Bains Report (SGLAMS, 1972) placed emphasis on the corporate approach to management. It was felt that, in this way, an authority could formulate more realistically its long-term objectives covering all services, and make forward planning projections. The Local Government Act, 1972 and the Local Government (Miscellaneous Provisions) Act, 1976 provided the framework for local authorities with respect to the provision and administration of facilities for sport and recreation with the emergence of leisure and recreation services in their own right. Central government placed a duty on local authorities (in England and Wales) to provide in only three specific areas: library services, youth and adult education facilities and allotments, but in each case, no indications of the scale of provision were given. Yet, in

Scotland and Northern Ireland, local authorities had a duty to make provisions in areas of sport and recreation.

Recent legislation and effects on leisure management

Central government, as indicated earlier in this chapter, has the most powerful effect on public leisure service. New Acts of Parliament in the late 1980s included:

- Compulsory competitive legislation
- Education Reform and
- the Children Act.

Compulsory competitive tendering

The Local Government Housing and Finance Act, 1988, containing provisions for the uniform business rate and compulsory competitive tendering (CCT), had the most dramatic effects on the management of local government. The Local Government Act, 1988 (Competition in Sport and Leisure Facilities Order 1989) imposed upon local authorities the necessity to offer the management of their sports and leisure facilities to competitive tendering; there were certain exceptions, such as dual use centres, which combine education and public recreation provision. This was compulsory but not out-and-out privatization; local authorities still had control over aspects such as pricing, programming and opening hours. CCT resulted in economic savings and improved financial performance by local authority direct service organizations (DSOs) and generally satisfactory results from management contract companies, non-profit distributing organizations (NPDOs), leisure trusts, management buy-outs and other management hybrids. The results of CCT indicated improved efficiency, but were the services more effective? Did they meet the needs and expectations of the people they are there to serve? Some leisure academics and professionals did not believe so. However, what is beyond doubt is that local authority leisure services had changed forever.

Many processes and procedures of CCT survive and are of relevance today. TUPE is one example. European procurement rules require all prospective contractors to be treated equally and are implemented in British law by secondary legislation which sets down transparent criteria for selecting tenderers and awarding contracts. These regulations and guidance also deal with the Transfer of Undertakings (Protection of Employment) Regulations, 1981 (TUPE) and the European Union Acquired Rights Directive. In a sense, a contractor was 'taking over' a business and much uncertainty existed as to what constitutes a 'transfer of undertaking'. The 1988 Act introduced the concept of anti-competitive behaviour; the 1992 Act helped to define it in law and the 1993 Regulations assisted local authorities in conducting competitive tendering and avoiding anti-competitive behaviour. The thrust of the rules was to ensure that no anti-competitive practice entered into the process. The DoE circular, *Guidance on the Conduct of Compulsory Competitive Tendering* (DoE, 1996) focused on five key principles of good tendering practice:

1 Transparency Authorities should require the same standards of performance from a successful in-house team as from an external contractor.

2 Removing obstacles for good market response Authorities needed to demonstrate that a reasonable range of prospective tenderers had been considered.

3 Focusing on outputs Authorities should specify the output to be achieved, rather than the way the service was to be performed.

4 Evaluating quality and price Authorities should adopt clear procedures for evaluating tenders to ensure that the quality being sought could be achieved.

5 Fairness between in-house and external bids Authorities must act fairly to ensure that tendering did not put any provider at a disadvantage.

The Education Reform Act and recreation

The leisure and recreation resources to be found in educational institutions in the United Kingdom make up the largest volume of built facilities available to the public. Indeed, half of the newly-built leisure complexes of the past three decades are linked in some way with education. Moreover, schools are often the birthplace of our feelings about music, art, crafts and sport: some of young people's future potential leisure time interests. In the United Kingdom, relatively few young people play a musical instrument, draw and paint for pleasure, and although most play sport, a significant proportion take little exercise outside school. Anything that affects the provision and management of education, therefore, affects the scope and delivery of leisure and recreation to the community.

Major education Acts have each had substantial effects, not only on schools, but on leisure: community education in its widest sense. The Education Acts of 1918 and 1944, arising out of world wars and looking to new horizons and better deals for all citizens, helped develop community sport and recreation. The Education Acts of 1986 and 1988 likewise made changes of substance. In common with apparent Conservative government policy, the Education Acts aimed to make the education service 'more responsive to consumer needs', devolve responsibility to local levels and reduce bureaucracy.

While many schools currently have good community use of premises, the 1986 Act encourages greater use. The 'market forces' approach, however, poses problems which can restrict a co-ordinated policy, resulting in different arrangements and standards from district to district, and from school to school. A policy, agreed and understood, between district schools and district leisure departments can do much to assist local organizations and clubs. One-off 'wheeling and dealing' may make for an individual school winning out in the marketplace, but is likely to be a short term measure, lacking continuity and making it difficult to inculcate an integrated, comprehensive approach to the management of community recreation.

In terms of leisure and recreation management, the impact of the 1988 Act is felt under two main headings: the National Curriculum and local management of schools (LMS). In addition, there are further, far reaching implications, including:

- the option for schools to 'opt out' and become a grant maintained school (GMS)
- 'open enrolment'

- devolved budgets
- performance indicators such as examination results
- school governing bodies with greater powers and
- legislation on charging for school activities.

Some schools have become far more 'commercial' in their approach, seeking to maximize income from community leisure uses and limit costs. Adding to the difficulties, activities requiring travel – field visits, outdoor pursuits, sports centres, theatres – have been restricted. Schools are prohibited from charging children for activities which take place off the school site, during the school day. Those with inadequate resources and staff, which have been making use of the local swimming pool, sports centre and theatre, now have to convince the Borough or County Council of the need and, therefore, gain a subsidy, or else pay for the facilities out of their allocated budgets. In a climate of limited budgets, the activity is often cut out of the programme. Business obligations call for a pragmatic, cost-centred, market approach. If school governors are to fund use of community sports halls, swimming pools, outdoor pursuit centres, visits to museums and so on from their delegated budgets, then it is likely that activities beneficial to pupils will be excluded on purely financial grounds. It is hard for school governors and head teachers to balance curriculum requirements against financial requirements. Education continues to face change with new regulations emerging almost year by year.

Most people will agree that children and young people need a balanced education – mental, spiritual, physical and social – in order to become balanced, positive citizens. But as teachers are required to address certain curriculum and attainment issues, less time is available for extra-curricular activities. It is these activities which shape the leisure and recreation skills and interests of children and young people now and for the future. Healthy children and young people, who have social skills and skills for leisure, have a better chance of enjoying fulfilling lives, compared to young people without skills and interests. Inactive children, for example, are likely to become inactive adults. Therefore, the Leisure Manager in a local authority now has an even more important role to play in positive links with schools both in school time and after school.

School and community funded facilities

It makes sound educational, social and economic sense to provide for the community within existing community structures, whether in community schools or in dual use or jointly-provided facilities. There can be benefits for all parties, but only given appropriate policies, facilities and management. Providing for leisure in these ways needs careful investigation and planning. One of the problems, for example, with these facility collaborations is the extent to which the facilities are 'school' facilities or 'community' facilities. Who owns and has management responsibility for sports halls, swimming pools, ice rinks and theatres on school campuses, when these have been partly or wholly paid for by district councils? There is a distinction between what is termed 'dual use', 'joint provision' and 'community school'.

Where the facilities have been provided solely under local education authority powers, they form part of the school and the governing body is empowered to control such use and is responsible for financial inputs and outcomes. Under the Act, community use must not be subsidized from the delegated budget which can only be used for school purposes and curricular activities. Such community use has to be seen to be self-financed.

Joint provision Joint provision, as distinct from dual use, is where the facility, whilst forming part of, or adjacent to, the school and used by the students, has been provided to standards appropriate for general public use and has been part financed from other agencies. Under the legislation, the opportunity exists to allow these other agencies to become involved in the day-to-day running of the facilities. The facility may be totally managed and maintained by another department of the local authority, as when a sports hall is managed by the recreation department. The school pays the recreation department for its use of the facility during school hours, and the governing body will not have management control over the facility. If the school manages and maintains the premises, the governing body will have the power to control its use by the community.

The Community School The Community School is a school which engages in non-school activities and in which the governing body has control as well as the responsibility for those members of staff who are wholly or partly engaged in non-school activities.

Leisure services departments and Leisure Managers can play an important role in achieving the best from the new legislation. For example they can:

1 provide an advisory service to school governing bodies and/or informally provide help and advice on community recreation, sharing with schools ideas and systems relating to marketing, programming, pricing, and operational management
2 achieve levels of parity, for example, in pricing, between different agencies
3 provide joint programmes and/or collaborative programming
4 offer to manage the non-educational use on a contract basis
5 organize courses for leaders and coaches; and courses for those teachers responsible for facility operation
6 in collaboration with the LEA, Sports Council, Arts Council and the local authority, appoint Development Officers to work with schools
7 promote links between school and clubs
8 provide collaborative promotion, awareness and publicity of the facilities and activities offered at the school
9 advise on applications to the National Lottery, grant-making bodies and sponsors
10 include the school resources in district cultural strategies and local leisure plans.

The Children Act and leisure services

The Children Act, 1989 came into force on 14 October, 1991. It is the most significant legislative change on behalf of children in a hundred years. The Act can be perceived as a unifying Act, replacing in part or whole 55 other Acts of Parliament, one going back a hundred years. How does this new Act affect the management of leisure, play and recreation? Leisure Managers will be involved as:

- providers of services for children
- providers of facilities
- employers of paid staff and volunteers
- providers of information and
- a body of expertise.

Leisure Managers, therefore, have to work with other departments, particularly Social Services and take a co-ordinated viewpoint. The Children Act contains regulations, duties and powers that affect everyone who is responsible for planning, managing and delivering services to children, particularly to children under the age of eight. The clear direction and commitment behind the legislation is to put children at the heart and give priority to their needs in all those processes which affect their lives. Of greatest significance is that a duty is placed on all people and organizations involved with young children and for all children 'in need', under the terms of the Act. The Act lays down four duties:

- to provide services
- to publish information
- to review and
- to register.

The key principles of the Children Act include the recognition of the child as having an important place in the community, and the right of the child to be cared for in the context of the family. The Act directs local authorities to consider preventative services and calls for the provision of a range of day care facilities which must be provided for children in need, but may also be provided for all children. The Act, therefore, encompasses a number of wider issues which apply to the public, voluntary and commercial sectors:

1   the needs of different age groups, not just those up to the age of eight
2   the needs of all children, including those with disabilities, and those from different ethnic and cultural backgrounds
3   adequate procedures between tiers of local government and different departments and
4   clearly defined standards of good practice so that children have a good, safe and creative experience.

For the first time in the sphere of play and recreation, the local authority has a statutory duty to provide. The main implications are that local governments should positively plan for children rather than taking a narrow departmental and traditional perspective. One of the practical outcomes of the Act is the requirement for registration. Any person or organization providing services for children under eight years old, whether in public, voluntary or commercial sectors, must register, if those services are provided for more than two hours a day. (The temptation is for some services to last just one hour and fifty minutes.) The process takes into account four main factors:

1   the body or organization applying for registration
2   the people who are being proposed to look after children under eight – paid or voluntary – are 'fit', that is, suitable to do this work
3   premises: the local authority will need to satisfy itself as to the 'fitness' (suitability and physical condition) of the premises
4   inspection: local authorities have a statutory duty to inspect premises.

The Children Act itself, unfortunately, does not mention play, recreation and leisure as such, which is a major difficulty in understanding the Act. Guidance notes to the Act, however, give an indication of where play and recreation play a part. The Act, by implication, does affect leisure and recreation providers in all sectors. Those facilities affected by the Children Act include:

- crèches; playgroups; child-minding services
- before and after school clubs
- playschemes outdoors and indoors
- activities in leisure centres: mini-gymnastics, ballet, trampolining, football and swimming classes
- activities in museums, art galleries
- adventure playgrounds
- commercial play centres
- city farms
- theme parks
- play spaces in shopping malls and supermarkets
- holiday schemes in libraries, theatres and sport centres.

These 'persons' (people and organizations) need to be reviewed, inspected and registered. In many cases, staffing, volunteers, programmes, equipment and facilities will need increase or improvement.

One major concern of recent times in the wake of the Children Act is that of child protection (see Protecting children at play and leisure, p. 89, Chapter 5). This has implications for all leisure and recreation services whether in the public, private or voluntary sectors. For those involved in sports clubs, for example, there is, however, increasing concern at the level of bureaucracy it entails for all voluntary leaders and helpers, such as vetting by the police. In researching this matter in consultation with club volunteers in 2004, a former colleague wrote to me:

> My cricket and football clubs are now required by the governing bodies to appoint Child Protection Officers and to have Child Protection Policies in place. Similarly local authorities are required to have detailed policies in place and to undertake staff training and awareness. Coaches and volunteers have to be vetted and police checked. As ever, this is a fundamentally sound process, but one which has had some hysterical by-products. At many leisure centres, simply walking in with a camera will have the staff jumping on you and innocent photography of, say, a school swimming gala is now banned in case you put the photos on the internet. There

are often lengthy delays in checking and vetting and some people simply refuse to get involved because of the hassle.

In June 2003, the government created a new Minister for Children within the DfES, responsible for:

- the Sure Start Unit
- the Children and Young People's Unit and
- the Connextions Service National Unit.

In Wales, the Assembly Government has a Minister for Education and Young People. There has been a Minister for Education and Young People within the Scottish Executive since November 2001.

The Green Paper *Every Child Matters* (see Useful websites) was published in September 2003 to protect children from neglect and harm, promote their well-being and support all children to develop their potential. *Every Child Matters* was published alongside *Keeping Children Safe*, a detailed response to the recommendations made in the Victoria Climbie inquiry report. In March 2004, the DfES published *Every Child Matters: The Next Steps* and a young people's version, *Every Child Matters: What You Said*.

The legislation in relation to these matters is contained within the Children Bill which received royal assent in November 2004 (see Useful websites). Under the Bill, local authorities, police and social services are obliged to work together to ensure child welfare. The Bill ensures that there will be a record of every child's involvement with social services or trouble with the police.

The Children's Commissioner for England is also created to champion the rights of under-18s and there are powers to intervene in failing services.

The government and leisure into the present

The years leading up to the turn of the century saw acceptance by government not only of the benefits of leisure for people and communities, but also for the economy. For the first time leisure was given a place in the Cabinet, with a Minister of State and a department, at first called the Department of National Heritage (DNH), then the Department for Culture, Media and Sport (DCMS). Along with the creation of the National Lottery, these were significant landmarks for leisure and recreation at the close of the twentieth century.

Central and devolved government in the United Kingdom

Leisure then is an extremely important modern industry of social and economic benefit to the United Kingdom. Central government has a critical role in its development for the country as a whole, and for the delivery of leisure at a local level. Central government makes decisions on major policy and sets out the legal framework for its regional and local network, its agencies and institutions and regulates the way local government can act and deliver services at the local levels. The legal framework laid down by central government regulates how the country is run; its laws apply to most aspects of

United Kingdom central government

The United Kingdom is a parliamentary democracy and is also a constitutional monarchy. However, unlike all other modern states, the UK does not have a written constitution. Hence it relies on statute law, common law and conventions, that is, rules and practices which are not legally enforceable but which are essential in the working of government. Parliament has three parts: the elected House of Commons, the appointed House of Lords and the Sovereign. They meet together only on major ceremonial occasions, such as the State Opening of Parliament.

life, including our social lives and leisure whether inside or outside the home. For example, the law sets down the rules governing radio, television and press coverage, what age you have to reach before watching certain films at the cinema, or drink alcohol in a public house, what standards of hygiene are enforced in restaurants, and a whole range of safety standards for fun fairs, rides and slides, sporting events, concerts and festivals. Central government is enormously powerful and influential in the way leisure is provided for and managed.

The UK Parliament makes primary legislation, other than for matters devolved to the Scottish Parliament and the Northern Ireland Assembly. Following devolution, the responsibilities of the Secretaries of State for Scotland, Wales and Northern Ireland changed, though they retain their positions in the UK Cabinet. The House of Lords, the 'Upper Chamber' has long been under scrutiny, being largely made up of hereditary and life peers. On gaining power from the Conservatives in 1997, the Labour Government in its first term of office announced that it wanted the House of Lords to be more representative of British society; it passed legislation in November 1999 to reduce the number of hereditary peers from 750 to 92. In April 2001, non-political life peerages were given to fifteen people selected from 3,166 applications. A White Paper, *The House of Lords – Completing the Reform*, was published in November 2001. In September 2003, the government published the consultation paper *Constitutional Reform: next steps for the House of Lords*. However, in March 2004, the government announced that it would not proceed with legislation to enact the proposals in the consultation paper.

The UK is divided into 659 constituencies, each of which returns one member to the House of Commons; 529 in England, 40 in Wales, 72 in Scotland, and 18 in Northern Ireland.

As representatives of the citizens of our nation, Members of Parliament and all those in positions of trust are expected to live up to high standards of public life. A number of safeguards ensure the probity of individuals in carrying out their public duties. The Committee on Standards in Public Life was set up in 1994 under Lord Nolan. Its role is to examine the standards of conduct of holders of public office. The post of Parliamentary Commissioner for Standards was created in 1995. The financial interests of MPs and Members of the House of Lords must be declared when speaking in the House or in Committee, when giving notice of a question or motion and they must also disclose any relevant financial interests.

The population in the United Kingdom in 2001 was around 59 million, according to the Office of National Statistics, the third largest in the European Union (EU) after Germany and France. Nearly 84 per cent of the total population of the UK lives in England, by far the most densely populated part of the UK. In contrast to Northern Ireland, Scotland and Wales, England does not have an elected national body exclusively responsible for its central administration. Government departments carry out its administrative affairs. However, central government policy has moved in the direction of regionalization. Regional Development Agencies came into operation on 1 April, 1999 to co-ordinate regional economic development and enable English regions to improve their competitiveness. The government is also committed to establishing elected Regional Assemblies in those regions that want them.

The United Kingdom and the European Union

Government in the UK is certainly complex. National and regional devolved government, on the one hand, are 'pulling away' from central government and, on the other hand, elected representation in the European Parliament means being 'pulled towards' Europe. The United Kingdom, formerly one of fifteen Member States of the European Union, on 1 May, 2004 became one of 25 Member States, ten additional nations joining on that day. What is the relevance of this membership to leisure management?

Earlier in this chapter we saw the implications of European legislation on the TUPE regulations. There is a great deal more. The EU is a source of funding from bodies such as the Regional Fund, the Social Fund and the European Coal and Steel Community; grants and loans are primarily for areas of deprivation, high unemployment, and areas in need of regeneration. These funds have been granted to a number of leisure projects in the UK. Another example concerns the Common Agricultural Policy, with the halting of subsidies where overproduction exists. Instead, farmers have been encouraged to convert land to non-agricultural purposes and leisure provision is an alternative. In terms of leisure management, being part of the EU has meant having to comply with a range of European standards pertaining to areas as diverse as children's playgrounds and tourism destination facilities. In terms of tourism, Britain has an extensive, often stunning coastline and some wonderful beaches, the envy of many inland European countries. However, many of the beaches had high levels of pollution and did not conform to EU standards; indeed, Britain was taken to court by the European Commission and found guilty in 1993. In 1994, 80 per cent of Britain's 457 designated beaches passed the minimum EU standards. The EU also has other standards for high quality beaches, including visitor facilities. On achieving the standards, the resorts are awarded the EU's Blue Flag. Examples of councils with Blue Flag awards are Herne Bay, Margate and Ramsgate and Ryde Sands on the Isle of Wight. This is an important award to help in the promotion of Britain's seaside resorts, many in great need of renewal.

> Failures in 1994 to reach EU standards for beach quality included some of the most famous resorts, including Brighton and Blackpool, the most-visited seaside resort in Europe.

Another link with Europe and on a wider international level concerns human rights. Universal respect for human rights is an obligation under the United Nations Charter. Other international instruments the United Kingdom is party to, and which have implications on leisure, include those on the elimination of racial discrimination, the elimination of all forms of discrimination against women, and the rights of the child. The United Kingdom is also bound by the Council of Europe's Convention for the Protection of Human Rights and Fundamental Freedoms (ECHR). The rights of the ECHR were enshrined in the UK law in 2000 upon implementation of the Human Rights Act, 1998. These rights apply to all aspects of leisure and its management.

The links between central government and local government

In recent years leisure has gained a far higher profile in government, although it has far less to spend than other departments. Nonetheless, the Secretary of State has a Minister of State (Sport), a Minister of State (Arts) and a Parliamentary Secretary. The Scottish Parliament has a Deputy First Minister with a mandate for Sport, the Arts and Culture. The National Assembly for Wales has a Deputy First Minister/Minister for Culture, Sport and the Welsh Language.

Currently, the main link between central government and local authorities in England is the Office of the Deputy Prime Minister (ODPM). In May 2002, the ODPM was separated from the Cabinet Office and established as a central government department taking responsibility for policy areas from the Department of Transport, Local Government and the Regions (DTLR) and the Cabinet. The ODPM has an extremely wide remit including:

- housing
- planning
- devolution
- local government
- the fire service
- the Social Exclusion Unit
- the Neighbourhood Renewal Unit and
- the government offices for the regions.

The ODPM therefore has substantial influence on leisure and recreation management. For example, in aiming to improve delivery and value for money the Department implemented Comprehensive Performance Assessments (CPA), such as engaging with authorities in planning improvements, monitoring local Public Service Agreements (PSA) and supporting the electronic delivery of services. Other departments influence include the Department for Education and Skills and the Department of Health. In Scotland, Wales and Northern Ireland, local authorities now deal mainly with the devolved Parliament and Assemblies.

Local government

In the United Kingdom there exists a range of different local authorities. There are two main types: single-tier and two-tier authorities. Reorganization of local government in Great Britain in 1974 brought unitary authorities into Scotland and Wales and into some parts of England. Scotland has 32 unitary authorities, the largest in Glasgow and Edinburgh and the smallest in the Shetland and Orkney islands. Wales has 22 unitary authorities, the largest in Cardiff and the smallest in Merthyr Tydfil. Northern Ireland has 26 unitary authorities.

In England there are three different types of single-tier authority: London Boroughs, Metropolitan Councils and Unitary Councils. There are:

- 33 London Boroughs with populations ranging from over 300,000 to under 150,000

- 36 Metropolitan Councils with populations of around 150,000 to over one million, the largest in Birmingham, Leeds, Sheffield, Bradford, Liverpool and Manchester
- 44 Unitary Councils, the largest in Bristol with 400,000 residents to Rutland with only 34,000 and the Isles of Scilly with just around 2,000.

> According to the Local Government Association (LGA), just under 21,300 councillors represent communities across England and Wales, around one-third of whom are employed on a full- or part-time basis.

Two-tier authorities in England consist of 34 County Councils, with populations from around 1.3 million in Kent and Essex to around 277,000 in Shropshire. There are 238 District Councils, with populations of approaching 200,000 in Northampton to the smallest in Teesside of around 25,000. Some districts have the ceremonial title of borough or city, both granted by royal authority.

Local authorities work within the powers laid down under Acts of Parliament. Some powers are mandatory: local authorities must do what is required by the law. Other powers are discretionary, allowing an authority to provide services if it wishes. As a consequence of mandatory and discretionary powers, authorities deliver services and provide facilities in different ways, including:

- direct provision and management
- contract management
- enabling other organizations through planning, grants, rate relief, and
- partnerships with institutions and with private and voluntary sector organizations and clubs.

Local government expenditure accounts for about 25 per cent of public spending. Local authorities in Great Britain raise revenue through the council tax, which meets only about 25 per cent of their revenue expenditure. Their expenditure is financed

> Education is the largest locally-provided service, with around 0.9 million full time equivalent.

primarily by grants from central government or the devolved administrations and by the redistribution of revenue from non-domestic rates, a property tax levied on businesses and other non-domestic properties. Local councils, particularly unitary councils and county councils, spend the largest proportion of their budgets on education services and social services. Local government employs 2.15 million people in England and Wales, three-quarters of whom are female and likely to be part-time employees, according to the LGA.

Local government and leisure

Local authorities have long promoted and provided for leisure and recreation in their districts. Statistics from the ODPM and the LGA in 2003 paint a broad picture.

- Approximately 7.5 million adults and 2.1 million children use parks for sporting activities each year.
- Local councils provide an estimated total of 21,000 playgrounds and play areas.
- 77 per cent of adults attended at least one arts event in 2000.
- During the same period more than four out of five adults participated in an arts or cultural activity.
- 24 million adults are public library members.

- Around 120 million volumes were estimated to be held in local council provided libraries in England and Wales.

However, there is little legislation that requires local government to be involved in leisure and recreation. Its involvement is largely discretionary and motivated by social and political objectives. The justification for leisure provision is made by local authorities on a whole range of perceived benefits to the community:

- adding to the quality of life
- providing for the socially disadvantaged
- supporting the education of children and young people especially
- attracting tourists
- developing civic pride; reducing crime
- promoting health and
- preserving heritage and the cultural uniqueness of the district.

As a result of these discretionary powers, there is a wide difference in the quantity and quality of services and facilities provided by different authorities. Moreover, in many, if not most authorities, expenditure on leisure has a relatively low priority in budgets.

The largest expenditures on leisure are libraries, outdoor open space and sport and recreation, particularly swimming pools. The arts, including museums, have relatively low expenditure, as does tourism, except for tourist destinations such as popular seaside resorts. In two-tier authorities, arts expenditure is distributed fairly evenly between counties and shire districts. Traditionally, going back from before and after the Second World War, recreation expenditure (leisure was not a term used then) was largely on amenities: 'parks, pitches, and pools'. Even with the advent of the modern leisure centre and income from social recreation and fitness centres, a substantial part of the leisure budgets is still spent on parks and open spaces, sports pitches and swimming pools. Traditionally, also, County Council expenditure is dominated by the libraries sector. Libraries are one of the very few leisure areas where legislation puts a statutory duty on local government to provide.

Modernizing local government and Best Value

Over recent years, the government has been in the process of modernizing the traditional systems which have operated in local government for over a century.

The framework for modernization in England is set out in the White Paper, *Modern Local Government: In Touch with the People*, which was published in July 1998 (HMG, 1998). The first steps were taken through the Local Government Act, 1999, which introduced a new duty for councils to provide Best Value in their delivery and management of services to their communities. The Deputy Prime Minister, in his foreword and introduction to the White Paper, said:

> People need councils which serve them well. Councils need to listen to, lead and build up their local communities. We want to see councils working in partnership with others, making their contribution to the achievement of our aims for improving people's quality of life. To do this,

councils need to break free from old fashioned practices and attitudes. There is a long and proud tradition of councils serving their communities. But the world and how we live today is very different from when our current systems of local government were established. There is no future in the old model of councils trying to plan and run most services. It does not provide the services which people want, and cannot do so in today's world. Equally, there is no future for councils which are inward looking – more concerned to maintain their structures and protect their vested interests than listening to their local people and leading their communities.

HMG, 1998

Probably the most significant recent Act of Parliament relating to local authority services is the Local Government Act, 2000. Part 1 of the Act came into force on 18 October, 2000 giving English councils new powers which enable them to work in partnership with other bodies to improve the quality of life in their local communities in order to promote or improve economic, social and environmental well-being.

The Act requires all councils to move from the traditional committee system, to improve accountability and efficiency for decision making, implement scrutiny committees who are not part of the executive, to examine decisions and to improve consultation with the public. Four models were put forward by the government:

Option 1 Directly elected mayor with cabinet

Option 2 Leader and a cabinet

Option 3 Directly elected mayor and council manager and

Option 4 Councils with less than 85,000 population allowing for only five small, politically balanced, decision-making committees, with scrutiny committees to review all decisions.

Writing in the *Municipal Year Book, Guide to Political Modernisation*, 2001, Robin Mosley (2001) states:

The original concept was clear; full council would set the budgets and policy framework. Executives would implement policies and drive through best value and be held to account by the overview and scrutiny committees. Translating this concept into practice is far from easy.

Sandy Blair, in the same issue of the *Municipal Year Book*, from the perspective of a chief executive, was guided by two fundamental principles: 'public entitlement' and 'democratic responsibility', and wrote that the public as individuals and collectively are entitled to high standards and good performance of all services. The elected members are responsible for 'the uniqueness of local government; they provide the difference; they reflect the shape and culture of their community; their presence is the defining feature which distinguishes local government from other services'.

Best Value

The statutory duty of Best Value was introduced following the Local Government Act, 1999 and came into effect on 1 April, 2000. Local authorities, police, fire and national parks authorities were required to make arrangements to secure continuous improvement in the services they manage.

Part of the government's modernizing agenda, Best Value championed an entirely new culture in local government administration and in so doing also replaced the Compulsory Competitive Tendering regime.

The Labour Party's manifesto in 1997, *Because Britain Deserves Better*, contained a commitment to introduce Best Value. The White Paper, *Modern Local Government – In Touch with the People*, then set out how it intended to improve local services through Best Value. Local authorities would have to deliver services to clear standards, covering cost and quality, by the most effective, economic and efficient means available. In carrying out this duty, local authorities would be accountable to local people and have a responsibility to central government in its role as representative of the broader national interest. Local authorities would have to set standards for all the services for which they were responsible. Delivery would be through four channels:

- clear standards
- targets for continuous improvement
- more say for services users and
- independent audit and inspection.

All new decision-making structures are required to incorporate rigorous arrangement for review and scrutiny of councils' policies and the decisions they make. Some decisions, such as the acceptance of the budget, are reserved for the full council, but most of those relating to the implementation of policy are for the executive. The executive is responsible for preparing the policies and budget to propose to the council. The new arrangements are designed to ensure that people know who in the council is responsible for taking decisions, how they can make their input into the decision-making procedures, and how to hold decision makers to account. Furthermore, the public, including the press, is admitted to meetings of the executive when key decisions are being discussed. They also have access to agendas, reports and minutes of meetings.

Compulsory Competitive Tendering was generally unpopular but it forced local authorities to review their services and through competition achieve the best financial results. CCT had made the cost of services more transparent and tightened budgets, but had been so definitively subscribed within tight time limits that the competition led to unimaginative tendering. Ways were found to circumvent the rules and splits were formed in the councils themselves between clients and contractors. The government's intention with Best Value was to have an approach based on partnership rather than on confrontation.

Best Value was structured around six key components:

Performance indicators National indicators would be developed and each authority would be expected to set targets in respect of these indicators and publish both the targets and the performance in annual local performance plans.

Performance standards Government leadership where national interest requires it.

Performance targets Locally set for strategic objectives, efficiency, cost, effectiveness, quality, and fair access.

Performance reviews To ensure that continuous improvements to all services are made.

Competition An essential management tool; ways to test competitiveness include: benchmarking; core service in-house with top-up support from the private sector; contracting out services after competition between external bidders; partnership or joint-venture; asset disposal or sell-off.

Audit and inspection New arrangements with rigorous external checks on the information provided in local performance plans. Quality schemes such as Investors in People and Charter Mark could also have important roles in achieving Best Value.

These 'best value' arrangements included the annual preparation of performance plans and a five-year cycle of reviews that cover all the functions of the local authority. The Local Government Act, 1999 identified 4 'Cs' as key aspects of the best value process:

- challenge whether the authority should be 'exercising the function now and in the foreseeable future', at what level, and the way in which it should be carrying out the service
- compare the authority's performance by reference to the performance of other organizations using a range of relevant indicators
- consult with stakeholders, including providers, users and non-users of the services, employees, and elected members at all stages of the review
- apply tests of competitiveness to determine the 'optimal way of delivering services against agreed targets and objectives'; the reviews employ the tools of challenge, consultation, comparison and competition.

In summary, the duty of Best Value requires local authorities to deliver services by the most economic, efficient and effective means available to meet the requirements of local communities and to provide ways and means to secure continuous improvements. Councils have to review their functions, monitor their performance against national and local indicators and publish an annual performance plan which is subject to audit. These new duties and their results are all subject to close annual inspection (see Local Public Service Agreements, p. 154).

Beacon Councils

Another initiative in the government's modernizing programme was the introduction of Beacon Council. The scheme was introduced in November 1999 to create pacesetters and centres of excellence. The scheme aims to raise standards in all councils by spreading best practice. It is not possible for any national programme to deal with a whole range of councils' work at any one time; therefore, the programme focuses on a few services and 'cross-cutting' services areas each year. The selection is undertaken in consultation with the LGA, the Improvement and Development Agency (IDeA) and the beacon scheme advisor panel. In the year 2001/2, 43 beacon awards were made to 39 councils covering services such as:

- accessible services
- competitiveness and enterprise
- independent living for older people and
- regeneration through culture, sport and tourism.

153

Round three of the scheme saw Beacon Councils being appointed in eleven new service areas from April 2002 to March 2003, including libraries. In 2003, 58 round four beacon awards were given in ten new service areas, including Community Cohesion and Social Inclusion, areas where leisure and recreation are of value.

Beacon Council status is a prestigious award and councils are able to use the Beacon Award logo in promoting their authorities. More than a status award, however, is the aim to spread best practice across the country, which is co-ordinated by IDeA. One of the requirements on a council being awarded Beacon status is that it has to help spread its experiences through the production of literature and hosting seminars and events and visits to other authorities.

Community strategies

Part 1 of the Local Government Act, 2000 gave English councils new powers which enable them to work in partnership with other bodies to improve the quality of life in their local communities in order to promote or improve economic, social and environmental well-being. Part 1 of the Act also places a duty to prepare community strategies in partnership with other local service providers. Community strategies should be aimed at improving local well-being and at contributing to the achievement of sustainable development in the UK. Local authorities are allowed to work out the best way of approaching the task of preparing a community strategy, but they will be expected to base their strategies on a proper assessment of local needs and to involve local communities in establishing priorities for action.

Local Government Minister at that time, Hilary Armstrong, said:

> The new well-being power is good news for local people. It gives councils a clear remit to engage in a broad range of activities in the interests of their community. It places the initiative squarely with local councils, empowering them to take new action to respond to local needs voiced by local communities. The new power will help councils and other local stakeholders to work together and respond to the needs and aspirations of their communities.

Leisure directors and managers need to ensure that their cultural strategies and leisure plans dovetail into the partnership community strategies and are not 'left out on a limb' financially and politically (see Local Cultural Strategies, p. 234, Chapter 12).

Local Public Service Agreements

The government has also introduced a policy to implement performance assessment in local government. Its object is to enhance Best Value and deliver 'thriving, inclusive and sustainable communities in all regions'.

> Our aim is to improve delivery and value for money of local services through implementing Comprehensive Performance Assessment (CPA), engaging with Authorities in improvement planning, negotiating and monitoring Local PSA agreements, providing a package of freedoms and flexibilities, developing capacity building programmes and supporting the electronic delivery of services.
>
> ODPM web pages

In the Green Paper, *Modernising Local Government Finance*, local public service agreements (PSAs) were proposed to complement Best Value and encourage continuous improvement. The subsequent Local Government White Paper set out proposals to integrate current performance assessment regimes under a new Comprehensive Performance Assessment. This process builds on the existing audit, inspection and external assessment, and introduces a framework for corporate assessment by the authority in partnership with the Audit Commission. These assessments will be the cornerstone of the government's performance framework for local government. They will provide government, councils, and the public with a clear profile for each council.

One of the major changes is the requirement to produce an annual Best Value Performance Plan (BVPP) which reports on what a council has achieved during the last year and set targets for the year ahead. It then has to report on how it did against these targets in the following year's plan. This was seen as being part of making councils more open and transparent. Part of this process is seen as reporting on how an authority was rated when inspected on a service-by-service basis.

The legislation created the Best Value Inspectors within the Audit Commission Inspection Service. This was part of the Audit Commission, but separate from other parts such as District Audit. These have now been joined together and the Audit Commission is responsible for local government service improvement.

The original Best Value Inspections of services have begun to be replaced by 'assessments' of how an authority functions as a whole. Comprehensive Performance Assessments (CPA) were carried out for single-tier authorities in 2002 and introduced for district councils in 2003 and 2004. These involve combining the work of the District Audit, Benefit Fraud Inspectorate and a general inspection to rate a council either excellent, good, fair, weak or poor. If an authority gets a very low score, the ODPM can, in theory at least, send in a 'hit squad', as happened with Hull City Council. If an authority scores highly, it gains future freedom from inspections and there is talk of some financial incentives.

The thrust of inspections is meant to be production of an Improvement Plan by the council and Audit Commission working together. The council will then have to report on how it has delivered this plan and the benefits local people have derived from it. Single service Best Value reviews and inspections are likely to be a thing of the past. Instead, authorities will be encouraged to do larger reviews either of cross-cutting services such as 'young people' or 'the environment' or of larger service groups such as 'cultural services'.

In January 2003, the ODPM brought out its Consultation Paper on Best Value Performance Indicators (BVPIs) for 2003/4. It proposed that the government specify 101 national service delivery Best Value Performance Indicators for principal authorities for 2003/4.

Local Government Finance Bill and leisure

Substantive local authority issues require funding. An important theme of Best Value is the notion of partnership: between local government and central government, between local government and the local community, and between local government and business. The Conservative Government launched the Private Funding Initiative (PFI) in 1992 as a means of pumping new money into the public sector. The PFI

Initiative has since become part of the Private/Public Partnership (PPP), which in turn has led to the creation of Partnerships UK (PUK).

At the time of writing, the Local Government Finance Bill is going through Parliament. It is another feature of the government's modernization: that of making partnerships with the private sector far easier. In April 2005, all businesses will face a revaluation. Of particular interest in the leisure field is the ODPM announcement that it will offer 80 per cent mandatory rate relief for clubs who register as Community Amateur Sports Clubs (CASCs). Voluntary sports clubs who own property need to register as CASCs in order to receive the new rate relief. A further feature of the new Bill is the introduction to the UK of Business Improvement Districts (BIDs). Brigid Simmonds of Business in Sport and Leisure (BISL) which represents the interests of private sector companies writes:

> Business Improvement Districts (BIDs) have worked well in America. The idea is that encouraging businesses and local authorities to work together can be very successful and can have many mutual benefits. The vast majority of business rates are collected by central government, which then redistributes them to local authorities, taking into account many different factors in their assessment. The idea behind BIDs is that local authorities will agree with the majority of businesses in a particular area and will contribute additional rates to help the BID.
>
> There are currently 22 pilot schemes for BIDs waiting to be introduced once the Bill becomes an Act. BIDs are a new development, which businesses and local authorities should strive to support. Improving public services, as the government has found out, is a long haul, but the contribution sport, leisure and hospitality can make to this process is immense. It should not be underestimated how important leisure time is to residents and how the environment they live, work and play in makes a difference to their whole attitude to life. Working with local authorities to make this happen, whether it be through planning, liquor licensing or BIDs, is hugely important and both private and public sectors should strive to understand each other's needs as this Bill becomes an Act.
>
> Simmonds, 2003

Improving services through legislation is not an easy task, however. The process of getting legislation through Parliament is a long and usually a tortuous road. To understand the process, we need to become familiar with terms such as 'Green Paper', 'White Paper', a 'Bill' and an 'Act'.

Government agencies and leisure and recreation

In providing for recreation, the government works with and through a number of quasi-statutory institutions, quangos and agencies. Some have been established by Royal Charter, some by legislation and others by ministerial direction. Central government, therefore, carries considerable weight and influence on national agencies. The DCMS provides funding, mainly through grant-in-aid, to a large number of executive and advisory Non-Departmental Public Bodies (NDPBs). These bodies play a role in the process of national government, but are not government departments. They operate to some extent at 'arm's length' from ministers as regards decision making, although they are expected to account for their decisions to government. Executive NDPBs have executive, administrative, regulatory or commercial functions. They

Case study: Local Government (Financial Provisions) Act, 2000

To get an Act through the system required years of work. The government published a Green Paper, a proposal by a government for public comment, in September 2000 on *Modernising Local Government*. This became a White Paper – a government report – in December 2001 and was called *Strong Local Leadership, Quality Public Services*. This became the Local Government Bill – the draft of a proposed law. To become an Act, any Bill has to go through a dozen or so stages: the Bill is proposed in the House of Commons and goes through a First Reading, a Second Reading, then to the Committee Stage; then to a Report Stage; and to a Third Reading. The Bill is amended and passes to the House of Lords when it goes through exactly the same system as in the House of Commons. The Commons then consider the Lords' amendments and some Bills pass back and forth between the two chambers. The final stage of the legislative process is the Royal Assent at which point the Bill becomes an Act of Parliament. Even when an Act is passed, it is often years before it becomes a law that all must obey. For example, in this particular Act, new business rate revaluations and mandatory rate relief for voluntary sports clubs will not come into force until April 2005. Another example is the Disability Discrimination Act, 1995 which came fully into force in October 2004.

usually carry out a variety of prescribed functions within government guidelines, but the degree of their operational independence varies. The department provides funding to and is responsible for 38 executive NDPBs, including:

- Arts Council of England
- British Film Institute
- Crafts Council
- Museums and Galleries Commission
- Sports Council
- British Tourist Authority and
- English Heritage.

National agencies assist government at all levels and provide help at local level in planning, provision and management. Countryside recreation, for example, is fraught with conflicts of interest between planning, agriculture, forestry, tourism, water resources, sport, recreation and conservation.

In addition to government agencies, there is a whole range of national, regional and local organizations which assist in providing for leisure and recreation. They are often voluntary bodies or hybrid organizations, in collaboration with government agencies and local authorities. While it is not their primary function to provide facilities, some of them do, and all of them influence provision through grants, loans, technical advice or support of some kind.

Department for Culture, Media and Sport

Central government is not a single entity, but a federation of separate ministries, each with its own ministers and policies. The Department of National Heritage (DNH) was formed

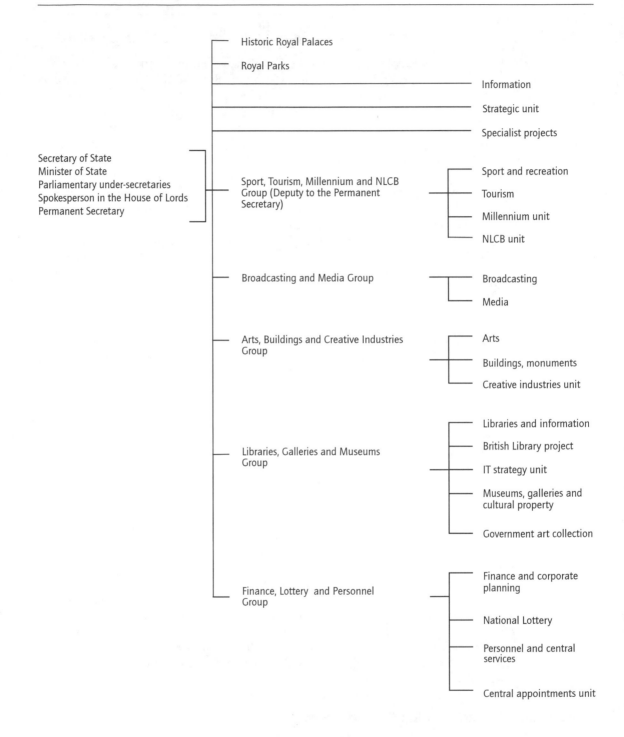

Figure 9.2 Department for Culture, Media and Sport: organizational structure

in April 1992 with responsibility for the arts, museums and galleries, libraries, heritage, film, sport, tourism, broadcasting, the press and the National Lottery. The areas covered by the DNH were formerly the responsibility of other departments: the arts, museums and galleries, libraries, and some aspects of film were dealt with by the Office of Arts and Libraries; heritage by the Department of the Environment; film and export licensing of art, antiques and collectors' items by the Department of Trade and Industry; tourism by the Department of Employment; broadcasting, press and the safety of sports grounds by the Home Office; and sport by the Department of Education and Science.

Following the general election, with a change of government, in July 1997 the department was re-named the Department for Culture, Media and Sport (DCMS). The reason for the change was given in *The Times* on 15 July, 1997 in a letter from the new Secretary of State: 'The name of Department of National Heritage was as inadequate and as partial as its unofficial alternative, the Ministry of Fun. Worse, it was inaccurate. Heritage looks to the past. We look to the future.' However, the word 'culture' conjures up an image of arts-related and intellectual pursuits, rendering other pursuits, therefore, non-cultural and in a way inferior. This is a long way from the concept of culture as the way of life of a people. In the first DCMS Annual Report, the then Secretary of State, Chris Smith, concluded:

> I want to see the Department for Culture, Media and Sport as a dynamic force at the centre of government, making a significant addition to the quality of life in every community in Britain, providing jobs, generating wealth, contributing to the perception of our country, at home and abroad, as a nation which recognises and celebrates creativity and talent in all its people. The work of this Department contributes to the government's determination to deliver on its manifesto commitments, and to build a modern Britain built on a stable economy with a fair society, with everyone playing a full part, and opportunities for all. Our four aims: promoting access, ensuring excellence, nurturing education throughout life, fostering creativity in our economy; these four provide a sound basis for carrying out the commitments we have made to the British people.

The DCMS is responsible for government policy on the arts, sport, the National Lottery, libraries, museums and galleries, broadcasting, film, press freedom and regulation, the historic environment and tourism. It is also responsible for the listing of buildings and scheduling of ancient monuments, for the export licensing of cultural goods, for the management of the British Library and the Government Art Collection, and for two agencies – the Historic Royal Palaces Agency and the Royal Parks Agency. The organizational structure of the DCMS is outlined in Figure 9.2.

The National Lottery

The National Lottery was launched on the 14 November, 1994 to raise money for a variety of good causes which are beneficial to the public and enhance the quality of life of people living in the United Kingdom. It is now an established part of Britain's national culture and is said to be the most successful national lottery in the world. The National Lottery, etc. Act, 1993 established five areas to benefit from the Lottery:

- sport
- the arts
- heritage
- charities and
- to promote the year 2000.

In addition, the National Lottery Act, 1998 created a sixth good cause to fund innovative programmes in education, health and the environment called NESTA. This came about as a result of the government's proposals in July 1997 for reform in a White Paper, *The People's Lottery*, with the focus shifting from buildings to people, supporting initiatives in health, education and the environment. NESTA – the National Endowment for Science, Technology and the Arts – is a national trust endowed from the Lottery, but operating independently of government. Its aim is:

- to help talented individuals (or groups of such individuals) to achieve their potential;
- to help people turn inventions or ideas into products and services; and
- to contribute to public appreciation of science, technology and the arts.

The Lottery is regulated by the National Lottery Commission and the Office of the National Lottery (OFLOT) is responsible for regulating the conduct of the operator – Camelot. Camelot was given a seven year contract to run the National Lottery. After examining competing bids, the Commission awarded Camelot the next seven years on completion of its first contract.

The Department for Culture, Media and Sport (DCMS) has responsibility for the policy framework for the National Lottery, but remains at arm's length from the regulation and operation of the Lottery. The National Lottery Commission (NLC) is a non-departmental public body, headed by five commissioners appointed by the Secretary of State. The NLC has no role in the distribution of proceeds from the Lottery, nor any responsibility for making Lottery awards.

The responsibility for distributing proceeds from the Lottery rests with several independent distributing bodies:

Four national Arts Councils
- Arts Council of England
- Scottish Arts Council
- Arts Council of Wales
- Arts Council of Northern Ireland

Four national Sports Councils
- Sport England
- Sport Scotland
- Sports Council for Wales
- Sports Council for Northern Ireland

UK Sport
Heritage Lottery Fund

Big Lottery Fund (formed from the merger of the Community Fund, formerly the Charities Board, and the New Opportunities Fund)

Millennium Commission

Film Council

Scottish Screen

The early years of the Lottery resulted in substantial sums being raised and exceeding expectations, but there has been an equally substantial drop in ticket sales in recent years. At least three clear messages for change have been identified:

1 too many grants were being awarded to large prestigious projects
2 certain geographical areas in the United Kingdom were benefiting more than others
3 certain types of activities and organizations, particularly those that were well organized in terms of being able to handle the whole application process, were being successful and other well-deserving causes were not coming forward or were not getting through the process.

To ensure a greater spread of distribution, the Lottery distributors are now committed to focusing funding into areas not previously funded. To benefit areas that have found it difficult to meet the criteria of application, Sport England, for example, runs a Priority Areas Initiative targeted at deprived areas in the inner cities and in deprived rural areas. Recently, small projects have benefited from the introduction of the Grants for All awards. The Community Fund gives grants which benefit charities, voluntary organizations and community groups. The Fund has a main grants programme, grants for projects costing up to £60,000, research grants, international grants and Awards for All.

Awards for All is a scheme aimed at small groups involved in arts, sports, heritage and charity activities, who are seeking grants of between £500 and £5,000 and priority is given to groups with an annual income of less than £15,000. The Awards for All scheme is funded by distributors in England, Scotland, Wales and Northern Ireland. In June 2004, the New Opportunities Fund (NOF) and the Community Fund merged to form a new single lottery distributor called the Big Lottery Fund which builds on the experience of both organizations to simplify funding in those areas where the two bodies overlap. This will establish the biggest National Lottery distributor delivering half of all good-cause funding to communities across the UK, estimated to be between £600 and £700 million a year until 2009.

Although lottery funding to local authorities can be significant, it is increasingly very difficult to obtain, as competition for funding mounts and available funds decrease. Local authorities can apply for direct financial assistance for projects at council-owned facilities and also enable organizations within the district to obtain funding for projects which complement existing provision and fit into local strategies. To harness these opportunities effectively requires a co-ordinated and focused approach by local authorities. The creation of a leisure strategy (or wider cultural strategy) is crucial to ensure effective use of total resources.

> The NOF, by early 2004, had given over £2 billion in grants to projects such as school and community sports facilities, free access to a gateway of 150 websites, nursery provision in deprived areas, education projects and childcare.

161

Partnership between central and local governments

To achieve greater partnership between central and local government, the government and Local Government Association (LGA) agreed a set of seven shared priorities for local government, focusing on improvement to public services, fulfilling a commitment made in the White Paper *Strong Local Leadership: Quality Public Services* to define a single list of main aims for local government. The key priorities are:

1 raising standards across schools
2 improving the quality of life of children, young people, families at risk and older people
3 promoting healthier communities by targeting key local services, such as health and housing
4 creating safer and stronger communities
5 transforming local environment
6 meeting transport needs more effectively and
7 promoting the economic vitality of localities.

This remained the situation in local government at the time of writing. The leisure and recreation services provided directly or indirectly by local authorities have a role to play of significance in terms of quality of life and healthy communities.

Summary

This chapter has looked into how central and local governments work and their influence and effects on leisure across all sectors and primarily in the public sector. The government's influence on the voluntary and commercial sectors is covered in Chapters 10 and 11 respectively.

Discussion points

1 Public sector leisure and recreation services and facilities should be founded on principles concerned with serving the greatest number and those in greatest need. Discuss.

2 The government in the UK has set out four principles of public service reform and modernizing government: high national standards, devolving decision making, greater flexibility in service delivery and greater choice. What effect is this modernizing programme having on your council's leisure services?

3 There has been a significant growth in the health and fitness industry. Successful private clubs now set the standard for services and facilities. However, many public sector centres and clubs are not far behind, offering comparable services at prices not too dissimilar. But should the public sector be competing in this way? Should those who can afford private facilities use them, leaving the public sector to provide for those who cannot afford them, by providing an affordable 'no frills' service? Debate the issues.

Further reading

For concise histories and descriptions on the work of governments read, for example:

UK 2004: The Official Yearbook of the United Kingdom of Great Britain and Northern Ireland, TSO, London.

For pre-Best Value regimes:

Adams, I. (1994), *Leisure and Government* (2nd edn), Business Education, Sunderland.

Coopers and Lybrand Deloitte (1992), *Local Government's Role in Leisure and Recreation*, Association of County Councils, London.

White, J. (1992), *Leisure: The Cornerstone of Local Government*, University of Birmingham, WMCLOA, Birmingham.

Useful websites

Cabinet Office: www.cabinetoffice.gov.uk

Central government: www.ukonline.gov.uk

Children Bill: www.publications.parliament.uk/pa/pabills/htm

National Assembly for Wales: www.wales.gov.uk

Northern Ireland Executive: www.northernireland.gov.uk

Office of the Deputy Prime Minister: www.odpm.gov.uk

Scottish Executive: www.scotland.gov.uk

Central Office of Information (COI): www.coi.gov.uk

Department for Culture, Media and Sport (DCMS): www.culture.gov.uk

Department for the Environment, Food and Rural Affairs (Defra) (Formerly Ministry for Agriculture, Fisheries and Food): www.defra.gov.uk

Department for Education and Skills (DfES) (formerly Department for Education and Employment DfEE): www.dfes.gov.uk

www.dfes.gov.uk/everychildmatters

Department of Health (DoH): www.doh.gov.uk

Department of Trade and Industry (DTI): www.dti.gov.uk

Department for Transport (DfT) (formerly Department of Transport, Local Government and the Regions DTLR): www.dft.gov.uk

Department for Work and Pensions (DWP) (formerly Department of Social Services DSS): www.dwp.gov.uk

HM Customs & Excise: www./hmce.gov.uk

Information for Local Government from Central Government: www.info4local.gov.uk

Information and Development Agency (I&DeA): www.idea.gov.uk

Local Government Association (LGA): www.lga.gov.uk

Local Government information Unit: www.lgiu.gov.uk

The Institute of Leisure and Amenity Management (ILAM) Factsheet *Best value terminology* provides a range of definitions being used by the leisure industry when referring to best value: www.ilam.co.uk

Leisure provision in the voluntary sector

Introduction

Chapter 9 focused on the public sector. We now turn to aspects within the non-public sector, which is large, complex and diversified, and to one of the main providers: the voluntary sector.

The voluntary sector can be viewed from two different angles. From one perception the sector is a body of volunteers: people doing unpaid work in their own leisure time, using their energy, skills, and often their money because it gives satisfaction and because they want to. In this sense, volunteering – giving service to others – can be seen as a leisure activity in itself, particularly in light of the definitions of some leisure philosophers and sociologists. Leisure, according to Kaplan (1975) 'provides opportunities for recreation, personal growth and service to others'. Godbey (1994), within one definition, perceives leisure as 'intuitively worthwhile and provides a basis for faith'. A great deal of volunteering, whether in caring for the needy, protecting the environment or teaching and coaching others, is motivated in large measure by doing these things for love and not for money; that they are worthwhile is self evident with the benefits accruing to individuals and the community.

Another perception of the voluntary sector is that of not-for-profit providers: a collection of societies, charities, associations, organizations and clubs of many kinds and in many fields with leisure and recreation a significant element. Hence the voluntary sector can be seen as a 'institution' of organizations providing services with paid and unpaid staff and vast numbers of volunteers.

The term 'social capital' is being used of late by government and agencies to convey investing in each other and the community. Social capital is associated with community spirit and cohesion, citizenship, neighbourliness, trust and shared values. As such, community involvement and volunteering in leisure and recreation play significant roles.

Voluntary organizations in historical context

Voluntary recreation and leisure groups have existed for centuries but not in the number and variety of recent times. In the eighteenth century the coffee-house was, for gentlemen of leisure, a social group that was nearly a club. Coffee-houses in cities such as London and Bath were, in theory, open to all, but often developed into clubs for a specified group, with restricted membership. Today in the United Kingdom we still find that many private and institutional bodies *and* voluntary organizations confine the use of their facilities to certain groups of people.

In early-industrial Britain, recreations were often communal affairs based on seasons, festivals and commemorative events. The sports, dances, processions and ceremonies were within the context of the whole community, as they are in unsophisticated societies today. It was the rationalization of work that led to a separate and identifiable sphere of social life (Thompson, 1967). Unions, factories and schools established their own football clubs; YMCAs and the Sunday School movement created clubs for recreation. Most national governing bodies for sport were also formed from the creation of interest groups of like-minded people such as the MCC (Marylebone Cricket Club), the founders of the game of cricket as it is played today.

> Some leisure interest groups have been established for a long time, such as the Royal Horticultural Society, founded in 1804; the Cyclists' Touring Club was formed in 1878.

Clubs featured in the eighteenth and nineteenth centuries as important organizations in the recreative and social life of the community. The great expansion of clubs took place in the last quarter of the nineteenth century but this was not a long-term trend. Working men's clubs developed through several stages from the last quarter of the nineteenth century. The most significant development was the move towards professionally based entertainment. The switch produced a change in the membership participation from producer to consumer patterns.

Many voluntary movements and associations arose out of the Great Depression as responses to social injustice. For example, the National Association of Women's Clubs arose in that way. Many were pre- and post-Second World War outlets for wives of unemployed men, and for unemployed women themselves.

> One in three eight-year-old UK girls is a Brownie.

Today, voluntary organizations generally are as strong as ever, though some traditional movements, for example, young people's church groups, have witnessed a decline in numbers. Scouting and Guiding remain popular. There are more than 28 million Scouts, youth and adult, boys and girls, in 216 countries and territories. There are approximately 500,000 Scouts in the UK, according to the Scout Association. Girlguiding is the UK's largest voluntary organization for girls and young women, with 600,000 members in 2003. Girlguiding UK reports that the association members and adult helpers give ten million voluntary hours a year, equivalent to 5,500 full time jobs.

Historically then, voluntary organizations have had a long and significant influence on the foundations of today's leisure and recreation. Moreover, work in the voluntary sector, particularly in the community sector, is ever-increasing.

Today, voluntary organizations are as important as ever – internationally,

nationally and locally. What then are the reasons for volunteering and what role do the individuals and groups have to play?

The nature of volunteers and voluntary groups

People go to extraordinary lengths and exhibit wide variations of behaviour in expressing their individual and collective needs in their leisure. There are religious, community and welfare groups, men's, women's, old people's and young people's groups, advisory and counselling groups, para-medical and military groups. Some people join clubs and associations that are cultural or educational. Some join acting, ballroom, jazz, line dancing, keep fit, slimming, singing, operatic or pop groups; large numbers play sport in groups, sail the seas with yachting clubs and climb with mountaineering groups. Many leisure groups identify themselves by wearing badges or special clothing like tracksuits and T-shirts; others have a uniform to create an alternative identity: a leisure identity. Some uniforms identify a way of living, for example, that of members of the Salvation Army, who in their own leisure time give help to the needy.

Is volunteering all about good neighbourliness, giving of ourselves for the good of the community? Although they like to think they are, volunteers often gain something for themselves. Consider volunteers on committees of governing bodies or local government councillors wielding power, or coaches (particularly parents) looking for glory from the achievement of their team, and think of the status conferred upon presidents and chairmen and women in clubs and societies. Volunteering is undertaken with different motives and in pursuit of different purposes. Stanley Parker (1997) identifies four types of volunteer, each sharing certain elements with one or more of the others:

- altruistic volunteering as giving of time and effort unselfishly to help others
- market volunteering as giving something 'freely', but expecting (later) something in return
- cause-serving volunteering as promoting a cause in which one believes and
- leisure volunteering as 'primarily' seeking a leisure experience.

> I say 'primarily' because motives are often mixed. Who is to say a particular act of apparently altruistic volunteering does not also provide a leisure experience for the volunteer? Some leisure activities enable people to feel they are doing something worthwhile and serving a cause, while at the same time enjoying themselves.
>
> Parker, 1997

Motives are seldom pure, as Parker muses: 'Perhaps there is sometimes an element of self-delusion, as when giving something apparently without thought of return, but secretly expecting some quid pro quo.'

In volunteering, people want to retain their own individuality, yet many want to belong to groups. A good deal of volunteering, therefore, encompasses elements of 'leisure' – doing something we like to do, accomplishing something. By and large, in volunteering, we feel we are contributing, for example, in community action, civic responsibility or environmental concern. In the arts and sports, we experience the satisfaction of bringing out the talents of other people, enabling the band or choir to perform at the music festival, to coach the sports team to success. Volunteers tend to give their service in the field of 'organized' leisure, as distinct from 'casual' leisure. Robert Stebbins (1996) identifies ongoing involvement with a voluntary organization as serious leisure. Others label it as 'formal volunteering' and 'constructive leisure'. Stebbins presents the idea of what he terms 'serious leisure' which acknowledges the presence of a serious orientation to leisure. Since many volunteer roles offer 'special careers and a distinctive set of rewards to the individual', these roles can be viewed as serious leisure, falling between work and casual leisure.

The work of volunteers in society and citizen participation is undergoing change. Susan Arai (1997) believes that empowerment theory can help in understanding this change. She explores the relationship between empowerment, volunteering and serious leisure. She concludes that while volunteering is often in the form of serious leisure, it can have both desirable benefits and undesirable elements such as tensions and power relationships at both a personal level and a community level. Among the benefits community volunteers described, were:

- opportunities for shared learning
- opportunities to contribute to community
- development of camaraderie, feeling connected to community and
- enhancement of individual knowledge about the community.

Thus volunteering is connected not only to psychological empowerment (self-conception, self-efficacy, locus of control), but also to social empowerment (increased access to information, knowledge, skills and resources; increased social connections) and political empowerment (access to decision-making processes, power of voice and collective action).

Table 10.1 Key dimensions and categories in definitions of the volunteer

DIMENSIONS	CATEGORIES
Free choice	1 free will (to choose voluntarily)
	2 relatively uncoerced
	3 obligation to volunteer
Remuneration	1 none at all
	2 none expected
	3 expenses reimbursed
	4 stipend/low pay
Structure	1 formal
	2 informal
Intended beneficiaries	1 benefit/help others/strangers
	2 benefit/help friends or relatives
	3 benefit oneself (as well)

Source: Cnaan, R., Handy, F. and Wadsworth, M. (1996)

167

Cnaan, Handy and Wadsworth (1996) considered four key dimensions and categories in defining the volunteer (see Table 10.1). Jarvis and King (1997) point to the traditional meaning of volunteering which is composed of three elements:

- the gift of time
- the element of free choice and
- the lack of payment.

Although this definition is undermined by the spread of paid volunteer schemes in recent years, the core premise remains that volunteering involves spending time, unpaid, doing something which benefits others.

General Household Surveys have shown that, generally, women are more likely to volunteer than men, particularly in raising or collecting money personally and marginally more in organizing or helping a group or serving on committees. Yet with more women now in full- or part-time work, in addition to looking after homes and families, volunteer commitment may be eroding. For certain kinds of voluntary groups, particularly women's organizations, membership levels have been in decline as reported in *Social Trends 2003*. Writing on the experience in America, Tedrick and Henderson (1989) in *Volunteers in Leisure* considered the role of women:

> A problem concerning volunteerism as a feminist issue will continue to arise as long as society devalues the work of women and as long as value is measured solely in economic terms. On the other hand, the contributions made by women to society through voluntary efforts are becoming more widely acknowledged. In addition, volunteer opportunities have provided a way for women to enrich their lives and to learn skills that can be directly transferred into paying jobs. The conception of volunteers being white, middle-class 'do-gooders' has also changed greatly. Today, people of all races, classes, sexes, and ages are volunteering. Many volunteer agencies have been concerned about the number of women returning to the paid workforce and how this has affected the volunteer ranks. While more women do work today, many women still find the time to volunteer.

Jarvis and King's study of the Guide and Scout Associations in Sheffield reports that there appears to be a general disillusionment among volunteers. In this regard, the loyalty of leaders is a strength of the Associations, and the degree to which they are involved in 'serious leisure' commitment appears higher than in other voluntary organizations. However, the fact that a few people do everything has implications for the recruitment and retention of volunteers. Leaders complained there were not enough people to volunteer. Those who might volunteer may be put off by the image projected by these apparent super-humans. In some cases, current and potential volunteers believe that an open-ended commitment is expected of them, which clashes with family and job responsibilities. Most of us have been in the position where we have felt obliged to volunteer; we have not been able or willing to say 'No'. Volunteers who felt obliged to join can be found in almost all branches of leisure activity and organizations. However, Stebbins warns that too much coercion can at times 'obliterate' for some people the leisure and volunteer components that other people find there. In other words, if we *have* to do something, it is not leisure.

Voluntary groups: differences and similarities

At first glance, each club appears to be decidedly different from another. A ladies' darts club meeting in the local pub, for example, might appear very dissimilar to the ladies' choral society meeting in the church hall. Hutson (undated) has shown, however, that there are many basic similarities between all forms of clubs and voluntary associations: there are similarities in patterns of activity and the ways in which clubs develop and decline. She has shown how organizers tend to form a distinct, closely connected, élite within a town or region. Social class, life cycle, physical mobility, kinship and sex roles affect both patterns of attendance and leadership. Voluntary associations tend to reflect 'the economic and social milieu' and tend to be dominated by a group of people of similar type. This leads to a proliferation of many small groups. Like-minded people tend to gather together and form associations. Recruitment is normally along lines of friendship or kinship. Most clubs are social clubs, whether the primary activity is social or not. People who are felt 'not to belong' to the predominant group are often kept out through formal procedures. In the areas in Swansea studied by Hutson, there were often internal political pressures and several examples of cliques leaving a club as another clique took over. These may be some of the reasons why newcomers, if they are in any numbers, tend to set up their own associations rather than join existing groups. While youth clubs were more socially mixed, and some associations claimed to draw members from all social categories, most clubs did not.

Study of the differences and similarities of clubs and associations reveals important factors for the Leisure Manager to consider.

- All the clubs tend to be, at least partially, exclusive. Many clubs, theoretically open to all in principle, have been able to 'guarantee' their exclusiveness with high enrolment fees or membership systems, requiring sponsors and seconders.
- Clubs are not static, but changing, organizations. The Wolfenden Committee Report on voluntary associations (1978) found that, 'New organizations are formed to meet newly discerned needs, others die. Yet others change their emphasis or venture into fresh fields ... There is nothing static about the scene.' The Leisure Manager should bear in mind therefore that new clubs, in particular, are likely to change in membership and will have different leadership patterns within the first few years. Such clubs may need shorter-term initial bookings of facilities and flexible and supporting management roles.
- Clubs display similarities in behaviour: they are social groupings. Sports clubs may be somewhat less exclusive than some other clubs, but just like other leisure groupings, sport generates separate groups and activities for different social categories.
- Clubs are often dependent on support services. Local authorities, commercial bodies and institutions can help by providing support services and premises. The local authority's enabling role plays an important part in this respect.

How many volunteers and voluntary organizations?

There are few definitive answers, and these vary depending on methods of calculation. Voluntary bodies vary greatly from neighbourhood groups to national and international organizations. The range of organizations is wide and diversified and no adequate classification has yet been made to cover all that exist. Several different types of grouping can, however, be identified; some of these are listed in Table 10.2, but the overlaps are many. For example, many uniform groups are youth groups; many women's groups are welfare groups, and so on. The list is by no means an attempt at classification or taxonomy; it is simply a means of showing the range and diversity of voluntary leisure organizations.

It is not possible, without some clear definition and methodology, to be precise about the number of people who can be labelled volunteers: most people give some unpaid service. However, 32 per cent of adults in Great Britain interviewed in the 2001 Office for National Statistics Omnibus Survey had volunteered, that is, given unpaid help to a group or organization, at least once in the past twelve months. Half of these had undertaken voluntary work of some kind in the previous four weeks prior to interview. Voluntary activity increases with age; 64 per cent of adults aged 70 years and over had volunteered in the last four weeks.

> In 2003, 22 million adults were involved in formal volunteering; 90 million hours of formal voluntary work takes place each week.

The Institute for Volunteering Research report on the economic value of formal volunteering which is in the region of £40 billion per year. (The Home Office, similarly, provides a figure of £36 billion.) The total public sector support for volunteering is estimated to be about £400 million per year and that for every £1 volunteer organizations spend supporting volunteering, they can expect a notional payback of up to 14 times. Contrary to popular thinking, young people do support the idea of volunteering.

Table 10.2 Range of voluntary organizations

COMMUNITY ORGANIZATIONS	Community associations, community councils
COMMUNITY ACTION GROUPS	National Council for Voluntary Organizations, Inner City Unit, Inter-Action Trust Limited, Gingerbread
CHILDREN'S GROUPS	Pre-School Playgroups Association, Toy Library Association
YOUTH ORGANIZATIONS	Scout Association, Girl Guides' Association, National Council for YMCAs, National Association of Youth Clubs
WOMEN'S ORGANIZATIONS	National Federation of Women's Institutes, National Union of Townswomen's Guilds, Mother's Union, Women's Voluntary Service (WVS)
MEN'S GROUPS	Working men's clubs, servicemen's clubs
OLD PEOPLE'S GROUPS	Darby and Joan Clubs, Senior Citizens
DISABLED GROUPS	Gardens for the Disabled, Disabled Drivers' Motor Club
ADVENTURE ORGANIZATIONS	Outward Bound Trust, Duke of Edinburgh's Award, National Caving Association
OUTDOOR ACTIVITY ORGANIZATIONS AND TOURING GROUPS	Camping Club of Great Britain and Ireland, Youth Hostels Association, Central Council of British Naturism, Ramblers' Association, British Caravanners' Club
SPORT AND PHYSICAL RECREATION ORGANIZATIONS	Keep Fit Association, British Octopush Association, National Skating Association of Great Britain, Cycle Speedway Council, GB Wheelchair Basketball League

As well as the difficulty in calculating volunteers, the number of volunteer-involved organizations is also subject to considerable estimation. One would need a clear definition of what constitutes a group and organization. Moreover, the numbers would fluctuate weekly. However, the *Official Yearbook of the United Kingdom, UK 2004* states that there are over 500,000 voluntary and community groups across the United Kingdom ranging from international, national and local bodies, giving service to improve the quality of life in their communities. A large proportion of these organizations is concerned with social and community work; the National Council for Voluntary Organizations (NCVO), for example, has a membership of over 3,400 voluntary organizations from large charities to local community groups. Findings from the 2001 Home Office Citizenship Survey suggest the vast majority of citizens recognize that they have rights and responsibilities towards the community. Yet formal volunteering and civic participation activities are highly concentrated within more affluent social groups. The survey suggests that 'more encouragement is needed toward the contribution of poorer, deprived communities, and people lacking qualifications'.

While volunteering can be regarded as a leisure pursuit in its own right, and in areas as diverse as social welfare and education, this chapter is focused on volunteers in leisure and recreation.

National voluntary organizations

The voluntary sector has a number of national bodies representing almost every main field of voluntary enterprise. Leisure has a wide range of national organizations including those for children's play, physical recreation, sports, arts, heritage, tourism, conservation and the environment. Most of these areas and their national bodies are mentioned in their respective chapters in this book. Others that are not included, for example, are the National Federation of Voluntary Bodies (providing services to people with intellectual disability), and the Voluntary Action History Society (a registered charity formed in 1991 to advance the historical study and understanding of voluntary action). Taking just one of these national bodies provides a picture of the committed volunteer.

Case study: The British Trust for Conservation Volunteers (BTCV)

The British Trust for Conservation Volunteers (BTCV) is the UK's largest practical conservation charity founded in 1959 and supports the work of over 130,000 volunteers each year.

BTCV received £6.5 million from the New Opportunities Fund to run the People's Places Award Scheme in England. This five-year programme was launched in October 2001. It is designed to help up to 1,000 local communities, which due to location or circumstance are less advantaged, create or improve green spaces. The scheme is run in partnership with English Nature.

An example of the government's 'cross-cutting agenda', BTCV's Green Gym project enables people to get fit and improve their health while doing practical conservation activities. This claim is said by BTCV to have been confirmed by Oxford Brookes University on the physical and mental health benefits of the project.

Table 10.3 Membership of selected environmental organizations

UNITED KINGDOM	THOUSANDS			
	1971	1981	1991	2002
National Trust[1]	278	1,046	2,152	3,000
Royal Society for the Protection of Birds	98	441	852	1,020
Civic Trust[2]	214	–	222	330
Wildlife Trusts[3]	64	142	233	413
World Wide Fund for Nature	12	60	227	320
The National Trust for Scotland	37	105	234	260
Woodland Trust	–	–	63	115
Greenpeace	–	30	312	221
Ramblers Association	22	37	87	137
Friends of the Earth	1	18	111	119
Council for the Protection of Rural England	21	29	45	59

1 Covers England, Wales and Northern Ireland
2 Latest Civic Trust data is for 2001
3 Includes the Royal Society for Nature Conservation

Some types of organizations, such as environmental organizations, have experienced very high levels of growth in membership. The National Trust had a membership of 3 million in 2002, more than ten times the 1971 figure (see Table 10.3).

Engaging the public and private sectors

Although not part of the sector as such, a number of bodies provide for the voluntary sector. Chapter 9 on the public sector shows how important is the partnership between local government and voluntary organizations to local leisure and recreation. There are many other joint arrangements. Private and institutional bodies, such as landowners, companies, universities, schools, colleges and institutes, make an important contribution to provision and services for recreation. Many firms provide social and sporting facilities. University extramural departments provide adult education classes. Many universities and colleges provide holiday residential courses, partly as a means of keeping residential accommodation and services open throughout the long vacations. The growth of the 'activity holiday' has been rapid in recent years. Private schools, such as Millfield, have become famous for their 'schools of sport'. Private landowners also play a significant part in the provision for informal recreation. They own much of the rural land in the United Kingdom which is the setting for outdoor leisure and recreation. They also own and manage facilities for public leisure through historic houses, country parks and many of the great tourist attractions.

In many cases, voluntary bodies are inextricably linked to public providers and public money. Charitable trusts are often partly sponsored by local authorities and, in some cases, largely subsidized. Advisory and counselling services such as the Citizens'

Advice Bureau, while volunteer based, are part-funded by local authorities. Local councils support and initiate many thousands of voluntary groups and projects and, in many cases, fund and staff them. The interdependence between many voluntary bodies and public authorities is part and parcel of the wide framework of public community services, including leisure and recreation.

Some voluntary organizations are also dependent upon commercial bodies. Some sports clubs might perish without the financial backing and marketing skills of commercial companies. At local level, many clubs rely on the local printer and shops, and on the brewer's contribution of the room at the back of the pub. Further complicating the issue is the problem of demarcation between what is commercial and what is voluntary. Some private institutions and voluntary organizations adopt a style of management which, in certain elements, is wholly commercial. With some private landowners, the earning of income is a major objective and therefore in terms of management they can be considered similar to commercial bodies.

The Leisure Manager has an important role in helping groups of people to negotiate with public bodies, planners, architects and other organizations. Supporting organizations, by helping them to run their own projects, may be more important than providing directly for them. With the advent of the National Lottery in the United Kingdom, the National Funding Bodies ensure that voluntary bodies part-fund their own projects; this helps to spread funds more widely and, importantly, encourages self-help and volunteerism.

The government and volunteerism

The government is keen to encourage links between the statutory, voluntary and community sectors. Government, increasingly, is recognizing the massive role played by the voluntary sector, particularly in community and 'caring' organizations. Also an increasing number of public and community services are delivered by voluntary organizations on behalf of the government at national level and on behalf of local authorities at local levels. Formal volunteering, encouraged by government and its agencies, has both economic and social benefits. The UK government's 2002 Spending Review allocated £125 million for the creation of a new investment fund to help voluntary and community organizations in their public service work. In September 2002 the Treasury completed a review of the role of this sector and recommended ways in which the government could work more closely with volunteers, for example by involving organizations in the planning of services, moving to a more stable funding relationship, and ensuring that the cost of contracts for services reflects the full cost of delivery.

The government's voluntary and community policies are implemented by the Active Community Unit at the Home Office. Further evidence of the government's reliance on the voluntary sector is shown in the Home Office project, the State of the Sector Panel. Over three years, 2003–06, the Panel will be surveyed on a regular basis to monitor progress in increasing voluntary and community sector activity in England, as set out in the Public Service Agreement 8, which is 'to increase voluntary and community sector activity, including increasing community participation, by five per cent by 2006'. The Home Office will also explore additional matters of concern to voluntary organizations, including sustainable funding, multi-agency partnerships, support for infrastructure organizations, recruitment and training of staff and volunteers and information technology.

Funding is made possible in a variety of ways such as grants and awards from the National Lottery, which have helped to provide projects across a range of activities (see The National Lottery, p. 159, Chapter 9). Charities can receive tax relief and tax exemptions. The Gift Aid scheme provides tax relief on one-off and regular cash donations and under the Payroll Giving scheme employees and those drawing a company pension can make tax-free donations from their earnings. The Charities Aid Foundation (CAF) is a registered charity that works to increase resources for the voluntary sector in the UK and overseas.

The Youth Service is a partnership between local government and voluntary organizations concerned with the informal personal and social education of young people aged 11 to 25 (5 to 25 in Northern Ireland). Local authorities manage their own youth centres and clubs and provide most of the public support for local and regional organizations. In its booklet, *Young People Make a Difference*, the government's plan of action was set out to provide grants to volunteer bureaux and to local youth volunteer facilitators and funding for the National Volunteering Helpline.

Volunteering in sports and the arts

Sport, Raising the Game (DNH, 1995) stressed how the mobilization of competent volunteers provides scope for enhancing the support given to coaching and sports development. Then the report *England, The Sporting Nation: A Strategy* (ESC, 1997) recognized the contributions made to sport by volunteers. *Game Plan* (DCMS, 2002) the report of the DCMS and the Cabinet Office, acknowledges the vital contribution volunteers make and sets out plans to extend their contribution (see National plan for sport, p. 356, Chapter 17). Sport depends on a blend of voluntary, public and private sector delivery. Organized sport is largely the responsibility of the voluntary sector and the vast majority of organizers, coaches and officials are unpaid volunteers and the majority of participants do so in an amateur capacity: 'For every champion, there will be hundreds of unpaid enthusiasts who make that success possible.'

The Sports Council defines a volunteer as: 'An individual who helps others in sport through formal organizations such as clubs or governing bodies whilst receiving no remuneration except expenses.'

LIRC estimate the total value of the UK sports volunteer market to be around £1.5 billion with about 1.5 million people involved.

A major study was undertaken for the Sports Council by the Leisure Industries Research Centre (LIRC) in the mid-1990s (Gratton *et al.*, 1997). Prior to this, empirical research into the voluntary sector was limited.

Chapter 17 on sport provides estimates to show that there are around 110,000 voluntary sports clubs, about 1.5 million volunteers and that the government, in partnership, plans to recruit and train 60,000 young voluntary leaders. Likewise the arts, community arts and craft and cultural activities in their variety are catered for largely through local voluntary societies, associations and groups, many supported by the Arts Council and regional arts boards.

The European Swimming Championships held in Sheffield in 1993 involved 700 volunteers working an average of 8 hours a day for up to 17 days: a total of about 95,000 hours.

Chapter 16 shows the immense contribution of volunteers, for example, in museums and galleries and the work of VAN, the Voluntary Arts Network.

Volunteers are essential in the running of minor and major events. The Olympic Games in Sydney and Commonwealth Games in Manchester called upon an enormous number of volunteers because of the size and scale of these multi-sport events.

In *A Sporting Future for All* (DCMS, 2001), the government recognizes that coaching is central to the development of sport at every level and that sport relies on 'an array of volunteers'. National governing bodies are encouraged to identify and appoint a national Volunteer Manager to implement strategy throughout sport.

Volunteers also provide essential assistance in schools (particularly primary schools) and youth and community organizations and play an indispensable role in the support of disabled sport. The British Paralympic Association has a high concentration of a small volunteer workforce donating high levels of hourly support.

Volunteers are usually highly motivated people, but if they neglect the needs of their family, friends or themselves, they could be lost to their sport. The Sports Council/LIRC identified a number of issues.

- The biggest problem faced by volunteers (cited by 74 per cent) is that there are not enough people to help.
- The second highest concern was work being increasingly left to a few people.
- Coaching training is needed, with courses viewed as too expensive in terms of cost and travel.
- The increase of professionalism within clubs places an additional burden on administrators.

Riding for the Disabled is supported by volunteers with an average of one helper for less than two riders.

- Legislative changes such as The Children Act, 1989 and Health and Safety requirements continue to demand stringent standards of procedure and operation. The Activity Centres (Young Persons Safety) Act, 1995 has implications for a number of adventure and outdoor pursuits clubs.
- Junior development was viewed as a problem area, with transport cited as a key deterrent.
- Attracting sponsorship and funding is a major task; many clubs require help and advice in making application for Lottery funding.

A number of reports have suggested that as volunteers were so vital for sporting success, there should be an understanding of the characteristics of volunteers and the motivations that lead to their involvement in their chosen sport (see, for example, Nichols, 2003; Shibli *et al.*, 1999; Sports Council 1996; Nichols *et al.*, 1998). However, volunteers and voluntary groups differ. In a detailed study of characteristics of volunteering and lessons from the sport of cricket, Richard Coleman (2002) contends that sports volunteers are not a homogeneous group. They differ according to the level within sport at which they volunteer.

The current investigation was able to demonstrate consistencies and subtle differences between systematic volunteering at middle level for a county youth cricket team and club level.

The volunteer county youth cricket managers fulfil multiple roles (varying from coach to committee work), tend to be better educated than sports club volunteers and volunteers in general and consistent with club level volunteers are likely to be in employment with no dependent children. The managers tend to be aged 35–59, with volunteering intensity increasing with age and a far greater incidence of retired volunteers than at club level. The majority of managers volunteered elsewhere in sport, possibly at club level with almost all having played club level cricket, suggesting that the managers come from within the sport and are a self-help group.

Time contributions in the county youth team were greater than those of systematic club level volunteers and represented a year-round commitment. Many volunteer managers volunteered for their own benefit rather than for altruistic reasons, although a significant number did want to help improve things. Managers in employment were likely to be asked to help whereas the economically inactive were more likely to offer their services. At middle level, the major problems encountered were consistent with those reported by sports club volunteers: work was increasingly left to a few people. Managers in employment were likely to feel that their efforts were sometimes wasted due to poor organization, and were also likely to experience conflicts with family commitments.

> The most common perception was of a dedicated few doing a large proportion of the work – leading to multiple roles in the club – though the dependency on key individuals was also seen as normal practice within clubs, providing a more effective and stronger nucleus for the club ... The widespread feeling is that it is harder to attract volunteers to take on roles in clubs. This had led to problems in recruitment and retention which has deterred others from becoming involved as volunteers.
>
> Coleman, 2002, p. 220–38

Coleman's study demonstrated the multi-functional role of the sports volunteer at middle level and also identified unqualified volunteers in positions of considerable responsibility relative to the development of young cricketers,

> which could potentially have deleterious effects on their continued participation and this should be addressed by governing bodies of sport. The implication is that volunteers need training, which may not fit comfortably alongside the conventional view of the volunteer as a non-specialist.
>
> Coleman, 2002, p. 220–38

Nichols *et al.* (1998) comment that pressures on volunteers may leave a hole in the Sport England strategy.

> Those who have been most likely to volunteer in the past may be feeling increased pressures from time at work; more two-income families means less time to give to volunteering; the propensity to volunteer may be reduced among young people for whatever reason; (and voluntary coaches were more likely to be younger volunteers); there may be more retired people to volunteer, but have they got the aptitude, empathy and energy to promote opportunities for young people? Even if sufficient volunteers can be found, their contributions need to be co-ordinated in a way that facilitates a young person's progress through the sports development continuum ... This important role

is made more difficult by the small and fragmented nature of sports clubs in Britain: an officer may set up a good relationship with a club which then collapses within three years or key people leave the committee. The small size of British sports clubs, in contrast to much larger multi-sports clubs on the continent, makes it harder for them to support junior sections.

Other problems identified include the lack of skills and capacities some inner-city and socially-disadvantaged groups might have to run a club efficiently, particularly with the increased level of administration and 'red tape'.

Volunteers, then:

- have a key role to play in United Kingdom sport
- need assistance to help motivation, retention and recruitment
- need ongoing support at local, regional and national levels and
- need opportunities for training and development.

The Sports Leader Award (described in Chapter 17) and the Step into Sport projects are ways forward.

Without volunteers, some of the most beneficial work carried out in leisure and recreation would not be possible. As in sports, volunteers are a substantial support network for active and passive participation in the arts. Voluntary organizations, collectively, with tens of thousands of members, are promoted by the Voluntary Arts Network (VAN), which provides a means of encouraging wider participation, promoting standards and supporting initiatives. VAN recognizes that the arts 'are vital to our health, social and economic development'. The range of art forms is wide and includes folk, dance, drama, literature, media, music, visual arts, crafts and applied arts, and festivals. Libraries, hospitals and some local radio stations make use of volunteers. Local libraries, even though a mandatory local authority service, use volunteers to deliver library materials to the housebound and assist in library projects. Local historians undertake research for local libraries. Hospital and student radio stations operate almost exclusively through volunteers.

The Royal Commission on the Historical Monuments of England uses volunteers to help carry out some of the survey work involved in recording the UK heritage. The Historic Royal Palaces agency uses volunteers on conservation work, and the Royal Parks benefit from the work of community service groups such as the British Trust for Conservation Volunteers. The Museums and Galleries Commission published *Museums Among Friends* (Heaton, 1991) to raise awareness of volunteer groups. English Heritage is increasingly making use of volunteers at its properties and, through its local management initiative, has delegated management of some of its sites to local managers, including volunteer groups, in order to make its sites more relevant to local communities and, one suspects, more financially viable.

> Twenty-five thousand volunteers work in museums and art galleries across the country.

One of the differences between the sports and arts sectors is that the 'registered' voluntary sports club coach is likely to have a coaching qualification endorsed by the National Governing Body; in comparison, there appear to be few equivalent 'coaches' in the arts, which draws heavily on those with talents and qualifications in proficiency, but it does not provide measured data with which to quantify volunteerism. However, the point made in this chapter is that every activity under the umbrella of culture, leisure, play and recreation relies on volunteers to sustain it. It is an area of immense importance to leisure management, yet not given the prominence, training or recognition it merits. Leisure Managers are needed in the voluntary sector in both the charitable and non-charitable organizations. It is to the charities that we turn next.

Charities and leisure trusts

The Charities Commission is the agency responsible for the registration, regulation and support of organizations that are charitable under the law of England and Wales. It has a statutory responsibility to ensure that charities make effective use of their resources. Many charitable organizations are not required to register, for example some churches and schools.

At the end of March 2003, the total annual income of all registered charities in England and Wales was estimated at over £30 billion. Approximately 6 per cent of charities receive 90 per cent of the total annual income recorded; two-thirds have an income of £10,000 or less a year and account for less than one per cent of the annual total. Cancer Research UK is by far the highest fundraising charity with total annual income of around £263 million, the National Trust around £201 million and Oxfam around £189 million. According to the Charities Aid Foundation, there are several charities with total income of over £100 million and they include: British Red Cross Society, RNLI, British Heart Foundation, Salvation Army and the NSPCC with over £90 million. Hence, once the National Trust is taken out of the figures, there are no leisure and recreation charities anywhere near the top twenty fundraisers.

> At the end of March 2002 there were approximately 186,000 charities registered in England and Wales.

The origins of charities go back centuries. The church encouraged people to give money or property to benefit the poor. With the 'nationalization' of church property by Henry VIII, there followed The Act of Charitable Uses, 1601 to protect property given to charity, an Act which still has an influence (though no power) even today. The abuse of charities led eventually to the Charitable Trusts Act, 1853, which set up the Charity Commissioners. Its work culminated after the Second World War, following the ideas of Lord Beaverbrook and the subsequent Nathan Committee, in the Charities Act, 1960, which applies to England and Wales and extended Charity Commissioners' powers, including the provision for the registration of charities. The register, which is primarily intended to inform the public about charities, provides conclusive evidence that the registered institution is a charity in law.

The Charities Act, 1960 gave local authorities power to carry out reviews. The 1985 Act places a stricter duty on trustees and enables small charities to be wound up. It is also concerned with the transfer of property to another charity.

In 2004, a new Charities Bill was going through Parliament. There will be a new definition of a charity and it is likely to include the need for organizations clearly to demonstrate public benefit as well as 'charitable' objectives. In addition, the Charity Commission could be given greater powers to strengthen its role as regulator, rather than rely on its advisory role. The Charities Bill was announced in the Queen's Speech in November 2004 as part of new legislation before the next general election.

There is no legal definition of the word 'charity'. Yet, an organization must be considered 'charitable' by law if it is to be registered with the Charity Commissioners. To become a charity, the Charity Commission must be satisfied that the purposes or objects of the organization fall entirely under one or more of the four 'heads of charity'. These are:

1 the relief of poverty
2 the advancement of education
3 the advancement of religion
4 other purposes beneficial to the community. Here, a decision has to be made whether there is a benefit to the community within the spirit and intent of the 1601 Act, long since repealed.

Leisure and recreation, generally, fall into the 'other purposes' category, though some elements, particularly in the arts, can fall into the advancement of education. Sport has difficulties in falling into any category other than 'other purposes'. Even here, the registration of sports groups is problematic. For example, sport for entertainment is certainly not charitable, it must fall into the 'interests of social welfare'. These aspects are addressed in the Recreational Charities Act, 1958.

Under the Recreational Charities Act, 1958, it is charitable: 'to provide or help to provide facilities for recreation or other leisure-time occupation', but the facilities must be provided 'in the interests of social welfare'.

It is clear that bodies are *not* charitable:

- which exist to promote an individual sport or art
- which exist to promote excellence or professionalism
- which exist to benefit only their members.

In this context, most clubs are set up to benefit their members and so are not charitable. These are more likely to fall within the non-charitable 'not for profit' group. However, designated 'community sports clubs' (CASCs) can now apply for the financial benefits of charitable status. Any sports clubs which meet the statutory definition are eligible. The clubs must be:

- open to the whole community
- organized on an amateur basis and
- provide facilities for, and promote participation in, one or more eligible sports.

The government has budgeted £10 million revenue and £60 million capital for community club development between 2003 and 2006, and £28 million to implement recommendations of the Coaching Task Force (see p. 358, Chapter 17).

Leisure and recreation trusts

A number of management systems exist in the delivery of leisure services. One system has become known as the trust system. The term usually applies to charities, or more widely to non-profit-making organizations, which can be charitable or not. Before starting down the road to becoming a charity, organizations need to think very carefully about reasons and motives behind the proposal: is it to save money, or to circumvent legislation or keep the local authority at bay? These are not good moral reasons, even if they are legal. It must be asked why a charity is needed. Is there a similar charity already doing the job? Are the objectives charitable in law? Are there calibre trustees to carry out the business?

There are many advantages in being registered as a charity: social, managerial and financial. However, the law also limits what a charity can do (see Further reading). Let us first consider the advantages in becoming a registered charity and forming a Leisure Trust.

Advantages of charitable status

- Choice of organizational structure. The trust system is flexible. The governing body can be built up on a widely representative basis.
- Tailor-made governing instrument and constitution. The purpose of the business can be written to suit its primary aims and objectives within its legal framework.
- Management autonomy, empowerment, independence, control, and faster decision making. The organization can be master of its own destiny, rather than have decisions imposed upon it. Being a non-political body, the trust can be free of undue bureaucracy and capital controls and establish a system of key member stability.
- The opportunities for partnership are easier to establish.
- Fiscal benefits. Registered charities can take advantage of financial benefits such as mandatory relief from 80 per cent of national non-domestic rates and the rating authorities have discretion to allow relief on such part of the remaining 20 per cent as they think fit under Sections 43 and 45 of the Local Government Finance Act, 1988.
- Financial and forward planning. Monies can be borrowed and invested with greater flexibility, provided the governing instrument permits it.
- Fundraising. Charities can plan fundraising to support both capital and revenue. With tax relief on charitable donations, they are better able to attract grants and sponsorship.
- Voluntary endeavour and community commitment. As a voluntary enterprise, it can encourage a strong spirit of belonging and community endeavour. Many paid staff, too, can feel a greater sense of personal commitment. Voluntary endeavour can produce economies in operation. As self-governing projects, trusts attract leaders in commerce, industry, the professions and the community who want to be associated with them.
- Low level bureaucracy. There can be direct access by management to executive control, cutting down levels of bureaucracy and streamlining decision making.
- Pioneering. Being flexible, the system lends itself to experimentation, new ideas and pioneer projects.

While there are advantages in adopting a trust system, the advantages pre-suppose that the organization has the resources, finances and capability for funding and managing capital and revenue budgets in the short and long term. In reality, most trusts experience financial and other problems and the need for partnership with local authorities or others becomes vital. Hence, trusts also carry difficulties and some disadvantages.

Disadvantages of charitable trust status

- Non-charitable activities. Charities cannot undertake certain political, campaigning and pressure group activities. They cannot trade 'permanently' and persons running the organization cannot benefit personally.
- Raising capital resources. Often, there are insufficient capital resources, and a need to raise substantial sums of money.
- Meeting operational expenditure. Often, there are insufficient operational resources. A voluntary body can be at the mercy of local councils, needing to apply for assistance every year.
- Constant fundraising. Trusts constantly need to raise money and some are having to sell/lease land to help fund projects.
- Staff over-commitment. There may be too few staff or staff on too low wages, many giving service beyond the terms of their employment.
- Public misconception. The public now have high expectations of recreation facilities. People may not know, or even care, that a theatre or sports centre is being run by a trust. To the public, it is a 'public' facility.
- Ultimate heavy trustee commitment. Trustees – all involved in the management committees – carry a heavy burden of responsibility. Key people are usually very busy, already engaged in many causes in the community.

The recreation trust for community recreation provision and management came into prominence with the creation of the Harlow and District Sports Trust in 1959. It was registered as a charity, having to prove its bona fides as an organization committed to community and humanitarian values and charitable objectives. A small number of similar charitable trusts, such as in Basingstoke, followed in the 1960s and 1970s. These remained but a few until the advent of Compulsory Competitive Tendering (CCT). Thereafter, a spate of trusts were formed, some no doubt with altruistic and charitable motives, but many were created primarily to circumvent the strict rules and CCT specifications and/or to benefit from substantial rate relief. Genuine trusts could be the way forward and organizations such as Greenwich Leisure now have experience of running a wide range of facilities.

Other large trusts include city-wide services such as Edinburgh Leisure. It is best to follow the advice of Michael Collins who wrote an article in *Recreation*, 'The Trust Experience – do it for the service, not the money!' .'Trusts may be the only mechanism to be able to do this in the current climate where leisure is losing out as a non-statutory service with no major performance indicators that represent its real value to its users' (Collins, 2003).

Although they are not-for-profit organizations, many trusts apply management and operational techniques and practices in order to compete with the private sector. This has benefits for local government funding, but is a dubious model within the charitable sector, particularly when the organization's facilities and infrastructure are provided in the main from rates and taxes.

Different types of legal structure

The term 'trust management' is used here as a system of control and management by a registered charity for the purposes of community welfare, as distinct from the management of facilities by a local authority, commercial organization or institution. However, in the legal documents that apply to charities the word 'trusts' carries a more specific understanding.

These types of organization are described briefly.

The most common types of legal structure

Type of organization	Governing instrument
Trusts	Trust, deed or will
Unincorporated associations	Constitution or rules
Incorporated organizations: companies	Memorandum and articles of association
Non-charitable industrial and provident society	Registered rules approved by registrar
Charitable industrial and provident society	Registered rules approved by registrar
Royal Charters	Charter

Declaration of trust Charities can be created by a 'declaration of trust'. Property can be given for charitable purposes by trust deed or by will. The trust document should set out the purposes of the trust and include provisions for managing it. However, trustees' liability is not limited.

Unincorporated associations There are many kinds of unincorporated organization, including associations, friendly societies and trusts. These are free of the statutory controls to which companies are subject, and, therefore, can be less expensive to run. The group adopts a constitution or rules which sets out, for example:

- the purposes or objects
- the constitution of the committee of management and
- the rules for governing the membership.

Many charities are established as unincorporated trusts or associations. Their main disadvantage is that their trustees have unlimited personal liability. Therefore, in terms of running leisure and recreation services and facilities for the benefit of the community at large, being an incorporated organization would appear to be essential.

Incorporated organizations: companies A legal difference between unincorporated and incorporated organizations is that an incorporated organization has a corporate legal existence independent of the individuals who are its members. It acts through its members, but has rights and duties in its own right. Charities may be incorporated under the Companies Act, 1985 as companies limited by guarantee. There are two main forms of limited company. The most usual in the field of commercial activity is the company limited by shares. This is likely to be an unsuitable format for a charity 'for social welfare' to adopt. The appropriate form is a company limited by guarantee;

there are no shareholders, but the members agree to guarantee to pay any debts of the company, up to a limit of normally £1 each. These members elect the directors to run the company. Company governing instruments consist of a memorandum of association and articles of association. The directors of a corporate charity are in broadly the same position as the trustees of a charitable trust, and are also subject to the provisions of the Companies Acts.

Industrial and provident society Under the Industrial and Provident Societies Act, 1965, societies can be registered with the Registry of Friendly Societies. It is an accepted method of creating a new charity, and is currently an 'exempt' charity, by the Charity Commissioners, as are companies. Non-charitable industrial and provident societies are being used in the creation of new housing associations and have been used for an employee-controlled transfer of leisure facilities from local authorities, for example, in Greenwich and in Bristol.

There is no statutory definition of a bona fide co-operative society, but such a society will normally be expected to satisfy conditions relating to:

- the business of the society conducted for the mutual benefit of its members
- control of the society vested in the members equally and
- matters relating to shares, profits and non-restriction of membership.

To qualify for registration, otherwise than as a bona fide co-operative society, a society must satisfy two principal conditions: that its business will be conducted for the benefit of the community, and that there are special reasons why it should be registered under the Act rather than as a company under the Companies Act.

Royal Charters Royal Charters, considered by the Privy Council, are only granted to large 'significant' bodies such as Sports Councils and Arts Councils. A Charter, however, does not confer charitable status. The English Sports Council (branded Sport England), for example, is not charitable; it has a separate charitable trust established by means of a Company Limited by Guarantee.

Financial benefits to registered charities

Charities can benefit in the context of their own tax and in the tax paid by their supporters such as personal and company donations through Gift Aid. Subject to certain qualifications, charities are entitled to relief from income tax, corporation tax, capital gains tax and inheritance tax. There are other tax benefits, for example, payroll giving schemes are not counted as taxable income, and if a trade is charitable, the expenditure qualifies for exemption. A charity is exempt from tax on monies used only for charitable purposes and have actually been spent or saved up for such purposes.

Trading profits are exempt from tax so long as the trade carries out a primary purpose of the charity or the work is done by beneficiaries of the charity. Trading and making profits are increasingly having to be debated in light of charitable status. A charity can charge reasonable prices, but they should not be so high that the charity endangers its status by ceasing to benefit a sufficient section of the public.

183

A local charity, like a recreation trust, will find that even though there may be a surplus or apparent 'profit', it is not making a true net profit. If a true profit were to be made, doubt may be cast upon the 'public benefit' of what the charity is doing. The Inland Revenue might interpret it as a trading profit, on which corporation tax should be levied. Although trade as such is not a charitable object, increasingly, charities need to trade in order to provide the funds for the charity to do its work. Some trade, therefore, is allowable by charity law, and exempt under tax law. One is where the trade is a direct and necessary implementation of the very object of the charity: this applies in part to community leisure and recreation projects. However, many recreation trusts run their facilities in such a way that it is difficult to distinguish them from other businesses. This throws into question whether their activities can be construed as exclusively charitable purposes in law. One potential way out of this dilemma is to set up a separate trading company: usually a company with limited liability. This new company, not subject to the laws of charity, is free to trade like any commercial company. The trading company can covenant its profits to the charity. It is important that the activities of the two companies are kept separate otherwise the charitable status of the charity could be put into jeopardy. As the two organizations may well share premises and facilities, rents and wages and other costs involved, these should be fairly divided between the charity and the trading company. In this way, no hidden subsidy of the trading company takes place at the expense of the charity. It would be a breach of its constitution for its funds to be used to subsidize the trading company.

The role of local authorities and charities

Local authorities may be involved in the work of charities in a number of ways:

- trusteeship
- land and property
- rates; grants
- fundraising and
- changes to charities.

In some cases, local authorities can be trustees: as holders of property for the benefit of the people it is to serve. In some cases, the governing instrument of a charity may give a local authority power to appoint or nominate some, or indeed most, of the trustees of the charity.

A good deal of land used for recreation is owned by charities. In some cases, such as rural parishes, the property can be transferred to the parish or community council or an alternative group, provided the Charity Commissioners and councils consent. Where a local authority has given money, goods or services to, say, a charitable recreation ground, the authority has power to make by-laws for the land. In terms of open recreational space and preserving amenities such as playing fields, the National Playing Fields Association provides advice and assistance to local authorities and can also act as custodian.

The permission of a local authority may be needed for fundraising. A good deal of legislation, strengthened by the Charities Act, 1992, exists concerning a wide number of activities carried out by charities. These include house-to-house collections, street collections, competitions and gaming and lotteries, including bingo, tombola and 'race nights'. A licence is needed, not just for house collections, but to go collecting in pubs, factories and offices and to sell things on behalf of a charity. Most local authorities also have regulations for street selling on behalf of charity.

Clearly, it is important for charities and local authorities to work together. Both have legal powers to co-ordinate their activities in the interests of the people who benefit from their services, bringing benefits to both charity and local authority. For the local authority, benefits can be:

- direct and indirect cost savings
- less use of central resources
- enterprise to involve new capable people with fresh ideas for provision and funding and
- opportunity to promote a successful recreation facility and safeguard community provision.

However, local authorities need to tread carefully in the role they can play in charitable work and particularly with companies. For example, forming a trust involving local authorities is limited by regulations relating to companies 'influenced by' local authorities. The Department of the Environment Consultation Paper, Local Authorities' Interests in Companies and the Local Government and Housing Act, 1989, provides a statutory framework to govern local authorities' interest in companies. The government considered that it was an anomaly that local authorities had influence or control of companies outside the rules governing the conduct of local authority business. Three types of company were identified.

Local authority controlled companies These form part of the public sector and their expenditure must, therefore, be treated, for the purposes of controlling public expenditure, as part of the public sector.

Arm's length companies These companies have directors whose status protects them from undue influence, the relationship between the authority and company is clearly regulated to avoid deficit funding and the company is in competition with a market.

Local authority influenced companies Action was deemed to be necessary to control companies over which a local authority has a dominant influence, either in 'personnel relationships' or 'financial relationships'. For example, a local authority is only permitted to have up to 20 per cent of places on a board of directors held by council members or officers.

In setting up a charitable recreation trust, key aspects have to be considered and satisfied.

- The Charity Commissioners have to be convinced of the need for and the bona fides of the organization and its 'governing document'.
- The Inland Revenue needs to be persuaded that tax exemptions are justified.
- The Acts governing companies need to be adhered to.

- The Acts governing local authorities and their influence on companies need to be satisfied to show that no undue subsidies or benefits accrue to companies.

Industrial and company recreation provision

Industrial and company recreation, by and large, is the provision of private facilities, ostensibly not provided for commercial gain, but for the workforce as private individuals. It is conceded at the outset that a happy workforce may achieve greater efficiency and output and thereby greater profits, but in terms of management, company leisure provision is more akin to the private members' club than to commercial enterprise because its *raison d'être* is for employee recreation, not for financial profit.

The development of the industrial sports and social club in the latter part of the nineteenth century has often been attributed to the philanthropic motives of benevolent and paternalistic employers, influenced by religious and humanitarian ideals. However, underlying this, more practically orientated motives may have been at work, and certainly the development of industrial recreation into the twentieth century is unlikely to be attributable solely to the altruistic behaviour of the employer.

A number of factors have been put forward as being influential in or motivating the decision by an employer to contribute capital and recurrent expenditure towards leisure provision. These include:

- philanthropy
- fitness for work
- reduction in staff turnover
- company image; company prestige and
- employee pressure.

The provision of company services and facilities is likely to have been influenced by a combination of these and other specific factors, not all of which will have been relevant at any one time.

Historical perspective of industrial recreation provision

Whatever the motivation, the beginnings of industrial recreation provision in the United Kingdom started in the latter part of the nineteenth and the early part of the twentieth centuries. The early days were dominated by such pioneers as Pilkington, Cadbury and Rowntree. The establishing of Pilkington's Recreation Club in 1847 was one of the foundations of the movement (SCSG, 1968). The government-initiated Clarendon Report, going back to 1864, extolled the virtues of sport participation as a means of developing comradeship, team spirit and loyalty to an organization. Following the First World War, many industrial clubs sprang up, often associated with religious and welfare organizations. However, the Great Depression caused a decline in the number of clubs owing to the closure of companies and impetus was only once again regained after the Second World War. In general terms, there was a boom in industrial recreation provision in the 1950s, when profits were high and a spirit of altruism led to a spate of companies 'investing' in sports and social clubs. In the 1960s responsibility for the organization and management of many of these clubs changed from employer to employee, under the guidance of a sports and social secretary and/or committee structures. Finance remained a joint effort with the employers often providing for capital expenditure and an annual block grant. The employees contributed by membership subscriptions, lotteries, and bar and vending profits.

Over the years, with some notable exceptions, there has been a general decline in the movement. Changes in the British economy with a decline in the country's manufacturing base, allied to changes in employee lifestyle and choice in leisure, have led to the closure of many sports and social clubs. And it is not just in manufacturing. In banking, for example, the demand by employees to use the sports and social facilities provided by the banks has declined, with Saturday closure of the banks and escalating house prices in the suburbs of major cities where many of the sports clubs are located. It is also due to changing leisure habits, family shopping, increased travelling inconvenience and the cost involved. The declining number of participating members has coincided with the increasing cost of maintaining the grounds and the indoor facilities. Drink-drive legislation and the trend, particularly in the south-east, for more people to live some distance from their workplace, have exacerbated these trends.

However, there remain exceptions to this generality. The types of clubs vary enormously from industrial 'giants' and large companies to local industry. The programmes vary from a few activity sections to as many as thirty in a club and there are considerable differences in funding. The type and size of the company have a bearing on provision. With its greater financial and physical resources, a firm with two thousand or more employees can offer a wider range of activities and opportunities; one of the largest in the United Kingdom, the Shell Lensbury Club, is such an example. Most of these larger clubs have excellent playing pitches and courts and social facilities. The Bank of England Sports Club is another example.

Where companies have outdoor sports grounds and indoor recreation facilities with declining attendances, it raises the contentious issue of under-use of recreation facilities, and the potential for shared use with the community. In general, shared use has been limited, though hiring out of certain facilities, such as playing pitches, has increased. While there may be a willingness by some companies to share, the majority of sports facilities are often maintained with the help of weekly contributions from employees; they are jealously guarded by the company club members themselves. The practical problems of preservation of standards, employee safeguards, cost of additional use, bar and excise licences, security, staffing costs and legal and insurance problems are put forward as reasons against involvement with the community, as is the problem of community use clashing with company use, particularly in those industries where shiftwork is prevalent. Also, industrial sector provision offers recreational experiences which are different in kind from those offered in the public sector; reports speak of 'identification', 'small units', 'belonging', 'minority groups' (e.g. 'aero modelling catered for') and 'getting together with work colleagues' (see Further reading).

Club secretaries, like managers in the public and private sectors, have managerial responsibilities. As well as a knowledge of management techniques, licensing laws and financial control, the company Leisure Manager should also be providing a programme relevant to the needs of the company's workforce. The manager may perform an administrative role, letting out the facilities to worker-organized clubs, or perform the role of enabler, actively promoting and encouraging participation through coaching schemes, special events and leagues, and for the unattached as well as the club user.

Roles are likely to differ from organization to organization. With exceptions, however, most programmes revolve around the traditional games and social activities, particularly with low-cost bar and catering facilities, often to far higher standards than provided in the public sector and more akin to the private members club.

Joint provision involving industry

Earlier it was suggested that there was limited use of company premises by the community. Facilities provided between companies and local authorities are rarer still. Yet this was being advocated over 80 years ago. Joint provision of recreation facilities by industry and local authorities for use by both employees and the community was advocated by B. Seebohm Rowntree, in 1921, when in *The Human Factor in Business* he wrote:

> That adequate opportunity for wholesome recreation is desirable for all workers, especially in view of the shortening of the working week will not be disputed. The question is whether an employer has any responsibility in connection with the matter. I think the right answer is that if many of his workers live near the factory he should satisfy himself that adequate recreational facilities exist for them. He may do this in two ways: either he may provide adequate recreational facilities for his own employees only, or, by his influence and possibly also his financial help, he may assist communal effort to provide such facilities for the community as a whole. Strong arguments can be brought forward in favour of either course. In the case of a town where voluntary committees or local councils are seeking to provide playing fields, clubs and similar amenities for the general public, it is certainly a disadvantage if large employers refuse to co-operate in the public effort because they are concerned merely with their own employees.

This view was endorsed in *The Pilkington Report* (SCSG, 1968):

> the Study Group was firmly of the opinion that, in the logical development of sociological planning following all the improvements in the overall standard of living, it is no longer the function of private or public industry to provide recreational facilities for the exclusive use of their own work people but that they might well combine their resources with those of the local authorities in order to provide facilities which could be used and enjoyed by all. There have been a few successful collaborative projects – though too few to mention, with exceptions such as the Sedgwick Club in London. One is left to ponder whether companies could apply the same drive and imagination in discharging responsibilities to employees and the community, as they do in meeting responsibilities to shareholders. If so, there could be a brighter future, but all the signs show a move away from the traditional company sports and social provision and use by their premises by outside players and teams.

Philanthropy, a major early influence on the development of individual sports and social clubs, is no longer a common motive for provision of employee facilities. Economic realism has become the hallmark and corporate fitness concepts are slowly infiltrating into the boardrooms of the larger British companies. The arguments are strong: the economic benefits can be substantial and company image and prestige can be enhanced at no major cost.

Employee health and fitness

The concept of 'corporate fitness' has been gaining momentum – though slowly – in the United Kingdom as statistics become more widely publicized regarding the poor health of British workers and executives. The World Health organization shows British workers at the top of the table when it comes to heart disease and lung cancer. British industry loses over 27 million days per annum due to heart-related problems and a further 13 million days per annum are lost due to back-related problems.

A significant number of large corporations in the United Kingdom, including BP, Shell, Glaxo SmithKline, Marks and Spencer, British Airways, British Telecom, the Bank of England and most of the major banks offer employees extensive and often luxurious sports and social facilities in recognition of the mutual benefits of corporate well-being to the employer and the employee. City firms in London and elsewhere include corporate health club memberships within their remuneration packages. Exclusive London sports, health and leisure clubs, such as Cannons, Holmes Place, Lambs and Cottons, have a very high proportion of corporate memberships.

People's tastes are changing – more sophisticated leisure experiences are now in demand, boosted by television advertising, the fashion industry, and the concept of fitness and 'wellness'. Just as many of Britain's manufacturing industries have declined, industrial sports and social clubs in the traditional sense belong to a fast-fading age. In general terms, many of the more traditional clubs are only used regularly by the older or retired employees for whom the style of facilities remains appropriate and attractive. The younger, more affluent and mobile employees have tended to forsake the sports and social clubs for alternative, more dynamic venues such as the night-clubs, the wine bars, the private health or sports clubs and the restaurants. Clearly, sports and social club committees and their sponsoring companies need to be addressing these trends and defining the future role and nature of recreation facilities for their employees *and* their local communities.

A partnership approach with the local leisure managers could lead to a partnership between the company, the schools and the local authority and trusts in the area to the benefit of all partners.

Discussion and summary

One of the characteristics of leisure-time participation is that a considerable proportion of people take on new leisure roles; indeed, they are no longer factory worker, bank clerk or housewife. They become instead leader, coach, club chairperson, golfer, sailor, youth worker, lay preacher or sergeant-major, where the uniform is the symbol of the organization; it gives identity, and image: it stands for something. The taking on of new roles in leisure time is an interesting phenomenon and may be significant. There is commitment, purposefulness and responsibility. Are these meaningful roles absent from other aspects of everyday life? What does it tell us about having clearly defined group norms and cultures? These are questions for the Leisure Manager to ponder and come to grips with in planning programmes for people (see Chapter 21).

Voluntary organizations give people both the chance to participate and the opportunity to become involved in all levels of organization and management. They also give the opportunity to serve. In terms of community recreation, in its widest sense, managers must be aware that the voluntary sector, more than other sectors, holds many of the keys to individual self-fulfilment, one of the main goals of effective leisure and recreation management. It is important, therefore, for Leisure Managers to understand something of what it means to be a volunteer.

The voluntary sector is extremely large and diversified and is linked with the public, institutional and commercial sectors. It is dominated by clubs, societies and associations. As a result of the sheer volume of organizations and numbers of people, there are more people involved in the management of leisure and recreation in the voluntary sector than in the other sectors. The range and diversity of voluntary leisure groupings, the motivations of people and the need to belong and to participate with others, are significant factors and as such should be studied by leisure academics and Leisure Managers. Clubs offer individuals a group identity. Inter-club competition and rivalries reinforce the identity and sense of belonging. Membership can confer status, and offer purposeful activity and a sense of importance. Voluntary organizations hold one of the keys to personal self-fulfilment; leisure and recreation professionals need to harness their assets and public authorities should enable and encourage their development.

Not-for-profit organizations linked to local authorities have been a feature of recent years. A charitable trust has considerable advantages. It can forge ahead through its own enthusiasm and initiative. It encourages community and commercial support and can save public money. But it needs support from authorities in the way of subsidy, grants, technical advice and help especially towards capital development costs. The days of community service organizations having to beg for financial assistance should end and can do so if local authorities and voluntary organizations collaborate. The trust system can be the bridge between voluntary bodies and statutory authorities; it represents partnership. There are precious little land, money or resources available for organizations and authorities to pay and develop facilities themselves without the widest consultation, co-operation and co-ordination. Projects are often well managed where authority lies in a small, strong, high calibre, independent committee, with wide terms of reference and complete control of day-to-day management. This may be easier to achieve in a recreation trust. However, it is important that the committee is independent, has strong powers and is not constantly blown off course by undue political pressure.

Industrial companies provide a large share of the nation's sport facilities. They offer considerable perks to employees and their families and contribute to company cohesion. If these facilities could be more widely available, they would contribute greatly to community recreation. Companies possessing good sports facilities with spare capacity have a ready-made opportunity to demonstrate their goodwill.

A note of warning is provided by Tedrick and Henderson (1989, p. 111), who say that we should not look to the voluntary sector to solve all the problems in communities and fill the gaps in services. Nor should we expect volunteers to do the work of leisure professionals and Leisure Managers.

> Volunteers are sometimes seen as the panacea for the problems of social service organizations. While they can do much to help, the limitations of using volunteers must also be recognised. This caveat is offered simply to foster a realistic approach to the use of volunteers. Volunteers are good and helpful, but a recreation, park, and leisure service agency cannot expect that the

use of volunteers will solve all its problems. Volunteers can expand, enhance, and extend services, but they cannot do the planning and administration that paid staff are trained to do. Staff should listen to volunteers, but the volunteer role should not administer a programme. The major drawback of working with volunteers is that it takes time, money, and energy to work with them. Volunteers do not drop in off the street, ready to teach a class or coach a team. They require recruiting, training, supervision and recognition, all of which involve personal contact. Unless an agency is willing to make the commitment to providing volunteer management on an ongoing basis, its volunteer programme will not be successful. Volunteers cannot supplant staff. They need direction and guidance from professional staff members. This need for guidance must be paramount when working with volunteers. How many volunteers can a leisure service staff member effectively supervise? This question needs to be considered in planning for enhancing leisure services through volunteers.

Volunteers represent the 'community' from which they are drawn and they can serve as excellent ambassadors for that community or their special interest.

Leisure management has an important part to play in the network of voluntary bodies and agencies; the Leisure Manager is part of a multi-disciplinary framework for leisure planning and management. The growth area for the profession in the early twenty-first century could be the management of voluntary sector leisure and recreation organizations and facilities.

Discussion points

1 'The most successful societies are those that harness the energy of voluntary action giving due recognition to the third sector of voluntary and community organisations' (Prime Minister, Right Honorable Tony Blair MP).

Voluntary organizations are increasingly becoming providers of services that are vital to a wide range of groups in society. While there are benefits in this trend, should the voluntary sector be providing essential services which have usually been encompassed with the public sector? Discuss in the context of play, recreation and leisure.

2 Leisure trusts enjoy tax and rate benefits. An increasing number of 'trusts', however, are not voluntary sector not-for-profit organizations, rather leisure management contractors sailing under flags of convenience. Some of these organizations win contracts a long way from their home base and, it can be argued, stretch their original objectives to beyond limits. Part of their competitive edge comes from financial factors such as rate relief that are not available to commercial operators. Discuss whether this should be allowed to continue and the implications of sealing up the legislative loophole.

3 The management of leisure organizations, services, clubs and special events usually requires volunteers. With professional staff, rewards come in the form of money and recognition; with volunteers, money is not a factor. Public and peer approval and recognition are therefore fundamental. How would you ensure this?

4 Competent volunteers are often difficult to recruit and keep. Increasingly, leisure and sports clubs rely on loyal, long-serving, older volunteers. The trend if continued will result in still fewer volunteers and clubs. What can be done to arrest and reverse this decline?

Further reading

Charity Commissioners for England and Wales (1997), *A Guide to the Charities Acts 1992 and 1993*, Charities Commission, London.

Lawrence Graham (undated), *Charitable Trusts for Local Authorities*, (3rd edition) Lawrence Graham, London.

Evers, S. (1992), *Managing a Voluntary Organization – Guidelines for Trustees and Committees*, British Institute of Management, Corby.

Useful websites

The National Council for Voluntary Organisations (NCVO). (*The Voluntary Sector* magazine is published by NCVO): www.ncvo-vol.org.uk

The Voluntary Skills Council: www.voluntaryskillssector.org.uk

Scouts: www.scouts.org.uk

Guides: www.girlguiding.org.uk

11

Leisure provision in the commercial sector

Introduction

In Chapters 9 and 10 attention was focused on the public and voluntary providers, and it was shown that there is a level of integration and overlap between them. This chapter is concerned with the commercial sector, which also has a relationship with the other sectors and also with the not-for-profit businesses.

The major difference between a commercial organization and a public or voluntary organization is that the primary objective of the commercial operator is to achieve financial profit or an adequate return on investment, even though the means of profit-making usually calls for giving valuable services. The other sectors may also make financial profits, but they are established primarily for other reasons. Yet profit-making and not-for-profit organizations in leisure have similarities: they must both attract sufficient clients, consumers and customers or they will fail. Leisure Managers in the public sector have to work within the limitations of local government laws, directions, duties and powers and public accountability. Although they can use some of the skills and techniques of commercial operators such as market research, product development and targeted promotion, they are not free agents. Commercial managers also have constraints, but they have wider freedoms for entrepreneurial enterprise.

However, the commercial leisure sector does not have a concise identity. There is a range of commercial providers from owners and operators of multinational companies to small local companies. There are operational commercial companies whose business is to manage services and facilities provided by others. A number of public leisure facilities, for example, are managed by commercial operators in return for a management fee. Many of these operating companies were created specifically for that function. Then there are public, institutional, independent and voluntary organizations running some of their activities profitably to meet revenue income targets. Many clubs and not-for-profit organizations run activities that make financial surpluses such as bars, catering, health suites and fitness areas, to provide the finances to keep their businesses solvent.

How then do we define commercial leisure? There appear to be three main strands or kinds of business.

1 Commercial operators managing commercial activities for profit
2 Commercial operators managing not-for-profit facilities/activities such as contract companies
3 Not-for-profit operators managing some activities commercially to improve financial performance, for example, to help repay capital costs, meet investment targets, run the business at break-even levels, and to subsidize non-profitable community activities. Leisure trusts are having to adopt this robust business approach. But these businesses are not commercial, *per se*. They may pay their directors and managers well and some may make surpluses to plough back into the business, but they do not make profits for directors or shareholders.

A commercial leisure company could be described as one where the capital investment and running costs are met from the activities of the private company.

The commercial leisure sector, therefore, can take many forms. This chapter focuses to a greater extent, though not exclusively, on these companies and their activities, the public sector and voluntary sector providers having been covered in the previous chapters.

The commercial leisure sector: an overview

People's residual income is taken up in large proportion with commercial products and services. Leisure 'activity' is an attractive and lucrative market.

Commercial organizations do not have an intrinsic interest in leisure and recreation, in and of itself, but in leisure as a source of profit. This is not to say that many organizations and managers are not deeply involved in leisure, nor is it to say that there is no altruism on the part of the providers. Indeed, patronage has long been an element in recreation provision, and commercial support has kept alive many activities which would not otherwise have survived. In addition, the mass media have been responsible for increasing interest and participation in a whole range of leisure pursuits, such as football, rugby, cricket, snooker, darts, bowls, golf, gardening, DIY and collecting

The leisure market was worth £35 billion in 2002, which was 5 per cent of total consumer spending.

antiques. However, while there is a desire to increase the popularity of a number of leisure pursuits, commercial operations (outside the realm of patronage) will only maintain their interest if there is benefit to the organization and its shareholders.

A large proportion of spending on leisure is in the commercial sector. In terms of numbers, millions of people buy sports equipment and cinema tickets, eat out socially, drink, smoke, gamble, watch television and are entertained in their leisure time through services and products provided commercially. The objective of the commercial provider is to make money by serving the public in the belief of 'giving people what they want'. However, does the commercial sector always provide the products that the public actually needs or wants, or is the public persuaded to want them? Is the public obliged to take what is on offer? Product choice is often limited in order to streamline production. For example, a few large breweries control the majority of Britain's public houses. Without voluntary consumer organizations such as CAMRA (Campaign for Real Ale) the specific wishes of people could become secondary to products and distribution efficiency.

The commercial provider is therefore, in essence, different from other providers: being, literally, in it for the money to both survive and prosper. Yet many private businesses are not always 'commercial'; they do not make profits. Of all American commercial ventures apparently 40 per cent never make a profit, but break even or go under, and 50 per cent of the rest of the companies make only marginal profits, the major problem being the mounting capital repayment debts. In such a climate, many private or commercial leisure organizations find it hard to stay in business and, compared to public sector business, competition is fierce and many companies and services may fail. Leisure is a volatile market and changes in leisure spending add to this uncertainty. The commercial leisure industry is made up of many thousands of businesses, from the neighbourhood sports or hobbies shops to the giant multinationals. While the industry is widely diversified and contains many retailers with only a few full-time staff and Saturday part-timers, the large companies predominate. The commercial sector is dominant in the provision of hotels, amusement parks, theme parks, leisure parks, holiday camps, cinemas, theatres, bowling alleys, ice skating rinks, horseracing, greyhound and speedway tracks, bingo clubs, restaurants, public houses, night-clubs, casinos, ballrooms and, increasingly, health and fitness centres, country clubs and even children's play and adventure centres. Despite major developments by relatively large companies, however, these providers are dwarfed by the expanding leisure giants: the multinational companies.

Ryanair's low cost airlines are one of the most successful in Europe, with over 120 routes to 84 destinations in 16 countries.

The most significant change over the past two decades has been the increase in the size of the multinational companies through mergers, takeovers and diversification of interests. Multinational companies have power and influence on people's leisure, supplying what we want and are willing to pay for. Entrepreneurial and risk-taking qualities are often the hallmarks of its leaders such as Ryanair's Michael O'Leary and Virgin's Richard Branson. Branson's empire includes Virgin Trains, Virgin Atlantic airline, megastores, mobile phones, credit card and internet services.

Although the Internet is a relatively new phenomenon, it is having a dramatic impact on life in the United Kingdom. In particular, e-commerce is growing rapidly and all commercial sectors are actively examining the opportunities and threats it brings.

Leisure activities in and around the home and commercial leisure

Commercial providers have enormous influence in home leisure pursuits. The nature of home-based activities and their enjoyment will be affected by factors such as housing conditions, availability of a garden and standard of living. Leisure time use will vary according to the home itself, home improvements, family interests and hobbies, and material possessions of the household, which may be leisure 'instruments' in themselves (television, computer) or may be time-saving appliances (dishwashers) which release members of the household from various tasks, so creating greater leisure time. Another often underrated factor pertaining to leisure at home is the keeping of pets. A dog, in particular, is often the main reason for regular walking and taking time away from the home.

> There are estimated to be more than 7 million cats and 6 million dogs in the UK and about 1 million budgerigars.

A large proportion of all leisure activities take place in the home. Activity in the home dominates life in all social groups, especially women, single parents, retirement and pre-retirement age groups, the professional classes and the unemployed. People's satisfaction with their homes relates to some extent to what they are able to do there and to how well the home accommodates their hobbies, equipment and activities.

The media and leisure in the home

The media probably have the most influential effect on leisure in the home. Media usage in the home includes not only television viewing but also radio, records, computers, discs, tapes, video, DVD, newspapers, books and magazines. The motivations for watching television are likely to include a mixture of needs: entertainment, information, education, social cohesion (e.g. watching television may become a 'family activity') or simply because there is, through either lack of opportunity or apathy, nothing else to do. Furthermore, television is cheap. Viewing appears to be the most frequent among children and the elderly, although overall there has been an increase in the time spent watching television.

The commercial sector's direct involvement with television includes:

- the commercial stations which make the programmes, advertise on them, and manufacture the television sets themselves
- the expansion of the DVD market
- the use of the television for active participation (i.e. video games)
- the use of the television as an information service, for example, Ceefax, Oracle and TeleText.

More sophisticated systems in development will provide information about leisure pursuits such as concerts, sporting events, theatre and entertainment, and even clubs and organizations specializing in particular activities or hobbies. Through them it will also be possible to book and pay for tickets, via the same system. Some have suggested that the growth of home-based leisure could be the embryo of an introverted society. Even twenty-five years ago in 1979, a Finnish social psychologist wrote 'The family is alive but not well!' (Tolkki-Nikkonen, 1979). With the Internet and new technologies as fixtures in the home, one wonders what he might say today.

And what of the radio? How much time spent in listening to the radio is purely for leisure, and in fact how much is actually home-based? Often the radio is on when we are doing the housework, cooking or driving to work. Listening to recorded music is another booming home-based leisure pursuit, often used as 'background noise'. Because they are portable, we can listen anywhere at any time, making the concept of leisure almost indefinable. The increasing versatility of the mobile phone adds further to a concept of lifestyle rather than leisure.

The written word, as with the radio, is by no means just a home-based pursuit. Publication of newspapers, magazines and books is primarily the prerogative of commercial organizations, although private, voluntary and government organizations publish technical and research material that can be read for pleasure. Direct commercial involvement can also be found with the organization of book clubs, while indirectly leisure behaviour may be influenced by the content of magazines, both in terms of their advertising and the values they promote.

The house, garden and leisure

The house and garden – for those who have them – can in themselves offer opportunities for leisure activity, depending on whether home improvement and gardening are viewed as leisure or as an unwelcome commitment. Whatever the motivation, undoubtedly, there is an increase in activity in this area, galvanized by hugely popular television home and garden 'makeover' programmes. Home improvements entail considerable expenditure on supplies, do-it-yourself tools and equipment. The popularity of the garden, for growing things or relaxing in, is reflected in the growth in the number of gardening books, programmes on television and garden centres, and in the associated increase in the range of products sold.

> Of men, 58 per cent like cooking, while only 50 per cent like DIY; more women than men like decorating; and 21 per cent of women like DIY (UK 2000 Time Use Survey).

The home can be used as a base for recreation and social activity, informal gatherings, parties, hobbies and other celebration activities. The commercial sector has all the necessary props. Guy Fawkes and bonfire night, 5 November, now overlaps with Halloween and children can choose from a huge range of goods for kitting out witches, ghosts and vampires. Adults don't have to wait for a celebration event; the increasing popularity of home drinking is indicated by the increase in supermarket alcohol sales, and the rise in the number of off-licences.

Home-based leisure in terms of playing traditional indoor games has been a declining market, but the developing 'technology' games and the demand for more updated board games stimulate commercial investment. The latest and most powerful addition to home-based leisure is the computer, with computer games and its uses as a new-found interest and hobby. 'Surfing the Net' is now commonplace and is potentially the most captivating and powerful and equally the most dangerously anti-social of all home leisure interests.

Household expenditure and leisure

Household expenditure since 1971 has increased steadily by an average of 2.8 per cent per year in real terms (ONS, 2003). Communications, spending abroad and recreation and culture, however, have risen more sharply, reflecting higher levels of disposable

Table 11.1 Household expenditure, United Kingdom

	INDICES (1971 = 100)			£BILLION
	1991	2001	2002	2003
Housing, water and fuel	138	152	154	118.4
Transport	181	242	251	98.3
Recreation and culture	283	545	570	79.5
Restaurants and hotels*	167	194	199	76.6
Food and non-alcoholic drink	117	137	138	60.8
Household goods and services	160	268	296	43.3
Clothing and footwear	187	340	371	37.8
Alcohol and tobacco	92	89	91	26.3
Communication	306	790	828	15.0
Health	182	175	179	10.1
Education	199	250	218	8.4
Miscellaneous	230	280	290	82.0
Less expenditure by foreign tourists, etc.	187	210	219	−14.3
Household expenditure abroad	298	669	715	24.6
All household expenditure	167	227	235	666.9

* Includes purchase of alcoholic drink.
Source: Office for National Statistics

Table 11.2 Household expenditure by family type

	2001/2002 − £ PER WEEK			
	COUPLES WITH DEPENDENT CHILDREN	COUPLES WITH NO CHILDREN	SINGLES WITH DEPENDENT CHILDREN	SINGLES WITH NO CHILDREN
Restaurant meals	12.70	14.70	5.00	7.00
Take-away meals	5.90	3.70	3.70	2.10
Holiday abroad	17.20	21.50	5.90	6.90
National Lottery and scratchcards	2.50	2.90	1.10	1.30
Newspapers	1.60	2.00	0.70	1.10
Cinema and theatre	1.70	1.30	0.90	1.10

Source: Office for National Statistics

income. The most dramatic rise in household consumer expenditure during the last quarter of the twentieth century was in the leisure sector (theatre, cinema, sports admissions, TV licences, holidays, gambling payments, but excluding alcoholic drink). In Table 11.1, when recreation and culture are added to restaurants and hotels, it can be seen that together they represent by far the highest level of household expenditure. It is of no surprise that household expenditure when analysed by socio-economic classification, shows that the managerial and professional occupations spend by far the highest amount on recreation and culture and restaurants and hotels, and indeed on household goods, clothing, education and health. Household expenditure by family type is shown in Table 11.2. Those who are single with dependent children have limited residual income to spend on leisure.

Half of all consumers' money spent on leisure outside the home, not including holidays and eating out, is on drinks at public houses.

Table 11.3 illustrates the growth in real consumer spending on leisure. Eating and drinking are the predominant expenditures followed by holidays and tourism.

Table 11.3 Growth in real consumer spending on leisure and value

CONSUMER SPENDING ON LEISURE	MARKET VALUE £BN	VOLUME OF SPENDING % CHANGE		
	2002	2002	2003	2004
Leisure in the home	48.03	6.4	4.0	4.3
Reading	7.01	0.7	2.5	0.0
Home entertainment	20.05	8.2	4.4	6.7
House and garden	13.59	6.0	4.6	3.5
Hobbies and pastimes	7.39	5.6	2.8	1.3
Leisure away from home	139.34	4.2	3.0	1.7
Eating out	36.78	2.1	1.5	1.1
Alcoholic drink	39.04	3.1	1.7	1.5
Eating and drinking	75.83	2.6	1.6	1.3
Local entertainment	4.92	4.6	1.6	0.6
Gambling	7.64	5.2	2.1	0.6
Active sport	9.14	9.5	3.7	2.5
Neighbourhood leisure	21.71	7.0	2.7	1.5
Sightseeing	0.98	−0.9	0.7	1.4
UK holiday accommodation	7.33	−0.7	3.0	1.8
Holidays overseas	29.70	6.8	6.1	2.1
Holidays and tourism	41.81	5.2	5.2	2.3
All leisure	*187.38*	*4.8*	*3.3*	*2.5*

Source: Adapted from *Leisure Management*, September 2003

In 2002, £17.6 billion was spent on pub drinks, over twice as much as was spent on the cinema, theatre, museums, galleries and bingo halls put together (Mintel, 2004).

The largest increases in spending are predicted to be in the home environment: home entertainment, house and garden. Away from the home, the greatest increases in expenditure will be in active sport, holidays overseas and holidays and tourism.

The away-from-home expenditure accounts for nearly three-quarters of leisure expenditure. However, the in-home leisure sector is growing faster at the current time.

Provision of social recreation away from the home can be divided up in a number of ways, for example visiting a pub and eating out, gambling, cinema going, 'clubbing', window shopping, leisure goods shopping, visiting attractions, weekend breaks and many more. Age is an important factor in the commercial market, with young people far more likely than older people to visit a night-club, disco, cinema or fast food restaurant. There is a steep decline with age for cinema going, with an even steeper drop for discos. Gender also leads to different levels of participation with men more likely to visit a pub and attend a sports event than women. Women, however, are more likely to visit a library, attend the theatre, or play bingo. The commercial leisure sector is a lucrative market with a major share going to large corporate commercial providers.

UK corporate commercial leisure providers

Granada	TV, motorway services, hotels, health clubs
Scottish & Newcastle	Breweries, pubs, holiday parks
Bass	Hotels, tenpin bowling, bookmakers
Whitbread	Restaurants, health clubs
Hilton	Hotels, bookmakers, health clubs
Rank	Gambling, publications, cinemas, restaurants, holidays
Pearson	Internet, publishing, theme parks
Virgin	Air, rail, shopping, music

Public houses and eating out

One institution which performs a unique and distinctive function in Britain is the public house. Going to a pub remains the most common free-time activity outside the home among adults. As a focal point for social activity, the selling of alcohol and food, and often staging live music events, the pub caters for a variety of demands. The breweries not only cater directly for leisure activity via their own outlets, but also give financial aid to private clubs in the form of grants and loans for the improvement or expansion of premises, usually in return for sales of their brewery's products.

The alcohol industry is dominated by the few major breweries, although consumer demand, focused through consumer organizations, has led to the growth of some small, independent breweries. In 1989 the Monopolies Commission examined a system which permitted six breweries to control the market. Breweries with over 2,000 pubs were forced to cut the brewery 'tie'. The smaller, unprofitable pubs were sold and the number of pubs decreased. Much has changed since that time with brewery sales and acquisitions and with government intervention with new laws governing the sale of alcohol.

The pub has had to meet competition and challenges on many fronts, including:

- take-home beers and wines from supermarkets and off-licences
- drink-driving laws
- health-conscious eating and drinking and
- for pubs in the south of England particularly, cheap purchases from across the Channel.

> Of all alcohol sold in the UK 40 per cent is for home drinking.

Leading pub groups at the end of 2003

Enterprise Inns PLC
Pubmaster Ltd
Punch Taverns PLC
Scottish & Newcastle PLC
Regional Brewers

The public house market has seen a growing diversification of products and segmentation of the market brought about by the growth of pub food. Food expands the market to a wider public and profit margins on food are greater than on drinks. Pub brands of catering such as Beefeater (Whitbread PLC) are highly attractive to the family market. Family pubs are increasingly characterized by the provision of indoor and outdoor play areas and children's soft play facilities so that families can enjoy meals out.

Pubs have had to adapt to these new markets, and are no longer the preserve of men, now having more women customers. Design, decor and image have been changed so that the buildings meet the expectations of women and families as well as men. Along with these changes has also come the nostalgia for the traditional pub, with real-ale brands providing a wider choice. Operators have to develop new brands and new ways of attracting customers in order to keep or expand market share. Indeed, a number are turning into 'gastro pubs', given the changing role of the public house in the community.

Pub food sales have risen steadily over recent years but net profit is still dominated by alcoholic drink, especially beer, though there have been rising sales of wine and bottled mixtures of alcohol and juices which has captured the female and young people's market.

The Department for Culture, Media and Sport (DCMS) is responsible for the laws relating to licensing in England and Wales. As part of the government's 1997 manifesto commitments, the Licensing Bill was introduced in Parliament in Autumn 2002. On 10 July, 2003, the Bill received Royal Assent and became the Licensing Act, 2003 modernizing the archaic licensing laws of England and Wales and providing for flexible pub licensing hours. Under the Act, a new 'personal licence qualification' is introduced to ensure licence holders are aware of the law and the wider social responsibilities attached to the sale of alcohol.

About 111,000 premises in England and Wales hold on-licences, allowing them to sell alcohol for consumption on or away from the premises. A further 45,000 premises hold off-licences, allowing them to sell alcohol for consumption only away from the premises. About 23,000 registered members' clubs hold a registration certificate, allowing them to supply alcohol to members and guests on their club premises.

Fast food chains emanating from the USA have a high market share of UK's eating out sector. Branded restaurants account for 24 per cent of market share. When the market leader, McDonald's, opened its restaurants in the 1970s, people drove some distance to the restaurants, but people wanted to eat at places convenient to them. McDonald's 1,116 outlets in the UK are now distributed in city centres, neighbourhoods, stations, airports and shopping centres. Demand for fast food outlets is strong, but they have been criticized for selling unhealthy foods and been the subject of protesters' actions as symbols of globalization and capitalism. Nonetheless, the M symbol is said to be the most recognized worldwide.

> McDonald's has about 29,000 franchisees worldwide in 120 countries and territories.

In the UK, there are over 50,000 enterprises in the licensed restaurant industry, including fast-food and take-away outlets. Total turnover in Great Britain in 2002 was £19.1 billion (ONS, 2003). Chinese, Indian, Italian, French, Greek and Thai restaurants are among the most popular restaurants. Fast-food restaurants, many of them franchised, specialize in selling burgers, chicken, pizza and a variety of other foods. Traditional fish and chip shops are another main provider of cooked take-away food. Sandwich bars are common in towns and cities, especially in areas with high concentrations of office workers.

Major fast-food companies

Burger King Corporation
City Centre Restaurants PLC
Compass Group PLC
McDonald's Corporation
Kentucky Fried Chicken
PizzaExpress PLC
Six Continents PLC
Wimpy International Ltd
Yum! Brands Incorporated

Betting and gambling

Another favourite area of social recreation is that of gambling. NOP/Mintel report that 70 per cent of all adults gamble, 73 per cent of men and 68 per cent of women. Gamblers are from all age groups, all social classes and whether in full-time work, part-time or not working. Some people with limited means gamble in the expectation, rarely achieved, of making a fortune. Gambling in the UK includes the National Lottery, amusement and gaming machines, the football pools, bingo, on- and off-course betting, casinos, and even Stock Exchange dealings on the outcome of the World Cup finals. Gambling turnover – consumer expenditure minus winnings – has increased over the past decade. Over the next few years, with the onset of satellite information service systems, technological advances and improved amenities, gambling is set to further expand, unless regulations intervene.

Gambling is a substantial part of the leisure industry and provides around 180,000 jobs, according to the Gaming Board of Great Britain. The Board, sponsored by the DCMS, is the regulatory body for casinos, bingo clubs, gaming machines and all local authority lotteries. As it stands, the law is complex and inflexible and has failed to keep pace with changes in public expectations and in technology. New legislation is being introduced to support the industry, but within regulatory objectives to keep gambling crime-free, to ensure players are not exploited and to protect children and vulnerable people from the dangers of gambling.

The main gambling outlets in the United Kingdom

The National Lottery
Casinos
Gaming machines
Horseracing
Greyhound racing
Bingo
Football pools

Hence, gambling spans a wide field, from gaming with 'serious money' in Monte Carlo to a 'flutter' on the Grand National. The launch of the National Lottery in the United Kingdom in November 1994 has witnessed an unprecedented increase in this form of gambling. The Family Expenditure Survey (FES) found that around 70 per cent of households participated. The traditional gambling sector has been hit hard by the National Lottery Saturday and mid-week draws and by the Lottery scratchcards. However, the industry has massive earning power and has adapted to the new environment. This is being helped by an easing of the Gaming Act sanctions, with less constraining rules and some elements of deregulation.

Licensed betting offices account for around 90 per cent of off-course betting revenues. Growth areas are betting by telephone, Internet and the television. The intro-

In 2003, there were approximately 3,600 bookmakers' permits and 8,800 betting office licences in force in Great Britain.

duction of the National Lottery led to the closure of a substantial number of betting offices, but numbers are growing again according to the DCMS. Three companies own half of the bookmakers: Ladbroke, Coral and William Hill. However, a number of changes to the law have enabled betting shops to keep customers and attract new ones, for example, up to two amusement machines can be installed and a daily draw which is televised to betting shops.

Horseracing accounts for 70 per cent of betting shops' turnover and is now second to football as the most televised sport. It is shown seven days a week on the Internet and terrestrial television channels. There are 59 racecourses in Britain staging about 7,000 races each year. Race meetings attracted 5.5 million attendances in 2002/3. Racing and breeding supports 60,000 jobs.

The National Greyhound Racing Club has 32 licensed stadia and there are 24 non-licensed stadia; 4 million attendances were recorded in 2002. The sport employs around 20,000 people including owners, trainers, stewards and operators.

The Football Pools industry has been in decline since the introduction of the National Lottery. However, there are still 2 million regular weekly players and there are signs of a renaissance. Littlewoods dominates the market with an 80 per cent share, and a door-to-door collector network of 13,000 agents. Prospects were buoyed by the lifting of Pools Betting Duty in April 2002. Pools companies have donated over £330 million to the community since the early 1990s through the Foundation for Sports and the Arts.

Following the report of the independent Gambling Review Body in July 2001 (led by Sir Alan Budd), the government published a White Paper in March 2002, *A Safe Bet for Success*. The draft Gambling Bill builds on this work. The key principles behind the Bill are:

- a crime-free gambling industry that can meet the challenges of the technological age
- regulation through a new Gambling Commission with wide-ranging powers
- an industry offering more choice for punters, and
- greater protection for children and vulnerable people.

In October 2004, the Gambling Bill was published which dramatically updates gambling laws in the UK. Critics are concerned with the implications for land-based gambling through large US investment in regional Las Vegas-style casinos, and the threat of increased addictive and underage gambling.

Publishing the Bill, the Secretary of State for Culture, Media and Sport, Tessa Jowell, said (see Useful websites):

> It is nearly 40 years since Parliament has had the opportunity to take a serious look at our gambling laws and it's not just attitudes that have changed since then. The technological revolution has touched all our lives and the gambling industry is no exception. Internet gambling and roulette machines in bookmakers are just two examples of where laws introduced nearly ten years before the first home computer hit the shelves are no longer able to protect children or vulnerable people properly.

National Lottery
- Started 19 November, 1994
- Ticket sales 1994–2003: £40 billion
- Total to good causes 1994–2003: £12 billion
- Ticket sales down from £5.5 to £4.6 billion per year
- Scratchcards down from £40 million peak to £10 million
- Average grant from £270K in 1995/6 to c.£50K in 2002

Casinos
- 123 casinos in 2003 in England, Scotland and Wales
- 23 casinos in London
- 12 million visits in 2002
- 12,000 staff employed
- £3.6 billion exchanged for gaming chips
- Roulette accounts for 60 per cent of sales
- 1400 casinos on the Internet; only a few in sterling

Gaming machines

- In Great Britain there are three types of authorized gaming machine: jackpot machines, higher-value cash amusement with prizes (AWP) machines, and lower-value coin or token AWP machines.
- 255,000 gaming machines sited in Great Britain: 221,000 are AWP machines; 25,000 club/jackpot; and 8,000 pinball machines
- Played in pubs and clubs, and amusement and seaside arcades
- 80,000 AWP machines in pubs
- Around 23,000 people employed directly
- About £10 billion wagered, about £9 billion paid out

Horseracing

- 59 racecourses in Britain
- 7,000 races each year
- 5.5 million (approx) attended race meetings 2002/3
- 3,600 bookmakers' permits
- 8,800 betting office licences in Great Britain
- 60,000 employed in racing and breeding
- £7.5 billion was bet (mostly off-course)

Greyhound racing

- 32 National Greyhound Racing Club stadia
- 24 non-licensed greyhound stadia
- 4 million attendances in 2002
- £2.2 billion was bet in 2002
- Represents 4 per cent of UK gambling market
- 20,000 people employed in the industry

Bingo

- 700 licensed and operating bingo clubs in Great Britain in 2003
- 90 million (approx) admissions
- 3 million people play regularly
- Bingo industry employs over 20,000 people
- National Bingo Game (NBG) first played in June 1986
- 500 licensed bingo clubs link up to National game every night
- Over £1 million a week in NBG prize money
- Total NBG prize money 1986–2003 c.£750 billion

Football pools

- Decline since introduction of the National Lottery
- Still 2 million regular weekly players
- £135 million staked in 2002
- £30 million winnings
- £330 million to community in the decade through Foundation for Sports and the Arts

Source for all figures: Department for Culture, Media and Sport, National Office for Statistics, and British Institute for Sport and Leisure

Casinos

There were 123 casinos in 2002, operated by sixteen companies in England, Scotland and Wales, of which 23 were in London. Casinos are not permitted in Northern Ireland. During 1995–6, nearly 11 million separate visits were made to them and this increased to 11.8 million by 2002, according to Mintel. Casinos employ 12,000 staff. The annual drop – the amount of money exchanged for gaming chips – was £3.6 billion. Roulette accounts for 60 per cent of sales. Over 70 per cent of all licensed casinos are owned by five public limited companies:

- Rank (31 Grosvenor casinos)
- Stakis (21)
- London Clubs International (7)
- Ladbroke (4) and
- Capital Corporation (2).

Changes in the law have benefited casinos through, for example, longer licensed drinking times, a shorter 'cooling off' period (the time between joining a club and being allowed to gamble) reduced from 48 hours to 24 hours and payment for chips with debit cards. However, the rise in the top rate of gaming duty from 33 per cent to 40 per cent in 1998, and the growth in competition, has led to a downturn for some operators such as London Clubs.

UK Casino Advice Online estimates that there were 1,400 casinos on the Internet at the end of 2003, but currently only a few play in pounds sterling.

The British Institute for Sport and Leisure (BISL) reports that the growth in unregulated on-line casinos could provide competition, but the introduction of technology-driven games inside casinos is proving popular. Deregulation of permitted areas, the lifting of advertising restrictions and immediate membership should lead to growth in this sector. New types of casino are being developed to capture market share, for example, with a purpose-built stage for live music and electronic roulette, targeted at the 18–40 age group. Gala plans to convert some bingo clubs into 'gaming sheds' offering casino and bingo under one roof.

Bingo and amusement machines

First developed in the sixteenth century in Italy as a game for the intelligentsia, bingo became regarded as an undemanding 'working class' pursuit. However, bingo requires levels of concentration that may strengthen the brain's neural pathways in older people, and can improve the accuracy and speed of short-term memory, according to findings presented at the British Psychological Society conference in 2002.

The Gaming Board reports that Great Britain had 688 licensed bingo clubs operating in 2002, and this has since risen to around 700. Bingo clubs have an estimated three million members with 89 million annual admissions, and employ 21,000 people. This is a formidable turnaround, bingo having been in decline. The game reaped the benefits of refurbishment, rationalization and the national game link-up. Bingo is also altering its 'older generation' image with new young players entering the game.

The trade association which represents the licensed bingo industry is the Bingo

Association. It is difficult to keep pace with the number of bingo units – clubs and premises – as the industry changes year by year and there is a range of providers including many small, independent companies. However, the industry is dominated by two operators, Gala Clubs and Mecca, who have nearly 80 per cent of the licensed units, Gala with nearly a half and Mecca nearly one-third. Other operators include Carlton Clubs, Top Ten Bingo, Walkers Group, County Properties and Development Ltd and other independents. Mecca and Gala report admissions of around 33 million in 2002, a turnover of £300 million and an average spend at nearly £9 per head.

Bingo was revolutionized by an amendment to the 1968 Gaming Act. The Gaming (Bingo) Act, 1985 permitted games of multiple bingo to be played, where pre-selected numbers were 'called' within the same time window in each of the participating clubs. Combined with high speed computer technology, this helped create The National Bingo Game (NBG). The NBG is the UK's second largest computer controlled game, the national lottery being the largest. It was first played in June 1986. Approximately 500 licensed bingo clubs link up every night of the year, except Christmas Day, to play, and over £1 million a week in prize money is distributed (see Useful websites).

As with other sections of the commercial entertainment industry, the National Lottery had an immediate effect, with 70 bingo clubs closing down in the 18 months following the introduction of the Lottery. However, advertising restrictions were lifted on bingo operators in 1997 and the major companies invested heavily to increase market share. Legislative changes in 2002 increased the number of prizes in multiple bingo and allowed clubs to mix Jackpots and AWP machines which have been the main income growth area. Bingo, offering a strong social context, appears to be the only gambling activity where women are more likely to play than men. While spending per head is up, and the average age of bingo players continues to drop, the bingo sector experienced falls in admissions between 2000 and 2003.

Amusement machines are a major source of income for pubs, clubs, bingo and others. They are the dominant, highly lucrative, products of the amusement sector – in terms of manufacturing, distributing and operating. Prize machines earn substantial sums of money for their owners and operators. BACTA, the trade association for the amusement sector, estimates that they can generate up to 30 per cent of public house income. There are about 220,000 prize amusement machines in various venues: 38 per cent in public houses, 17 per cent in inland arcades, 14 per cent in seaside arcades and 14 per cent in bingo clubs. They are also in places such as betting shops, restaurants, roadside service stations and leisure complexes.

There is also a range of other machines: skill machines, pinball machines and video games with an increasing variety of challenges. Skill machines with prizes, however, slumped in business when a £250 amusement licence duty was imposed in 1994. With the introduction of the National Lottery, followed soon after by the scratchcard Lottery, the amusement sector turnover reduced substantially. However, with so much money at stake, changes to the Gaming Act and deregulation, the sector is recovering. Changes to the law have included:

- increases in cash payouts
- amusement machines in betting shops
- increase in the number of machines on one site for casinos, bingo clubs and members' clubs.

New ways of winning back market share are also being developed. Video games, with advanced technologies, are being created which can compete with the home video market.

Tenpin bowling

Games of bowling balls against pins date back thousands of years. Modern tenpin bowling was developed in the United States during the nineteenth century. The first indoor centre in Britain opened in 1960. Tenpin bowling became popular in Great Britain during the 1960s, but declined during the 1970s. The 1980s witnessed a resurgence, especially as a recreational activity. The game received recognition by the International Olympic Committee and was included as a demonstration sport in the 1988 Seoul Olympics. Tenpin bowling is especially suited to people with disabilities and many centres have facilities available for disabled people and people with learning difficulties. The sport was included in the 1990 European Summer Special Olympics.

The World Tenpin Bowling Association is based in Kuala Lumpur, Malaysia. The British Tenpin Bowling Association (BTBA), founded in 1961, is the governing body responsible for the game in the United Kingdom. It was formed as a trade association for owners and operators of tenpin bowling centres in Great Britain. The first commercial bowling centre was opened in 1960 at Stamford Hill, North London. The National Association of Youth Bowling Clubs (for those aged 5 to 18) is also part of the BTBA and in 1984, the BTBA formed the Young Adults' Club to cater for the needs of participants aged between 17 and 23 years.

It is almost foolhardy to provide data on the numbers of bowling centres as they change every year and at times monthly. However, at the end of 2003, there were nearly 100 bowling centres, with over 2000 bowling lanes, in membership of the TBPA –Tenpin Bowling Proprietors Association of Great Britain, operating as Go Tenpin. This represents around half of the centres and includes the major chains. There were three major operators: Megabowl, AMF and Mitchells & Butler. Apart from a few other firms with a handful of sites, as shown in Table 11.4, the rest of the market is made up of single-site operators. Like the brewing industry, tenpin bowling is dominated in terms of market share by the major chains. However, it is not the number of centres, *per se*, but the number of lanes which dictate the position in the market, Megabowl having double the number of lanes compared to its nearest competitor, AMF.

The number of bowling centres more than halved between 1960 and 1973, but the image of bowling centres has changed radically as a result of substantial investment in refurbishment and new buildings. Improved design and advanced technology combined with improved bar and catering facilities have contributed to the increasing popularity.

Tenpin bowling centres are being developed as part of wider family entertainment centres with supporting features to encourage tenpin bowling as 'a good outing for the family', or 'an evening out', rather than a sport. Indeed, a good proportion of participants go as part of a friendship group. The development of social facilities is significant: bar and catering, amusement machines, snooker tables, American pool, laser adventure games, satellite television, soft play and at some centres, a crèche. The key target group is 15–35 year-olds, though children and senior citizens are also being attracted to fill off-peak sessions.

Table 11.4 Major bowling operators 2003

No.	Operator	Venues	Total no. of lanes
1	Megabowl	50	1,560
2	AMF	34	783
3	Mitchells and Butler	23	608
4	Bowlplex	12	214
5	Allied Leisure	9	174
6	Newbury Leisure Ltd	8	158
7	Namco	6	106
8	Keith Brown Properties	5	122
9	No. 10 Group	5	134
10	Leisurebox	3	40
11	David Lloyd Lanes	3	78
12	City Limits	3	82
13	Quattro Leisure	3	76

Source: Colin White in *Leisure Management*, Nov/Dec 2003

Tenpin bowling, then, is another leisure pursuit that has been transformed over the past decade, largely as a result of computer technology with visual scoring displays and through a change of image from the structured, dull facilities dominated by league and club events, to an activity that presents itself as a family-based pursuit in facilities that are bright and relaxing, with associated support services. Although the game itself has changed little over the years, innovative additions have been glow-in-the-dark coatings for lanes and balls, coupled with good sound systems for 'disco bowling' and bowling lane additions to assist children and people with disabilities. Popular centres attract over 1,000 people per day.

Cinema-going

In 1895, the Frenchman, Louis Lumière, invented the first successful portable motion camera, which led to the motion picture. The hundredth anniversary of the cinema was celebrated in 1997. In 1897, the moving picture was one of the earliest forms of packaged entertainment for the masses, the 1903 film *The Great Train Robbery* breaking new ground. Then came the talkies. During the 1930s, the 'Golden Age' of Hollywood produced the legendary *Wuthering Heights*, *Gone with the Wind* and *The Wizard of Oz*. Cinemas were built all over the world, one screen in one building, and this continued until the creation of the multiplex, and we are now moving into the era of the megaplex. Cinema-going is now classed within a commercial leisure category called the cinema exhibition market.

The peak audiences for cinema-going in the UK were in the years immediately after the Second World War. However, with the invention of television came a decrease in cinema ticket sales. Attendances fell dramatically from a

The UK British Board of Film Classification exists to classify films that can be shown to the public to reflect public decency and to protect children and young people.

Table 11.5 Attendances at cinemas in Great Britain, 1986–2003

	% AGED 15 AND OVER ATTENDING 'THESE DAYS'
1986/87	31
1996/97	54
1998/99	57
2000/01	55
2001/02	57
2002/03	61

Source: Adapted from TGI/BMRB International/Cinema Advertising Association

peak of 1,635 million in 1946 to 156.6 million in 1972 and then to an all time low of 54 million in 1984. Yet cinemas, like tenpin bowling and bingo, experienced an upturn in their fortunes, so much so that by 2003 cinema-going was more popular than it had been at any time since the slump in attendances decades before, with double the attendances of the 1980s with nearly two-thirds of the adult population going to the movies (as shown in Table 11.5).

There were an estimated 176 million cinema admissions in the United Kingdom in 2002, the second highest in the European Union after France, with 185 million admissions. In terms of rates per head of population, Ireland has the highest rate of admissions at 4.2 per head, compared with 2.6 in the UK and the highest level in the United States at 5.4 per head.

Young adults, people aged 15 to 24 years, are the most likely age group to go to the cinema. In 2002, 50 per cent of this age group reported that they went to the cinema once a month or more, compared with 17 per cent of those aged 35 years and over (ONS, 2004). There has also been a growth in the attendance by over a third of the 7 to 14 age group, a tenth accompanied by a grandparent.

The multiplex and megaplex cinemas

What brought about such a dramatic change? In a word, the multiplex: an attractive cinema environment, providing a choice of films. The cinema revival began in 1985 when AMC opened the United Kingdom's first multiplex at The Point in Milton Keynes with ten screens. The development of multiplex cinemas, with well designed comfortable surroundings, car parking, and computerized booking, and which offer choice of films, food and merchandise has contributed to maintaining and increasing admissions in the United Kingdom.

Although with the multiplex there has been a decline in the number of cinema sites, there has been a corresponding increase in the number of screens; this was brought about by the division of many of the existing cinemas into multi-screen units. However, the decline in the number of cinema sites has left many small towns without cinemas. This can cause problems in districts and new housing estates where there is insufficient population to support a multiplex cinema, particularly as new areas tend to have a high proportion of young people, an important cinema-going market sector.

The growth in multiplex cinemas is set to continue, though estimates vary as to the number of screens operators are likely to require. Some consider 12 to 16 screens an optimum size. Others see 6 to 8 screens as appropriate for town centre sites providing for a catchment population of at least 150,000 within a 20-minute drive time.

Megaplexes of around 20 to 30 screens need very large catchments and will overlap with other towns and cities and with other megaplexes. Hence, developers and planners need to consider proposals with extreme care to avoid flooding the market, leading to unsustainability.

Not only is the number of screens per site increasing, but cinema-going is developing into a night-out experience with bars, wine bars, 'cappuccino cafés', and merchandising: videos, CDs and amusement machines. However, they need substantial populations to draw on and could challenge other multiplexes for business. To build such structures requires large amounts of space and car parks. Location within leisure 'parks' adds to the attraction. Other facilities on the site at large complexes might include restaurants, tenpin bowling, health and fitness club, supermarket, children's play area, fast-food outlets and a petrol station.

Despite the growth of multiplexes, the United Kingdom is still under-screened compared to many other countries, with less than 40 screens per million people compared to 50 per million in Ireland, 77 per million in France and nearly 100 per million in the US. Annual visits per head are also lower, about 2.1 in the United Kingdom in 1996 compared to about 4.82 per head in the USA. The researchers Dodona forecast that 200 million admissions per year are sustainable between 2005 and 2010. It would appear that at present new multiplexes do not take much business away from existing cinemas, but create a new audience. Currently, as more multiplexes open, admission figures rise.

However, if operators open huge megacentres, then smaller units may stand little chance in the face of such dominating competition. Given the choice of different film centres within their catchments, customers will decide which to go to, not necessarily on the basis of which film is showing – they are likely to be showing the same films – but on other factors, such as accessibility, ambience, and ancillary attractions.

Cinema operators and new technologies

Over recent years, there have been many changes in the owners and operators in the cinema industry. Statistics relating to the operators, the number of sites and number of screens change year by year, primarily as a result of mergers and takeovers in ownership. Every major provider of cinema sites and screens in the UK currently has an expansion programme.

Currently, UGC Cinemas is Europe's leading cinema operator with over 90 sites in 2003 across six countries: United Kingdom, Ireland, France, Belgium, Spain, and Italy.

While cinema-going is a buoyant industry in Europe, 'Bollywood', the name given to the industry in India, dwarfs all others, boasting billion-strong audiences worldwide. India's film industry is the biggest in the world.

The growth of the large 3D format theatre network, dominated by IMAX, is fast outstripping the number of films available for exhibition, according to Euromax. The IMAX product is relatively new. It uses a completely different cinematic technology with a 15 perf/70mm film format and a film some ten times the size of a traditional 35mm movie. The films can be either in 2D or 3D. There are essentially three levels of product:

Leading UK cinema chains in 2004

Odeon Cinemas Ltd
UGC Cinemas Ltd
UCI (United Cinemas International)
Cine-UK Ltd
Vue (merger between SBC and Warner Village Cinemas)

- the large screen/large theatre format which normally seats 400–500 people
- the IMAX Dome which provides 360-degree projection and
- smaller, 80–100 seat, motion-based theatres which provide seat movement co-ordinated with the film (this is not the same as the smaller, capsule based simulators which can be found at theme parks and fairgrounds throughout the country).

The films for IMAX theatres are extremely costly to produce and there is a limited range of product available. The duration of the films is generally no more than forty minutes, and for the smaller, motion-based theatres from five to fifteen minutes.

The location of IMAX theatres tends to be in areas which either:

1 have a high throughput of people, for instance the IMAX at the Trocadero in London which has an annual passing footfall of 45 million people, half of whom are tourists, or

2 are part of a larger heritage or theme park attraction, such as the IMAX at Bradford at the National Museum of Photography, Film and Television.

Although cinema audiences have increased in the UK in recent times, only around 10 per cent cinema capacity is reached from Mondays to Thursdays. Another revolution, however – digital technology – provides an opportunity to increase usage and revenue in off-peak times. For example, it is now possible to screen sporting events and pop concerts and to hold business conferences linking up with other cities and countries. The 2003 Rugby World Cup was screened at Odeon UK in London, Cardiff, Leicester and in Scotland. Manchester United Football Club has its own theatre: the Red Cinema at the Lowry Centre.

Screen Digest predicts that there will be around 10,000 digital cinema screens worldwide by 2005; film reels will disappear in time and film data will be stored digitally and sent to cinemas by satellite, DVD or cable. This should lead to substantially reduced costs.

In terms of Leisure Management, multiplex cinemas have a relatively stable future for trainee managers in the commercial sector. They combine decades of cinema management and operational experience with the latest technology to provide leisure experiences sought by increasing numbers of people.

Theatre-going

Commercial leisure provision for entertainment and the arts outside the home covers a number of areas, although these can be divided into two basic categories:

- those which encourage active participation (e.g. ballrooms, discos, drama, music and dance schools) and
- those in which provision is generally geared towards audience and spectators.

This section deals primarily with the latter.

In the United Kingdom, commercial theatres are in large measure centred on London. According to Albemarle of London, in 2003, there were 54 theatres in London's West End with around 61,000 seats, of which 40 theatres with around 47,000 seats, were included in the category commercial West End theatres. Excluded in the calculation of commercial theatres were theatres such as the Barbican, Royal Opera House, Sadler's Wells and Shakespeare's Globe.

The largest commercial venues of over 2,000 seats

Apollo Victoria (2208 seats)
Dominion (2001 seats)
Drury Lane Theatre Royal (2237 seats)
London Apollo (3485 seats)
London Palladium (2298 seats)
Lyceum (2075 seats)

The largest West End owning and managing theatre companies in 2003 were:

- The Really Useful Group and Partners with 13 theatres and 15,713 seats, including the Adelphi, Apollo Shaftesbury, Cambridge, Drury Lane Theatre Royal, Garrick, and the London Palladium
- Clear Channel Entertainment with only 4 theatres but with 9,769 seats, including Apollo Victoria, Dominion,, Lyceum and London Apollo (formerly Hammersmith Apollo)
- Ambassadors Theatre Group with 11 theatres and 7,859 seats, including Albery, Comedy, Duke of York's, Phoenix, Piccadilly
- Cameron Mackintosh currently manages three theatres, The Prince Edward, The Prince of Wales and the Strand and will acquire further theatres from the two leading companies.

A number of large theatres not included in the commercial theatre sector include:

- Barbican (1162 seats) owned by the City Corporation
- London Coliseum (2356 seats) owned by English National Opera
- Old Vic (1067 seats) owned by the Old Vic Trust
- Royal Opera House (2100) owned by Royal Opera House Covent Garden
- Sadler's Wells (1500 seats) owned by Sadler's Wells Trust
- Shakespeare's Globe (1500 seats) owned by Shakespeare's Globe Trust.

Other smaller theatres are owned by the Arts Council, and include the Cottesloe,

Lyttelton and Olivier; other independents own the Aldwych, Criterion, Gielgud, Haymarket Theatre Royal, Open Air, Peacock, Playhouse, St Martins, Savoy, Shaftesbury, Vaudeville, and Victoria Palace.

Attending the cinema and theatre, going to popular and classical concerts, visiting art galleries or going to shows and festivals are all part of the audience and spectator activities provided by the commercial sector. Going to the theatre is not as popular as going to the cinema, and only a small percentage of the population attend the theatre, opera or ballet. Half of the professional theatres in Britain are owned or rented by commercial companies. Of these, nearly one-third are found in London; but West End theatres are finding it difficult to make a profit, owing to competition from subsidized national theatres and civic suburban theatres, and there is a declining number of commercial theatres in the provinces to accommodate touring plays and musicals. In addition, world events such as wars and terrorism affect the tourist market, particularly visitor numbers to the theatre and visitor attractions.

Children's indoor play centres

The idea of adventure play was pioneered by the Adventure Playground movement after the Second World War. The outdoor facilities were in inner-city areas and gave children adventure and fun, but they resembled junk yards (see Chapter 5). The same ideas are behind commercial children's indoor adventure play centres, but they are a relatively new sanitized version.

The needs of children and the family market which have stimulated demand are:

- indoor facilities when it is too cold or wet to play outside
- a safe place for young children
- healthy physical and adventurous activities and
- the social aspect of leisure and play activities.

These play centres go by many different names: Playworld, Adventure World, Pirates and so on. Different areas can be developed for different ages, such as soft play adventure for under-5s, and for 6–12s a large area with sufficient height for 'jungle gym' activities, on different levels, fitted out with slides, rope ladders, soft landings and ball pools. Lighting and sound effects can be included. The success of such centres will depend on many factors:

- the range of activities and equipment
- the setting and attractiveness of the play centre
- the location and accessibility for regular usage, particularly places such as town centres, and leisure centres, that are busy day and evening, all year round
- the catchment area and the market competition (not just from play centres but also other opportunities for children and families)
- operational management, pricing and customer service
- catering and social elements and party opportunities
- facilities and services for parents and adults accompanying children
- adjacent or nearby car parking.

The range of venues for children's play centres varies enormously. They can be found in leisure parks, shopping centres or where large numbers of children are likely to be attracted. However, they are also to be found in smaller towns, attached to leisure centres and also constructed in warehouses and converted barns and most recently at family eating out spots, supermarkets and pubs. Their long-term viability is yet to be determined. However, at present, they are proving to be attractive for young children and for groups for special treats, such as birthday parties.

Sport

Government policies towards sport, sport agencies, public services, facilities, and participation are covered in Chapter 17, Sport and recreation. Here, we briefly deal with some of the commercial elements.

Sport is an expanding market. More people are playing sport, more sports are being played and consumer spending on goods and services is likely to keep rising. Commercial providers are concerned in sport in a number of key areas, for example, in spectator sport, sports sponsorship and sports goods and equipment. However, the commercial sector is involved in the provision of facilities for participants in only a limited number of sports. Of the outdoor sports, only top class football, golf, tennis and water sports are provided in any great numbers, and in the case of golf and tennis, these are also provided by the public sector. The growth in golf, however, throughout many parts of the world, has largely been private-enterprise led. Of the indoor sports, snooker, tenpin bowling, ice skating, indoor tennis and, more recently, health and fitness clubs are being provided by commercial organizations, and the latter are covered in the section to follow.

> Soccer is still the most popular spectator sport in the United Kingdom.

Commercial enterprise tends to deal with only a few sports in terms of spectatorship. These sports, however, such as motor sports and horseracing, attract large numbers of spectators and huge television audiences. Association Football is still the most popular spectator sport in the United Kingdom (here 'spectator sport' refers to actual attendance, rather than watching via television: a leisure activity which is forecast to increase dramatically with digital TV). Soccer spectatorship has declined since the postwar years, when spectators amounted to 41 million attendances in the 1948/9 season dropping to 16.5 million by the end of the 1985/6 season in the English Football League matches. Since then, there has been a small increase in attendances. The reduction in the Premiership (the top league) attendances may be in part a result of disasters such as occurred at Hillsborough and the policy to turn the standing terraces into seated stands and, in part, the sharp rise in admission charges. Average gates at this top level are less than 30,000. Only Manchester United can sustain a 50,000-plus gate on average. No other clubs achieve anywhere near this. Arsenal, Liverpool and Newcastle United record the next highest admissions. However, football remains the most popular spectator sport on television, well ahead of cricket, rugby union, horseracing and motor racing, though with England's win in the 2003 Rugby World Cup final, the sport has witnessed a resurgence in interest.

Spectator sports in the UK, apart from some Premier League football, rugby and cricket internationals and events such as Wimbledon, are generally not lucrative in terms of receipts from attendance, although many popular indoor spectator sports such as indoor tennis, indoor show-jumping and boxing lend themselves to viewing by comparatively large audiences. There are, however, some indoor sports, snooker and darts in particular, which cannot accommodate large audiences on-site, but which become popular spectator sports through the medium of television, though coverage has declined in recent years. Indoor bowls is another sport which has gained popularity through television as has curling with Scottish Olympic success, but whether this will be sustained is unknown. While terrestrial television broadcasts may not cover the minority sports, cable and satellite stations have dedicated sports channels and these create interest in certain sports.

Hence, although there has been a decline in the traditional spectator sports, others have increased in following, many as a direct or indirect result of television coverage and commercial sponsorship. Tennis and golf are examples and ice hockey and basketball seem set to follow.

A substantial industry to supply leisure goods, clothing and equipment has developed.

Consumer sports expenditures

Sports services in 2003 (65 per cent of expenditure)	Sports goods (35 per cent of expenditure)
gambling (15.8 per cent)	clothing and footwear (20 per cent)
television	sports equipment (6.6 per cent)
radio	boats (4.9 per cent)
videos (11 per cent)	publications (3.5 per cent)
health and fitness (10.5 per cent)	
travel (6.3 per cent)	
spectator sports (5.2 per cent)	

Sport Industry Research Centre

Health and fitness centres

The fitness sector is diverse, fragmented and fast changing; it is provided by the public, voluntary and commercial sectors. It is an important part of the government's policy towards improved health so is included in Chapter 17, Sport, recreation and physical activity, which covers public-related provision. Here, we deal with some of the commercial aspects.

Health and fitness centres as we know them today have evolved over the past 40 years into a widespread sophisticated market leader. At the start of this modern fitness movement (there have been different physical training and keep fit movements in times past), sports centres and clubs included areas called 'weights rooms'; they were male dominated and involved body building as an important element. These developed into fitness areas or suites with machines as well as weights, and attracted larger numbers of men and women who wanted to get and keep trim and fit. To these areas were added small halls for aerobics, dance, yoga and activities that did not require equipment. With a move towards individual health and fitness, a burgeoning market sector grew in the private and public sectors with new kinds of equipment – resistance, cardio-vascular, treadmills – and these have led to highly sophisticated machinery, computerized and incorporating club members' personal workout information.

The commercial sector attracted a large share of the market. At the lower end of the market, there are clubs with basic fitness rooms and changing space. These are likely to go out of fashion. There are clubs with larger workout space, better equipment and some have a sauna, spa and pool. The growth is in the upper-end-of-the-market clubs, all with pools and with higher levels of luxury. In addition, there are health clubs at hotels, most of which are open to the public and run by the hotel or by outside contractors.

There are a reported 3.8 million private health and fitness club members in Britain, double the number of a decade ago. The rate of growth has slowed down since its peak in 2001, but is expected to continue to increase in number over the next few years (*The Times*, 8/1/04). Moreover, sports and leisure businesses, spawned by the fitness boom, are growing at a faster rate than ever before. In 2003, the number of keep fit, cycling, personal training and health clubs that were created increased by nearly 50 per cent from 2002 to 66,300 in 2003 (*The Times*, 31/3/04). It is a volatile industry, so numbers and statistics change almost month by month. In the autumn of 2003, there appeared to be about 20 leading private sector owners with membership numbers ranging from 20,000 to 340,000 and with numbers of sites ranging from 10 to 150, most of which were in the United Kingdom (Keynote and HC Management, 2003). At the top end of the scale, with memberships of around 300,000 and more were:

> Private fitness clubs grew from under 2,000 in the mid-1990s to nearly 3,000 in 2004.

- Cannons Group Ltd including the Harbour Club
- Whitbread PLC including David Lloyd and Marriot brands and
- Fitness First PLC.

Other major operators included Esporta PLC, Holmes Place PLC, Hilton Group PLC (LivingWell), De Vere Group PLC, LA Fitness PLC, Bannatyne Fitness Ltd, JJB Fitness Club, Next Generation Clubs and YMCA (England).

In a MORI survey in May 2003, people were asked what would motivate them to join a health club. Half said lower prices and one-third said a fitness regime to suit lifestyle and ability, a free trial and more information.

The nature of some clubs has been moving from physical fitness to health and well-being – wellness – and this shift is evolving still further. Two likely directions are into spas and holistic well-being. Advocates of the holistic approach argue that traditional medicine deals with the body, mind and spirit as separate entities. The holistic approach to health sees the need to treat all three together and to seek underlying causes and prevention of physical and health problems. On a larger scale, holistic principles embody a way of life.

It is not uncommon today to find private health companies with a range of services, providing not just physical activity, but also treatments and therapies, including acupuncture, Alexander techniques, aromatherapy, chiropractic, homeopathy, hypnotherapy, massage, meditation, osteopathy, reiki, reflexology, relaxation training, sports injury clinics, t'ai chi, yoga, Pilates and others. Such health centres, however, are not the majority. Rather, while providing a few of such services, the trend in the private sector is more towards the concept of 'wellness' and health spas, which have been extremely popular in parts of Europe for the last hundred years. The American 'wellness' market sector has also moved towards provision of health spas and holistic approaches. And the UK is likely to follow.

However, it is not only in the commercial sector that some health and fitness centres are moving to a holistic approach. The whole idea behind the government and National Lottery backing to the concept of Healthy Living Centres is to provide a range of opportunities that deal with the needs of 'the whole person'. Links with the National Health Service and Healthy Living Centres are discussed in Chapter 17.

Theme parks

Tourist attractions are covered in Chapter 14 on tourism. Here, brief mention is made of theme parks as distinct commercially developed projects.

Theme parks have become popular since the creation of Disneyland which resurrected the amusement park industry in 1955 in the United States. Their philosophy has been one of providing excellence, cleanliness, courtesy and safety. They create an atmosphere of fantasy, glamour, escapism, prestige and excitement. These parks have been successful in other countries such as Summerland in Tokyo, and Tivoli in Copenhagen.

Britain's first theme park was Thorpe Water Park at Chertsey, with a theme of maritime history. The predominant theme is water, with activities such as water skiing and tourist attractions such as *Bluebird* and Viking longships. Today, it boasts the first ten-looping rollercoaster. Its development encouraged the provision of other themed facilities elsewhere in the United Kingdom. However, many of the theme parks have not been resounding success stories. Britain's world-rated theme park is Alton Towers, in Staffordshire. It offers a combination of magnificent surroundings and heritage with fun and fantasy. Alton Towers has been transformed from a stately home and gardens into one of the finest in Europe.

Theme parks in the United Kingdom

Alton Towers, Alton, Staffordshire
Thorpe Park, Chertsey, Surrey
Chessington World of Adventures
Legoland, Windsor, Berkshire, an attraction aimed at younger people
Blackpool Pleasure Beach, for the traditional British holidaymaker
Pleasureland, Southport
Pleasure Beach, Great Yarmouth
Flamingo Land, North Yorkshire
New Pleasurewood Hills Leisure Park, Corton, Lowestoft, Suffolk
Oakwood Theme Park, Narberth, South Wales
Flambards Village Theme Park, Helston, Cornwall
Loudoun Castle Theme Park, Galston, Ayrshire
Sundown Children's Theme Park, Rampton, Nottinghamshire

Theme parks are a magnet for children and young people and, therefore, attractive for day trips and family outings. Theme parks take up large amounts of land so need to be located at distances from urban settings, requiring longer travel times than to local facilities. The large theme parks also attract over one million visitors a year, a heavy throughput of traffic and people; these require substantial infrastructure.

Free admission theme parks, Blackpool Pleasure Beach and Pleasureland, Southport, attract around 6.5 million and 2.1 million respectively. The highest admissions to paid admission theme parks are Legoland, Pleasure Beach Great Yarmouth and Flamingo Land (ONS, 2002).

The United Kingdom theme market is extremely competitive. Britain's history provides numerous ready-made themes. Britain has a day-trip tradition and it is densely populated. There must, however, be a limit to development. Moreover, some heritage attractions funded through the National Lottery Millennium Fund have faltered. The effects of the Single European Market and the opening of the Channel Tunnel on the theme park industry have yet to be fully determined. However, the opening of EuroDisney near Paris indicates the level of competition that the market in the United Kingdom is having to face.

Family entertainment centres and night-clubs

Family Entertainment Centres (FECs) represent a relatively new addition to existing leisure markets. They tend to provide technology-based activities which have evolved from the amusement arcades, but which appeal to a wider-based family market rather than exclusively adolescent males. The traditional amusement arcades were not attractive to the family market and had a somewhat 'sleazy' image. FECs created a new, attractive image. The first major company into the market was Sega, the Japanese computer games leader, when it opened a centre in the toy store, Hamleys, in London in 1992. Sega now has a number of United Kingdom venues with its flagship Sega World, described as an 'urban indoor electronic theme park', in the Trocadero Centre in London's West End. Namco opened its first centre in the Meadowhall shopping centre on the edge-of-town site in Sheffield, and its second in Soho in London targeted to the youth market. Allied Kunick's Smilin' Sam's entertainment centres focuses on the adult market with amusements, food and bars. Some bowling centres have refurbished their premises to accommodate the family entertainment concept.

A significant development influencing leisure habits is a move away from stand-alone facilities to integrated centres, offering a range of leisure activities to consumers and for providers, economies of scale in the form of central services and car parking. For example, in multi-leisure complexes with a synergy between the cinema, tenpin bowling and night-clubs, the activities expand the leisure experience, widen the base and add appeal to the 'night out' market. Of particular interest is that each activity has improved its products to meet new public expectations. Cinemas and tenpin bowling centres both suffered slumps in the recent past, but by improving facilities, re-development, re-packaging and image-making, they have re-built these former flagging leisure activities.

Night-clubs and discothèques

The movement towards a leisure-experience package – a night out – is also to be seen in the redevelopment of the conventional night club. The value to commercial opera-

> Clubbing is thought to be a sector with a £3 billion turnover.

tors of the night club/discothèque sector has continued to increase because of high demand and sustained high levels of admission. Admissions in Britain rose from 137 million in 1991 to 173 million in 1996, according to Mintel's 1996 Night-clubs and Discotheques report, and estimates of 250 million are forecast. Around two-thirds of expenditure is on drink and this has led to the negative images of clubbing. Drug-related deaths among teenagers led to the passing of a private members bill, the Public Entertainment (Drugs Misuse) Act, which contains powers to close a club immediately if it is considered to have a 'serious' drug problem. The night-club sector's trade body, the British Entertainment and Discothèque Association (BEDA), however, is campaigning to have introduced a nationwide register of door supervisors (formerly called bouncers). BEDA is also attempting to have Sunday dancing legalized. In night-clubs it is still illegal to dance on a Sunday night outside London: a law that dates back to 1780.

Like other sectors of the commercial leisure industry, night-club ownership has major players and a wide range of independents, some 1,800 of them. A recent innovation has been to have two clubs at the one venue, for example, one for under-25s and one for over-25s. Getting the mix of activities right for more discerning markets has seen leisure companies updating old concepts: finding new combinations and being innovative. Independently owned clubs are generally smaller than the major clubs and tend to be conventional in terms of disco nights. The major clubs need large regular throughputs and run a number of special events and promotions to increase business on quiet nights, that is, early in the week.

The rise in the number of young people drinking regularly, binge drinking, the risks to health and links to anti-social behaviour and crime, are estimated to cost the UK £20

> The NHS reports that it spends around £3 billion on alcohol-related admissions, about 150,000 each year.

billion a year. The government's alcohol strategy launched in March 2004 aims to tackle these problems as the industry has failed to do so. However, the problem is more complex than it might appear. One of the anomalies of this massive lucrative market is in the clash of cultures. On the one hand is the promotion of sales of alcohol, tobacco and fast foods and the encouragement to gamble as these make for profitable business for the industry and through taxes also for the exchequer. Yet on the other hand the profits from some of these activities are used for 'healthy living' projects. Some health clubs are owned by brewers; how does the ethos of healthy living and the drive for alcohol profits sit together when it comes to boardroom decisions about shareholder investments? The Licensing Act, 2003 makes it easier for pubs and clubs to stay open whatever hours they wish. One side of the debate believes that this will encourage alcohol abuse; the other side believes that it will help eliminate last-minute heavy drinking and the exit from pubs and clubs *en masse* leading to fights and crime.

Leisure Managers and other professionals need to identify ways in which leisure and recreation can help to alleviate some of the problems. Leisure education, in its widest sense, is one of the means of helping young people to make their own alternative choices which can meet their needs for excitement, fun and self-esteem.

Leisure parks

So far in this chapter, we have considered the influence of the commercial sector in the home environment and going out locally. There are many other commercial leisure interests. Hotels, holiday centres, travel and tourism are included in Chapter 14. Those health and fitness centres which are more akin to sport and physical fitness are included in Chapter 17.

We move on from here to cover the development of large-scale schemes such as 'leisure parks', a concept which needs explanation in that they have little to do with parks and the outdoors: they are the opposite.

Developers of leisure schemes take close account of demographic changes and trends in leisure behaviour. With an ageing population, allied to early retirement, a larger percentage of people will have more leisure time. Generally, for most households, there is also increasing disposable income and higher expectations. Leisure experiences in attractive, safe environments attract families, the older age groups and provide an alternative to home entertainment. However, different groups in the community have different demands; these are largely age-related and lead to a fragmented market. To cater for each separate market would be costly and less attractive to the family market. Multi-facility leisure schemes are increasingly being developed to attract a wide range of users within one complex.

In the 1990s interest from developers in the leisure park market has been stimulated by evidence of increasing numbers of cinema-goers, greater interest in tenpin bowling and bingo and the popularity of night-clubs and FECs. As a result, nearly all leisure parks designed during this time are anchored by multiplex cinemas which then become a catalyst for bingo, tenpin bowling, night-clubs, restaurants and family entertainment centres. At some leisure parks, sports facilities and health clubs have been part of the leisure mix.

Leisure parks have been defined as: 'A purpose-built development comprising at least two leisure occupiers and usually anchored by a multiplex cinema. To qualify, the park requires a prominent, visible frontage with adequate forecourt style customer car parking. They can be located out-of-town, in fringe locations or town centre sites'
(Estates Gazette UK)

or 'a purpose-built development with at least three units covering 30,000 sq ft or more of lettable floorspace, mainly comprised of leisure occupiers and usually, but not always, dedicated car parking'.

The classic marketing cycle of new schemes and products sees a fast rise, followed by a levelling out of production. Inevitably this is happening in the leisure park market. In 2003 only ten new parks were opened compared with 31 openings in both 2000 and 2001. Of significance also is the shift from the out-of-town leisure parks to half the new 2003 parks being developed in town centres. The trend towards town centre developments has in part been as a result of the government's planning guidance to enhance town centres whenever possible.

The top ten largest leisure parks in 2003
(excluding hybrid shopping and leisure schemes)

1 Star City, Birmingham
2 The Printworks, Manchester
3 The Mailbox, Birmingham
4 Junction 10 Leisure Park, Walsall
5 Broadway Plaza, Birmingham
6 Cross Point, Coventry
7 Gunwharf Quays, Portsmouth
8 Parrswood Leisure Park, Manchester
9 Fountain Park, Edinburgh
10 Skydome, Coventry.

FPD Savills and TW Research Associates

The four top owners and/or investment managers of UK leisure parks and schemes were: Xscape Properties, National Amusements, Morley Fund Management and Legal & General Investment Management. Like other products in commercial leisure, a few major players hold a significant share of the market. On the tenant side, the largest by numbers of units on leisure schemes are the fast food retailers.

The trend towards town centre schemes is likely to divide the market into in-town and out-of-town schemes. The latter will be targeted to the car-orientated, family market with cinemas, FECs, tenpin bowling and restaurants. With drink-driving laws and schemes dependent on alcohol sales, the town centre schemes are more likely to target the younger adult age group with night-clubs and discothèques.

The scale of leisure parks means that the impact of a development extends far beyond the boundaries of the local authority providing the planning permission. A strategic county-wide approach is therefore needed (see Key planning processes, p. 229, Chapter 12). The larger the scheme, the greater the impact on smaller towns in the catchment area of the leisure park.

Hence, local authorities faced with decisions on planning have to take into account a number of factors, including:

• the local development plan
• the effect on nearby town centres
• the consideration of alternative locations – the 'sequential test'
• the demand for the proposed development and
• accessibility by public transport.

The sequential test must demonstrate that all sites capable of accommodating the development have been examined in the following order of preference, as outlined in government planning guidance:

• town centre
• edge of the centre
• out of the centre and
• out of town.

There are well over 100 large-scale Leisure Parks in the United Kingdom, up to a third of which are Retail and Leisure Parks. There are also a number of hybrid schemes: commercial leisure schemes which do not fit into any pattern or definition of what constitutes a 'leisure park'. Some large shopping centres and malls have for the past two decades included leisure facilities, particularly multiplex cinemas. There are also large retail schemes with leisure facilities. There is therefore a distinction between a Leisure Park, a Retail and Leisure Park and a large shopping complex containing leisure facilities. In addition, there is a wide range of hybrid or one-off schemes.

Case study: Xscape centres

An example is schemes developed by Xscape Properties, by far the largest owner/investment manager in this area of commercial leisure at the time or writing. Milton Keynes in 1985 was the first town to develop a multiplex cinema in the United Kingdom. Xscape's first entertainment centre opened in Milton Keynes in July 2000 with a real snow indoor ski centre, multiplex cinema, shopping, bars and restaurants. Xscape's second centre opened in Castleford in October 2003 and houses a 175-metre long indoor snow slope, climbing walls, including an ice climbing wall, skate park, a 14-screen Cineworld cinema, tenpin bowling, an air park, shops, bars and restaurants.

Xscape schemes have been designed by architects FaulknerBrowns, well known for their design of international sports facilities such as Ponds Forge International Swimming Centre in Sheffield. The Castleford project is reported to have cost £56.5 million; and the next scheme is planned for Glasgow. At these capital costs, a high throughput of customers is needed at prices to make revenue surpluses and inroads into the capital expenditure. A one hour ski and snowboard lesson was set at £26 (adult) and £22 (junior) at peak times, and £20 and £17 for recreational skiing. Of interest to Leisure Managers is that despite prices at what the market can bear, the Milton Keynes scheme attracts around 6 million admissions a year. If the product and service provides the right experience then people will want to buy it.

Xscape Braehead in Scotland to be opened in 2006 will be alongside Braehead Shopping Centre Retail Park and Leisure facilities. It will combine an Odeon Multiplex Cinema, 20 lanes of bowling and anchored by a 170m real snow slope all under one roof.

Summary

The major difference between the commercial operator and the public or voluntary operator is the *raison d'être* of the business, the primary objective of the commercial operator being that of financial profit or adequate return on investment. Other sectors may make profits but are established and in being for other primary purposes.

Commercial providers of facilities, services and products for leisure consumption have by far the greatest influence on people's use of leisure time, compared to other providers. This is seen particularly in leisure in and around the home and in social recreation. The holiday and tourist industry is an expanding commercial market and the continuing rise in active recreation has expanded the leisure and sports goods markets. Sponsorship (covered in Chapter 20, Marketing) has made it possible to promote many sports and arts events and has helped to bring major sporting and entertainment attractions of the highest calibre into the homes of millions of people through television (see Chapter 22, Event management).

Commercial businesses have to make profits or in the end they go out of business. In order to achieve the best profits and returns on investment, management policies, approaches and techniques often differ from those used in the public sector, though the gap is closing. A Leisure Manager should recognize the differences and learn which approaches and techniques are best applied to specific situations. Many general management principles apply to all leisure provision, be it public, private or commercial. However, many specific differences will apply to different management situations and to meet different objectives. Leisure management is thus both general and specific.

Commercial leisure is a massive industry. It is limited, however, in what is likely to be provided through its market. Capital investment must produce an adequate return on investment and this therefore excludes many costly land-based resources such as parks and open spaces (apart from 'resort' attractions inland and on the coast) and community and social service elements. At a local level particularly, the need for co-ordination between the public, commercial and voluntary sectors is of immense importance. Such co-ordination should fall upon local government in general, and upon leisure professionals in particular. Local leisure plans, for example, need to take account of all resources and all providers.

Discussion points

1 The commercial, public and voluntary sectors often compete for the same markets and must attract customers/ clients or else fail. For example, similar leisure facilities/programmes are now being provided in the United Kingdom by each sector. What differences and what similarities are there between the commercial sector and the not-for-profit sectors ?

2 Facilities such as health and fitness, theatres, and indoor play centres could be provided by the commercial or public sector. What factors might influence the development by the commercial sector? What key elements will a commercial leisure developer or operator have to consider in deciding whether to invest in a new leisure facility of this nature?

Further reading

Mathiason, N. and Kochan, N. (2004), 'Fear and loathing of Las Vegas', and Hughes, D. (2004), 'Capital Complex on a loser Down Under', *The Observer*, 31 October

TW Research Associates and Lunson Mitchenall have produced reports on shopping and leisure, leisure parks and retail and leisure parks. Dodona Research is a research publishing and consulting firm specializing in the cinema industry.

Useful websites

Bingo: www.national-bingo.co.uk
Screen Digest research company: www.screendigest.com/about_us
BACTA: www.bacta.org.uk/bacta
Odeon: info@odeonuk.com
UGC: ugccinemas.co.uk
UCI: www.uci.co.uk/index
Vue: www.myvue.com/corporate/home

12

Planning for leisure and recreation

Introduction

The planner's dream is to provide the right facilities, in the best location, at the right time, for the people who need them and at an acceptable cost. Leisure planning must, therefore, be predicated on a base of knowledge of leisure and the needs of the community.

Planning is one of the most important processes involved in providing facilities for people in their leisure time. Leisure Managers and Town and Country planners need to work together with a range of other professionals to assist in providing the best possible outcomes for their communities.

This chapter is written from the perspective of a Leisure Manager. It is not a text for planners; rather it provides information about the planning system, the context in which planners work and raises issues that leisure practitioners need to be aware of. The context for planning involves legislation, government regulation, direction and guidance, public debate and consultation, the geography of an area, land use, planning obligations and the need for facilities and amenities to fit within community plans and cultural strategies.

From a purely planning perspective, a range of texts is recommended by the Royal Town Planning Institute (see Useful websites). For an excellent comprehensive text on policies and the wide issues involved in planning for leisure, read Tony Veal's *Leisure and Tourism Policy* (Veal, 2002).

Planning in historical context

Planning laws in the United Kingdom date back to 1909. The current system dates from the Town and Country Planning Act, 1947 and subsequent acts. The Town and

Country Planning Act, 1990 and the Planning and Compensation Act, 1991 brought about sweeping changes in the planning system. In terms of leisure and recreation in England and Wales, other Acts of Parliament have placed statutory responsibility upon local authorities to provide only allotments, libraries, youth facilities and Adult Education facilities. However, no recommendations have been made with regard to the scale of provision required to fulfil this statutory obligation. This, coupled with the 'permissive powers' that relate to other forms of leisure provision, have resulted in considerable variation in the range and scale of provision made by different local authorities. The political philosophies of councils have further exacerbated the situation, with traditional Labour councils generally perceiving provision for recreation, sport and the arts to have a greater social service orientation compared to traditional Conservative councils, but the differences have narrowed as a result of financial constraints on local government.

Historically, a paternalistic concern for the health and welfare of the community was the major influence on recreation planning. The standard response was the provision of facilities such as parks, playing fields and swimming pools, and these remain today primary areas for local authority provision and finance. Early planning policies appear to have been based on three philosophies or a combination of two or more: equitable distribution, expressed demand and social control.

Equitable distribution This policy sounds fair, but equity is not the same as equality: equal distribution of facilities does not necessarily provide either equal opportunity or equal participation. Often, the more affluent people are the most predominant users of public sector facilities, despite attempts to provide amenities in disadvantaged areas.

Expressed demand Planning policies based on the expressed demand of its residents are attractive to local politicians. The use of petitions, staging public meetings or having media-inspired campaigns can influence planning decisions, particularly when a council election is imminent. Pressure groups, however, tend to be represented by the more articulate, and their influence is far greater than the proportion of the electorate they represent. In contrast, those with perhaps the greatest leisure needs are unlikely to be heard without the advocacy of the professional leisure leaders.

Social control There is a strong and instinctive belief that the provision of sports and leisure opportunities will alleviate anti-social behaviour and other problems. This belief has been well established in the minds of local authority members and at central government level since the government White Papers, *Sport and Recreation* (DoE, 1975), *Policy for the Inner Cities* (DoE, 1977) and the *Report of the Scarman Inquiry* (Lord Scarman, 1981). Local authorities, agencies and researchers are being asked by the government to provide robust evidence as to leisure's contribution to health, crime reduction and social cohesion.

Planning has always been concerned, albeit often peripherally, with the provision of facilities for recreation. The evolution of the planning movement was closely associated with the nineteenth-century fight for the retention of open spaces and commons which were threatened by unplanned urban development. The movement has evolved from a concern for public health, education and moral standards to problems of inner cities and countryside recreation and conservation. Since the Public Health Act, 1848, which authorized local authorities to provide public walks and pleasure grounds, successive Acts of Parliament were formulated to meet changing demands. These included:

- Physical Training and Recreation Act, 1937
- National Parks and Access to the Countryside Act, 1949
- Countryside Act, 1968.

In this evolution, the planner's role has been strengthened by the profession's wide powers over the control of land use. Leisure planning as a discipline in its own right is not a new phenomenon. Indeed, leisure planning was to the forefront in the planning of the Garden Cities by Ebenezer Howard at the turn of the last century; he also recognized the economic and social benefits associated with the dual use of school facilities. The first of many recreational standards of provision was established by the National Playing Fields Association in 1925.

Planning is not a static process, but a dynamic and changing one. Town and Country planners need to work with all the disciplines involved in creating leisure amenities and opportunities for people in neighbourhoods, villages, towns, cities and in the countryside. Planners themselves are only part of the planning process. They do not directly acquire and manage land and amenities. They identify locations for facilities according to acceptable planning principles. They seek to minimize conflicts of interest, traffic, noise, pollution and congestion. Planners help to make towns functional, attractive and healthy places; they also have to safeguard public interest and help to conserve (and foster good use of) the countryside. Gold (1981) defines recreation planning as:

> a process that relates people's leisure time to space. It is both art and science, using the methods of many disciplines ... into developing alternatives for using leisure time, space, energy and money to accommodate human needs. The process results in plans, studies and information that condition the public policy ... to provide leisure opportunity.

The social dimension of leisure planning emphasizes the difference between it and general planning. Leisure facilities, outside the home, in comparison to housing, retail outlets, roads, and so on, are non-essential facilities. Assessing the demand for a particular leisure amenity is therefore a complex process, since there is a range of competing attractions for a person's leisure time. This is where leisure professionals can help.

The Leisure Manager should be involved in the planning process at the earliest stage to assist in assessing need and demand, identifying gaps in provision and in proposing appropriate services and facilities. Unfortunately, however, there are too many examples of poor planning. The most common failure is that leisure facilities are often placed on land which is owned by the local authority, but which is not in an appropriate location. In such circumstances, they are unlikely to achieve optimum levels of usage and hence require increased levels of subsidy. Community built facilities located on the periphery of centres of population or away from main transportation routes or alongside physical barriers, such as rivers, or difficult road systems, suffer from poor access and inevitably result in a restricted catchment.

The role of government in planning

Planning systems regulate development and land use and contribute to the government's strategy for sustainable development in towns, cities and the countryside. Planning is part of the remit of the Office of the Deputy Prime Minister (ODPM). In England there are just over 400 planning authorities including county councils, district councils, unitary authorities and National Park authorities.

There are several tiers in the planning system: national, regional, county and district. Regional Planning Bodies prepare regional planning guidance (ultimately, it is issued by the Secretary of State). County Councils develop Structure Plans and District Councils develop Local Plans. In December 2002 the Planning and Compulsory Purchase Bill was introduced aiming to simplify the system and make it fairer and faster to speed up the process. The Planning and Compulsory Purchase Act, 2004 received royal assent in May 2004. The first Commencement Order brought a number of sections of the new Act into force which amends and adds to the Town and Country Planning Act, 1990. The changes are substantial. Out go:

- Regional Planning Guidance
- Structure Plans
- Local Plans
- Unitary Development Plans
- Minerals Plans and
- Waste Plans.

In come:

- Regional Spatial Strategies and
- Local Development Documents (LDD.)

However, the following guidance is given:

It will not be possible to take any of the formal steps leading to adoption of LDDs until commencement of the relevant provisions of the Act. In the meantime, it will be necessary to continue to rely on development plans that have been adopted or approved before commencement ... whatever constitutes the development plan in an area will retain development plan status ... for three years from commencement of the new Act.

Issues in Wales are covered in *Planning Policy Wales* published in March 2002; in November 2002 the consultation paper 'Planning: Delivering for Wales' was produced which involves the Welsh Assembly and the 25 local planning authorities. In Scotland there are 33 planning authorities. Legislation is contained in the Town and Country Planning (Scotland) Act, 1997. Scottish Planning National Planning Policy Guidelines statements of Scottish Executive policy are provided on nationally important land use. The *Review of Strategic Planning Conclusions and Next Steps* was published in June 2002. In Northern Ireland a consultation paper in February 2002 'Modernising Planning Processes' presented a wide range of proposals for improving the planning system in Northern Ireland.

The town and country planning system aims to ensure that development occurs in the right place and that inappropriate development is prevented. The system helps to plan for homes, schools, factories, roads, etc. and in doing so protects the natural and man-made environment and ensures that planning decisions do not damage the environment for future generations.

A number of factors have been brought to bear on local authorities in recent times including:

- the National Lottery funding new facilities
- Best Value legislation
- revision of policy planning guidelines and
- the instruction to local authorities to prepare Local Cultural Strategies.

The word 'culture' encompassing leisure is of significance in that only relatively recently was the concept of leisure itself accepted as the umbrella term.

Leisure professionals need to be aware of key planning processes:

1 Statutory Plans
2 Planning Policy Guidance
3 Planning Obligations
4 Development Plans and Development Control
5 Planning Inspectorate
6 Environmental Impact Assessments
7 Regeneration and Sustainable Communities
8 Local Leisure Strategies.

Key planning processes

Statutory plans

The planning system is referred to as 'plan-led' because decisions are taken in the context of plans drawn up by local councils in consultation with local communities and other organizations.

Planners have a legal duty to conform to statutory planning regulations. In parallel, they have to try to meet local needs. The views of local councillors may well conflict with the planner's statutory role.

There are different kinds of local authority plans. Upper-tier local authorities such as county councils produce 'structure plans'; lower-tier local authorities such as district councils produce 'local plans' with more detailed and site-specific information.

Structure plans set broad targets for development of housing, industry and transport in relation to predicted changes in the population and the economy of the area. For leisure, structure plans identify strategic land use policies for major initiatives, such as community forests, and projects affecting large areas or populations.

District Plans or Local Plans designate the approved uses of different sites within the local area. Local Plans need to address local needs for leisure and recreation. To do this, deficiencies have to be identified, sites found and policies adopted to balance the requirements of landowners, developers and residents. Local Plans tend to deal with open space allocations and they tend to be site specific. One of the problems for local councils is that a structure plan may demand allocations for industry and housing, thereby utilizing space for local councils' leisure plans.

Unitary development plans in London Boroughs, Metropolitan Districts and Unitary Authorities are formed by combining structure plans and district plans.

Whilst it is the statutory duty of County and District Councils to produce structure and local plans, the borough or district leisure strategies are discretionary. However, the most effective local authorities incorporate their leisure strategies in their local plans. The new Local Cultural Strategies (see p. 234) will now be taken into account in the preparation of the local plans.

Planning Policy Guidance

National policy is set out in Planning Policy Guidance Notes (PPGs) which apply in different aspects of planning. These form the basis for policies contained in local development plans which each local planning authority must produce for its area. In 2004, there were 25 Policy Planning Guidance Notes, most of which have implications for leisure and some of which are significant to leisure planning (for details, see Useful websites):

PPG 1: General policy and principles
PPG 2: Green belts
PPG 6: Town centres and retail development
PPG 7: Countryside
PPG 9: Nature conservation
PPG 12: Development plans
PPG 13: Transport
PPG 15: Planning and the historic environment
PPG 16: Archaeology and planning
PPG 17: Planning for open space, sport and recreation
PPG 21: Tourism.

Planning Policy Guidance (PPG) 17: *Planning for open space, sport and recreation*, is the guidance which has been of greatest interest to leisure, sport and recreation professionals. It was first published in 1991. The government's main planning objectives were to promote sustainable patterns of development, social inclusion and urban renaissance; local authorities were expected to adopt a strategic approach to the provision of new facilities and to plan positively for their effective maintenance. The government expects all local authorities to carry out assessments of needs, audits of existing facilities and to adopt local standards for provision. The government believes that open space standards are best set locally and that local standards should include quantitative elements, a qualitative component and accessibility. These standards should be included in development plans. Local authorities should:

- assess local needs
- identify deficiencies
- encourage the development of suitable sites for additional sport and recreation and open space provision
- ensure that provision is co-ordinated with other development and land use
- protect open space with recreational or amenity value.

Of concern is that the National Playing Fields Association Six Acre Standard (see Assessment of demand, p. 238) is not specifically mentioned in PPG 17 and no funds are available from central government to enable local authorities to carry out assessments of need, undertake audits of existing facilities and develop their own local standards. There is also a lack of guidance on measures to be used, pending the adoption of local standards.

The protection of open space and sports facilities is prominent in the Guidance. Their protection however should be based on 'a robust assessment of need and on locally derived standards of provision'. Similar principles would also apply to the retention of recreational buildings. The potential to exchange land was possible provided such exchange was equivalent in terms of size, quality, accessibility, usefulness and attractiveness. The government was 'firmly committed' to protecting playing fields used by schools or by the wider community. This commitment has been challenged by many agencies, especially by the National Playing Fields Association (NPFA).

PPG 17 also provides guidance on a number of other issues: allotments, indoor sport, dual use, maintenance of facilities, rights of way, Green Belts, Agenda 21 implications and commercial providers as partners in the development of sport and recreation facilities.

The loss of playing fields and open spaces

In August 1996, Article 10 of The Town and Country Planning (General Development Procedure) Order, 1995 was amended to require a local planning authority to consult Sport England on any application for planning permission for development that:

(i)   is likely to prejudice the use, or lead to the loss of use, of land being used as a playing field; or

(ii)   is on land which has been:
        used as a playing field at any time in the five years before the making of the relevant application and which remains undeveloped; or
        allocated for use as a playing field in a development plan or in proposals for such a plan or its alteration or replacement; or

(iii)   involves the replacement of the grass surface of a playing pitch on a playing field with an artificial, man-made or composite surface.

When consulted on an application for planning permission, Sport England considers the proposals in the context of the 1997 A Sporting Future for the Playing Fields of England (ESC, 1997). The Town and Country Planning (Playing Fields) (England) Direction, 1998 requires that before any local planning authority in England proposes to grant planning permission for the development of a playing field against the advice of Sport England, they must consult the Secretary of State.

In its recent campaigning, the National Playing Fields Association has drawn attention to the crisis facing the nation because of the loss of playing fields, which are being sold for alternative development.

> Very little of the recreational land bank in the United Kingdom is protected through charity; an approach strongly advocated by the Association. The campaign to protect threatened recreational land is not helped when playing fields are declared surplus to the requirements of local education authorities or when facilities become concentrated in fewer, and sometimes less accessible, locations like the urban fringe. To safeguard recreational land through the planning system, local authorities should adopt policies that allow for disposal only in the most exceptional circumstances.
>
> NPFA

Green Belts are areas of land that are intended to be left open and protected from development to control the unrestricted sprawl of large built-up areas, prevent towns from merging and preserving the countryside. In PPG 2 Green Belts, one of the objectives for the use of land in Green Belts is 'to provide opportunities for outdoor sport and outdoor recreation near urban areas'; however, the construction of new buildings inside a Green Belt is inappropriate unless it is for one of a number of specified purposes including 'essential facilities for outdoor sport and outdoor recreation'. Examples of such facilities include small changing rooms or unobtrusive spectator accommodation for outdoor sport.

Planning obligations

There has been much debate over the proposed reform of the planning system and whether planning obligations should be replaced by a tariff-based approach (see Useful websites). Currently, local authorities may enter into planning obligations, under Section 106 of the Town and Country Planning Act, 1990, 'to secure the provision of public open space and sporting, recreational, social, educational or other community facilities as part of larger mixed developments'.

Planning obligation is the process whereby planning permission may be granted provided certain obligations are fulfilled. *Planning Obligations for Sport and Recreation – A Guide for Negotiation and Action* sets out ways in which councils can use the powerful tool of planning obligations (formerly referred to as planning gain) to improve the provision of sport and recreation facilities by agreements with developers, planning applicants and landowners.

Sport England encourages local authorities to use planning obligations to benefit sport and recreation in addition to locally developed district sport and recreation strategies and development plans. Developers can help when recreational land or open space is lost through development. They can provide facilities both on and off site and councils can demand a contribution to nearby sports and recreational open space or community provision. Thus, planning obligations give councils another means of securing facilities for the community.

Department of the Environment (now with the ODPM) Circular No. 1/97 'Planning Obligations' states that among other factors the Secretary of State's policy requires planning obligations to be sought only where they meet the following tests by being:

(i)   necessary
(ii)   relevant to planning
(iii)   directly related to the proposed development
(iv)   fairly and reasonably related in scale and kind to the proposed development
(v)   reasonable in all other respects.

Development plans and sustainability

Development Plans, explained in PPG 12, shape land use and provide a framework for consistent decision making. They set out the policies and proposals for the development of use of land over a period of ten years. Development Plans provide a statement of the types of development which would and which would not be acceptable. They must have regard to national policies and regional guidance. Members of the public have a number of opportunities to comment on the proposed development plan before it is adopted.

Local planning authorities, usually local councils, take about 98 per cent of all planning decisions. However, Local Planning teams in the regional government offices become involved in scrutinizing draft development plans and also have a Development Control function, the process for regulating the development of land. The *Official Yearbook of the United Kingdom, 2004* reported that in 2002/3 district planning authorities in England received 634,000 applications for permission, granting 86 per cent of applications. Scotland received 47,600 applications and granted permission to 94 per cent of these. If planning permission is refused or is granted with conditions attached or an application is not determined within eight weeks, the applicant has a right of appeal to the Secretary of State, the Welsh Assembly or Scottish ministers.

The Planning Inspectorate serves the ODPM in England and the National Assembly for Wales on appeals and other casework. In 2002/3 over 15,000 planning appeal cases were determined. The Inspectorate's main work is processing of planning and enforcement appeals and holding inquiries into local development plans. Planning appeals are made in England to the Secretary of State. Under the Town and Country Planning Act, 1990, almost all appeals can be decided by planning inspectors. These are called 'transferred appeals', the decision being transferred from the Secretary of State to the Planning Inspectorate.

The Planning Portal – the first port of call – offers a range of services and guidance on the planning system advising on planning permission, on-line planning applications, appeals and how the planning system works. There is a wide range of other planning casework including:

- listed buildings where English Heritage is the statutory adviser
- Conservation Areas
- Tree Preservation Orders and
- Compulsory Purchase Orders.

Environmental Impact Assessment (EIA) is an important technique for ensuring the likely effects of new development are fully understood and taken into account before the development is allowed to go ahead. It generally falls to Local Planning Authorities to consider whether a proposed development requires EIA. Proposals

233

normally fall into two broad categories: Schedule 1 and Schedule 2 developments. Schedule 1 developments such as railways, motorways, airports, inland waterways, oil refineries and so on always require EIA. Schedule 2 developments include a wider range of developments which may or may not require EIA; leisure and tourism fall into this category.

In the autumn of 2002 the largest ever regeneration conference was held in England: the Urban Summit. The Summit aimed to promote commitment to urban regeneration and identify progress made on the 2000 Government White Paper on urban policy *Our Towns and Cities: The Future – Delivering an Urban Renaissance*. The Summit lent support to the Sustainable Communities Plan.

Regeneration policies enhance economic and social development through part-nership between the public and private sectors. Run-down areas in the United Kingdom benefit from European Union Structural Funds which assist in a variety of projects including leisure and recreation. The UK government initiatives include Sure Start, Health Action Zones, Crime Reduction Partnerships and the work of the Social Exclusion Unit. The most innovative community regeneration schemes can be given the Sustainable Communities Award.

Central to the work of the ODPM is the government's commitment to sustainable communities. The Communities Plan (*Sustainable Communities: Building for the Future*) was launched on 5 February, 2003. The Plan sets out a long-term programme for deliv-ering sustainable communities in urban and rural areas. The Plan (or the programme, that is, proposals) at a cost of £22 billion includes major reforms, modernizing and speeding up the planning system. Housing shortages in the South-East of England and low demand in the North and the Midlands are to be tackled. The Plan's themes include protecting the countryside and in the urban context improving the local environment with cleaner streets, improved parks and better public spaces. Key funding initiatives include investing £5 billion to regenerate deprived areas and an extra £201 million to improve parks and public spaces.

Local Cultural Strategies

There are social, health, community, economic and environmental benefits in devel-oping opportunities for and participation in cultural activities. *Local Cultural Strat-egies: Draft Guidance for Local Authorities in England* (DCMS, 1999) was published in June 1999 by the Department for Culture, Media and Sport in partnership with the Local Government Association (LGA) and the Chief Culture and Leisure Officers' Association (CCLOA). Following pilot projects in fourteen local authorities, the final guidance, *Creating Opportunities: Guidance for Local Authorities in England on Local Cultural Strategies* (DCMS, 2000), was published in December 2000.

Local authorities are being encouraged to provide opportunity to all people in their community to engage in cultural activities and for the strategy to support social and economic regeneration, lifelong learning, environmental sustainability and the development of healthy communities. However, the concept of culture, generally considered as activities pertaining to the arts, is difficult to communicate to the wider sports and leisure audience. The DCMS is at pains to stress the all-embracing nature of culture and emphasizes that culture has both a value dimension and a material dimension.

The value dimension incorporates for example:

- relationships
- shared memories, experiences and identity
- diverse cultural, religious and historic backgrounds
- standards
- what we consider valuable to pass on to future generations.

The material dimension includes for example:

- the performing and visual arts, craft and fashion
- media, film, television, video and language
- museums, artifacts, archives and design
- libraries, literature, writing and publishing
- the built heritage, architecture, landscape and archaeology
- sports events, facilities and development
- parks, open spaces, wildlife habitats, water environment and countryside recreation
- children's play, playgrounds and play activities
- tourism, festivals and attractions
- informal leisure pursuits.

The Guidance sets out underpinning principles. Local Cultural Strategies should:

- be guided by a vision
- promote the cultural well-being of the area
- meet needs, demands and aspirations
- ensure fair access for all
- develop a cross-departmental and inter-agency approach
- take a holistic rather than a service viewpoint
- have clear links with other national, regional and local strategies and plans
- ensure meaningful active consultation
- take account of the wider central and regional government context
- contribute to the government's key objectives.

The LCS should be viewed as overarching, focusing on strategic choices, priorities and forward planning and ensuring that the strategy document contains an Action Plan.

The wider context being referred to includes: central government, Regional Development Agencies and Cultural Consortiums, government-sponsored agencies and their regional offices, Regional Arts Boards, Regional Offices of Sport England, Regional Tourist Boards, Area Museum Services, English Heritage, Countryside Agency, English Nature, Environment Agency and others.

The government's key objectives include: sustainable growth and employment, promoting fairness and opportunity and modernizing public services, including the cross-cutting agendas of: public health, community safety, social inclusion, environmental sustainability, regeneration and lifelong learning. Developing a Local Cultural Strategy is complex and takes time. The Guidance document illustrates a 'Seven-stage strategy development process' (Figure 12.1) taking at least a year to complete but no

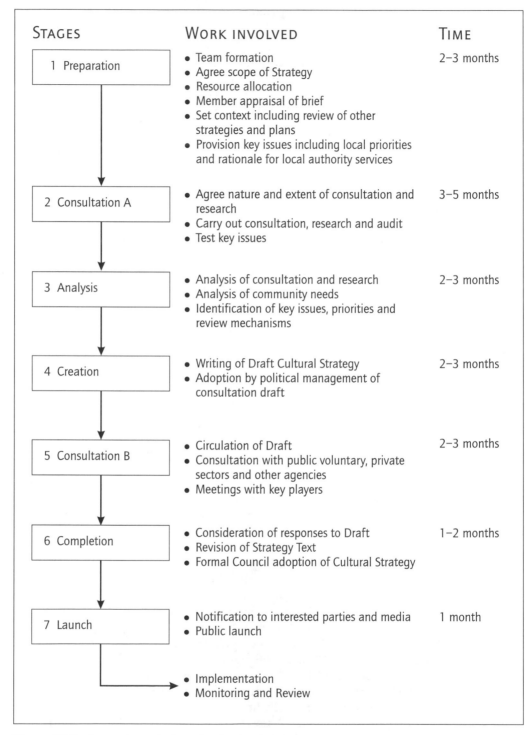

Figure 12.1 Seven-stage strategy development process

one model will suit all authorities. Different local authorities have designed different models, much depending on whether the strategy is for a district, city, borough, county or region.

The LCS Guidance sets out two main approaches to developing the strategy:

- service specific approach and
- the thematic approach.

The service-activity approach is the more traditional and more easily understood approach: culture consists of a number of activities such as arts, sports, tourism and so on. A strategy based around the services therefore may appear to make common sense.

Local authorities can decide which approach to adopt. However, the Guidance states, 'Given the inclusive nature of an LCS, the need to foster linkages and partnerships and the need to advocate the contribution of cultural activities to the wider community agenda, the thematic approach is favoured.'

For traditionalists the thematic approach loses the appreciation that activities – sport, music, dance – are indulged in and are satisfying in their own right; people play the guitar or play sport for the fun of it, not because it is good for social inclusion. Moreover, trying to explain to the local soccer team that they are part of the cultural strategy is challenging to say the least. Yet, the thematic approach takes in the wider, policy-based, inclusive picture; it is more complex and asks more questions. The thematic approach promotes partnership, encourages social inclusion, cultural diversity, lifelong learning, and supports healthy communities, economic regeneration and environmental sustainability. Moreover, it addresses the government's agenda for culture, education, the environment, health, law and order, planning, social services and community initiatives.

The LCS Guidance is in two sections – Section A: Guidance, and Section B: General Advice.

Section A: Guidance

Scope: reflect the local community, local history and geographical identity.

Aims: to promote the cultural well-being of the area.

Benefits which the strategy should seek to achieve.

Principles which should underpin Local Cultural Strategies.

Context: take into account national and regional context.

Best Value: linked to Local Cultural Strategies.

Community strategies: Local Government Act, 2000 requires local authorities to prepare a community strategy. Need to be linked with and inform the LCS.

Other government initiatives: be aware of their development to inform the LCS.

Regional Cultural Consortiums: develop a Regional Cultural Strategy.

Links with other plans and strategies: essential to link LCS with the local authority's (e.g. Local Development Plan) and partner agencies' strategies.

> ### Section B: General Advice
>
> Practical help to authorities developing their own Local Cultural Strategies based on good management practice. The section discusses the process, content and monitoring and review of local cultural strategies.
>
> Process: the guidance details the seven stages of strategy development, from preparation to launch.
>
> Monitoring should be in place to ensure that the Strategy remains on course.
>
> Content: this section gives proposals for the overall structure and content of Local Cultural Strategies – core sections; benefits of cultural activities; strategic context.
>
> Monitoring and review: monitoring; financial planning and corporate management framework; linked with Best Value and for library authorities complement the Annual Library Plan.
>
> Use of external consultation also used to monitor.
>
> Most strategies have a lifespan of five years and are reviewed after two to three years.

Assessment of demand

Leisure behaviour is by no means fully predictable and there is no single correct method of assessing potential demand. Provision should not therefore be based upon a simple set of measurements, criteria or rules. By using different approaches to the same problem, greater confidence can be attached to the solution. A range of methods include the following:

1 standards of provision
2 spatial or geographic analysis and hierarchy of provision
3 national participation rates
4 matrix-grid approach
5 need index approach
6 expressed demand and playing pitch strategy
7 facilities planning model
8 public consultation.

Standards of provision

One of the most developed and widely accepted approaches to the 'equitable' distribution of recreational services is the use of scales of provision, standards and norms (Table 12.1). Many standards are not based on empirical research, but on long-accepted assumptions of what is needed. Standards appeal to politcans and planners: someone in authority has done the thinking for you. The advantages of standards are:

- they are simple and efficient
- they can lead to the same level of provision area to area
- they act as an external authoritative source and
- they can be measured, monitored and assessed.

Standards are important and useful when they have been based on sound methodology and are used with flexibility and local knowledge. Tempered with wise judgement they

Table 12.1 Standards or guidelines of provision (many are undergoing change)

Category/Facility	Standards	Recommended by:
Outdoor recreation 'playing' space	6 acres (2.42ha) per 1,000 population	National Playing Fields Association
Outdoor equipped playgrounds	0.5–0.7 acres (0.2–0.3ha) per 1,000 population	National Playing Fields Association
Casual or informal play space within housing areas	1.0–1.25 acres (0.4–0.5ha) per 1,000 population	National Playing Fields Association
Athletics and miscellaneous	0.5 acres (0.2ha) per 1,000 population	National Playing Fields Association
Sports pitches	Playing Pitch Strategy	Sports Council/NPFA/CCPR
Golf courses	One 9-hole course per 18,000 population	Sports Council
Metropolitan parks	150 acres (61ha minimum) within 2 miles (3.2km) of population	GDLP – Greater London Development Plan
District parks	50 acres (20ha) within 0.75 mile (1,200m) of population	GDLP
Local parks	5 acres (2ha) within 0.25 mile walking distance (400m)	GDLP
Small local parks	Under 5 acres (2ha)	GDLP
District indoor sports centres	One per 40,000–90,000 population, plus one for each additional 50,000 population ($17m^2$ per 1,000 population) [Former guideline: now use Facilities Planning Model]	Regional Sports Councils
Indoor swimming pools	One 25m pool and one learner pool per 40,000–45,000 population ($5m^2$ per 1,000 population) [Former guideline: now use Facilities Planning Model]	Regional Sports Councils
Squash courts	One court per 5,000 population	Squash Rackets Association
Indoor bowling rinks	4-, 6- and 8-rink centres to serve populations of up to 30,000, 44,000 and 59,000 respectively [Guideline]	Regional Sports Councils
Ice skating rinks	One in conurbation if 250,000 within a 5-mile radius [Guideline]	National Ice Skating Association of the UK
Artificial turf pitches	One per 60,000 within 20 minutes drivetime [40,000 long term]	English Sports Council
Libraries	One service point within 20 minutes on foot or public transport. Mobile library at least one every 2 weeks. Housebound visits every 4 weeks, minimum	Library Association

have considerable advantages. They give yardsticks against which to measure existing provision, they are easy to understand and communicate and they cover many of the facilities provided by local authorities.

However, while standards have advantages, they also have disadvantages.

- Standards can become institutionalized and unmovable and be given greater strength and importance than they merit.
- Standards vary. Most major pursuits have standards for pitches, pools, indoor sports centres, libraries, and so on, but sometimes the same activity has different standards, so which one to choose?
- The validity of some standards is open to question. Playing space standards, for example, are based on participation rates, but participation is largely dependent on the level of supply. For example, the number of swimmers will depend on the number of pools, their location and accessibility, whether they are all open to the general public, the type of pool and the quality of provision, whether instruction is good, the level of costs and so on. The growth of indoor bowls and fitness centres, the decline in squash and the decline and re-birth in tenpin bowling, all show how misleading fixed standards can be. Some standards of just a decade ago are no longer valid or appropriate.
- Standards should always be tempered by local knowledge and circumstances. If they are unrealistic, they will be ignored; for example, national open space standards cannot be achieved in inner city areas.
- While standards are easy to understand, they can be misinterpreted and used as a justification for taking no further action. Some authorities have been known to interpret standards to suit their own purposes. For example, they may show that they have more than adequate indoor playing space but analysis might reveal that most of the total space is made up of small units unsuitable for activities in demand, or that access by the general public is restricted.
- Standards are inanimate, inhuman. They are concerned with quantitative and not qualitative aspects of provision. They take no account of the leisure potential of the specific areas: local needs, local priorities, local differences and local environments.

Many leisure pursuits are amenable to standards of provision, but many are not. Water recreation, tourism, heritage, entertainment and arts have no comprehensive basis for evaluation.

In summary, standards of provision can be a crude assessment of demand. As they are based on national information, they can often bear little relationship to local circumstances; they deal in quantities, thereby ignoring the quality of provision, aspects of distribution, use and management. Their ready acceptance prevents planners from considering the unique possibilities of each situation. However, standards of provision can be used as a starting point by providing a benchmark for measuring the adequacy of facilities and for identifying under- or over-provision, while recognizing that most standards indicate minimum levels of provision. From this initial assessment, more detailed standards of locally formulated criteria can then be used to test the feasibility of particular schemes. The National Playing Fields Association has gone to great lengths to overcome many of the difficulties in applying its own Six Acre standard.

The Six Acre Standard

The National Playing Fields Association's Six Acre Standard per 1000 head of population does not apply to open space *per se*, but is concerned with public-availability playing space standards (NPFA, 2001).

Prior to 1925, the supply of public recreational facilities was a local matter with provision being spasmodic and held back by lack of central direction. The National Playing Fields Association (NPFA), a voluntary body, was founded in 1925 to offer such direction by encouraging the provision of adequate playing fields and recreation facilities throughout the country. The association was incorporated by Royal Charter in 1933, and in 1963 it was registered as a national charity. There are affiliated Playing Fields Associations and a branch in Wales and Scotland. The NPFA is responsible for the protection of over 2,000 playing fields, including 374 King George's Fields presented to the nation in memory of King George V. The Association campaigns for the protection of recreation grounds and keeps a register of fields known to be under threat of development.

> The NPFA recommends a minimum standard for outdoor playing space of 2.4 hectares (6 acres) for 1000 people.

Since its inception in 1925, the NPFA has recommended minimum standards of provision throughout its history. These have been reviewed at intervals since that time, the latest reviews in 1989, 1992 and 2001.

> Outdoor playing space is not the same as public open space. It is space that is safely accessible and available to the general public, and of a suitable size and nature, for sport, active recreation or children's play. It is a significant component, but not the only form, of open space.
>
> NPFA, 2001

Although the metric system is used as the main form of measurement in the NPFA publication, the title The Six Acre Standard has been retained because that name is familiar and well respected and it has stood the test of time. A breakdown of the Standard is shown in Table 12.2.

The NPFA acknowledges the potential disadvantages with standards, saying they are 'used as a crutch by planners', have limited empirical evidence, lack monitoring, take no account of catchment characteristics, or quality of provision. However, the NPFA believes that:

> Such disadvantages do not invalidate the use of a standard. Rather, awareness of these potential problems provides a note of caution against inappropriate use and a reminder that, if used in isolation, it will lead to inappropriate land use policies. The absence of an adopted standard is likely to result in inadequate levels of new provision and be of benefit to those who argue for the disposal of existing facilities.
>
> NPFA, 2001

The Six Acre Standard includes the provision of children's play areas; all local authorities provide play areas for children. Before applying standards, it is important at the outset to have an appreciation of the different needs of children at different stages of life. Play provision needs to match the ages, abilities and motivations of children: toddlers; preschool; primary school age; older children; and adolescents and young people.

Table 12.2 The National Playing Fields Association Six Acre Standard

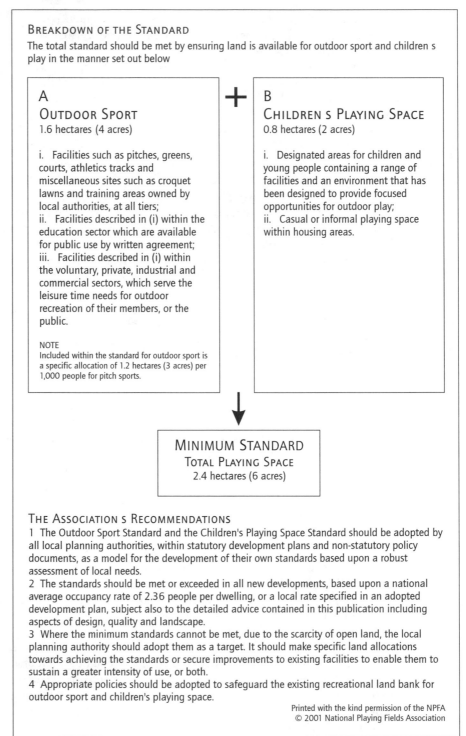

BREAKDOWN OF THE STANDARD
The total standard should be met by ensuring land is available for outdoor sport and children s play in the manner set out below

A
OUTDOOR SPORT
1.6 hectares (4 acres)

i.   Facilities such as pitches, greens, courts, athletics tracks and miscellaneous sites such as croquet lawns and training areas owned by local authorities, at all tiers;
ii. Facilities described in (i) within the education sector which are available for public use by written agreement;
iii. Facilities described in (i) within the voluntary, private, industrial and commercial sectors, which serve the leisure time needs for outdoor recreation of their members, or the public.

NOTE
Included within the standard for outdoor sport is a specific allocation of 1.2 hectares (3 acres) per 1,000 people for pitch sports.

+

B
CHILDREN S PLAYING SPACE
0.8 hectares (2 acres)

i.   Designated areas for children and young people containing a range of facilities and an environment that has been designed to provide focused opportunities for outdoor play;
ii. Casual or informal playing space within housing areas.

MINIMUM STANDARD
TOTAL PLAYING SPACE
2.4 hectares (6 acres)

THE ASSOCIATION S RECOMMENDATIONS
1 The Outdoor Sport Standard and the Children's Playing Space Standard should be adopted by all local planning authorities, within statutory development plans and non-statutory policy documents, as a model for the development of their own standards based upon a robust assessment of local needs.
2 The standards should be met or exceeded in all new developments, based upon a national average occupancy rate of 2.36 people per dwelling, or a local rate specified in an adopted development plan, subject also to the detailed advice contained in this publication including aspects of design, quality and landscape.
3 Where the minimum standards cannot be met, due to the scarcity of open land, the local planning authority should adopt them as a target. It should make specific land allocations towards achieving the standards or secure improvements to existing facilities to enable them to sustain a greater intensity of use, or both.
4 Appropriate policies should be adopted to safeguard the existing recreational land bank for outdoor sport and children's playing space.

There is also a need for features, fixtures and equipment in stimulating play areas. The range and type of equipment provided can influence the level of attraction, particularly if the opportunities provided contain elements of uncertainty, complexity and novelty (see Chapter 5). In the circumstances, it is hardly surprising that, to children, adventure playgrounds and challenging or interesting open spaces are perceived as being more attractive than the traditional static playground.

In 1992, while the NPFA's minimum standard for outdoor playing space remained unaltered, three new categories of play provision were introduced to meet the needs of children of different age groups. These were:

- a local area for play (LAP)
- a local equipped area for play (LEAP) and
- a neighbourhood equipped area for play (NEAP).

The main characteristics of a LAP are that it caters for children up to six years of age and is within a walking time of one minute from home.

> A LAP is a small area of open space specifically designated and laid out for young children to play close to where they live. Located within a walking time of one minute from home, the LAP provides essential play opportunities for toddlers and young children in locations that are overseen by parents, carers and the local community. The space within a LAP contains demonstrative features rather than equipment and is designed to encourage informal play and social interaction. It also provides opportunities for children to bring and to use their own toys and games.
>
> NPFA, 2001

The main characteristics of a LEAP are that it caters for children four to eight years of age, is within a walking time of five minutes from home and is positioned beside a pedestrian pathway on a route that is well used.

> A LEAP is a piece of open space that is designated and equipped for children of early school age. Such areas need to be located within a walking time of 5 minutes from home. As children begin school, their play activities occur more frequently in a group and tend to become more boisterous. This can lead to parents and carers seeking an alternative to the private garden (assuming there is already access to one of sufficient size). At the same time, children are progressively given greater freedom to roam from home. Therefore, there is a need to provide children with a safe environment in which they are able to experience new activities and other stimuli.
>
> NPFA, 2001

Play equipment is an important part of the attractiveness. A LEAP should include at least five types of well-designed, stimulating pieces of equipment.

The main characteristics of a NEAP are that it caters predominantly for older children, is within a walking time of fifteen minutes from home, and is positioned beside a pedestrian pathway on a route that is well used.

A NEAP should contain at least eight types of play equipment. It can be subdivided with one part comprising a range of playground equipment and another part containing a hard surfaced area for ball games or wheeled activities.

Once children have reached 8 years in age, their use of traditional play equipment begins to diminish. Older children require a greater number and a wider range of stimuli. Initially, they engage in wheeled activities and informal ball games, some of which may develop later into more formal and recognised sport. As they enter their teenage years, children actively choose to meet away from their home environment and look for places to congregate and improve their social awareness.

NPFA, 2001

A summary of the characteristics of these children's play areas is at Table 12.3.

Catchment areas and location

Spatial analysis In recent years in the United Kingdom, extensive user surveys have been taken of many leisure facilities, and from these an indication of the size of a leisure facility's catchment area can be made. By using this approach, the geographical area covered by the facility's perceived catchment area can be identified, with areas beyond that, theoretically, not being served. This is a useful planning tool, but it has limitations.

- No consideration is taken of the quality of the existing facility or whether it has spare capacity, or if the demand exceeds supply.
- It assumes that the density of population is evenly distributed, while in reality there may be pockets of heavily populated areas and other areas where fewer people reside.

Table 12.3 The National Playing Fields Association summary of the characteristics of children's play areas

Facility	Time	Walking Distance	Radial (Straight Line) Distance	Minimum Size Activity Zone	Nearest Dwelling	Characteristics
LAP (Local Area for Play)	1 min	100m	60m	100m^2	5m from Activity Zone[1]	Small, low-key games area (may include 'demonstrative' play features)
LEAP (Local Equipped Area for Play)	5 min	400m	240m	400m^2	10m from Activity Zone[2]	Five types of play equipment, small games area
NEAP (Neighbourhood Equipped Area for Play)	15 min	1,000m	600m	1,000m^2	30m from Activity Zone[3]	Eight types of play equipment, opportunities for ball games or wheeled activities

[1] To forwardmost part of dwelling that faces the LAP
[2] To property boundary
[3] To property boundary

- The catchment areas of leisure facilities are not circular but are distorted by many factors. Physical barriers such as rivers, railway lines and busy roads can restrict a catchment area, while access to a facility along a major road can extend the catchment area along its route.
- The assumption that similar-sized facilities will have identical catchment areas is problematic as the respective populations may differ in size, affluence, mobility and social composition.

All these factors, however, can be taken into consideration in undertaking a spatial analysis.

Location and attraction factor of leisure facilities When asked what were the three most important factors in the development of hotels Conrad Hilton cited 'location, location, location'. This equally applies to most leisure facilities. Ideally, a public leisure facility should be located near a main road that is well served by a public transport system, in close proximity to other facilities. In this way, the accessibility of the facility is improved and the catchment area is extended along the main road. People travelling along the route will have a high level of awareness of the facility, and this can be exploited in terms of promotion.

Locating a facility alongside other facilities will benefit from a degree of spin-off that will not be available for 'stand alone' facilities. Also, a cluster of facilities is likely to appeal more to family groups because their divergent interests and preferences are more likely to be met. In order that the main road does not act as a physical barrier, good pedestrian access should be provided.

The more attractive a facility is perceived to be, the greater distances people are prepared to travel and the more frequently they are likely to use it. The perceptual capacity of a facility can be both an attraction and a distraction. In a country park setting, for example, a large number of people in a person's view can be a distraction.

Large facility versus distribution of smaller facilities In an ideal world, both centralized and localized facilities are provided. However, with scarce resources, often a choice has to be made. This is a debate that is of primary importance to any strategy: whether to provide a large centrally located facility or numerous smaller facilities strategically placed throughout the district. There will probably be savings in the capital costs if only one large centre is provided as the economies of scale would apply. However, the closer a person resides to a leisure facility such as a swimming pool, community centre, library or sports centre, the more likely the person concerned is to use the facility as compared to a person who resides some distance away as distance decay curve principles apply. Further, the person living closer is also more likely to use the facility more frequently. Hence, in terms of a strategy, the greater the distribution of facilities, the more accessible they become to more local people. A large centre has a larger catchment area because of the 'attraction factor' and the range of activities on offer, but most users have to be mobile.

Travel time The development of out-of-town shopping and family entertainment centres has shown that people are prepared to travel, but that travel time is a key factor. People make longer journeys to specialist facilities such as theatres, ice rinks, leisure pools and indoor tennis centres, than to conventional swimming pools and sports halls. The greater the number of competing facilities in an area, the smaller the catchment becomes for a specific facility. Eighty per cent of users of conventional swimming pools and sports halls, for example, travel within journey times of 20 minutes or less. Once the time and effort of travel exceeds the satisfaction to be gained from the activity, motivation is diminished.

Hierarchy of facilities A modified version of the standards approach is the hierarchy of facilities approach, normally applied to a range of facilities for a given population size. It has been used in the development of new towns where the planning of leisure facilities is seen as a prerequisite of attracting people to the towns. For example, a town might have a 3-tier hierarchy for sport:

1 at a school level using facilities for school and community: a grass-roots tier
2 specific club facilities such as hockey or tennis at a second tier and
3 a third tier of flagship central facilities.

However, the approach is of value also in small communities. An example of a hierarchy of facilities is given in Table 12.4 which was developed specifically for use in the small communities along the Lambourn Valley in Berkshire (Torkildsen and Griffiths, 1987). Such an approach is more beneficial when used for small-scale communities; if it is used for large-scale projects, the limitations associated with the use of standards equally apply to this approach.

Table 12.4 Suggested hierarchy of leisure provision for rural communities based on a specific location in Berkshire

COMMUNITY SIZE	RECOMMENDED FACILITIES THAT COULD BE OFFERED	EXAMPLES OF ACTIVITIES RELATING TO LOCATION	ADDITIONAL COMMENTS
1 Hamlet/small village, 100–500 population	1 Village hall suitable for social functions. Kitchen, snooker table depending on demand and local tradition	1 Meetings, dances/discos, concerts, table tennis, youth club, voluntary organizations, e.g. scouts, adult education classes	1 Centrally located – preferably linked to community open space
	2 Community open space, 2–3 acres, with children's play area with equipment	2 Children's play, football and cricket, informal recreation, village festivals, carnival, etc.	2 Location – central, avoiding the necessity for children to cross main roads. Possibly linked to primary school
	3 Mobile library service – van	3 Books, records, tapes, etc.	3 Preferably linked to form focal point of village

Community size	Recommended facilities that could be offered	Examples of activities relating to location	Additional comments
2 Medium-sized village, 500–1,500 population	1 Community hall (15–20 × 10 × 6.7m) with kitchen, toilets, temporary stage, changing facilities, storage areas. Bar facilities depending on demand, car parking	1 Recreation, badminton, keep-fit, yoga, aerobics, meetings, drama, concerts, dances/discos, youth clubs	
	2 Community open space, 3–7 acres, including football pitch with pavilion (or linked to community hall), children's play area with equipment, seats, floral beds. Space for tennis and/or bowls, depending on local demand	2 Children's play, football club level, informal cricket, informal recreation, village festivals, carnival, pony club	
	3 Mobile library service – trailer library	3 Books, records, tapes, etc.	
	4 Community mini-bus – availability for hire – provision dependent on public transport service and facilities available within village	4 Organized visits in connection with sporting, art, entertainment and social events	4 Hire costs and maintenance schedules important
	5 Mobile recreation service	5 Offering sports and arts activities, particularly for the very young, females, etc., unemployed and the elderly	5 Depending on the range of opportunities available and the degree of initiative and leadership within the village. One half-day visit per week
3 Large village, 1,500–2,500 population	1 Community hall (20 × 10 × 6.7m), marginally larger than that required for a medium-sized community, plus bar facilities	1 A range of sports (including gymnastics, martial arts, badminton, possibly 4-a-side soccer, etc.), arts and social recreation	1 Location – central, focal point of public transport

Community size	Recommended facilities that could be offered	Examples of activities relating to location	Additional comments
	2 Community open space, 9–14 acres, 2 or more football pitches,1 cricket square, bowling green, 2 hard/tarmacadam surfaced tennis courts/ netball courts. Pavilions for changing, plus bar refreshments facilities. Children's play area with kick about and equipment	2 Activities to include club football/rugby, cricket, bowls, tennis, netball	2 Depending on the availability of open space, it might be necessary to have the facilities at more than one location. Each site should have pavilion with changing facilities
	3 Library - fixed accommodation	3 Books, records, tapes, etc.	3 Opening times staggered throughout week to meet different people's needs
	4 Mobile recreation service – depending on the facilities within the village and whether they are professionally managed	4 Sport and recreation activities	4 Visit restricted to half-day a week
4 Small country town, 2,500–6,000 population	1 Sports hall (26 × 16.5 × 7.6m), depending on the size of community, consideration to be given to ancillary facilities such as weight training area, 2 squash courts	1 Increased range of sporting activities, including 5-a-side football, cricket, indoor bowls, basketball, volleyball, weight training, squash, archery, tennis	1 For economic reasons dual use with a secondary school or a large sports club/ voluntary organization should be explored
	2 Swimming pool (20–25m)	2 Swimming, life-saving	2 As above; provision only if dual-use arrangement can be achieved
	3 Community hall/arts centre – to include stage and projection facilities, plus meeting rooms, kitchens, bar, toilets, craft workshop	3 Meetings, drama, concerts, cinema, whist drives, bingo, table tennis, adult education classes, displays	3 Linked to other community provision – improve spin-off and awareness

COMMUNITY SIZE	RECOMMENDED FACILITIES THAT COULD BE OFFERED	EXAMPLES OF ACTIVITIES RELATING TO LOCATION	ADDITIONAL COMMENTS
	4 Community open space (15–40 acres), including park area, children's play areas with equipment, 4 football/rugby, hockey pitches, 2–4 tennis courts, bowling green and pavilions with refreshments, I cricket square, multi-purpose floodlit hard all-weather area	4 Children's play, town show, carnival, soccer, rugby, cricket, bowls, tennis, netball, 5-a-side football, training purposes	4 Children's play areas, easy access to housing estates. Playing pitches best located near sports hall – economies of scale and spin-off
	5 Library facilities – branch library	5 Books, cassettes, records, video, pictures	5 Permanent accommodation – spread opening hours
	6 Mobile recreation service	6 Sports/recreation activities	6 Programmed to meet specific market segments, e.g. unemployed – off-peak times/one day per week

National participative rates

Large-scale national or regional participative surveys such as the General Household Surveys (GHS) and British Market Research Bureau surveys can be used to help determine what the potential demand may be for a given community. However, the level of participation is largely dependent upon the level of provision and does not take into consideration potential or deferred demand. Additionally, such surveys do not normally indicate the participation rates within different types of neighbourhood.

Another national survey that can be used in this approach is the Target Group Index (TGI), which is a national consumption survey funded by the British Market Research Bureau. The advantage of using the TGI is that it is linked with ACORN (which is the acronym for A Classification Of Residential Neighbourhoods). By using the activity index for each ACORN type of household, the potential demand for a particular activity can be determined. There are disadvantages, however. While the GHS determines what activities the respondents participate in during the four weeks prior to being interviewed, the TGI is more open-ended, asking whether respondents take part 'these days'. The consequences of the different approaches are reflected in the results, with some of the participation rates in the TGI sample being substantially higher than those found by the GHS.

Matrix-grid approach

This approach is more of a management technique than a planning approach, but it has an important function in specific situations, for example, where planning criteria have been established for a range of possible developments on a particular site, or where the facilities within a park or geographical zone have to meet the demands of all sections of the community. By dividing the community into different categories, such as pre-school, young children, teenagers, adults and so on, listing their needs and matching these against facilities available, deficiencies can be determined. A further application can be used to place a list of facility and/or service deficiencies into a priority ranking list or to select the most appropriate site from a range of possibilities.

The following list suggests a range of questions that could be asked to achieve a community recreation priority–criterion ranking system for new developments.

- Does the proposed facility meet an unfulfilled local leisure need?
- Has there been a high level of expressed demand for the facility?
- Does the facility replace or renew a facility with a high value to the community?
- Will the facility specifically benefit persons from a leisure deprived area?
- Will the facility benefit priority target groups?
- Is the facility likely to attract a high level of usage and meet the needs of different age groups?

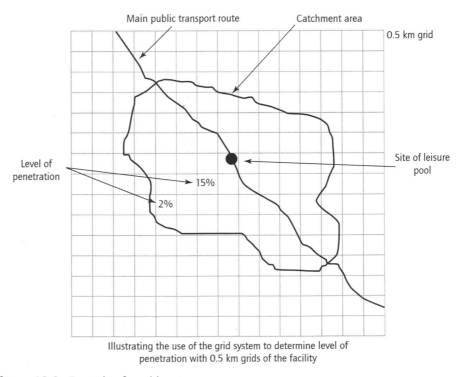

Illustrating the use of the grid system to determine level of penetration with 0.5 km grids of the facility

Figure 12.2 Example of a grid system

- Will the facility involve the council in best value for money capital investment?
- Will the facility involve the council in minimal or best value revenue expenditure?
- Will the facility attract substantial grant aid and/or sponsorship?
- Is the facility likely to make a contribution to increasing levels of health and reducing levels of anti-social behaviour in the area?

Figure 12.2 illustrates how a matrix-grid system can be used to measure the level of penetration from different parts of the catchment area.

Need index approach

The need index approach determines whether a deficiency exists, and places the different deficiency areas into a priority ranking. The basic concept behind this approach is simple and is illustrated in Figure 12.3.

At present, most of the methods of assessing demand concentrate upon the relationship between resources available and potential users and little emphasis is attached to the concept of need. It is logical to assume that those areas with a low resource level, as well as a high level of need, should have a higher priority than areas with a high level of resources and a low level of need.

This approach is well illustrated when applied to the provision of children's playgrounds. First, it is necessary to assess the needs and measure the resources. Factors that affect children's opportunity to play, together with indicators of social deprivation, should be examined. These include, for example, the number of children, incidence of high-rise flats, lack of gardens, dwellings lacking basic amenities, number of unemployed, working mothers and lone parenthood. In measuring the resources, factors to be taken into account include: location of the play area, size of the playground, range and nature of the equipment and whether the playground is supervised.

A case study using the need index approach in Basingstoke and Deane (LMGT, 1996) is described below.

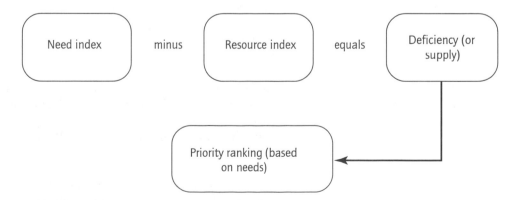

Figure 12.3 Need index approach

Case study: The need index approach

Basingstoke and Deane Borough Council commissioned a study to design a system for awarding funding for children's play areas by ward, equitably. The result was a 'needs minus resources' model which provided an index to establish gaps in provision and priorities.

The Need Index

In 1994, the Department of the Environment produced a set of indicators to measure the relative degree of deprivation to be found in the 366 local authority areas of England, using various sources, but largely based on the 1991 census. The Index of Multiple Deprivation is now often used (see Useful websites). There were 13 indicators, 7 of which apply to ward level:

1   unemployment;
2   overcrowded housing;
3   lacking or sharing basic amenities;
4   children in low income households;
5   no car within a household;
6   children living in 'unsuitable accommodation', e.g. flats;
7   17-year-olds not in full-time education.

Three indicators specifically refer to children and a fourth, overcrowding, rarely occurs without children. The other factors – unemployment, lacking basic amenities and no car – provide a picture of lack of affluence and mobility, thereby restricting access to play areas beyond a child's walking distance.

The closer focus through analysis of enumeration districts (EDs) is more useful in deciding priorities, as it is possible to identify levels of need in a few streets or an estate. The problem was that there were 25 wards in Basingstoke and Deane and over 300 enumeration districts. Therefore, the formula was based primarily on wards and supplemented by ED information.

The theory is simple; the practice is more complex. To make for a relatively easy transfer from theory to practice, four key aspects were identified:

1   the number of children under the age of 16 years within each ward;
2   the social deprivation indicators within each ward, giving weighting where necessary;
3   children in 'unsuitable accommodation' in each ward;
4   children in low-earning households in each ward.

The number of children in each ward is of critical importance as it is logical to assume that the areas with the greatest number of children will have the greatest demand for the use of playgrounds provided, all other variables being the same. Moreover, where the social deprivation is high, it is safe to assume that the need for the provision of play facilities will also be high.

Resource index

The resource index measures the play areas by ward. Giving a score value to playgrounds is a difficult exercise, as there is a wide range of factors to consider, many requiring subjective analysis, best carried out by experts. Specialist consultants to the National Playing Fields Association were used to carry out inspection of around 180 sites.

Key factors taken into consideration when developing the resource index were:

1 the scale of play provision within each ward
2 the quality of provision, facilities and equipment
3 the distribution of playgrounds within each ward
4 the size of the playgrounds: small, medium, large and extra large
5 the range of equipment, capacity, attraction of the playgrounds and the quality of the provision
6 the maintenance and condition of the playgrounds and their equipment
7 the safety factors, taking into consideration whether the playgrounds have impact absorbing surfaces, are enclosed by a fence, and are safe from passing traffic
8 the play value of the play area: an assessment of the overall physical, social, creative, educational and motivating features to be found.

Units per play area were allocated to these factors. Statistical steps were used to combine the indicators into an index. One key step was that of 'standardization'. Standardization alters values to make them of equal worth. To make comparisons between different wards, it was necessary to convert the data and points allocated to a comparable form. A statistical tool known as the 'C' Scale was used. To convert a range of data to a 'C' Scale each range was set against a scale of 0–100. As an example, consider the following range of hypothetical data – 50, 200, 225 and 500. This range is 0–500 (500 units) and, therefore, each unit on the 'C' Scale (0–100) or 100 units, represents 5 units on the range data. Thus, the figures are converted as follows by dividing the base data by 5:

Data	50	200	225	500
'C' Scale	10	40	45	100

The key is to reduce every range of data to the 0–100 of the 'C' Scale. The best way of converting data to a 'C' Scale is by using a range of numbers rather than percentages.

Applying the model

The resulting index was used to place the wards in order of priority need. The Council initially allocated funding to the top twelve wards on the basis of areas in greatest need. Wards lower down the priority scale move up as their needs become greater in relation to those areas already refurbished. By using this method, areas (wards) with a high level of need and a low level of resources were given a higher priority than areas with a high level of resources and a low level of need.

Refining the formula

The formula is a broad, and hence crude, method of placing wards into priority order. It has limitations. This approach involves interpreting need, a difficult concept.

The resource index is limited in that some elements require a subjective judgement. However, subjectivity was minimized by awarding the most 'units' to factual information, i.e. actual provision. In terms of play area distribution, enumeration district numbers can be used to supplement ward analysis.

Priority ranking

The formula of 'Need – Resource = Deficiency = Priority' also provides a need ranking by ward and resource ranking by ward. In determining ward priority, it will be useful to also bear in mind the relative ranking in the two indices. A ward with low ranking in both indices could achieve higher priority although it may have a similar overall index score to other wards.

In summary, the formula results in a Play Area Index, giving a ranking by ward. This ranking, in computer spreadsheet form, will change as ward demographic data change or resources change for better or worse. Information needs updating regularly and the formula should be reviewed on at least an annual basis.

Source: The index for Basingstoke and Deane was devised by George Torkildsen, Gwynne Griffiths and Pat Kendall; the play area inspection was carried out by consultant to the NPFA, Tony Chilton.

Expressed demand: a strategy for playing pitches

The level of demand for existing facilities can provide a useful guide as to whether additional facilities are required in an area. The analysis of sports facilities' booking sheets, for example, can reveal the amount of spare capacity available, or whether the demand for specific facilities exceeds the supply available. This section describes an approach which assesses the demand for outdoor playing pitches

There is wide variation across the country in the level of provision of adult-sized pitches (including secondary schools) for all sports (Table 12.5). Football accounts for about half of the provision and cricket a quarter, with rugby and hockey sharing a balance.

The Register of Recreational Land in England was produced in 1993 by the Sports Council, now Sport England, as a result of a joint initiative with the Central Council of Physical Recreation (CCPR) and the NPFA. The Register records playing pitches and playing field sites in excess of 0.4 hectares used for competitive play, irrespective of ownership. The Register grew out of a need for accurate and comparable data on playing fields at the local and national level, to improve decision making and monitor change. The Register collected information on over 73,000 sports pitches in England across 24,500 sites, covering a total of 150,300 acres of land. Information on ownership, type of usage (for example, public, schools, private), size, type of surface, floodlighting, ancillary facilities and threats from development were detailed. However, concern over reliability of the data and that it has not been updated since 1993, has led to scepticism about its value for planning.

Table 12.5 Population per pitch

	AVERAGE	RANGE
Football	1,840	1,274–8,640
Cricket	4,243	2,216–6,750
Hockey	8,271	3,683–31,963
Rugby	8,968	3,320–24,000

The Playing Pitch Strategy (PPS) published in 1991, was a guidance document written by The Sports Council, the NPFA and the CCPR. This was reviewed during 2001 and 2002 and re-published, with the title *Towards a Level Playing Field: A Guide to the Production of Playing Pitch Strategies* by Sport England and the CCPR in February 2003 (SE/CCPR, 2003). The guide recommends a model approach for assessing the demand for playing pitches based on the expressed demand as indicated by the number of teams requiring pitches within the study area.

Local authorities have been slow in adopting this approach, perhaps because it is time-consuming, perceived as complex, and it adds to the workload and constrained budgets. Indeed, in some cases, responsibility for playing pitches has been delegated to local clubs in exchange for peppercorn rentals.

The strategy takes a different line from other conventional approaches, starting with actual participation; it is, therefore, sensitive to local situations. The strategy provides a process of calculating the demand for pitches based on current and latent demand. The difference to previous approaches is that, instead of using land area per head of population as the basic unit, it measures demand (at peak times) in terms of teams requiring pitches and then compares this with the pitches available. Basic information required to employ the methodology involves calculating demand and supply:

Demand
- number of teams in an area
- whether adult or junior team, male or female
- each team's home ground
- day and time of week when home games are played
- number and type of home games played in a season
- number of weeks of the playing season
- demographic data for study area (actual and projected).

Supply
- size and surface (grass/artificial) of each pitch
- sports for which it is used
- ownership of the pitch: public, private or educational
- availability at different days and different times.

In addition to these quantitative elements, other qualitative information and trends in demand can be gathered. Given this basic information, there are sequential stages in the process:

1 identifying teams/team equivalents in the main pitch sports
2 calculating the number of home games per team per week
3 assessing the total home games per week
4 establishing the demand for games at different times
5 calculating the number of pitches used or required on each day, or the peak day in the week
6 recording the total amount of pitches available
7 addressing problems and issues arising from the above and

8   developing a range of policy options to overcome the problems identified, i.e. finding solutions.

It is essential that the methodology is used as a means of understanding the relationship between the demand for pitches and their supply; its outputs should be tempered by detailed local knowledge and common sense. However, as it will be firmly rooted in the local circumstances, its calculations and the resultant findings will be unique to that area, and should enable policy makers to deal confidently with the issues raised. Solutions for one sport are likely to have repercussions for the others since there may be competing demands for scarce resources; therefore, decisions on one sport are best not taken until all sports have been assessed. Herein lies a problem in that the strategy provides local authorities and others with a method of assessing the need for only one type of open space (i.e. playing pitches). In contrast, the Six Acre Standard embraces a wider range of activities (e.g. provision for athletics, tennis, bowls and children's play). The NPFA suggests that a playing pitch strategy fits within the Six Acre Standard which, in turn, contributes to the evolution of local standards for provision required by PPG 17. While the guide recognizes that the production of a strategy can be time-consuming, as with PPG 17, it fails to provide guidance on what to do in the interim.

Facilities planning model

The Sports Council's Facilities Planning Model (Sports Council, 1998) is a method of assessing the demand for sports facilities at the community level of provision. The basic structure of the model is to compare demand for facilities with supply, using the same unit of measurement: this being number of visits per week at peak times. The approach has three components: demand, supply and catchment areas.

1   The demand is measured by the rate and frequency of participation using local and national data, e.g. from surveys.
2   The supply side is measured by working out the number of attendances a facility can accommodate in a specified peak period.
3   In terms of catchment, calculations are based on identifying the distance travelled by the regular participants (70–80 per cent of users).

The model is based on comparing demand and supply, applying that to a specific geographical area and thereby:

●   identifying where demand is located
●   whether, and to what extent, demand exceeds supply
●   whether, and where, spare capacity exists.

Local demand is measured on the basis of the number of visits per week in peak period for any particular sports facility, determined by:

●   the total number of people resident within the study area

- the demand rate: the proportion of residents who want to use the facility type for particular sports
- the desired fequency of visits: how often they want to visit
- the proportion of visits which arise in the normal peak periods per week.

The benefits of the model include the fact that it is based on actual participation, applies to a local population, a discrete geographical area, and that different facilities can be assessed using the same approach; the model can also be used in urban and rural settings. The model, therefore, is a substantial improvement on standards *per se*. The model, however, deals only with known demand and not with latent demand, nor visitor demand, nor demand created by marketing or innovative management. The model relies on consistent information about existing facilities and is a technique (the Sports Council's description) not a policy making instrument. The model has been used principally to help make decisions on the provision of sports halls, swimming pools and synthetic turf pitches. Whether its application can go further to playing fields is at present not known.

Public consultation

Public consultation, after expressed demand, is arguably, the most important indicator of public demand. The weakness is that people may demand facilities but never use them; in addition, the more articulate and organized leisure groups are often the most vocal. Nevertheless, public consultation remains invaluable in gauging local feeling and opinion. Not only is it politically desirable to consult the people, but also the planning process itself is incomplete unless people are consulted about their leisure needs and demands, their perception of existing facilities and services and their expectations of future provision. Without such consultation, the planning process is one of dictating provision for people, as opposed to planning with the people.

As with other methods, public consultations are not without their shortcomings. These are normally associated with the expressions of demand not being representative of the community, as a whole, and with the subjective nature of many of the responses made.

The major methods of consulting with the public include:

1 community demand surveys
2 user surveys
3 organization surveys
4 public meetings
5 working parties
6 interviews
7 focus groups.

Community demand surveys Four types of survey used regularly are: household interviews, street surveys, postal surveys and telephone surveys. The face-to-face household interview is a sound approach, but can be both time-consuming and expensive to administer. In order to avoid unnecessarily alarming residents, particularly the elderly, household interviews are best undertaken following an introduction, which requires even more time. A face-to-face alternative is the street survey. This requires achieving randomized quota sampling, e.g. a reasonable cross-section of males and females, different age groups, and so on. It also calls for trained, sensitive interviewers. The postal survey is much easier and cheaper to administer, although it has limitations. The response rate can be very low unless some interest has been created in the local media or an incentive is associated with a return of the questionnaire. A telephone survey using skilful, sensitive researchers, is comparatively easy to undertake, provided the questionnaire is short and simple. The problems are those of contacting the selected people and getting accepted. Many sales personnel use the telephone in an attempt to sell products such as double glazing and kitchen refurbishments. Hence, there is resentment to this form of consultation.

Leisure facility user surveys User surveys conducted in a face-to-face approach or by self-completing questionnaires can be informative, providing information on the user profile, the facility's catchment area (and also the areas not being served), participation data (e.g. activities, frequency), perceptions of the facility and how it is managed and expectations for the future. User surveys, where the questionnaires are self-administered, tend to be less representative and the response rate is reduced, though this method is easier and cheaper. Identifying users also provides a broad picture of the non-users.

Survey of clubs, societies and organizations The voluntary organizations for sports and arts are the backbone of leisure groupings in the United Kingdom. Hence, in any leisure planning process, their contribution is essential. A survey of local clubs and societies can provide valuable information regarding membership levels, resources and current and future requirements. The drawbacks are that often databases are out of date with changes in club officials and there is often a delay in the responses because of the seasonal nature of some clubs. Further, too many clubs are inward looking and are not prepared to look at aspects beyond those that directly affect their members. Responses tend to be low.

Public meetings Although opinions given at public meetings are not necessarily those representing all the community, they do give an indication of the strength of the support or opposition to a particular proposal. Good promotion is necessary to ensure that adequate representative attendances are achieved at the meetings and that those who 'shout loudest' or have vested interests do not hold sway. Working with the press to give balanced reports requires good public relations.

Working party approach A much under-used approach is that of a working party, whereby members of local clubs, residents associations, etc., together with officers and members from the local council are formed into a working party that has delegated authority to propose recommendations. Examples of where such an approach has been used include the designing of a new park and the conversion of an old school into a community centre. It is important, however, that such working parties have authority to influence decisions, or they simply become talking shops and soon lose enthusiasm.

The advantages associated with this approach are considerable. It is democracy at work and, hopefully, the realistic expectations of the local community can be fulfilled.

Unfortunately, in such a situation, decision making can be slow and the commitment of its members will wane if progress is not seen to be made. But the greatest problem may be associated with many members making unrealistic demands that require excessive amounts of space and finance to fulfil.

Interviews Interviews with community leaders can be an invaluable source of information. The group might include politicians, teachers, leisure leaders, playworkers, youth leaders, social workers, police, ethnic minority representatives, disadvantaged and disabled groups and the business community. Likewise, informal interviews with shopkeepers, publicans, postal workers – all those who come into contact with a wide range of residents – helps to build a picture of how different people perceive the current provision and how it is managed and what deficiencies they think exist. A 'living-in' approach for some of the research time will assist in identifying issues and deficiencies from a resident's viewpoint.

Focus groups Focused interviews originated in America in the evaluation of audience response to radio programmes. They were adapted into focused group interviews after the Second World War. The pioneer was Robert Morton (Stewart and Shamdasani, 1990). The 'focused interview' differs from others in four ways:

- all those interviewed have been involved in a practical 'concrete' situation
- the 'content' has been previously analysed and hypotheses have been arrived at
- an interview guide has been fashioned and
- the interview itself is focused on the subjective experience of the persons exposed to the pre-analysed situation.

The focus group interview generally involves eight to twelve individuals who discuss a particular topic under the direction of a moderator who promotes interaction and assures that the discussion remains on the topic of interest. Smaller groups may be dominated by one or two members, while larger groups are difficult to manage. A typical focus group session will last for one and a half to two and a half hours.

Depending on the intent of the research, the moderator may be more or less directive with respect to the discussion, but more often is non-directive. The moderator might begin with a series of general questions but direct the discussion to more specific issues as the group proceeds.

Other consultations There is a range of other methods, including consultation clinics for individuals or small groups, stakeholder panels, local press and media, and via a website.

It is clear that, at present, there is no one way of determining the level of potential leisure demand for a particular activity. All the approaches described in this section have different degrees of limitation, and in order to be able to make a fairly accurate projection of the likely demands, it is necessary to use a range of different leisure planning techniques. Planning for people means putting people into the planning process. To make future leisure provision more appropriate and meaningful, a greater understanding is required of people's needs and demands, what leisure means to people and the role it plays in their lives. The government's new policy under Best Value calls for greater public consultation: a step in this direction.

Ideally, longer-term in-depth studies could be undertaken to understand people's needs, leisure interests and preoccupations. Such studies could add to demand analysis at a deeper level.

In *Leisure and the Family Life Cycle* (Rapoport and Rapoport, 1975), the Rapoports and Strelitz, thirty years ago, looked beneath the surface of leisure planning and revealed underlying predispositions towards leisure. Planning should not be by 'feasible' extensions of what already exists and is known to be workable and on hunches about what people's needs are, but begin from the 'people's side of the equation'. By learning about people's motivations, preoccupations, interests and activities and injecting their knowledge into the planning process, decision makers will have a broader platform on which to plan policies.

Brandenburg *et al.* (1982) developed this model further towards an understanding of why a person adopts a particular activity. The process commences with preoccupations and interests. Four conditions – opportunity, knowledge, favourable social milieu and receptiveness – were deemed necessary and sufficient to enable an interest to be expressed through adoption of a specific activity. These conditions are focused upon a specific activity by one or more key event(s), which may at the same time, modify the conditions themselves. While various research projects have revealed much about the conditions that influence actual participation, further research is required for a greater understanding of the impact of the 'key events'.

A ten-stage leisure planning process

The leisure planning process, in conceptual terms, is a simple model based on identifying leisure needs and demands and providing services and facilities to meet those demands. In reality, however, the process is far more complex. Set out below is a ten-stage leisure planning approach based on leisure theory and current practical application from a leisure management perspective (Figure 12.4). This runs parallel to, and in collaboration with, the formal planning process and Local Plans. The process suggested is similar to preparing a marketing plan (see Chapter 20).

Stage 1: Determine council policies, goals and objectives This concerns the philosophical basis of providing for the community and the roles of the council (e.g. as provider, enabler, partner, and so on).

Stage 2: Evaluate current leisure provision and services This stage identifies the type, range and ownership of facilities, whether public, voluntary or commercial. It also evaluates effectiveness and efficiency, usage and management. It determines levels of demand and spare capacity. A population study will identify resident concentrations and specific sections of the community that require special consideration, while a transportation analysis will highlight the accessibility of existing and potential leisure sites.

Stage 3: Consult widely This stage provides the opportunity to find out whether what is to be provided and how it is delivered are appropriate for those it is intended to serve. Consultation is needed with local residents, workers and organizations. A range of techniques should be used. Consultation is also needed with agencies such as arts and sports governing bodies, with education authorities and schools, and with neighbouring authorities to avoid overlap and duplication.

Stage 4: Assess known and potential demand Although there is no single leisure planning technique that can accurately indicate what the potential demand may be for a particular activity or facility, a good indication can be obtained by using different leisure planning techniques, including demand modelling. These include national and, more specifically, local data, population profiling, the results of consultation and identifying known and latent demands.

Stage 5: Determine deficiencies and surpluses This stage analyses the supply–demand relationship. Comparing the level of potential demand with the actual provision should, theoretically, produce a list of deficiencies. It would be unrealistic for any authority to contemplate redressing all the perceived deficiencies, rather the deficiencies should be ranked in order of priority.

Stage 6: Identify and assess resources available It will be necessary to examine all potential sites for leisure development and these should be assessed in terms of their suitability (e.g. size, terrain, accessibility, environmental considerations). A feasibility study should be undertaken which should lead to a business plan encompassing capital and revenue costs, management and use. Grants and planning obligation opportunities will need to be considered.

Stage 7: Select management approaches There now exists a range of management options and it is incumbent on local authorities to provide best value. Options include competitive tendering, not-for-profit organizations, trusts, buy-outs, buy-ins, concessions, partnerships and hybrids. Different facilities and services may well require different management approaches.

Stage 8: Produce or revise the authority's Cultural Strategy and local leisure plan Local authorities are obliged to produce a Local Cultural Strategy. Leisure Managers will also need to prepare a local leisure plan or series of specific plans (e.g. Arts, Sport and Recreation), incorporating short- and medium-term development plans for the area, with the council's role in these developments being clearly defined. The LCS will set out the roles of the council, the policies, the development and management objectives, and a plan of actions.

Stage 9: Action plan To implement the strategies, it will be necessary to produce an action plan with clear objectives, targets and methods of measurement. Areas of responsibility will need to be assigned to key committees and officers with delegated areas of responsibility. In order to ensure that the tasks are completed on time, it is advisable that a detailed critical path analysis network be drawn up.

Stage 10: Monitor and evaluate The progress made will need to be monitored and results measured. This should include the effect of the actions upon the community.

The strategies will need periodic review in the light of economic, social and environmental changes.

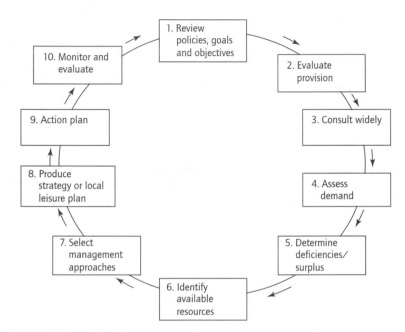

Figure 12.4 A leisure planning process

Summary

Leisure planning has now become an important discipline. This should result in eliminating previous examples of poor leisure planning in the United Kingdom and elsewhere. Leisure planning differs fundamentally from general planning, as leisure outside the home is made up of an extremely wide variety of activities and choices and leisure behaviour is not always predictable.

In this chapter, Leisure Managers have been encouraged to learn about the planning process and their involvement in it. The role of the government, the tiers in the planning system and the planning processes have been briefly considered: planning policy guidance, development plans, structure and local plans, the planning inspectorate, planning obligations, regeneration and sustainable communities and Local Cultural Strategies. A suggested ten-point planning process for Leisure Managers to consider was put forward as a way of identifying what roles they might play in the process.

An integral, but often ignored, stage is the evaluation of current provision and services which can identify areas of spare capacity and where the demand exceeds the supply available.

The nature and scale of leisure provision by many local authorities is the result of inheritance and possibly this may be the reason why many councils had no philosophy for the allocation of leisure resources – no stated purpose for the expenditure on leisure services – which in most large councils represents many millions of pounds each year.

This has now changed largely due to the advent of CCT, superseded by Best Value and due also to the direction by the DCMS that local authorities should prepare Local Cultural Strategies. However, in terms of facility planning, there is no one method of accurately determining the demand for a particular activity or facility. In this chapter we have examined different methods of assessing demand: standards of provision, spatial demand, hierarchy of facilities, national participative rates, the matrix-grid approach, the need index approach, expressed demand and public consultation. Although these approaches have their limitations, used appropriately, they can provide a good indication of the level of deficiency. To develop a more accurate method of assessment, greater research is needed into why people choose a particular activity and the extent to which it is the facilities themselves and the extent to which community leadership, management and marketing direct choices and enable people to take up the opportunities.

Discussion points

1 The planning profession must act as the conscience of local government because those involved in leisure and education services, politicians and officers alike, are too often driven by the short term and view outdoor land for sport and play as a significant potential capital funding source for other service priorities. Discuss.

2 The provision of opportunities for play meets a universal need, whereas the provision of leisure facilities for the adult population should be demand led and based on informed choices. Discuss and assess the implications of the statement for leisure facility planning.

Useful websites

Royal Town Planning Institute: www.rtpi.org.uk

The National Playing Fields Association: www.npfa.co.uk

Sport England: www.sportengland.org

For the Index of Multiple Deprivation, see www.go-wm.gov.uk/regionalintelligence/deprivation

ODPM website (www.odpm.gov.uk) contains consultation draft revisions of two Planning Policy Guidelines (PPGs). They are now published as Planning Policy Statements (PPSs).

13

Trends in the leisure industry

Introduction

In recent years the pace of change in our quality of life, including our use of leisure, has been rapid. We are now enjoying higher standards of living filled with goods, services, activities and opportunities that in past years seemed unimaginable. Underlying this growth have been several major trends related directly or indirectly to leisure and recreation.

A trend is defined as: 'a tendency or general direction'.

Exploring the past and predicting the future in terms of leisure provision and participation is itself a major growth area. The study of trends is now an essential planning and management tool. Leisure commentators, forecasters, social scientists and researchers provide information on trends in areas such as leisure time, leisure participation, consumers' expenditure on leisure, travel, and economic, social and demographic changes which all impinge on leisure provision and participation.

Trends are used in numerous ways in leisure management, including:

- to predict the most likely future leisure activities of consumers
- to reduce the element of risk in decision making on future policy
- to plan leisure services and facilities strategically
- to draw attention to specific declines or likely growth areas
- to monitor the reaction of customers to a service, facility or activity over several years
- to provide information for use in the marketing of future facilities, services and programmes.

Sources of information on trends in leisure

There are a number of sources from which readers can obtain information about trends in leisure, both general sources and specific leisure-related sources. General sources of information include a wide range of reports from:

- the Office of National Statistics (ONS)
- the General Household Survey (GHS)
- Annual Abstracts of Statistics
- Social Trends and Regional Trends
- British Market Research Bureau (BMRB)
- Target Group Index (TGI) and
- private companies such as the Mintel Group and Key Note.

Specific sources for leisure-related trends come in the form of annual reports from the Department of Culture, Media and Sport (DCMS), its sponsored agencies such as the Arts Council, Sports Council, VisitBritain and the tourist boards, and from university and independent sources such as the Leisure Industries Research Centre (LIRC) and Sports Industries Research Centre (SIRC). A few of these sources are now briefly described.

General Household Survey The General Household Survey (GHS) was started in 1971, and apart from breaks for re-design, has been a continuous survey carried out by the Social Survey Division of the Office for National Statistics (ONS) to collect information on a range of topics from people in households in Great Britain. A sample of approximately 13,000 addresses is selected each year from the Postcode Address Files. All adults aged 16 and over in these households are interviewed. Data from the GHS is widely used in other publications such as *Social Trends* and *Regional Trends*. Among the topics of importance to leisure researchers and managers are: demographic information, household income, household and family information, employment, health issues and consumer durables including vehicle ownership.

The GHS is an important national source of data on participation in sport and leisure activities. The GHS has included a section on sport and leisure activities at roughly three-year intervals since 1973 with methodology changes, for example, in 1987. Sporting activity by children, which is important in assessing total demand for facilities, is not covered by the GHS. The survey also excludes the use of facilities by people on holiday from outside Britain, although sports undertaken by respondents when abroad are included.

Two measures of participation are available:

- four-week participation rate: the percentage of people aged 16 or over who took part in an activity in the four weeks before interview
- twelve-month participation rate: the percentage of people aged 16 or over who took part in an activity in the twelve months before interview.

Twelve-month rates are likely to be higher than four-week rates because some of those who have participated during the year will be interviewed about a four-week period in which they did not participate. This is most likely to occur if the activity is highly seasonal or attracts infrequent participants.

Social Trends Social Trends draws together social and economic data from a wide range of government departments and other agencies and organizations. It provides a broad picture of British society and how it has been changing over the years. There are 13 chapters, each focusing on a different social policy area. Possibly of greatest interest to leisure researchers and managers, in addition to population, households, education and training, labour market, income and wealth, environment and transport, is the chapter on lifestyles and social participation. The 2004 edition includes a section on ageing and gender.

Mintel International Group The Mintel International Group (see Useful websites) produces a range of reports. Each year, Mintel's flagship report, *British Lifestyles*, looks into consumer spending and attitudes and focuses on a particular lifestyle trend. *British Lifestyles*, with 20 years' experience, has become an important marketing tool in helping to predict consumer behaviour.

Key Note Key Note is a long established marketing research company (see Useful websites). It has produced over 600 reports across 27 market sectors. Marketing sectors for leisure include, for example, drinks, food and catering, leisure and entertainment, lifestyle, transport, travel and tourism.

In addition to these general surveys, there are specific surveys of direct relevance to leisure researchers and managers.

Leisure Industries Research Centre The Leisure Industries Research Centre (LIRC) (see Useful websites) is a joint research centre of the University of Sheffield and Sheffield Hallam University. The Centre is made up of specialist research teams whose collective experience spans the leisure industry, including environment and outdoor leisure, food, hospitality, tourism and cultural change, leisure management, leisure statistics and sport.

The Sport Industry Research Centre (SIRC) (see Useful websites) covers a broad range of issues relating to the sports market. Alongside economic impact studies of sporting events, SIRC also evaluates voluntary sector and public sector subsidies to sport. The company works overseas on international projects and in the UK, with clients such as UK Sport and Sport England.

Making use of trends reports

The sources described above, and others, provide information which help in forecasting. Trends are important indications of future needs and demands. However, they are normally indications of national movements. It is important for leisure planners and managers to remember that what is happening nationally may not be occurring locally. National trends need to be supplemented by local traits, and local situations, needs and demands, to ensure a substantial degree of success in interpretation. Moreover, some of the 'trends', so called, are short-lived, emphasizing the volatility of the leisure industry. Also, forecasting future trends can be dangerous. It was predicted in the 1960s that by now, we should have moved to the 'three 30s': 30 years of working life, 30 working weeks per year and a 30-hour working week. This has only been achieved in part, and for the very few. Indeed, many people in full-time employment are working longer hours now than a decade ago and the UK is known to have the longest working hours in Europe.

Trends analysis should also be undertaken locally by all leisure service organizations. Annual surveys, as part of performance measurement and in the writing of strategic reports, need to be undertaken and the results compared to previous years and with national and local performance indicators.

Recent trends in the UK

The population in the United Kingdom has grown steadily over the decades and at mid-2002 was 59.2 million. Of these, 49.6 million people lived in England, 5.1 million in Scotland, 2.9 million in Wales, and 1.7 million in Northern Ireland. *Social Trends 2004* records that increases in population are likely to continue slowly to 2021, when there will be 62.4 million. Projections suggest that the number of people aged 65 and over will exceed the numbers aged under 16 by 2014.

The United Kingdom is also becoming more multi-racial, and not as a result of in-migration or asylum seekers, which in fact comprise a very small minority. The balance of ethnicity in the population is to do with age structure reflecting past immigration and fertility patterns.

One of the biggest changes in social behaviour over the past two decades has been the general tendency for women to delay having children. This tendency is linked to participation both in higher education and in the labour force. In addition, many women start a second family following breakdown of marriage or partnership. Another striking change in social behaviour is the increase in one-person households. The reasons are:

- the growing number of 'never married' men and, to a lesser extent, 'never married' women
- the increase in separations and divorces (the highest rates in the European Union) and
- the increased number of elderly widowed women.

A fifth of dependent children lived in lone parent families, almost twice the proportion as in 1981. Such dramatic changes have implications for leisure. Different age groups and different cultural groups have different fashions and tastes. Older groups have more time, and generally greater affluence and higher expectations than ever before. Health care is a growing industry and in terms of Leisure Management, the health and fitness sector has to adapt and cater for different market segments. This is considered in Chapters 11 and 17 on the commercial and sport and recreation sectors respectively.

The United Kingdom had the highest rate of births to teenage girls in the European Union in 2000–2003.

Over the past decade the volume of spending on leisure goods and services has grown at a faster rate than spending on non-leisure goods and is likely to continue to do so, particularly if the levels of service, facilities and customer services continue at the same pace as they have over the past several years.

People's expectations of leisure are rising rapidly. Attitudes to and perceptions of leisure and its relationship to work are shifting; consumers are becoming more discerning and knowledgeable and want value for money. In terms of community leisure, therefore, residents expect to be provided with good facilities and a quality of service that would be expected from the private sector.

Leisure provision and choice of activity are increasingly affected by outside variables: health, fitness, food, fashion and concern about the environment. The catering industry is faced with making decisions about organic and GM foods. Those leisure activities that result in harming the environment, for example, motor sports, may suffer falls in participation unless active measures are seen to be taken to alleviate the problem of pollution. Developers applying for planning permission, particularly in the Green Belt, will continue to face strong objections from local pressure groups and a less favourable attitude from local authorities. Leisure planners and developers will have to consider how provision of facilities and services fit in with prevailing political and community expectations.

Provision for young people, in the lucrative commercial sector, used to be the key target market for many operators. Now targets are more diverse. With the youth market no longer predominant, adjustments in leisure provision towards the older markets have needed to be made. For example, at leisure centres, provision may need to be made for some environments with a quieter, slower tempo and atmosphere, enabling people to carry out activities at their own pace. Leisure providers have to move away from the standardized, mass-market provision, towards more flexible provision, for more segmented markets.

The presence of children in the family is an important influence on both the extent and type of chosen leisure activity: swimming, holiday centres and theme parks, for example, are orientated towards children and families.

> Coastal retirement areas have the largest proportion of elderly people.

Where people live can also affect the leisure pursuits that they engage in. Many rural populations can be as disadvantaged as inner urban areas. Around a fifth of the population of Great Britain now lives in rural areas. In contrast, the population living in mining and industrial areas has fallen. The number of people living in resort and retirement areas has increased, reflecting the general ageing of the population.

Clearly, demographic change should be taken into account by planners, developers and Leisure Managers.

Income: wealth and poverty

The leisure industry is a growth industry, employing around 2.5 million people. Income and wealth are important measures of the standard of living of individuals and the country as a whole. They also directly influence leisure behaviour. One of the most commonly used measures of living standards is household disposable income, which has generally increased over the past decades, along with the gap between high income and low income earners. Couples with non-dependent children have the highest gross household income in the United Kingdom. Lone parents with dependent children receive nearly half their income in the form of non-contributory cash benefits. They are among the poorest. Retired households receive their income either from investment income, such as personal pensions, or from contributory cash benefits.

The amount households spend on goods and services provides an indication of their standard of living and material well-being. However, the ownership of goods is not a true reflection of wealth; many poor people own considerable goods, whether they can afford them or not. Household expenditure is considered more fully in Household expenditure and leisure, p. 197, Chapter 11.

It is essential for businesses to have an understanding of underlying price change patterns and the real changes in prices affecting leisure participation; these can be established from the wide range of price statistics available from National Statistics Retail Price Index (RPI) business unit. Not unexpectedly, the households with the lowest incomes spend a higher proportion of their income on essentials such as food, fuel, light and power than other households. Conversely, those with the highest incomes spend a higher proportion of their income on leisure goods and services.

Leisure itself, therefore, could become either the social equalizer or a social divider. Although an over-simplification, leisure may become dominated by two groups, those with the money, but not the time, and those with the time, but not the money, unless home computers and digital technology are used by busy, time-harassed people to create greater freedom and time for more leisure. However, at the other end of the scale, poverty seems always to be with us. The Rowntree inquiry into Income and Welfare depicted the United Kingdom as the second highest nation, behind New Zealand, in the 'rising inequality' league. One disturbing statistic is that life expectancy England and Wales for professional, managerial and technical men and women is far higher than for manual workers.

Some poor people may be caught in a vicious circle of bad housing, unemployment or low pay, poor diet and poor schools. There are significant health inequalities; obesity is increasingly a cause of concern, particularly in children and young people. With adults, stress is the modern disease. The National Lottery New Opportunities Fund (NOF) has opened new avenues to help poorer communities and the NOF funding targets initiatives around health and lifestyle (see Healthy Living Centres, p. 364, Chapter 17).

Prescriptions for anti-depressant drugs dispensed in England alone more than doubled, from 9 million items in 1991 to 24 million in 2001.

The use of time: leisure at home

The amount of time people spend in work and on essential tasks impacts on the amount of time they have for leisure activities and upon their lifestyle. For most people, around a third of each day is spent sleeping. How people use their time for the rest of the day is related, among other things, to gender and economic status. Both men and women who are not working spend more time than their counterparts who are in work on domestic chores and on watching television, listening to the radio and socializing. However, it appears that the traditional gender division of labour is still strong. Women still do the majority of household chores, despite their increased participation in the labour market. Overall, women from all social classes spend more than three times longer than men on average on cooking and routine housework and more than twice as long on caring for children and adults.

Concerning leisure in the home, recent General Household Surveys report that almost all respondents had watched television (99 per cent) or visited or entertained friends or relations (96 per cent) during the four weeks prior to interview. Adults aged 16 and over completing the *UK 2000 Time Use Survey* spent 20 hours a week, or just under 3 hours a day, watching television. Listening to the radio (88 per cent) and records or tapes (78 per cent) were the next most popular activities. The popularity of television viewing is reflected in the fact that the most widely read monthly magazine was the *Sky TV Guide* and *Take a Break*, the most popular women's weekly. Video tapes are now more likely to be bought than rented, and this may be linked to the expansion of the distribution of pre-recorded videos in such places as supermarkets.

Playing music on home music systems is another popular activity and the technology has changed rapidly: from records to cassettes, to compact discs (CDs) to digital versatile discs (DVDs), which can play music, video and games. DVD was launched in the United Kingdom in April 1998. Since then, both hardware and software sales have increased rapidly. According to the British Video Association, the DVD is the fastest growing consumer electronics format of all time, selling faster than the video and CD players did at the same stage after their launch. The rental market showed 87 million DVDs compared to 69.1 million videos. However, in early 2004, 91 per cent of homes in Britain had a video player, while only 54 per cent had a DVD player.

> In January 2004 sales of DVDs accounted for up to 85 per cent of the market compared to videos.

The major recent trends in the UK are in the advances in technological equipment available to individual people, including the versatility of mobile telephones, personal computers and access to the Internet. The computer is destined to be the greatest invention of all time. The power of the Internet is illustrated with top class sport and sports teams with websites carrying advertisements for on-line gambling, ticket sales, sponsorship and merchandising. At the 2003 Wimbledon tennis championships, over 4 million 'unique users' logged on to the website, visited over 27 million times, and stayed for an average of over two hours.

> In 2002, £100 million worth of bets were placed on the Grand National; 10 per cent of these were on-line betting.

Technology for downloading music from the Internet is fast developing, with a growing number of websites offering this facility. The singer George Michael recorded a top-selling single in 2004 and distributed it on his website for free downloading. The effect of such dramatic initiatives are yet unknown, but there is little doubt that technological advances will change the conventional delivery of both leisure services and products.

Reading for pleasure, interest and information is for most adult people a consuming leisure time activity. Over half the population are members of their local library and in Great Britain over 400 million books are borrowed from public libraries in the United Kingdom. Many libraries have collections of CDs, records, audio and video-cassettes, and DVDs for loan to the public. Nearly all public libraries now have personal computers for public use; in May 2002, 70 per cent had Internet connections. The library sector is included in Chapter 16.

Reading newspapers is an important part of many people's daily routine. On an average weekday, around 55 per cent of people aged fifteen and over in the United Kingdom read a national morning newspaper, 59 per cent of men and 50 per cent of women. Over 80 per cent of adults read a regional or local newspaper every week. The *News of the World* is the most popular Sunday paper, the *Sun* the most popular daily paper. The more serious daily newspapers, such as *The Times* and *Guardian* and *The Observer on Sunday*, are read by only a small number relative to the popular newspapers.

There are marked variations in the spending patterns of income groups on different types of reading material. Households in the highest income group spent more than three times as much on books and magazines as on newspapers; the lowest income group spent more on newspapers than books or magazines.

Commercial leisure services and equipment in the home environment are included in Chapter 11, Leisure provision in the commercial sector.

The use of time: leisure away from home for social interests

The most common leisure activity outside the home among adults in Great Britain is visiting a public house, with 65 per cent of all adults, more men than women, saying that they had done so in the three months before being interviewed. Seven in ten of those aged between 16 and 24 had gone to a night-club or disco in the previous three months. Fast food was also more commonly eaten by those in the younger age groups. These aspects of leisure and activities such as cinema- and theatre-going, gambling, tenpin bowling, eating out and other commercial services are also covered in Chapter 11.

Figures from the Henley Centre show that social grade affects participation in some leisure activities, for example, among those in the non-manual social grades a meal in a restaurant is more popular than a visit to the pub. They also participate more frequently in most of the main leisure activities outside the home. The exceptions include visits to a disco or night-club, betting shops and bingo. Activities which were much more popular with men than women include watching a sports event and going to a betting shop and a pub. Activities more popular with women than men were visiting a library, going to the theatre and playing bingo.

Chapter 16 considers participation and trends in the arts. It shows that the proportion of adults that attend most types of cultural events has not changed much over the last decade or so. The exception is going to the cinema; whereas three in ten adults said in 1986/7 that they went to the cinema, five in ten did so in 1995/6 and in 2003, about six in ten said they did so.

Visits to theme parks and leisure parks are discussed in Chapter 17. Visits to other leisure destinations and tourist attractions and holidays are covered in Chapter 14 on tourism. The United Kingdom Tourism Survey found that one in five holidays taken in the United Kingdom had an activity as their main purpose, with swimming and walking/hiking the most common activities. Nearly 60 per cent of people participated in an activity of some sort while on their holiday; visiting museums and heritage sites was also popular.

Day visits which are not made on a regular basis and which last for three or more hours away from home are called tourism leisure day visits. The United Kingdom Day Visits Survey collects information on round trips made from home or work for leisure purposes. Around 70 per cent of day visits are to a town or city, around 25 per cent to the countryside and less than 5 per cent to the seaside or coast. The two most popular reasons for this all-year-round activity are visiting friends and relatives and going out for a meal or drink. The car was the main form of transport used for leisure day visits, although travelling on foot accounts for around three in ten of all visits. Most visits involved total travelling of less than ten miles away from home.

Other leisure-related activities

Leisure is not just about filling time for enjoyment, but includes a wide array of activities, many of which could be termed 'serious leisure', for example, hobbies, formal leisure learning, doing good works, religious activities and all manner of volunteering. Volunteering is covered in Chapter 10 and serious leisure is also explained in Chapter 24. There appears to be an insatiable demand from a growing number of people to continue to learn through courses of instruction and attendance at leisure classes. Women predominate over men, though the gap lessens year by year. The likelihood of attending classes varies with the economic status, socio-economic group and educational qualifications of men and women. Men and women in non-manual socio-economic groups were twice as likely as those in manual groups to be going to classes and the likelihood of attending a class also increased with the person's educational level.

Religious activities take up a good deal of 'free time' and form an important part of many people's lives. The 2001 Census figures in the UK showed that 77 per cent of people in England and Wales, 67 per cent in Scotland and 86 per cent in Northern Ireland said they identified with a religion. The most common faiths after Christianity were Islam, Hinduism, Sikhism, Judaism and Buddhism. Well over 90 per cent of respondents who identified with a religion said they belonged to the Christian faith.

According to Christian Research, around 60 per cent of people active in their religion in Great Britain are female. Those people aged under 15 and over 45 are over-represented while those aged between 15 and 44 are under-represented. There has been a fall in church-going. Only 11 per cent of adults questioned in the British Social Attitudes Survey said they attended church once a week or more.

Summary

Main indicators of social change include a steadily increasing population, a growing multi-cultural nation, falling birth rates, middle-ageing population, life longevity, single and smaller households, increasing disposable incomes for some market segments but growing differences between rich and poor, flexible work patterns, more women in the workplace and greater emphasis on personal independent lifestyles. Women still undertake traditional household roles. Couples having families later and also having smaller families allows these relatively young people more time, freedom and money for leisure.

It is important for Leisure Managers to understand and be able to use information about trends in leisure. They need to know, not just what leisure activity people are engaged in at leisure centres, parks, swimming pools and theatres but also about people's time for leisure, their social situations and their disposable income. Leisure Managers need to know the market and the trends.

Of the three main providers of leisure services and facilities – local government, voluntary organizations and commercial companies – the commercial sector is the most volatile and it is in this sector therefore that changes in leisure spending can be discerned as shown in Chapter 11.

Discussion points

1 Trends in leisure behaviour are usually based on national data. To what extent are they of value in your local situation and what else needs to be done to make best use of them?

2 When examining leisure statistics and data from a variety of sources and comparing results, you are likely to find differences. Why might this be the case?

Further reading

Social Trends and the *General Household Surveys* contain questions relating to the lifestyles and leisure habits of people living in the UK. This text used:

ONS (2003), *Social Trends 34*, TSO, London.

ONS (2003), *Living in Britain – Results from the 2001 General Household Survey*, TSO, London.

ONS (2003), *Annual Abstracts of Statistics*, 2004 edn, TSO, London.

ONS (2003), *UK 2004 – The Official Yearbook of the United Kingdom*, TSO, London.

The Office for National Statistics also produces *Population Trends* quarterly, and *Regional Trends* annually.

Useful websites

Office for National Statistics: www.statistics.gov.uk

British Market Research Bureau: www.bmrb.co.uk

National Centre for Social Research: www.natcen.ac.uk

Mintel International Group: www.mintel.com

Key Note: www.keynote.co.uk

Leisure Industries Research Centre (LIRC): www.sums.ac.uk/leis-mgt/lirc.html

Sport Industry Research Centre (SIRC): www.shu.ac.uk/schools/slm/sirc.html

Part 3

14

Tourism, heritage and leisure

In this chapter

- Tourism: an international perspective
- Tourism in the UK
- The government and tourism
- Tourist visit profiles
- Promoting tourism and destination attractions
- Tourism and heritage worldwide and in the UK
- Tourism, hospitality and accommodation

Introduction

Tourism functions at many levels. It is a global, international, national and local phenomenon. It is vast and increasing in size and in the world economy. Tourism is of significance in most countries and of substantial importance in the United Kingdom.

There are many segments in the tourism market, including holiday tourism, business tourism, eco-tourism, cultural tourism, spiritual tourism, sports and activity holidays tourism, extreme sports and 'experience' tourism, education tourism, destination tourism, event tourism and also sex tourism, regrettably. Scientists are even talking about space tourism. More down to earth, visiting friends and families, away days to the countryside or seaside, leisure shopping to other cities and across the Channel, all add to the tourism market.

Tourism, travel, destination management, attractions and hospitality are growth areas in Leisure Management with thousands of new people seeking qualifications and employment in the industry. The United Kingdom has a rich historic environment and tourists visit to share in the nation's tangible and intangible heritage. To try to cover even a small part of this industry in one book would be a challenge. To attempt this in one chapter would be totally unrealistic. This chapter, therefore, provides a broad picture of what makes the United Kingdom a great destination for both international and domestic tourism.

Tourism: an international perspective

Tourism 2020 Vision is an assessment by the World Tourism Organization (WTO) of the development of tourism in the first 20 years of the new millennium. International

Table 14.1 International tourist arrivals and receipts

INTERNATIONAL TOURIST ARRIVALS (MILLION)		INTERNATIONAL TOURISM RECEIPTS (US$ BILLION)	
WORLD	703	WORLD	474
1 France	77.0	1 United States	66.5
2 Spain	51.7	2 Spain	33.6
3 United States	41.9	3 France	32.3
4 Italy	39.8	4 Italy	26.9
5 China	36.8	5 China	20.4
6 United Kingdom	24.2	6 Germany	19.2
7 Canada	20.1	7 United Kingdom	17.8
8 Mexico	19.7	8 Austria	11.2
9 Austria	18.6	9 Hong Kong (China)	10.1
10 Germany	18.0	10 Greece	9.7

(Data as collected by WTO, September 2003)
Source: World Tourism Organization (WTO)

arrivals are expected to reach over 1.56 billion; 1.18 billion will be intra-regional and 377 million will be long-haul travellers, according to the WTO. The top three receiving regions will be Europe (717 million tourists), East Asia and the Pacific (397 million) and the Americas (282 million). East Asia and the Pacific, South Asia, the Middle East and Africa are forecasted to record growth rates.

International travel is affected by global economic conditions, wars and conflicts in different regions and, increasingly, terrorism. The fateful day imprinted in the minds of people everywhere is 11 September, 2001, which had an immediate down-turn effect on international tourism. Yet, in relatively few years, for much of the world, travelling is getting back on track. Data collected by the WTO in September 2003, reported that in 2002, there were 702,600,000 international arrivals – 399,800,000 to Europe, particularly Western and Southern Europe; 131,300,000 to Asia and the Pacific; and 114,900,000 to the Americas, predominantly to North America. Table 14.1 shows the top ten countries visited and also the international tourism receipts with the United States by far the largest in the world.

In 2002, the UK ranked the seventh country in international tourism earnings behind the USA, Spain, France, Italy, China and Germany.

Britons are great travellers overseas. Spain and France are the top countries visited with over 12 million each year. The USA is still the top long-haul destination, with Australia, New Zealand, South Africa and Thailand still popular. Short break holidays have increased and account for 15 per cent of overseas holidays (National Statistics, 2003).

Tourism is one of the largest industries in the United Kingdom. It is worth approximately £80 billion. In 2002, over 24 million trips were made by overseas visitors spending around £11.7 billion (see Table 14.2).

A breakdown of the distribution of overseas tourism in 2002 is shown in Table 14.3. England attracted 20.54 million visitors, Scotland 1.58 million,

Table 14.2 Overseas visitors to UK: visits and expenditure, 1964–2002

	Total visits (000)	Expenditure (£m)
1964	3,257	190
1974	8,543	898
1984	13,644	4,614
1994	20,794	9,786
2000	25,209	12,805
2001	22,835	11,306
2002	24,180	11,737

Source: International Passenger Survey, Office for National Statistics

Table 14.3 Distribution of overseas tourism in 2002

	Visits (millions)	Nights (millions)	Spending (£millions)
Cumbria	0.18	1.0	41
Northumbria	0.53	3.9	169
North West	1.37	9.5	466
Yorkshire	0.86	7.5	303
Heart of England	2.59	21.1	881
East of England	1.66	13.6	616
London	11.60	75.4	5,788
South West	1.43	11.5	526
Tourism South East	3.85	31.4	1,504
England unspecified	0.07	0.4	19
TOTAL ENGLAND	20.54	175.3	10,313
TOTAL SCOTLAND	1.58	15.0	806
TOTAL WALES	0.86	6.6	252
NORTHERN IRELAND	0.28	1.7	126
Oil Rigs/Travelling	0.22	0.4	15
Isle of Man	0.02	0.2	5
Channel Islands	0.02	0.1	9
Other UK	0.01	0	2
Nil Nights	1.87	0	89
TOTAL UK	24.18	199.3	11,618

Note: Non-addition within the visits column because some visitors stay in more than one.
Source: International Passenger Survey (IPS)

Wales 0.86 million and 0.28 to Northern Ireland. In England, London attracts over half the tourists. Tourism is hugely important to the economy of the United Kingdom and provides direct and indirect employment.

Tourism in the UK

The majority of tourists in the United Kingdom are UK residents at 167.3 million in 2002 compared to overseas residents at 24.2 million. Business travel accounted for around 30 per cent of all overseas visits. In 2002, UK residents took:

- 101.7 million holidays of one night or more spending £17.4 billion
- 23.3 million overnight business trips spending £5.6 billion
- 39.6 million overnight trips to friends and relatives spending £3.4 billion.

The distribution of domestic tourism in 2002 is shown in Table 14.4 and differs from the pattern of overseas tourists. London – an expensive city to stay in – is not the main choice. The South East, the Heart of England and the South West are the most popular regions in which to stay.

Table 14.4 Distribution of domestic tourism in 2002

	TRIPS MILLIONS	NIGHTS MILLIONS	SPENDING £ MILLIONS
Cumbria	4.3	13.0	728
Northumbria	4.8	13.4	868
North West	14.5	39.3	2,316
Yorkshire	12.2	36.3	1,595
Heart of England	24.6	64.8	3,166
East of England	14.5	44.3	1,704
London	16.1	35.4	2,818
South West	21.0	87.1	3,901
Tourism South East *	25.5	77.3	3,420
– Southern *	14.6	45.8	2,065
– South East *	10.9	31.5	1,355
TOTAL ENGLAND	134.9	415.8	20,787
Scotland	18.5	64.5	3,683
Wales	11.9	39.8	1,543
Northern Ireland	2.8	9.3	525
TOTAL UK	167.3	531.9	26,699

Note: *On 1April, 2003 the Southern Tourist Board and the South East England Tourist Board merged to form Tourism South East. Separate figures are shown to allow comparisons with previous years.
Source: United Kingdom Tourism Survey (UKTS)

The government and tourism

Tourism is an industry with shared provision between many providers. Largely, it is the job of national and local government in collaboration with the private and voluntary sectors. Central government provides grant-in-aid to statutory tourist boards. Within central government, the Department for Culture, Media and Sport (DCMS) has lead responsibility, working through its agencies.

In 1995, a government action plan *Tourism: Competing with the Best* (DNH, 1995) resulted in advice to over 40,000 accommodation operators on standards and customer expectations. Building on this plan, in 1997 the government department of the day, the Department of National Heritage (DNH), launched a strategy for tourism, *Success Through Partnership* (DNH, 1997). The report *People Working in Tourism and Hospitality* set out an agenda to spread good management practice. The ETB, AA and RAC jointly announced details of the new harmonization rating scheme for serviced accommodation, designed to raise standards. In 2000, the Wales Tourist Board produced a strategy for tourism in Wales (Wales Tourist Board, 2000), and in 2001, the English Tourism Council published a strategy for sustainable tourism in England (English Tourism Council, 2001). Two of the most recent national reports are *A Tourism Plan for Scotland 2000–2005* (Scottish Executive, 2002), and the DCMS publication on the structure and strategy for supporting tourism in the UK (DCMS, 2003). VisitBritain published *EnjoyEngland - the strategy* in 2003 (VisitBritain, 2003). In addition, there is a wide range of reports coming out from all the regional tourism bodies (see Useful websites).

The role of government is to provide a framework within which tourism can best develop. The DCMS champions good quality and services for tourists from the UK and from overseas. *Tomorrow's Tourism Today* (DCMS, 2004) sets out the government's ambition for meeting the needs of customers and the aims for growth in jobs and prosperity in tourism. It is self-evident that tourism is concerned with the movement of people whether within the UK or overseas. Governments, therefore, must work in co-operation to achieve the best results for all. Europe attracts more visitors than other continents; the UK government and the European Commission are to report on how to enhance the sustainability of tourism in Europe. VisitBritain has a representative in Brussels to work specifically with officials of the EU on matters which affect tourism.

On 1 April, 2003 the English Tourism Council merged with the British Tourist Authority to form VisitBritain. The new organization markets Britain to the rest of the world and England to the British. VisitBritain has a statutory duty under the Development of Tourism Act, 1969, to advise government and public bodies on issues affecting British tourism and to provide that advice freely and independently. VisitBritain work with and through Regional Tourist Boards of England who provide detailed information on visiting their respective regions: Cumbria, Northumbria, North West, Yorkshire, Heart of England, London, South West, Southern and South East England. Since 1999, tourism has become the responsibility of the UK's devolved national administrations.

The United Kingdom has four tourist boards:

- VisitBritain (formerly the English Tourism Council and the British Tourist Authority)
- VisitScotland (formerly the Scottish Tourist Board)
- Northern Ireland Tourist Board and
- Wales Tourist Board.

The Tourist Boards in England, Scotland and Wales were set up under the Development of Tourism Act in 1969 (the Northern Ireland Tourist Board was set up under separate legislation). The Act aimed to co-ordinate the diverse interests that make up the tourism industry and provide it with a single voice, a task made harder by the fact that the Boards report to different authorities:

- VisitBritain reports to the Department for Culture, Media and Sport (DCMS)
- The Wales Tourist Board reports to the National Assembly for Wales
- VisitScotland reports to the Scottish Executive.

VisitBritain has the major responsibility of marketing Britain abroad; links are maintained between VisitBritain and the other boards and their reporting authorities. Tourism activity is also influenced by other government departments. Here are some examples of the relevant activities of certain departments:

- Department for Transport: aviation, railways, roads and so on
- Department for Education and Skills: sector skills councils, National Training Organizations
- Department for Environment, Food and Rural Affairs: forestry, sustainable development, conservation and environmental protection and water and countryside issues
- Department for Trade and Industry: bank holidays, small and medium sized businesses, e-commerce
- Office for the Deputy Prime Minister: local government, planning
- HM Treasury: taxation
- Home Office: liquor licensing.

There are also many other non-governmental organizations that have an interest in tourism. VisitBritain, however, is the leadership and co-ordinating arm.

In July 2003, VisitBritain published a consultation document, *England Domestic Marketing Strategy 2003/4 to 2005/6* (VisitBritain, 2003), with a mission 'to grow the value of domestic tourism throughout England' by improving awareness of perceptions of holiday brands, products and destinations, and spreading the season of domestic tourism, among a number of 'added value' goals. Five strategies were proposed:

1 insights: understanding market potential
2 relationships: engaging with public and private stakeholders
3 products and brands: communicating destination appeal
4 distribution: making it easy to access information
5 resourcing: aligning organization and culture.

VisitBritain will provide the focal point and co-ordination; however, Tourist Boards, Regional Development Agencies and EnglandNet will be important strategic partners in the implementation of this strategy.

Tourist visit profiles

As one might expect, visitors from overseas and UK tourists have different visit profiles. As shown in Table 14.5, more than half the UK residents are on holiday when they travel for overnight stays, compared to overseas visitors who come for holiday or business in roughly the same number.

Table 14.5 Purpose of tourism in the UK 2002

	UK RESIDENTS		OVERSEAS RESIDENTS	
	TRIPS MILLIONS	SPENDING £ MILLIONS	VISITS MILLIONS	SPENDING £ MILLIONS
Holidays	101.7	17,352	7.7	3,702
Business	23.3	5,552	7.2	3,573
Visiting friends or relatives	39.6	3,428	6.4	2,514
Other	2.7	365	2.9	1,910
All purposes	187.3	28,699	24.2	11,737

Sources: United Kingdom Tourism Survey (UKTS)/International Passenger Survey (IPS)

Table 14.6 lists the main paid-admission attractions. Large numbers will visit these, whether paid or not, though numbers rise when no charges are made which is no surprise. Britain's government-sponsored museums and galleries have proved this point, as illustrated in Table 14.7 which shows that visitors to the National History Museum, Victoria & Albert Museum and Science Museum more than doubled on lifting charges. Seaside resorts and 'pleasure' beaches, particularly Blackpool Pleasure Beach, with 6.5 million visits, are major attractions; others include Pleasureland in Southport, Eastbourne Pier, Pleasure Beach in Great Yarmouth and Flamingo Park in Hastings.

Promoting tourism and destination attractions

In the recent past, tourism was defined by government agencies as visits away from home with at least one overnight stop. Day visits did not feature in tourism economics and visiting friends and relatives was not viewed as significant. That view has changed over the years in light of what actually occurs; day visits and visiting friends and relatives are now seen as important market sectors and of economic value.

Table 14.6 Major paid admission attractions

ATTRACTION	LOCATION	VISITS 2002	VISITS 2001
British Airways London Eye	London	4,090,000	3,850,000*
Tower of London	London	1,940,856	2,019,183
Eden Project	St Austell	1,832,482*	1,700,000
Legoland Windsor	Windsor	1,453,000	1,632,000
Flamingo Land Theme Park and Zoo	Kirby Misperton	1,393,300*	1,322,000*
Windermere Lake Cruises	Ambleside	1,266,027	1,241,918
Drayton Manor Family Theme Park	Tamworth	1,200,000*	960,000*
Edinburgh Castle	Edinburgh	1,153,317	1,126,680
Chester Zoo	Chester	1,134,949	1,060,433
Canterbury Cathedral	Canterbury	1,110,529*	1,151,099*
Westminster Abbey	London	1,058,854	986,354
Kew Gardens	Richmond	969,188	989,352
Windsor Castle	Windsor	931,042	904,164
London Zoo	London	891,028	906,923
Roman Baths	Bath	845,608	864,989
New MetroLand	Gateshead Metro Centre	810,000*	650,000*

* = estimate
Source: Survey of Visits to Visitor Attractions (data from attractions which responded to the Survey of Visits to Visitor Attractions and gave permission)

Tourism was defined by the former Department of National Heritage as signifying 'all aspects of the visitor experience, whether the visitor is on a day trip, a short holiday or a long holiday, visiting for leisure or business from this country or overseas'. This broad definition holds good today.

Marketing tourism has developed into a 'mini-industry' of its own. However, tourism has many different markets which need different approaches. Chapter 20 delves more fully into marketing processes. Here a brief mention is made of one important feature of marketing: that of segmentation. Domestic tourism, for example, has some different market segments to those of international tourism and each segment is made up of different time durations:

- short break holidays
- visiting friends and relatives (VFR)
- business tourism
- longer stays
- day visits.

Table 14.7 Major free admission attractions

ATTRACTION	LOCATION	2002	2001
Blackpool Pleasure Beach	Blackpool	6,200,000	6,500,000
Tate Modern	London	4,618,632	3,551,885
British Museum	London	4,607,311	4,800,938
National Gallery	London	4,130,973*	4,918,985*
Natural History Museum†	London	2,957,501	1,696,176
Victoria & Albert Museum†	London	2,661,338	1,446,344
Science Museum†	London	2,628,374	1,352,649
Pleasureland Theme Park	Southport	2,000,000*	2,000,000*
Eastbourne Pier	Eastbourne	1,900,000*	2,000,000*
York Minster	York	1,570,500*	1,600,000*
Pleasure Beach	Great Yarmouth	1,500,000*	1,500,000*
National Portrait Gallery	London	1,484,331	1,269,819
Tate Britain	London	1,178,235	1,011,716
Kelvingrove Art Gallery and Museum	Glasgow	955,671*	1,031,138
Somerset House	London	900,000*	700,000*
Flamingo Family Fun Park	Hastings	900,000	900,000*

* = estimate.
† National Museums and Galleries that changed admission policy from paid admission to free admission in 2000 or 2001
Source: Survey of Visits to Visitor Attractions (data from attractions which responded to the Survey of Visits to Visitor Attractions and gave permission)

VisitBritain is targeting short breaks, VFR and business tourism as these are perceived as the areas of growth. Short breaks (1–3 nights) represent the largest area of growth and there is opportunity to encourage long weekends or a second holiday. Holiday travel is expected to continue to dominate the domestic tourism market, rising by 27 per cent by 2005. However, the VFR and business sectors are predicted to increase proportionally by even more, according to VisitBritain. In terms of marketing, UK demographics show that the market for tourism is changing. Middle-aged and older people are becoming more active and mobile and more travel-sophisticated than in times past. The growth in the affluent retired market offers opportunity to promote year-round tourism. Also those in employment, particularly the 'cash-rich, time poor', segments will be attracted to more short break holidays but require value for money and value for time, such as easy booking and accessibility to quality accommodation, travel destinations, attractions and events.

The tourism product in the United Kingdom

Core ingredients of the tourism 'product' are transport, accommodation and meals. The tourism 'experience', however, calls for a wider portfolio serving different market segments, including: hospitality, visitor destinations and attractions, events, shops catering for visitors, hotels and guest houses, pubs and restaurants, theatres, museums and galleries, theme parks and urban parks, swimming pools and sports facilities, conferences, exhibitions, access to coastal paths, canal tow-paths, resorts, the country-side, landscape gardens, and heritage sites, and all elements of travel by road, rail, water and air.

Innovation and new ideas of what constitutes a tourist attraction are helping to open up new markets and with them, economic growth, particularly in areas unable to support traditional tourism. Television series such as *Coronation Street*, *Last of the Summer Wine* and *Heartbeat*, and period dramas such as *Wuthering Heights*, *Jane Eyre* and *Pride and Prejudice*, have created demand for visiting studios in Manchester, the Brontë's village of Haworth in Yorkshire, and Jane Austen's home in Chawton in Hampshire. The classic film *Brief Encounter* now attracts visitors to Carnforth station in Lancashire, recently restored to its original design and décor. Films such as *Braveheart* promote the Highlands of Scotland. British-made, low budget, films such as *The Full Monty* and *Calendar Girls* provide interest in the county and the 'Yorkshire grit' and determination in overcoming difficulties. *Shakespeare in Love*, linking heri-tage, the Globe Theatre and a visit to London appeals to target audiences. The VisitBritain 2002 campaign around the Harry Potter theme led to the highest-ever number of email enquiries to the agency in one week. Durham Cathedral, already a major tourist destination, now attracts even more to see the setting for many of the scenes for filming Harry Potter's Hogwarts School of Witchcraft and Wizardry. The Lake District is not only visited for the striking scenery and walking holidays, but to experience the area in which William Wordsworth lived and wrote his poetry. Themed attractions such as Legoland in Windsor have a dual appeal for families; children can enjoy Legoland, while the parents can visit Windsor Castle.

Creativity and culture provide powerful means not just to promote attractions but to also market regions, cities and towns. Cities short-listed for the European Capital of Culture 2008 – Birmingham, Bristol, Cardiff, Liverpool and Newcastle/Gateshead – promoted their cities, not just as having good accommodation, services, vibrant night life and events, but cities with a strong sense of identity and culture across a broad scale of interest. The pop culture of the Beatles, the famous Royal Philharmonic and the city's cathedrals, were all highly marketable products for the winning city Liverpool. The symbolism of reconciliation between the Anglican Cathedral and the Roman Catholic Cathedral facing each other along Hope Street, adds to the distinctiveness of the city. Liverpool is also a ferry ride to the slow-paced, hospitable and quiet beauty of the Emerald Isle or a drive south into Wales, the legendary land of song, with its rugged mountains and valleys, a history of coal mines and a passionate national culture with its own language.

The UK's historic cities and towns, rural and costal areas continue to have appeal and reflect the interest in British heritage and culture. Tourists are not just interested in the big destination attractions but in many of the relatively small things and the ways of life of people. However, in terms of the mass tourist market for domestic and international tourism, the destination attraction is the magnet. Destination management is set to be an even more significant growth area for the British economy and for managers in leisure and tourism.

Destination attractions

The DCMS reports that around 257 million visits are made to attractions in the United Kingdom and that there are more than 6,400 'registered' attractions in the UK. Museums, galleries and historic properties make up just over half the known and recorded attractions. The sector includes cathedrals, gardens (over 500), wildlife sites, country parks, farms, steam railways, themed exhibitions, leisure parks and a host of other attractions. Of the top twenty paid admission attractions in Britain, London has a major share. In 2002, British Airways London Eye was by far the single most popular attraction with over four million customers, more than double those for the Tower of London, the next most popular. It is of interest that tourism is not only about the traditional experiences but of new ones also. The London Eye, the Tate Modern, the Magnum, Sheffield's themed industrial discovery centre, and the Eden Project which attracted nearly two million visits in 2002, have expanded the market for international and domestic tourism.

> In 2001, free and paying attractions combined received around 452 million visits.

Tourism For All was a national scheme to improve accessibility of accommodation for disabled people. Disability awareness within the tourist industry is a growing feature. Under the terms of The Disability Discrimination Act, 1995, it is unlawful to provide a lower standard of service or offer less favourable terms to those who are disabled.

London and royalty are prime destination attractions. Why London? Because not only is it one of the world's most famous cities, it receives double the number of overseas visitors than the top twenty visited cities in the United Kingdom. The Passenger Survey 2002 recorded 11.6 million overseas visitors to London, 850,000 to Edinburgh, 670,000 to Birmingham and 590,000 to Manchester. Other cities with between 200,000 and 400,000 overseas visitors were Glasgow, Oxford, Bristol, Cambridge, Cardiff, Newcastle-upon-Tyne, Brighton and Hove, York, Bath and Nottingham.

Why royalty? Because every year, millions of visitors from the United Kingdom and from overseas, visit places and enjoy events associated with today's royalty and with the lives of earlier kings and queens, with pageantry, and with traditional pomp, ceremony and custom. The top royal attractions in terms of visitor numbers are:

- The Tower of London
- Windsor Castle
- Hampton Court Palace
- Buckingham Palace
- The Palace of Holyrood House.

These five destinations alone attract four million visits each year. Other royal visitor attractions include: Balmoral, Kensington Palace, Sandringham House, and Clarence House which will be the Prince of Wales' official London residence and was opened to the public in 2003.

Members of the Royal Family themselves are principal ambassadors, not just for

287

visiting royal houses, but visiting the United Kingdom. The Duke of Edinburgh hosted part of VisitBritain's programme for the World Travel Leaders Summit ensuring that Britain was a safe place to visit after the foot-and-mouth outbreak in 2001. The Queen's Golden Jubilee celebrations in 2002 with television pictures of one million people cramming into the Mall and around Buckingham Palace and the televised pop concert in the gardens of the palace, were massive boosts to international tourism.

Economic impact of tourism

The extent of the economic impact upon a community from tourism will vary according to the type of visitor attracted and their length of stay. Generally, hotel guests spend the most and their spending has the greater 'multiplier' effect, with conference delegates amongst the high spenders. The development of tourist facilities tends to be 'supply-led' with local authorities initially investing public money, which in turn attracts investment from the private sector.

Government influence and legislation have a considerable effect on tourism. The transport infrastructure is a key factor in making journeys a pleasant part of the leisure experience. Government-sponsored attractions such as museums and galleries boost indirect spending. The loosening of the rules on gambling makes it easier to gain access to a casino. The liberalization of English licensing laws enables pubs to stay open for longer hours. The campaign Daylight Extra seeks to bring the United Kingdom in line with Western Europe and extend the tourist season.

Co-operative marketing is a growing feature of cost-effective tourism promotion: day trips packaged with household goods; colour film processing with tickets to visitor attractions; and 'child goes free' vouchers to pantomimes. Successful advertising campaigns have generated substantial new business. The former ETB estimated that, for every £1 it spent, an additional £13 was created for the industry.

In 2002, the average spend per trip by UK residents was £160 compared to overseas residents at £480. Total tourism expenditure, however, by UK residents was double that of overseas visitors as shown in Table 14.8.

Tourism, by definition, involves travel: leisure transport. Travel and the mode of transport can be a leisure activity in itself, whether that travel is by cycle, motor cycle, car, coach, boat, barge, ship, train or plane. The importance of the commercial sector and leisure travel was summed up by Roberts 25 years ago and holds good today:

> Transport as a leisure activity in itself (pleasure motoring, from home, canal boat tours, sea cruises etc.) as a linkage between home and leisure destinations, or a means of enlarging their destination's attractions (coach tours, car trips, boat trips, fishing excursions etc.), forms a high proportion of leisure expenditure. The commercial sector is directly or indirectly involved in all leisure transport modes in addition to the private car. The sector owns and operates shipping lines, aircraft, coaches, some railways in continental Europe, taxis, pleasure boats and others. It supplies cars and bicycles for hire; provides catering services; provides the boots for hikers, and the shoes for less ambitious walkers. The supply of equipment generally (for example bicycles) is the prerogative of the commercial sector. Finally, it provides marinas and often owns seaside piers which provide landing stages for shipping.
>
> Roberts, 1979

Table 14.8 Tourism expenditure by category 2002

	UK RESIDENTS		OVERSEAS RESIDENTS	
	% OF TOTAL	£ MILLIONS	% OF TOTAL	£ MILLIONS
Accommodation	30	7,960	33.3	3,908
Eating out	21	5,680	20.6	2,418
Total shopping	17	4,100	26.0	3,052
Travel within the UK	19	5,060	9.2	1,080
Entertainment	8	2,190	2.9	340
Services, etc.	2	470	4.0	469
Other	3	790	4.0	469
Total	100	26,700	100	11,737

Sources: United Kingdom Tourism Survey/International Passenger Survey

Two aspects are worth noting. First, there are a number of personal and social reasons for travel which may be as important as the destination itself. Second, travel is normally expensive and those who can afford it can go further and in greater comfort. Poorer people travel less. Even a simple journey across a large city with a young family could be formidable. For people with disabilities, it can be impossible. More than most forms of leisure, travel is shaped by cost, both direct and indirect.

Tourism and heritage worldwide and in the UK

When we use the word 'heritage' we often think of historic sites, castles, monuments and museums: a tangible heritage of physical structures. However, there also exists an intangible, non-structured heritage, which is passed on from generation to generation and structures our ways of life.

An intangible heritage

Many tourists are not just interested in destinations and sites but in how people live now and how their forebears lived in the past. In Chapter 3, Cultural heritage, particularly in the United Kingdom, was discussed and its influence was still seen in leisure and recreation today. In many parts of the world, however, traditions and heritage are lived out in current times. Leisure Managers need to be aware of, and manage, cultural differences. These are not just of language, geography and history, but of values, belief, attitude and behaviour. Compared to the highly competitive nature of much of Western and other societies, epitomized in Olympic Games and World Cups, some nationalities have no great wish to win at all costs, nor to excel over and above all others. In sport, for example, in one tribal culture, the home tribe is always declared 'the winner', whether it has won the game or not. Having provided the facilities and lavish hospitality for the annual festival, the home tribe is praised and declared the winner, and peace between the tribes continues. Different value systems need to be respected. All over the world, religious values and activities take the form of festivals and celebrations, which are major leisure events.

Clearly, what is handed down over the years is not just the tangible heritage of historic buildings and sites, but an intangible heritage. In February 2003, UNESCO promoted a conference, Towards a Convention for the Safeguarding of Intangible Cultural Heritage.

> Whether on land, underwater, cultural or natural, mobile or immobile, humanity's tangible heritage is safeguarded, in times of peace as in times of war, by four international conventions adopted by UNESCO's Member States in 1954, 1970, 1972 and 2001. However, in just about every part of the world, another very important element of peoples' cultural legacy, their intangible heritage – for example, oral traditions, customs, music, dance, rituals, festivities and traditional medicine – runs a risk of disappearing unless appropriate safeguard measures are taken.
>
> UNESCO, 2003

To ensure that such safeguards are effective, UNESCO proposed the creation of local and national management bodies, educational programmes, legal and funding initiatives.

Heritage from this perspective is perceived as the cultures of nations and territories, local traditions and customs. Even in a relatively small country such as the United Kingdom, there are many different cultural identities – Scottish, Welsh, Irish and English – and within these are regional and local identities. In the West Country, indigenous Cornish people are trying to rekindle the old Cornish language; some parents want their sons to be born in Yorkshire so they may be entitled to play cricket for their county; and in the East End of London, there exists the proud heritage of Cockneys, particularly those born within the sound of Bow Bells.

However, heritage can also be viewed from a global perspective which removes the barriers of nationality and draws the world together in a shared heritage of millions of years of physical development and thousands of years of human development. One factor which enhances this world view is the designation and listing of World Heritage Sites.

World Heritage UK Sites and tourism

The World Heritage Convention is the international legal instrument which provides a framework for the conservation of cultural and natural heritage considered to be of outstanding universal value. The major players involved in the Convention are:

- the 176 State Parties who have ratified the World Heritage Convention
- UNESCO and its World Heritage Centre
- the World Conservation Union and
- other advisory bodies such as the International Council on Monuments and Sites.

World Heritage Sites are inscribed on the nomination of the national government who must adhere to the 1972 World Heritage Convention. Under Article 4 of the

Convention, national governments have an obligation to care for their natural and cultural heritage.

The World Heritage List includes 754 'properties' from 129 States Parties as at 2003 – 582 cultural sites, 149 natural sites and 23 mixed properties. Some of the sites are well known landmarks such as the Taj Mahal, the Great Wall of China and the Galapagos Islands famous for their unusual animal life, giant tortoise, iguana and birds and their association with Charles Darwin's theory of evolution. The list also includes national parks containing globally significant biodiversity such as the Serengeti National Park and Mount Everest, and ruins and monuments of bygone civilizations.

In the UK, Stonehenge is one of the sites known worldwide. Another is Hadrian's Wall, the only Roman World Heritage Site in Britain and the largest of all the British examples. It is the most complex and elaborate of all the frontier works of the Roman Empire. Hadrian's Wall was the first UK site to complete its Management Plan. Of interest to Leisure Managers is that its Management Committee has to deal with two main areas of potential conflict, one of different industries: the interests of tourism, farming and forestry, and one of different authorities: Hadrian's Wall crosses twelve local authorities, including two national parks. Fortunately, English Heritage has a remit over the whole site. Although a relatively small country, geographically, it is little known that by 2003 there were 24 World Heritage Sites in the United Kingdom and like nearly all other sites, their listing adds to their appeal as tourist destinations, given good marketing and promotion. The World Heritage Sites in the United Kingdom listed under the Convention between 1986 and 2003 are shown in Table 14.9 overleaf.

Management of historical sites

The United Kingdom, as well as being a signatory to the World Heritage Convention, is part of the Council of Europe's efforts to conserve and manage Europe's heritage. The Council's second summit in 1997 reaffirmed its commitment to the protection of European cultural and natural heritage. The subsequent campaign, Europe, A Common Heritage, was launched in September 1999. This is enshrined in two documents: *Convention for the Protection of the Architectural Heritage, 1985*; and the *European Convention on the Protection of the Archaeological Heritage (revised), 1992*. Aware of the growth in urban development projects, the Convention sought ways of protecting the archaeological heritage through integrated conservation methods. Pickard (2001) studied ways in which heritage sites could best be managed, bearing in mind the principles enshrined in Council of Europe and World Heritage Conventions, under four main headings:

- management and regeneration action
- environmental management
- tourism and heritage management and
- sustainability.

The management of a historic centre will require the formulation and implementation of some form of plan mechanism and may include a specific 'conservation plan' or 'action plan' and the use of an economic development and regeneration strategy to encourage the maintenance and

Table 14.9 World Heritage Sites in the UK 1986–2003

YEAR OF DESIGNATION	WORLD HERITAGE SITES
1986	Giant's Causeway and Causeway Coast
	Durham Castle and Cathedral
	Iron Bridge
	Studley Royal Park
	Stonehenge
	Castles and Town Walls of King Edward in Gwynedd
	St Kilda
1987	Blenheim Palace
	City of Bath
	Hadrian's Wall
	Westminster Palace, Westminster Abbey and St Margaret's Church
1988	Henderson Island
	Tower of London
	Canterbury Cathedral, St Augustine's Abbey and St Martin's Church
1995	Old and New Towns of Edinburgh
	Gough Island Wildlife Reserve
1997	Maritime Greenwich
1999	Heart of Neolithic Orkney
2000	Historic Town of St George and Related Fortification, Bermuda [Listed under UK jurisdiction]
	Blaenavon Industrial Landscape
2001	Dorset and East Devon Coast
	Derwent Valley Mills
	New Lanark
	Saltaire
2003	Royal Botanical Gardens, Kew

re-use of historic buildings and environmental improvements. The improvement or rehabilitation of buildings for housing, and the encouragement of compatible businesses, are likely to be two basic objectives of conservation as they may help to ensure that an area is kept alive. In this respect, action taken to preserve single monuments as well as groups and sites will be equally important ... National and Local authorities and other agencies may need to take part in the management process and this may involve the establishment of specific management agencies (public, private and joint venture) for the co-ordination of policies to revitalize a historic centre.

Pickard, 2001

Agenda 21, the UN Conference on Environment and Development, known as the Earth Summit held in Rio de Janeiro in 1992, called for 'indicators of sustainable development'. Pickard's study, while not providing precise indicators (which would be extremely difficult to define), provides some guidelines:

> However, some general principles may be identified that are relevant to the sustainable management of historic centres:
>
> - respect community life
> - improve the quality of life
> - maintain identity, diversity and vitality
> - minimize the depletion of non-renewable heritage assets
> - change attitudes and perceptions – the process of managing change involves wider interests and should involve different actors from the public and private sectors; property owners, investors, residents, and other community and voluntary interests; in other words, the process should become part of everyone's conscience
> - empower community action and responsibility through involvement
> - provide a suitable policy framework for integrating conservation objectives with the aims of sustainable development
> - define the capacity by which the historic centre can permit change.
>
> In order for the built heritage to be included in the aim of building a sustainable society, the 'static' goal to protect must be married to the managed 'process' of change within a community framework of planning and negotiation. The capacity of the historic centre to accept change will depend on relative values that are placed on heritage assets and the priorities of society.

Preserving UK heritage sites

Preserving our tangible heritage is not new. Apparently, 2,500 years ago, the city of Athens required its citizens to swear an oath including the agreement to leave the city of Athens not less, but greater, better and more beautiful than it was left to them. The principle should not be lost on today's generations.

Historical buildings, landscapes and artifacts, preserved as symbols of the nation's heritage, date from the earliest prehistoric monuments such as Stonehenge to those of Roman Britain, Anglo-Saxon England, medieval Britain, the Tudors, Stuarts, Georgian Britain, and the Victorian period. Great cathedrals stand today like Durham Cathedral which was founded in 995 and is regarded as one of the finest examples of Romanesque architecture in the world. Ironbridge stands as the birthplace of the Industrial Revolution. In addition to these two World Heritage Sites, and the others in the UK and Northern Ireland, there were 500,000 listed buildings, 17,700 scheduled monuments and 8,500 conservation areas in England alone in 2003.

In the UK there are 48 wreck sites under the Protection of Wrecks Act, 1973.

Britain's built heritage is a prime national asset. And it is not just buildings and monuments from the past that are so valuable. Heritage includes many different things that have been, and can be, passed on from one generation to another. Heritage, therefore, includes countryside, parks and gardens, battlefields and other sites. It includes historic building, museum and gallery collections, objects and sites linked to industrial, transport and maritime history, and records and archives, and photographic collections. Conservation contributes to economic regeneration, and an attractive environment draws more economic activity to an area, underpins sustainable development strategies and helps maintain a sense of community.

In preserving the past, every year hundreds of buildings are added to a statutory preservation list. This represents more than just old buildings: the listing process increasingly includes relatively modern architecture. Anyone can ask the DCMS to consider a building for listing and this could have a huge impact on those seeking to knock down leisure buildings of the recent past: pre- and post-war swimming baths and more recent 1960s sports centres. The National Sports Centre at Crystal Palace opened in 1964 was added to the list in 1997.

The DCMS has the responsibility for the identification, conservation and enhancement of the historic built environment in England. This includes listing and scheduling historic buildings and ancient monuments, protection of conservation areas and management of the DCMS historic buildings. It carries out European and international work and is involved in the selection and arrangement for the care of World Heritage Sites in the United Kingdom. *The Historic Environment: A Force For Our Future* (DCMS, 2001) is the statement of government policy on the historic environment.

English Heritage is the national body created by Parliament in 1984 charged with the protection of the historic environment and with promoting public understanding and enjoyment of it. It is the government's official adviser on all matters concerning heritage conservation, and is provided with substantial funding for archaeology, conservation areas, and the repair of historic buildings, and is responsible for some 400 historic properties in the nation's care. English Heritage makes grants under the Historic Buildings and Ancient Monuments Act, 1953 towards the cost of the repair of buildings of outstanding historical or architectural interest.

English Heritage's principal aims are:

- to secure the conservation of England's historic sites, monuments, buildings and areas
- to promote people's access to, and enjoyment of, this shared heritage
- to raise the understanding and awareness of the heritage and thereby increase commitment to its protection.

The Treasure Act, 1996, the first ever reform of the medieval law of treasure trove, came into force on 24 September, 1997. Within the first three months of the Act's operation, 40 finds were reported as treasure compared with 30 during the whole of the previous year. All finders of gold and silver objects, and groups of coins from the same finds, over 300 years old, have a legal obligation to report such items under the Treasure Act, 1996. Now prehistoric base-metal 'assemblages' found after 1 January, 2003 also qualify as treasure.

The Portable Antiquities Scheme is a voluntary recording scheme for archaeological objects found by members of the public. Every year thousands of objects are discovered, many of these by metal detector users, but also by people whilst out walking, gardening or in the construction business or home building. Such discoveries offer an important source for understanding our past. The Scheme had a database of over 55,000 finds and 13,000 images by 2003, ranging from prehistoric flints to post-medieval buckles.

Heritage Counts 2003 is an audit of the state of the historic environment. It is a guide as to what can be argued is the country's greatest asset: its heritage. English Heritage states:

> Above all, Heritage Counts 2003 delivers the resounding message that in our small, crowded and ancient country, the historic environment is all around us and that the vast majority, whatever their ethnic, social and cultural background, cares passionately about it. But statistics in the Report show that much of our heritage is in peril – despite the evidence of its contribution to core government policies such as social and economic regeneration, sustainability, social inclusion, tourism, education and citizenship.
>
> English Heritage

A MORI poll for Heritage Counts 2003 revealed that 92 per cent of people thought it important to keep historic features when regenerating towns and cities and 90 per cent said heritage meant their local area as well as castles and stately homes. The Report makes housing and the streets where people live its main theme. It demonstrates the contribution that historic housing can make to projects such as the Pathfinder schemes for housing market renewal. Where new housing is required, Heritage Counts 2003 shows that the new can be knitted closely to the old and valued. Account must be taken of what is already there if communities with a sense of place and identity are to flourish.

The Heritage Lottery Fund (HLF) is having an increasing impact on the heritage sector. Notable recent awards which have made a particular impact include £6 million towards Conservation Area Partnerships. These schemes are operated in conjunction with English Heritage and local authorities.

The Heritage Lottery Fund distributes money raised by the National Lottery to support all aspects of heritage in the UK, from historic buildings and museums to archives, nature conservation and oral history. The Fund:

- provides both capital grants (for buildings and equipment) and time-limited activity grants
- supports buildings repairs and conservation work, buying items, land or buildings, and making it easier for people to gain access to experience heritage
- supports activities that increase learning, that broaden the involvement of a wider range of people, and those that involve volunteering.

Two schemes – Awards for All and the Local Heritage Initiative – support heritage projects run by small local groups.

Tourism, hospitality and accommodation

Hospitality, literally, is being hospitable and providing friendly and generous treatment to guests or strangers.

Hospitality is an important and growing industry in many parts of the world, including the United Kingdom. It is concerned with management excellence: giving quality services to customers. Providing welcoming and quality service is good for customers, therefore, good for business and good for the prosperity of the country.

Tourism involves travel from one location to another, visiting destinations that provide facilities, activities and experiences, and have as their core accommodation and/or food and drink: the principal business of the hospitality industry. The industry, therefore, is inextricably linked to transportation, travel agents, tour operators, visitor attractions and customers and clients from the tourism market sectors: leisure, visiting friends and relations and business.

Tourism needs excellent hospitality services. The tourism and hospitality industries are interwoven. The DCMS seeks to promote good quality and service for all tourists, domestic and international. *Tomorrow's Tourism* sets out the government's ambition for customer service, growth in employment and prosperity in tourism.

As indicated earlier, Britain is one of the world's leading destinations, but global competition is growing rapidly. In real terms, the UK's market share of world tourism has been slipping since the mid-1990s and expenditure by overseas visitors fell from a high of nearly £13 billion in 2000 to less than £12 billion in 2002. The profile of our visitors is also shifting, and there is a trend towards independent travel, shorter breaks and business-related travel.

Good attractions and hospitality, therefore, are extremely important economically, both centrally and locally. Hospitality, however, is not just about government and the economy, nor is it just about tourism. Hospitality – giving good service – is important in a whole range of enterprises, whether in the public, voluntary or commercial sectors, and can generate repeat business, increased turnover and employment.

Statistics concerning the number of jobs in the tourism and hospitality sector vary considerably depending on when they are calculated and what facilities and services are taken into consideration. Hotels and guest houses in the UK range from major hotel groups to small guest houses, individually owned. Holiday centres, including traditional holiday-camps with full board, self-catering centres and caravan parks, are run by hundreds of companies. Restaurants and cafés, where employment has increased substantially in the past decade, are included in government agency figures, but a significant proportion will not be related to tourism. Figures from the DCMS show that the UK tourism industry consists of around 127,000 businesses, 80 per cent of which have a turnover of less than £250,000 per year. Around 2.1 million people were employed in the tourism-related industries in June 2002, a considerable increase with the Department's figures of a little less than 1.8 million in March 2000.

Around 2.1 million people were employed in tourism-related industries in June 2002.

In *UK 2004*, the Official Yearbook of the United Kingdom, figures are given for the hotel and restaurant trades, which include pubs, wine bars and other licensed bars

Table 14.10 Employment in tourism-related industries, Great Britain, June 2002

	THOUSANDS
Hotels and other tourist accommodation	418
Restaurants, cafes, etc.	545
Bars, public houses and night-clubs	536
Travel agencies/tour operators	134
Libraries/museums and other cultural activities	81
Sport and other recreation activities	413
TOTAL	2,127
of which: Self-employment jobs	163

Source: Department for Culture, Media and Sport

in addition to all kinds of business offering accommodation and prepared food. Around 52,600 enterprises exist in the licensed restaurant industry, including fast-food and take-away outlets alone.

Jobs in the hospitality industry are seasonal, often relatively low-paid and tend to attract more young people, women and a wider ethnic mix than other industries. According to the Hospitality Training Foundation (HTF), the hospitality industry employs just over 1.6 million people and accounts for about four per cent of GDP. Around half of unfilled vacancies remain unfilled and there has been a severe drop in the number of students enrolling onto hospitality programmes. The need for chefs is the main pressing problem. There were approximately 266,000 in the UK in 2002 with around 20,000 notified vacancies according to the HTF.

As shown in Table 14.10, 134,000 people are employed in the travel agency and tour operation business. Of the high-street travel agencies, 70 per cent are members of the Association of British Travel Agents (ABTA).

ABTA's 830 tour operators and 1,700 travel agency companies have over 7,000 offices and deal with more than 90 per cent of UK-sold package holidays.

ABTA operates financial protection schemes to safeguard its members' customers and maintains a code of conduct drawn up with the Office of Fair Trading. It also offers a free consumer affairs service to help resolve complaints against members, and a low-cost independent arbitration scheme for members' customers. The British Incoming Tour Operators Association, founded in 1977, represents the commercial and political interests of incoming tour operators and suppliers to the British inbound tourism industry.

In March 2004, the Tourism Minister at the DCMS announced that £1 million was to be given to develop the next phase of EnglandNet: an e-business structure that will revolutionize the way tourist information is accessed, developed and marketed.

Holiday accommodation

Long before there was any thought of a profession of leisure management, services were being provided and managed for people's leisure. Hotels, for example, have been

The British Holiday and Home Parks Association provides an on-line guide to 2,600 holiday parks in the UK.

market leaders in a number of specific aspects of leisure management. Hotels, as well as being essential for business, are also essential for holidays and leisure travel. There is hardly a new hotel built or extended which does not now include leisure elements including, in some cases, swimming pools, spas and fitness facilities, and where space is available, tennis courts, lawns, gardens and walks.

The hotel industry is greatly affected by the economy and the tourist industry. World travel has been greatly affected in recent years by terrorism. In addition, in the UK, the consequences of the foot-and-mouth disease outbreak and BSE have had their negative effects. At the time of writing, the strength of the pound is such that it is expensive for overseas tourists to visit the UK, particularly London. A drop in the number of visitors occurs at times like these. The corollary to this is that Britons going to overseas destinations benefit financially from attractive exchange rates.

Like other sectors in the commercial leisure industry, a few major companies dominate at the top end of the hotel market. There are three major hotel chains in the United Kingdom: Granada, which became the market leader after acquiring Forte in January 1996, Whitbread and Thistle Hotels. At the other end of the scale are a vast number of independent establishments. In 2001, there were just under 12,000 hotels and motels (826,000 bedplaces) in the United Kingdom; there were nearly 23,000 (1.8 million bedplaces) other accommodation establishments; and around 4,300 short-stay and camping sites.

The range of budget, lodge style hotels were developed in the UK when Forte and Granada, learning from their success in continental Europe, opened up accommodation for those on the move as extensions to their roadside service stations. These budget hotels focus on the core of the business to provide quality bedrooms at a cheap price, without the frills of service and ancillary facilities. Economies of scale are realized, with hotel guests eating and purchasing goods at the service stations which have increased in both range and quality of products and services.

The concept of the holiday centre is a growing market, particularly for short-break holidays. The number of holidays taken by British holidaymakers has increased for both holidays in Britain and holidays abroad. Approximately 60 per cent of British residents in the United Kingdom now take a holiday (National Statistics, 2003). Short breaks, including family activity holidays, are becoming popular as second and/or seasonal holidays. This trend has helped to increase the popularity of holiday 'centres' in the UK.

In 1936, Billy Butlin created the most recognized holiday company in Britain: Butlins. The first Butlins Holiday Camp was opened in Skegness and introduced the now famous Redcoats. The Butlins Holiday Worlds of today are a far cry from the Butlins Holiday Camps of post-war Britain, familiar through television comedies. Butlins now offers year-round holiday and leisure facilities to meet today's expectations at its centres in Bognor Regis, Minehead and Skegness. Butlins also inspired a number of other holiday centre enterprises. Haven have 21 holiday parks and Pontins is a major player in this market, operating along similar lines to Butlins with 8 Pontin family centres at seaside resorts including Blackpool.

Over the years, standards of provision have risen with improved accommodation, leisure facilities and services. One of the most innovative and significant developments has been the introduction of Center Parcs into the UK.

The first Center Parcs holiday village, opened in 1987, revolutionized the holiday centre market in the United Kingdom. It was in a secluded, wooded, countryside location in Nottinghamshire with lakes, quality outdoor and indoor leisure facilities and chalet-style lodge accommodation. Center Parcs in Sherwood Forest, Elveden Forest in Suffolk, Longleat Forest Village in Wiltshire, and Oasis Whinfell Forest in Cumbria, are examples of a holiday and short break village in 400 acres of woodland, which has at its hub a very large domed leisure water facility. This type of outdoor and indoor activity holiday is becoming extremely popular particularly with family groups. The Center Parcs concept, founded in The Netherlands, has been a significant leisure development that provides the opportunity not only to experience indoor tropical water facilities but also to participate in a number of recreational sporting and non-sporting pursuits, in a clean, friendly, informal atmosphere. These centres are open all the year with near full capacity.

In part, the holiday centre market has followed the classic commercial route of major players coming into the market, investing in it and acquiring facilities or going concerns. However, some unique characteristics are evident. The first is building on the tradition of the 'working-class' holiday camps, particularly Butlins and Pontins, which have been acquired and developed, thereby widening the market. The second is the advent of the holiday village concept of Center Parcs, a major landmark in market positioning in a very short space of time. The third is the diverse field of large numbers of holiday 'parks' and caravan sites. What they all have in common in the first years of this century, is a buoyancy in the market and the potential for growth and development.

Summary

In this chapter an attempt has been made to provide a broad picture of the tourism market and particularly what attracts people from overseas and home to visit places all over the United Kingdom.

The role of the government and its agencies is significant as tourism is of great value to the economy. Tourism needs a wide range of services, including transport, travel agencies, hotels and other accommodation, food and drink and hospitality. It needs a wide range of facilities, attractions and events. These are covered in greater detail in Chapter 11 on the commercial sector. The UK's historic and natural environment, historic sites and the built environment of the past and present are attractions for tourists from home and abroad. These attractions need good maintenance, management and promotion.

Tourism needs well qualified leisure and tourism managers and other professionals. Tourism has many market sectors, and each require capable personnel. It is an attractive and fruitful area of work for aspiring Leisure Managers.

This chapter was written before the Asia tsunami disaster on 26 December 2004, which will have substantial impacts on the tourism market.

Discussion points

1 Tourism means different things to different people. To some, it is thought of only as travel and a holiday destination – an activity pursued in leisure time. However, it is far broader, more complicated and has a significant impact on the world's economy. Discuss these contrasting perceptions.

2 Tourism contributes to changes in value systems, lifestyles and relationships of tourists to the communities that they visit and vice versa. Sustain or reject this assumption.

3 Tourism is essential to the life of nations because of its effect on social, cultural, educational and economic development. A more cynical view is that it is but an extension of politics and economics. Discuss these differing viewpoints.

4 From the consumer's perspective, tourism is usually that of leisure and holiday activity offering a range of experiences and opportunities. From the producer's perspective, tourism is a system of commercialized travel and hospitality. Discuss the potential benefits and problems arising from these viewpoints.

Further reading

The British Library, local libraries, colleges and universities are prime sources of publications relating to tourism in the UK. VisitBritain and the Tourist Boards recommend and supply information.

A brief selection of titles covering some of the market sectors in tourism and cover concepts, issues and practice are:

Locum Destination Review, Summer 2003.

Lockwood, A., Baker, M. and Ghillyer, A. (eds), (1996), *Quality Management in Hospitality,* Cassell, London.

Hall, C.M. and McArthur, S. (1998), *Integrated Heritage Management*, TSO, London.

Boniface, P. (1995), *Managing Quality Cultural Tourism*, Routledge, London.

Weaver, D. and Lawton, L. (2002), *Tourism Management*, Wiley, Milton, Australia.

Witt, S. and Moutinho, L. (eds) (1994), *Tourism Marketing and Management Handbook* (2nd edn), Prentice Hall, New York.

Office for National Statistics, *Travel Trends* 2003 edition. This is a guide to travel patterns and trends in the UK based on the 2002 International Passenger Survey which collects information from passengers as they enter or leave the UK.

Useful websites

British Hospitality Association: www.bha-online.org.uk

VisitBritain (formerly British Tourist Authority/English Tourism Council): www.visitbritain.com

www.englishtourism.org.uk

Hotel and Catering International Management Association (HCIMA): www.hcima.org.uk

World Tourism Organisation: www.world-tourism.org

English Tourist Board: www.travelengland.org.uk

Northern Ireland Tourist Board: www.discovernorthernireland.com

Scottish Tourist Board: www.visitscotland.com

Wales Tourist Board: www.tourism.wales.gov.uk

StarUK, the National Tourist Board's tourist statistics website: www.staruk.org.uk

Guide to Internet Resources in Hospitality, Leisure, Sport and Tourism: www.altis.ac.uk

Resource Discovery Network: www.rdn.ac.uk

15

The environment, countryside and open space

In this chapter

- Protecting heritage and the environment
- Countryside: national policy and administration
- National parks
- Protection of use of forests and woodlands
- Open spaces and urban parks

Introduction

'Natural heritage and the countryside' includes major landscapes, features, places and attractions for people to enjoy in their leisure time. They attract millions of local leisure users and domestic and international tourists and visitors.

In Chapter 14 we looked at world heritage sites, including those in the United Kingdom. These heritage sites, designated to be of outstanding universal value, are a great cultural asset to the country. The uniqueness of the UK, however, can also be found in its natural heritage. It is 'to be at leisure' to walk in the countryside and along the coastal paths, to enjoy the hospitality of local towns, rural villages, pubs, restaurants, hotels, inns and bed and breakfast establishments – getting 'off the beaten track'. To enjoy the green spaces in and around our towns is also to be at leisure.

Protecting heritage and the environment

Protecting the environment has become a major issue at all levels of government – local, national, European and worldwide. The United Kingdom is a signatory to several international conventions relating to conservation and environmental protection.

International conventions

Worldwide convention

Protection of the World Cultural and Natural Heritage (ratified 29 May, 1984)

European conventions

Conservation of Wild Birds

Convention on the Conservation of European Wildlife and Natural Habitats

The European Environment Agency (EEA) provides decision makers with the information needed for making policies to protect the environment and support sustainable development. This is gathered and distributed through the European Environment Information and Observation Network (EIONET), which has over 300 environment bodies in the public and private sectors across Europe. The Agency has 31 member countries.

In addition to world heritage sites in England, Scotland, Wales and Northern Ireland, in England alone there around one million archaeological sites recorded, and English Heritage's *Monuments At Risk Survey* of England estimated that there are around 300,000 monuments – prehistoric, Roman, medieval, post-medieval, a few modern monuments, and around one-fifth of uncertain date. English Heritage assesses those that should be afforded statutory protection and the Department for Culture, Media and Sport (DCMS) maintains a schedule of ancient monuments. In 2001 the government published *The Historic Environment: A Force For Our Future*, the statement of government policy on the historic environment.

> In 2003 there were 461,000 listed buildings and 32,000 scheduled monuments in the United Kingdom.

Government organizations

English Heritage is responsible for the maintenance and presentation of 409 historic properties in public ownership or guardianship. Most of English Heritage's properties are open to the public, with around 5.5 million visits to staffed properties in 2002/3. Government funding for English Heritage in 2003/4 was £122 million.

Historic Scotland cares for over 330 monuments, and in Wales, Cadw cares for 127 monuments. There were nearly 3 million visitors to Historic Scotland's properties where admission is charged and 1.1 million visitors to monuments in Wales in 2002/3. The Department of the Environment (DoE) in Northern Ireland has 182 historic monuments managed by the Environment and Heritage Service (EHS). These received an estimated 150,000 visits in 2002.

Local planning authorities have designated more than 9000 conservation areas of special architectural or historic interest in England and there are 513 in Wales, around 600 in Scotland and 58 in Northern Ireland. Many of the royal palaces and all the royal parks are open to the public; their maintenance is the responsibility of the DCMS and Historic Scotland. Around one-quarter of trips to the countryside are to heritage sites, gardens and heritage centres.

The Environment Agency is a non-departmental public body, whose aim is to protect and improve the environment. With a budget of £800 million in 2003/4, it is responsible in England and Wales for conservation, regulating and controlling pollution, managing water resources, and improving flood defences. It manages and maintains fisheries and waterways. The Scottish Environment Protection Agency carries out similar responsibilities. Created on 1 April 1996, the Environment Agency merged the National Rivers Authority, Her Majesty's Inspectorate of Pollution, the Waste Regulation Authorities and other smaller units from the Department of the Environment. The Environment Agency is

Over 20,000 boats are registered with the Thames Region alone. Every pleasure boat must be registered and every boat with an engine must have a licence.

now one of the most powerful environmental regulators in the world with the aim of protecting and enhancing the whole environment. As such, the EA has a strong influence upon leisure and recreation, particularly in areas such as water recreation, fishing, camping, canoeing and enjoyment of the countryside.

Non-governmental and voluntary organizations

Non-governmental organizations (NGOs) have an important role in conservation in the United Kingdom. A large proportion of the statutory protected areas are owned or managed by NGOs.

Campaigning bodies include: the Council for the Protection of Rural England, the Association for the Protection of Rural Scotland, and the Ramblers' Association. The Environment Council acts as an umbrella body for a large number of the NGOs. The Council for National Parks is a national voluntary organization set up to promote the conservation of natural beauty and the promotion of the parks for the enjoyment of the public.

In the United Kingdom, there are also a number of independent and private bodies involved in countryside conservation and environmental protection, such as the National Trust.

 THE NATIONAL TRUST A registered charity, independent of the government, the National Trust was founded in 1895 by three Victorian philanthropists, concerned about the impact of uncontrolled development and industrialization. They set up the Trust to acquire and protect threatened coastline, countryside and buildings.

The National Trust owns and protects places of historic interest and natural beauty for the benefit of the nation. The Trust cares for around 250,000 hectares of land in England, Wales and Northern Ireland, including forests, fens, moorland, downs, farmland, nature reserves and stretches of coastline. In total, it is responsible for 200 historic houses, 160 gardens, 40,000 ancient monuments and archaeological remains, and 46 villages.

A separate National Trust for Scotland owns 127 properties. Established in 1931, it has a membership of around 260,000 and over two million visitors each year.

Non-governmental organizations

Other NGOs include:

The Royal Society for Nature Conservation Wildlife Trust Partnership
The Royal Society for the Protection of Birds
The Woodland Trust
The Wildfowl and Wetlands Trust
The World Wide Fund for Nature UK
The British Trust for Conservation Volunteers
Scottish Conservation Projects

Some 12 million people visit National Trust properties each year and about 50 million visits are made to its coasts and countryside properties.

Most of these properties are held in perpetuity. The vast majority are open to visitors. The Trust has over three million subscribing members and other supporters. Claimed as the world's leading conservation charity, it is also concerned for the long-term future of the nation's garden heritage and cares for the largest collection of historic gardens and cultivated plants.

Countryside: national policy and administration

The countryside is an exceptional resource for leisure and recreation, but the countryside also has to accommodate the pressing needs of work, housing, agriculture, conservation, protection of the environment and natural heritage. Moreover, the range of providers, owners, agencies and organizations involved, together with the legal and administrative structures, renders countryside management extremely complex. Countryside recreation, therefore, is far from simple in terms of its planning and management. Fortunately there are abundant resources to cater for the diverse needs, provided there is:

- sound policy
- good planning
- co-ordination of the range of interested parties
- appropriate provision and
- excellent management.

It is the sector of leisure management that merits greater consideration.

Bodies involved in countryside issues

In England these include:
    Environment Agency
    Countryside Agency
    English Heritage

In Wales there are:
    Environment Agency Wales
    Countryside Council for Wales
    Cadw Welsh Historic Monuments Executive Agency

In Scotland there are:
    Scottish Environment Protection Agency
    Scottish Natural Heritage

In Northern Ireland there is one agency:
    Environment and Heritage Service

To laymen and women, including many leisure managers, there appears to be a range of overlapping bodies involved in countryside issues. For example, there are government departments, government sponsored agencies, non-departmental public bodies, and independent, private and voluntary organizations.

305

Complicating the issue further, over relatively short periods national agencies may change or become integrated, particularly with changes in legislation and government. For example, in the Environmental Protection Act, 1990, the duties of the Nature Conservancy Council were transferred to four bodies:

- The Nature Conservancy Council for Scotland
- The Countryside Council for Wales
- English Nature
- The Joint Nature Conservation Committee (JNCC) for Great Britain.

The Department for Environment, Food and Rural Affairs (Defra) is responsible for policy on the countryside and wildlife in England.

The Department's *Strategy 2003–6* describes how it aims to deliver six priorities:

- Sustainable development
- Rural England: opportunity for all
- Climate change
- Farming and food
- Animal health and welfare
- Less waste and more recycling.

The Department for Environment, Food and Rural Affairs (Defra) is the government's main environmental department, whose mission is to deal with 'the essentials of life: water, food, air, land, people, animals and plants'.

Defra sponsors three of the non-departmental public bodies: the Countryside Agency, English Nature and the National Forest Company. The devolved administrations in Wales and Scotland sponsor similar bodies. Responsibilities in Northern Ireland rest with the Environment and Heritage Service (EHS). Defra also sponsors the Joint Nature Conservation Committee (JNCC) comprising English Nature (EN), Scottish Natural Heritage (SNH) and the Countryside Council for Wales (CCW). The Department's main strategic focus does not include leisure specifically. However, the agencies responsible to Defra have wide-ranging roles encompassing leisure and recreation.

Protecting the countryside and habitats is essential, and there are a number of designations given to these important areas. However, their designation does not exclude their use for leisure and recreation.

The primary conservation legislation in Great Britain is the Wildlife and Countryside Act, 1981, which provides for a range of measures to protect plants and animals. It was strengthened by the Countryside and Rights of Way Act, 2000, which gave government departments in England and Wales a statutory duty to the conservation of biological diversity and contained new measures for the conservation and protection of habitats and wildlife. It also created a new statutory right of access, giving people greater freedom to explore the open countryside, while also providing safeguards for landowners.

The Scottish Executive published the draft Nature Conservation (Scotland) Bill in March 2003. It includes proposals to strengthen the protection of SSSIs in Scotland to promote biodiversity, and for new legislation to tackle wildlife crime. The Environment (Northern Ireland) Order 2002 includes measures which allow for the increased protection and management of ASSIs.

Protected areas

Protected areas as at 31 March, 2003 include the following:

Sites of Special Scientific Interest (SSSIs) in Great Britain – 6,586 sites
Areas of Special Scientific Interest (ASSIs) in Northern Ireland – 196 sites
National Nature Reserves (NNRs) – 399 sites
Local Nature Reserves – 903 sites
Marine Nature Reserves – 3 sites
Special Protection Areas (SPAs) – 240 sites

National Statistics, 2003

Scotland has 40 National Scenic Areas (NSAs) and four regional parks. The main purpose of NSAs is to give special attention to the best scenery in Scotland when new development is being considered. Certain developments are subject to consultation with Scottish National Heritage and, in the event of a disagreement, with the Scottish Executive.

There are 50 AONBs in the United Kingdom, covering 10 per cent of the total land area.

The primary objective of Areas of Outstanding Natural Beauty is the conservation and enhancement of the natural beauty of the landscape, although many of them also fulfil a wider recreational purpose. Designation started in 1956 with the Gower peninsula in Wales and the most recent is the Tamar Valley in Cornwall. Northern Ireland has nine with two more proposed – Erne Lakeland and Fermanagh Caveland. AONBs in England and Wales are designated by the Countryside Agency and Countryside Council for Wales.

ENGLISH NATURE

English Nature is the government-funded body whose purpose is to promote the conservation of England's wildlife and natural features. Its main duties and powers are given in a number of Acts of Parliament:

- National Parks and Access to the Countryside Act, 1949
- Countryside Act, 1968
- Nature Conservancy Council Act, 1973
- Wildlife and Countryside Act, 1981 (amended 1985)
- Environmental Protection Act, 1990 and
- Countryside and Rights of Way Act, 2000.

English Nature promotes the conservation of wildlife and natural features such as Sites of Special Scientific Interest (SSSIs). The Scottish Executive sponsors Scottish Natural Heritage (SNH) concerned with nature conservation and the countryside. The Countryside Council for Wales (CCW) has responsibilities for landscape and nature conservation and for countryside recreation. In Northern Ireland, the EHS protects the natural and built environment.

The Countryside Agency

The government has had an agency for the countryside for nearly a century. The Rural Development Commission dates back to 1909.

Funded by Defra, with an annual budget of around £100 million, the Countryside Agency has over 600 countryside specialists and support staff. The Agency brings together all aspects of the countryside – economic, environmental, community and recreation – into a single body. The Agency advises the government and public bodies, provides information to the public to prevent damage to the countryside and informs people of their rights and responsibilities. The Countryside and Rights of Way Act, 2000 also requires the Agency to map open countryside and 'prepare for its enjoyment by the public'. The Agency's work revolves around five main programmes:

- open access, for example, to mountains, moors and registered common land
- diversity: reviewing equal opportunities and access
- healthy walking
- countryside recreation and 'Greenways' and
- National Trails.

The Countryside Agency was established by the government in 1999 as the statutory champion and watchdog working to make 'the quality of life better for people in the countryside and the quality of the countryside better for everyone'.

In 2003, the government published the report, *The State of the Countryside 2020 – A Green and Pleasant Land* (Moynagh and Worsley, 2003). What will it be like to live, work and visit the countryside in the year 2020? The way the government and its agencies act now will shape the answers to these and other important questions. The need for homes in the countryside continues to rise. Commuter countryside continues to expand and country towns are becoming increasingly desirable for new or relocating businesses. What will this social fragmentation do to the traditional strong sense of community in rural areas? The Agency is working on its Countryside Quality Counts project developing national indicators for change in the character and quality of the countryside in England.

> The Hadrian's Wall Path National Trail opened in May 2003, and visitors are able to walk along an unbroken path 135 kilometres long.

England has about 190,000 kilometres of rights of way and bridleways. There are 15 long-distance walking routes in England and Wales, designated as National Trails. There are five Long Distance Routes in Scotland. Around 80 per cent of common land is privately owned, although only 20 per cent has a legal right of public access.

The *Common Land Policy Statement*, published by Defra and the Welsh Assembly Government in July 2002, contained proposals relating to the registration and protection of common land and village greens. The Land Reform (Scotland) Act, 2003, established a right of access to land and inland water for recreation and passage in

Scotland. In England and Wales, the Countryside and Rights of Way Act, 2000 created a public right of access to mountain, moor, heath, down and registered common land. The Act requires local highways authorities in England and Wales to take account of the needs of people with disabilities. Of interest to Leisure Managers is the Countryside Agency's production of good practice guidance on how to improve access for people with mobility and sensory impairments.

Coast and waterways

Britons have an affinity to water with a link to the sea, rivers and inland waterways.

Local planning authorities are responsible for planning land use at the coast; they also aim to safeguard and enhance the coast's natural attractions and preserve areas of scientific interest. Certain stretches of undeveloped coast of particular beauty in England and Wales are defined as Heritage Coast. There are 46 Heritage Coasts protecting 1555 kilometres, about 35 per cent of the total length of coastline. The National Trust, through its Neptune Coastline Campaign, raises funds to acquire and protect stretches of coastline of natural beauty and recreation value. The National Trust for Scotland cares for more than 400 kilometres of the Scottish coastline and protects other stretches through conservation agreements.

> The coastline of Great Britain is 18,843 kilometres in length, including 163 estuaries; about 75 per cent of the European chalk coast is located in the United Kingdom.

A good deal of the coastline is given statutory protection or non-statutory protection. In Wales, non-statutory protection has been given to heritage coasts which cover a large area of undeveloped coastline; these receive special attention in development planning.

British Waterways is the custodian of 2000 miles of a network of canals and inland waterways which were built to service the transport needs of the world's first industrial revolution. Much of the system is over 200 years old. Still part of the country's land drainage and water delivery systems, and used for transporting coal and other materials, the waterways network's industrial and trading operations have been in decline for some time.

> The waterway network includes 3,200 km of canals, 4,763 bridges, 397 aquaducts, 60 tunnels, 1,549 locks, 89 reservoirs, nearly 3,000 listed structures and ancient monuments, and 66 SSSIs.

The network is undoubtedly an important part of our history and heritage, which is an attraction to domestic and international tourists. Today, the waterways are valued as a leisure and recreation resource for millions of people. British Waterways report that the network is visited each year by 10 million people, of whom only a small proportion own boats or take holidays on the canals. In addition to activities on the water, the waterways are used for walking, angling, cycling, wildlife pursuits and visiting heritage buildings.

British Waterways is required under the Transport Act, 1968, to maintain its canals and rivers in a safe and satisfactory condition and to carry out this mandate receives grants from the government. Following British Waterways' *Our Plan for the Future 1999–2003*, which highlighted the need for considerable renovation and maintenance to the network, the government, British Waterways, local councils and the private sector are working on a plan of restoration, for example, on improvements to canal tow-paths and other infrastructure which will benefit the local area.

National Parks

The National Parks Commission was established under the National Parks and Access to the Countryside Act of 16 December, 1949; it became the Countryside Commission under the Countryside Act, 1968, and in 1982 the Commission was granted the status of an independent agency funded by the Department of the Environment. National Parks were mostly set aside by the government in the 1950s and 1960s because of their natural beauty and as sites and landscapes of ecological, archaeological, geological and recreational value.

National Park status, designated by the Countryside Agency and Countryside Council for Wales, recognizes the national importance of the area concerned in terms of landscape, biodiversity and recreation. However, a National Park does not signify national ownership; most of the land in National Parks is owned by private landowners. Each park is administered by an independent National Park Authority.

The first two National Parks in England and Wales, the Lake District and the Peak District, were designated in 1951. There are now eleven parks in all in England and Wales. The New Forest and the South Downs are in the process of designation.

Scotland's first National Park, Loch Lomond and the Trossachs, was inaugurated in July 2002. A second, the Cairngorms, was inaugurated on 1 September, 2003.

The National Parks are among the most valued landscapes in the British Isles, containing some of the finest scenery, rare wildlife and cultural heritage. The National Parks are visited by millions of people each year who visit to enjoy the peace and tranquility, to experience 'living landscapes', and to spend leisure time. This peace and haven for rare wildlife has to be preserved, yet the National Parks are also attractions for people's sport and recreation. National Parks have to be managed effectively; sound planning and sensitive management are essential to ensure the right balance between protecting the environment and providing opportunities for people's leisure. The National Parks of England and Wales receive over 100 million visitor days a year, with the greatest number visiting the Lake District and Peak District national parks. Unlike some other countries, National Parks in the British Isles are not publicly owned land, but operate in a similar way

National Parks in England

The Norfolk Broads	Northumberland
Dartmoor	North York Moors
Exmoor	Peak District
Lake District	Yorkshire Dales

National Parks in Wales

Snowdonia	Brecon Beacons
Pembrokeshire Coast	

National Parks in Scotland

Loch Lomond and the Trossachs	The Cairngorms

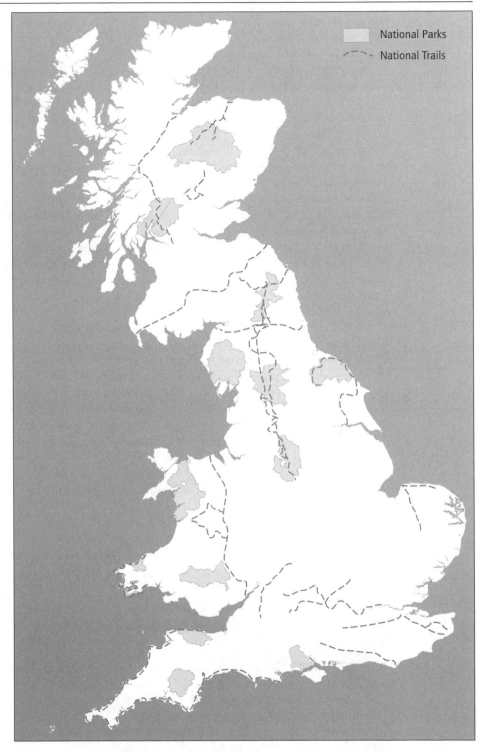

Figure 15.1 National Parks and Trails

to Areas of Outstanding Natural Beauty, which have special protection conferred on them and restrictions apply to any developments and use. Resources are available to promote and manage tourism and recreation within the parks.

National Parks in Scotland are a little different. The first was designated only in 2002 under the National Parks (Scotland) Act, 2000. Other national parks soon to be designated are the South Downs National Park, New Forest National Park and Cairngorms National Park. The Mournes is to become Northern Ireland's first national park.

There are key policy and managing bodies with responsibilities for and within the National Parks including National Park Authorities, the Council for National Parks, the National Trust, the Countryside Agency, English Heritage and others. National Parks are run by the National Park Authorities. These are similar to local councils and have many of the powers that councils have including controlling development. The Authorities are funded by central government. The balance between conservation and recreation is a sensitive one, but greater priority is given to conservation than to recreation. The Council for National Parks (CNP) is the charity that works to protect and enhance National Parks of England and Wales and areas that merit National Park status. It promotes the conservation of national beauty and also the parks for the enjoyment of the public.

National Park Authorities have a planning and enforcement section, an estate management or up-land management service, a ranger and/or warden service, information and interpretation section, and an administration section. Norfolk and Suffolk Broads are administered by the Broads Authority, while the New Forest is largely administered by the Forestry Commission under a mandate from the Minister of Agriculture.

In addition to National Parks, there is a wide range of inland and coastal areas of outstanding natural beauty and heritage. Public rights of way and common land have been part of the British countryside for centuries. There are 15 long-distance walking routes in England and Wales, designated as National Trails. Thirteen have been fully developed and two are in the process of completion. The Hadrian's Wall Path National Trail opened in May 2003: an unbroken path 135 kilometres long. There are five Long Distance Routes in Scotland.

Pressures on the National Parks come from tourists and visitors and numbers are increasing. On the one hand, there is damage caused by an excessive amount of traffic by road and on foot – an impact on the environment, and on the other hand, there are the people who want to visit the Parks to experience the beauty and peace of the areas and for their recreation.

National Trails in England and Wales

Cleveland Way	Pembrokeshire Coast
Cotswold Way	Pennine Bridleway and Pennine Way
Glyndwrs Way	South Downs Way
Hadrian's Wall Path National Trail	South West Coast Path
North Downs Way	Thames Path
Offa's Dyke Path	The Ridgeway
Peddar's Way and Norfolk Coast Path	Wolds Way

Protection and use of forests and woodlands

In the long and distant past, two-thirds of the country was covered by forest. The relatively few small areas of ancient forest which remain have mostly been extensively modified by centuries of coppicing and other activities.

The first laws pertaining to natural resource protection were the Forest Laws of King Canute in around 1014. The oldest protected area, the New Forest, was declared a Royal hunting preserve in 1079 and the oldest in Scotland dates from the twelfth century. In the nineteenth century, control of forests was vested in the Commission of Woods and Forests. The first areas to be given legal protection for nature conservation were a number of bird sanctuaries declared in the nineteenth century. Today the Wildlife Trusts and the Royal Society for the Protection of Birds (RSPB) play an important part in protecting wildlife throughout the United Kingdom. The Wildlife Trusts have over 2,500 nature reserves covering 82,000 hectares. The 47 independent trusts have over 413,000 members in total. The Wildlife and Countryside Act, 1981 and the Wildlife and Countryside (Amendment) Act, 1985 have a number of sections on protected areas.

> In total, forests cover about 2.81 million hectares or 11.6 per cent of the total area of the UK.

On a broader front, the Countryside Act, 1968 and the Countryside (Scotland) Act, 1967 required all departments and agencies of government to have regard to conserving the natural beauty, flora, fauna and geological features and amenities of the countryside. Country Parks are designated under these acts; they are sites established by local authorities primarily for their leisure and recreation value. The Countryside Agency recognizes 267 country parks in England; there are 35 in Wales, recognized by the CCW, and 36 in Scotland. Northern Ireland has 11 country parks.

The Forestry Commission (see Useful websites) was established under the Forestry Act, 1919 originally to promote forest industry, rather than for nature conservation purposes; its duties and powers are now mainly defined under the Forestry Act, 1967. The Commission operates as a cross-border public body within Great Britain. In each country, it serves as the forestry department. It provides grant aid for the stewardship of existing woodlands and woodland expansion in the private sector.

The Forestry Commission is the largest landowner in Britain, with 3 million acres. Its primary role is that of timber production. In 1935, the Commission recognized the public's need for greater opportunities of access to its forests for recreational purposes and opened the first of its forest parks in Argyll. In 1970, the Commission set up a conservation and recreation branch at its headquarters and established eleven recreation planning officers in each of its conservancy regions. In 1998, the report *Forestry Strategy for England* (DETR, 1998) was published setting out the government's priorities and programmes.

The problems resulting from the conflicting interests of forest management and recreation, need policy sensitivity and diplomatic management. In addition to the user problems, the commission must make a return on investment. The greater the provision for public recreation, the more difficult it becomes to show the level of profit required. However, major forest developments which include leisure and recreation within their remits are The National Forest, Community Forests and Forest Parks.

> A total of 5 million trees had been planted in the National Forest by the end of March 2003; 30 million will be planted eventually.

The National Forest Company was established in April 1995 to oversee the creation of a new forest: The National Forest. The founding members were

313

the then Secretary of State for the Environment and the Minister for Agriculture, Fisheries and Food. The new National Forest, covering 520 square kilometres in parts of Derbyshire, Leicestershire and Staffordshire, provides landscape improvement, recreation, education and nature conservation. In doing so it is a catalyst in regenerating the economy of the area it covers.

Community Forests

Community forests are part of a national programme of major environmental improvement and reaches half of England's population. Community forests were initiated in 1989. Each forest contains hundreds of green spaces, including parks, woodlands, wetlands and recreation areas: all places for local people to visit and enjoy in their leisure time, providing an appreciation of the countryside, their heritage and surroundings and improving their quality of life.

Table 15.1 Community Forests

NAME OF FOREST	LAND AREA (HA)	POPULATION* (MILLIONS)
COMMUNITY FORESTS		
Forest of Avon	57,300	1
Forest of Mercia	23,000	4
Forest of Marston Vale	15,800	1
Great North Forest	24,870	1
Great Western Community Forest	39,000	1
Greenwood Community Forest	43,800	2
Mersey Forest	92,500	4
Red Rose Forest	76,000	4
South Yorkshire	50,530	2
The Tees Forest	34,970	1
Thames Chase Community Forest	10,406	5
Watling Chase Community Forest	18,800	3
OTHER COMMUNITY FORESTRY INITIATIVES		
Black Country Urban Forest	36,000	1
Central Scotland Forest	160,000	1
Elwood (East Lancashire)	126,000	0
The National Forest	50,200	10
White Rose Forest	202,100	2
TOTAL	1,061,276	42

* Total area designated as extent of Community Forest
Source: Forestry Commission

The 12 community forests in England and five other community forestry initiatives in Great Britain cover a land area of 1.1 million hectares.

The creation of Community forests is the result of development partnerships between the Countryside Agency, the Forestry Commission, 58 local authorities and other national and local organizations. Community forests aim to:

- revitalize derelict landscapes
- enhance biodiversity and
- provide opportunities for recreation, cultural activity, education, health and social and economic development.

Since their inception in 1991, the community forests have helped to revitalize areas around many of England's towns and cities, delivering economic, social and environmental benefits to local communities. A total of 21 thousand hectares of new planting had been achieved by March 2003. This has increased the woodland cover in these forests from an initial 7 per cent to 9 per cent of the total area by March 2003, according to the Forestry Commission.

Table 15.2 Forest Parks

		HECTARES
ENGLAND	New Forest	27,000
	Forest of Dean	11,000
	Delamere	700
	Sherwood Pines	900
	Thetford	19,000
	North Riding	12,000
	Whiniatter	1,200
	Grizedale	2,500
	Kielder	61,000
		135,300
SCOTLAND	Glenmore	3,500
	Tay	17,000
	Queen Elizabeth	20,000
	Argyll	21,000
	Galloway	77,000
	Tweed Valley	4,900
		143,400
WALES	Afan Argoed	2,700
	Coed-y-Brenin	3,100
	Gwydyr	6,500
		12,300

Source: Forestry Commission

Forest Parks

There are 17 Forest Parks in Great Britain administered by the Forestry Commission. They cover around 143 thousand hectares in Scotland, 135 thousand hectares in England and 12 thousand hectares in Wales. The largest is Galloway Forest Park, which covers a total area of 77 thousand hectares, followed by Kielder Forest Park, at 61 thousand hectares.

Forest Parks are a relatively recent creation; they are large areas of forest and open land in which provision for public recreation is a main management objective. However, forest nature reserves are of considerable conservation value also; these require effective management in order to conserve their areas of special nature interest, yet also offer recreational amenities.

Recreational use of woodlands

The UK Day Visits Surveys found that more visits were made to local authority woodland, but that infrequent visitors tended to go to Forestry Commission woodland. In the Public Opinion of Forestry Survey 2003, respondents were asked to identify the factors that were important to them when choosing to visit a woodland. In percentage terms, the most frequently stated reasons were peace and quiet (65), wildlife (65), attractive scenery (62) and a safe environment (57).

Almost one-half of the visitors surveyed in the national programme lived locally (within 15 miles of the site), a further one-third were holidaymakers and the remainder were on a day trip from home. In some areas a charge has been levied to enter forests and woodlands. This does not appear to deter most people.

Forests provide opportunities for walking, cycling, horse riding, orienteering, camping, caravanning, fishing, bird-watching and a whole host of other activities enjoyed by people of all ages. The Commission encourages private woodland owners to manage their forests for public access and also provides grants to those owners through its Walkers Welcome initiative to help pay for those activities.

Information on Forestry Commission recreation facilities and activities were advertised on the Forestry Commission website in August 2003. A total of 549 sites were featured. Almost half (48 per cent) of these sites were in Scotland, over one-third (35 per cent) were in England and the remainder (17 per cent) were in Wales. Almost all sites (88 per cent) had parking facilities and over three-quarters (77 per cent) included walking activities.

Table 15.3 Number of day visits to woodland

JOURNEY STARTING POINT	MILLIONS OF VISITS			
	GB	ENGLAND	SCOTLAND	WALES
1994	303	273	18	12
1996	346	308	26	11
1998	355	321	22	11

Source: UK Day Visits Survey (not National Statistics)

The Forestry Commission obtains information about woodland visits and visitors from the UK Day Visits Survey, Public Opinion of Forestry Survey and on-site monitoring programmes. It is estimated that around 355 million day visits from home were made to woodland in Great Britain in 1998. Of these, 321 million (90 per cent) day visits originated in England, 22 million (6 per cent) in Scotland and 11 million (3 per cent) in Wales.

National Cycle Network

The National Cycle Network currently provides more than 7,000 miles of cycling and walking routes throughout the United Kingdom. By 2005, this will be extended to 10,000 miles. About one-third of the network is on paths which are free from traffic; the rest on quiet minor roads and traffic-calmed streets. The network is ideal for cycling holidays and family rides, and the routes are also favoured by many people as an alternative to roads for local trips to work, school or for shopping.

The network is co-ordinated by the charity Sustrans and involves hundreds of organizations: local authorities, businesses, landowners, voluntary organizations and environmental bodies. The first 5,000 miles were supported by Millennium Commission funds and funding has been provided by national and local government, charitable trusts, companies and, importantly, from voluntary donations which demonstrate support from the general public.

Also to be run by Sustrans is the 'Green Routes, Safe Routes' programme funded under the New Opportunities Fund (NOF) Green Spaces and Sustainable Communities Programme. It will deliver a range of sustainable transport projects targeted on disadvantaged areas across England, including:

- Green Transport Corridors creating safe cycling and walking routes to and within green spaces
- Safe Routes to Stations providing cycling and walking links to bus and rail stations and
- Safe Routes to Schools enabling children to cycle and walk to school safely.

The NOF Green Spaces and Sustainable Communities initiative is providing £100 million in England to help urban and rural communities to understand, improve or care for their natural and living environment.

The Green Spaces and Sustainable Communities Fund is also working in partnership with a number of other partners on a range of programmes, including:

- Better Play (Barnardo's and the Children's Play Council)
- People's Places (British Trust for Conservation Volunteers – BTCV)
- Wildspace! (English Nature)
- The Social Economic and Environmental Development (SEED Programme – Royal Society for Nature Conservation)
- Doorstep Greens (The Countryside Agency)
- Playing Fields and Community Green Spaces (Sport England) and
- Sustrans programmes.

317

According to the Countryside Agency, over half of all visits to the countryside are within only five miles of home, and 80 per cent of the population of England lives in towns and cities. The countryside around towns is also the home and workplace for many people and it can also provide great opportunities for improving the quality of life for many people living in the towns and cities and for visitors from further afield. The rural urban fringe is a space that is often neglected as an open space amenity that can provide leisure and amenity for millions of people. Many urban fringe ideas and initiatives are being developed. Major initiatives include the completion of Millennium Green projects, Doorstep Greens, and Community Forests which have been covered earlier.

One important innovation is the introduction of Millennium Greens: a £20 million project. In 1995, a bid was submitted to the Millennium Commission for the creation of Millennium Greens throughout England. A grant of £10 million was awarded and £10 million was raised which is being used to complete 250 Millennium Greens – a new area of open space, small or large, in urban or rural locations, within easy walking distance of people's homes, which is owned and managed by the community through the establishment of a local Millennium Green Charitable Trust – developed by local people.

Doorstep Greens is another initiative. The Countryside Agency, in association with Groundwork UK and with the help of Lottery funding from the New Opportunities Fund (NOF), is assisting 200 communities in creating green spaces near to people's homes, particularly in places where people experience disadvantage and in places where regeneration of the local environment is badly needed. The objective is to create 200 Doorstep Greens by 2006.

The Green Gym initiative was pioneered by the British Trust for Conservation Volunteers (BTCV) in 1997 as a new approach:

> to create healthier communities and a healthier environment. It offers people the opportunity to improve their physical fitness through involvement in practical conservation activities. As well as improving physical fitness, the Green Gym provides other health benefits through social contact and being outdoors.
>
> BTCV website

Experienced co-ordinators provide training in practical skills and healthcare professionals play a vital role in referring patients, and people can also refer themselves. The kinds of work involved include footpaths, maintenance, vegetation clearance, resurfacing, drainage creation and repair.

Open spaces and urban parks

The government's Urban Green Spaces Task Force looked into the decline of urban parks and open spaces and made 52 recommendations in its report in May 2002. At the Urban Summit, the government, in response to the report, launched *Living Spaces: Cleaner, Safer, Greener* (ODPM, 2003).

The report recommended a single organization to champion and campaign for open space. CABE, the Commission for Architecture and the Environment was chosen. CABE has concern with the outside environment and streets in towns and cities. CABE established a unit with a remit to cover all outside spaces including parks and streets, with an initial focus on parks and green spaces. Hence, CABE Space was created in 2003, funded by the Office of the Deputy Prime Minister. It was established for the following reasons:

- parks and green spaces are as essential to our cities as roads and sewers, breathing life into communities, bringing charm, beauty, character, nature, and wildlife
- 30 per cent of the public say they won't use parks, usually because they do not feel safe
- even fewer people who are elderly or from minority ethnic groups used parks
- if you live in a deprived area, your parks are likely to be in a worse condition than if you lived in a wealthier area
- children's play areas are often unsafe, empty, and have broken equipment
- one-third of all people never walk alone in their area after dark, even fewer women or older people go out after dark.

CABE Space aims to bring excellence to the design, management and mainte-nance of parks and public open space in towns and cities. It encourages local councils to think holistically about ready access to their green spaces and their contribution to their residents' health and well-being. A major issue for CABE Space is the under-investment in local parks and green spaces. Local authorities have to spend more, but a great deal can be done for minimum expenditure such as good practice. The Green Flag Award Scheme is one way of improving the quality and attraction of parks and open spaces.

The Green Flag Award Scheme

The public has high expectations of parks and makes exceptionally good use of them. An important feature of our heritage for over 150 years, they have evolved from 'green lungs' needed in industrial cities; they are of social, recreational and economic value to local communities. They are for all ages and they offer a mix of facilities for play, walking, sport and contact with the natural world. But many parks do not meet these expectations. The Green Flag Award Scheme started in 1996 as an environmental award to promote ways of managing public spaces. It represents the national standard for parks and green spaces across England and Wales. The scheme is not yet available in Scotland and Northern Ireland, though plans are in hand to extend the scheme to these areas.

In a detailed report for the Local Government Association, John Taylor and Fred Coalter debate the case for urban parks, spaces and the countryside in realizing the potential of cultural services. The original purpose of the Green Flag initiatives was to generate public confidence in well run public parks:

> The Green Flag Parks Award was established by the Pesticides Trust in 1996 to draw attention to, and reward, good environmental practices in park management. This was subsequently ex-tended to include broader criteria following the development of partnerships with the Char-tered Institution of Water and Environmental Management (CIWEM), the Civic Trust, English

Nature, Institute of Amenity Management (ILAM), KMC Consultancy, and Liz Greenhalgh. Here are some criteria for consideration for a Green Flag Park Award.

Environment Parks should support a variety of habitats, encourage conservation ... environmentally sound maintenence practices ... a low dependence on chemical pesticides ... and the designation of wildlife areas.

Community Parks should contribute to the locality and provide facilities suited to the needs of the community. The park should be a focal point of local activities such as children's shows and other events. The community should look to its park as a true asset, and be actively involved in its management and development.

Landscape Parks should be aesthetically pleasing places which provide active and passive recreational opportunities in ways that take account of a park's size, location and catchment area.

Safe, clean and accessible A park must be a safe place for everyone to use. It should be well maintained and managed. Access to a park and its facilities must be available to all members of the community.

Taylor and Coalter, 2001

Green Flag is an independent award that sets standards for management and promotes the value of parks and green spaces as social places as well as places for walking, play, recreation and for contact with the natural world. Although the Award was set up for public parks, a wider range of green spaces needed to be included to improve green spaces across the United Kingdom.

The Green Flag Award has become the benchmark against which the quality of public parks and green spaces can be measured. It now extends across a range of community open spaces:

- town parks
- country parks
- formal gardens
- nature reserves
- local nature reserves
- cemetery and crematoria
- water parks
- open spaces
- millennium greens
- community run greenspace
- doorstep greens.

Successful parks and green spaces are eligible to fly the Green Flag. The award is open to any freely accessible park or green spaces and application is made by the organization that manages the facility. The Green Flag Award Scheme works on a 3-year cycle with the first year being a new application and the subsequent 2 years a re-application. However, if a park or green space is to retain the award, it has to maintain and improve on the standards that gained it the award in the first place. Criteria by which the parks and green spaces are judged are as follows:

1   A welcoming place: how to create a sense that people are positively welcomed in the park.
2   Healthy, safe and secure: how best to ensure that the park is a safe and healthy environment for all users.
3   Clean and well maintained: what people can expect in terms of cleanliness, facilities and maintenance.
4   Sustainability: how a park can be managed in environmentally sensitive ways.
5   Conservation and heritage: the value of conservation and care of historical heritage.
6   Community involvement: ways of encouraging community participation and acknowledging the community's role in a park's success.
7   Marketing: methods of promoting a park successfully.
8   Management: how to reflect all of the above in a coherent and accessible management plan or strategy and ensure it is implemented.

However, the criteria are not prescriptive, but allow for the distinctness of each park and green space. We are not looking for the perfect park, but a park or green space that is well run. Judging is done on a points system covering a desk assessment and site visit and any entry that reaches the benchmark standard will be eligible to fly a Green Flag.

In terms of leisure management, the award scheme encourages efficient and effective common-sense programming, maintenance and management, for example, planning sports uses without destroying quiet areas for contemplation. Natural and historical features can be sensitively exploited to the benefit of the community.

Summary

This chapter has taken in a broad span of countryside issues in the United Kingdom. It began with world heritage sites and ended on doorstep greens. As such, no one area was covered in depth. The purpose was not to do this, but to provide a panoramic overview which revealed the opportunity for leisure and recreation in nearly all settings and also showed a need for careful planning and management and exceptional, sensitive negotiating and operational skills.

In most settings, appropriate balances need to be struck between conservation, protection, peace and tranquillity, leisure and recreation and economic considerations. Many countryside areas cut across not only physical barriers, but potential political, ownership, administrative and social barriers also. Management skills are needed to negotiate these potential problems, to recognize the needs of all parties involved and to harness the goodwill and support of the community. Stewardship of the countryside needs professional managers and able staff. It also calls upon the sustained commitment of thousands of volunteers who need to be attracted, organized and managed. It is an immense field of work for Leisure Managers with an interest in leisure and recreation in the countryside, rural areas, the urban fringe and open space settings.

Discussion points

1 A mass trespass on Kinder Scout and other moors in the Peak District took place in 1932 and helped bring about the formation of national parks. The Countryside and Rights of Way Act, 2000 (Crow) will extend by nearly 3,200 square miles the amount of land available to walkers in England and Wales. The Act gives walkers the right to roam over mountain, moor, heath and downland without having to stay on paths. It excludes cultivated land, improved grassland, golf courses and racecourses. The Act, effective from 19 September, 2004 in the Peak District, will extend across England and Wales. Consider the implications from the perspective of countryside conservation, the landowners and the walkers.

Further reading

National Statistics (2003), *UK 2004: The Official Yearbook of the United Kingdom*, TSO, London, p.267.

Moynagh, M. and Worsley, R., for the Countryside Agency (2003), *A Green and Pleasant Land*, Countryside Publications, Wetherby.

ODPM (2002), *Living Places: Cleaner, Safer, Greener*, Office of the Deputy Prime Minister, London.

The Institute of Leisure and Amenity Management (ILAM) Fact Sheet *Open Space Terminology* provides a wide range of terms applying to open space, together with a number of references.

Useful websites

Department for Environment, Food and Rural Affairs (Defra): www.defra.gov.uk/environment/index.htm

The Welsh Assembly Government: www.wales.gov.uk

Scottish Executive Environment and Rural Affairs Department (SEERAD): www.scotland.gov.uk

Department of the Environment (Northern Ireland) (DoE): www.doeni.gov.uk

Department of Agriculture and Rural Development (DARD): www.dardni.gov.uk

Environment Agency: www.environment-agency.gov.uk

Environment Council (independent UK charity): www.the-environment-council.org.uk

Environment and Heritage Service (Northern Ireland): www.ehsni.gov.uk

Association of National Park Authorities: www.anpa.gov.uk

Council for National Parks (national charity): www.cnp.org.uk

British Waterways: www.britishwaterways.org

Countryside Agency: www.countryside.gov.uk

Countryside Council for Wales: www.ccw.gov.uk

English Heritage: www.english-heritage.org.uk

Scottish National Heritage: www.snh.org.uk

English Nature: www.english-nature.org.uk

Joint Nature Conservation Committee: www.jncc.gov.uk

Forestry Commission: www.forestry.gov.uk

Green Space (incorporating the Urban Parks Forum): www.green-space.org.uk

National Trust: www.nationaltrust.org.uk

National Trust for Scotland: www.nts.org.uk

British Trust for Conservation Volunteers: information@btcv.org.uk

16

The arts, museums and libraries

Introduction

Most of us in the leisure profession used to have a clear understanding of what was meant by 'cultural activities' and 'the arts'. Of late, however, some confusion has crept in. This may be partly as a result of the naming of the Department for Culture, Media and Sport (DCMS), which separates culture from sport; but then sport is included as one of the major components in Local Cultural Strategies. It may be because the government now uses 'the arts', 'cultural activities' and 'the creative industries' at times differently and at times to convey the same things. Or it may be because in official national reports such as the *Official Yearbook of the United Kingdom*, under the heading 'cultural activities', only the traditional arts are listed: plays, classical music, ballet, opera and contemporary dance (see for example Table 16.1).

Chapter 3 provided an insight into the rich and diverse cultural history of the United Kingdom and its traditions. The word 'culture' is used to encompass our heritage, traditions, customs and ways of life, in similar vein to the DCMS cultural strategy approach. This chapter, however, deals specifically with the arts, museums and galleries and libraries and uses as a starting point the definitions of the Select Committee report on Public and Private Funding of the Arts and the DCMS, which show considerable similarity.

The term the arts includes, but is not limited to, music (instrumental and vocal), dance and drama, folk arts, creative writing, architecture and allied fields, painting, sculpture, photography, graphic and craft arts, industrial design, costume and fashion design, motion pictures, television and radio, tape and sound recording, the arts related to the presentation, performance, execution, and exhibition of such major forms, and the study and application of the arts to the human environment (DES, 1982).

The creative industries are: 'those industries which have their origin in individual creativity, skill and talent and which have a potential for wealth and job creation through the generation and exploitation of intellectual property. This includes advertising, architecture, the art and antiques market, crafts, design, designer fashion, film and video, interactive leisure software, music, the performing arts, publishing, software and computer games, television and radio.' (DCMS)

The DCMS sees its role as 'to assist the creative industries by raising their profile and helping them achieve their full economic potential'. The emphasis on 'industry' and the economy is a notable departure from the idealistic concept of 'art for art's sake'.

National policy and the arts

The Arts Council of Great Britain (ACGB) was established by Royal Charter in 1946. The impetus for its creation was the success of the Council for the Encouragement of Music and Arts which had been established during the Second World War. Regional Arts Associations, later called Regional Arts Boards (RABs), were established in 1950 to work with the Arts Council, but independent of it.

The recommendations of the Wilding Report (Wilding, 1989) shifted the emphasis, particularly in terms of funding and organization, to the Regional Arts Boards. In 1994, ACGB's responsibilities and functions were transferred to the Arts Council of England, the Scottish Arts Council and the Arts Council of Wales. The Arts Council of Northern Ireland was already established as a separate body. Each was responsible for development and funding in their respective countries, receiving grants from government, though operating 'at arm's length' from central government.

The 'arts' cover a wide and diverse range of pursuits. The public, voluntary and commercial sectors are all involved in the provision of facilities and in arts-related activities and events. In 1992, *Towards a National Arts and Media Strategy* (NAMMG, 1992) called for a strong partnership between the public and private sectors: 'The arts and culture are at the core of citizenship; they are central to the individual and in society and to community and national life.' *A Creative Future* (Arts Council, 1993) promoted a clear message: the arts do not exist in isolation; to be involved with the arts is to be involved with society.

Today, the arts and creative industries are very much involved in society and permeate into our lives and daily living, particularly through the television, radio, and from the written word. Half the population engages in arts and crafts, hobbies and interests in arts-related voluntary activities. High proportions of the public also attend events.

Table 16.1 illustrates that the percentage of the population that attend cultural events has remained relatively stable over the past decade, apart from going to the cinema which has risen dramatically from less than half to nearly two-thirds of the population between 1992 and 2003. Visits to some of the major museums and galleries in England also rose with the largest rises to the Natural History Museum and the Victoria & Albert Museum. The first major museum in the United Kingdom devoted to Britain's colonial past, the British Empire and Commonwealth Museum opened in September 2002 and is housed in the old Bristol Temple Meads railway station.

Table 16.1 Attendance[1] at cultural events, Great Britain

	1991/92 %	2001/02 %	2002/03 %
Cinema	44	57	61
Plays	23	24	24
Art galleries/exhibitions	21	22	24
Classical music	12	12	13
Ballet	6	6	7
Opera	6	6	7
Contemporary dance	3	5	5

[1] Percentage of resident population aged 15 and over asked about their attendance 'these days'.
Source: Target Group Index, BMRB International

What the attendance figures do not tell us about is the market and audience for popular music, country and western, folk, rock music and the huge appeal to young people of pop music. It is of course the commercial music world that leads these markets, whereas many other forms of music need funds from government, voluntary organizations and the public, in order to survive.

Churches and cathedrals are an important part of the UK's cultural heritage and in addition to their congregations and events, attract large numbers of visitors. York Minster and Canterbury Cathedral receive over 1 million visitors.

Festivals and live performance events are held in their hundreds in the UK each year, some for days and for weeks.

Theatre and drama go back centuries; the first permanent theatre building was opened in London in 1576. In 2001, 11.7 million attendances were recorded at the commercial and grant-aided theatres in central London alone. Long-running West End productions at March 2004 include *The Mousetrap* (51 years), *Les Misérables* (19 years), *The Phantom of the Opera* (18 years) and *Blood Brothers* (16 years).

The DCMS reports that the creative industries grew by an average of 8 per cent per annum, between 1997 and 2001, and exports contributed £11.4 billion to the balance of trade in 2001. In 2002, there were around 122,000 companies in the industry on the Inter-Departmental Business Register and around 1.9 million jobs in the creative industries.

The administration of the arts

The arts and creative industries in the United Kingdom are delivered through a wide range of central government-supported agencies, local authorities, institutions and through the voluntary and private sectors. Local authorities maintain many museums and art galleries and provide public libraries.

The responsibilities of the DCMS include amongst its portfolio the national policy for the arts, public libraries and archives, museums and galleries, the built heritage, the creative industries and the National Lottery, all of which impinge on leisure and its management.

Government expenditure on the arts is distributed through the DCMS, the devolved administrations in Scotland, Wales and Northern Ireland have responsibilities in their areas. The department's expenditure in 2002/3 on museums and galleries (England), libraries (UK) and museums' library archives (UK) was around £500 million. Expenditure on the arts in England was around £300 million. The DCMS objectives in relation to these areas are:

- creating an efficient and competitive market by removing obstacles to growth and unnecessary regulation
- broadening access to cultural events and to the built environment
- raising the standards of cultural education and training and
- ensuring that everyone has the opportunity to achieve excellence in areas of culture and to develop talent, innovation and good design.

The National Assembly for Wales has responsibility for the arts in Wales and has a cultural strategy called Creative Future. The Scottish Executive administers cultural policy in Scotland. In Northern Ireland, responsibility for the arts rests with the DCMS.

Arts Council England (ACE), the Scottish Arts Council, the Arts Council of Wales and Arts Council of Northern Ireland (see Useful websites) are independent bodies that distribute government grants and Lottery funding to visual, performing and community arts and to literature. ACE funds national organizations such as the Royal Opera, the Royal Ballet, the Birmingham Royal Ballet, the Royal Shakespeare Company and others.

The Scottish Arts Council is an executive non-departmental public body (NDPB), which is one of the main channels for government funding for the arts in Scotland, receiving its funding from the Scottish Executive. The Council distributes National Lottery Funds received from the DCMS. As a non-departmental public body, the Scottish Arts Council is independent from, but accountable to, the Scottish Executive. It funds a range of arts organizations for annual programmes of work and makes project and lottery grants to individual artists and arts organizations.

Arts Council England

Arts Council England (ACE) is the national development agency for the Arts in England, distributing public money from government and the National Lottery. ACE operates under a Royal Charter which sets out its constitution, describes its membership and gives the organization three objects:

1 to develop and improve the knowledge, understanding and practice of the arts
2 to increase the accessibility of the arts to the public
3 to advise and co-operate with departments of government, local authorities, the Arts Councils of Scotland, Wales and Northern Ireland and other bodies on any matters concerned, whether directly or indirectly, with the foregoing objects.

ACE works within the DCMS Secretary of State's four overriding priorities – children and young people, communities, the economy and delivery – to improve the quality of life through the arts. It provides annual funding to over 1,200 regularly funded organizations. ACE's stated aims are to:

- broaden access for all to a rich and varied artistic and cultural life
- ensure that the artistic activity we fund aspires to be world class in terms of standards and innovation
- ensure that everyone has the opportunity to develop artistic talent and to achieve excellence in the arts
- develop the educational potential of all the nation's artistic and cultural resources
- raise standards of artistic and cultural education and training
- ensure an adequate skills supply for the arts and cultural sectors
- reduce the number of those that feel excluded from society by using the arts
- to carry out our work using best management practice and reflecting and using the diversity of those who work here and those with whom we work outside the department.

Ambition for the Arts (ACE, 2003) sets out the ambition of ACE to 'promote the arts at the heart of our national life'. This is the start of a new era of expansion for the arts in England with a major increase in public investment. Between 2003 and 2006, the government is investing £2 billion of public funds in the arts in England, including funding from the National Lottery. ACE, therefore, aims to:

- prioritize individual artists
- work with funded arts organizations to help them thrive rather than just survive
- place cultural diversity at the heart of our work
- prioritize young people and Creative Partnerships
- maximize growth in the arts
- as well as creating a modern and progressive Arts Council.

In the past, the Arts Council had policies and strategies; in *Ambition for the Arts*, it now has a manifesto which states what it wants to do and replaces other general policy statements.

> We believe in the transforming power of the arts – power to change the lives of people throughout the country. Our ambition is to place the arts at the heart of national life, reflecting the country's rich and diverse cultural identity as only the arts can. We want people throughout England to experience arts activities of the highest quality. We believe that access to the arts goes hand in hand with excellence.
>
> ACE, 2003

ACE works with nine English Regional Arts Councils (RACs); these were formerly the Regional Arts Boards (RABs). Together they make up the integrated system for arts funding and development in England.

ACE and the RACs are constitutionally independent from one another, but their successful operation relies on close working relationships and their roles are complementary and interdependent. The regional bodies receive their core funding from several sources: ACE; local authorities; the British Film Institute; and the Crafts

Council. The RACs in turn provide funding to arts organizations and artists working in the performing and visual arts, literature, film and video, and crafts in their region, through regular grants and one-off Development Funds.

Working with local authorities

Local government plays a vital role in supporting the arts. For local authorities in England and Wales, funding of the arts is discretionary; that is, although authorities are empowered to support the arts, they are not mandated to do so. There are a number of motivations for local government funding of the arts, for example, a wish to enhance the quality of life for residents, attract visitors and tourists and the contribution of the arts to the local economy. Support for the arts is provided by local authorities in a number of ways, including, for example:

- providing and operating arts venues; there are over 200 arts centres, generally managed professionally, but invariably supported by an array of volunteers
- funding of independent arts organizations, artists, performers and venues
- funding 'in kind': reduced rent and rates
- funding of their local Regional Arts Board
- providing venues for other events: community centres, town halls, and often the organization of promotion of such events
- promoting festivals and other arts events
- funding of Percent for Art schemes: a percentage of the cost of new building or environment schemes is allocated to commission artists and craftspeople
- public art projects: art works that are in public places
- providing outreach resources and programmes; rural areas suffer more than urban areas in provision for the arts, not just because of isolation, but also because of low incomes, high unemployment, poor transport and higher costs to local authorities, with most funds targeted towards urban centres.

As local authorities do not have a statutory obligation to provide arts funding, new developments have tended to be *ad hoc* and opportunity-led. Lottery funding has been demand-led, which makes development more sporadic than strategic. Local authorities are encouraged to link voluntary organizations with the Voluntary Arts Network (VAN). VAN aims to promote participation in the arts and crafts, recognizing that they are a key component to elevating our health, social and economic development.

According to the Crafts Council, over half the UK adult population is involved in the voluntary arts and crafts: 'those arts and crafts that people undertake for self-improvement, social networking and leisure, but not primarily for payment'. The range of art forms is wide and includes folk, dance, drama, literature, media, music, visual arts, crafts and applied arts, and festivals.

There are large numbers of artists, craftspeople and art-involved enthusiasts, but provision and opportunity are in a variety of pockets. However, small specialisms may well thrive by being separate. The performing arts, on the other hand, need to be co-ordinated because each cannot have its own performing venue.

Creative Partnerships

The arts are also an important part of education, are included in Key Stages 3 and 4 in the National Curriculum for schools, and arts for young people have been given added impetus by government and through the National Lottery in recent years. *Setting the Scene: The Arts and Young People* (DNH, 1986) committed public funding to the arts and widening choice, engaging communities and tapping the skills and interests of young people. Meeting children's needs must now take account, not just of the National Curriculum, but also of the delegation of budgets to schools. Artsmark is an ACE national award scheme for schools committed to the arts.

Creative Partnerships (CPs) is the DCMS and Arts Council England's flagship programme in the cultural education field, to give schoolchildren aged 5 to 18 and their teachers the opportunity to explore their creativity by working on sustained projects with creative professionals. Creative Partnerships, a DCMS-sponsored initiative with additional support from the Department for Education and Skills (DfES), was started in 16 local partnership areas in 2002/3 with around 15 to 25 schools in each partnership taking part. An additional £70 million funding for the scheme was announced in June 2003, bringing the total available to £110 million. The additional funding will allow schools from 20 new partnership areas to become involved in the project over the next two years.

DCMS and the DfES see this programme as the government's response to the National Advisory Committee on Creative and Cultural Education report *All Our Futures: Culture, Creativity and Education* (DCMS/DES, 1999).

A 'Partnership' is the relationship between an organization such as a theatre, TV studio, arts centre, library or museum, and the school(s) which they work with on a basis of understanding and shared learning. The government believes that the Creative Partnerships model will be effective in reaching young people most at risk of exclusion, who are often turned off by more academically based approaches.

> Creative Partnerships will embrace a multiplicity of cultural, creative and artistic activities. Benefits for school children will include having unprecedented opportunities to work with creative practitioners to learn about and develop new skills in creative activities such as fashion design, television and radio writing, internet style, choreography, directing or producing videos and plays. The creative teaching and learning programmes will provide opportunities for pupils and young people to develop their objective, critical and analytical skills within a creative and cultural environment as well as having fun in the process ... As well as supporting formal learning, taking part in creative activities will help increase pupils' confidence and motivation. This is particularly significant for disaffected young people who may feel they are a failure at school. Creative Partnerships will also stretch our most gifted young people by giving them the opportunity to work with talented professionals from the creative and cultural sectors.
>
> DCMS/DES, 1999

The problem with a number of government-sponsored projects introduced over many years is that they often start with money and enthusiasm, but once core-funding ceases or is reduced and key workers move on, the projects lose momentum and many do not survive. However, the DCMS proposes that each Partnership area will be led by a Creative Director, supported by an Advisory Group. They will identify ways in which CP programmes can be self-sufficient and sustainable.

The arts and business and Lottery funding

The introduction of the National Lottery in 1994 significantly altered the funding of arts in the United Kingdom. During the early years of the Lottery, the focus of arts funding was chiefly on major capital projects and some of these provoked negative public reaction. Shift in emphasis occurred from 1998 onwards, with the allocation of funds to smaller, local projects. In addition, the National Endowment for Science, Technology and the Arts (NESTA), uses the income generated by £295 million of Lottery funds to support projects and inventions in the arts and sciences.

> By June 2003, the arts councils across the United Kingdom had awarded over 27,000 grants worth a total of over £2.1 billion.

The Awards for All scheme – operated by a number of distributors and managed by the Community Fund – makes available grants of between £500 and £5,000 to community groups with a turnover of less than £15,000.

The Business Sponsorship Incentive Scheme promotes growth in sponsorship on the basis of matching funds from government. The Pairing Scheme for the Arts is a competitive scheme which provides an incentive to businesses to sponsor the arts. Managed on behalf of the DCMS by ABSA, the Association for Business Sponsorship of the Arts, now called Arts & Business Ltd (A & B), the scheme is to help build communities through developing partnerships between business and the arts. It encourages businesses to sponsor the arts for the first time, and existing business sponsors to increase their support, by offering matching funds, at different ratios, for new sponsorship money. Additional incentives are in place to encourage long-term commitment by sponsors, and for those sponsorships which generate easier access to the arts. Since the scheme's inception in 1984, it has succeeded in bringing in new money to the arts. In one year, 1999/2000, commercial investment reached £150 million. London, not surprisingly, generates the largest sums of business investment, around 60 per cent, followed by Scotland at around 12 per cent. The most attractive art forms to investors were museums and galleries and opera. Twenty-four businesses each generated more than £1 million in investment.

A & B is said to be the world's leading not-for-profit organization working in this field, with 18 regional offices in the UK. It has over 350 business members and manages the Arts & Business New Partners Programme on behalf of Arts Council England and the DCMS. A & B conducts an annual survey of UK arts organizations supported by ACE and the DCMS. The latest results show UK business investment in the arts in 2001/2 was £111 million, compared with £114 million in 2000/1. Business help for new developments rose from £9 million to £15 million. Sponsorship in kind fell from £18 million in 2001/2 to £14 million in 2002/3.

Visiting Arts is the national agency for promoting the flow of international arts into the United Kingdom and developing cultural links abroad. Visiting Arts is a joint venture of the Arts Council of England, the Scottish Arts Council, the Arts Council of Wales, the Arts Council of Northern Ireland, the Crafts Council, the Foreign and Commonwealth Office and the British Council. It promotes and facilitates the inward flow of foreign arts into England, Scotland, Wales and Northern Ireland.

Crafts and films

The Crafts Council, established in 1971, is a registered charity which receives an annual grant from government, and is the national organization for promoting contemporary craft in Great Britain with priority given to innovative work. The object of the Crafts Council is to advance and encourage the creation of works of fine craftsmanship and to increase the interest of the public in the works of craftspeople. Its objectives include:

- raising the profile of crafts in England and abroad
- strengthening and developing the craft economy in support of craftspeople
- organizing the annual Chelsea Crafts Fair and other programmes
- co-ordinating British groups at international fairs.

Craft Forum Wales supports craft business groups in Wales. Craftworks, an independent company, is the craft development agency for Northern Ireland. The Arts Council of Northern Ireland funds crafts promotion. The Scottish Arts Council has a Crafts Department which promotes crafts and craftworkers.

The Crafts Council receives most of its funding from the DCMS through ACE. In turn, it distributes funds to the Regional Councils for allocation to crafts projects in their regions. It also offers financial support by means of grants to individuals and organizations. The Council exercises most of its relevant powers through the Regional Councils. Twenty-five thousand people are involved in crafts professionally; the number engaged in crafts in an amateur capacity is, of course, hugely greater.

The Crafts Council offers a range of services to makers and the public. As well as exhibitions and selling crafts and books, it provides a specialist Reference Library and a national register of over 4,000 UK craftspeople.

The UK Film Council oversees public funding for film production in the United Kingdom. It advises government and is the principal funder of the British Film Institute (BFI), which promotes audience appreciation of film. The BFI was established in 1933. The UK Film Council is the government-backed strategic agency for film in the UK. Its main aims are to stimulate a successful UK film industry and to promote the enjoyment and understanding of cinema. It works with Scottish Screen, the Northern Ireland Film and Television Commission and Sgrin, the Media Agency for Wales. The former British Film Commission operates as the international arm of the UK Film Council. The UK Film Council distributes Lottery and government grants. The British Board of Film Classification (BBFC) is responsible for classifying films and videos. (The commercial film industry is covered in Chapter 11.)

Museums and galleries

The United Kingdom has some of the finest museums and galleries in the world. The world's first national public museum, the British Museum in London, celebrated the 250th anniversary of its foundation in 2003. There is no exact figure on the total number of museums in the United Kingdom: there are a large number of independent and private museums and estimates vary. The DCMS estimates that there are between 2,000 and 2,500, though many curators believe that this number is high bearing in mind the difficulties facing a number of small independent museums. While there has been a high number of museums that have opened, this is offset by a high number of closures particularly in the category of small museums of 20,000 visitors or less. However, the DCMS reports that the introduction of free admissions to its sponsored museums and galleries has increased the number of visitors to over 30 million a year.

Table 16.2 Visits to national museums and galleries, 2002/03, England

	NUMBER OF VISITS (MILLION)
Tate Gallery[1]	5.2
National Gallery	4.6
British Museum	4.4
National Museum of Science & Industry	3.1
Natural History Museum	2.8
Victoria & Albert Museum (V&A)	2.4
Imperial War Museum	1.9
National Portrait Gallery	1.3
National Maritime Museum	1.2
National Museums Liverpool	1.1
Royal Armouries	0.4
Wallace Collection	0.2

[1] Combined figures for Tate Britain, Tate Modern, Tate Liverpool and Tate St Ives.
Source: Department for Culture, Media and Sport.

Sponsored museums and galleries include the Museum of Science and Industry in Manchester, Imperial War Museum, Tate Gallery and National Portrait Gallery (see Table 16.2).

Over 80 million visits a year are made to the 1,860 registered UK museums and galleries which include the national museums and about 1,000 independent museums, according to the *Official United Kingdom Yearbook* (ONS, 2003). While numbers have fallen, the sponsored museums and galleries have flourished, accounting for around one-third of the visitor market. When another one-third accounts for visits to London museums alone, a picture emerges of one healthy end of the sector and a corresponding diminishing market for the larger number of museums across the United Kingdom. Sightseeing Research, 2000 reported that 66 per cent of museums attracted less than 20,000 visits each, and are thus unlikely to have exceeded 65 visits on any one day. Another salutary finding reported by Resource is that overseas visitors to the UK represent around 40 per cent of visits to London Museums and that children under 16 years make up 30 per cent of all museum visits. If overseas visitors and children were excluded from the market statistics, then the scene could be relatively bleak in terms of UK adult visitors to museums, and gives a different slant from the often quoted 'headline' figures of more visitors than spectators at Football League matches.

> Taking all museums into account, the total visitor figures are likely to approximate 77 million.

Resource and government support

Resource, the Council for Museums, Archives and Libraries, is the strategic agency working with museums, archives and libraries across the United Kingdom, and advising the government on policy issues. Resource (see Useful websites) was launched in April 2000 as the strategic body replacing the Museums and Galleries Commission (MGC) and the Library and Information Commission (LIC) and now includes archives within the scope of its work. Its core role is reported as fourfold:

- to provide strategic leadership
- to act as a powerful advocate
- to develop capacity within the sector and
- to promote innovation and change.

It is currently in the process of establishing regional agencies in each of the nine English regions. It provides funding through these agencies and their predecessors (which include the Area Museum Councils). It has responsibility for a number of other initiatives, including:

- the portable antiquities scheme, set up to record archaeological objects
- schemes for museum registration and designation of collections
- Renaissance in the Regions, a major new government investment programme to tap the potential of England's regional museums and
- the Acceptance in Lieu Scheme, whereby pre-eminent works of art may be accepted by the government in settlement of tax and allocated to public galleries.

The Museums Association Ethics Committee in 1999 stated: 'Museums belong to everybody. All members of society have a right to visit and use them.' These principles are enshrined in the Museums Association's ethical guidelines on access: museums have a duty to provide access today. Unlike other cultural organizations, they equally have a duty to safeguard for future generations their collections and other resources, including information and expertise. Museums and galleries help us to understand our culture and our heritage, they are important for education, and they are venues that we visit in our leisure. According to Sightseeing Research 2000, over 77 million visits are made to museums and galleries per year. MORI in 2001 reported that nearly a third of adults resident in the UK claim to have visited a museum or gallery in the past year. Museums also act as a focus for their local communities and also involve the community. They are costly to preserve and manage and nearly two-thirds of them rely on volunteer work and support.

Local authorities provide and manage about 650 museums. The relevant legislation concerned with museums is discretionary. Spending priorities, therefore, come into play. The threat to museums – exemplified in many districts and boroughs – is financial. Short term economies and inadequate maintenance create longer term problems. Two major reports in 1991 have shaped changes to the museum service: a report by the former Museums and Galleries Commission, Local Authorities and Museums and *The Road to Wigan Pier?* (Museums and Galleries Commission, 1991), a report by the Audit Commission. Other initiatives were the establishment of Area Museums Councils and the introduction of the Registration Scheme for Museums, prescribing minimum standards.

Since that time, two major influences have been brought into play: the National Lottery, and the amalgamation of central government services, museums and galleries and libraries. The National Lottery led to unprecedented levels of capital investment into the nation's museums and galleries.

The National Heritage Act, 1997 gave the Heritage Lottery Fund (HLF) new powers with which to assist a wider range of museum projects. The HLF is now able to support projects relating to access, education and Information Technology, as well as heritage.

Museums and galleries count for the largest amount of the DCMS direct funding, with an estimated £353 million in 2002/3, a sum greater than the arts and three times greater than sports from central government. When funding from other government departments, local authorities, and the National Lottery are taken into consideration, and another £32 million in business sponsorship, and upwards of £37 million in consumer spend (Selwood, 2001), plus £4 million plus from its Friends' organizations, museums could receive up to £500–£600 million of public funding (British Association of Friends of Museums, 2001).

The Museums and Libraries Sponsorship unit within DCMS provides advice to both government and the museums and galleries sector. The Department's sponsored museums and galleries are run by independent Boards of Trustees, the majority of whom are appointed by the government. The Department also works alongside a number of other bodies, such as the Regional Agencies, Resource and the Department for Education and Skills (DfES) to take a strategic role in the wider sector including museums run by universities, local authorities and independent providers.

Despite their popularity, as reported earlier, the number of visits to museums in the United Kingdom has fallen in recent years, particularly regional and local museums. Local authority museums are subject to Best Value (see Modernizing local government, p. 150, Chapter 9), designed to ensure that local government services are of high quality and delivered at the most economical costs. However, under-resourced museums have had to reduce expenditure on caring for collections, marketing, programming temporary exhibitions and with their education and outreach work. Should they receive low grading, the local authorities may well find justification for funding them difficult. Independent museums (if grant funded by local authorities) may also fall within the Best Value guidelines and any reduction in their funding could cast doubt on their future.

Museums, lifelong learning and accessibility

The DCMS works with the DfES in taking a strategic role in the museums sector, which includes universities, local authorities and independent museums and galleries. Museums and galleries can be hugely important facilities for education and lifelong learning. The Campaign for Learning through Museums and Galleries (clmg), formed by some of the UK's leading museums, galleries and educational institutions, was launched in 1997. It started as a result of the report called *A Common Wealth* (Anderson, 1999) which investigated the state of education and learning in UK's museums and galleries. It found that learning opportunities were abundant but were yet to be unlocked. David Anderson wrote, 'museums and galleries at their finest are universal educational institutions of immense power and authority. They communicate with us across boundaries of language, culture and time'.

Among many achievements clmg has co-ordinated the £3 million DfES Museums and Galleries Education Programme which involved 65 museums in ground-breaking projects to support the National Curriculum and the further £1.5 million phase two.

335

The mission of 'museums for all' is epitomized in the Museums and Galleries Disability Association, a not-for-profit organization, part-funded by Resource, promoting the use of museums, galleries and heritage sites to people with disabilities. MAGDA encourages all visitor destinations to achieve access for all. Access is not just physical access, however: there needs to be a whole change of attitude towards disability. However, access for all implies access for those with disabilities of any kind, whether they be physical, educational, social or financial. Museum visits by adults, in general, tend to be by market sectors that have 'higher' social backgrounds and educational attainment, are 'white', and frequented in large proportion by students and people over the age of retirement.

Organizations which form clmg

Arts Council for England	Campaign for Learning
Resource	Group for Education in Museums
Association of Independent Museums	Engage
Museums Association	Cultural Heritage National Training Organisation
Visual Arts and Galleries Association	

In terms of quality leisure management, visiting experience shows that a large proportion of museums have a long way to go to meet the customer service expectations consumers find in many other leisure facilities. This subjective assessment by leisure managers is supported by the Selwood Report (Selwood, 2001) which found that even in registered museums which are expected to meet minimum standards:

- one in five had no labels and one in four no interpretation panels
- two out of three had no plan of the museum
- two out of three had no café
- one in three had no temporary exhibition space
- one in five had no toilet facilities and most had no baby change facilities
- less than half had staff trained in visitor care
- a majority had no member of staff specifically responsible for visitor care, nor a member of staff with specific responsibility for education
- only one in five had a marketing policy and
- less than half had carried out visitor research in the previous five years.

Changes in the museums sector and e-culture

Some professionals have suggested that a number of museums are unlikely to survive and that as many as one-third are unlikely to meet the more exacting standards required. The most vulnerable museums are those with low attendances, poor standards of visitor care and poor marketing. A Resource funding officer indicates the prevailing professional view:

... there are too many museums in the UK and new ones should be discouraged because they may put even more pressure on the limited public funds available and supply will outstrip visiting demand. More recently, it has been suggested that too many poor quality museums are diluting the strength of the brand and these should, in some way, be distanced from the 'better' ones. Unfortunately, this does not square well with the pressure from communities to create their own museums.

On a more positive note, as the population becomes older, the museum sector could improve services and marketing to attract this growing market. The family market, if catered for, is also a key sector. More of the population is entering higher education and museums have a strong education potential. The emergence of e-culture could have mixed blessings: it could stimulate visits to museums and galleries, but on the other hand, some may find more enjoyment in surfing the web for museum experience from around the world. 'Virtual' museum connections are already a rapid growth market.

The use of multi-media is already a feature of museums providing a wider range of interest and information. The next decade is likely to see the emergence of an 'e-culture' with electronic cultural services. This should provide a focus for museums' marketing and enhance prospects for delivering lifelong learning. However, not all the population will be reachable. At present, people over 45 and especially those over 65, are increasingly being left behind by the new technologies. Increased access for some, however, should not dilute the principle that public museums are for all. Indeed, the disadvantaged, one could argue, need far more and far easier access. A further long-term argument is the question of whether technology and virtual museums will rob individuals of the desire to see and experience the real thing.

In 2003 the 24 Hour Museum database included over 2,800 museums, galleries and heritage attractions.

The 24 Hour Museum, a charity funded by the DCMS through Resource, promotes UK museums, galleries and heritage attractions. The Internet site, launched in May 1999 as a partnership between the Museum Documentation Association and the Campaign for Museums, became independent in April 2001. The 24 Hour Museum is the UK's national virtual museum. The 'virtual attraction' (see Useful websites) encourages people to visit the real attractions.

The world wide web Virtual Library museums pages (VLmp) is a directory of on-line museum-related resources. The original site, founded in 1994, has seen many changes: the Internet is a changing and volatile market. Virtual visitors are becoming an immense market, with well over 6 million visitor personal numbers allocated to this site alone from August 1994 to November 2003. VLmp pages are supported by the International Council of Museums. At least one museum per day is being added to the museum pages and these are being split into sub-lists by country or region.

Books, libraries and leisure

Despite the availability of huge amounts of information today from alternative sources, the demand for books is as strong as ever. In 2002, UK publishers issued around 125,390 separate titles, and the UK book industry exported books worth £1.2 billion (ONS, 2003). Authors whose sales have reached one million and over are presented with Platinum Awards and those granted by September 2003 included: Louis de Bernières (*Captain Corelli's Mandolin*), Helen Fielding (*Bridget Jones's Diary: A Novel*), Frank McCourt (*Angela's Ashes*), five of J.K. Rowling's Harry Potter books and others.

Public libraries attract a wide range of people: shoppers dropping in to exchange a book, retired people spending time browsing the daily newspapers, business people using resources or students studying. There are also homework clubs, lessons in computing, parents choosing a new video for themselves or their children, young children at storytelling. Libraries are also the first point of contact for information. However, some public libraries are closed when people most want to use them. The introduction of Sunday opening at many libraries has increased attendances significantly, and visits at weekends are now greater than during the week at some central libraries. Public libraries, however, have to deal with commercial competition. For many people, those who can afford it, the best way to get a popular book is to buy one, particularly since paperbacks are relatively cheap and there are holiday offers of '3 for 2'. Books, however, can also be purchased at some libraries.

Public libraries need to respond to this and other changes. Currently, public libraries offer electronic options, but these will soon be available in other sectors. In addition, with Local Management of Schools (LMS), many schools are now buying direct from suppliers, rather than through centralized purchasing schemes. As Ken Worpole of Comedia comments: 'The worlds of the bookshop and public library are drawing closer together.'

Local authorities in Great Britain and education and library boards in Northern Ireland have a duty to provide a free lending and reference library service. In Great Britain, more than 34 million people (58 per cent of the population) are registered members of their local library, and of these, 20 per cent borrow at least once a week. Many libraries have collections of CDs, records, audio- and video-cassettes, DVDs and musical scores for loan. Most libraries hold documents on local history, and all provide services for children.

Nearly all libraries have personal computers with Internet connections for public use. A government initiative under the New Opportunities Fund is providing £50 million for enabling library material to be stored and accessed in digitized form and £20 million for staff training in information and communications technology.

Public libraries, like public museums and galleries, now fall within the remit of Resource. There are different types of library in the United Kingdom:

About 406 million books and 39 million audio-visual items were borrowed from UK public libraries in 2000/1 (ONS, 2003).

- national libraries: British Library, National Library of Scotland, National Library of Wales and National Art Library
- Research Council libraries
- university and college libraries
- public libraries
- private and independent libraries.

The exact number of libraries is not known because there are many independent and private libraries that do not appear on the main registers. However, the UK 2004 *Official Yearbook of the United Kingdom* reports that there are around 5,000 public libraries. There is a also a wide range of electronic communications: the Electronic Libraries Programme, and electronic books and journals.

This wide picture shows the importance and place of libraries, particularly public libraries, in the nation's culture, education, business and leisure. Going to the local public library appears to be the fifth most popular away-from-home pastime, after going to a pub,

Facts about UK libraries

4,759 public libraries, including 693 mobile libraries
210 Open Learning Centres attached to public libraries
19,136 public library service points in hospitals, prisons, retirement homes etc.
900 secondary school libraries
835 libraries and learning resources in further education colleges
600 library service points in higher education institutes
200 library service points in government departments and related agencies
200 archive facilities for public records in England, including central government, local
    authority, museums, universities, military and business archives.

public library statistics

eating out in a restaurant, driving for pleasure and eating in a fast food outlet. More people go to libraries than to professional football matches, estimated by the football associations in England, Wales, Scotland and Northern Ireland at around 33 million spectators.

The main organization speaking for librarians and the library service is the Library Association, a registered charity formed in 1877. The Chartered Institute of Library and Information Professionals was formed in April 2002 unifying the Insititute of Information Scientists and the Library Association. Before the amalgamation, the association had 25,000 members working in local and central government and its agencies, business, higher education, schools, national public libraries and in the voluntary sector. Over 100 members work overseas.

More library statistics

377 million visits made to public libraries
551 million items issued
58 per cent of the UK population hold public library memberships
78 million visits to higher education libraries and 61 million items issued

New Library: The People's Network (Library and
Information Commission, 1997)

The government and the libraries sector

In such a large section of public life, it is not surprising to find government, its agencies and many organizations operating. At central government level, there have been major changes relating to the national structure. The DCMS Secretary of State has a statutory obligation under the Public Libraries and Museums Act, 1964 to ensure that local library authorities in England provide a comprehensive and efficient public library service. All library authorities are now (since 1998) required to produce Annual Library Plans in a common format to help the DCMS to carry out the statutory obligation. Public libraries fall within the remit of county councils and unitary authorities. However, borough and district councils need to work in close collaboration because libraries, potentially, can be the hub of communication, in addition to being one of the major leisure facilities.

In 1995 the Library and Information Commission (LIC) was set up by the DCMS. It was a national source of expertise, advising government on issues relating to the library and information sector. In October 1997, the LIC published *New Library: The People's Network* which recommended the establishment of a national public library IT network. On 31 March, 2000 the LIC was replaced by Resource, described earlier in this section of the book.

In 2002, the largest investment in public libraries made the Internet available to all, with computers provided in nearly all public libraries through the Lottery-funded People's Network project. In February, 2003 the government published *Framework for the Future* (DCMS, 2003), a ten-year vision for public libraries, outlining how they can best serve their communities in the twenty-first century. 'Framework aims to promote public libraries, give them improved visibility, and set out why libraries matter.'

The central themes of Framework are:

- books, reading and learning: knowledge, skills and information are at the heart of economic and social life
- digital citizenship: access to more information than ever before through the Internet
- community and civic values: libraries are safe, welcoming, neutral spaces open to all the community.

Resource has prepared a three-year Action Plan with a range of partners to fulfil the aims of the DCMS. The Action Plan is funded by a £3 million investment over three years. The full report of Turning Vision into Action for Public Libraries is available on the Resource website (Resource, 2003) and see Useful websites.

The report concluded that there is an urgency to prepare for development of the information society, based on lifelong learning. Barriers to this development were the lack of universal access to the information superhighway. There is a need to create awareness, training, universal access and infrastructure. Public libraries are seen to be the means and the major component of this development.

> In the 21st century, the basis of all wealth and achievement will be knowledge and culture. The cities which contribute most to human civilization will be those which are best able to educate and organize their people, attract talent from all over the world, make use of available existing knowledge, originate new knowledge and apply these sensibly. Public libraries of a new kind will play a vital role in creating and sustaining such dynamic human communities.
>
> Resource, 2003

Libraries, as facilities that have to be managed, fall into general management principles as do other leisure facilities. However, librarians are a good deal more than technical experts. Technically handling printed and electronic materials, videos and the like, is but one dimension. Librarians have to understand the reading, leisure and business habits and needs of their communities and, in the public sector, the requirements of government. Indeed, strategic management of public libraries takes place in the arena of government.

> While managing a public library has much in common with managing any other enterprise, at least at tactical and operational levels, the public library's relationship to political authority sets

constraints on strategic management and complicates the process. The legitimacy of the public library is based in almost all instances on political authority ... virtually all public libraries rely on public money for the biggest share of their budgets.

Hayes and Walter, 1996

Libraries, technology and strategic management

'Do you think me a well-read man?'
'Certainly', replied Zi-gong, 'Aren't you?'
'Not at all' said Confucius, 'I have simply grasped one thread which links up all the rest'.

The one thread which could link up all the rest in the twenty-first century is electronic communication, part of a future e-culture. Frances Hendrix wrote, 'If the public libraries in the UK do not act as the bridge between the new electronic information world and the language and history of print, then no one will, and we risk losing our culture, heritage and education.'

In the twenty-first century, greater desire for knowledge, for fast communication and access to information, far from making the library service redundant, make the service even more vital than in times past. Public libraries are becoming the hub for co-ordinating access to information. Libraries, however, are still perceived by many people as institutions that are built around books. Will public libraries change sufficiently and fast enough to cope with the wider and broadening needs of education, business and leisure consumers? With rapid changes in technology current and future generations need to embrace the changes or sections of the community will find themselves in a way isolated. Every hour of every day we are advised to 'log on to www dot ... for further information'. The Internet has the capability of linking every home, business, school, institution, and organization with the local public library.

One extremely important sector of society – children and young people – needs to be nurtured in new technologies. The children's library service therefore will have to 'continually reassess services and plan strategically' (Blanshard, 2000).

The use of new technology in libraries will inevitably change the way libraries are run. The library can be the nerve centre of the community, providing information, knowledge and service. Links with schools and the higher and further education sectors are essential. For the public as a whole, the concept of 'a library without walls' is based on any member of the public being able in a public library to call up on a screen, and have printed, information held in the British Library or any other internationally important reference collection. It could also encompass library resources accessed from computers and digital TV equipment in the home.

The British Library (see Useful websites), the national library of the United Kingdom, is custodian of one of the most important collections in the world. It is housed in the largest wholly publicly funded building constructed in the United Kingdom in the twentieth century. The basements, the deepest in London, have 340 kilometres of shelving for fifteen million books. There are 11 reading areas, three exhibition galleries and a conference centre.

The British Library holds 150 million items spanning 3,000 years.

Greater than even the British Library, however, the Internet is said to be the most significant achievement in the history of mankind (Shuman, 2001).

341

Whether or not this is true, it is having a colossal impact worldwide, has revolutionized communication and given access to information and knowledge unprecedented.

Discussion points

1 The government uses the word 'culture' at times to encompass the arts and creative industries and at times to convey the mores and ways of life of people – a very wide interpretation. Discuss the perceptions of 'art', 'arts', 'culture' and 'the creative industries' in order to provide your local authority with an understanding of the terms.

2 Many claim that public art has impacts beyond its aesthetic value but the government report, *Culture at the Heart of Regeneration* (June 2004) found little evidence of this. Make a case to support or reject the claim.

3 Activities which provide challenge, raise curiosity and make for discovery, are an attraction for people. From your experience, discuss the extent to which museums management take these factors into consideration.

4 Electronic communication and access to information at home, in the workplace and in a range of organizations, far from making public libraries redundant, make the service even more vital than in times past. Discuss.

5 The Internet is the most significant achievement in the history of mankind. Discuss this assumption and its implications upon people's leisure.

Further reading

Ambrose, T. (1993), *Managing New Museums*, HMSO, Edinburgh.

Moore, K. (ed) (1999), *Management in Museums*, Athlone Press, London.

Ambrose, T. and Paine, C. (1993), *Museums Basics*, ICOM/Routledge, London.

Fopp, M. (1997), *Managing Museums and Galleries*, Routledge, London.

DCMS (Department for Culture, Media and Sport) (2003) *Annual Report 2003*, CM 5920, The Stationery Office, 2003.

Useful websites

Department for Culture, Media and Sport: www.culture.gov.uk

Arts on line: www.artsonline.com

Arts Council England: www.artscouncil.org.uk

Arts Council of Wales: www.ccc-acw.org.uk

www.artswales.org.uk

Scottish Arts Council: www.scottisharts.org.uk

Arts Council of Northern Ireland: www.artscouncil-ni.org

National Archives: www.nationalarchives.gov.uk

Arts and Business (formerly ABSA): www.aandb.org.uk

British Film Institute: www.bfi.org.uk

British Broadcasting Corporation: www.bbc.co.uk

National Endowment for Science, Technology and the Arts (NESTA): www.nesta.org.uk

Voluntary Arts Network (VAN): www.voluntaryarts.org

British Library: www.bl.uk

National Library of Scotland: www.nls.uk

National Library of Wales: www.llgc.org.uk

Chartered Institute of Library & Information Professionals (previously the Library Association (LA) and the Institute of Information Scientists (IIS): www.cilip.org.uk

Museums

24 Hour museum: the national virtual museum: www.24hourmuseum.org.uk

Cornucopia: Discovering UK collections (database of UK museum collections) Initiative taken on by Resource: www.cornucopia.org.uk

Council of Museums in Wales: www.cmw.org.uk

Heritage Lottery Fund: www.hlf.org.uk

Museums Association: www.museumsassociation.org.uk

National Museums and Galleries of Northern Ireland: www.magni.org.uk

Resource, The Council for Museums, Archives and Libraries: www.resource.gov.uk

Scottish Museums Council: www.scottishmuseums.org.uk

Standing Council on Museums and Archives (Partnership: Museums Association, Society of Archivists and the Association of Independent Museums): www.hmc.gov.uk/scam

Museums and Galleries Disability Association: MAGDA.org.uk

17

Sport, physical recreation and physical activity

In this chapter

- Sport and cultural identity
- A brief recent history of sport policy in the UK
- Administration of sport in the UK
- The Sports Councils
- Major national independent organizations
- National plan for sport
- Provision and participation in sports and physical activities
- Sport, leisure and healthy lifestyles

Introduction

Leisure Managers need to have an understanding of sport, physical recreation and physical activity and their promotion and management. Sport-related activities, facilities and organizations are important when considering the number of participants, spectators, employees or volunteers, the number of facilities and amenities, or sport in the context of community, health and economic benefits.

In Chapters 2 and 3, dealing with the history of leisure and culture, it was shown that the United Kingdom has a long tradition of sporting invention, participation and achievement. In 2003, UK sportsmen and women held over 50 world titles. However, important as it is, sport is not just about winning or even about being the best. Participating at a club or recreational level and watching in person at an event or on television, are important forms of leisure activity.

The Council of Europe defines sport as: 'all forms of physical activity which, through casual or organized participation, aim at expressing or improving physical fitness and well-being, forming social relationships, or obtaining results in competition at all levels.'

The Sports Council is a major advocate:

Sport and physical recreation have a vital role to play in today's society by giving a sense of pride, by helping to alleviate the consequences of social and economic disadvantage and by having a positive effect on the mental and physical well-being of individuals and the nation. Sport also enables people to participate in activities which can bring together those of different races, gender, social class, age, ability, or religious belief.

Sports Council, 1995

Trevor Brooking, then chair of Sport England, wrote in *Best Value Through Sport*:

Sport is part of the culture of this country. It touches us all, whether we are participants, spectators or volunteers. Our quality of life is significantly enhanced by it. Sport entertains us; it gives us the opportunity for self-expression; it provides us with a sense of camaraderie and friendship; it enables us to stretch ourselves mentally and physically; it teaches us how to win and how to lose; it enables us to appreciate and value our natural environment.

However, sport needs to demonstrate tangible benefits to individuals, communities and the nation as a whole, if it is to compete with many other worthy causes for a share of limited public resources.

Brooking, undated

For those involved in sport, there is no question that sport can and does provide these benefits. However, for some politicians, researchers and scientists, there is yet insufficient evidence to prove the case categorically.

What is not disputed is the fact that sport is good for business and the British economy. It is estimated by the Department for Culture, Media and Sport (DCMS) that 400,000 jobs are related to sport, and that consumers spend over £10 billion a year on sports goods and activities. Even with the Lottery Sports Fund, sport gives back to the taxpayer nearly £5 for every £1 it receives in grant. Above all, however, it is also undisputed that sport, physical recreation and physical activity give pleasure to millions of people.

This chapter considers a number of aspects in the field of sport, physical recreation and physical activity. Data on sport and leisure provision and participation change regularly and often rapidly; indeed some aspects will have changed before publication of this book. In addition, some readers may not realize that national data and statistics often take years to produce and publish. Readers, therefore, need to be circumspect about published data and statistics. Even Internet websites can be out of date, in some cases by years.

Sport and cultural identity

Sports are part of every culture, past and present. Different cultures have their own definition of what constitutes sport. The importance of sport in the lives of people everywhere is shown in the work of sociologists, anthropologists, economists, geographers, historians, physical education teachers, political scientists, social psychologists and the medical profession. The sociology of sport examines the role and meaning of sports in the lives of individuals and in society and writings were first published in Germany back in the 1920s.

Leisure professionals today are being urged by the government to produce evidence that sport and physical activity contribute to the health of the nation. Yet Hippocrates, the Greek physician, over two thousand years ago, is believed to have said that 'sport is a preserver of health.' He said:

> All parts of the body which have a function, if used in moderation and exercised in labours in which each is accustomed, become thereby healthy, well-developed and age more slowly, but if unused and left idle they become liable to disease, defective in growth and age quickly.

The broadcaster Ron Pickering was well known for his advocacy of sport, an activity handed down over thirty centuries; he was often heard to say, 'Sport is the most precious commodity we can hand on to the next generation.' Nelson Mandela, at the Rugby Union World Cup in South Africa in 1995, announced, 'Sport has the power to change the world.' Zinedine Zidane, one of the world's finest footballers, was brought up in poverty in Marseilles. In describing the ascent for him and his family that football had given him, he said, 'We came from nothing; now we have respect.' Sport has the potential to give people an even chance: a level playing field.

The construction of a national identity is based on a range of characteristics. Sports are well placed to contribute to the formation of identity. Sometimes the nationhood of countries is viewed as indivisible from the fortunes of national teams of major spectator sports. Sports became 'patriot games' in the late nineteenth century and their significance has grown ever since, often involving governments at the highest levels, for example, governments' intervention in boycotting the Olympic Games in Moscow, and even in the 'bodyline' series of Test Matches in Australia (the English cricket team's dangerous and intimidating 'bodyline' bowling controversy in 1932–33), seventy years ago, is still brought up when England tour Australia in a Test Match series. At that time it was so serious that it brought both governments into the furore. Some commentators believe that it was one of the catalysts which moved Australia further towards a lobby for greater independence from the British Crown. And sport is also drawn into the 'theatre' of war. Following the Soviet invasion of Czechoslovakia in August 1968 in response to the 'Prague Spring', the Soviet and Czech ice hockey teams faced off in that year's Winter Olympic Games. A violent and bloody contest was won by the Czechs, providing the nation with a symbolic defeat of its subjugator.

More friendly rivalry, though of symbolic national significance, is the passionate desire of many countries, particularly Scotland, Wales, All-Ireland, and France, to beat the 'old enemy', England; and for Australia, India and Sri Lanka to take revenge on their colonizers. England's rugby team before a 'battle' against France, listened to the reciting by Sir Laurence Olivier of a passage from Shakespeare's *Henry V* before the battle at Agincourt. The epic clash between Australia and England in the Rugby World Cup Final in Sydney in 2003 was a classic reversal of fortune with England winning in the closing seconds of the match which had gone into extra time. The effect on both nations will ripple on for years to come.

Scotland's rugby team was taken to see the film *Braveheart* before one of their internationals against England.

National identity, politics and major international sport are interwoven so much so that it is perhaps naïve to say 'leave politics out of sport'. Indeed, government interest from an economic perspective is substantial; millions of pounds are needed for infrastructures to hold world events and the potential revenues or losses can be considerable. Sport today is beamed across the world engaging the interest of billions of people worldwide. The 2008 Summer Olympic Games will be in Beijing. China alone has a population of 1.3 billion. Mass media and professional sport are now inextricably merged and economically dependent. Sport, at one end of the scale, is very big business and a few powerful companies dominate the market with lucrative broadcasting rights: News Corporation Limited, Disney Corporation, AOL Times Warner for example. And only a few sports attract the 'big money': the trinity of sports in the USA, American Football, baseball and basketball; and in the UK, Association Football, rugby and cricket. A few powerful individuals and companies also have their own clubs with their own television stations such as Manchester United Football Club, one of the most famous and successful sports clubs in the world. The introduction of cable and satellite delivery systems gives 24-hour access to sports channels and pay-per-view audiences who, as it were, go through turnstiles in their own homes by paying to watch the match. Sport is undoubtedly a global phenomenon.

The development of sport as a global institution

The largest mega-sports event in recent times in the UK was the 2002 Commonwealth Games in Manchester. It had a global television audience of over 1 billion; 750,000 tickets were sold in the UK alone, and 5,900 athletes and officials took part (see Chapter 22).

The globalization of sport, in large measure, stems from modern sports and the amateur rule 'exported' from the British Isles to most other areas of the world. Many of today's major international sports were invented in Britain including association football, boxing, cricket, golf and rugby football. Even though tennis began in Renaissance France, the sport was modernized and given its rules by the British. France had a strong global influence, not only with tennis but also in cycling and the modern Olympic Games. In 1894 at the conference in Sorbonne in Paris, Pierre de Coubertin selected the first Comité International Olympique which arranged for the first Olympic Games of the modern era which was held in Athens in 1896.

With British rule in far flung areas of the world, cricket, for example, was said to follow the Union Jack, so that we find cricket the main sport in the West Indies and Sri Lanka and rugby and cricket main sports in Australia and South Africa. English contains many expressions about fairness and team spirit: 'come on, play the game', 'be a good sport' and 'that's not cricket'.

It was only in the late nineteenth century that the United States of America rivalled Britain as an industrial power and an inventor of modern sports: basketball in 1891 and volleyball in 1895 under the auspices of the YMCA. YMCA workers took with them these sports to China, Japan and the Philippines. American Gridiron football evolved from rugby, providing the modern professional sport in the USA. Association Football (soccer) is the sport played and followed most throughout the world, except where the American economic and cultural influences are strongest. Hence, baseball is strong in Cuba and Japan.

A brief recent history of sport policy in the UK

Sport, historically, was promoted by individuals, clubs and associations and the governing bodies that they founded. Today, the government plays a crucial role in terms of policy, through its sponsored agencies and its funding.

347

For leisure and recreation management, a watershed document was published 45 years ago. The Wolfenden Report of 1960, commissioned by the Central Council for Physical Recreation (CCPR), identified the need for a Sports Development Council. In order to satisfy this need, the Sports Council was eventually established in 1965. Originally, it was simply an advisory body, closely linked to the government through the civil service, with a government minister as its chairman. However, in 1972, it was granted independent status by Royal Charter, taking over both the staff and the assets of the CCPR and assuming responsibility for the Technical Unit for Sport (TUS) which prior to this had come under the auspices of the Department of Education and Science.

In addition to the Sports Council, there were three national councils. The Scottish Sports Council and the Sports Council for Wales were set up as independent executive organizations by Royal Charter in 1972. They received annual grant-in-aid direct from central government and performed similar general functions to those of the Sports Council. The Sports Council for Northern Ireland was established by statute in 1974 to advise government on capital expenditure and financially to assist voluntary sports organizations.

In parallel with the setting up of the Sports Council, the second report from the Select Committee of the House of Lords on Sport and Leisure (House of Lords, 1973) called for action to remedy deficiencies in sport provision. It was a turning point in sport and leisure policy:

> The state should not opt out of caring for people's leisure when it accepts the responsibility of caring for most of their other needs. The provision of opportunities for the enjoyment of leisure is part of the general fabric of the social services.

Central government was also of the belief that the provision of sports and leisure opportunities could help to alleviate anti-social behaviour and many ills of the world. This belief was stressed later in *Policy for the Inner Cities* (DoE, 1977) and the report of the Scarman Inquiry (Scarman, 1981). In 1974 the government produced a White Paper on sport and recreation, which proposed substantial changes (DoE, 1975).

In 1976, regional sports councils took on extended remits. These councils supplied a forum for consultation among local authorities, local sports councils, various regional bodies of sport and recreation and other interested parties. They were concerned with the planning of facilities and the promotion of opportunities for participation in organized sport and recreation, as well as with informal countryside recreation and the conservation problems inherent in its development. They were independent, autonomous bodies with representatives from organizations which had a major role to play in the development of sport and recreation. Following the DoE Circular 73/77, *Guidelines for Regional Recreational Strategies July 1977*, the regional councils were also responsible for the production of strategy plans for the development of recreation within their regions. The direct link between the GB Sports Council and the Regional Councils for Sport and Recreation came to an end on 1 January, 1996.

In July 1994, the then Minister for Sport announced a major reorganization of the Sports Council. The Great Britain Sports Council's Royal Charter was revised by the Secretary of State to bring about the separate United Kingdom and English Sports

Councils. The government's responsibility for sport since then has been based upon five autonomous councils: the United Kingdom Sports Council, the English Sports Council, the Sports Council for Wales, the Scottish Sports Council and the Northern Ireland Sports Council.

Then in November 1994 came the launch of the National Lottery, one of the most influential decisions ever made for the sustained development of sport and physical recreation in the United Kingdom. In England, over £1 billion of Lottery funds had been invested in over 3,300 community facilities. In Scotland over 6,000 awards totalling more than £200 million had been made to July 2003 and the Sports Council for Northern Ireland had made 1,000 awards worth over £50 million. Facilities funded by the National Lottery must be available for use by the whole community.

> Between the start of the Lottery and June 2003, the Sports Councils awarded 23,175 grants worth around £1.9 billion.

The Department of National Heritage published a sports policy document, *Sport: Raising the Game*, in July 1995 (DNH,1995). Sports participation in schools had declined and *Raising the Game* aimed at reversing the trend, promoting closer links between schools and sports clubs and establishing a new British Academy of Sport that would serve as a pinnacle of a national network of centres of excellence. During 1997, the Academy was redefined, following consultation with athletes and sports organizations. Redesigned as the United Kingdom Sports Institute (UKSI), it provides support services throughout the country through a network of national, regional and sport specific facilities.

Association Football is the UK's premier sport in terms of numbers of spectators; the sport brings much pleasure to millions of players and supporters, but also brings problems of administration, crowd safety and hooliganism. The Football Task Force was launched in July 1997, to consider and advise ministers on issues facing football. A funding package of £55 million for the Football Trust was announced by the Minister for Sport in June 1997 to help League clubs complete the safety work required by the government in response to the Taylor Report into the Hillsborough disaster. Funding was provided by the Lottery, the Football Association and the FA Premier League.

The administration of sport in the UK

The structures for administering and delivering sport in the United Kingdom are complex and interrelated at four levels:

1 national (government)
2 national (non-government)
3 regional
4 local

National (government)

In government, a 'Sports Cabinet' consisting of the Secretary of State for Culture, Media and Sport (DCMS) and the four home country ministers (England, Scotland, Wales, Northern Ireland) with responsibility for sport, determines strategic priorities for sport in the United Kingdom.

A number of other government departments are also involved in sport: Office of the Deputy Prime Minister (ODPM), Home Office, Department of Trade and Industry

(DTI), Department of Health (DoH), Department for Education and Skills (DfES), HM Treasury and others concerned with transport and the environment.

National (non-government)

- UK and home country Sports Councils in England, Scotland, Wales and Northern Ireland
- UK Sports Institute
- Home Country Sports Institutes in England, Scotland, Wales and Northern Ireland
- National Governing Bodies of Sport (NGBs)
- National Sports Organizations (NSO), e.g.
  British Olympic Association (BOA)
  British Paralympic Association (BPA)
  Central Council of Physical Recreation (CCPR)
  Youth Sports Trust
  SportscoachUK
  Women's Sports Foundation
  National Association for Sports Development (NASD).

Regional organizations include:

- Government offices
- Sport England Regional Offices
- Regional Cultural Consortia
- Regional Sports Boards
- Regional Federations
- County Partnerships
- NGBs at regional and county levels.

Local organizations include:

- Local authorities
- Schools
- Further and Higher Education institutions
- Local trusts and not-for-profit organizations
- Private sector owners and operators, e.g. health and fitness clubs
- Local Sports Councils, sports clubs and associations.

Funding for sport

Funding for sports comes from a variety of sources, including:

- central government
- local government
- National Lottery
- Sponsorship
- SportsAid (formerly Sports Aid Foundation)
- Foundation for Sport and the Arts
- Private sector companies
- Voluntary sector, benefactors, donors and the public.

The ODPM funds sport through allocations to local governments; the DfES funds physical education, school sports, joint-provision and dual use of schools. The Home Office funds joint initiatives, for example, the role of sport in crime prevention and community leadership.

In addition to central government, there are several main sources of funding for sport. Local government is by far the major funder, providing thousands of facilities, employing thousands of people in sport and sports-related activities, awarding grants to sports clubs and organizations and assisting in kind.

Governing bodies that receive funding from the Sports Councils are required to produce development plans from grass-roots to international levels. In order to have access to funds from the National Lottery for their top athletes, they need to prepare World Class Performance Plans.

Most sports benefit from sponsorship, which is encouraged by a number of bodies including the Institute of Sports Sponsorship which includes around 100 UK companies. Sponsors in the United Kingdom invest more than £1 billion annually in sport according to the *Official Yearbook of the United Kingdom 2004*. SportsAid raises funds and supports talented young people usually aged between 12 and 18 and disabled people of any age. The Scottish Sports Aid Foundation, SportsAid Cymru and the Ulster Sports and Recreation Trust play similar roles to SportsAid.

> Since 1975 SportsAid has distributed over £20 million in grants.

The Foundation for Sports and the Arts, set up by the football pools promoters in 1991, has made awards of £330 million to over 100 sports for sports projects on a relatively small scale compared to some of the large Lottery projects.

Sports public bodies

The main sports public bodies

United Kingdom Sports Council, operating as UK Sport
English Sports Council, operating as Sport England
Scottish Sports Council, operating as sportscotland
Sports Council for Wales
Sports Council for Northern Ireland
(see Useful websites)

The Sports Councils in the UK form a link between the government and sports organizations. They also distribute National Lottery grants (see The National Lottery, p.159, Chapter 9). As non-departmental public bodies (NDPBs), they operate at arm's length from government but are accountable to Parliament. This means that they carry out their day-to-day functions independently of ministers, but for which ministers are ultimately accountable. Politics cannot, therefore, be left out of sport.

In England there are nine Regional Sports Boards (RSBs), grant aided by Sport England. They work in partnership with Regional Development Agencies and Regional Assemblies. The establishment of County Partnerships (45 in England), overseen by

RSBs, deliver Sport England programmes in partnership with local authorities, county level NGBs and others.

There are other public bodies funded by the government. The Football Licensing Authority is funded by the DCMS. The FLA is an independent public body set up under the Football Spectators Act, 1989. Its main functions are to license league and international football grounds in England and Wales and to oversee the control of safety at these grounds by local authorities. Its objectives are to ensure the reasonable safety and management of spectators through, for example, all-seated Premiership and First Division grounds.

Individual sports are run by independent governing bodies, the majority of which are 'recognized' National Governing Bodies (NGBs). Some have a UK structure, some a GB structure and most are constituted on a home country basis. In Northern Ireland, around half of the sports are part of an all-Ireland structure.

National Sports Organizations are independent of government. They are not-for-profit organizations, most are charitable and rely on funding from the Sports Councils. Each sport has at least one NGB and, according to the Central Council of Physical Recreation (CCPR), there are around 265 NGBs for just over 100 sports recognized in the UK. The same sport can, therefore, have different NGBs competing for funds.

The Sports Councils

The Sports Councils are independent of the government but responsible to it, and work to its policies and strategies. Each of the Sports Councils has its own autonomy and remit. However, each is generally responsible for three functions:

- encouraging people to take part in sport and physical activity
- the achievement of excellence and
- the provision of sports facilities.

Other priorities concern encouraging sport in deprived areas; enabling more ethnic minorities to be involved, and enabling people with disabilities and more women to participate. One initiative aimed at meeting these objectives is Sport England's Sport Action Zones.

The United Kingdom Sports Council – UK Sport – was established on 1 January, 1997 and receives annual grant-in-aid from the DCMS. UK Sport operates under a Royal Charter. It is an independent body with the objects of fostering, supporting and encouraging the development of sport and the achievement of excellence in the United Kingdom. Its functions are:

- the co-ordination of support to sports in which the UK competes internationally (as distinct from the four home countries competing as England, Wales, Scotland and Northern Ireland)
- tackling drug misuse in sport
- co-ordinating policy for bringing international sports events to the UK and
- representing UK sporting interests overseas at international level.

UK Sport's overriding aim is 'for the UK to be in the top five sporting nations by 2012, measured by athletic performance at World Championships, Olympic and Paralympic Games'. UK Sport is also a Lottery Sports Fund distributor through its World Class Performance and World Class Events programmes.

Initially, an anomaly existed concerning the distribution of Lottery funding. The four home country sports councils were distributors of the Lottery Sports Fund, while UK Sport was not. In the summer of 1998, with the transfer of the chairman of Sport England to the chairmanship of UK Sport, the change was accompanied by additional resources, including making UK Sport a Lottery distributor.

The English Sports Council – Sport England – was established in January 1997 as an independent body which fosters, supports and encourages the development of sport and physical recreation and achievement of excellence in England. Sport England operates under a Royal Charter. It is the government funded agency responsible for providing the strategic lead for sport in England. It receives annual grant-in-aid from the DCMS for core expenditure and specific programmes. The aim is 'to see more people involved in sport, more places to play sport and higher standards of performance in sport'. Sport England is undergoing a radical modernization programme and has adopted a new vision, mission, role and business objectives. Its vision is 'to make England an active and successful sporting nation' and its business objectives are:

- to increase participation in sport to improve the health of the nation, with a focus on priority groups
- retain people in sport and active recreation through an effective network of clubs, sports facilities, coaches, volunteers and competitive opportunities and
- promoting sporting success at the highest level.

The Sports Councils for Wales, Scotland and Northern Ireland have the same general priorities as those in Sport England and they undertake similar functions, but have their own specific objectives.

The Sports Council for Wales' local development work is focused on creating opportunities for school-age children to take part in sport, while nationally concentrating on raising standards of performance and excellence.

SPORTLOT, the Lottery Sports Fund for Wales, manages the money coming in from the National Lottery. A major difference in Wales is the reorganization of local government which resulted in 22 unitary authorities replacing entirely the two-tier government system and establishing the Welsh Assembly. These changes affect the way public money is prioritized and spent. The current strategy for sport in Wales is addressed in *Sport and Active Recreation in Wales: Climbing Higher, Dringo'n Uwch: Strategy for Consultation*. One of the priorities of Dragon Sport aims at increasing extra-curricular and sports club membership among 7 to 11 year-olds. Since the scheme started, over 400 schools have joined the programme and over 100 after-school clubs have been established.

Likewise in Scotland and Northern Ireland, more rapid progress towards meeting objectives is made possible through their role as distributors of National Lottery funds. The Scottish Sports Council Lottery Sports Fund has made a substantial improvement in the country's facility infrastructure. More than £250 million is invested each year by Scotland's local authorities. The current strategy for sport in Scotland is in *Sport 21*

2003–2007 Shaping Scotland's Future, the updated National Strategy for Sport. One key target is that Scotland should have 150,000 volunteers contributing to the development and delivery of Scottish sport.

A problem faced by Sport England, sportscotland, the Sports Council for Wales and the Sports Council for Northern Ireland relates to their role in international sport. UK Sport has an overall United Kingdom remit to bring together the many elements and national 'preserves' for the future benefit of British sport. The effective relationships between UK Sport and the home country Sports Councils and between the UK Sports Institute and the Sports Institutes in the home countries are crucial. Devolved governments such as the Scottish Parliament add to the complexity *vis-à-vis* Scottish sport.

The United Kingdom Sports Institute (UKSI) helps the country's top sportsmen and women to win medals in major tournaments such as the Olympics and the World Athletics Championships. It provides world class facilities and a higher standard of co-ordinated support services than the UK has ever had before.

The Institute is made up of four Home Country Sports Institutes: English Institute of Sport, Scottish Institute of Sport, Sports Institute Northern Ireland and UKSI CYMRU. These are supported by the Performance Directorate of UK Sport on areas such as coaching, sports science, technology and innovation.

The English Institute of Sport (EIS) is a network of world class training facilities and support services. It features nine regional multi-sport hub sites, supported by 35 satellite centres: an investment of more than £120 million of Lottery money in high performance training venues plus the facilities of Manchester's Commonwealth Games facilities, an investment of £135 million.

In addition to funding and facilities at national and local levels, the Sports Councils need support services to achieve their objectives, especially excellent coaching, sports medicine and sports science. The National Sports Medicine Institute of the United Kingdom serves as the national focus which is funded through contracts with the Sports Councils and others. Sports science support – biomechanical (human movement), physiological and psychological – is being promoted by the Sports Councils in collaboration with the British Olympic Association (BOA) and Sports Coach UK with a view to raising standards of the performance of national squads. Sports Coach UK (formerly the National Coaching Foundation), supported by the Sports Council, works closely with sports governing bodies, local authorities and higher and further education.

Drug misuse is an area of worldwide concern and UK Sport has the responsibility of tackling the problem in the United Kingdom. UK Sport's Anti-Doping Directorate co-ordinates an independent drugs-testing programme. Such is the complexity of the problem that in January 2002, UK Sport launched an on-line database of information from 102 sports, listing 3,000 substances and 5,200 products.

To promote excellence in sport, the national Sports Councils undertake a range of functions, including running National Centres of Excellence in their own countries, with the primary objective of meeting the top-level requirements of select sports. The centres are:

- Crystal Palace (athletics, swimming and other major sports)
- Holme Pierrepont, the National Water Sports Centre
- Lilleshall (soccer, gymnastics, cricket, etc.)

- Bisham Abbey (tennis, hockey, rugby, etc.) and
- Plas y Brenin, the National Centre for Mountain Activities.

Sport England has also grant-aided the development of national facilities including the National Indoor Arena, Birmingham, the National Cycling Centre, Manchester and the National Hockey Stadium, Milton Keynes.

Major national independent organizations

Two major organizations are the Central Council of Physical Recreation (CCPR) and British Olympic Association (BOA).

The CCPR was formed in 1935. After the transference of the CCPR's staff and property assets to the Sports Council in 1972, the member bodies of the CCPR voted to retain the CCPR's independence as a forum for the national and governing bodies of sport and recreation. In addition, the Royal Charter setting up the Sports Council specified the need for a 'consultative body' to the Council, and the CCPR has been accorded this role.

The CCPR (see Useful websites) is reputed to be the largest sport and recreation federation in the world and represents 265 national governing and representative bodies (NGBs) and an estimated 110,000 voluntary sports clubs, many of which are affiliated to NGBs. They are mostly run by volunteers, numbered around 1.5 million, but the CCPR estimates that the number of sports clubs has declined by 40,000 since 1996. The British Sports Trust was established by the CCPR as a charitable trust with the primary function of administering the volunteer Community Sports Leaders Award Scheme. The Scottish Sports Association and the Welsh Sports Association and the Northern Ireland Sports Forum are the home country equivalent organizations.

To fulfil its role of representing the interest of sports governing bodies and clubs, the CCPR has a wide network of key contacts. In Europe, the CCPR has links with the European Parliament Sports Intergroup and the European Non-Governmental Sports Organization. The Institute of Sports Sponsorship (ISS) (set up in 1985 following the Howell Report), in conjunction with the CCPR, drafted a model sponsorship agreement, A Model Contract, to the benefit of all parties. The Institute of Professional Sport (IPS) was launched in 1992 demonstrating the influence professional sports players have on the public at large and the need to enhance the reputation of the players and the sport.

The CCPR's directional and policy formulation is achieved through a framework of six divisions:

- major spectator sports
- games and sports
- movement and dance
- outdoor pursuits
- water recreation and
- interested organizations.

The British Olympic Association (BOA) (see Useful websites) comprises representatives of the 35 national governing bodies of Olympic sports and organizes the participation of British teams in the Olympic Games. The BOA is supported by sponsorship, by donations from the private sector and the general public and works closely with UK Sport. It arranges training camps and has programmes to support national governing bodies and their athletes. The BOA's Olympic Medical Institute for example provides services for competitors before and during the Olympics. This institute is distinct from the National Sports Medicine Institute of the UK (NSMI) which serves as the national focus for those concerned with sport and exercise medicine. The NSMI is funded through contracts with the Sports Councils and also generates income from its services.

In addition to the national structures for sport in the United Kingdom, a number of international federations have their headquarters in the UK, including the Commonwealth Games Federation which has close ties to the BOA, UK Sport and the CCPR.

National plan for sport

The government's Plan for Sport is *A Sporting Future for All* (DCMS, 2001). In September, 2002, the Strategy Unit published *Game Plan: a Strategy for Delivering Government's Sport and Physical Activity Objectives* (DCMS, 2002).

The DCMS aim is: 'to improve the quality of life for all through cultural and sporting activities, support the pursuit of excellence, and champion the tourism, creative and leisure industries.'

Within the DCMS's aim, there are four priorities linked to four Public Sector Agreement (PSA) targets. Priorities 1 and 2 relate to sport:

- to enhance access to a fuller cultural and sporting life for children and young people, providing opportunity to develop talents and
- to open up institutions to the wider community to promote lifelong learning and social cohesion, particularly through coach development officers and community sports coaches.

Total government and lottery expenditure on sport and physical activity in England alone is estimated to be roughly £2.2 billion a year, a significant proportion distributed by local authorities. However, money from the National Lottery and television rights income is decreasing and local government leisure budgets are tightly controlled. The major exception is the amount of public investment into school sports facilities.

Since coming into power in 1997, the government has introduced the £60 million Capital Modernization Fund for Sport; invested £130 million in Space for Sport and the Arts; with the DfES invested £450 million into physical education and sport in schools; and injected £750 million into school and community sports facilities. Millions of pounds will also go into the UK's bid to host the Olympic Games in 2012.

However, in national sports administration over only a few years, there have been reorganization and different plans and strategies, so much so that one can be forgiven for not knowing which plan or strategy we are in at any one time. Even the DCMS admits that, 'currently, multiple statements of strategy lead to confusion and complex structures lead to inefficiency'. *Game Plan* is the long-term view: the 20-year plan. In *Game Plan*, the Strategy Unit concluded that government should set itself two over-arching objectives:

- a major increase in participation in sport and physical activity, primarily because of the significant health benefits and to reduce the growing cost of inactivity
- a sustainable improvement in success in international competition, particularly in the sports which matter most to the public, primarily because of the 'feel-good factor' associated with winning.

In order to achieve this, recommendations were made in four areas:

1 grass-roots participation: focusing on economically disadvantaged groups, in particularly young people, women and older people
2 high performance sport: better prioritization of which sports are funded at the highest level; better development of talented sportsmen and women; and service delivery more focused on customer needs
3 sporting mega-events: there should be a more cautious approach to hosting these events, including a clear assessment of the benefits
4 delivery: organizational reform before further increases to its investment in sport, with less money going to bureaucracy and more to the end user.

The government invests in sport for four main reasons, set out in the Executive Summary of *Game Plan*:

1 for health benefits
2 for educational benefits
3 to generate the feel-good factor
4 for economic and regeneration benefits.

Given this justification the government's long term vision for sport and physical activity by 2020 is:

to increase significantly levels of sport and physical activity, particularly among disadvantaged groups; and to achieve sustained levels of success in international competition. The message is simple: get more people doing more and increase our success rate in top level competition.

The Plan for Sport Second Annual Report, published in April 2003, includes objectives for education, sport in the community and the National Governing Body and World Class Programmes.

By 2005, 400 specialist sports villages and academies will be created. Community sports clubs can now apply for the financial benefits of charitable status. Funding for community club development and implementation of recommendations from the Coaching Task Force will be put in place. National governing bodies will be funded for Elite Sports and the World Class Performance Programme and World Class Events Programmes.

In 2003, the government implemented one of the key *Game Plan* recommendations. The Activity Co-ordination Team (ACT) has brought together eight government departments to co-ordinate the delivery of aims in health, education and community cohesion through sport. The DCMS and DoH are jointly leading a cross-government team to develop a national delivery plan to meet *Game Plan* targets to increase participation in sport and physical activity to 70 per cent of the population by 2020, particularly among economically disadvantaged groups, school-leavers, women and older people. ACT will involve the public, private and voluntary sectors to determine how community sport and recreation, education, workplace, travel, environment and healthcare might contribute to the 70 per cent target.

Sport 21 2003–2007 Shaping Scotland's Future is the updated strategy for sport in Scotland published in 2003. The Welsh Assembly consultation strategy was launched in July 2003, entitled *Sport and Active Recreation in Wales: Climbing Higher, Dringo'n Uwch*, covering the period to 2023.

Coaching at all levels

Coaching is central to the development of sport at every level, from beginner to élite athlete. Following the government's *Plan for Sport*, a Coaching Task Force was established to review the role of coaching. The Task Force report was published in July 2002 and the government has committed £28 million over three years to implement its key recommendations, with a Coaching Project Board to oversee the process. The objective is to tackle the shortage of coaches, professional and voluntary, and recognize coaching as a profession, with accredited qualifications and a real career-development structure.

In 2001/2, nearly 60,000 students enrolled in a British Sports Trust (BST) Sports Leader Award.

It is essential also to encourage voluntary leaders, young and old. The CCPR and British Sports Trust (BST) have for many years run the successful Sports Leader Award.

A new government-sponsored project, Leadership and Volunteering in School and Community Sports Programme – Step into Sport – will add to this success. It is a leadership and volunteering project for young people aged 14 to 25 and older volunteers. The project aims to raise the profile of volunteering in sport, and provide support and training to organizations that rely on volunteers.

The project is a DCMS/Home Office (HO) Active Communities Unit initiative; it is being managed by a consortium of the Youth Sport Trust, the British Sports Trust and Sport England. The consortium is working with local partnerships of schools in 150 education authority areas. It is also working closely with the local education authorities themselves, 45 County Sports Partnerships and 16 National Governing Bodies.

The objectives of the first stage of the project are:

- to train and support 60,000 young people to develop leadership skills and to volunteer
- to train 8,000 adult volunteers to mentor, lead, officiate and coach sport locally
- to assist NGOs to produce strategies and provide support for clubs to receive leaders.

Sports development

At the time or writing, sports development was under scrutiny by agencies and organizations involved in sports development, including the Sports Councils, SportsCoach UK (the former National Coaching Foundation), the Youth Sports Trust (YST), the Central Council of Physical Recreation (CCPR), SportsActive (the national training body), the National Association for Sports Development (NASD), the Institute of Sport and Recreation Management (ISRM), the Institute of Leisure and Amenities Management (ILAM), and local authorities, colleges and universities such as the University of Loughborough. Discussions in early 2004 on an amalgamation between the ISRM and NASD and the potential merging of ISRM and ILAM had foundered.

There are different definitions and models of what constitutes sports development. In previous years, sports development was being driven by the Sports Council's Sports Development Continuum. This identifies four levels of involvement in sport with an emphasis on pathways of progression from one area to the next: Foundation; Participation; Performance; Excellence. The National Junior Sports Programme included TOP Play (4–9 year-olds), Champion Coaching (11–14 year-olds), TOP Club (developed by the English Sports Council and the YST), and Sports Fair directed at youth groups, incorporating Sports Train for training of youth workers. Today the Active Sports Model appears to be favoured.

Bev Smith, adding to the debate, feels that there is a misconception by some in the field:

> People believe that sports development is what local authority sports development officers (SDOs) do. I subscribe to the view that sports development is about systems and structures that enable people to progress through sport and therefore, by inference, I believe that sports development officers are enablers, not deliverers.
>
> Smith, 2003

This viewpoint suggests that SDOs are not enabling sport, rather delivering; delivering – the coaching – should be left to coaches.

There are potential tensions between all the people involved: PE teachers running after-school activities, school-sport co-ordinators making links with the community, SDOs employed by the district council running separate programmes and governing body sports coaches, often highly trained and passionately focused on their sport, able to attract and inspire young people, yet focused to the exclusion of all else. Young people can be pulled in different directions and become confused. Policies, objectives and strategies to meet their needs should be the guiding principle.

Sports development should also be about sports equity, that is, fairness in sport, equality of access, recognizing inequalities and taking steps to redress them. It is about changing the culture and structure of sport to ensure that it becomes equally accessible to everyone in society, whatever their age, race, gender, disability or level of ability.

There is not yet equality of opportunity in sport. One example is a gender imbalance. Modern sport was invented by and for men. Although today there have been strong moves to even up opportunities between men and women, there is some way to go. At the Olympic Games in Sydney in 2000, men participated in 48 more events than women and it was rare to find countries from around the world with an equal number of men and women in their national teams. UK Sport organizes a UK Co-ordinating Group on Women in Sport to raise participation by women and girls at all levels of sport and increase numbers involved in coaching and managing sport. The Women's Sports Foundation promotes opportunities for women and girls in sport.

Provision and participation in sports and physical activities

Participation depends to a large extent on facilities, opportunities and accessibility – physical, financial and social – and the schools, clubs and organizations. The former athletics national coach, Geoff Dyson, is remembered for his saying, 'where there are no polevault pits, there will be no polevaulters'.

The United Kingdom now has a range of world class sporting facilities including 13 National Sports Centres, including venues for the National Institutes for Sport. Many national facilities have been improved, including the Millennium Stadium in Cardiff, the Wimbledon tennis complex and several football stadia. New facilities were built and used for the Commonwealth Games in Manchester, including the stadium (now the home of Manchester City FC), and the national indoor cycle velodrome. The Wembley Stadium in London is being rebuilt to seat 90,000 and is due to open in 2006.

Estimates vary and statistical data change month by month. However, across most of the regions in the UK, facilities for sport have increased substantially over recent times.

Sports facilities in England

1,300 public pools (excluding school pools)	1,270 eighteen-hole (or equivalent) golf courses
1,500 indoor sports halls	282 artificial turf pitches.
500 indoor tennis courts	3,000 sport and leisure centres
300 indoor bowls clubs	2,500 of these have health and fitness centres,
40 ice rinks	gyms or fitness rooms.
100 dry ski slopes	3,000 private health clubs
410 athletic tracks (around half synthetic)	

Besides the professional sports clubs, as mentioned earlier, there are in excess of 100,000 voluntary sports clubs affiliated to the national governing bodies of sport in the United Kingdom. The clubs are predominantly run by leaders and coaches who give freely of their time. It is estimated by the Central Council for Physical Recreation that 6.5 million people play sport in such clubs, many run by professional staff funded by the club members.

An estimated 1.5 billion visits are made to public parks each year and 7.5 million adults and 2.1 million children are said to use parks for formal or informal sport. An estimated 80 million visits are made to local authority swimming pools and sports halls each year. Football is the UK's main sport when spectator figures are added to those who play the game. There are around 42,000 football clubs; and England's Premier League is said to be the finest or one of the finest in the world.

Estimates vary depending on definitions and systems of measurement, but around half the adult UK population say they take part in sport or physical activity. Compared to some countries, participation at around 46 per cent (participation in sport or physical activity more than 12 times a year) is relatively high, but nowhere near as high as in Scandinavia (70 per cent in Sweden and nearly 80 per cent in Finland) (DCMS, 2002).

Analysis of participation in sport and physical activity shows some clear patterns of behaviour.

- Participation in the UK has been relatively stable over the past decade as shown in successive General Household Surveys.
- Participation is closely correlated with age with participation levels dropping as individuals age. *Game Plan* suggests that this need not be the case, again comparing the UK with Sweden and Finland.
- There is a substantial drop in participation of young people on leaving school and this appears always to have been the case.
- Participation amongst women is low. The gap between males and females is greater than in other countries apart from Scandinavia where the gap is in the other direction, with more women participating.
- Participation varies with socio-economic group. Participation generally decreases down the socio-economic line from professionals to unskilled workers and this is more defined in women. For men, the 'intermediate/junior non-manual' workers participate at the same levels as the professional groups.
- The lowest participation rates recorded in General Household Surveys were for men and women who were economically inactive.
- Ethnicity and disability affect levels of participation. Women are affected to a greater extent than men.

Table 17.1 Participation in sport and physical activity

	% AGED 16 AND OVER	
	MEN	WOMEN
Walking/hiking	22	24
Snooker	17	4
Swimming	15	18
Cycling	14	7
Football	12	1
Golf	10	1
Weights/fitness	10	4
Keep fit	9	19
Running/athletics	7	3
Racket sports	7	4
Darts	5	2
Bowls	3	2

Percentage of people reporting participation in the four weeks before the survey
Source: UK 2000/2001 Time Use Survey, Office for National Statistics.

The General Household Survey (GHS) is an important national source of data on participation in sport and leisure activities (see Chapter 13).

Sports participation in the United Kingdom, according to recent General Household Surveys, is dominated by walking: 45 per cent of adults said they had been for a walk of two or more miles in the previous four weeks (as shown in Table 17.1). If walking is excluded, the proportion of adults who took part in at least one sport in the four week reference period was 47 per cent. After walking, swimming was the most frequently mentioned activity: 15 per cent of adults said they had been swimming in the four weeks before interview. Only three other activities attracted more than 10 per cent of adults in a four week period on average through the year; these were cue sports (snooker/pool/billiards), keep fit/yoga and cycling. However, the statistics reveal a decline in the more traditional pub-based recreations of darts, snooker, pool, and in the traditional sports-centre sports, such as badminton, squash and table tennis. Following a significant increase between 1987 and 1990, overall rates of participation in sport have stabilized.

Swimming has remained the most popular sport. Factors that contribute to this include the very strong attraction of water, its mass participation appeal, individual or family orientation; it is inexpensive, no equipment is required and it is easily available to the majority of the population. The traditional swimming market has, however, been segmented into those that wish to swim, dive, splash and have fun; and those who want to improve health and fitness. The design of a proportion of swimming pools has, therefore, changed considerably in recent years from the standard rectangular shape to the modern free form with the addition of flumes, slides, islands and spas. However, the demand for conventional swimming pools is strong with 'lane swimming' on the increase.

Sport, leisure and healthy lifestyles

Successive governments have been warning of the dangers to health brought about by lack of physical activity. Back in 1992, the Sports Council and Health Education Authority published *The Allied Dunbar National Fitness Survey* (Sports Council/HEA, 1992) which found that in terms of physical activity, seven out of ten men and eight out of ten women fell below their age-appropriate activity level necessary to achieve a health benefit; even among 16–24 year-olds, 70 per cent of men and 91 per cent of women were below target. A growing number of the population were overweight. In July 1992, the White Paper, *The Health of the Nation* (DoH, 1992), provided a strategic approach to focus on health as much as health care, with the aims of 'adding years to life' and 'adding life to years'. The concepts are integral to the aims of the World Health Organisation.

Health services are only one part of the strategy. Of importance are public policies (considering the health dimension in a number of public services), healthy surroundings, including physical environments and leisure, and healthy lifestyles through increasing knowledge, understanding and opportunity. Physical activity is a factor which may reduce early mortality and ill-health and contribute to healthy living. A lack of physical activity is accepted as a main risk factor for heart disease and stroke. With the decline in physical activity in everyday life and work, sport and physical recreation now account for most vigorous activity that a person engages in and they are central to the future health of the nation, as well as providing pleasure to millions of people of all ages and abilities.

DoH, 1992

Almost three-fifths of men and just under a half of women aged 16 and over in England were classed as overweight or obese in 1994. Alcohol consumption above 'sensible' levels and smoking were also a recognized health risk. Alcohol abuse and smoking among young people were of particular concern. Inactive children are likely to become inactive adults, increasing the risks of obesity and heart disease. The report, *Sport: Raising the Game* (DNH, 1995) also focused on the decline in interest by the young in traditional team sports. In 1998, the government published the White Paper, *Our Healthier Nation – A Contract for Health* (DoH, 1998):

Good health is treasured. It is the foundation of a good life. Better health for the nation is central to making a better country. We have major opportunities to improve people's health. Almost 90,000 people die every year before they reach their 65th birthday. Of these, nearly 32,000 die of cancer, and 25,000 die of heart disease, stroke and related illnesses. Many of these deaths could be prevented. Health inequalities are widening. The poorest in our society are hit harder than the well off by most of the major causes of death. In improving the health of the whole nation, a key priority will be better health for those who are worst off. There are sound economic reasons for improving our health. 187 million working days are estimated by industry to be lost every year because of sickness – a £12 billion tax on business.

One of the latest specific pronouncements from the government is in *Game Plan*:

The benefits of physical activity on health are clear, well evidenced and widely accepted. 30 minutes of moderate activity five times a week can help to reduce the risk of cardiovascular diseases, some cancers, strokes and obesity. Estimates put the total cost to England of physical inactivity in the order of at least £2bn a year. Conservatively, this represents about 54,000 lives lost prematurely. A 10 per cent increase in adult activity would benefit England by at least £500m a year (saving about 6,000 lives). These estimates exclude the costs of injuries. The burden of physical inactivity is an increasing problem, as the continuing rise in obesity and other inactivity-related health challenges demonstrates. As these escalate, so will the costs of physical inactivity.

Health and fitness centres

Health and fitness centres have been covered in part in Chapter 11 on Commercial leisure. Here, we focus on public-related facilities and participation.

The increase in positive awareness of health and fitness has meant a boom in the market and considerable interest from all sectors: public, voluntary, institutional and commercial. In the public sector, nearly all large leisure centres now provide fitness centres, aerobics studios and health suites; to provide more space, some squash courts all over the United Kingdom have been converted into fitness facilities. In the voluntary sector, sports clubs have installed fitness machines and new tennis facilities rely on the fitness centres to help ensure their financial stability. At not-for-profit leisure centres where limited subsidy is provided by the local authority, health and fitness centres have become essential in reaching financial break-even targets, often achieving three-quarters of a centre's income. For example, the first community multi-sport centre, Harlow Sportcentre, owned by a charity, is an example of how an ageing centre (where all local authority financial support has been withdrawn) can cover the operational costs from its health and fitness programme, bringing in around the £750,000 needed to break even. It also delivers one of the most successful GP referral schemes in the country.

What has brought about this level of interest? Vanity and health are prime reasons for individuals; money-making is the major business driving force. People want to look good and feel good. The drive for fitness, however, has not been based in sport but in health and lifestyle. In the commercial sector, the Fitness Industry Association (FIA) has been active in spreading the 'gospel of fitness for life'. BUPA has joined forces with the FIA to form the BUPA-approved Health and Fitness Club Network. Successful GP referral schemes, pioneered at leisure centres, illustrate that when the doctor tells you to exercise, you are far more likely to do so, than when exactly the same message comes from elsewhere.

So explosive has been the fitness centre market that it is difficult to be precise as to the extent of the industry. The overall market is dispersed and mainly in the hands of relatively small operators. Part of the difficulty in measurement is the fragmented nature of the market, its expansion and its volatility, with acquisitions at the top end of the market. In addition, some commercial operators work in the public, voluntary and private sectors.

Despite a developing and changing market, in terms of design, there are discernible 'bankers' in a successful fitness business.

- A fitness gym with cardio-vascular and resistance machines. The size of the gym has a direct bearing on the number of members that a club can accommodate. Provision of 'women only' gyms is also increasing as part of a mixed club, particularly for those new members who are self-conscious about their shape and who may be 'working out' for the first time.
- Dance/aerobics studios. Most clubs have at least one or two studios for aerobics, step classes, yoga, etc. These activities are an important element in attracting female members.
- A swimming pool providing an ambience of quality is the single most attractive facility a health and fitness club can offer. Few major commercial new developments being built are without a pool of some size.
- A health spa with steam, sauna, water therapy pool, are adjuncts to clubs with a holistic approach to health. Areas for treatments and essential relaxation add to overall experience (see Health and fitness centres, p. 216, Chapter 11).
- Health and beauty salon. Areas for health and beauty treatments: facials, massage, aromatherapy, hairdressing, etc.
- Support facilities such as catering, bar, health drinks and food, and a crèche to attract the daytime family market.

Healthy Living Centres

The government Green Paper, *Our Healthier Nation*, outlined initiatives and targets for improving the health of the nation by 2010. One of the main thrusts was for the establishment of Healthy Living Centres. The proposed network of Healthy Living Centres was one of the first initiatives to be funded by the government and an estimated £300m was allocated from the New Opportunities Fund (NOF). Lottery cash was targeted to areas of urban deprivation and social exclusion. This initiative contrasted to the traditional selection criteria for the siting of a private health club, where investors look for ready access to a large population of relatively well-educated and better-off individuals who respond more readily to health promotion messages.

Hence, the Healthy Living Centres initiative was aimed at helping to reduce the variations in health that arise as a result of differences in people's income, housing, education, employment, age and ethnic background.

Examples developed with Lottery funding include Peckham Pulse in London and the LIFE project on the Wirral. Activity for Life at Harlow Sportcentre was developed without external funding. Peckham Pulse Healthy Living Centre comprises a main swimming pool, hydrotherapy pool with adjustable floor, gym, spa, crèche and a health suite with a National Health Service clinic. The Wirral national award winning LIFE project was a collaborative scheme aimed at reducing coronary heart disease. Following its success, the Council and Health Authority provided joint funding to Wirral's Health Links programme: the Health Promotion School Scheme, Health Promotion Training Programme, Healthy Living Courses and a Health Information and Research Centre.

The Harlow project, linked to its GP Referral scheme, involved every GP in the town, health promotion, health education and primary healthcare. The centre works with the Cardio-rehabilitation Unit of Princess Alexandra Hospital (the town hospital) and with health visitors. Ideally, managers at the centre would like it to be the town's 'one stop shop' for sport, exercise, health treatments, pharmacy, holistic therapies, and an advice centre for lifestyle issues.

These are a few examples of initiatives being carried out in many parts of the UK. They demonstrate the strong potential links between physical activity and healthy lifestyles and also demonstrate why central government and local authorities are anxious to provide these facilities. However, it should not be forgotten that most people taking part in sport and recreation do so for the fun, comradeship and the enjoyment of taking part. Physical activity, like play, can be enjoyed for its own sake.

Summary

Sport is a major industry in the United Kingdom. At the international level, it is better placed than we often think. Based on an index of success in over 60 sports across 200 countries, the UK is ranked third of the world's sporting nations behind the USA and Australia. At international level, some national sportsmen and women compete for the United Kingdom and/or Great Britain and also as home countries. This has led to some difficulties. The government is currently involved in radical reforming of the national structures and systems in order to meet its twin goals of increased mass participation and improved international success. Participation in sport and physical activity compares unfavourably with that in the Scandinavian countries.

The government has an important role to play as a partner with the voluntary and private sectors. It does so mainly for the health benefits they yield to the nation. The national administration and structures of sport in the UK are complex and funding is fragmented. In terms of policy, there is a national plan, but changes and revisions over relatively short periods of time have added to the complexity. However, sport is delivered at a local, not a national level. Local government oversees schools, further education, and higher education; national governing bodies of sport oversee sports clubs, and the private sector also has a role. The health sector is also becoming important in order to meet government targets.

Sport, recreation and physical activity is an area with the greatest potential for employment in leisure management. Quality Leisure Managers are likely to be in demand for many years to come.

Discussion points

1 In the United Kingdom, billions of pounds of National Lottery and other public money have been spent on sport and physical activity at grass-roots level. Critics claim that participation has not risen accordingly. Discuss why this may be the case.

2 In setting priorities for the nation, make a case for 'sport for all' and/or a case for sporting excellence.

3 A Chief Executive Officer of a national agency remarked on Olympic and world sporting events: 'Failure is an orphan. Success has many parents!' Discuss.

4 Staging sports mega-events can cost billions of pounds. Should the home city be responsible for funding them, when there are benefits to the region and the country? Or do city events benefit the city in the main? Debate the issues.

Useful websites

UK Sport: www.uksport.gov.uk

Sport England: www.sportengland.org.uk

sportscotland: www.sportscotland.org.uk

Sports Council for Northern Ireland: www.sportni.org

Sports Council for Wales: www.sports-council-wales.co.uk

British Olympic Association: www.olympics.org.uk

Central Council of Physical Recreation (CCPR): www.ccpr.org.uk

Women's Sports Foundation: www.wsf.org.uk

English Federation of Disability Sport: www.efds.net

Physical Education Association of the United Kingdom: www.pea.uk.com

National Council for School Sport (NCSS): www.schoolsport.freeserve.co.uk

SportsCoach UK (previously The National Coaching Foundation): www.sportscoach.uk

The Sports Industries Federation (TSIF): www.sportslife.org.uk

The National Association for Sports Development (NASD): www.nasd.uk.com

Part 4

18

Management principles and foundations

Introduction

Management is a word that can be applied to most situations of life: it is the act or art of managing. It tends to be used most often in business, industry and commerce, with 'managers' and 'staff' or 'workers' being considered side by side, yet they are often worlds apart in some industries. A number of institutions claim management as their *raison d'être*, for example, in the United Kingdom, British Institute of Management, Institute of Leisure and Amenity Management and Institute of Sport and Recreation Management. Many of these kinds of organizations also focus on specialist technical knowledge.

The management of leisure requires the effectiveness and efficiency which is needed in all good management; the core elements of management will be the core elements of 'leisure management'. Managing leisure will also have its own specialisms.

This chapter introduces the concept of general management to show that there are core elements which apply to all branches of management, including leisure. Management is viewed from an historical perspective of early management thinkers to the management gurus of today before focusing on the management processes and practical management in the leisure environment.

Management: what it is and what it does

Management is both an active human occupation and a process by which people and organizations achieve results. Management is a distinct type of work. The ability to do a job is not enough. The good physical education teacher, swimming coach, librarian, park ranger or sports or arts administrator does not automatically make a good manager. While technical 'know-how' is important, management is more: it concerns the work of people, effectiveness and accountability for end results.

What is the distinct type of work which relates to the manager? Management is not a science, with precise laws and predictable behaviour. No foolproof rules exist which can replace the need for experience, judgement, and common sense. Management is not an art, if by that we imply only intuition and individual judgement, on the thesis that 'managers are born and not made'. Management is not a profession, even though a code of ethics and standards has been established, for example by the British Institute of Management. Management appears to be a bit or a blend of each: 'It is the sum of art and science that makes a manager.'

While management, fundamentally, is concerned with human behaviour, behaviour is not constant. Management situations vary. Management is concerned with change; it is continually flowing and interacting and few areas of life change as much as the world of leisure: a volatile profession if ever there was one. Peter Drucker emphasized this aspect of management:

> The job of management is never to be concerned with restoring or maintaining normality because normality is the condition of yesterday. The major concern of management, if they are to make their business effective, must be in the direction of systematically trying to understand the condition of the future so that they can decide on the changes that can take their business from today into tomorrow.
>
> Drucker, 1965

Discussions on management often start with a search for the best definition of the word. In its earliest usage, managing, from the Latin word for a hand, meant handling something such as a sword or a supply of money. It was used in handling or training a horse, which was put through the exercises of the *manège*, the French for the riding school. So, from handling things and animals, today we use the words 'manage', 'managing' and 'management' in a variety of ways including handling people and organizations.

A cursory look at dictionary definitions illustrates the breadth of usage. The verb 'to manage' can mean to direct, to handle, to influence, to exert control, to make submissive, to contrive or to cope with. One can 'manage to succeed in one's aims', 'manage on a small budget', 'manage our time well or badly', 'manage to make a mess of it all', or have the inability to 'manage a drinks party in a brewery'. One of the *Oxford English Dictionary* definitions of 'management' is 'the application of skill or care in the manipulation, use, treatment, or control of things or persons, or in the conduct of an enterprise, operation, etc.'. In business, terms which are commonplace include Management by Exception and Management by Objectives.

When we refer to Leisure Management, we convey that we are in business to manage people, resources, organizations, services, facilities and programmes for clients and customers in their leisure time, including specifically the range of leisure products such as play, recreation, the arts and culture, sport, festivals, celebrations and events, health and fitness and travel and tourism. This chapter, however, deals with the fundamental principles and core ingredients of management.

Management thus depends on a variety of factors such as the situation, the people involved and the organization. In significant measure, management depends on the person, or persons, doing the managing. Management relates to people's behaviour.

This conditions any definition of management. The qualities found in the good manager are therefore important in any definition of management.

What appears to be abundantly clear is that there is no one way, no one 'instant brew' for instant, effective management and no one management principle that is right every time. Management is malleable, amenable to change and flexible in organization. It has many functions. The manager is not just a creator, but he or she is also a planner and forecaster, setting objectives, motivating, leading, deciding, checking and monitoring performance. Management – in the simple idiom of today – is getting things done with and through people, and as such management is a social process.

The profit orientation of management

Management is usually considered in terms of economic efficiency; it can only justify its existence by the economic results it produces. There may be greater non-economic results, such as the contribution to community welfare, but management has failed, according to Drucker (1955), if it fails to produce economic results. It must supply goods and services which the public wants, at a price the consumer is willing to pay.

However, good management can make 'profits' in a wide variety of ways which are not tied to economic results. 'People service' programmes, including many aspects of leisure management, differ in some fundamental respects from a commercial profit-orientated company. While local authorities, trusts and other not-for-profit organizations have to be concerned with economic viability, 'profit' needs to be defined in terms not just of money but in terms of a range of criteria. For example, at a public leisure facility, good management should result in meeting performance targets such as:

- the range of users attracted, including the socially disadvantaged and the disabled
- improving performance
- improving health
- the numbers attracted from the locality it serves and
- other benefits to individuals and the community.

Hence, there are 'profits' of many kinds, in addition to the level of financial viability aimed for. Extending this idea, some have tried to place an actual financial value on recreation participation. David Gray (1977) says:

> We desperately need a method of planning that permits social cost–benefit analysis. Lacking such a system we are turning control of our social enterprises over to the accounting mind. The accounting mind reaches decisions by a method in which short-range fiscal consequences are the only criterion of value. Recreation and park services will not survive in that kind of environment. Most of the great social problems that disfigure our national life cannot be addressed in a climate dominated by that kind of value system.

Similarly, Robert Wilder (1977) states: 'The modern day name of the game seems to be quantification, justification, competition and cost–benefit analysis.' In search of a management tool by which to measure recreational benefits in terms of 'profit',

Wilder presented his 'economic equivalency index' (EEI), which attempts to quantify recreation value in financial terms.

Good management, therefore, is needed to achieve objectives: financial and social. Leisure managers need above all else to be good managers, with both generalist and specialist skills. In whatever branch of management, they need to be 'profit' orientated.

The founding principles of modern management

Contemporary management practices have been influenced by many schools of management thought. Management understanding has progressed from the 'scientific movement' instigated by Frederick Taylor (see Wren, 1972) a hundred years ago, through the 'human relations movement' influenced by Elton Mayo (1933), through the 'classical movement' stressing organization and administration and influenced by Henri Fayol (1930) and Max Weber (see Wren, 1972), to the behaviourist view of management put forward by Douglas McGregor (1966) and Frederick Herzberg (Herzberg et al., 1959), who built on the inspiration of Abraham Maslow (1954; 1968).

Leisure Management can benefit from the experience and knowledge of eminent thinkers. The management of people, organizations, societies and nations has been part of history over thousands of years. The management of the state, economics, property and social cohesion go back beyond Greek civilizations. Some power struggles and takeover bids of today exhibit the kind of thinking set out in Machiavelli's *The Prince*, written at the time of the Renaissance in Florence. However, management strategies, systems and structures found in business today owe much to ideas developed early in the twentieth century.

Beginning of modern management

Management as we know it today has its beginnings at the start of the twentieth century. Four examples from the first half of the twentieth century are: the 'scientific movement'; 'classical' theory; bureaucracy; and human relations. We then look at the 'behaviourist' view of management.

The 'scientific movement' Frederick Taylor, an American engineer, dominated the beginning of what has become to be known as the 'scientific movement' from the turn of the last century until the 1920s. Taylor's ideas are management foundation stones for many organizations and enterprises that sprang up in the earlier part of the twentieth century. The term 'time and motion study' emanates from Taylor. His was a system of reward: the higher the productivity, the higher the pay. The belief was born that optimum work environments would enhance productivity. In *Principles of Scientific Management* (Taylor, 1947), he set out four foundations of his principles:

1   the development of a science of work and meeting goals, with pay linked to productivity: a fair day's work for a fair day's pay
2   the scientific selection and training of each employee to fit the task
3   bringing together the science of work and the selection of the workers for the best results and
4   equal division of work and responsibilities.

'Classical' management theory Classical management theory is concerned with the efficient design and structure of organizations: the administration of the business. Building on Taylor's theories, the French mining engineer, Henri Fayol, had an important influence on management thinking, although his work was not published in English until 1949 (he died in 1925) in *General and Industrial Management* (Fayol, 1949). He emphasized five management processes: planning, organizing, commanding, co-ordinating and controlling. In addition to these five foundations, he developed fourteen general principles of management, including the influential 'unity of command' in which each employee should have only one boss, without conflicting lines of command and the 'scalar' or hierarchical chain of command.

Classical theory is thus concerned with structures and hierarchy, principles which have had profound effects on government and industry. Local government, and hence public recreation services, conform to formal structures, organizational charts, hierarchical structures: people know their station, role and authority; their jobs are defined. Classical management structuring, however, appears to neglect the people-orientation. It is often mechanistic, bureaucratic and red taped. Formal structures tend to put work into tight categories; departments tend to be sub-divided into units; labour is divided into specialisms; inflexibility is instilled and top-to-bottom chains of control – chains of command – become sacrosanct. In public recreation services we find that comprehensive departments, so called, may well be a series of demarcated administrative boxes and specialisms. For example, a large 'leisure' or 'culture' department may have sections called Administration, Finance, Activities and Events, Catering and Bar, and Maintenance. Or they may be divided into Parks, Pools, Sports, Arts, Youth, Aged, all acting out separate roles in separate units.

Bureaucracy German sociologist and political economist Max Weber studied the role of the leader in an organization and how individuals respond to authority. Today we talk about charismatic management, yet it was Weber who recognized this quality in an individual's personality. Despite this finding, Weber believed that the bureaucratic organization, from a purely technical point of view, was the most efficient to run a business. However, as Wren (1972) points out: 'Bureaucracy was conceived as a blueprint for efficiency which would emphasise rules rather than men.' In terms of leisure and recreation management, the bureaucratic model has been the norm through Europe, including the United Kingdom. In the public sector, the greater the government 'rules', whether central or local government, the greater the bureaucracy in leisure departments.

The management of people

Management is more about people than about organizations and systems, if these are to be effective.

The 'human relations movement' The long-held theories of 'scientific' management and bureaucracy were challenged by writers such as Chester Barnard and Elton Mayo. Barnard recognized that large organizations were made up of smaller groups, which were made up of individuals with personal motivations. Ahead of his time, in *The Functions of the Executive* (Barnard, 1938), he saw the distinction between efficiency and effectiveness. To be effective, the aims of an organization must be accepted by those contributing to its success; in other words, authority in an organization only exists while employees are willing to accept it. He perceived the Chief Executive in an organization as a 'value sharpener' as distinct from the former authoritarian styles of management.

One of the founders of industrial sociology is Australian-born Elton Mayo, who studied in Australia and in Britain. He emigrated to the USA in 1923 and spent much of his career at Harvard. Mayo is best remembered for the Hawthorne Experiments which were conducted in Western Electric's Hawthorne Works in Chicago from 1927 to 1932. The tests were conducted following earlier experiments with two work groups. An experimental group of women worked in one room; a control group of women worked in another room. Lighting conditions were varied in the experimental group. It was discovered that not only did improved illumination result in improved productivity, but that all changes to illumination resulted in improvements, including levels of illumination which were highly unfavourable. In addition, it was discovered that as well as increased production in the experimental group the same improvements occurred in the control group. Researchers from Harvard led by Elton Mayo were called in to continue the studies (Mayo, 1933). After the illumination experiments, other variables were also manipulated. For example, the experimental group were given scheduled work breaks, shorter working weeks and other benefits. Again, productivity increased both in the experimental group *and* the control group. Mayo's researchers then removed all the benefits from the experimental group. Yet again, production increased in both groups!

What were the reasons for these effects? Why had attitudes to work changed in this situation? Each group was found to be reacting to being an 'object of study', the consequence of the presence of researchers. Mayo's methodology was to spend considerable time in interviewing both the experimental group and the control group. Employees were made to feel that the company genuinely cared for them, cared about their problems and their feelings. Management was seen to be concerned about employees as people. The improved social conditions appeared to be more important than improved physical and environmental conditions. Hence came the dawn of the 'human relations movement' and the discovery that the informal organization and the quality of supervision had a significant effect on morale and productivity. This realization was one of the pivots in the human relations school of management: interpersonal relationships are important; management is a people-orientated business.

The paternalistic concern of management in relation to industrial recreation may well be one of the products of this management movement. Many businesses try to provide a good working environment, offer fringe benefits, social benefits and appear to show genuine concern for workers at work and away from work (see Industrial and company recreation provision, p. 186, Chapter 10).

Employees' dissatisfaction with businesses in the United Kingdom today, which may be seen on the surface as wanting better conditions, tea-breaks, etc., may have more to do with lack of management sensitivity and involvement of employees emotionally. Hence, the Taylorist philosophy of self-interest was disapproved of by Mayo. While the experiments were said to have scientific flaws, they have shown the importance of the peer group in the workplace and that within each formal organization there are many informal ones, which, far from being discouraged, should be welcomed. These discoveries make it possible to work towards motivating and encouraging employees or fellow colleagues to achieve corporate goals. For the leisure industry, it illustrates that managers should develop understandings and communications within and between all people involved in the leisure enterprise: policy makers, managers, staff, clients, and customers.

The 'behaviourist' view of management One of the post-Second World War management movements is a 'behaviourist' approach, which has been in vogue since the early 1950s. It arose, in part, in opposition to the rigid structuring and organizational character of classical methods. It was felt that organization structures should be tempered with flexibility and a greater concern for employee involvement. The inherent discord within closed systems needed to be eliminated; harmony would lead to improved work and work relationships. McGregor (1966), Herzberg (Herzberg *et al.*, 1959), Argyris (1957), Likert (1967) and others have enlarged management thinking within the behavioural approach, inspired by the work of psychologists such as Erich Fromm and Abraham Maslow and the human relations work of Elton Mayo. Probably the best known management theorist in the area of human psychology is Abraham Maslow, famous for his theory of the hierarchy of needs in motivating people, set out in his classic *Motivation and Personality* (Maslow, 1954). People have needs, some are basic to survival, some are social and some are self-fulfilling. Basic, lower levels, must be satisfied first. Maslow believed that once needs are satisfied, they no longer motivate. In those parts of the modern Western world free from warfare, most people are fed, sheltered and have security. These things are no longer motivators. But in war-torn countries, survival is an immensely strong motivator. (See Chapter 6.)

World terrorism of the twenty-first century has motivated world leaders to take strong security measures. However, by and large, in an affluent society, most physical and safety needs have been consistently satisfied; consequently, it is the social and ego needs which are dominant. Maslow's concern that people should be 'self-actualized', whether at work or play, led to the kind of thinking which stressed working patterns that encouraged people to express themselves, not only in their free time, but in work also. Leisure Managers, like most other people, want to be recognized as individuals, to have some measure of control over the decisions in their working environment and their own jobs, to accomplish something worthwhile: in other words, to see themselves in something that is successful and meaningful.

Management motivators The value system of the way in which managers handle colleagues and staff has changed and continues to change. Douglas McGregor, an American social psychologist, made management history with his famous 'Theory X' and 'Theory Y': authoritarian and participative management approaches set out in *The Human Side of Enterprise* (McGregor, 1966). How you manage people has a deep impact on their behaviour. Management methods need to change to suit different people and in different situations, if people are to be motivated to manage themselves.

Theory X, whereby staff carry out instructions, is the traditional view of direction and control. Most people have to be coerced, controlled, directed and even threatened before effort is made towards the achievement of organizational objectives. The theory also suggests that people prefer to be directed, respond when disciplined, wish to avoid responsibility, have relatively little ambition and want security above all else. In essence, Theory X is the 'stick and carrot' approach, the carrot being money or reward and the stick being the threat of financial insecurity. McGregor believes that this must be replaced by Theory Y.

Theory Y, whereby staff act on their own initiative, is the theory of the integration of individual and organizational goals. Effort in work is as natural as play or rest. External controls are not the only means for bringing about effort towards objectives. People can exercise self-direction and self-control when commitment is high. They respond to honest praise and resent punishment. Moreover, people learn, under proper conditions, not only to accept but also to seek responsibility; the capacity to exercise a relatively high degree of imagination, ingenuity and creativity in the solution of organizational problems is widely, not narrowly, distributed in the population, as the old-style management of 'leaders' and 'followers' suggests.

Theory X managers will tend to push people to achieve a task. Theory Y managers will tend to lead people to achieve a task. McGregor claimed that those managers operating predominantly towards the principles of Theory Y were generally more successful in the following ways: their departments had higher outputs; staff showed greater motivation; and there were fewer labour problems, lower labour turnovers, less waste and greater profits. However, greater robust scientific evidence is needed to confirm these findings. In management, is there sometimes a need to mix Theory X and Theory Y in order to motivate and inspire and also to challenge, so that peak performance is achieved?

McGregor's work has been enlarged by Likert, an American social psychologist (Likert, 1967), whose concepts are presented in four management systems:

- System 1, exploitative authoritative
- System 2, benevolent authoritative
- System 3, consultative and
- System 4, participative.

He claimed that the nearer the management system is to System 4, the more productive the organization. It produces lower costs, higher earnings, better union relations, more positive worker attitudes and higher morale. Conversely, the nearer the management is to System 1, the more it results in lower productivity, higher costs, poorer union relations and lower morale. The problem with these theories, unfortunately, is that productivity alone is an insufficient measurement; it is the trade mark of factory conveyor-belt management and at its worst is seen in exploitative systems such as in the production of leisure goods from developing countries.

However, the findings of McGregor and Likert confirm that more effective results can be obtained by a people-orientated approach to management. That being the case, the implications for leisure service management are considerable. If humanistic approaches to management can prove more effective in product-orientated industries, they should also produce more effective results in service-orientated organizations, such as those found in the leisure industry.

Frederick Herzberg, an American psychologist coined the term 'job enrichment'. His theory of motivation (Herzberg et al., 1959) relates to two main job satisfaction parameters: hygiene factors and motivators. Herzberg's study of satisfaction and dissatisfaction at work was first published in *The Motivation to Work*. He found that those aspects leading to feelings of satisfaction included achievement, recognition and personal growth and he called these 'motivators'. Dissatisfaction mostly related to what he termed 'hygiene' factors, such as working conditions, salary, status, and job security. These things in a modern context of, say, conditions of service, company car, car parking space, luncheon vouchers, incremental rise in pay and so on, keep us from being unhappy, they do not necessarily provide happiness: job satisfaction. Herzberg believes that as jobs become enriched, the need for job supervision lessens. Hence, today, employees in many organizations can be trusted to work at times and places more suited to their needs, leading to flexi-time or home-based work.

Hygiene factors then are not part of the actual job, but relate to the work environment: policies, conditions, fringe benefits, and so on, which may affect job performance. Motivators, on the other hand, are concerned with the job. Is the job challenging? Does it carry responsibility, recognition for achievement, give prestige and esteem? Herzberg is concerned with job enrichment but his theory is limited by being preoccupied with two strands of employment.

Other 'behaviourists' have taken the ideas forward. Reg Revans, at one time a United Kingdom local government officer in the education field, is thought to be the 'inventor' of Action Learning: managers educating each other through shared working experiences. Action Learning is a method well suited to leisure management. The German economist E.F. Schumacher, who worked for the Coal Board in Britain, coined the phrase 'small is beautiful'. People need to be involved in the decision-making process in small units. Later, management theorists were to extend this idea to include delegating authority to far wider groups within an organization and to dub this approach 'empowerment'. Leisure, with its vast range of choice, offers great opportunity for work in small units, with high levels of delegated authority, for example, decentralized service units on a geographical or neighbourhood basis, such as local parks and open spaces and neighbourhood community provision.

Argyris, building on Maslow's self-actualization theme, believes that job enrichment will increase employee initiatives and self-direction. There would appear to be much in common between Argyris, Maslow's hierarchy of needs, Herzberg's job enrichment, McGregor's 'Theory Y', and Likert's 'System 4'. They are all concerned with job enlargement, job enrichment and self-fulfilment.

It is important that we learn the lessons of the past. They affect the present and can point to the future. However, we now turn to more contemporary thinking by learning from the management gurus: the 'pop stars' of management.

The management gurus

In recent times management experts have been fêted with the equivalent of management 'pop idol' status. A thumb-nail sketch of some of their insights is provided in this section and owes much to the highly informative book by Carol Kennedy, *Guide to the Management Gurus* (Kennedy, 1991). This section considers briefly the contributions of Drucker, Mintzberg, Argyris, Adair, Peter, Handy, Bennis, Peter and Waterman, Moss Kanter, Deming and Juran and Blanchard.

The modern 'guru' status owes much to one of the founders of modern management, Peter Drucker. Drucker was born in Vienna, came to Britain in the 1920s, worked as an economist in London in the 1930s and emigrated to the USA in 1937. Working as a consultant with General Motors, he wrote his first book in 1942, became a prolific writer and has had profound influence in the spread of management thinking for the past five decades. Drucker's basic principles of management have been sustained over time: setting objectives; organizing; motivating and communicating; measuring performance; and developing staff. One of his most influential books is *Concept of the Corporation* (Drucker, 1946), in which he sought to discover what made large companies successful. He believed that these companies knew what businesses they were in, what their competencies were, and how to keep focused on their goals. In *The Practice of Management* (Drucker, 1955), which remains a classic, Drucker identified management by objectives as the first of seven primary tasks. In the United Kingdom, John Humble turned the principle of management by objectives into a system of management: MBO. Regarded by some as somewhat dated, MBO remains a key to the involvement of a workforce in setting and achieving an organization's goals.

To Drucker, management is central to life, not just business. Chief executives are like conductors of an orchestra. Extending this perspective, there are few fundamental differences between managing a business, a hospital, a ship, a government agency, or a leisure service. Currently, local authorities in the United Kingdom are asking themselves whether they should be providers, organizers or enablers. Drucker advocates that government should govern, not 'do'.

The Canadian professor of management Henry Mintzberg (1983) takes a different viewpoint. He suggests that chief executives, far from planning, organizing, controlling and being an orchestral conductor, jump from topic to topic, thrive on interruptions, meet a steady stream of callers, read few reports fully and spend as much time dealing with people outside the organization as within it. He believes that chief executives favour intuitive thinking, creative strategies, 'right-brain thinking'.

American psychologist Chris Argyris is best known for his work in developing individual potential within organizations. Each individual has potential which can be enhanced or stunted depending on the way in which an organization is managed. Managers have to deal with conflicts. Chris Argyris and Donald Schon examined these kinds of conflicts and provide potential solutions in *Organizational Learning: A Theory of Action Perspective* (1978).

A pioneering British thinker on leadership, John Adair is a strong advocate of training; he believes that leadership is a learned skill, rather than an inborn aptitude. Leadership is about a sense of direction; it is about achieving a task with a team. Leaders inspire others with their own enthusiasm and commitment. Adair is best known for his concept of action-centred leadership, and the overlap between the task, the team and the individual. In *Understanding Motivation* Adair (1990) lists the functions of leadership as planning, initiating, controlling, supporting, informing and evaluating. He suggests that 50 per cent of success depends on the team and 50 per cent on the individual; 'the ultimate cure of the "us" and "them" '. His latest work is referred to in Chapter 19, Leadership (Adair and Reed, 1997).

In *The Peter Pyramid* Laurence Peter (1986) demonstrates the ways bureaucracies sap human resources; major organizations are constructed upside down, with the point of the operation all but invisible beneath the bulk of a top-heavy administration. The bureaucrat is so busy keeping his job that he has no time to do it! Peter suggests that we simplify meaningless complexity and stop the procession of the 'blind leading the blind'.

The world of management has changed in recent times as a number of current management thinkers have sought to revolutionize management practice. Charles Handy has a concern with how companies reach goals far beyond financial profit levels. He believes that organizations are more than structures and systems. He sees the need to move to a process of 'upside-down thinking', a process similar to the psychologist Edward de Bono's lateral thinking, which he described as generating new ideas and escaping from old ones.

According to Handy in *Inside Organizations* (Handy, 1990), companies are increasingly taking on a shamrock shape. The Irish clover, the national emblem, was originally used by St Patrick who demonstrated that the three leaves were still part of one leaf, so the three aspects of God were still the same God. Handy uses the symbol to postulate that in today's business there are three different types of workforce: the core workforce, the contractual fringe and the flexible labour force. Each is a part of a larger whole.

The core workforce is made up of those people who are essential and give the organization its uniqueness. They are increasingly precious. There are fewer of them; each is responsible for more; they are not easily replaced and they carry a large slice of the organization's know-how with them. The contractual fringe are specialist organizations. They have the resources and they are geared to undertake specialist tasks in their fields. However in leisure management, it is not easy to decide what to contract out and what to keep in the core, as one's uniqueness. For example, in a private health club, is it good business to contract out the cleaning, catering and beauty treatment? Core workers and specialists are expensive. Can leisure make better use of a flexible labour force, e.g. for events and holiday programmes?

Clichés now abound in management literature and current jargon. Warren Bennis, an industrial psychologist, is remembered for his: 'Managers do things right. Leaders do the right thing.' Strongly influenced by the motivational theories, he sees the need to move from 'bureaucracy' to 'adhocracy', the opposite of bureaucracy, describing small, flexible groups that operate freely across departmental boundaries. He sees the leader as the bridge-maker between the now and the future: a person who can transform an organization. A prolific writer, Bennis identifies 'vision' that provides a focus to guide personal and organizational activities (see Bennis, 1984; 1989; 1985). He perceives effective leadership in four areas of management:

- attention (drawing others into his/her vision through a supreme focus)
- measuring (communicating meaning, directing and aligning staff to work in harmony)
- trust (conveying the leader's integrity and reliability) and
- self (the leader's ability to understand and accept his/her and staff's personal limitations and thus exploit their strengths).

Vision and mission have now become business trade marks. Three powerful books to hit the management scene in the 1980s were Tom Peters and Robert Waterman's *In Search of Excellence* (1982), Tom Peters and Nancy Austin's *A Passion for Excellence* (1985) and Peters' *Thriving on Chaos* (1987), which Peters calls a 'handbook for a management revolution'. Peters' previous books were written against a background of stability and predictability. That no longer exists: we are in a time of accelerating change. Aspiring only to be excellent is not enough, says Peters. Businesses must continually create new market niches and add new value, quality to their products. Leisure is an expanding industry also. It too needs constantly to look for new quality niches.

In *The Art of Japanese Management* (Pascale and Athos, 1981) the authors identified the reasons for Japanese post-war success. From this they invented the acclaimed Seven S Model. This is made up of three 'hard' S factors (strategy, structure and systems) and four 'soft' S factors (style, shared values, skills and staff) in which the Japanese excelled. It was the soft S factors that made the difference and the best firms linked their purposes to human values as well as to economic measures.

In the changing management scene, 'empowerment' has become a buzz word. Empowerment goes beyond delegation. Rosabeth Moss Kanter, an American sociologist and a professor of Harvard, has become an authority on managing change. She sets out future organizations as 'post-entrepreneurial', empowering individuals as a force for change. She sees new corporations, for example, as leaner and fitter, with fewer management levels and able to do more with less. Moss Kanter's vision is to make fundamental changes within organizations, providing greater power to a wider range of employees, including clerical staff, and creating intermediate jobs to bridge the gap to top management. Hence, she calls for 'empowering' strategies leading to flatter hierarchies, decentralized authority and autonomous working groups. Her essential skills for future managers are set out in *When Giants Learn to Dance* (Kanter, 1989). Given opportunities and resources, decentralization and empowerment could work well in a number of leisure settings: library business units, sports development units, arts groups and so on.

Every few years, new sounding themes and new ways of managing come into vogue. The early 1990s resounded to the word 'quality' and abbreviations like TQM (Total Quality Management), the symbol of the ideal organization and its management. There were also BS5750/ISO 9000, testimony that the organization has reached a certain standard of management, and 'Kite Marks' to denote quality. (See Quality frameworks and award schemes, p. 535.)

> An important quality standard today is the award Investors in People which has been achieved by many leisure organizations.

Yet the 'quality movement' had been instilled into Japanese management thinking in the post-war years by management consultants such as Americans W. Edwards Deming and Joseph Juran. Later, the Americans were anxious to copy the successes of Japanese industry. Deming's management philosophy was perceiving the customer as 'the most important part of the production line'. Profit in business comes from repeat customers. Hence, management must stay ahead of the customers, anticipating needs in the years to come (Deming, 1986).

A leading American management consultant and author, Kenneth Blanchard, has become best known for a series of popular texts including *The One Minute Manager*, (Blanchard and Johnson, 1983), *Leadership and the One Minute Manager* (Blanchard *et al.*, 1986) and *The One Minute Sales Person*. These easy to read texts are noted for their strap lines, for example 'Help People Reach Their Full Potential – Catch Them Doing Something Right'; 'Situational Leadership Is Not Something You Do To People But Something You Do With People'. Blanchard with his co-authors dismisses the idea that a person's age and service are the best qualification of management; they demonstrate that the ability to manage one's own behaviour and attitudes is an essential prerequisite to managing other people. This is a huge lesson for leisure managers and is a theme taken up later in Chapter 19.

Implications for management today

Up to this point, we have looked at lessons from the past and also what the management gurus of recent times have had to say. What do these findings imply for today's management?

The management of most businesses and public leisure services in the UK appears to be based on classical management theory. Many writers have revised Fayol's original model but generally the framework and logic have remained intact:

- planning (policies, forecasting, objectives)
- execution (systematic implementation of policies, co-ordination) and
- control (monitoring performance).

More recent writers have added to Fayol's model with additional functions such as motivation, communication, budgeting, and staff development.

The functions of management are seen as important because they are the constituents of every management job. The emphasis they receive, however, will vary according to the type of job, the level of the manager, the nature of the environment and many other factors. It would appear that the classical principles of management theory, adapted and modified to meet the needs of different organizations, can be used as a basic framework for the management of leisure services, facilities and programmes, namely:

1 conceptualizing, having a mission, direction, goals and marketing strategy
2 setting measurable objectives
3 organizing, establishing a structure and system
4 recruiting, training and developing staff
5 carrying out the plan (e.g. a leisure service or programme) and obtaining results through people
6 assisting subordinates and inspiring and motivating them
7 seeking improvements and appraising results.

There appears to be a core of knowledge and skills that is needed for management at all levels; MacKenzie's classic 3-D management process illustrates his 'ideas–people–things' model (MacKenzie, 1969). These core management tasks are basically of three types: conceptual, human and technical.

- The conceptual skills are developed on an understanding of the overall situations, the nature of the problems and complexities, and the abilities to think clearly, analyse problems and plan carefully.
- The human skills are concerned with people, and include the abilities to select, develop, motivate, lead, decide, control and monitor performance. Managers must have good judgement and be able to work with and through people to meet objectives.
- The technical skills are needed to incorporate experience and knowledge of the subject area, and the methods and techniques which are needed to perform the tasks. In the leisure facility environment, for example, technical skills are needed for operating and maintaining parks, pitches, swimming pools, theatres, leisure centres, plant and equipment.

All managers, supervisors and group leaders need all three skills – conceptual, human and technical – but they are needed in different quantities, depending on their level of authority and the tasks in hand. Generally, the higher up the managerial ladder, the greater the need for conceptual skills, while the more 'sharp end' workers will need to have greater technical skills. The pools supervisor, for example, will have greater concern for the number of staff on poolside, safety, the quality of the water, and the correct procedures and standards, and less on, for example, the demographic profile of those using the swimming pool. However, all staff need human skills and it is these skills of dealing with other people that are critical to effective management practice.

It is important to appreciate that management is nothing without something to manage. In this context, that 'something' is leisure and recreation, which need both general and specialist management, and quality in both.

Quality management

Three 'movements' in modern business have gained ground during recent years: the computer-technology revolution worldwide, quality customer care, and, increasingly, empowerment. If organizations are going to be leaner and fitter, with fewer management levels, and more decision-making power is to be delegated, then teamworking needs to become the preferred practice in many businesses, including leisure, as traditional structures give way to flat, multi-skilled workforces. Markets, including leisure and tourism, have become increasingly competitive. Quality, pricing and delivery have been key determinants in satisfying customers and thereby increasing market share. Whether managing in the commercial, public or voluntary sectors people have to be attracted to the services and facilities and these should be managed with excellence – that is, with quality. But quality does not just happen. It has to be worked for. It has to be managed.

Total Quality Management (TQM) is an approach to improving the effectiveness of a business as a whole, that is, a process from top to bottom, bottom to top, which involves every person in an organization, in order to ensure customer satisfaction at every stage. TQM thus focuses on customer needs and builds a logical linkage between these needs and the business objectives.

If quality is synonymous with meeting customer requirements, then this has fundamental implications for leisure management. The first item on the agenda will be to find out who are the current and potential clients and customers and what are their needs and requirements. Then, services and products have to be developed to meet their needs and delivered with excellence.

The principles behind such total quality are identified by Pip Mosscrop and Adrian Stores (1990):

- excellence as the objective and getting it right first time
- everyone is a customer or a supplier in every transaction; every transaction in the business, every link in the chain, has a supplier and a customer
- absolute clarity about customers' needs: customers' perceptions are paramount
- commitment from the top
- measurement of all key outputs: 'We are convinced that control through measurement of key outputs in terms of ratios against past trends, standards and/or targets must become a way of life for all those employed in the leisure sector'

- prevention not blame; sharing responsibility, preventing future occurrences
- training and education from top down
- integration of total quality into the business: a core business activity which permeates every aspect of leisure operations.

In other words, excellence is called for and is worked for by every person in all aspects of the operation. All activity throughout all operations is continuously directed at satisfying client and customer requirements.

> *The British Quality Association provides a definition of TQM:*
>
> *Total Quality (TQM) is a corporate business management philosophy which recognizes that customer needs and business goals are inseparable. It is applicable within both industry and commerce. It ensures maximum effectiveness and efficiency within a business and secures commercial leadership by putting in place processes and systems which will promote excellence, prevent errors and ensure that every aspect of the business is aligned to customer needs and the advancement of business goals without duplication or waste of effort. The commitment to TQM originates at the chief executive level in a business and is promoted in all human activities. The accomplishment of quality is thus achieved by personal involvement and accountability, devoted to a continuous improvement process, with measurable levels of performance by all concerned. It involves every department, function and process in a business and the active commitment of all employees to meeting customer needs. In this regard the 'customers' of each employee are separately and individually identified.*

John Oakland (1989) believes that Total Quality Management is concerned with moving control from outside the individual to within, the objective being to make everyone accountable for their own performance, and to get each person committed to attaining quality in a highly motivated fashion:

> While an intellectual understanding of quality provides a basis for TQM, it is clearly only the planting of the seed. The understanding must be translated into commitment, policies, plans and actions for TQM to germinate. Making this happen requires not only commitment, but a competence in the mechanics of quality management, and in making changes.

All the theories set out in this section ultimately point to the need for a manager to have motivational and leadership skills as key components in their management armoury. A better understanding of these skills is developed in Chapter 19.

A study of successful facility managers in the public and private sectors (Torkildsen, 1986) found that five essential criteria were almost universal: sound leadership, objectivity, staff motivation, care of customers and operational excellence.

In addition to these 'bankers' within the 'effective operational model', management, to be effective, needs to be flexible to accommodate changing circumstances, and to meet the needs of different people.

Summary

This chapter has considered the founding principles of management, including the scientific, classical, bureaucratic and human behaviour stages in the development of modern management. Lessons were gleaned from some of the most recent thinkers in the field.

Good management is the result of good managers, individuals who have the responsibility for providing leadership to an organization and the ability to move it towards its goals.

There are many differences between the public, voluntary and commercial providers, but the similarities – in terms of core management skills – are fundamental. All managers must have conceptual, human and technical ability. Managers in all sectors are getting things done with, and through, people to provide opportunities for people in their leisure time. The efficient operation of facilities and the specific technical tasks are essential. However, the excellent management of people is needed to be effective and to meet organizational objectives. It is to these human aspects of leadership and decision making that we turn next.

Discussion points

1 Can leisure be managed? If leisure is about personal experience, and management is about organization and control, do we have a contradiction in terms? If leisure is defined as personal experience, how can it be managed by someone else? Does it defy management? Discuss how management can be used to provide for people's leisure experience?

2 As long as they have a good understanding and grasp of the principles of management, anyone could manage a leisure service or facility. Discuss.

3 Consider the following statement: empowerment cannot be decreed by top management from on high, nor simply bought from consultants; empowerment must develop over a period of time, and arises from mutual trust, through beliefs and attitudes of participants.

4 The management of change is ever present. In this climate, the job of management, in the words of Peter Drucker, is 'never to be concerned with restoring or maintaining normality because normality is the condition of yesterday'. How credible is this statement in the context of leisure and recreation management?

5 'If it can't be measured, it can't be managed' is the well-known cliché. How true is it in terms of leisure management?

Further reading

Robinson, L. (2004), *Managing Public Sport and Leisure Services*, Routledge, London.

Useful websites

The Institute of Management Services: www.ims-productivity.com

British Institute of Facility Managers: www.bifm.org.uk

Institute of Leisure and Amenity Management (ILAM): www.ilam.co.uk

Institute of Sport and Recreation Management (ISRM): www.isrm.co.uk

19

Leadership and decision making

In this chapter

- Leadership versus management
- Leadership, vision, inspiration and direction
- Leadership styles
- Leadership behaviour models
- Deciding how to lead
- Team building
- Group behaviour in the leisure management setting
- Entrepreneurial and inspirational leadership
- Decision making
- Communication
- Coaching, mentoring and motivational leadership
- Delegation

Introduction

Good leadership in leisure management requires an understanding of the goals of the organization, its services, facilities, programmes and resources. It also requires understanding of the people involved: ourselves, colleagues, clients and customers. We also need to understand what motivates staff to do a good job, willingly. The handling of people and communications are probably the most important ingredients for harmony in management. Thus of the three core elements of skill needed by the manager – conceptual, human and technical – this chapter concentrates on the human factors.

Leadership versus management

Leadership cannot be separated from management, though management is not leadership *per se*. An unorganized group can have a leader, but managers only exist in an organized structure where specific roles have been created. Leadership is an important aspect of management: the ability to lead effectively is one of the factors that produces an effective manager. Leadership has been described as a mixture of art, craft and humanity. It is an essential part of a manager's job.

In *Not Bosses but Leaders*, Adair and Reed (2003) point to the need for leadership:

Management has the overtone of carrying out objectives laid down by someone else. Moreover, there is nothing in the concept of management which implies inspiration, creating teamwork when it isn't there, or setting an example. When it is the case that inspiration and teamwork exist, you may well have managers who are in effect leaders, especially if they are the source of the inspiration. But it is, I believe, unfortunately more often the case that management does not ring bells when it comes to people.

A good leader is concerned both with people and results. Leadership is a word with positive connotations. We look to leaders to inspire, direct and pave the way. In leisure management, there is a need for excellent leaders at all levels: policy makers, executives, middle-managers and operational personnel.

The Chinese philosopher Lao-tzu is reputed to have said: 'To lead the people, walk behind them.' The suggestion here is that not all leadership is waving a flag up at the front. Henry Miller, in *Wisdom of the Heart* (Miller, 1942), captures the same spirit: 'The real leader has no need to lead – he is content to point the way.' John Adair (Adair and Reed, 2003, p. 59) spotlights some of the distinctive features in the concept of leadership:

- direction (a way forwards which may be new objectives, markets, etc.)
- inspiration (kindling motivation and energy)
- building teams (transforming groups into teams which look for leaders not bosses) and
- example.

Effective leaders see the 'big picture' and long term goals, yet handle the smaller issues as needs demand.

Leadership, vision, inspiration and direction

Good leaders create a vision and define a strategy to get there; they provide:

- inspiration: communicating a clear vision and its underlining principles
- direction: pointing the way, setting objectives and eliminating uncertainty
- support: listening, encouraging, facilitating and involving others in problem-solving and decision making
- drive: giving motivation, inspiring confidence and building team cohesion
- leading by example
- communication and representation: to the outside world and from outside to the team.

Vision – the power to see far – should 'picture' where the organization is now, what direction it is travelling in, and where it is going. However, in leisure, success is often in the journey, not just in the destination.

But not everybody wants to be a leader. Moreover, some managers at all levels, including the top level, are poor leaders: they really need to be called 'administrators'.

As the biblical saying goes, 'If the blind lead the blind, both shall fall into the ditch'. A number of managers can be good at some functions of management, but may not be good leaders. Generally, however, in leisure, a highly visible 'profession', managers without good leadership qualities cannot be said to be good managers. As a leader, you are visible; incredibly visible.

One of the arts of leadership is to instil in staff the desire to want to do what the leader wants to do. Most people involved in leisure need very little motivation. Leisure directors, managers, supervisors, trainees, sports and arts teachers and coaches, countryside rangers, music directors, museum curators, play leaders, tourism managers and holiday activity organizers, in the main, are highly motivated to begin with. This gives leisure leaders a head start over salespeople selling used cars and double glazing.

Leadership is often thought of in terms of the qualities that a person has – one's personality – and effective leaders tend to possess certain qualities which are expected of them in their particular professions, businesses and organizations. In the leisure industry, the director of the arts would most likely exemplify enthusiasm and knowledge of some art form such as theatre, music, painting, etc.; a physical education teacher, an inspiring interest in physical activity and healthy lifestyles. But, as Adair points out, leadership is more than possessing the qualities required and respected in our way of life (Adair and Reed, 2003, p. 9). There are certain qualities that are the hallmarks of good leaders:

- integrity (trust is of central importance)
- enthusiasm
- warmth ('a cold fish does not usually make a good leader; a warm personality is infectious')
- calmness and
- toughness with fairness.

Another strong perception of leadership, handed down through the ages, is that of the generals leading the troops into battle. Whether it is a Winston Churchill, defending an island nation in war, or a Boudicca, assembling an undisciplined and ragged mob into an effective force to defeat the Romans, leadership is seen as an ability to galvanize support and commitment to a cause and to direct and lead from the front, handing orders down the chain of command. In much the same way, we talk about the leaders or 'captains' of industry, such as Henry Ford or a modern 'captain' of the leisure industry, such as Richard Branson.

Leadership, fortunately, covers far wider territories than leading from the front into battle, waving a flag and beating a drum. There are other facets to leadership. Sometimes, managerial leadership skills are from within the team or exercised so subtly that they are not always overtly discernible. We can see evidence of this with some conductors of an orchestra, directors of a theatre production, or with some captains in sport, who quietly get the best out of their players without shouting from the rooftops.

In earlier decades there appeared to be a clear demarcation between 'leaders' and 'followers', based on tradition, class and upbringing, which divided 'boss' and 'workers'. In business management the leader was portrayed as a person, normally male, who was endowed with initiative and the authority to lead men. The Military Academy of Sandhurst joke is of the commanding officer who says of one of his recruits: 'This young officer is not yet a born leader', illustrating a myth that has been perpetuated that leaders are born, not made. Certainly, some people are born with greater potential than others; fortunately, however, for most of us, leadership can be a learned skill.

In distinguishing leadership from other management functions, it has been suggested that most management functions can be taught, whereas leadership skills must be learned. We learn through doing. Leadership stems largely from a manager's personal dealings and personal influence over others. Leaders then need to inspire and communicate, support and direct.

In the management situation, leadership could be said to be 'people power': the powerhouse of most organizations. Leadership moves the organization along a chosen route towards its goals. Leadership provides the drive and the direction. Good leaders must also have the ability to inspire followers through the use of appeal and persuasion. Some inspirational leaders have taken on apparently hopeless causes and have succeeded through the strength of loyalty and devotion that they have been able to instil in their followers. The civil rights leader Martin Luther King, who gave the famous 'I have a dream' address, and won the Nobel Peace Prize in 1964, was an example of such a leader.

Leadership styles

There are several appropriate leadership styles. It is not always possible to define, precisely what good leadership is, but unlike good leadership, poor leadership exhibits a wide range of easily recognizable traits in a person: aloofness, insensitivity to others, intimidating manner, abrasiveness, overbearing, over-supervising, failing to delegate, seeking praise first instead of giving praise to colleagues, blaming, finding scapegoats, indecision and so on.

Yet, in given situations, highly autocratic leadership may be needed to achieve desired results, for example in the military. Clearly, there are different styles of leadership.

In *Leadership and the One Minute Manager* (Blanchard *et al.*, 1986), four styles are described: directing, coaching, supporting and delegating (see Figure 19.1). Different styles will be appropriate to different situations. The late Ted Blake (2003) used to say in circumstances, not of the military nature, 'if you are going to bark every time you stand up, people will soon fail to listen'. This raises the question of how a manager can be 'democratic' in dealings with subordinates and yet maintain the necessary authority and control. Over the past few decades, social scientists have developed the concept of group dynamics, which reveal the importance of employee involvement and participation in decision making.

Democratic leadership began to be thought of as solutions coming from the ground floor and autocratic leadership attributed to the boss who makes most decisions himself or herself. Generalizations, lacking research evidence, spoke in simplistic terms of leadership being either 'democratic' or 'autocratic', and even more misleading, these terms became for some, synonymous with 'right' and 'wrong' styles of leadership and, for others, 'strong' leadership and 'permissive' leadership. In this context, a leader should not be confused with the role of the 'head', who is imposed upon a group or organization from above.

The notion of styles of leadership, particularly simplistic styles like autocratic, authoritarian, democratic, *laissez-faire*, has led to misunderstandings about leadership. Adair (Adair

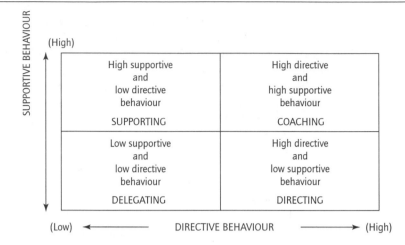

Figure 19.1 Leadership styles

and Reed, 2003, p. 45) suggests that terms such as autocratic and democratic are political in origin. 'They have limited currency in the world of work.' It is unhelpful and could be dangerous to suggest that one style is more correct or appropriate for all situations,

> simply because there has been a general shift over the past fifty years from control and direction to the idea that modern or new leaders should be coach, mentor, teacher, and 'stewards of the vision'. The required skill is more one of being able to use behaviour appropriate to the urgency, technical complexity or difficulty of the prevailing situation.

Style is nonetheless significant, but more a matter of personality, temperament, attitudes and values; it is a personal way in which a person leads, 'It's like your style of handwriting. Although there are recognizable styles – copperplate or italic, for example – most of us develop our own style of writing. The issue is really whether it is effective or not.'

In answer to the question: 'what is leadership?', there appear to be three main schools of thought.

- Leadership is a matter of personal traits, such as initiative, courage, charisma and intelligence. These traits must be possessed by individuals and then they are able to lead in most situations.
- Who becomes the leader of a group, and what the leadership characteristics are in the given case, are a function of the specific situation but one person emerges as the leader.
- Leadership is a function. Any or all of the members of the group may perform, at various times, specific leadership acts or functions which are necessary if the group's objectives are to be realized. The latter two views of leadership appear to have greater credence; however, all three views are relevant in given situations.

In informal groups, particularly in voluntary sector leisure management, the emergence of a leader is needed to move the business along and to satisfy the needs of the group. A leader is needed as a focal point for concerted action, as often many groups are pulling in different directions. In these groups, representation, the voice of the organization, is also of importance. With special tasks of leadership, such as in running an event or the maintenance of premises, certain people will emerge as leaders. Different leaders for different situations is a concept worth pursuing in all diverse organizations and of value to leisure management with its wide areas of activity, depth of people's interests and abilities and range of facilities and activities.

Leadership behaviour models

There are many leadership models. First, we look at the classic leadership continuum, then, as examples in the range of systems, two other models: a managerial grid and the Five 'C' Model.

Continuum of leadership and decision making Robert Tannenbaum and Warren H. Schmidt (1958) studied the range of behaviour adopted by leaders and presented a continuum or range of possible leadership behaviour available to a manager. In their model (Figure 19.2) each type of action is related to the degree of authority used by the manager and to the amount of freedom available to the subordinates in reaching decisions. Actions on the extreme left characterize the manager who maintains a high degree of control, while those on the extreme right characterize the manager who releases a high degree of control.

The continuum demonstrates that there are a number of ways in which a manager can relate to the group. However, there are implications. First, in any given situation, the manager must expect to be held responsible for the quality of the decisions made, even though operationally they may have been made on a group basis. Second, delegation is not a way of 'passing the buck'. Third, it is important for the group to recognize what kind of leadership is being adopted. For example, if the manager has already decided what to do and wishes to inform them, then he/she should do so; to adopt a façade of involving the group in the decision-making process would be counterproductive, and lead to antagonism and frustration. Fourth, the democratic manager is not one who gives his or her subordinates the most decisions to make. That may be

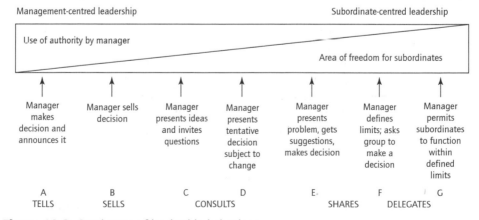

Figure 19.2 Continuum of leadership behaviour

391

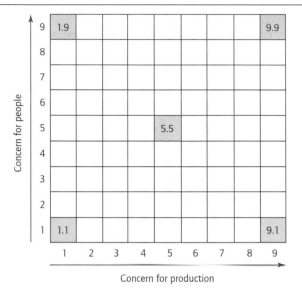

Figure 19.3 Concept of the managerial grid

entirely inappropriate. There may be other more important priorities for them. The quality of involvement and decision making is important. Involvement only in low levels of decision making may simply prove to be patronizing to some members of staff.

The managerial grid Another theory suggests that managers combine two styles simultaneously, but in differing proportions. One style is job- or task-centred. The other style is employee-centred. The managerial grid developed by Blake and Mouton (1981) plots the two dimensions on a chart on scales 1 to 9 (Figure 19.3). The vertical axis represents increasing concern for people, and the horizontal axis, an increasing concern for production.

A manager rated at 1.1 is wholly ineffective. A manager at 1.9 has great concern for people, but is ineffective in achieving the task. A manager at 9.1 is task-driven with little concern for people. Managers at the midpoints (5.5) show balance. The ideal is 9.9, high regard for people, combined with optimum focus on results.

Five 'C' Model James Weese (1996) developed what he calls the Five 'C' Model of Leadership. His synthesis of leadership identifies 'trait', 'behavioural' and 'situational' theories: personal traits and characteristics separating leaders from others; behaviour measuring the leader's orientation to the task and to the relationships with subordinates; and situational theories where time, place and circumstance had been overlooked in the trait and behavioural theories.

The work of several academics underpinned Weese's model, in particular Bernard Bass (1985; 1990) who identified four characteristics of 'transformational' leaders:

- 'individualized consideration' (for each person's situation and genuine concern for staff)

- 'intellectual stimulation' (appealing to the intellectual capacities of followers and challenging them)
- 'inspirational motivation' (charismatically inspiring ownership) and
- 'idealized influence' (showing respect and influencing by example).

Warren Bennis uses the term 'visionary leadership' rather than 'transformational leadership'.

The Five 'C' Model incorporates:

C1 credible character: leaders must have the respect of those they lead and be perceived as trustworthy and reliable

C2 compelling vision: followers need to believe in the leader and in the vision and know that they are doing a worthwhile job and their efforts are appreciated; these leaders provide support and extend the horizons of their followers

C3 charismatic communicator: charisma is linked to communication, emphasizing effective speech patterns and non-verbal actions which heighten a leader's standing in the eyes of followers

C4 contagious enthusiasm: leaders excite and inspire others to go above and beyond the call of duty; they challenge intellectually and emotionally

C5 culture builder: beliefs, values and attitudes shape and help interpret the behaviour of a group or organization.

Deciding how to lead

A leader's style should be flexible enough to change to suit the situation. Leaders have to balance the big picture – the vision – with the details. What they find is that little things matter: sensitivity, care, attention to detail. A false assumption is made that one is either an autocratic, a democratic or 'free-rein' leader. Most leaders tend to use many styles but with a leaning towards one. Much will depend on the circumstances. In emergencies and critical situations – swimming pool safety or problems in opening a major event on time – authoritative, autocratic leadership is eminently suitable. The authoritarian style can also be very effective when toughness is needed under certain conditions, even at some personal emotional cost to the leader. Leadership is not an easy option. It requires commitment. As one guru said: 'Leadership is a foul-weather job.' There is another American saying that 'nice guys don't win ball games' and there is a germ of truth in this, in tough situations. However, in longer-term organizational situations where leadership is an ongoing 'craft', and where the manager is working with and through other staff, then there are four major factors which help to determine the style of leadership which is most appropriate: the characteristics of the manager, the ability of subordinates, the type of organization and the nature of the problem.

The leader-manager The manager's behaviour occurs as a result of his or her attitude, belief, personality, knowledge, ability and experience. Among the significant internal forces are the leader's value system and the trust and confidence shown in the subordinates. External forces are also exerted upon the leader, and in order to retain the confidence and allegiance of his or her staff, the leader has to be aware and accepting of the norms and rules of the 'group'.

393

The subordinates Assistant managers and staff will have expectations of the manager. Each member of staff has his or her own personality and ability factors: the better the manager understands these forces within the group, the better he or she can determine the role to play in achieving the best for subordinates and the organization. Generally speaking, under the leadership continuum, the manager can permit subordinates greater freedom if the following conditions exist:

- assistant staff have high needs for independence
- there is a readiness to assume responsibility
- they prefer a wide area of freedom rather than simply clear-cut directives
- they have considerable interest in the problem and feel it is of importance
- they appreciate the goals of the organization
- they have sufficient knowledge
- they have been 'educated' to expect to share in decision making
- there is a climate of mutual confidence and respect.

The organization Management situations vary enormously. Much will depend on the organization itself, its aims and objectives and the efficiency of the group in given situations.

Organizations such as a local government district council will have traditional roles, procedures and kinds of behaviour which are approved of and other kinds which are not. Its leisure services department may have dispersed sections and sites which preclude effective participatory decision making. In contrast, a commercial leisure club manager may have to decide prices and controls yet meet tight financial external targets.

The nature of the problem The most important consideration is the problem itself, which will determine the kind of leadership style to be adopted. The problem may need specialist information only available from, say, the librarian or museum curator, or be of a complex nature involving many disciplines: sports, parks maintenance and school physical education. The manager will need to be sure all the necessary – essential – knowledge is acquired within a given time. The pressure of time is often said to be the biggest headache, even though such pressures are often self-imposed. With crisis decisions, a high degree of autocracy is needed. When time pressure is less intense, it becomes easier to bring others into a situation where group dynamics – skilfully handled – will become one of the tools to good management.

Day-to-day housekeeping in the leisure field, such as the maintenance of the buildings and grounds, duty rosters, the regular programme, the handling of stock and the accounting for cash from entry systems, will be more routine and administrative. An organizational, well-established pattern is likely to have been set and leadership choices will, therefore, be limited; changes, short term, are inappropriate. However, long-term decision, strategies and solutions to new long-range problems give opportunity to involve others in achieving goals more effectively. For example, a leisure centre's programme and system may have been fixed for the coming twelve months, but a survey has indicated that only 25 per cent utilization is being made by females and that the daytime use by shift workers, the unemployed and the retired is negligible. The manager, anxious to increase the proportions of these customers to meet the aims of the organization, should confer with the assistant managers, initially, and discuss with them the scope of the problem, the constraints to time and money and the need to acquaint and involve the staff and user groups with the problem and the opportunities.

It is in the strategy and the tactics of handling the problem where the manager's leadership skills are put to the test: can he or she raise the level of employee motivation? Can staff and key user groups be persuaded to accept change readily? Can the quality and effectiveness of managerial decisions be improved? Can teamwork, morale and staff development be enhanced along with increased levels of satisfactions for the clients and customers?

Team building

While leisure managers should be leaders, leaders are not necessarily organizational managers. Leadership is needed at all levels. Leadership should not depend on positions in the hierarchy of the organization. Leisure leaders are often community workers, youth leaders, playworkers, sports coaches, department representatives: those who are responsible for the essential face-to-face work. The leader is usually employed to get a job accomplished working through a group of people. The leader should:

- achieve the task
- develop the individuals in the team and
- maintain and motivate the team.

There are many kinds of teams: formal and informal, structured and loosely controlled, each best suited to carrying out and completing certain functions and tasks. Formal 'teams' are fundamental to most leisure organizations usually under the headings of sections or departments, for example, Buildings, Grounds Maintenance, Catering and Bar, Sports Development. They are often permanent, have defined remits and routine procedures and duties. There are also structured teams for one-off or special tasks, such as organizing a major event. In addition, there are informal teams or groupings formed on an *ad hoc* basis to, for example, 'brainstorm' creative programming or inter-group personnel groupings.

The more formal the group, the more disciplined the leadership tends to be, with organization regulations and procedures adhered to. These teams tend to meet on a regular basis and record the results of their meetings formally. Although informal teams are less structured, leadership must be results-orientated to be effective and not a 'talking shop'.

Effective leadership in leisure management has much to do with team building. A lighter weight tug-of-war team, trained and well led, can beat heavyweight teams who lack the knack of working together. The precision team works in concert and pulls only when it has to. The leader directs operations like the conductor of an orchestra.

Good team leaders are likely to exhibit the following traits:

1 enthusiastically accept responsibility for leading the team
2 accept responsibility for achieving objectives
3 ensure that each team member knows his or her job and what is expected of him/her
4 ensure that the team understands and accepts its role in achieving objectives

5 have concern for individual welfare and the inner goals of members of the team and will face up to individual problems at the earliest opportunity

6 listen to members of the team and understand both the overt and underlying messages being given

7 be open with the team, showing loyalty to them and to the organization

8 instil confidence into the team and the individuals within it; highly motivated staff can put up with a good deal of upheaval, show resilience and come through crises more quickly than less motivated staff

9 have a job training plan for each person, each job and for the team

10 walk the job every day; in this way, leaders are less remote, they are close to the team and, hence, close to customers; they show they care.

Teams fashioned in these ways are more likely to be both efficient and effective, both functionally and psychologically. Moreover, they will exude the essential feature of successful teamwork: trust. Mutual trust can be promoted through openly sharing information, successes and failures, and through the delegation of tasks with authority to carry them out. All teams need good coaches, an area we turn to later in this chapter.

Adair, addressing the hallmarks of leadership, states that effective leadership has an end-product: the high-performance team which exhibits the following characteristics:

- clear realistic objectives
- shared sense of purpose
- best use of resources
- atmosphere of openness
- reviews progress
- builds on experience
- rides the storm.

A distinction needs to be made between the Manager as the Leader and leaders of discrete teams within the organization. Heller (1998), in *Managing Teams*, offers the advice:

> A leader must always be aware of the ultimate goals of the organization, and know how their own objectives fit in with them. Once these goals have been established, you must ensure that your team understands the direction in which they are heading and why, and the purpose of their own activities within the overall plan. The ultimate objective should be broken down into attainable, yet challenging goals that ideally will be inspiring and motivating for the whole team. Aims should also relate directly to the specific skills of each individual within the team. Working together towards a shared goal gives people a sense of ownership and responsibility, and builds an atmosphere of team spirit.

> All successful teams demonstrate the same fundamental features, strong and effective leadership; the establishment of precise objectives; making informed decisions; the ability to act quickly upon these decisions; communicating freely; mastering the requisite skills and techniques to fulfil the project in hand; providing clear targets for the team to work towards; and – above all – finding the right balance of people prepared to work together for the common good of the team.

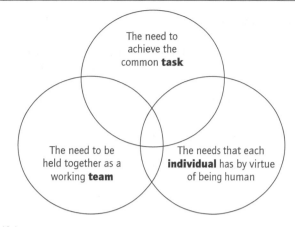

Figure 19.4 Unifying a team

Meredith Belbin (1981) identified nine team roles: problem-solver, resourcer, co-ordinator, shaper, evaluator, team worker, implementer, finisher and specialist. He found the teams that are likely to perform best are the ones that have the best blend of team members with these traits and abilities to play off against each other. The team is built up on the strengths we bring to the collective. No individual is perfect, but by putting together and developing different, yet competent, people, you can build the perfect team for the right job.

People, unlike machines, are flexible, and leisure management calls for stepping into other roles when the need arises. Then staff look upon it as 'our job'. When flexibility is needed, the team can stretch. (Bamboo scaffolding around Hong Kong tower blocks bends with typhoons; the rigid metal poles cannot cope when the pressure is on.)

Heller, in similar vein, suggests that for a team to function most effectively, there are key roles that should be filled, including co-ordinator, ideas person, critic, external contact, implementer, team leader and inspector. It is vital that all members of a team work together to maximize team performance. Each member should be able to cover the role of at least one other member; members should be given responsibility to act on their own initiative within a team, but a large task will be better handled by the whole team being responsible for the entire project. Along similar lines to Adair, Heller places emphasis on unifying a team. He suggests that most teams place too much focus on the task and not enough on the individual. His model, shown in Figure 19.4, illustrates an 'ideal situation in which the needs of the individual, the dynamics of the group, and the requirements of the task coincide at four strategic points to produce a unified, effective working team' (Heller, 1998, p. 16–17).

Group behaviour in the leisure management setting

In business, including the management of leisure programmes and services, it is likely that the important decisions are taken in consultation with others. Managers must therefore develop skills in understanding the behaviour processes at work. Some behaviour assists in this work, and some behaviour hinders progress. What types of behaviour are relevant to the group's cohesion, collective resources and strengths?

What types of behaviour detract from group cohesion and are self-orientated rather than group and/or task-orientated?

Two main types of group can be classified as primary and secondary. Primary groups are made up of a relatively small number of people in a common task. Secondary groups are made up of a larger number and no one member has a clear picture of all the others. These groups can be further classified by their development; formal groups are those deliberately created, and informal groups are created by accident.

Primary groups are made up of individuals engaged in a common task who have regular face-to-face contact with one another, such as the family, the playgroup, the parent-and-toddler group, the work group, the club, the church and the youth group. The primary group is the setting through which individuals acquire many of their attitudes, opinions and ideals and one of the sources of control and discipline. The primary group can be one of the main satisfiers of an individual's need for status and emotional security. In the leisure context, the role of club leader, the society secretary and the sports coach fulfil status and emotional needs.

Primary groups tend to 'appoint' or have a natural leader. Generally speaking, the more harmonious the group becomes, the more efficient will be its performance in most respects. The experience of team spirit, of belonging and sharing defeats and successes, make for extremely strong bonds. Disharmonious groups tend to be less effective. Leisure Managers dealing with groups need to understand primary and secondary group behaviour and respect their standards, traditions and collective needs. Harmonious groups working together, helping the newcomer and maintaining good relationships, are the groups likely to aid, not inhibit, the fulfilment of managerial goals.

As illustrated in Adair's model, working in teams requires the getting together or fusion of three things:

- achieving the task
- good relationships within the team and
- consideration of the needs of the individual.

The modes of behaviour within groups have been termed task-orientated, maintenance-orientated and self-orientated. Both 'task' and 'maintenance' of the team are important in varying situations, depending on the objectives of management, whereas the behaviour within self-interested and self-orientated groups hinders or obstructs the achievement of common goals. This behaviour can arise, for example, because individuals may be faced with problems of identity, and personal goals and needs, rather than the group goals and needs. These undercurrents should not be ignored; they should be recognized and attempts made to integrate the individual needs with the group's goals.

As a guide, Argyris and others (Argyris, 1966; 1976) have put forward ten criteria, based on empirical research, that they see as necessary for group competence and effectiveness.

1   Contributions made within the group are additive.
2   The group moves forwards as a unit, is team-spirited and there is high involvement.
3   Decisions are mainly made by consensus.
4   Commitment to a decision is strong.

5   The group continually evaluates itself.
6   The group is clear about goals.
7   It generates alternative ways of thinking about things.
8   It brings conflict into the open and deals with it.
9   It deals openly with feelings.
10 Leadership tends to go (or move) to the person most qualified.

Leaders have to deal with conflict and co-operation within and between groups. Conflict is not in itself undesirable; only through expression of differences can good problem solving take place. For everyone to agree is as unrealistic as expecting that no agreement is possible. But conflict so severe as to disable the participants and prevent the continuation of problem solving is undesirable and unacceptable.

What happens when two (or more) groups are faced with a problem of some kind involving their interest? The problem may be unsatisfactorily 'solved' by maintaining isolation between the groups, or by enforcing unification of the two groups, or by allowing one group to take over or destroy the other. The more the inter-group situation is defined as win-or-lose, the more likely we are to see certain effects leading to confrontation. However, the more it is defined as problem solving, and win–win, the less likely the adverse effects. Win-or-lose situations often result in the winning group becoming 'fat and happy', but less effective, and the losing group becoming 'lean and hungry', re-grouping, re-organizing and becoming fitter for future 'battles'. How can these negative effects be reduced? The answer is to find an overriding goal – one which both (or all) groups accept as essential to reach and which all can reach – thus both groups win, and can be satisfied with their achievement. In recent years, the use of groups such as Quality Circles has become an accepted procedure for problem solving within an organization. In this way, a group that has a range of abilities and knowledge is more likely to identify all the possible options available, provided that the group environment is receptive to suggestions from all its members and that the size of the group is manageable.

Entrepreneurial and inspirational leadership

Entrepreneurial leadership, usually seen as a domain of the private sector, is gaining momentum in the public sector as never before, in part due to success experienced in the private sector and the policy requiring local authorities to optimize income and decrease net expenditure. Commercial managers primarily have to be accountable for financial performance – or go out of business – and hence use entrepreneurial skills to increase income. This form of leadership was almost diametrically opposed to operating in government agencies which relied on the system, rather than the managers and staff, to provide services. The current climate in leisure management calls for entrepreneurial, creative managers who are prepared, within budgets, to be bold and take action and lead, rather than simply react to what happens.

Leisure professionals and managers must be able to 'teach' and inculcate the skills of leadership to assistant managers, supervisors and community leaders. They will need to learn to accept responsibility for leading their teams, have loyalty to the organization and to the team, ensure that each team member knows his or her job, face up to individual and situational problems and 'walk the job' every day. The results of good leadership then permeate throughout the organization. This ethos is much easier to inculcate through a sense of 'mission' and vision from the top. Hence leisure managers need more than entrepreneurial skills. They need vision and the maturity to delegate leadership responsibilities to the young as well as to the experienced staff. One of the most successful captains of England's Rugby Union teams was the youngest in the side of fifteen players, when he was given the captaincy.

Visionary leaders have principles and values. Their principles of personal leadership stem from inner convictions. These convictions, enthusiastically projected, influence others positively. The ability comes from the personal vision that is large and clear enough to be shared. Harry Alder in *The Right Brain Manager* (1993) believes that such a person is a leader, not because he or she leads, but because people tend to follow. And, as Henry Mintzberg suggests, the processes 'seem to be more relational and holistic than ordered and sequential, and more intuitive than intellectual'. In *On Becoming a Leader* (Bennis, 1989) Warren Bennis's ingredients for a leader today include a guiding vision, passion, integrity, trust and curiosity and daring.

'What lies behind us and what lies before us are tiny matters compared to what lies within us' (Oliver Wendell Holmes).

In *Please Don't Just Do What I Tell You! Do What Needs to be Done* Nelson (undated) introduces what he calls 'The Ultimate Expectation':

You never need permission to do great work. Wherever you work, whomever you work for, management expects that you will *always* use your own best judgement and effort to do what needs to be done for the organization to be successful. I call this The Ultimate Expectation. It's a message that every employee needs to hear, but one that few employers explicitly state.

In this vision of effective management, staff take the initiative to do the right things without being asked. Such a work colleague can be dropped into a work situation and take independent action. Leisure Management, with its range of services and programmes, needs among its employees those members of staff who can easily work in others' shoes, from receptionist to 'front of house', from supervisor to duty manager.

Servant leadership

For people to benefit from leisure, other people, paid and voluntary, have to give service. The concept of the 'servant-leader' – caring leadership – fits well into many aspects of the profession of Leisure Management. The founder of what has today become a movement in leadership circles in the USA is Robert Greenleaf. The servant-leader is servant first: he or she has the desire to serve; the servant-leader also has the aspiration to lead. It is based on the needs of people. The object is that the service given to them enables them to grow into healthier, wiser and more fulfilled people and contributing citizens.

There is a revolution underway. In corporate boardrooms, university classes, community leadership groups, not-for-profit organizations and elsewhere, change is occurring around the ways in which we, as a society, approach the subject of work and leadership. Many people are seeking new and better ways of integrating work with their own personal and spiritual growth. They are seeking to combine the best elements of leadership based upon service to others, as part of an exciting concept called 'servant-leadership'. It has been, to be sure, a slow-growing revolution – but one which is now sending deep roots throughout society.

Spears, 1994

A great deal depends on what we want to accomplish. As Stephen Covey (1992) says: 'Begin with the end in mind.' Adair in *Not Bosses But Leaders* (2003) has a similar brief chapter entitled 'Humility': leadership as a form of service. 'Humility comes from "humus", the earth. Humility means being on ground level with others.' Adair uses the strapline: 'the task of leadership is not to put greatness into humanity, but to elicit it, for the greatness is already there.'

In summary, the manager must be a successful leader in order to be effective. The manager must understand himself or herself and the staff and the customers. The manager recognizes that a high degree of subordinate-centred behaviour in helping to run an organization raises employee teamwork and morale. But this does not mean that a manager leaves all decisions to the staff. Situations vary and staff vary. Staff readiness and ability are important. The successful leader will behave appropriately in the light of his or her perceptions of the people and the situations, and cannot therefore be categorized as 'strong' or 'permissive'. He or she must have the insight and ability to act appropriately, remaining firm on cardinal principles, yet being flexible to permit degrees of freedom to the greatest advantage. In addition to leading personally, the manager must recognize that many subordinates fill important leadership roles themselves. They too need training in the 'art' of effective leadership. Leadership may result in the successful completion of a task, but effective leadership occurs when the team of staff not only complete the task, but also do so willingly and find its accomplishment rewarding.

Good leadership is required for effective management. It is concerned with both results and relationships. Good management is largely the result of good managers. They are individuals who have the responsibility for providing leadership of the organization and the ability to move it towards its goals.

One of the most important areas of work for leaders and managers is that of decision making.

Decision making

One key function of management is decision making and a significant proportion of a manager's time is spent in handling situations and making decisions. Decision makers are people responsible for making judgements between alternatives or choices. How decisions are made is of importance. Hence, the process of decision-making, as well as the content of the decision, is important for success. The manager and his or her group, or groups, should have an awareness of alternative decision making procedures and processes.

Management has moved, and continues to move, from an intuitive 'art' with its 'rule-of-thumb' approach, to decision making on a more scientific or reasoned basis. Science, however, is not solely the science of economics, physics or mathematics, but the sciences of people: the psychological processes which affect decision making.

Traditionally, decision making has been seen as being undertaken by only those 'at the top'. This has been shown to be wholly undesirable and inadequate. Decisions should be made at all levels of management. Robert Townsend, in *Up the Organization* (1970), goes further still: 'All decisions should be made as low as possible in the organization. The Charge of the Light Brigade was ordered by an officer who wasn't there looking at the territory.'

Types of decision

There are three main types of decision identified by Video Arts, namely emergency decisions, routine decisions and debatable decisions. Heller's (1998) categories are similar and include decisions which are routine, emergency, strategic and operational and the most demanding form of decision making involves strategic choices, for example, deciding on aims and objectives and converting these into specific plans.

Emergency decisions are needed under crisis. They require clear, quick and precise actions, for example, to evacuate the building given a security alert, to break up a fight at the discothèque or to make the call for ambulance, fire service or police.

Routine decisions revolve around the everyday running of an organization. Changes to the duty supervisor rota, the change of menu, or giving the blessing for additional staff for the forthcoming major events, are all within an organization's policy framework. Many of these routine decisions simply require a Yes or No to maintain the status quo and staff are delegated to make such decisions.

Debatable decisions are debatable because they change the status quo. They mean changes for people and their work. They are debatable because the chances are that they will be improved through consultations, given effective leadership. They are debatable, too, because there may be a number of different ways of handling the particular situation.

A leisure manager's operational decisions, especially those concerned with staff, clients and customers – the human problems – need sensitive handling, particularly those involving change, such as staff change of duties and different programme times for clients and member groups.

While routine problems and decisions can be delegated by managers to other staff, long-term problems or changes, such as new programming initiatives, ways of substantially increasing income or reducing expenditure, call for skills in developing a strategy, building staff morale and cohesion and solving the problem with commitment by all. It is these debatable decisions which should occupy a manager's time more than others. It is these decisions which generally lead to harmony or disharmony; it is these decisions with which the following section is concerned.

Debatable decisions usually involve a series of other decisions. The decision to extend or reduce a leisure programme, for example, will involve decisions on timing, resources, implications on staff and clients and more. Concerning timing, does the decision have to be made now or later; is there a deadline? Heller advises that if decisions can be taken quickly, then usually, the sooner the better. Never postpone vital decisions. However, common sense reminds us not to make important decisions when under extreme pressures; a little time of calm reflection may be needed.

Involving others, discussing problems and sharing decisions with colleagues – seeking consensus – is the most effective way of arriving at non-routine decisions.

The decision-making process

We often make decisions intuitively. After all, we are managers paid to make them. However, effective decision makers tend not to allow their personality to dominate. There is a need to balance hunches with logical analysis.

> One side of the brain is believed to be the location of emotion, imagination, intuition, and creativity; the other is the site of logic, language, maths, and analysis. Though people tend to have a dominant side, this does not mean that decision-makers fall into two separate categories: the intuitive decision-maker deciding creatively and spontaneously, versus the logical decision-maker working rationally on fact-based judgement.
>
> Whichever side your natural decision-making style leans towards, always aim to achieve a balance between both sets of faculties ... Whatever your decision-making style, there are advantages in being systematic. Systematic methods of reaching a decision ensure that all the correct issues are addressed: necessary information is gathered, all alternatives are properly considered and compared, difficulties are identified and feasibility assessed, and consequences are taken fully into account. A systematic approach enables you to prepare a logical and effective plan of action so that your decision process can be explained clearly to any colleagues or clients who are affected.
>
> Heller, 1998. p. 10

Balancing hunches with logic is, however, but one part of the process. Much will depend on the decision-making environment. Leisure Managers operate in different cultures: public, voluntary trust, private club, large commercial enterprise. The organization culture affects the options available to the manager. A local authority leisure manager will need to conform to local government systems of bureaucracy; radical decisions may need to be curtailed. A plea of a local council chair in the party's promotional material reads: 'Every decision requires communication, planning, tact, negotiation, compromise, and sensitivity to the mood of the debate. Next time you see a council committee chair, offer them a pitying smile and an aspirin!'

Decision making of a complex nature can be perceived as having phases: causes, potential decision options, their consequences, evaluation and making a choice. The technique of perceiving decision making in this way helps to highlight the need for information and factual data and the relevance of it to the problem. It helps to analyse logically and so assist in effective decision making. Decision making is therefore a process which can be divided into a number of stages. A variety of texts suggest a different number of stages, though much the same logic is apparent. For the purposes of this chapter, nine simple stages are identified.

1 Defining the problem Defining the problem is so obvious that it is often overlooked. It can be one of the hardest things to do (as many students writing theses will testify), but having defined the specific problem, we are a long way forward in finding solutions. We have to be clear; what is the real situation: the symptoms must not be confused with the problem itself. What is the decision supposed to achieve?

2 Gathering and examining information and identifying possible causes What facts and information are needed? When are they needed by? What are the constraints and limiting factors? Are there cash limits, time pressures or staff shortages? Only valid and useful information should be used.

3 Consulting with people and considering their views Others may think of ideas which you have not thought of. The Leisure Manager needs to identify who will be affected by the decision and to discuss with the group the facts and their implications.

4 Considering choices or alternatives Consider all possible courses of action. A brainstorming session would help, in this respect, for we often stumble on important ways of achieving results by keeping our minds open to all the possibilities.

5 Considering the implications The implications of certain decisions may solve the problem but cause even greater problems. Compare different solutions. One may work in the short term, but not in the long term or vice versa. Major decisions often involve risk; changes could have negative results. Managers should consider the outcomes, the knock-on effects. Recently a leisure organization was advised by financial advisers that having fewer staff would make for financial savings. The organization decided, however, to keep staff, take steps to provide an even better service and 'live' with the expenditure. The decision boosted morale, increased income and cut deficits. The staff had been treated not as an accountant's cost, but as an organization's asset.

6 Making the decision and deciding a course of action The decision should be clear and unambiguous, and needs to be taken at the right time. Thinking and planning ahead, however, are not substitutes for getting things done. We have all witnessed committees putting off making decisions for want of more information. But when do we know we have all the facts? A well-known cliché is 'paralysis by analysis' to describe decision-making procrastination; it was often used by management trainer, Ted Blake (2003). A project in London's docklands took so long in debating political issues and planning, without decisions being taken at the right time, that huge accounting and legal costs were incurred so that as a result, the project could not be afforded.

7 Communicating the decision In communicating the decision, the manager must be prepared to persuade people of its 'rightness'. This is made all the easier if staff (and clients) have been involved in the decision-making process or if the decision has been made by the representative group. Communicating decisions must be undertaken sensitively. For example, receptionists at leisure centres, often working part-time at unsocial hours, are rarely part of the decision-making team; they should not have to learn about forthcoming events from the local newspapers or through the grapevine.

Communicating the decision needs care, timing, sensitivity and, above all, the reasons why the decision has been made. Some leisure managers are careful to inform the staff of the reasons but fail to tell the customers why. How often have we seen 'No entry' and 'Cafeteria closed'? And it is not just in the public sector. Parents who were members of a private health club in Essex arrived with their children to use the pool in half term to be met with a notice 'Our sincere regrets, but the club is closed today.'

As a board member of an international organization, I found that decisions were taken by the core group, but not widely circulated, giving the false impression of secrecy and creating misunderstanding. Organizations are often reluctant to give out too much information; while this may be understandable, too little or no information, is worse still:

> When communicating a decision, lean towards releasing rather than suppressing information – and towards telling everybody involved, not just a chosen few. In traditional hierarchies, decisions are often reached behind closed doors, with the result that rumours may abound. This creates anxiety and uncertainty, and lowers morale. Sometimes, it may be necessary to keep good news under wraps, perhaps for reasons of security, but delaying bad news, understandable though it is, is always counterproductive.
>
> Heller, 1998, p. 55

People tend to be more understanding and co-operative when they know why, and more so when they have been consulted. In communicating decisions, true sincerity and enthusiasm are important. You generate enthusiasm in others only if you give decisions and reasons with conviction. How it is done is important. When briefing the staff team, it is often best to undertake it collectively in order to show an open and frank situation and avoid the grapevine, contrived gossip and the subsequent miscommunications and misunderstandings.

Managers often hide behind memos or emails in communicating decisions. They feel, in this way, that everybody knows, because the written word is clear. However, the written word is sometimes most unclear. It is conceived differently by different people; hidden messages might be imagined; and there may be an air of mistrust. Communication is a two-way process: 'no one can ask questions of the memo'. When preparing the brief – spoken first, then written – the manager needs to envisage how people will feel on the receiving end of the decision. Managers have to place themselves in the position of the receiver, into the shoes of the other person.

8 Implementing and following up the decision This requires briefing people together, whenever possible, being ready and willing to sell the decision with enthusiasm and belief and then confirming the decision in writing. Many 'debatable' decisions need a framework on which an evaluation can be made, such as timing, targets and implementation. It is important that the manager monitors progress and that new problems are alleviated, particularly where people's feelings are concerned.

9 Evaluation, feedback and modification Most debatable decisions need time to see whether they have been successful or unsuccessful, and to what extent. Even the best preparation may result in the wrong decision being made. Hindsight is a luxury we do not have in decision making. Once proof of its 'wrongness' is substantiated, managers need the courage to admit the fact and try again.

Having considered just one form of communication, in decision making, we now turn to a fuller consideration of communication in the wider management process.

Communication

The novelist George Eliot wrote: 'The people of the world are islands shouting at each other across a sea of misunderstanding.' Good communication is essential for the internal functioning of an organization, enabling co-ordination of its managerial functions and a focus on common objectives. A leisure manager must also communicate with external organizations – clients, customers, the community, government agencies and so on.

Communicating is far more important than just transmitting a message. The way it is done can affect the attitudes and performance of staff and the relationship with customers. The purpose of communication is to ensure that whoever receives the message understands what is in the mind of the sender; what is obvious to the sender may be obscure to the receiver. One-way communication is fraught with such difficulties: it is impossible to know if your message is getting through. Many problems of management, in industry and in leisure services, stem from the misunderstanding, misconception, mistrust and underlying feelings of not being put clearly in the picture which arise from one-way communications. One-way messaging is quick and satisfying for the sender, but often frustrating for the receiver and it can lead to misunderstanding. Mobile texting, emails, fax and answerphone communications can carry with them perceived underlying messages. Managers must beware the dangers and use 'one-way' only for emergencies and when autocratic communication is essential. If the goals of communication are to be understood by others, to get clear reception or perception, to get understanding, to get acceptance in order to get effective action, then two-way communication is essential.

Staff should, therefore, be trained to handle work through greater levels of two-way communication for more effective achievement of the task and greater harmony within the team. While two-way communication takes longer and may be frustrating for the sender, it is essentially more sensitive and more accurate. To communicate, we must understand others. Each one of us is different from everyone else. We are different psychologically; we vary in intelligence, education, political and religious beliefs, social background and experience. These experiences create different frames of reference with the result that people look at the world around them in a particular and unique way. Our physical and mental make-up and our environment have a direct effect on our perception and judgement. All too often, when interpreting information, we see or hear what we are taught 'ought' to be there and/or what we want to see or hear. Thus there are barriers to communication in ourselves, and these barriers also exist in our subordinates, our peers and our bosses.

The late Ted Blake (2003) taught that effective communication needs to be built upon an understanding of people. Ted's analysis was:

> Every person is like ...
> All other people
> Some other people
> No other person
> Identifying in which respect helps Communication.

He was a great communicator. His slogan was A.I.D.A.: gain Attention, hold Interest, and stimulate a Desire to instigate an Action. He said:

> Communication is the initiation, transmission and sharing of information, meanings, understandings, conclusions, decisions and responses. It is never the message sent out that counts – only the message received. By definition, all effective communication has to be self-serving, to produce for the communicator a specific outcome or effect. The purpose, i.e. the why of communication, is to contact, measure, maintain, or change, i.e. to influence others.

The argument for two-way communication is not only a moral one, it is also a practical one because the manager will become more effective by encouraging the group members to make full use of their abilities. Peter Drucker put the argument against the purely persuasive approach to communication in the following way:

> In many cases human relations has been used to manipulate, to adjust people to what the boss thinks is reality; to make them conform to a pattern that seems logical from the top down, to make them accept unquestionably what we tell them. Frankly, sometimes, I think it is better not to tell employees anything rather than to say 'We tell them everything, but they must accept it, and it is our job to make them accept it'. Forcing one-way communication on to people without their understanding and without understanding them, makes for poor management.

As Samuel Butler, the seventeenth-century poet observed: 'He that complies against his will is of his own opinion still.'

One-way communication problems can frequently arise if the sender and receiver are not on the same emotional level. The advantages of two-way communications are considerable. In small groups, such as those which apply in leisure settings (community arts centres, sports centres, recreation offices or community associations), the advantages can lead to greater harmony, understanding and effectiveness.

In today's world, we communicate in many more ways than in the past, including: meetings, memos, faxes, emails, notice boards, newsletters and the press and media. The telephone is used in different ways: mobile, texting, answerphone and tele conferencing. However, the most effective method is likely to be informal, direct conversation: old fashioned, but effective. To encourage this, staff, ideally, should have easy access to each other.

Communication 'models' and networks

All communication 'models' are simple illustrations of different basic theoretical concepts, the reality of which is far more complex and diffuse. Nevertheless, they serve to demonstrate that some methods of managerial communication serve particular circumstances better than others. The illustrations, however, do not show up the informal communications network which, far from being pushed underground, should be seen as essential for the gelling together in informal as well as formal processes.

Personal communications are usually one-to-one and face-to-face. Managerial communications, on an organizational basis, call for a variety of communication channels: downwards, upwards, sideways, crossways and informal communications. All have merit in different situations. However, most organizations tend to keep to downward communications through hierarchical channels. This can lead to misunderstandings or a regimented response and also activate the 'grapevine'. It is far better to have these essential cross-communications out in the open, as necessary, and informal.

There are different channels of communication and each has merit in different situations, but closed systems are more restrictive and centralized (Figure 19.5). Kent (1981) identified three closed models:

- the chain: the straight line, with the manager at the top
- the Y formation: simple gatekeeping, with the manager controlling at the centre and
- the wheel: large control span, gatekeeping, with the manager at the centre 'calling the shots'.

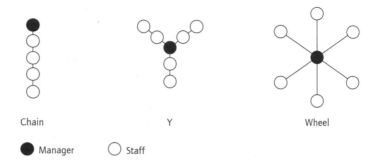

Chain   Y   Wheel

● Manager   ○ Staff

Figure 19.5 Closed systems

The concept of 'line management' and 'chain-of-command' is typified by the military; there are generals at the top and the foot soldiers on the ground. Generals don't order the troops. They tell the brigadiers and colonels who tell the majors and captains who instruct the sergeants who order the corporals who order the soldiers who carry out the commands.

In addition to line management, organizations, including hierarchal ones, incorporate 'line and staff'. 'Staff' exist at various levels. They perform specialist functions and should complement 'the line', for example, finance and personnel officers. Staff need to understand the problems of the line and provide the back-up services. Managers hold the team – line and staff – together.

These restricted networks can work fast and efficiently in tasks requiring simple mechanical processes, tightly controlled specifications and routine procedures. It is so much easier to give and carry out instructions. Alternatively, where there is a free range of ideas, such as in organic structures (growing and evolving) and where decentralized and horizontal structures are to be found, then open networks are to be encouraged (Figure 19.6). They include the circle, with the manager as one member of the decision-making team, and the web, where the manager is central for strategic work, delegates operational functions to groups and is a team member where appropriate.

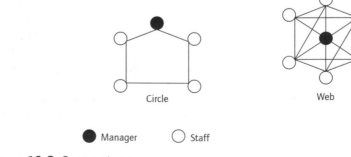

Circle   Web

● Manager   ○ Staff

Figure 19.6 Open systems

Given simple tasks, the wheel was consistently quicker and more accurate; the chain was the slowest and least effective. However, in terms of job satisfaction, the circle was most effective. The circle was also more adaptable in complicated and ambiguous tasks. The wheel with its central 'gatekeeper' inhibited adaptability to changing situations. Kent concludes that people never transmit information as well as they believe they do. He outlined commonly identified problems which restrict communication, for example, perceptual bias by the receiver, the distortion of information by the sender, the lack of trust on the part of both sender and receiver, too much information and power used to secrete rather than share information. The answer is to use more than one communication network.

> A lateral rather than a vertical direction of communications in an organization will avoid the problem of one person becoming the 'gatekeeper' of all information, a gatekeeper being a person who can withhold or pass on information as he sees fit.
>
> Kent, 1981

In both public and commercial leisure management, a substantial level of communication is of the one-way kind. Orders come down from the civic centre, town hall or head office, sometimes by word of mouth through the chain of command and often via the written memo and, increasingly, email: a system subject to all the misunderstandings and misinterpretations imaginable. It is difficult enough at times to communicate at a face-to-face level. With that in mind, Leisure Managers need to understand physical gestures such as facial expressions, movement of eyes, or sitting positions, whether made consciously or unconsciously, which can convey much to the receiver of the sender's attitude and understanding, and vice versa.

In terms of organization, to improve communication and ensure all who need to know get the message, flatter hierarchies work better than vertical ones and also encourage two-way communication. Moreover, excellent ideas can be generated from those 'at the coal face' and sharing information has a positive effect on performance (see Chapter 23).

Coaching, mentoring and motivational leadership

Like sports players and teams, leisure management staff and teams need coaching. Why? Because learning takes place through practical experience and when learning experiences are guided by managerial leaders, then staff become self-managers and more effective, more quickly. Coaches give clear instructions as to what they expect. Coaching provides people with confidence in the job, as individuals and as valuable members of the team. Leisure managers have an abundance of practical situations and opportunities for inculcating in their staff fine leadership qualities. Cursory consideration of leisure's products confirms this: play, sport, recreation, arts and tourism, among others. Leisure management coaches have two key tasks: to ensure that staff know what to do and how to do it; and to motivate and instil confidence in staff so that they carry out the work willingly and effectively.

Staff can also be enabled to undertake new tasks, improve performance, develop new skills, learn how to solve problems and become even more valuable members of the team. No matter how good people are at their jobs, there is always need for improvement and often a need for confidence boosting. The world's finest sportsmen and women, musicians and artists are constantly looking to improve. Wimbledon tennis stars have coaches and psychological motivators to keep them developing and improving. Good leaders will challenge staff to realize their potential, praise them when it is deserved, and show concern for their individual needs and welfare.

Staff need to work at their potential – for themselves, for the team, and for the organization. If they do not, they can be an expensive liability to the organization and they weaken the team. A motivated workforce is more likely to be successful than a de-motivated team. Pulling together is better than pulling apart. When people work as a team, they motivate each other – no one wants to let the side down – and as a result, the team is more productive. Staff will feel, think and work like a team.

A leisure management 'coach' can also be a 'mentor'. However, it is important to understand that the three roles – coach, mentor and counsellor – have separate purposes. In Homer's *Odyssey*, Mentor was the friend whom Ulysses put in charge of his household when he left on his epic voyage to Troy. In particular, he was responsible for advising and overseeing development of Ulysses' son, Telemachus. Visionary leaders make good mentors because they have principles and values which stem from inner convictions. These convictions, enthusiastically projected, influence others positively. They have trodden the path before; they can empathize. The ability comes from the personal vision that is large and clear enough to be shared.

A mentor is an experienced guide – a believer, an understander, promoting the cause and showing the way – a teacher and coach who can make a lasting impression on an individual's life. College students will know the value of a good, sensitive and inspiring personal tutor. Mentors provide a helping hand, inspire mutual trust, loyalty and friendship. The bond between mentor and protégé is an emotional one. Professions such as law and accountancy include 'apprenticeship' periods, a time when recent graduates must work with qualified professionals to 'learn the ropes'. In this process, the apprentice absorbs an approach, a style, a life view, which can shape their future. The relatively young profession of Leisure Management needs to establish its own 'apprentice' scheme, shaping the careers of people, young and older, who have the passion and ability to deliver outstanding leisure and recreation services and products.

Mentors should not be line managers: line managers and mentors have different roles. Likewise, counselling is very different from coaching and mentoring. Counsellors are called upon to deal with personal problems whether at work or home. A counsellor is a sympathetic listener who, ideally, helps a member of staff to find his or her own solution, though in the work situations, suggestions and advice may be called for. External help from experts may be needed, though in most leisure management situations, financial resources for such 'fringe' services are not available.

Motivational leadership

People are capable of remarkable achievement if they are given the right motivational leadership. A key to motivating others is to communicate a strong sense of shared purpose. Inspiring other people often begins with a leader's vision – the long view and the principles underlying it. Receiving orders, however, is unlikely to be motivating. Participation in planning and decision making can help in motivating staff to achieve their ambitions, manage themselves and in doing so, meet the objectives: the desired results. Heller (1999) identifies ten motivating factors:

- self-fulfilment, enabling staff to take on challenges
- recognition, letting them know how well they are doing
- peer respect, celebrating an individual's success publicly
- expertise, encouraging special knowledge
- competence, training to develop key skills
- achievement, agreeing targets that are achievable
- autonomy, planning their own work
- self-confidence, ensuring tasks can be done well
- self-respect, increasing regard for oneself
- membership, ensuring staff enter the 'club' of co-workers.

The difference between leadership and organizational management is in the leader's ability to inspire and motivate people to achieve their best, willingly. Apart from being ordered to carry out actions under a military or similar regime, people – motivated, challenged and inspired – are capable of remarkable achievements. Vision is foreseeing an aim or a goal worth striving for; leaders need to communicate this clearly with strong underlying principles. People rally behind worthwhile 'causes', particularly those that are well promoted with reason and passion. Leisure Managers, therefore, need to understand the underpinning principles and the benefits of leisure and recreation – referred to in earlier parts of this book – to instil a vision, inspire and motivate staff and in doing so, better deliver services to clients and customers.

Delegation

A delegate is a person authorized to act as a representative for another or others. A manager can delegate authority, but not ultimate responsibility.

A leader cannot do everything himself or herself; if he or she could, there would be no point in having a team. Good leadership means handing over a task to others, then helping them to match or exceed your standards of performance. However, it is no use delegating without providing the authority and the means to achieve the best results. What is strategically desirable, needs to be technically possible with the resources that are available. Hence, delegation requires a leadership style combining directive and supportive behaviours. Delegation is not simply assigning work and off-loading tasks; it is assigning the delegator's work to others, and giving them the authority and the resources to get the job done. As Ted Blake says: 'Delegating is not giving others work to do, but results and goals to achieve.' Some jobs, however, should not normally be delegated. They are likely to include confidential matters, disciplining, buck-passing of unpleasant tasks and key areas in which only the delegator has the power.

Delegated decision making reduces pressure on senior management. Thus, delegation for the Leisure Manager can free up time for key priorities on the one hand, and build up competences of staff and enhance their professional growth and development on the other hand. It also allows decisions to be taken at the most appropriate level. However, there is need for delegation clarity: the person delegating should focus attention on the results and standards; allow staff the freedom to decide on how to achieve them, and be concise about the power being handed on.

In *The Seven Habits of Highly Effective People* (1992), Stephen Covey differentiates between 'gofer delegation' and 'stewardship delegation'. Gofer delegation means, 'Go for this, go for that, do this, do that, and tell me when it's done'. It spawns a creed which says: 'Tell me what you want me to do, and I'll do it.' This is inefficient and ineffective. Stewardship delegation is focused on results instead of methods. It involves mutual commitment to expectations: what, not how; results, not methods. It provides guidelines, identifying parameters, as few as possible to avoid 'methods delegation'. Delegation also requires performance standards and resources: personnel, financial, technical and organizational.

Summary

In this and the previous chapter, we have considered the different interpretations of management versus leadership and shown how important the human side can be to the effective management of leisure and recreation. Leadership, decision making, communications and an understanding of group behaviour are key components. Management must be appropriate to different situations, and the manager must adapt his or her style of management to be appropriate to changing situations. What has become clear is that a manager armed with only one style of management may be ill-equipped for the variety of different tasks and people to be handled: just like a golfer with only one club.

The business of leisure requires staff to be flexible and work unsocial hours, and it calls for styles of leadership in keeping with providing good customer service and care of staff. In these circumstances, the 'democratic' manager with a professional 'executive style' is more likely to succeed. He or she will see the job as effectively maximizing the efforts of others. This manager's commitment to both task and relationships will be evident to all. These managers often work with a team; ideas can come from any quarter; and the greater number of possibilities explored, the better the understanding of the problem. They still have to lead: they cannot hide behind the team; and they still have to make the ultimate decision but both manager and staff feel involved in the successes and failures. This style of management is an 'objective' art gained with experience and learning, allied to personal drive and flair. It is this quality of management leadership which is essential to the successful and harmonious leisure and recreation service.

This chapter has concentrated on the manager's need to understand people and the relationships between them, whether as individuals or in groups. Without this understanding, and without the ability to communicate, motivate and lead, the manager's chance of successfully and effectively undertaking a task or meeting the needs of his or her clients and customers is considerably reduced. Moreover, management and leadership must be situational and adaptable to change. Wess Roberts (1989), in *Leadership Secrets of Attila the Hun*, believes that it is a privilege to direct the actions of others. Leadership flexibility is crucial; no model can anticipate circumstances. The relatively less known concept of the 'servant-leader' has much to commend it to professionals in leisure. Quality management requires quality managers and leaders.

Discussion points

1 Why can't we all be leaders? What do effective leaders bring to the table?

2 Leaders are born, not made. Leaders are made, not born. Discuss the opposing assumptions.

3 Active-centered leadership focuses on what leaders actually have to do in order to be effective, rather than on the personal qualities that they need to be good leaders. Discuss.

4 Management control can be described as monitoring the performance of a delegated task so that the expected results are achieved successfully. Managers are encouraged to delegate to achieve more. How would you let go without losing control?

5 It is possible to communicate without a word being spoken. Provide examples from your recent work experience.

6 Consider a management decision in your recent experience that had to be changed or shelved because it was clearly the wrong or inappropriate thing to do. Was it because the decision was unsound or was not properly implemented? How could the problem have been avoided?

7 'Managers are appointed. Leaders are chosen.' Discuss.

20

Marketing of leisure and recreation

Introduction

Marketing is an essential part of good management practice. Marketing is a process of identifying customer needs, wants and wishes and satisfying them. It involves creating appropriate products and matching them to market profiles. Leisure services and facilities depend on satisfied customers or they go out of business.

This chapter deals with the concept, moving between theory and practice, with examples and anecdotes from working experience; it provides approaches, messages and clues to providing attractive leisure services to customers at a social 'profit'.

Development of the concept of marketing

Marketing is not selling, as such. It was developed for selling. It is concerned with the needs and demands of potential customers. Selling is one of its ingredients, but that comes late in the marketing process. Selling focuses on the seller; marketing focuses on the needs of the buyer.

In simple terms, what we are trying to do is to discover what our clients and potential customers need, and are prepared to buy, then to create products and services to suit the needs and to sell these 'profitably'.

Therefore, marketing, far from being the end activity of a business – selling the goods – is at the beginning and goes on as part and parcel of the business itself. The key is to match leisure services and products to the people: the marketplace. Indeed,

Leisure Management itself is essentially a marketing process: meeting the needs and demands of people through leisure opportunities.

The historical development of marketing is encapsulated in the growth of the car industry. At first there was no competition, then there was competitive selling,and then marketing. Henry Ford, in the early days of the industry, is believed to have said, 'You can have any colour of car you like, as long as it's black'. The growth in competition increased the need for promotion and selling. Later, the products (the cars) had to be adapted to the needs of the market (the buyers), hence, a number of different models were produced, a variety of choice to suit different tastes. Japanese business captured much of the car and motorcycle markets in the 1950s and 1960s by providing what customers were looking for: style, colour, speed, comfort and fuel economy, and at a lower price.

This industrial and commercial marketing base has expanded into not-for-profit institutions and into leisure, private and public. For example in the public sector, when the conventional local 'baths' were the only swimming facility in town and few people had cars, there was little choice. But today many of those same towns and cities have a choice of pools within easy travel distance: conventional pools, leisure pools, and private pools in health clubs, designed to meet the needs of different markets.

We are all influenced by marketing. In Western civilization marketing is part of the fabric by which we go about our daily business. 'It is part of the modern survival kit — because we depend on it' (McIver, 1968). Marketing is simple. There is no mystique about it. Some treat it as a formal, academic subject. Others take a more liberal and relaxed view. Robert Townsend (1970) in *Up the Organization* captures the latter spirit: 'If you can't do it excellently, don't do it at all. Because if it's not excellent it won't be profitable or fun and if you're not in business for fun or profit, what the hell are you doing here?' You don't need marketing departments, he argues: everyone in the organization is in the business of marketing.

Marketing: what it is and what it does

In the commercial world marketing has proved to be an effective means of staying in business and making greater profits. For leisure services in the public and voluntary sectors, it can also bring greater success.

Marketing is a beginning-to-end process. It is co-ordinating the activities of the business in the pursuit of adding maximum value at minimum cost. Its point of origin is consumer demand. In essence, marketing is that essential part of the management process that matches markets with the leisure 'products' and services. It:

- assesses the needs and wants of potential customers
- analyses the situation and the market profile
- creates and develops tailor-made products and services
- packages the products and services to increase sales and avoid price resistance
- promotes in ways to best reach the target markets
- distributes the products
- sells the products and services at a 'profit'
- analyses, evaluates and adjusts.

One feature of the concept of marketing is that of voluntary exchange: 'It calls for offering something of value to someone in exchange for something else of value' (Kotler, 1975, p. 5). For example, public recreation is provided for the community in exchange for people's money, time, rates and taxes.

Commercial 'product' marketing and public 'service' marketing have some aspects in common but there are conceptual differences. In the commercial field the product is the means of achieving financial profits. In the not-for-profit sector, there is a wider range of measures of profitability. However, many people still treat marketing with suspicion:

> It's an unfortunate fact that marketing – the profession, trade, way of life or what you will – is held in pretty low esteem by the public at large. It's probable, of course, that the public at large doesn't actually understand what marketing's about, but for many, the term has too close an association with the street trader, who would sell his sister if the price were right. The whole panoply of consumer persuasion, from advertising and PR, through sales promotion, packaging, point-of-sale display and salesmanship itself, is bundled together in many minds as *prima facie* proof that marketing is immoral, in practice if not in theory.
>
> *Marketing*, 1984

Although the extract is from an article written in 1984, the sentiments appear to still hold good today.

The marketing approach

Marketing is not a single function in a business or service organization. It is a business philosophy, a business way of life. It starts in the marketplace with customers.

Traditionally, many companies are process-led and product-orientated; they have a pre-determined product or service. They find customers and convince them they want the product. The approach is, 'This is what we've got, now sell it'. Local government services often work in this way. For example, facilities are built, equipment is installed, markings are put on to the floors, programmes are devised, times are decided, charges are determined, systems are established, and the council will proudly announce that the facility is open. Many councillors will then say of the facility, 'It is there for them to use; if they don't use it that is their lookout. We provide plenty of opportunity in our town'. This approach is concerned with providing pre-determined products.

The marketing way reverses the process and starts with the customer. It is market-led. It says, 'This is what the customer wants, now make it'. It then designs, produces and delivers the satisfactions for the customer, at a profit. Using the findings of a market research programme, that is, information received, management organizes its business to ensure that the product is tailor-made for the market. By knowing who your customers are and about their wishes and wants, it is possible to produce appropriate products. When wants have been ascertained, sales resistance is apt to evaporate. The Japanese perfection in mass production, efficiency and knowledge of what the public wants in design, looks, performance and price, at one time reaped a harvest in the motorcycle, car, home-based leisure and other industries. The question for Leisure Managers is: what does the public want from leisure services? Management trainer Ted Blake (1985) said: 'Sports centres, pools, theatres, art galleries, libraries, museums, gymnasia, are merely warehouses holding tangible and intangible products that have no value except that brought to them by customers.'

Potential customers need to know therefore about the 'products' and be attracted to them. Local authorities have to compete for a share of the market. The financial profit motive, however, is not normally an issue, although greater stress on viability and commercial approaches are being employed. Viable services are important but service to the public at large should be pre-eminent.

An emerging marketing myth is that local authorities can market public recreation in exactly the same way as one can market breakfast cereals, cameras or holidays. While local authorities have elements within their services which could be commercially orientated, and while marketing techniques can be used to promote recreation programmes, the overall purpose of the authority is not to make financial profit, but to meet need and demand. Moreover, the recreation product is extremely difficult to define and quantify, and quality of the service is difficult to measure, though the development of processes such as ISO 9000, Total Quality Management and Quest help towards this measurement. The aims and objectives, too, are decidedly different from many commercial undertakings: financial yardsticks are only one measurement and should normally be secondary to other criteria. Local councils have political, governmental, traditional and institutional constraints, in addition to social and moral obligations. Marketing is needed but the way in which it is processed should also be different because the commercial product and the local authority service 'product' are not identical. Public sector marketing is a hybrid of approaches which have evolved historically and are now caught up with commercial approaches, primarily to limit subsidy or to help make the facilities pay for themselves. With compulsory competitive tendering, and now Best Value in respect of public services, leisure managers are under far greater pressure to 'perform', that is, to perform financially.

The concept of social marketing

Marketing is typically defined in business terms as the planning, pricing, promoting, distribution and servicing of goods and products. It has been concerned with economic exchange of goods. As such it has been associated with business objectives to sell products and to learn about the kinds of product that the public would like to purchase. The concept of marketing, as suggested earlier, can be interpreted as much broader than just economic exchange and could also 'logically encompass exchanges dealing with social issues and ideas' (Laczniak *et al.*, 1979). Most people are familiar with recent attempts through marketing to project politicians and political platforms particularly coming up to an election. For example, an individual participating in an election exchanges his or her vote for the promise of particular policies and actions if the candidate is elected. Marketing, it is argued, includes the facilitating of social exchanges as well as goods and services.

Kotler and Zaltman (1971) define social marketing as: 'The design, implementation and control of programmes calculated to influence the acceptability of social ideas and involving consideration of product planning, pricing, communication, distribution and market research'.

Marketing, then, can encompass political campaigns, community programmes and social causes, such as environmental issues, pollution control, healthy living, child protection, disability issues, stop smoking campaigns, equal opportunities, and peace campaigns. The success of BBC's Children in Need and ITV's Telethon are testimony to the power of marketing social causes in recent years.

Any new trend is likely to have both positive and negative effects. Marketing can improve the chances of useful social and community programmes coming to fruition. However, marketing can also be seen as having potential ethical problems. Those who are economically powerful could use marketing techniques to enhance ideas which may promote causes that are not socially beneficial.

Social marketing can be utilized in the leisure field for causes and community projects and to assist in recreation planning. The purpose of the National Lottery is to help 'good causes'. Improved marketing could better promote the causes for which the Lottery was established. A wide range of causes could be brought to public attention, for example, retention of open space, recreation for the disabled, health and fitness, tackling the problems of obesity, 'sport for all', 'art for all' and 'music for all' campaigns. However, its sensitive application is enormously important, if we wish to avoid the criticism of indoctrination, for social marketing could be a powerful instrument which can affect the way people think, speak and act. This, of course, is the purpose of some marketing and this is why the causes and issues must be debated and adjudged by society to be beneficial. It is very important to put philosophy and principles first. Therefore, it is beneficial to start a marketing strategy with a vision or mission statement which tells everybody why we are in business and what we are in business for.

Leisure is a marketing service

The provision of leisure, whether in the public or private sectors, is a marketing exercise. Consider the following sequence of events:

- facilities like theatres, swimming pools and sport centres are built in locations where they are thought to be right for the market
- programmes are designed to attract people from the catchment area
- the activities are priced at levels to attract buyers and give value for money
- the 'packages' of activities are promoted and targeted
- the performance is evaluated.

This sequence illustrates the interwoven nature of management processes, marketing and programming. In other words, leisure – regardless of who manages – is a market-orientated business. There will be different goals and different nuances for different markets. However, the question needs to be asked: how well are we marketing?

Despite a radical 'sea change' by local authorities, in the wake of compulsory competitive tendering, and the advent of Best Value, towards a more commercial stance or 'economic approach', differences of principle behind the provision of leisure still exist. The way marketing is carried out will be different; local authorities will be more sensitive to political and general public reaction and will endeavour to comply with social policies.

There is a blurring of differences between public and private businesses particularly with the success of private contract companies managing local authority facilities, but local councils are still in control, accountable to the public, and managing facilities provided by tax and ratepayers' money. What has changed is the use of commercial techniques and the keener financial objectives of local authorities.

Local authorities provide a number of services such as housing, refuse collection, social services, and so on, and citizens have little choice in the matter, except at local election time. But they can choose whether or not to use local authorities' leisure facilities and services. The facilities are said to cater for the whole community. Some people, however, are not aware of the extent of provision; others are aware but are not motivated to use the facilities: either they are not prepared or not able to exchange what they have for what is on offer. Indeed, public leisure facilities are disproportionally used by those who are more mobile and more socially and financially advantaged. Marketing linked to balanced programming could help reduce the imbalance.

Local authorities, however, have problems in terms of marketing: providing for everybody's needs may make good political sense but is unlikely to make sound marketing sense where segmentation is used to attract target markets. Local government structures, like cargo ships, are not designed for speedy response to the marketplace and political interests cloud issues. Moreover, local authorities interpret their sport, leisure and recreation responsibilities differently from the private sector, even though the notion of recreation as a social service has lost ground in recent years (Cowell, 1978).

In the commercial sector financial profits are used as measuring criteria, bearing in mind capital and revenue costs. In local authorities, financial pressures lead to ambivalence. Panic measures may demand that income be maximized and expenditure minimized. This may mean that expenditure in one vital area is reduced, which could then work against achieving the objectives: a treatment least likely to effect a cure.

It is clear that, while marketing may have considerable benefits in local authority provision and management of recreation, the use of marketing approaches must be adapted to suit the social, political, economic and institutional structure within the local government setting.

Customers and the influences upon them

A caption in *Advertising Age* exemplified the susceptibility and vulnerability of potential customers to persuasive promotion: 'In very few instances do people really know what they want, even when they say they do.'

Customers have many similar needs. But their demands may vary as do their levels of disposable income. In addition, in times of economic recession, the disposable income of many people diminishes, while the costs of goods and services increase. Not only do customers vary one from another, but the same customers may vary from one situation to another, from one mood to another and from one inclination to another. Therefore in leisure we must market for both the similarities and differences in customers.

Customers come in all shapes and sizes, from tiny gymnasts to Sumo wrestlers, and from grandparents in the over-sixties keep fit classes to their grandchildren learning to swim. Different customers, however, may have many similar needs: young and old may be equally at home in the fitness centre using different fitness programmes. And similar types of customers may have different needs; not all young men want to play football; not all young women want to do step aerobics.

Customers are a variety of people. They include:

- individuals
- friends and families
- organizations (who buy for others)
- supporters
- spectators
- schools
- parents
- visitors.

Each link in the chain is a customer. The network is wider than we at first imagine; the chain is longer. Many factors affect demand, including:

- interests and motivations
- choices available
- home and upbringing
- social groups, pressures and attitudes
- age and peers
- family and friends
- education
- looks and abilities
- personal aspirations and confidence
- income and spending power
- job and status
- fashion and trends.

Customers are under constant pressure, whether as individuals or companies. In the past, there were small, concentrated and highly profitable markets. Now there are widespread mass markets with affluence. There is far greater choice. Because of this there can be constant changes in the market and in the buying habits of customers. The leisure market has seen many shifts in demand, from ballroom dancing to step aerobics and from trampolining to bungee jumping.

Customers are not static, unquestioning beings, but dynamic and often highly irrational people. They do not remain the same. Situations can change people. Therefore, there is a need for flexibility in management style. Managers must vary their responses so that they continue to be appropriate to changing situations. In leisure services we cannot satisfy all of the people all the time, but we can go a long way towards satisfying most people. As Ted Blake (2003) believes, we can satisfy most people by treating them with importance, attention and understanding. This underlines the importance of staff training in customer service. In leisure services there is often a tendency to treat managers, processes, systems and hierarchy in organizational structures as important. But most important should be a client and customer-orientation.

In order to market leisure successfully, we must sell benefits to clients and potential customers. Local authorities have special benefits to give, not only to those who can take up the opportunities readily but also to those who are least able to fend for themselves: some old, some young, the disabled, the unemployed and especially the jobless school-leaver. Here the problem is compounded, in that they have more free time, less disposable income and poor mobility. Young people need a favourable image of themselves; they need to realize some of their dreams. The marketing of leisure can assist in this image seeking. Yet the young are susceptible to marketing; commercial enterprise has been quick to seize the opportunity to provide what they are looking for. Pop culture, fashion, music and drink take a massive share of leisure spending. The pub is the leisure centre for many young people.

Suffice it to say that, in terms of marketing, the customer is key. However, potential customers can be influenced in a variety of ways. It is worth considering therefore some of the motivating factors.

Motivation and the depth approach to marketing

All of us can be influenced and manipulated, far more than we realize, through marketing. Efforts are constantly being made to channel our unthinking habits, our buying decisions and our thought processes through the use of sciences such as psychology. 'Typically these efforts take place beneath our levels of awareness, so that appeals which move us are often, in a sense, hidden' (Packard, 1965). Some 'manipulating' has been amusing, and some disquieting. The 'depth' approach, as Vance Packard calls it, is being used in a variety of fields and on a variety of unsuspecting people.

> The use of mass psychoanalysis to guide campaigns of persuasion has become the basis of a multi-million dollar industry. Professional persuaders have seized upon it in their groping for more effective ways to sell us their wares – whether products, ideas, attitudes, candidates, goals or states of mind.
>
> Packard, 1965, p. 11

The persuaders are looking for the 'whys' of our behaviour; for example why people are drawn into illogical purchases or fill shopping baskets in a supermarket as though under hypnosis, or why others buy certain drinks or cars. Packard believes that the persuaders see us typically as 'bundles of day-dreams, misty hidden yearnings, guilt complexes, irrational emotion blockages. We are image lovers given to impulse and compulsive acts' (Packard, 1965, p. 14). It seems that our subconscious can be 'pretty wild and unruly'. The persuaders stop at nothing. Nothing is immune or sacred. Agencies seek to discover the psychological effects of the female menstrual cycle on the purchasing of certain food products; psychiatric probing techniques have been used on impressionable young people anxious to be attractive; and public relations experts are advising church ministers on improving communications with their congregations. Cheskin (1965) adds support to Packard:

> Motivation research is the type of research that seeks to learn what motivates people in making choices. It employs techniques designed to reach the unconscious or subconscious mind because preferences generally are determined by factors of which the individual is not conscious ... Actually in the buying situation the consumer generally acts emotionally and compulsively,

unconsciously reacting to the images and decisions which in the subconscious are associated with the product.

Marketing is, then, potentially equally powerful and dangerous. What people tell interviewers at a surface, conscious level could have little bearing on how they will actually behave in a buying situation. The manipulators are working beneath the surface of conscious life. In contrast, most leisure research concerned with public sector provision has been based on surface-level surveys and questionnaires and on quantitative analysis. Research which is more qualitative and looks beneath the surface is required to help to understand people's motivation in making leisure and recreation choices.

What motivates people to 'buy' leisure and recreation?

What motivates people in making choices? The realization that there are 'hidden persuaders' makes us aware that there are factors of which the individual is unconscious and that people act differently from how they say they will. For example, impressions could decide the customer's response. First impressions count. Leisure facilities must therefore create the right impression. Marketing slogans preach: 'it is not the product but the promise'. There is a need in leisure to be selling both the product and the promise.

Music has been used cleverly to symbolize and promote products and messages. Pop singles are often marketed on what are called 'hooks' – those lines, rhythms or jingles which you cannot get out of your head. Puccini's 'Nessun Dorma' sung by Luciano Pavarotti was BBC TV's introduction to the 1990 World Cup in Italy. The single and LP were massive hits both for the records and for promoting the BBC and the World Cup. One of the best-selling hits of 1973, 'Tie a Yellow Ribbon', was revived in 1981 to welcome home Iranian hostages to the United States, and again in 1985 for the hostages from Beirut. The jingle had not been forgotten and so the message had not been forgotten. The ribbon symbolism was used years later as a mark of peace on the fortieth anniversary of Hiroshima and again after the Gulf War.

Some marketing slogans can become part of the product itself and hence a great deal of marketing can be undertaken at very little cost. Leisure equipment, clothing and fashion can carry slogans, messages and communications which become embedded in the minds of consumers. To return from shopping in London's West End carrying a Harrod's carrier bag confers a kind of status on the carrier. 'Carrying an Adidas sports bag and wearing an Adidas sports shirt confer status beyond what might be expected from association with the name of professional sportsmen' (Wilson and West, 1982). The McDonald's 'M' and the Nike tick illustrate that we are 'symbol minded', but, companies such as these have to be quick to change products and promotional methods. McDonald's had to deal with the United Kingdom beef scare and Nike has to deal with the footwear trend when trainers became less fashionable.

Co-operative marketing spreads the burden of promotional expenditure. Breakfast cereals, for example, support promotions of toys, video recorders, sports bags and bathroom scales. The television and radio media are flooded with advertising jingles. The jingles may remain in the head and promote products for an appreciable length of time. Wilson and West (1982) recall that, in 1971, Coca-Cola commissioned a jingle for a new advertising campaign. This was heard repeatedly on television and in cinemas throughout the world. The copyright was assigned to a musical company and a new lyric was written. The former commercial jingle entered the singles record charts as 'I'd Like to Teach the World to Sing'. But the pop song never lost its association with the Coca-Cola advertisement: 'So the company not only recovered much (if not all) of the original investment; it also continued to enjoy a promotional benefit.'

The leisure demotivators

Bad news travels fast. It is passed on more readily than good news. Marketers (in our case, Leisure Managers) must therefore not only have concern with what motivates people to recreation, but also with what demotivates. Nothing demotivates more than poor handling of customers: rudeness, a 'take it or leave it' attitude, double-bookings, ruined expectations, dissatisfactions and broken promises and the package holiday scandals of holidaymakers being sent to the wrong place. All these situations demotivate.

Leisure service is primarily concerned with clients and customers; it is about their needs. Townsend (1970) believes that good service is given and things get done because of men and women with conviction. In current leisure management, the light of conviction is often seen in the eyes of junior staff, who may not have the necessary experience but can, with enthusiasm, reach customers in a way that others cannot. They are the connectors. They should be encouraged, for leisure can be best marketed by people who are involved, committed and who undertake their work with conviction and enthusiasm.

Satisfying customers brings benefits. Success in selling leisure and recreation lies not in leisure departments, centre management, committees or even in the facilities themselves, but out in the market, in the minds and pockets of the customers.

Training for customer service

Who should do the selling to customers? The British Productivity Council estimates that in the vast majority of cases, there must be face-to-face selling. Commercial organizations spend considerable effort in training and briefing staff, teaching staff how to talk with, meet and communicate with customers.

Training of staff in public facilities is poor by comparison. Many who are in the greatest need of training are those who are the operational staff – those unlikely to be released for training by their authorities. It is these staff at the 'sharp end' – the receptionists, the caretakers, groundsmen, park keepers and supervisors of all kinds – who have the job of meeting and motivating the public. With some notable exceptions (such as many reception staff), face-to-face employees are often the least capable of communicating with and handling customers. They have not been trained, encouraged, motivated, made to feel important or supported. Yet it is they who are called upon to undertake the most important job, namely that of serving and communicating with people. Staff need help in carrying out this important function; they need training. Regrettably some leisure services, far from motivating people, sometimes serve to demotivate them, achieving the complete opposite of what was intended.

Customer care and quality of service in leisure are possibly more important than in any other service because the leisure 'product' we are dealing with is providing

423

satisfying experiences for customers. A visit to a leisure event which is badly managed and results in bad experiences is unlikely to be bought again. And the opposite is true: if people enjoy their experience or have found it worthwhile, they are likely to come again and they will let others know about it.

The marketing mix

Marketing is concerned with providing the right products and services and then forging the best relationships between customers and products and services. The Marketing Mix is the means by which that relationship is expressed. It has a number of ingredients, each of which will have a greater or lesser influence in different settings:

1 product (including service)
2 pricing
3 place
4 promotion (pre-purchase)
5 performance (post-purchase).

There are a number of factors which need emphasis in deciding how the ingredients are going to be mixed in order to be appropriate to the market. Sandy Craig (1989) points to some:

> Firstly, the nature of the product or service influences the balance of the ingredients. Products with a high fashion content, e.g. designer sportswear, emphasise the product itself through product development and design and promote heavily. Price and availability are not so important. By contrast, staple foods such as canteen food emphasise price and ready availability with promotion and product playing less important roles. If the 'canteen'/cafe in your facility provides fast food the availability becomes more important, product development (including packaging) becomes more important and price less important. If it provides health food (or healthy food) then product development (including packaging and presentation) becomes even more important, and price less important.

The emphasis on leisure products in the commercial sector and on products in community recreation services will be different. The sections which follow deal with the main ingredients in the 'marketing mix' and, first, the product.

The leisure product

The product (including the service) is the basis of all marketing. It is the unit of exchange with the client or customer. If it offers the customer satisfactions, he or she may continue to buy it. Products exhibit life cycles. With most commercial products, that life cycle revolves around:

- product start
- growth
- development and
- decline and the replacement by better products.

In leisure services many products have been with us for decades, but even well established activities like squash may currently be on the decline and have to be packaged differently to redress the present downward trend. What is needed is product development to provide a continuous stream of new or changing products.

It may be thought that the products are facilities (squash and tennis courts) and activities (theatre-going and aerobics). Yet, in reality these are the vehicles for getting to the 'real' product – experiencing satisfaction through leisure participation – which is the unit of exchange with customers. If customers do experience satisfactions or worthwhileness, they will want to 'buy' them again.

The leisure product, in essence, is the satisfying or worthwhile experience derived from participation in or involvement with an activity in a person's time for leisure which was described in Chapter 8 as 'pleisure'. Therefore the product is not goods, but the experiencing of satisfactions. Let us use the analogy of tennis. As Jim Johnson reminds us (1987) you can buy a tennis racket, feel and handle it, pay for it and keep it. It is tangible. But leisure is intangible until you experience it. The tennis racket not sold today can be sold tomorrow. The tennis court space or theatre seat not sold today is lost forever. Its sell-by date is in advance of the activity. Leisure, in this sense, cannot be stored. The product is perishable. If you are rich you might own a tennis court, but most of us simply rent it for an hour and we have a choice of waiting our turn at the park courts, booking in advance at the sports centre or taking part at a tennis club.

As well as being perishable, the product is fragile and unpredictable. It is easily damaged. John McEnroe can smash his racket on the ground and use another one. But a customer treated rudely at reception, double-booked on the court or unable to get a drink at the bar in reasonable time, can take her or his custom elsewhere. Leisure behaviour is less predictable than work behaviour. In leisure, customers have choice – and they can be fickle.

The leisure product therefore is somewhat of an enigma – diverse, changing, intangible, perishable, fragile and fleeting – and, in many instances, dependent on the person giving the service, namely the organizer, teacher, the arts and sports development officer, the coach, tour guide or entertainer.

In terms of leisure participation, people are in it for what they can get out of it. People want to enjoy, to be with friends, to learn, to look better, to feel better, to be somebody, to be skilful, to win. We need to sell success. We have in leisure management the means to make people into better players of the violin or football, better coaches, better administrators, keener supporters. We can help to make people happier, healthier, slimmer, fitter, better informed. We can sell glamour, risk, excitement and adventure, particularly for the young. The potential benefits are abundant.

Capturing interest is essential. Good marketers should encourage levels of originality and be prepared to take risks. They need to explore possibilities. Originals and 'firsts' capture interest and can also create a lasting impression. Who was the first to break the four-minute mile? Now, who was the second? Who were the first to climb Everest? Who were second? The first product to find a niche in the customer's mind is difficult to dislodge. The different types of synthetic sports surfaces by other manufacturers are still referred to as Tartan for tracks and Astroturf for artificial grass. Instant cameras by other suppliers are still called Polaroids. Spa baths are called jacuzzis. Good marketers must also experiment with new ideas, such as:

- fitness and swim packages, not just single lines
- extending leisure self-service (early swims; late squash) and
- self-booking systems: after all, we help ourselves to far more costly items at petrol filling stations.

Market research and product testing need to be undertaken to have the best chance of matching people with products. Leisure products need testing and changing to suit customer needs. Leisure products and services are provided by the public, voluntary and commercial sectors. Commercial leisure normally has a finite answer and a measurable target. For example, a health and fitness club may need to enrol 80 per cent of its projected 1,000 members on a direct debit basis of £50 per member per month. But along with this objective of selling memberships, there are many service elements – efficiency, attractive facilities, ambience – all of which go to make up the product and bring satisfaction to the user.

Demand for a product may arise out of choice, out of opportunity or from the facilities themselves. Facilities, opportunities and 'welcome' can stimulate demand and dramatically expand a leisure market. On the other hand, demand for a product can be stifled by restrictive policies, limited opportunities, high exclusivity of clubs, lack of choice, vested interests and other demotivators. For example, a sports facility requiring a playing-in standard, or an enrolling fee, or a proposer and seconder on an application form, may attract better players, and those who can handle the whole joining process; others may find the process itself intimidating and a major stumbling block to participation.

Most recreation programmes, even those designed with major speciality areas, tend to market more than one product. How many products are to be marketed? A combination of facilities can attract greater use, be more economical, and also provide the spin-off to other activities, expanding the market. Many commercial tennis centres are used more for health and fitness, swimming and social activities than for tennis.

Markets rarely remain static. Managers should therefore avoid putting all their eggs in one basket. Products exhibit life cycles, as we have seen. In leisure services, many products – theatre, cinema, golf, swimming – have been with us for decades. But some well established activities are on the decline, for example squash and cue sports, and have to be packaged and promoted differently to redress the trend. What is needed is product development to provide a continuous stream of new or changing products. Cinemas have changed from single to multi-screen. Tenpin bowling and bingo have changed to social 'nights out' venues with a wider range of products. Golf is played on golf driving ranges. Swimming includes water fun, water recreation and swim aerobics.

Some products will cease to contribute to profits or to provide benefits. New products may be the life-blood of some static leisure services. The answer may be to introduce new looking products to create new images, and which bring additional client and customer benefits. For example, products may decline, but demand for the type of product may still be rising. Skateboarding's rapid growth and decline hid the creation of new looking activities on wheels such as roller hockey and roller blading, which in turn have re-kindled skateboarding to a serious leisure pursuit for young people.

Product development and improvement are therefore of importance. Packaging different products can generate customer benefits at all levels of participation; for example a daytime leisure centre package might include sports activity, dietary clinic, sauna and a crèche for the children.

Pricing the products

We need to match people's needs with products at a price they are willing to pay. The pricing policy is an important factor in financial planning and in the overall strategy. It is a vital part of marketing. Should we price high and then reduce; price low for a quick penetration of the market; price at one rate for all the customers; or offer special rates, discounts and packages? Commercial business is profit orientated; therefore, it is price sensitive. Products must be gauged at the right price to attract customers to buy. Discussion is often centred on keeping prices low, but in many exclusive establishments pricing high can achieve the type of response aimed to meet objectives. The price of branded fashion goods becomes a secondary issue for young people's 'must have' products. Moreover, low pricing does not necessarily equate with increased participation.

Pricing policies remain a thorny problem in most local authorities. The private sector has a far easier choice. It sets its prices at what the market can stand and what is the most profitable. Whether public or private we need to ask: how can pricing help us to achieve objectives? Pricing strategies include:

- status quo
- price increase
- price decrease
- price offers.

Choice of strategy will depend on needs to:

- make financial profits
- cover costs
- cover part costs
- undercut competitors' prices
- win additional market share by low pricing
- win segmented market share by pricing high.

Pricing is only one factor in making choices. Price may not be as dominant a factor as we may think. Cheapness is one criterion, especially for the financially disadvantaged, but not necessarily the only criterion. Rambling, camping, public tennis, museums, and athletics, for example, are relatively cheap activities, yet they attract only certain small segments of the population.

Public tastes can be notoriously fickle. We can offer 'superior' products to enhance quality of life, health and fitness and provide them at no charge, yet many will prefer mediocre, expensive, even damaging-to-health alternative products.

The level at which prices are set can also be used to control the demand for a particular activity (e.g. high pricing exclusive health spas and golf courses). On the other hand, it can be used to extend the capacity of a facility (e.g. the indoor tennis initiative with lower pricing).

	← – – – – – – – – – – – – – – Subsidy	Profit – – – – – – – – – – – – – – →		
Type of charge	No charge	Some charge	Economic charge	Commercial charge
Basis of policy	Social service – all residents have a recreational need – facilities available to all	Many people and groups have needs for specialist activities for health and recreation	Participants are main benefactors – hence have to pay full costs	Benefits participants exclusively. Charges include full costs and profit charges based on what market can bear. Profit used to subsidize other facilities
Types of facilities	Parks Libraries	Swimming pools Public tennis courts Arts centres Community centres	Entertainments Golf courses	Indoor tennis Health and fitness Squash Sauna Sunbeds
Profile of users	Representative of neighbourhood	High proportion of local people Youths/young people	Middle income groups Young adults	Middle to high income groups

Figure 20.1 The charging policy continuum in the public sector

Local authority pricing is largely based on tradition, and what is an 'acceptable' level compared with other authorities. There are similarities between local authorities. These can be expressed in theory along a charging continuum, which extends from a social service approach, where no charges are imposed, to a commercial approach at the other end of the continuum. Figure 20.1 illustrates this charging continuum. The bulk of public sector leisure activities are priced at a subsidized level to make recreation accessible for all the community; swimming is a prime example.

The economic approach aims to charge at rates which will result in a break-even operational cost or minimal deficit. This is made possible by charging at higher rates for fitness, squash and event rentals and entertainment.

The profit approach is based on charges levied not only to cover operational and capital costs, but also to provide a profit. Thus at this end of the continuum, the charges made are what the market can withstand. Local authorities are increasingly using all three policies for different markets, but any return on capital investment is highly unlikely.

There is fierce competition in the commercial world. Competitive pricing and good margins are valuable weapons for sales personnel. There are special bonuses for the sales teams. For the buyer, there are attractions in the form of points, competitions, and incentive schemes. Promotional inventiveness is endless. Commercial marketing is not just concerned with the product (it is often quite secondary to other factors), but with the benefits: to the customers if they buy the product, and to the salespeople if they sell it.

Price therefore may not be as important after all. The level at which prices are set can also be used to control the demand for a particular activity, while at others it may be used to extend the capacity of a facility. Pricing has always been a vitally important element in commercial business. Now it is more important for local authorities because of the financial constraints imposed on local government. Local authorities will need to examine their marketing strategies in terms of subdividing their products by price and quality and consider the advantages and disadvantages of pricing high, medium or low and the implications of these policies on the service. Maintaining a principle of accessibility for all will be sorely tested. One of the keys may be price flexibility, allowing managers to gauge the sensitivities of the market.

Place

Products – facilities, programmes, activities – need to be accessible to the people they have been developed for. Therefore, the distribution policy should be based on the market research about customers, their home and work locations, transportation and accessibility factors in addition to the products and the prices.

It is therefore very important for services and facilities to be placed in locations which customers can easily reach. We need to make the facilities physically, socially, and financially accessible. The journey can be influenced with directional signs, maps, an attractive welcoming entrance, and by lighting the parking areas and walkways. The general awareness of the leisure facility can be reinforced with attractive displays and exhibitions in public places and with leaflet distribution. It is also important to locate key elements within facilities with customer convenience in mind, e.g. changing rooms near playing areas, crèche adjacent to outdoor play space, good viewing to activities. Programming of different activities, times, space and opening hours, all needs to be orientated, to best serve clients, customers and operational staff.

Services may well be available, accessible and at the right price but customers may still not take advantage of the opportunity. This is where promotion and communications come into play. Activities need to be in the right place at the right time. Information services often close in the evenings and weekends when they may be most needed. Many leisure facilities will be inaccessible to segments of the population. Some people will live in remote parts; some will be small children; some will be old. In these cases, needs can be met, for example, by managing mobile services – mobile library, toy library, play bus, travelling theatre – and by appointing artists in residence, 'animateurs' and sports development officers.

Promotion

Another ingredient of the 'marketing mix' is promotion. (Most people use the word 'marketing' when they really mean promotion and advertising.) Promotion provides awareness and seeks to attract customers to a particular service or product. It is a process of familiarizing, reminding and creating favourable images, attitudes and a willingness to buy. The process is one of pulling customers to the product using words, music, pictures and symbols to present an image of the product that is attractive, if not compelling.

We now realize that there are many factors affecting demand, some which we may be unconscious of. Impressions, for example, could decide our response. Leisure facilities must, therefore, create the right impression – the motivating impression. And first impressions count most. They can motivate or demotivate.

Promotional activity has been defined as: 'an exercise in communications. Its role is to facilitate exchanges with potential client groups by communicating the benefits offered by a programme or service; it seeks to inform, persuade, or remind' (Howard and Crompton, 1989).

Promotion consists of four key components:

1 Personal contact: this involves a verbal 'presentation' to one or more potential customers with the objective of selling a service or a product
2 Advertising: this represents a paid form of non-personal presentation about the organization and/or the programme of opportunities offered
3 Incentives: these represent a financial offer or 'gift' that is made to potential customers with the objective to encourage them to purchase a particular service or product
4 Publicity: this represents a favourable form of communication in the media (e.g. print or broadcast) at no direct cost to the organization concerned.

A fifth promotional vehicle is sponsorship, which is covered later in this chapter.

A new and powerful vehicle for promotion, advertising and publicity is the Internet and world wide web.

Personal selling

Leisure is 'sold' largely through people. The public's impression of a service or facility is often made on the first encounter with a member of staff. A warm smile says, 'You're welcome'. Looking elsewhere and talking to someone else says 'You're not welcome'. In most leisure businesses the staff, generally, have the right attitudes and many have an outgoing personality which enables them to interact well with people.

To be effective in personal selling, it is necessary that the person concerned does it with enthusiasm, so that he or she is perceived as being able, efficient and caring. The function of personal selling involves a two-way communication process and can provide valuable feedback about existing and potential recreation programmes and activities.

A promotional strategy should be built around a proper brief taking account of:

- the benefits of the products, e.g. for fitness and health
- the target markets, e.g. children and seniors
- the information and messages to be conveyed, e.g. relieve stress; look and feel good
- the media and promotional methods to be used
- the offers and inducements.

If the message does not reach people, there is no point in sending it. And if it reaches people, do they understand it? The message must be relevant to the market and also be expressed in such a way that it attracts, rather than repels. The media are a major vehicle by which managers can communicate their programmes. The more direct forms include television, radio, press and the cinema. The less direct include literature and packaging, sales gimmicks, incentives and sponsorship. But word of mouth and recommendation could be the most successful in that a large proportion of leisure facility users come with friends and like-minded groups of people. Different methods of communication and different messages suit different markets.

Advertising

Advertising encompasses many forms of communication and includes:

1 posters in prominent, eye-catching locations
2 brochures and leaflets that describe the facilities, services and programmes on offer
3 advertisements placed in the local media, such as newspapers and radio
4 newsletters and fully paid supplements in the local newspapers
5 direct mailing enclosing new information, such as offers of new benefits in new programmes
6 Internet advertising.

In comparison to publicity, advertising does not provide immediate feedback and can be an expensive form of promotion. Television advertisements are extremely expensive, as are paid advertisements in the press. In contrast, the local cinema can be a relatively cheap form of advertising. As cinema-going audiences are largely young people, the products, activities and services that appeal to young people could be effectively advertised in local cinemas. Local radio advertising can vary in cost but in getting across to young people local radio could pay dividends. Poster advertising can be very indifferent compared with face-to-face communication, which makes a greater impact. A mail shot using an agency address list or a compiled database is a good way of getting directly to a target audience but costs need to be compared to those of other methods.

The message to Leisure Managers appears to be to look at the whole variety of ways of communicating, to try out various forms and then act positively, measure results and make appropriate adjustments. In order to ensure that the communication messages are effective, there are general guidelines that can be helpful in attracting the attention of potential customers.

- Colour attracts the attention of the reader far more than black and white material. Unusual or novel design catches the eye of the reader.
- Taller shaped material appears to be more effective than wide shaped material.
- Large materials tend to attract more attention than small exhibits.
- Communications that involve more than one sense (e.g. sight and sound) appear to have the greatest impact.
- Headlines attract interest.
- Topical features hold interest and curiosity.
- Strap lines (e.g. 'Free this Week', 'Play in a Day') demand attention.

The importance of the headline in an advertisement cannot be over-emphasized. The headline must be catchy to stimulate the reader to read the full message. Often this takes the form of a question which is answered in the text below. Topical questions that touch on aspects of health, fitness and beauty tend to arouse adequate interest for potential customers of sports centres to read further. Also the text should demand action from the reader such as 'telephone now' or 'complete the attached form now'.

A self-testing criterion for an advertising communication is that it should produce positive answers to the following questions.

- Is it eye-catching?
- Is the layout attractive?
- Does the headline stimulate the reader to proceed further?
- Does it provide adequate information?
- But at the same time, is the message clear and simple?
- Is the text persuasive and credible?
- Does the advertisement create a favourable public image of the organization?
- Does it use corporate style: colour, typeface, logo, etc.?

Incentives and publicity

The 'offer' has become a prime means of persuading people to buy. In contrast to the other forms of promotional activity, incentives should not be used regularly and when offered should be restricted to a limited period of time. The main objective of using incentives is to stimulate participation from identified market targets. The incentives can take the form of an introductory offer, such as no joining fee for a specified period, discounts, two-for-one purchases, and gifts of CDs and T-shirts.

Financial incentives can be persuasive. We all like a bargain. The offer of discounts such as reduced off-peak pricing without adequate promotion and publicity, however, is unlikely to have a great impact. Permanent sales or discounts appear to have a minimal impact and can lead to questions being raised on whether the normal pricing levels are good value for money.

One of the cardinal principles of attracting a positive and warm response is to give freely and generously. A local authority leisure department may give free tennis courts, but that is usually because it is more costly to collect the money. But genuine giving has both direct and indirect benefits. Leisure managers, for example, could carry free tickets for visits to the centre, free 'have-a-go' tickets, free sampler-activity tickets, free sauna or a free second activity for those taking part in one activity only, and free tickets to events for disadvantaged groups.

Since most local authority leisure services departments have a minimal promotional budget, this has resulted in many concentrating more on publicity. This normally takes the form of press releases, feature articles and in some instances, a theatre or leisure centre may write its own weekly column in the local newspaper. It is a useful method of conveying information to clients and potential customers, informing the community of the results of programmes, fixtures and forthcoming events. To keep a facility continually in the public's mind, it is necessary periodically to have general interest stories relating to the facility in the local newspaper, since not everyone reads the arts and sports pages.

Although publicity does not directly involve financial expenditure, the true cost of preparing the publicity material may be considerable, particularly if many senior personnel are involved. Also the press editorial staff may reject the press release or prepared copy on the grounds that it is not adequately newsworthy. Coverage of a leisure programme or event or issue can fix an image in the mind of the public. Such an image is difficult to eradicate, particularly if the image is a poor one. The press can give a negative image in seconds; and the press is often seen as challenging, questioning and embarrassing to the local authority. Therefore, the only effective approach is to influence the control of the image-making and take a hand in managing the coverage. This can be achieved by informing and involving them and keeping them up to date with news. Good press coverage will help the public to say that their money on a leisure facility is well spent.

Promotional activity should be planned around a strategy. The messages must be appropriate to the target markets and the methods must be compatible with the characteristics of the market. Continued, modified promotion and sustained public relations campaigns are needed for long-term effects, with short-burst promotions for one-off events. Promotions will need to take into account the marketing research information, so that the most appropriate methods are used to target different market segments. These methods include, for example, advertising, packaging, sales promotions, public relations and in the leisure facility environment membership schemes, 'passport' schemes, discounted prices, price packaging and a host of others. It is said, 'if you don't promote the organization you either limit or diminish it.'

Mission, market position and segmentation

In constructing a marketing plan, an understanding is needed of three key concepts:

1   mission: what are we in business for?
2   position: how are we placed in the market?
3   segmentation: what segments of the market are we to target?

1 The mission Marketing starts with a cause – a mission. The vision and ethos of an organization can be encapsulated in a mission statement. As Ted Blake (1990) puts it in his succinct manner:

> Everybody is looking for meaning in their lives. The right kind of mission gives this meaning. Meaning, in addition to fair pay and good working conditions, inspires greater trust, co-operation, commitment and loyalty through better job clarification and satisfaction; better decision making; clearer communication; and greater ease of delegation with less need for supervision and inspection. Recruitment becomes less subjective and the mission makes it easier to define, recruit, promote and develop the 'right kind of people'.

The mission statement then becomes the organization's cause, its flag, its purpose.

2 Market position Positioning, like many marketing innovations, emanates from the USA with its highly competitive selling of products. 'Positions' are people's perception of products that can be retained and recalled instantly, and products with favourable positions can also be banked upon for continued sales.

Products and services have long-term 'personalities', just like people. For example, the Bank of England, normally safe and dependable; Wimbledon, the pinnacle of tennis and its traditional values; or Richard Branson's Virgin products, innovative, creative, daring, adventurous. McDonald's, Levi's, Nike, Kelloggs, Heinz, Harrods, Ascot and hundreds of other 'institutions' have a position in our minds and in the marketplace, as has Disney. Positions, however, can be favourable or unfavourable. Local authority leisure services are anxiously trying to throw off yesterday's perceptions. Despite many extremely successful services and good management, they are still tainted in the minds of some people with the tag of 'baths', the smell of chlorine, 'keep off the grass' signs and cheapness.

But market positioning can be re-positioned. The fizzy drink Lucozade used to be sold in chemists' shops for convalescents, but TV promotions using Olympic gold medal winners such as Daley Thompson repositioned it as a refreshing energy drink for athletes. Its marketing position changed from being a drink for the sick to a drink for the fit.

Positions, however, usually take time to establish, though television exposure has speeded up the process. For example, new activity holiday resorts like Center Parcs, have established a strong market position in a relatively short time. Insurance companies such as Cornhill and Axa Equity and Law improved their business ranking through sponsorship of cricket. Green Flag has achieved the same with football.

Positions are perceptions that linger in the public mind. They can be evoked, dramatized, and made more important and urgent by advertising and promotion. Leisure facilities that do not at present engender such perceptions need to work on their products and the presentation of them to win favourable market positioning.

3 Market segmentation Knowing our mission and the position of our products in the minds of potential customers, we need to decide where our best future opportunities lie. Which section or segment of the population should we target? There are basically four approaches which are illustrated in Figure 20.2.

1 selling to existing markets, which includes extending product life cycles, e.g. from aerobics to step aerobics (market penetration)
2 selling to new markets, e.g. incentives for new customers who try taster courses (market development)
3 selling new or re-modelled services to existing customers (product/service development)
4 selling the new services to new markets (market diversification).

A painter or a potter creating a work of art for a special gift provides an exclusive service. Teaching the piano or tennis through private one-to-one tuition also provides an exclusive product designed for the individual. With mass markets, however, it is impossible to provide exclusive products for each individual, but it is possible to tailor-make products for segments of a market. Low-income earners do not buy Rolls Royce cars, nor join the most expensive golf clubs, nor book seats at Covent Garden Opera House. However, there are many dissimilar individuals who can still be segmented

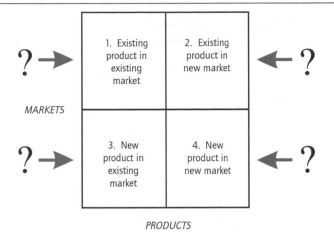

PRODUCTS

Figure 20.2 Increasing products and expanding markets

> Sir Thomas Beecham is reported to have said: 'God has yet to invent a faster way of spending money than putting on an opera'.

because of their similar social characteristics, e.g. the same age, the same sex. Targeting to like-minded segments, with appropriate products, is much more likely to achieve success than a hit-or-miss strategy. Local authorities tend to avoid market segmentation because they believe they should be providing for all their customers. The problem with this view is that the service given may not be wholly appropriate to any group in particular: in trying to suit everybody, they may suit very few.

A market segment, then, is any homogeneous subdivision of a market that is likely to be attracted to particular products or services. A local authority or a company can choose different kinds of segmentation to attract people to their products and services.

- Differentiated markets separate products and services for each segment (e.g. junior sports and senior citizens' 'Old Time Music Hall').
- Undifferentiated markets sell one product to all buyers within a catchment area (e.g. town festival which caters for all segments).
- Concentrated markets focus on one or just a few lucrative or popular 'brands' (e.g. health and fitness and aerobics in a sports centre or golf and tennis at a country club).

The process of segmentation needs good market research, understanding of groups and people's life cycle needs. It requires strategies and selection of segments which match particular products within the overall service.

Sponsorship

Companies are increasingly incorporating sponsorship into the marketing mix as it is a means of 'selling' what the company has to offer. Local authorities also can use sponsorship to enhance their leisure services.

Sports sponsorship has been defined in more pragmatic terms by Sportsmatch (see Useful websites):

Sponsorship is an agreement between a company and an event organizer where the company gives money – or the equivalent in kind – in exchange for rights to associate the company name with the event. This association can include the company name on team shirts, on advertising banners, in press advertisements or whatever is agreed in order to improve the awareness or image of the company.

Sponsorship has been defined as: 'the provision of financial or material support for some independent activity which is not intrinsic to the furtherances of commercial aims, but from which the supporting company might reasonably hope to gain financial benefits' (English Tourist Board, 1998).

Sponsorship differs from patronage where the financial, material or professional expertise is given by a commercial company to an activity for philanthropic reasons, without looking for any material reward or benefit.

Sponsorship can benefit leisure in many ways. For example, it brings in revenue, creates interest, increases participation, audiences and supporters. It can help to attract major 'players' in sports and arts and it can assist in bidding for events or schemes. Sponsorship can also support good causes, social and environmental. However, while there are benefits, there are also costs to the sponsor and the sponsored.

Sponsorship can benefit the company in a number of ways:

1 by increasing publicity
2 by helping to reinforce or change its corporate image
3 by improving public relations, improving trade relations
4 by providing a vehicle for the promotion of company products
5 by increasing market share and gaining competitive advantage
6 sponsorship can be integrated into other marketing communication such as advertising, direct mail and corporate hospitality.

The scale of sponsorship can vary enormously, from contributions of millions of pounds from a multinational company for national sports to the donation of a cup or prize from a small sports shop to a locally run competition. Indeed, most teams in sport have a sponsor. Sponsorship is now a high profile form of collaborative marketing between organizations which usually involves investment by the sponsor, in an event, team, competition, or facility in return for exploitable benefits, particularly favourable promotion and publicity.

Sponsorship growth, worldwide, can be attributed in large measure to increased television coverage of major and mega-events in both sports and arts, though sport predominates (see Chapter 22). Mega-events are extremely costly to the sponsor and potentially extremely beneficial; a World Cup can reach an audience of billions.

Companies want to promote favourable images of themselves and may want also to divert attention from less favourable company product images. With restrictions on tobacco and alcohol advertising, sponsorship offers an alternative. In some cases, the survival of professional sports is dependent on sponsorship. Spectators in any number will only come to watch top players and performers, so events need sponsorship to help pay for star appearances. Sponsors want television coverage which will only be attracted to events with large audience ratings and star players. Without sponsorship, many events would be uneconomic even with large audiences and ticket sales.

Sponsorship has the potential to promote greater awareness than advertising and can be more effective in changing perceptions and positioning an image. Sponsorship is being used not just to sell goods and services but to project a company and all it has to offer; international events can position a company on to a world stage. As Karen Sweaney (1997) wrote in *Australian Leisure Management*, 'sponsorship is no longer about sponsorship any more, it's about presenting the company with all its management expertise to the world'.

Sponsorship in sports and the arts

Sports sponsorship began to develop significantly in the United Kingdom in the early 1960s and expanded dramatically with the ban placed on television cigarette advertising. The cigarette companies had budgeted for television advertising, a large part of which was consequently redirected into sponsorship of sport, since sport had a wide appeal and helped promote a healthy image, thus attempting to counteract anti-smoking propaganda, and probably, most important, lending itself to surrogate advertising through the press and television. However, in 1977 the Minister for Sport placed a ceiling on the amount of sponsorship that cigarette companies could give to sport, and there has been a consequent withdrawal of some companies from this area of sponsorship.

Sponsorship has helped some sports to survive and others to flourish. Snooker and darts are cases in point, but other, once minority, spectator sports are now thriving. For example, basketball in the 1990s was sponsored by Carlsberg and with television exposure, turned from being an insignificant British spectator sport into an expanding one involving the import of American coaches and amalgamation of the top teams from the two main leagues. Ice hockey and indoor bowls experienced a similar growth pattern. However, sponsorship support is not secure and these sports have not yet achieved as high a profile as the major traditional popular sports played in the UK.

The exact amount of sports sponsorship is difficult to ascertain, many companies and governing bodies being reluctant to reveal information. Spending on sports sponsorship events in the United Kingdom is much greater than that for the arts, the latter accounting for approximately 10 per cent. However, there are signs that some sponsors are shifting their ground in favour of the arts. Popular television drama series are highly marketable. However, there is a considerable blurring of what constitutes sponsorship and what is advertising. Until recent years, the arts were more usually the subject of private and company patronage.

Although the majority of sponsorships are a success story, there are some financial disasters, or companies do not achieve expected targets; or the company's name no longer has benefits in one or another direction. The brief history of sponsorship has shown it to be a rapidly changing and fluctuating industry. Among the problems are that the larger the sponsorship investment, the greater the implications on the activity and the greater the harmful effects if sponsorship is withdrawn.

Although there are many hundreds of commercial companies sponsoring all manner of leisure pursuits and organizations, national and international sport and art events gain the most from sponsorship. It is the major companies investing heavily in sponsorship that dominate the market financially.

As might be expected, the major sports services and equipment companies have a considerable stake in sports sponsorship. However, in cash terms the major sponsors tend to be the national banks, the oil companies, and tobacco manufacturers. Brewers, insurance companies and of late computer and mobile phone companies have entered the field. The classic top sports events in the UK attract substantial sponsorship, for example, Test Matches, the Grand National, the Oxford and Cambridge Boat Race, and the London Marathon.

> Most multinational and national companies are involved in some measure with sponsorship.

Why do the 'big four' – banks, oil, tobacco and alcohol – need to be involved in sponsorship? Although commercially powerful, they are vulnerable to a tarnished public image. Banking and oil are connected with huge profits, drinking is linked with alcoholism and crime, and smoking with lung cancer. Sponsorship helps to buy respectability. Respectability means a good public image. Good images create favourable impressions to buy products and services. The major sponsor's main motive is not to aid sport and the arts *per se*, but to achieve maximum favourable publicity. Maximum publicity means exposure on television. The greatest sponsorship of sport and the arts is seen on the BBC television channels. The BBC's charter, however, explicitly forbids paid advertising. Commercial television cannot sponsor. However, the line between advertising and sponsorship is somewhat fragile. There appears to be a qualitative difference between the two. The publication of a company brand constitutes advertising; the company's name does not. The company nevertheless can obtain more exposure per hour for its name than would be achievable or permissible on the independent television network.

With technological advances such as cable and satellite television, sponsorship via the media will increase, and digital television will spread sponsorship further still. However, sponsorship is no longer of national significance only, it is international – worldwide. Sponsorship which is in place for a mega-event bid such as an Olympic Games or World tournament, can help to provide a favourable financial anchorage.

From a leisure management viewpoint, whether companies are advertising or sponsoring events and projects, they are all marketing to draw customers to their services and products by creating favourable impressions, so that people will buy what the company has to offer rather than a competitor's product.

Sponsoring good causes at a community level

Sponsorship is of local as well as national significance and sponsors can raise their respectability profile with the public and with government when sponsoring good causes, particularly those advocated by the government. For example, in 2003 an All Party Parliamentary Group on Obesity reported that overweight correlates with inactive lifestyles. Initiatives that tackle problems of inactivity or social and environmental issues, place a sponsor in a favourable light. Brief examples are provided to show how sponsorship is helping in tackling inactivity in children and young people illustrating how linkages can be forged between the government, organizations and sponsors. The examples include Sportsmatch, the Youth Sports Trust, Cadbury, Nike and BSkyB. However, they also show the potential incompatibility between business goals and good causes.

438

Case study: Sportsmatch

Sportsmatch is the government's grass-roots sports sponsorship incentive scheme. It is funded by the Department for Culture, Media and Sport (DCMS) via grant aid from Sport England and administered in England by the Institute of Sports Sponsorship. Established in 1992, Sportsmatch today receives around £3.5 million of government funding each year. Its objective is to use government funds to attract new and existing sponsors in sport. It has made over 3,800 awards in 73 different sports over the period 1992–2003. A lion's share has gone to Association Football, Rugby Union, cricket and multisport. Other main recipients include basketball, Lawn Tennis, athletics, rowing, rugby and field hockey.

Case study: The Youth Sports Trust (YST)

The Youth Sports Trust has several initiatives designed alongside its TOP Programme, which encourage and provide for physical activities for children and young people. Some of these are enabled through sponsorship. The YST works in partnership with business such as sports goods companies (Nike, Reebok, Pentland, Adidas) and these companies provide the YST with resources and national promotion; in turn the schemes meet the corporate brand and social responsibility objectives of the company.

Case study: Zoneparcs

In 2001, the Youth Sports Trust, Nike and the Department for Education and Skills (DfES) initiated a pilot programme to transform the environment of school playgrounds. YTS claim that the 13 pilot Nike Zoneparcs have resulted in better behaviour by pupils, less truancy and a more active school population.

Case study: Cadbury Get Active scheme

This scheme established three projects: Free Sports Kit 4 Schools, Resources 4 Teachers (resources and training for teachers from the YST) and Cadbury Get Active Event. Free Sports Kit 4 Schools has made inroads into 22,000 schools with £8.8 million worth of equipment. It offers schools a chance to obtain sports equipment, through special tokens printed on over 160 million chocolate bars. This undoubtedly creates interest and opportunity to get children involved in more physical activity; however it also opens up the debate on healthy eating. A headline in the *Guardian* read: 'How much chocolate do you need to eat to get a free netball from Cadbury?' The British Dietetic Association also said that the promotion went against all public health messages, with 31 per cent of children overweight and 17 per cent obese. The counter argument from the DCMS is that eating chocolate is not harmful within a balanced diet and an active lifestyle. The company suggests that the tokens collected are not just from the children at school but from the whole community.

Case study: Reach For The Sky (RFTS)

This long-term project is an initiative to support and inspire young people to achieve their potential. Three specific initiatives for 2004 were: RFTS Live, Youth Challenge and Living for Sport. Launched in September 2003, Living for Sport is an initiative from BSkyB and the Youth Sports Trust for young people aged between 11 and 16. RFTS Challenge, launched in January 2004, aims to help young people to develop new skills, and build confidence and self-esteem. It is aimed at young people 16 and 17 years of age and not in education, employment or training. There are four zones: Music, Dance, Drama and Video Production.

These brief examples illustrate how sponsorship can be used as one of the marketing tools to promote the sponsor and the organizations receiving sponsorship. It also illustrates the fusion between organizational objectives, management and marketing.

Leisure Managers need to be aware of the benefits and problems associated with sponsorship and also need an understanding of how difficult it can be in securing sponsorship. Sportsmatch offers the following advice in attracting a sponsor.

1   Appoint a co-ordinator for sponsorship through whom all communications are channelled.
2   Decide exactly what you are seeking sponsorship for using a sponsorship audit: what does the organization have to offer the potential sponsor and what are the potential sponsors seeking to achieve?
3   Draw up a shortlist of companies and find out how the marketing objectives of each company meet the organization's objectives.
4   Write the sponsorship-seeking letter with a view to setting up a meeting and follow up each letter with a telephone call.
5   Write a sponsorship proposal which should include the information gathered in the audit.
6   Secure a meeting and plan for it meticulously: its objectives, the organization of ideas and how delivery can be effected.

For sport sponsorships, information should be given to the potential sponsor of the Sportsmatch £ for £ scheme. For the arts, potential sponsors should be informed of the Arts and Business incentive scheme which helps in linking organizations to sponsors (see The arts and business and Lottery funding, p. 331, Chapter 16).

Up to this point in the chapter, having looked into the concept of marketing, positioning, segmentation and the marketing mix, we are now in a position to consider how to go about constructing a marketing plan.

Constructing a marketing plan

In order to market successfully there needs to be a marketing plan. We want to bridge the gap between where we are now and where we want to be. To do that, we need to match appropriate products and services to the different segments of the market. However, there are no exact formulas, no off-the-shelf marketing plans, no one-way-

A marketing plan is a document that incorporates a plan for marketing the services and products of an organization. It sets out the organization's marketing objectives and proposes strategies and the resources needed to achieve them. The plan is the result of marketing planning.

only strategies. Good marketing plans are tailor-made. The marketing process is flexible, able to adapt to changing situations, able to respond to opportunities.

Marketing planning is a process that involves:

- undertaking research within and outside the organization
- looking at the strengths and weaknesses of the organization, its services and products
- setting marketing objectives
- generating marketing strategies; defining programmes
- setting budgets and
- monitoring, reviewing and revising the strategies and programmes.

Figure 20.3 illustrates a ten-stage marketing plan: it is described briefly overleaf.

Figure 20.3 Process in writing a marketing plan

1 Set or confirm the organization's vision, mission and objectives.
2 Identify market demand through market research. This could involve demographic analysis of the perceived catchment area, studying the trends and market structure and whether it is expanding or contracting, measuring the level of competing services or facilities and their positions in the market.
3 Carry out internal research into the organization itself and its position in the marketplace, the services it provides, its performance and its capacity. Many managers still use the acronym SWOT to signify analysis that looks into the strengths, weaknesses, and the opportunities for the organization and potential threats to its success.
4 Set marketing objectives and targets. This is key to the plan. It states unequivocally in measurable terms what the plan aims to achieve.
5 Create marketing strategies and action plans – the methods that will be used to meet marketing objectives. These will relate to the elements in the marketing mix. For each marketing objective, strategies need to be developed relating to the elements in the marketing mix – product, price, promotion, and place. Sponsorship could be one of the strategies used for one or more of the objectives.
6 Define the programmes. This converts strategies into focused actions of what will be done, when, where, how and by whom.
7 Set budgets and identify resources. Programmes and actions need resources of the organization, its staff, time and money. This stage defines the resources required to carry out the marketing plan.
8 Prepare the written marketing plan. This should be concise and need only contain the essential information that needs to be communicated.
9 Communicate the marketing plan, especially to those who will be implementing it. The process leading up to this point should have involved consultation with the organization's personnel.
10 Monitor, review and revise. The marketing plan will need regular review and updating to take account of changing conditions and situations.

What follows is an example of how a marketing plan for a large new public leisure and recreation indoor centre might be written.

A ten-stage plan for marketing a new public leisure and recreation facility

Stage 1: Policy of the organization
- Write the 'mission statement' which sets out the purpose of the facility and the key overall objectives.

Stage 2: External research and market demand
- Determine potential of facility.
- Undertake demographic analysis of perceived catchment area (having taken location and accessibility into consideration).
- Study the market profile and different market segments.
- Examine the market structure and the range of competing facilities. Is the market expanding or contracting? What are the market trends? What is our share of the market? What positions do our services have on the market?

- Identify the segments of the market that need to be targeted.
- Undertake survey of programme requirements of the general public, local clubs, schools and organizations.

Stage 3: Internal research
- Look into the organization: its 'position', performance, services and products; undertake a SWOT analysis (strengths, weaknesses, opportunities and threats).
- Examine competence of staff to undertake promotional tasks.

Stage 4: Set market objectives and targets
- Having analysed the market structure, position and products and services, all we have achieved is to know where we stand. We need to decide where we want to get to and how.
- Set marketing objectives including the targets, the market segments, and the results to be achieved.

Stage 5: Market strategy
- Decide strategies to meet objectives.
- Provide centre with identifiable logo (potential for local competition).
- Establish programme guidelines to cover casual use by public, education, range of activities to be offered, club usage, courses, etc.
- Establish target groups: 50 plus, unemployed, disabled, mother and toddler, areas of disadvantage.
- Determine potential total attendances.
- Propose areas to secure sponsorship (to supplement promotional budget).

Stage 6: Programme (product)
- Produce practical suggestions for programming to meet council policy: range of activities, range and ability level of courses to be offered, proposed competitions, proposals for establishment of facility-based organizations, specific programme for different target groups, special events proposals.
- Suggest role in borough/district leisure development plan and cultural strategy.

Stage 7: Pricing strategy
- Produce proposals to ensure: value-for-money image, maximum penetration in local catchment area, maximum impact on target groups
- Consider: discounts for target groups, cost per participant for courses.
- Suggested prices for: peak/off peak, club use, hire of premises.
- Estimate gross profit levels on trading activities.

Stage 8: Promotions
8A Pre-opening phase
- Identify methods to create high levels of awareness amongst potential users.
- Maintain high level of press coverage throughout the development phase.
- Communicate with clubs and organizations and representatives of education service.

- Introduce newspaper pull-out supplement to enhance public image of facility (and obtain sponsorship and sale of advertising space).
- Produce brochures providing information relating to: scale of facilities, activities to be offered/opening hours, availability of courses, prices to be charged, programme for target groups, booking procedures.
- Distribute leaflets at locations accessible to public.
- Produce 'give-aways' e.g. stickers, badges and balloons.
- Produce design/layouts for posters and advertisements.
- Estimate gross cost of printing brochures, posters etc., advertising in local media, staff/personality fee, cost of artwork, cost of promotional 'give aways', staff costs and travel expenses.
- Estimate income from sponsorship to offset costs.

8B Opening phase
- Suggest programme for official opening, e.g. displays, competition.
- Obtain personality and resources to undertake official opening.
- Draw up list of official guests and VIPs and suggest hospitality.
- Draw up invitation list of local clubs and organizations.
- Place advertisements in local media.
- Organize house-to-house invitation drop.

8C Post-opening phase
- Consolidate early successes.
- Identify programme areas that are underperforming and reassess them.
- Organize and promote special events on regular basis.
- Review programme on regular basis and modify if necessary.

Stage 9: Project results
- Estimate: level of utilization, total attendances, total users (adults, juniors), club usage, attendance on courses, total income.
- Identify user profile and compare to market profile.

Stage 10: Monitor and review
- Assess effectiveness of promotional strategy.
- Compare facility performance with set objectives and targets.
- Obtain feedback, consult and amend programme if necessary.
- Introduce occasional new initiatives.

Summary and conclusions

This chapter has considered the marketing approach to leisure services and facilities and the benefits that can accrue to organizations. The concepts of the marketing mix, market positioning and segmentation were explained. It is suggested that marketing approaches to leisure products and services, using a marketing plan, will increase the probability of success in both public and private sectors. The marketing approach ensures that when a product or service is made available to the consumer, it has been planned, designed, packaged, promoted and delivered in such a manner that the customer is persuaded not only to buy, but also to repeat the experience as often as possible. While impulse buying, like attending an event or 'having a go' are important, repeat visits and repeat buying of the leisure experience are even more important. People get 'hooked' on products. Once bitten by the bug of pottery, painting, jazz, playing golf, fitness, squash, snooker, sauna bathing or yoga, we are anxious to participate even more. They become habit-forming.

Marketing needs a budget. Compared to the commercial sector, the amounts that local authorities spend, usually under the heading 'advertising', are minimal. The marketing process, however, needs to be adjusted to meet the conceptual differences to be found in private sector establishments and local authority services. Opportunities exist to meet community needs and demands through marketing, but sensitive handling of the process and selection of appropriate methods and messages are essential. Values and principles should be the foundations.

At the start of this chapter, it was stated that marketing is concerned with voluntary exchange and that leisure services are provided in exchange for people's money, time and rates and taxes. If the public does not want what is provided and is not prepared to pay the costs and give up the time, then local authority support could well be reduced. Therefore, Leisure Managers must be concerned with the questions: are the clients and customers satisfied with the leisure products, are they experiencing satisfactions? It is not just how many participated, but whether the market target groups were reached with satisfying results and whether objectives were met.

Marketing needs objectives, a plan, action and measurement. A marketing plan is a statement about what actions are to be undertaken to meet objectives. Marketing affects people's attitudes. It can affect the way they speak, look, think and behave. Managers of leisure should encourage people to look more favourably towards themselves and towards the products and services being offered by their organizations.

Discussion points

1 Marketing, on the one hand, can be an extremely powerful influence for 'good', on the other hand, it can be equally as dangerous. It can affect not only how we spend money, but also how we look and behave. Discuss in the context of leisure.

2 Marketing of social causes, including play, recreation and leisure, can have profound effects. But is marketing and advertising always honest and ethical? Discuss with examples for and against the question.

3 Marketing is often perceived only as advertising to sell goods and services. Explain how this perception is a long way short of understanding what marketing should be and should achieve.

4 Selling focuses on the seller, marketing on the needs of the buyer. Discuss these assumptions in light of leisure and recreation services.

Further reading

Torkildsen, G. (1993), *Marketing made simple – forget the myths and mysteries*, Torkildsen's Guides to Leisure Management, Longman, Harlow.

Courtis, J. (1987), *Marketing Services: A Practical Guide*, British Institute of Management, Kogan Page, London.

Kotler, P. (1990), *Principles of Marketing*, 5th edn, Prentice-Hall, Englewood Cliffs, NJ.

Kotler, P. (1996), *Marketing for Hospitality and Tourism*, Prentice-Hall, Hemel Hempstead.

Lovelock, C. (1991), *Services Marketing*, 2nd edn, Prentice-Hall, Englewood Cliffs, NJ.

McIver, C. (1987), *The Marketing Mirage: How to Make a Reality*, Heinemann, London.

Stone, M. (1990), *Leisure Services Marketing*, Croner, Kingston-upon-Thames.

Useful websites

Chartered Institute of Marketing (CIM): www.cim.co.uk

Advertising Association (representing advertisers, agencies, the media and support services): mailto:aa@adassoc.org.uk

Advertising Standards Authority (the independent, self-regulatory body for non-broadcast advertisements in the UK): mailto:inquiries@asa.org.uk

British Market Research Association ('representing and promoting the best in British market research'): mailto:admin@bmra.org.uk

21

Programming leisure and recreation services and facilities

In this chapter

- The what and why of leisure programming
- Programme classification
- Directional programme planning strategies
- Specific methods and approaches
- Co-ordinating the approaches to programming
- Targeting disadvantaged groups
- Programming multi-leisure centres
- Programming by Objectives.

Introduction

Programming and marketing go hand in hand in the process of managing leisure. Programming is the key element in the delivery of services. It is the means by which opportunities are provided for people to enjoy their leisure time. It is also the mechanism by which the aims and objectives of an organization are realized. Programming and event management are undertaken by Leisure Managers in the public, commercial and voluntary sectors.

This chapter concentrates on the programming process and the manager's role in that process. The leisure field is so varied and complex that in giving practical examples to support ideas, there has been a need for selection. Greater emphasis has been given to recreation services and facility programmes open to the general public.

The what and why of leisure and recreation programming

Programming is important. It is a highly underrated factor in leisure management yet the programme is the single most important product of a leisure and recreation organization. Everything that a service or department is concerned with – facilities, supplies, personnel, budgets, marketing, public relations, activities, timetabling and administration – is solely to ensure that opportunities exist for people to enjoy or experience leisure in ways satisfying to them. The opportunity is made available through the programme.

447

Programming must achieve optimal use of existing resources – facilities, personnel and finance – to meet the goals of the organization and the needs of people. The programming process is the delivery mechanism by which these objectives are met. There are other reasons for excellent programming.

1   There is a need to make the best use of resources: time, space, staff, money.
2   There is a need to resolve conflicting claims of time and space for available facilities.
3   Most leisure facilities have potential permutations in which to exploit and provide opportunities; the same space can often be used for different activities at different times.
4   Space which is not sold today is lost forever.
5   There is a need for balance in the programme and for fairness between a wide range of clients and potential customers.
6   Good programming is a means of achieving best results: optimum numbers, a range of different people and a choice of activities.
7   The programme provides order and structure; people know when to come, and what they can expect.
8   Without programming, there could be chaos, no order, no structure, no balance and unfairness, and resources will not be used to best advantage; even space available on a casual or first-come, first-served basis needs to be programmed.

Leisure programming consists of planning, scheduling, timetabling and implementing action. The process uses resources, facilities and staff to offer a wide range of services and activities – passive, active, routine, guided, graded, varied and special – within the reach of the community to be served. The programme is the essence of leisure and recreation services; it is their *raison d'être*.

Programmes will differ depending on the facilities and on the aims of the organization. A leisure facility may be run by different kinds of organization: it may be a community recreation trust, an arts or sports association, a private sports company or under local government contract management. Whether a public authority, a voluntary organization or a sports and leisure business, all have to attract the public, or they fail. Programmes are the tools of the Leisure Manager; they are the vehicles through which leisure opportunity is made available to the community.

One of the hallmarks of good programming is the extent to which individual satisfaction, individual welfare and the values of the participant are important aspects of the programme. While numbers are important, the individual rather than the aggregate must be the core of the service. Programmes are often judged on how many have attended; qualitative aspects are rarely brought into any evaluation. In order to programme for people, we should bring people into programme planning. Within the broad range of leisure programming, a fundamental aspect for public sector services, is community recreation.

Community recreation programming

Community recreation programming incorporates many social objectives, but local authorities in the United Kingdom, faced with economic difficulties, have now to programme within far tighter financial constraints than in the 1960s to 1980s, the growth years in public leisure provision. The Leisure Manager should strive to offer a programme which balances the needs of different people, different activities, together with the social and financial objectives. A balanced activity programme at a local authority leisure complex would have some of the following features:

1 opportunities to participate in a range of leisure activities on a structured and informal basis
2 opportunities to participate actively, passively and creatively
3 opportunities to be involved as an individual or with a club or group
4 time set aside for a regular core programme of activities as well as time set aside for a variable programme
5 competition, participation events and audience and spectator special events.

Programming in multi-use centres tends to be founded in tradition, convention and guesswork: on trial and error, common-sense approaches. These are inadequate substitutes for good programme planning. Leisure Managers, therefore, need to be leisure programmers, interpreting policy and having the organizational skills to deliver the bespoke programmes appropriate to the needs of different market sectors.

Which main agencies programme leisure and recreation?

There are many agencies and organizations involved in programming leisure and recreation services and facilities. They include local government, leisure trusts, leisure management contractors, commercial organizations, education authorities, schools, company sports clubs, institutions, HM Forces and a wide range of voluntary organizations, associations and clubs. There are, however, four broad categories:

- the commercial sector
- institutional sector
- voluntary sector and
- the local government sector.

The commercial sector has specified, defined activities, and segmented targets and user categories. It has cinemas, bingo halls, night-clubs, fitness centres, golf driving ranges, tenpin bowling centres, tennis centres, country clubs and holiday centres.

The institutional sector, such as universities, colleges and community schools, needs skilful programming, but, generally, there is a discrete main market – that of the institution first, and the community second. In the industrial sector, a variety of leisure and sports facilities have to be programmed, but here, again, high levels of exclusivity and club-based organization make for ease of programming.

In the voluntary sector, programming is largely for interest groups such as sports clubs or multi-activity groups. However, trusts and not-for-profit voluntary organizations, such as the YMCA/YWCA and large community associations, with a range of facilities, find themselves in similar situations to leisure managers at public leisure centres in terms of programming.

It is in the diversified local government public sector where broad-based programming skills are most needed, because of the range of facilities, the range of activities and the range of customers. Also, Leisure Managers have to effect a balance between on the one hand providing a social service, on the principle of equality of opportunity, and increasingly on the other hand providing a more economic service. Facilities such as swimming pools, leisure centres, playing pitches, theatres, community halls and dual use centres at schools, need programming to produce appropriate balances of opportunity. One of the main problems that public providers have is that balanced programmes giving equal opportunity to all is extremely difficult to fashion without sufficient resources and a range of facilities. One of the problems is encapsulated in the truism 'There is nothing more unequal than the equal treatment of unequals.'

What constitutes a programme?

What makes a programme? Does it have to be a schedule of activities, a timetable of bookings, or a list of events? Or can it be the planned availability of a supervised playground, a park, a school or venture trail? Or can it exist through the organized distribution of services such as a recreation and leisure information service which collates all that is going on? A programme is all these things and a good deal more. It can take almost any form in the framework of one's definition of what constitutes a leisure or recreation activity. However, in practical terms, programmes revolve around:

- activities
- amenities and facilities
- services
- staff and
- money.

Activities can range from the completely spontaneous variety to the highly structured and all stages in between. Informal activities can be anticipated within a community programme by creating opportunities, encouraging spontaneity, having resources available such as space, time and equipment – like a ball to kick about, a wall to scribble on or deck chairs to sunbathe on. Structured activities, for programming purposes, fall into several major categories such as arts, crafts, dance, drama, entertainment, games, sport and health and fitness, hobbies, music, nature, social recreation, travel and tourism, and voluntary service to the community.

Amenities cover open spaces, buildings, supplies and equipment within recreation. These can be designed and constructed for special purposes such as public arts centres or swimming pools; designed for self-directed or spontaneous activity like a park; or simply the natural resources available to the public such as riverside walks, forests and beaches.

Services cover all methods and means through which people are enabled to enjoy leisure and recreation, for example, information services, promotion and publicity, transport, passport schemes in local authorities, member credit card or direct debit schemes in private clubs, crèches and holiday services for parents with young children.

Staff are the enablers, connectors and controllers: duty managers, supervisors, coaches, countryside rangers, teachers, technicians, cleaners, stage hands, librarians, museum curators, sports development officers, youth and community workers and receptionists.

Money is needed for the investment to achieve financial profits or to break-even or to run services, facilities and programmes at an agreed subsidy level.

The Leisure Manager/programmer must use the available resources efficiently to deliver programmes that meet the aims and objectives of the organization. The recreation programme, however, is not a series of individual activities strung together. It is a carefully integrated and planned combination of many activities selected on the basis of individual and group interest, related ideas and themes, organized to achieve the objectives of the organization and the needs of individuals and groups it is intended to serve.

Programme classification

How a programme is classified is not of major importance. However, the type of programme needs to be known in order to communicate with the public and avoid misconceptions. Programme classification should describe and communicate the different activities in the programme. Classification is more than communicating what is on offer. It helps in providing programme balance through analysis of each category. The commercial sector is particularly adept at 'segmenting' market sectors for profitable outcome.

Simple classifications can aid communication and administration and make it easier for clients and customers to understand. 'Fun sessions' at a swimming pool will give a warning signal to serious adult swimmers that these sessions may not be for them. Programmes can be classified in a number of ways and four in particular are commonly used:

- by function: the most usual classification, normally by listing a number of activities or groups of activities such as sports, arts, crafts, social; often, the functional classification is linked to special groups of people, such as children, youth, disabled, aged, beginners, advanced and so on
- by facilities: pitches available, pool opening times, halls to be let
- by people: who the programme is intended for, such as casual users, members, family days, over 50s, parents and toddlers
- by outcomes: 'Learn to swim', improver courses, 'Keep fit', 'Slim and trim' sessions.

Sociologists and psychologists tend to group people for classification into life stages. Erikson (1963) identified eight stages – six stages up to young adulthood and two stages beyond. Meyer (1957) presented four adult stages. Farrell and Lundegren (1978) identified a range of activities through eleven life cycle changes. However, these can be merged for many programmes (e.g. youth, teenager and young adults can be grouped together), or the groups can be further broken down (e.g. pre-school into toddlers, infants and pre-school). Further classification can be made regarding the activities themselves: passive/active, structured/unstructured, planned/self-directed, high risk/low risk, and so on.

In summary, the community recreation programme is the means by which activities are delivered to clients and customers and the means also of meeting the aims and objectives the organization. It has been defined as 'the total experiences of individuals and groups resulting from community action in providing areas, facilities, leadership and funds. These experiences represent a wide range of activities, planned and spontaneous, organized and informal, supervised and undirected' (Butler, 1976, p. 231). Essential elements that influence the success or failure of the programme to meet its stated objectives are planning and management. Without these elements, programmes would be inefficient and ineffective. First, we consider the planning strategies.

Directional programme planning strategies

The two main strategic directions for public-related community recreation programmes, put simply, are:

1 social programming: planned programmes directed professionally by officers or authorities
2 community development: programmes which emanate from the community itself.

They could be termed 'other-directed' and 'community initiated' (Edginton *et al.*, 1980, pp. 28–43).

The social planning approach is the most common. The basic assumption underlying this process is that use of professional expertise and knowledge is the most effective way of meeting community needs and demands, balancing programmes and meeting objectives. Community development, on the other hand, is a method of organization in which the role of the Leisure Manager is one of enabling individuals and organizations to get involved in the programming process. The locus of control is the important factor. Leisure development occurs as a result of community intervention and involvement, not as a result of diagnosis by a professional or the authority. The process itself and the participation is part of the experience; participants assume initiatives for their own development. The social planning method is participant dependent and professional and authority controlled. The community development approach fosters participant independence. The distinction between the differing approaches is put cogently by Edginton *et al.* (1980, p. 38):

It is important to draw a distinction between the work of a community developer and the work of a social planner. Perhaps the most important difference concerns the view that each has of the participant. The social planner views the participant as a consumer of his services. The role is to isolate individuals with needs and then intervene directly with services. The community developer, on the other hand, views participants as citizens with whom he or she engages in an interactive process of problem solving. The social planner is primarily involved in fact gathering in an effort to determine the needs of the individuals being served. Once the appropriate information has been gathered, it is used in the decision making process to develop a rational plan for the distribution of available or acquired resources. The community developer, however, maintains a basic strategy of change in which the role is to help individuals identify and bring about change through their collaborative efforts. The community developer works with individuals and small groups, whereas the work of the social planner is primarily carried out in large, often bureaucratic organizations. The skills needed by the social planner are primarily those of management and administration; the community developer's skills should be particularly strong in the areas of communications and small group behaviour.

The adoption of a community development approach needs capable, trained men and women 'out in the field'. Community developers have become known by many names: encourager, enabler, catalyst, friend, adviser, activator and so on. The French use the words *animateur* or *animateur sociale*. Animateurs are well trained, capable and sensitive people who work towards stimulating individuals to think about their own development and also the development of other people in the community, through community programming. They work to develop the leadership capabilities of others. They assist by supplying information about methods and procedures; they enable others to act for themselves.

The relationship between the animateur and the group changes as the group matures. Initially, the animateur fulfils the role of the benevolent authoritarian leader and undertakes the necessary tasks associated with the activities of the group and its maintenance. With continued contact, the role of the animateur changes to that of a democratic leader; and as leaders emerge from the group, his or her role diminishes and the groups largely become autonomous but with support available, should it be necessary. This support is normally required if the natural leaders of the group leave and there are no immediate replacements.

The experience in the United Kingdom has shown that on the whole outreach programmes are only successful as long as the support is available over a sustained period of time. When the programmes cease, through lack of funding for example, the majority of the newly formed groups founder after a period of time due partly to the lack of physical and/or psychological support. In the United Kingdom, the current expansion of Sports Development Officers is creating new opportunities. The systems which are being put in place are also providing pathways and networks to maintain and sustain new programme developments.

Traditionally, local authorities have undertaken the social planning approach to programming, with much of the work being administered centrally, from the town hall away from the facilities. Such an approach, alone, has disadvantages.

1   The decision makers are remote from the potential users of the facilities.
2   There is generally a lack of consultation and sensitivity concerning the needs and demands of the community.
3   The facility staff are less likely to be involved in the decision-making process and this can lead to a lack of accountability and commitment at facility level; this can manifest itself in poor staff motivation and low job satisfaction.
4   Decision making tends to involve committees and may be slow, resulting in repetitive and unimaginative programmes. However, programme planning is increasingly decentralized and there have also been a number of programmes focusing on the community development approach (see Haywood and Henry, 1986).

Looking across the broad spectrum of recreation programming, it seems clear that to adopt one direction – social planning or community development – to the exclusion of the other would be inappropriate. Both strategies have merit. A blend of the two is not only possible, but also essential. In addition to the directional mixture, the actual specific approaches and methods can be selected to meet particular segments of the market or to suit particular requirements. To achieve a blend and balance of direction and of approach calls for high skills of management and for programme planning objectivity.

Specific methods and approaches

Within the broad framework of the two main directional strategies lies a range of specific approaches and methods of programming. Providing leisure opportunity is so diverse and complex that there is no one approach, system or method which is suitable for all organizations, all situations or all people. The different methods are known by a variety of names; most of them have no agreed formal titles.

Most methods appear to evolve as a result of the nature and the aims of the organizations themselves. From around thirty approaches which have been identified, including those of Farrell and Lundegren (1978), Edginton *et al.* (1980) and Kraus and Curtis (1977), this section groups some of these together into twelve broad approaches or methods.

The programming methods employed depend on the organization, the aims, the community to be served, the directional strategy, staff skills, money, facilities and a wide variety of other factors. Most recreation programmers do not use a single method. Most use a number of methods, but if they are poorly planned, they can be an untidy mix, lacking co-ordination. Specific methods include the following dozen, in no order of priority. They each have benefits if used along with other methods.

1 Lettings policy or *laissez-faire* approach is commonly found in the management of community centres; the facility is provided and made known; bookings and usage are awaited. Optimal usage and balance are seldom achieved.

2 The traditional approach, whereby what has gone on in the past and is generally successful is likely to be repeated. This is useful information. However, it relies on the same format for future programme planning. It is not necessarily based on needs, but on what has worked before. It does not take into account new ideas and changes in demand. As a single approach, it is ineffective. It can be a far more useful as part of a scheme which learns from the past and makes modifications for the future.

3 The comparative current trends approach relies on reacting to recent trends or activities in vogue. This has benefits in meeting some new demands. However, the approach is totally experimental. It is likely to serve only a segment of the market, and what may work in one area may be a total failure in others. Fads are important to provide for but must be seen in context. It is a useful method to include so as to test the market.

4 The expressed desires approach, by asking people through questionnaires and surveys and then programming for people's wishes, assumes we are providing what they want. But will this result in actual participation? And which activities will meet which desires? Such an approach is difficult to administer, but it is a valuable tool for the programme planner; it gives information about people's desires and wishes. This approach has its limitations, however, as many respondents may not

really know what they want until they try it and cannot predict with any degree of accuracy what their future leisure behaviour is likely to be.

5   The authoritarian approach, whereby reliance is placed on the judgement of the Leisure Manager. The assumption is that he or she understands what the needs are and what the community wants. This is a quick and tidy approach at its design and planning stage. However, participants are denied any involvement in the programme process. Such an approach makes it difficult to adapt to a more community-orientated strategy. The prescriptive approach (Edginton *et al.*, 1980), and perceived need approach (Kraus and Curtis, 1977) are very similar to the authoritarian approach. Programming by the manager's perception of what a community wants, is a tempting approach to adopt because it appears to be based on needs. However, without community involvement, it relies on professional expertise to diagnose other people's needs.

6   The political/social approach is where pressure from groups, often linked to social causes, is used as a basis for a community programme. Edginton *et al.* (1980), and Kraus and Curtis (1977), use the term 'sociopolitical'. Such causes are invariably grist to the political mill, and carry councillor support. For example, crime, poverty, deprivation, discrimination and social disorder may call for particular kinds of recreation planning and programming. Leisure Managers, particularly in the public sector, do not operate in a vacuum but have to respond to political and social pressure and to changing conditions. The approach, however, needs careful handling by an experienced, mature Leisure Manager and within the context of the overall goals of the organization.

7   Action–investigation–creation plan approach is a three-phase plan to programming which Tillman (1974) suggests is the most effective. The action plan is a reaction to the demands generated by the community. The investigation plan is concerned with fact-finding. The creation plan is the interactive relationship between participants and professionals. The professionals use their own expertise and actively seek the views and involvement of participants. Such a three-phase plan, allied to aims and objectives, could form a logical basis for programming.

8   External requirements approach is where the programme is basically dictated by an authority, an institution or a governing body. It tends to have uniform standards, leadership and resources and there is an external assessment for measuring. A Scout or Girl Guide troop, for example, will satisfy the association's requirements. Such organizations normally have vertical management structures, a hierarchical leadership pattern, similar resources, administration and an external reward system. Uniformed groups like British Red Cross, St John Ambulance Brigade and Girls' Brigade and Boys' Brigade, and newer groups like the Majorettes, are clear examples.

9   Cafeteria-style approach is where a variety of diverse choices are assembled. James Murphy is reported to have first termed this approach the 'cafeteria' style (Murphy, 1980). This is a useful approach, in that there is a variety of choice; people may not know what they want and can try things out. Additionally, such an approach can help to meet the diverse needs of clients, such as family groups where individuals can choose different activities. It is a safe approach but tends to be expensive. While appearing to be the answer to the Leisure Manager's dilemma, it is ineffective in the use of resources, in that it can create and provide services

which are unused because they have not been chosen. And in addition, it is very difficult to set objectives and measure success: some activities will be winners and others losers, but the reasons may not be known. For example, poor marketing, rather than the activity, may be the cause. Nevertheless, any comprehensive programming will need to indulge in a cafeteria approach for some of its recreation programmes.

10 The demand approach – offering what people want – is the most usual form of programming. Clubs, associations and interest groups make known their demands. Managers are faced with scores of applications requesting specific facilities. However, the most vocal, the most aware and the socially articulate will make their demands known most readily. The approach is not concerned with equitable distribution and may result in narrow segmental programming. Many people and groups will not be aware of the recreation options and benefits. Most comprehensive programmes, however, will and should include this approach within the overall plan.

11 The community orientation approach – this is a process where individuals are involved in the planning process. The approach is only possible by using professionals or capable amateurs to meet people on their own patch, for example, through outreach programmes, associations and community counsellors.

The discovery approach is an extension and continuation of community orientation. It assumes that people can work together, there being no superior or subordinate relationships. One's knowledge, skills, abilities and interests are used to meet another's needs without necessarily imposing value systems or external expectations. The approach is a people-to-people approach of interactive discovery requiring community face-to-face leadership.

12 Community leadership approach is where consumer input is made possible through advisory boards, user committees, tenants' groups and other action groups. They represent the concerns of the community. This approach assumes that individual interests are represented by their group. This, of course, is not wholly possible, but it does indicate community interaction and a level of democracy. As Edginton *et al.* emphasize, it opens channels of communication between providers and consumers. It is a valuable tool for the recreation programmer.

Few community recreation service programmes emanate from the community itself or from consumer input; this kind of programming is difficult, time-consuming and expensive in terms of paid personnel, usually requiring subsidy or to be managed by volunteers; hence, it is increasingly out of fashion with a growing commercial realism in local authorities.

Because there is lack of understanding of the complexity and importance of programming, community leisure services and facility programmes are often conventional and based on educated guesswork; they are not based on people's needs. A carefully selected mix of programming methods needs to be chosen to best suit the situation. This requires good leisure management.

Co-ordinating the approaches to programming

In terms of community recreation, organizations are faced with a twin dilemma: which strategic programming direction should be taken? Which methods should be adopted to meet objectives? The Leisure Manager is the key person in finding solutions. This is where the manager should come into his or her own. He or she will be trained and experienced to assess the situation. One of the guiding principles will be that programming must be situationally and culturally specific. There are different communities, different problems. The good manager must be a realist and use whatever approaches and options are open to meet needs and demands effectively and to be efficient in planning and operating the programme.

Needs assessment is complex (see Chapter 6). Part of the solution is gradually to make it possible for people to interpret their own needs and which types of programme best suit them. Managers must, therefore, involve people in programme planning. The Leisure Manager must:

- understand the lessons to be learned from the various strategies and approaches
- understand the problems and opportunities within current community recreation programming
- devise a logical and objective approach to the situation, bearing in mind the goals of the organization and the resources available.

The lessons to be learned from past mistakes

One of the hallmarks of good programming, whatever the organization, is the extent to which objectives have been met and client satisfaction has been paramount.

Managers should learn from the successes and the problems of many of the programmes currently practised. Outlined below are a number of problem areas which have been found at community leisure and recreation centres. They are a random collective and in no particular order.

- Demands and needs are not being assessed.
- Objectives, so called, are not measurable.
- Programmes tend to be too traditional and static, with much of the same activities, same methods and same people.
- Programmes lack variety and novelty.
- Often a 'take it or leave it' approach is adopted, regardless of whether the programme is appropriate to the target groups in the community.
- The advantages and disadvantages of different user systems (e.g. casual user, member) are not evaluated fully.
- The need to balance casual use with club use and events is based on not policy, but expediency.
- The need to analyse the benefits and problems of different activities is rarely considered.
- Client life-flow patterns such as regular, habit-forming activities (e.g. weekly sessions) are broken into by insensitive one-off programming which breaks into the pattern without consultation.
- Programme patterns, such as seasonality, are not given due consideration.
- Incompatible activities are sometimes programmed together.
- Insufficient flexibility to adapt to new demands is built into programming.

- Ways of expanding an already busy programme are insufficiently explored (e.g. early or late bookings).
- IT and computer systems are not being put to best advantage to aid efficiency (e.g. self service); bureaucracy and cumbersome administration systems still abound.
- Many programmes contain imbalance; there is a myopic view to a programme (e.g. 50 per cent of time and space to badminton and football in a sports hall).
- Programme worth is increasingly judged on numbers allied to financial viability; qualitative programming gives way under such strain.
- Risk avoidance leads to a lack-lustre approach, with a lack of creativity, stifled programmes, lack of adventure and non-appeal for young people.
- Some community facilities are used for single purpose or few purposes which occupy only a proportion of time and attract a narrow market segment.
- Programmes do not take into account outreach possibilities; many potential satellite resources remain unused for the community: schools, church buildings and club, business and industrial recreation facilities.
- Programme monitoring and systematic evaluation are rarely carried out to change and improve programme content and presentation.

Not all poor programmes can be changed overnight. It may well take several cycles of the programme, for example, because of established patterns and 'sitting tenants'. However, most problems can be ironed out by making changes in easy stages.

Targeting disadvantaged groups

Public sector leisure facilities are less used by those who have social, economic and other hardships than by those who are more affluent and mobile. Such social hardships, in relation to leisure participation, have been highlighted from a number of sources, including Griffiths's survey in Greenwich (Griffiths, 1981), the author's survey of lone parents in Harlow (Torkildsen, 1987) and in the work of a number of leisure researchers. Haywood and Henry's study (Haywood and Henry, 1986) offers insights into non-traditional ways of developing services for communities and targeting disadvantaged groups. Effective community recreation management can be measured in part by the degree to which a reasonable balance of the various population market segments within a community has been attracted across the range of services. The Harlow study found that those least likely to use leisure facilities are characterized by having low incomes, poor mobility and dependent young children. The problems are exacerbated if children are being cared for by a lone parent. Recreation and leisure do not appear to be of much relevance to the lot of disadvantaged people because of a combination of factors, for example, the unrelenting pressure of parenthood, lack of money, no use of a car, loss of confidence and for lone parents, lack of a partner.

It is the continuing theme of this book that positive leisure experience can lead to building up of self-image and self-confidence. Management flexibility, to cope with the different needs of different people, deserves far greater attention. Clearly, Leisure Managers need to make contact with, and communicate effectively with disadvantaged groups.

Providers can assist greatly by lightening the social and financial burdens that some members of their community face. This will also help managers to give a better

Table 21.1 Positive programming to encourage wider community use

FINANCIAL	OUTREACH
• Cost subsidies	• Assistance to self-help groups
• Reduced/free memberships	• Babysitting services
• 'Passports', 'Leisure Cards' or free passes (not just for children)	• Neighbourhood contacts
	• Neighbourhood facilities
• Avoidance of lump sum payments	• Mobile facilities
• Bus passes	
PROGRAMMES	**MARKETING**
• Playschemes and family holiday programmes	• Leisure counselling
	• Advertising benefits
• Women's programmes	• Helpline services
• Transport, e.g. minibus shuttle	• Leisure information service
• Crèches at minimal or no cost	• Links with other community services and voluntary groups
• Leisure skill learning – arts, crafts, sports	
• Taster courses	
• Family events	
• Open days and days out	
• Social and community programmes	

service. Authorities need to provide, and make known, concessions and opportunities on a far wider front. They need to support voluntary groups. They need to assist in a variety of ways – a helping hand, even in small ways, may be the catalyst that many people may need. Others will need more substantial help; as one professional worker put it: 'the disadvantaged need to be met more than half-way.' Or, as Ted Blake (2003) puts it: 'Throwing an eleven foot rope to a man drowning twenty feet away is not more than meeting him half-way!'

Concessions and benefits to disadvantaged people – and made known to them – will enable them to exercise greater choice and enjoy the relative freedoms which are open to people enjoying greater advantages.

The single most limiting factor for many disadvantaged groups is said by them to be the cost of taking part. Yet, even when providing facilities free of charge, the manager will still need sensitively to promote and provide support and backup services such as more crèche facilities, taster sessions, mother and child activities and more sessions and attractions for women generally, and women with children in particular. Attracting people through promotion and incentives, however, is not enough. Sensitive handling is essential, also. Many lone parent users felt that managers and staff could be far more helpful and sensitive to individual needs. The style of management and the in-house operational services are important. Those people lacking in confidence are the most vulnerable to 'take-it-or-leave-it' services and will be easily put off. First impressions count. The approach of leisure centre staff to some users was described as 'intimidating', particularly at receptions. Procedures, regulations, membership cards and having to ask for information about concessions, for example, can be daunting. An abrupt voice at reception can ruin a person's leisure experience. Disadvantaged people, who outwardly look perfectly capable, may need welcoming and encouraging. Managers and staff must be both sensitive and reactive to their needs. It is people who promote leisure, and the benefits of leisure are most successfully promoted by face-to-face communication. Therefore, staff training in customer service is of vital importance.

Programming multi-leisure centres

Leisure centres provide the most challenging grounds for leisure programmers. In the United Kingdom there are in the region of 2,500 leisure centres; these are a centres comprising at least a multi-purpose sports hall that is open to the community, whether provided by public, voluntary or private sectors. There are thousands of other pools, halls and outdoor leisure facilities that also need programming.

Multi-purpose leisure centres require programmes which use the same space in a variety of ways. Swimming pools, for example, can be programmed for 'lane swimming', 'water fun', 'water aerobics', 'water therapy', galas, canoeing and even sailing, using a wind machine at one end of the pool. Sports halls are used for concerts, antique fairs, dances, fashion shows and Christmas parties, in addition to their main sports function. Many redundant squash courts are being used for activities such as aerobics, fitness and snooker and can also be used as sports shops, classrooms or information centres.

Case study: Ponds Forge International Sports Centre, Sheffield

It is not just community facilities that need balanced programmes. International facilities also need to consider beginners and fun users. For example, Ponds Forge International Sports Centre in Sheffield is one of the most technically advanced centres in the world. It has three pools – a 52.6m by 25m by 2.3m pool, an international diving pool and a leisure pool – and a sports hall large enough for ten badminton courts and international volleyball, and has seating for up to 1,800. Programming the range of water activities highlights the need to have firm general policies, which include a balance between local and international, community and club, casual and group, training and recreation. Programming problems for the management to overcome include: competition demands versus participation; club squad and structured activity versus casual use; and income versus development of excellence; and social needs criteria.

It is not just the large centres that need good programming. Small centres with limited space and resources need even greater skill at times. For example, in a one-court sports hall (four badminton courts), programming may include sport (for schools, clubs, coaching, recreation), concerts, dances, exhibitions and antique fairs. In the early part of the last century, swimming pools were covered over to programme sports events, dances and dinners. Leisure programming is not new.

The programming of indoor arenas is included in Chapter 22, Event management, because their programmes generally are based on spectator or audience events. Even those with community programming are events-orientated. The National Indoor Arena (NIA) in Birmingham, for example, is committed annually to a substantial quota of events arranged by United Kingdom Governing Bodies of Sport.

Programming by Objectives

The basic assumption was made at the start of this chapter that programming is a process. It is logical therefore to make programming a systematic process, a system which takes a wide and open view of the variety of possibilities. First, the approach at public facilities must be capable of incorporating both major strategies: social planning and community development. Second, the approach must be capable of handling any of the options, from the wholly authoritarian-directed service at one extreme to the participant-controlled programme at the other.

Different approaches will suit different situations at different times. The Programming by Objectives method builds on the principles of Management by Objectives. MBO as a general management system is no longer in vogue but its focused systematic style can be of much value in improving programming performance. It is a planning approach to achieve measurable targets. It can be used to co-ordinate the network of several specific methods of programming; it sets targets, plans, implements, controls and monitors. It is a practical, objective approach which gets things done.

Essentially, programming (allied to promotion and good management) results in people taking part in leisure activities. One thing we know about leisure behaviour is that, if the experience is satisfying, it can become habitual. Programmes, therefore, need to offer levels of continuity. Once established, programmes are difficult to change in a hurry. Moreover, programmes need time to set up and they need resources and finances to promote and organize. Hence, community participation programmes need at least a few months to run, unless, for example, they are short-term holiday or one-off weekend programmes or tasters.

Leisure programming, therefore, in most cases is an on-going cyclical process. Once a programme has been set in motion, it can go on in repeated cycles like a long-running saga. While it may be easier to just let matters take their cyclical course with the same content, good programmers will constantly review the programme, introduce initiatives or refine, re-plan, implement afresh, run the programme, evaluate and then review again, and so the cycle goes on. Demands change, markets change and leisure managers have to match their products to the market.

The process outlined below is concerned with setting up the programme in the first place. But most programming deals with on-going programmes with regular cycles of review, forward planning, implementation and evaluation. The suggested stages for programming are based on operational experience and founded upon workable programming theory.

Community leisure and recreation programming planning guide

1 Interpret policy, establish aims and objectives Understand the purpose of your organization, its philosophy and its fundamental beliefs.

- Produce a mission statement or statement of purpose, stating the aims and goals of the organization.
- Produce programme policy guidelines and directional strategies.
- Where no written philosophy or policy exists, top managers should interpret the organization's purpose, communicate with others, produce a written policy statement and obtain endorsement.

461

2 Assess resources and current and potential demand Produce a profile of the current and prospective consumers and the type of services and activities meeting their needs and demands.

- Evaluate current resources, facilities, organizations, services, programmes and opportunities.
- Evaluate the current performance of facilities and services; determine the level of spare capacity, etc.
- Collate all marketing information. Use surveys, suggestions, community councils and recreation organizations.
- Evaluate the contribution made by other agencies: voluntary sector, commercial enterprise, education and industrial clubs.
- Establish a profile of potential users, the individuals and groups likely to participate.
- Assess the forthcoming year's new opportunities, e.g. historic celebrations, sponsorship and campaigns.
- Identify market gaps and determine areas of deficiency in terms of services and programmes.

3 Set objectives Translate policies and market demands into practical objectives, prioritize and make each objective measurable and within a time span.

- Involve policy makers, staff and community in the setting of objectives.
- Set short-range targets in each area within a precise time period: weeks (e.g. holiday programmes); months (e.g. leisure courses); and years (e.g. financial targets, social objectives).
- Set an appropriate balance between community-orientated and professionally-directed approaches.
- Set balances between passive and active leisure, between sport, recreation, art, social, entertainment, and so on, to meet the aims.
- Agree performance indicators, financial income/expenditure ratios, subsidies and targets.

4 Plan the programme Design a critical path network. Be guided by Murphy's Law: 'Nothing is as simple as it seems. Everything takes longer than you think. If anything can go wrong, it will.' Adopt the programmer's motto: Proper Prior Planning Prevents Poor Performance.

- Time is the basis on which most programmes operate. Establish hourly, daily, weekly and seasonal patterns of use.
- Consider both fixed and flexible timetables.
- Determine programme areas (arts, sports, social, etc.).
- Determine programme forms (clubs, courses, events, etc.).
- Recognize the different needs of different people: recreational, competitive, beginners, high standard, older, younger, etc.
- Balance the programme providing width and depth – balance implies diversity. Because of conflicting claims, it is necessary to establish priorities.
- Choose and analyse activities and methods which collectively are most likely, within resources, to meet objectives.
- Avoid totally exclusive use, it narrows the field.
- Avoid totally casual use, it also narrows the field.

- Build flexibility into the programme. It will lead to variety, wider use and greater balance.
- Consider how the programme fits into the marketing strategy, e.g. corporate approach to marketing, specific promotions.
- Consider the staffing implications and management style, division of labour, responsibilities, etc.
- Train staff teams and individuals to undertake responsibility so as to gain job satisfaction and professional skills. Train staff for a customer-orientated approach.
- Avoid administration problems by establishing easily handled and easily understood systems and methods. They should be easy for the user and easy for the organization.
- Make full use of information technology and modern computerized systems.

5 Promote, implement and control the programme Construct, promote and implement the programme with vitality, enthusiasm and charisma. Implement the agreed marketing strategy, using the most appropriate aspects of the marketing mix. Spend time on promotion (see Chapter 20, Marketing of leisure and recreation).

- Give sensitive care to staffing aspects, especially with regard to community development. Staff/helpers are needed to support newly formed groups until they become self-supporting. Consider some outreach programmes.
- Try new technologies for programming: video, computers, giant screen for information, visuals to show court availability, self-service, do-it-yourself bookings, etc. Use information technology to advantage.
- Flexibility is needed to meet changing situations. The flexible approach needs skilful management to enable individuals to participate in the way they want to.
- Control the programme through appropriate staffing and delegation of authority, financial and operational systems.
- Develop monitoring systems to provide management with information relating to current level of usage, profile of users and changing trends.
- Anticipate the likely problems; be ready with alternatives.
- Avoid incompatible activities in terms of health and safety, noise, age, level of play, etc.
- Expand the programme with new activities, new methods and new people.
- Sell packages, not only single items.
- Try some experiments; try out regional and national activity trends, yet always enhance local success.
- Extend product life cycles through changes, variety and new ways of selling.
- Use pricing flexibility as a marketing tool; consider the benefits of differential pricing.
- Keep all informed of what is going on. Use a variety of communication systems.

Programme control is a management function; it helps if one manager has overall responsibility. He or she must have the necessary ability and authority and be part of the policy making team. Ensure that the way the programme is being delivered meets the highest customer service and that staff are carrying out their own jobs efficiently. Programming success is often dependent on seemingly small items, administrative or technical. Double-bookings cause problems far in excess of the minor mistake. Deal with complaints immediately and turn them into opportunities for getting things right. Practical operational knowledge might show a need to adjust staffing levels, cover for staff sickness or obtain daily feedback. Walk the floor, check that the facilities and equipment are up to scratch; use a monitoring system on a day-to-day basis.

6 Evaluate the programme Evaluate; how else will you know whether you are doing a good job? To what extent has the programme been successful or unsuccessful? Measure its effectiveness: to what extent have objectives been met?

- Evaluate inputs – what has gone into planning the programme – resources, staff, time, costs.
- Evaluate the process – what has occurred in carrying out the programme from start to finish.
- Evaluate the outcome – the results. How did they compare to targets and performance objectives? Were clients and customers generally satisfied with the service?
- Measure the efficiency of the operation: how well has the job been carried out? How adequate has the staffing been; how well have staff performed?
- Use several criteria, not just financial, to measure profits, both quantitative and qualitative: throughput, social mix, use by less advantaged, age mix, income generation, subsidy per user, levels of sponsorship achieved, etc. Measure cost-effectiveness.
- Determine any changes in user profiles or catchment areas.
- Establish effectiveness of the marketing strategy.
- Determine effectiveness of the changes in the programme.

Who should do the evaluation? Evaluation can be undertaken in three main ways.

1 Inside evaluation can be more sensitive to staff feelings, but is more likely to be biased and less objective and more likely to justify failures, or to exonerate from blame.
2 Outside evaluation is likely to be more objective, but can be hampered by staff suspicion or worry about the outcome. External evaluations sometimes misinterpret complex relationships and common-sense know-how.
3 A combination of inside and outside evaluation makes better sense. Better still is involvement from all sources – from the policy makers, the officers, the clients, the contractors, the staff and the customers.

7 Obtain feedback and modify the programme appropriately Each programme cycle is likely to merit some modification.

- Obtain feedback from users (duty manager daily records; surveys; focus groups; user forums) and through the community network and community leader resources.
- Show appreciation to those running successful elements of the programme.
- If the programme or elements of it have been unsuccessful, first, determine the causes for failure to meet targets; second, consider staff training or retraining; third, consider changes in staff areas of responsibility; fourth, consider the effectiveness of the management style.
- Modify targets according to levels of performance.

Summary

Programming provides the leisure services and products which Leisure Managers are in business to deliver. It is the mechanism for meeting the needs of clients and customers and organizational objectives. Arguably, it is the single most important function of Leisure Managers. Programming is an on-going process characterized by repeated cycles of planning, implementation, evaluation and review.

Good programming can offer choice, provide balance, attract the markets being aimed at, and be responsive to the needs and wants of clients and customers. Conversely, poor programming results in not meeting organization objectives; choice is limited and too many clients and customers become dissatisfied.

There are many ways in which programmes can be classified, including by function, by areas and facilities, by social grouping and by the expected outcomes. The classification into functional activities is the most common. There are different approaches and methods to programming. Two major approaches or directions can be termed loosely as 'social planning', where the locus of control is with the authority and professionals, and 'community development', which is a more people-orientated direction. Within directional strategies, there exist a variety of specific methods of delivery. Good programming requires strategy, structure and co-ordination. Programming by Objectives is an approach which overcomes many of the inherent problems in other, more subjective methods.

Programming is perceived as a continuous process, and while there are steps in the procedure, different aspects of the programme will be at different stages of the cycle as the programme changes and evolves. This is why high-quality management is needed to co-ordinate and control the entire operation. Leisure and recreation programming needs quality Leisure Managers.

Discussion points

1 Explain why the effective programming of leisure facilities and services is fundamental to achieving the aims and objectives of the leisure organization and authority.

2 Programming is an underrated skill and little attention is given to it in the planning and management of leisure and recreation and is often omitted in leisure course curricula. Consider why this may be the case and what should be done about it.

3 Leisure managers have to provide a wide range of services to meet the needs and demands of different people and different organizations. Describe how you would endeavour to provide a balanced community recreation programme in a 'wet' and 'dry' leisure centre to meet the needs and demands of the catchment population.

465

22
Event management

Introduction

Event management has become an industry in its own right, featuring specialist event companies and event managers. Events have been part of the history of all cultures across the world to celebrate landmarks in public and private life. They are staged at international, national and local levels, in the public, commercial and voluntary sectors. Events are of many kinds. The terms 'major events' and 'special events' have been used to describe a very wide range of festivals, ceremonies, celebrations, sports competitions, arts spectaculars, and trade and public exhibitions. 'The field of special events is now so vast that it is impossible to provide a definition that includes all the varieties and shades of events' (Allen *et al.*, 2002).

International and worldwide events in leisure are more important than ever before. In most countries today major events are significant at all levels of society and institutions, whether it be national and local government, corporations, businesses, governing bodies or community organizations. Sporting events dominate large sections of the press, television and radio broadcasting. Major events are a global industry evidenced by the existence of a world body, the International Festivals and Events Association (IFEA), which has a number of national associations. In such a growth industry, it is of interest, therefore, to consider a little of the historical background, the broad spectrum of special events and the main categories of events and their features before moving into the planning and organization of those events which are part of the Leisure Manager's annual programme.

Events as landmarks of history

Special events are part of our history and culture and have been so for thousands of years in countries across the world. People have always celebrated or marked special occasions in their lives: births, deaths, tribal initiations, marriages, seasons, spring times, harvests, full moons. Myths, legends and traditions have been handed down over time and are still celebrated today with festivals, pageantry, ceremonies, parades, sporting contests, exhibitions and displays and often accompanied by music, song and dance (see Chapters 2 and 3).

In Ancient Greece, the pleasure-loving Athenians devoted over 80 days to spectacles. There were four great festivals of Olympian, Pythian, Isthmian and Nemean Games. A universal truce was observed during their celebrations. Family events marked the birth of children, their enrolment as citizens and their first exhibition in the gymnasium. The earliest festivals were in the autumn after gathering in 'the fruits of the earth'; offering up sacrifices and enjoying social festivities were the natural consequences of a time of plenty.

The Greek title Symposiarch (from *symposium*, a drinking party) was given to the Master of the Feast.

The Ancient Jews, whose history is diligently recorded, were prescribed 52 weekly Sabbaths and 30 holidays – 82 sacred days, 59 of which saw an entire cessation of work, according to Horatio Smith (1831). Like the ancient Greeks, the ancient Jews appointed their own 'Events Manager' – the Director of the Feast – whose duty it was to promote and organize these special events. Traditional events such as christenings and bar mitzvahs are important in preserving cultures. In the United Kingdom, the communities from the West Indies and Asia have established cultural carnivals such as the now world famous Notting Hill Carnival, Hindu festivals and the Chinese New Year. In Chapter 3, the traditions and cultural landmarks in the UK such as May Day and the Scottish Hogmanay were described.

The history of many other nations has been catalogued with dates of victories, celebrations, festivals and special events from the time when they were founded up to the present time. In *Festival and Special Event Management* (Allen *et al.*, 2002), the authors chart historical events in Australia from the arrival of the First Fleet in 1788, and describe how its history is mirrored with celebrations, for example the First Anniversary Day, First Melbourne Cup (1861), development of Australia Rules football, cricket Test Matches, Anzac Day, visit of Queen Elizabeth II (1954), First Gay and Lesbian Mardi Gras (1978), the Olympic Games in Melbourne (1956) and in Sydney (2000), the Rugby World Cup (2003) and the Commonwealth Games to be held in Melbourne in 2006.

The United States of America celebrates 'Home Coming' and Independence Day which commemorates the formal adoption of the Declaration of Independence by the Continental Congress in Philadelphia on 4 July, 1776, recalled in popular songs with lines such as being 'born on the fourth of July'. Canada Day, formerly Dominion Day, commemorates the formation of the Dominion of Canada on 1 July, 1867. It is celebrated with parades, fireworks, and display of the flag. French-speaking Quebec celebrates its separate history, and in 2008 marks its 400th anniversary.

Mega-events, hallmark and major events

The range of events is so wide that there is no one definition which encompasses all. Bowdin, McDonnell, Allen and O'Toole (2001) in their substantial *Events Management*, identify four main categories of event:

467

- mega-events
- hallmark events
- major events and
- local events.

Mega-events

Bowdin, McDonnell, Allen and O'Toole (2001) describe mega-events as 'those events that are so large that they affect whole economies and reverberate in the global media; these events are generally developed following competitive bidding. They include the Olympic Games, the Paralympic Games, the FIFA World Cup, the IAAF World Championships and World Fairs, but it is difficult for many other events to fit into this category'.

Getz (1991), in similar vein, adds that they 'yield extraordinarily high levels of tourism, media coverage, prestige, or economic impact for the host community or destination'. He defines such events as those attracting over one million visits, that their capital costs should be at least 500 million US dollars and that their reputations should be of a 'must see' event. Hall (1992) states that they are 'mega' by virtue of their size, attendance, public involvement, political effects, television coverage, construction of facilities and social and economic impact.

In his paper 'Mega-Events, Global Forces and Local Responses', Maurice Roche (2002) at the Seventh World Leisure Congress described the concept of mega-events:

The concept of 'mega-event' refers to specially constructed and staged international cultural and sport events and event genres such as Olympic Games and World's Fairs/Expos. They are typically publicly perceived as having an 'extra-ordinary' and memorable status, among other things, by virtue of their very large scale, the extent and intensity of their international public appeal and interest, the time-cycles in which they occur and their various impacts on their hosts. Mega-events are dynamic multi-dimensional phenomena – for instance they are simultaneously urban events, touristic events, media events, and international or global events – and are simultaneously the subject of collective and corporate discourse and action in each of these dimensions. To appreciate and grasp these dimensions in any particular case requires at least a broadly based context-sensitive sociological or social scientific approach by individual scholars and researchers. More idealistically, in principle, the multi-dimensional character of mega-events calls for a multi-disciplinary team-based approach to researching them, if possible organized at an international level, a situation which has never been realised in practice in mega-event case studies as far as I am aware. Mega-events are short-lived collective cultural actions, 'ephemeral vistas', as Greenhalgh calls them in his seminal study of Expos (Greenhalgh, 1988), which nonetheless have long-lived pre- and post-event social dimensions, in some respects for the international community, but particularly for the urban and/or national communities which host them.

Hallmark events

> *Ritchie (1984) defines hallmark events as: 'Major one-time or recurring events of limited duration, developed primarily to enhance awareness, appeal and profitability of a tourism destination in the short term and/or long term. Such events rely for their success on uniqueness, status or timely significance to create interest and attract attention.'*

Allen *et al.* (2002) add that these events become so identified with the spirit or ethos of a town, city or region that they become synonymous with the name of the place. They cite classic examples such as the Carnival in Rio de Janeiro, the Kentucky Derby in the USA, the Chelsea Flower Show in England, the Edinburgh Festival in Scotland. Such events provide competitive advantage for the host cities – cultural, physical, environmental, political, tourist and economic. However, events have many impacts both positive and negative and the cost of failure can lead to disaster socially, economically and politically.

Chris Gratton at the Sport Industry Research Centre (SIRC) has studied the economic importance of sport with events across a spectrum from competitor-driven to spectator-driven events, concluding that the more competitor-driven the event, the easier it is to forecast the economic impact. Major sports events can generate a significant economic impact on the local economy and the sports industry can drive local and regional economic regeneration. However, Gratton warns that major events require subsidy from local government and that cities often use too many resources attracting events which have little economic impact (Gratton, 2003).

Hundreds and sometimes thousands of unpaid volunteers are used in running mega-, major and hallmark events. Their collective contribution in terms of money saved is substantial. But does such volunteering detract from their commitment to other causes and events? Harry Arne Solberg (2002) used the 'opportunity cost approach' and the 'market price equivalency' to calculate the value of volunteers' work at a major sporting event, the 1999 World Championship in Ice Hockey. The survey showed no long term displacement of other voluntary work; indeed it enhanced motivation to volunteer further.

Major events

Major events are not on the scale of mega-events but are large enough and prestigious enough to attract the attention of the national media, attract large spectator numbers and provide economic benefits. In the sports world they are events in which international players are interested in participating, such as open golf championships, Grand Prix races, and international test matches. UK Sport defines a major event as having an international dimension:

- attracting a number of nations
- significant public interest through attendances and media coverage and
- features prominently on the UK's international calendar.

While sport is the dominant product for major events, cultural events and business events fall within the potential scope of leisure event managers. Cultural events in the United Kingdom include international music festivals such as Cheltenham International Jazz Festival, Glyndebourne Opera Festival and a variety of arts, literature and music festivals. Business events, agricultural shows, trade exhibitions and conferences are a substantial market. As the arena industry in the UK grows, so does the demand for events in indoor arenas.

Events in indoor arenas

The success of arenas is dependent on skilful programming (see Chapter 21). Indoor arenas are event orientated, and the range is extremely diverse. The United Kingdom indoor arena industry is smaller than US counterparts and more diverse in programmes compared to many American or European arenas (Shields and Wright, 1989).

An arena programme of events depends on a range of factors including:

1 the philosophy of use, aims and objectives: the National Indoor Arena (NIA) in Birmingham, for example, is committed annually to a substantial quota of events arranged by United Kingdom Governing Bodies of Sport
2 the targeted markets and balance to be achieved between sport, entertainment, exhibitions and conventions/launches
3 the extent of home-based teams: most US arenas depend on tenant teams for economic survival and Sheffield Arena and London Arena are experiencing similar financial positions
4 the contracts, for example, between the arena and governing bodies of sport, entertainment promoters, local authorities and commercial developers
5 the promoters: the extent of 'dry' hire, in which the premises are rented to a promoter at an agreed fixed price with or without profit sharing, joint promotions and own promotions; other than at the NIA, the most popular events in UK arenas are rock and pop concerts, exhibitions, conventions and rallies and then sport (unless there is a home-based team)
6 the flexibility of the arena design, e.g. the ability to change from a hard floor to a resilient surface or artificial turf, or ice, and changing from entertainment to sports participation
7 support services: the effectiveness of ancillary facilities and attractions to retain customers, maximize income potential ('secondary spend') and stagger arrival and departure times
8 set-up and break-down times.

Programme versatility must be coupled with management flexibility and operational experience. For example, the ambience and security issues for a rock concert or for a symphony concert call for quite different management solutions. At the opening event in the London Arena, Luciano Pavarotti was disturbed by the constant sound of footsteps on a hard non-carpeted floor, as latecomers arrived throughout the first half of the concert.

Programming events is affected greatly by design. A large space with a hard floor and strong walls and ceiling is often more flexible for programming large events of different kinds, compared with a purpose-designed building. All arenas need seating configuration permutations, good acoustic and lighting capability, ceiling catwalks, platforms and strong fixing beams, large staging capability, truck loading bays, etc. These factors emphasize the need for event managers and operators to influence design.

Income variables are affected by seating layouts, floor layouts, exhibition and sports layouts, changeover times, lettable space per event, and in large measure, dependent on the type of booking, whether 'dry' hire, joint hire or own promotion.

The simplest and most used form of hire is dry hire (or some variation on it). Wembley Arena and the National Exhibition Centre in Birmingham hire much of their programme time on this basis. Joint promotions are becoming more fashionable and there is considerable bargaining, particularly with pop concerts and sponsored events, and especially over the extremely thorny problem of television rights.

Major exhibitions

An exhibition is defined as a situation where: 'The main purpose of the audience is to attend an area where pre-booked space is allocated to ten or more businesses to display their products and services relating to a specified theme/sector for the objective of conducting business and/or demonstration for said products and services. An element of educational content exists for the visitor and the opportunity to visit exists only for a stated, and usually short, period of time. This includes all non-consumable products and services available for immediate sale' (Bulletin 100).

The United Kingdom is one of the world's leading centres for international conferences and exhibitions. Key venues are in most of the major cities. The Association of Exhibition Organizers (AEO) estimates that between 1999 and 2001, spending on exhibitions rose from £1.8 billion to £2.0 billion. Venues with 2000 square metres of space and over attracted 855 events in 2002 and 10.3 million visitors. In addition, there were 5 million visitors to 50 exhibitions held in outdoor venues in 2002. A further 787 smaller exhibition events, often regional, took place in 336 venues attracting 5.5 million visitors (ONS, 2003).

A number of factors influence an organizer's choice of venue for major events: size, location, accessibility to the target market, transport infrastructure, services available and costs. In the United Kingdom, the NEC, owned by Birmingham City Council, is the largest venue. In 2001, it held over 180 exhibitions, and over 450 conferences and seminars, resulting in three million visitors and 49,000 exhibiting companies. NEC's related venues are the NEC Arena, National Indoor Arena, International Convention Centre and Symphony Hall. At these major venues the events are usually promoted and organized by professional companies. Bulletin 100, an analysis of the United Kingdom's largest trade and public shows, reports that they are organized by 52 different sized companies. However, currently, around 40 per cent of the top 100 events are organized by just six companies. UK exhibition organizers also operate further afield, particularly in Europe.

> ## Associations of exhibition and event organizations
>
> The Event Services Association (TESA)
> Association of Exhibition Organizers (AEO)
> Exhibition Venues Association (EVA)
> British Exhibition Contractors Association (BECA)
> National Outdoor Events Association (NOEA)
> Association for Conferences and Events (ACE)
> British Exhibition Contractors Association (BECA) which has represented exhibition
>   contractors since 1913.

The primary revenue indicator for a trade exhibition is net stand space; for a public exhibition it is the number of visitors. The effectiveness of this marketing medium is shown by the fact that the largest 100 shows attract around five million visitors and these shows represent only five per cent of Britain's exhibition market. The most prestigious show, in terms of numbers, is the Daily Mail Ideal Home Show which in 2001 attracted nearly 427,000 visitors, double the number of the International Motorcycle and Scooter Show (c. 206,000), the Royal International Air Tattoo (c. 180,000), BBC Clothes Show (c. 170,000), and London International Boat Show (c. 160,000). Leisure, sport, travel and tourism are one of the three most significant industry sectors (Bulletin 100).

So far in this chapter, events have been seen in the context of mega-events, hallmark, major and large-scale indoor arena events. I now turn to the events most Leisure Managers have to plan and manage in the local and regional setting and at local facilities.

Special local events

Events are an important part of any comprehensive leisure and recreation programme. They have appeal; they capture the imagination. Events can involve the community, increase awareness and help put an organization or an activity on the map. Some events can attract top-class performers; other events can display the talents of beginners; some provide entertainment, novelty, adventure and fun; and some bring glamour to a programme.

Well organized events can therefore be a boon to any organization; badly organized, they can damage. Being out of the ordinary, events carry programme and promotional advantages. Community events, in particular, need the help of many people and usually large numbers of volunteers. However, they can attract unwieldy committees and lots of people with very good intentions, but with variable organizational skills. Some people take on too much and others let you down at the last moment. Events, therefore, need a competent co-ordinator. His or her role is of paramount importance.

The management of special events is receiving greater attention as people are increasingly exposed to professionally produced events, as the British arena event industry continues to develop and as more events are presented on television. The public has thus become more sophisticated in its taste when it comes to the organization of events whether national or local. Leisure Managers must be capable of leading or controlling the planning and execution of special events whether in a stadium, a leisure centre or a town park.

Whilst most top-level major events are organized by promoters or by governing bodies and associations outside the control of leisure facility managers, community related events, joint promotions and 'own' promotions call for considerable expertise on the part of Leisure Managers who have to present special events throughout the course of the year as part of the overall leisure programme. The principles and many of the methods will apply to all event organizers, but it is recognized from the outset that some organizations are set up as specialized event producers. In local authorities, too, there are specialized event departments and committees to stage the county show or annual festival. In national sports administration, committees and staff exist to administer national and international events. While all event organizers can take something from this chapter, it is the Leisure Manager, whose special events are superimposed on all his or her other tasks, that it is primarily intended to serve; attention is focused on the management of events at a local level. For the grand, celebratory spectaculars, read, for example, *Special Events: The Art and Science of Celebration* (Goldblatt, 1990).

For the planning and operation of special events read the excellent, concise, *Events from Start to Finish* by Sue Stayte and David Watt for the Institute of Leisure and Amenity Management and the government publication, *Guide to Health, Safety and Welfare at Pop Concerts and Special Events* (1993).

Special characteristics and functions of local special events

What is a local special event? It can be a special 'happening', project or attraction of any kind that is outside the ordinary programme. It usually attracts a crowd or an audience or draws the attention of the media. An event can include sport, art, music, drama, festival or tournament. It can be competitive, fund-raising, social or just 'plain good fun'. It can be the town annual show or the village fête, athletics championships or the Scouts' sports. It can be an exhibition, a meeting, a rally or a talk. The scope of local special events is as wide as the scope of the leisure and recreation spectrum.

Special events carry a number of features which distinguish them from other elements within a leisure and recreation programme, including the six outlined below.

1 Events have distinctive characteristics: all major events are perceived as being something special. All events have a starting and finishing point. They are tightly bound in time and space. They have fixed deadlines. For the Leisure Manager, these are usually superimposed on other work.

2 Events carry opportunities to improve programming and management: events can capture the imagination of both sellers and buyers. They can be a means of promoting the organization and creating favourable images. Their organization crosses administrative and departmental boundaries; hence they can unify the organization. They call upon all the resources of an organization and test them, revealing strengths and weaknesses. They may break new ground and could present the organization as a pioneer.

3 Events must conform to regulations: most special events have to meet stringent regulations involving aspects of health and safety and police matters. Licensing issues have become more complex and obtaining licences to hold large events is

now more complex than before. Events such as firework displays and pop concerts have to be very carefully planned, controlled, 'policed' and monitored.

4   Events pose many problems to all organizers: events are risky, so we have to expect the unexpected. Most problems can be anticipated but many will be unforeseen. The event, unlike the normal ongoing programme, is speeded up and delivered within a short space of time; this concentrates all the advanced planning and actions into specific hours and moments. Problems can thus be dramatic and could prove devastating. One problem is that managers and event organizers cannot depend on established routines. Another is that there are dangers in dates slipping by in preparation, targets not being met and budgets being overspent. In addition, there are dangers in lack of co-ordination, bringing inadequate linkages, miscommunications, omissions, duplications, wasted effort and inadequate controls.

5   Events lend themselves to certain management styles and methods. First, events need a co-ordinator; his or her role and style are paramount. Second, they need precision, deadlines and fast decisions and this differs from most normal programming issues. Third, tight administration, using flowchart organization and checklists can help to meet deadlines and objectives. Fourth, entrepreneurial skills, allied to good administration, can be put to best effect. Fifth, because events are task-orientated, a more authoritarian style of leadership or 'benevolent dictatorship' may be required in the late stages of detailed preparation and on the day itself, autocratic management, particularly hours before the curtain goes up, or the tape is cut, or the whistle blows.

6   Events have similarities in organization: in terms of management approaches, the similarities of different events appear to be greater than the differences. While policies, programme and content will differ, a planning sequence is the same for all:

- decision making
- planning and preparation
- presentation
- evaluation.

No one precise method of organizing a major event is best and all others second best. The method will depend on the organization and organizers, the nature of the event and the circumstances surrounding it. However, some ways are more effective than others. Events therefore are a specialized aspect of leisure and recreation management and an event planning approach is outlined in the sections that follow.

Local event planning process and organization

All events need good planning and organization. Regrettably, all events are not well planned and organized, even many of some significance, particularly in the voluntary and public sectors. Leisure Managers must guide and support event organizers in the basic principles of planning and organization.

The management approach to an event will depend on the particular circumstances, but it is worth recognizing seven interrelated planning stages in the life cycle of a major event:

1   formulating the proposal and the policy
2   examining feasibility and making decisions
3   setting objectives and budgeting
4   organization structure and key appointments
5   general and detailed preparation
6   the event presentation
7   feedback and evaluation.

Is the idea worth investigation; is it a worthwhile event? First, receive or formulate the idea. Debate, reason out and answer fundamental questions: why is the event proposed? What is it for? What are its aims? How will the event be run? Where will it be held? Who will be responsible for its planning and operation? When will it be held? If the idea is a good one, take the idea to the next stage of considering its feasibility.

Feasibility and decision making In considering the feasibility of an event it is important to explore in greater depth the questions already raised. What are the benefits? What are the costs, not just in terms of money, but also in terms of personnel, time and effort? Will the effort result in meeting the aims of the event? Can the problems be overcome?

If the event is not feasible, planners should have the courage to say 'no'. Regrettably, many events have taken place without considering their feasibility and they should never have been held. If the event is feasible, and there is positive commitment to the project, then it is important to make a firm decision, allowing ample time for forward planning and detailed planning. Coinciding with the decision to go ahead, certain crucial tasks should be undertaken.

- Announce the decision to hold the event.
- State clearly the nature of the event and the aims of the event; commit these to paper.
- Appoint an event working committee.
- Appoint the co-ordinator, the key figure in the planning and control of the event.
- Set objectives.

In setting objectives, be clear and unequivocal in stating them as measurable targets. Make them unambiguous. Include all main areas and units of the event. In particular, be precise about the financial estimates and budgeting. In formulating the objectives, the co-ordinator should consult with the policy makers and the key personnel involved in it, whether as representatives of organizations or as unit or team leaders. Set the dates, times, specific deadlines and critical dates in the planning stages.

Evaluating costs and setting budgets All major events need a budget. The extent to which they do depends on the nature of the event and on the objectives. Is the event designed to give a free service to the public: an open day in the park, free band concert, children's festival or a sports centre open day? Is the event designed as a crowd puller on a break-even financial exercise: an entertainment talent contest or a sports tournament? Is the event a sponsored event to draw in the crowds and capture the eye of the media: a national basketball tournament? Is the event totally sponsored, such as a leisure exhibition? Is the event primarily designed to raise funds for the organization or another charitable cause?

Most local authority events are heavily subsidized (by council tax). Town shows, concerts, free pop festivals in the park, old-time music halls, painting competitions, exhibitions and many thousands of events are run because they enhance the quality of life of citizens and are part of our heritage and traditions. Two key aspects concern evaluating true costs and setting budgets.

As far as the Leisure Manager is concerned, all events, even those totally subsidized, in reality, cost money. They must all have budgets and must all achieve the income/expenditure balance or ratio set in the objectives. Even more important is that the event be run with excellence. The principle for the Leisure Manager to work to is that of being professional. Regardless of whether the event is free, the facilities are free or the staff are already paid for, the manager should always evaluate the true costs.

It will normally cost money to use, hire or acquire facilities and make them functional and attractive for the event. There will be costs for electricity, water and technical and maintenance aspects. There will be costs of transport. Equipment may need to be hired, purchased, borrowed and transported. Additional staffing, stewards, voluntary helpers and personnel connected with the event will be required. Administration costs will include not only the promotion, printing, tickets, posters, financial costing and preparations, but also the whole office backup and administrative services, such as telephone, stationery and staff resources. There will normally be costs for mounting the event itself, the programme costs, the cost of artists, hospitality, the additional insurances and legal costs. The hidden costs of most events are enormous. The good manager should know what they are. They may not be of great importance to one event, but they could be to the next.

Most events will accrue some income. Even events which are free to the consumer will need to raise income from some sources such as grant aid from the local authority, from sponsorship and from advertising. Income can be derived from direct methods and indirect methods. The direct methods include gate receipts, programmes, bar and catering, car parking, cloakrooms and costs of other services. The indirect methods include advertising, donations, sponsorships, sales, raffles and fundraising of a variety of sorts. Sometimes the amount of effort put into running the annual dinner raffle is more than that put into the whole event itself!

Events, then, need a budget and all events need expenditure limits. A large proportion of events also need income targets. If budget targets are known to all from the outset and are included in the objectives of the event, then everyone is working to the agreed targets for the event. Many events lend themselves to a break-even figure. Although extra income might accrue, it will normally help to meet hidden costs.

The risk element with most events is very high, particularly when they are at the mercy of the weather, or the call of the television on Cup Final Day, or when new ideas are being tried or when dealing with an unknown quantity. There are risks enough without taking even greater financial ones such as overspending budgets or minimizing income. Events therefore need not only the budget but also a finance officer working with the co-ordinator to ensure that financial targets are met.

Event organization structures Events need an organization structure system and methods to achieve objectives. For most special events, the structure will show the

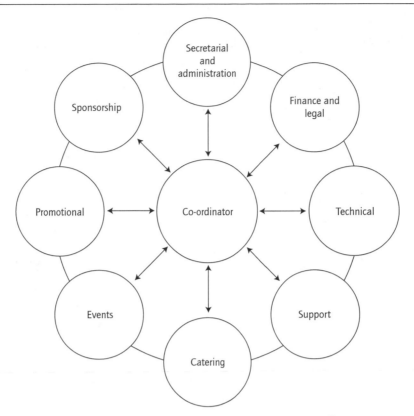

Figure 22.1 Major events structure with units/teams linked to co-ordinator

main elements and key personnel heading up discrete units, teams or working parties dealing with the various areas of work. The structure must cover the broad spectrum of the event. An event such as a festival involving community groups might have several units, for example:

- programme and content – activities, organizations
- budget – accounting, income and expenditure in all areas
- promotion – awareness, publicity, media, etc.
- personnel and staffing – contracts, duties, etc.
- administration – programmes, printing, box office, legal, etc.
- technical – resources, equipment, preparation, etc.
- services – parking, cloaks, information, first aid, etc.
- catering and social – routine, special entertaining, etc.

There should be a working team for each area and a section leader who accepts the responsibility and links with the main co-ordinator. It is important to agree the precise roles and responsibilities of each group and each leader, and the organization, tasks, target deadlines and dates. The events personnel structure for a large town festival is shown in Figure 22.1; the organization structure for a national sports championship is shown in Figure 22.2.

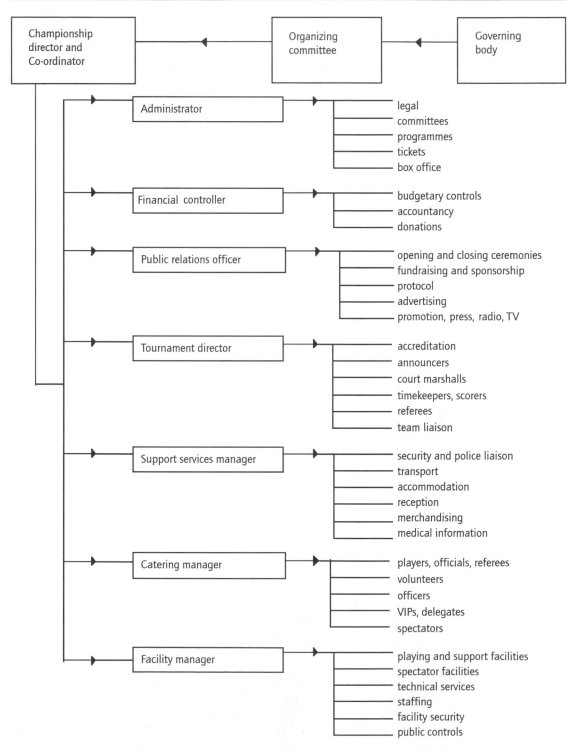

Figure 22.2 Organization structure for a national sports championship at a regional centre

Roles and responsibilities Everyone involved in an event should know to whom they are responsible, who is responsible to them, who they are working with and what exactly their function is in the organization. There must be sufficient, keen and knowledgeable people prepared to give time and effort to the tasks. People need an optimum amount of responsibility.

The use of an organization chart is helpful to clarify any ambiguities and provides an overall picture indicating the various responsibility areas. For major international events such as an international tournament, an organization handbook will be necessary, in addition to an organization chart.

In addition to the structure, a work flowchart indicating critical paths will be valuable for programming and timetabling the work of committees, task units and teams. It should indicate the flow pattern, the critical dates, the deadlines, the merging of sections at appropriate times and the interrelationships between sections.

Staff and personnel All events need personnel. The number and type will depend on the nature of the event. However, all events need a co-ordinator and support staff.

- The co-ordinator. The co-ordinator does not organize directly. He or she is the leader, the link person, the informer, the one person who knows what is going on in each unit, section or team. The co-ordinator does not have to know every detail, but needs to know who has the knowledge and whose responsibility it is. The co-ordinator must control and monitor progress using the most efficient methods, i.e. meetings, sectional heads reporting, work flowcharts. He or she needs to be an encourager, yet firm in handling situations. Towards the later stages of the planning, the co-ordinator will have to exert pressure and make authoritative decisions in order to meet the deadlines. He or she is the key figure in any event organization – the link, the controller and the communicator. Information disseminated to all concerned throughout the planning is essential to keep people motivated, involved and committed, in addition to keeping abreast of information. So often, those in the firing line are ill-informed.
- Support staff. For large events, the co-ordinator will normally work with a team of sectional heads. Each team head, and each discrete unit, will have its clear responsibilities, duties, times, deadlines and calendars, but all within the overall organizational design. Without linkages, it is possible for one unit to function independently, making its own contribution unilaterally, and sometimes competitively, without sufficient thought to the overall success of the project.

Events are run with many different types of staff and helpers. Large-scale events will have full-time staff, part-time paid staff, paid casual staff and volunteers and will also delegate certain functions to agencies, organizations, clubs or concession others.

Paid staff will need to know well in advance their pay, the times and the conditions; trade unions may well be involved; and there will be irregular hours, different rates of pay and insurance aspects. Volunteers will also need to know exactly where they stand, what their responsibilities are and how far these extend. Legal problems are always to be borne in mind with special events; contractual problems, health and safety issues, insurance details and promotional aspects will call for professional legal advice.

Staff and helpers must be highly committed and involved. This is the job of the co-ordinator and the team heads. The answer is never to be complacent, nor to take people for granted. Motivation, acknowledgement, praise and thanks are important. People want to see something of themselves in a successful venture.

Local events: learning from past mistakes

Reliance on the maxim 'It'll be all right on the night' is no substitute for good organization. There are sufficient examples of poor event management to provide material for a comedy series.

Real things that have gone wrong with events

- At one event there was no staging; the public address did not work; lights did not come on; the changing rooms were in the nearest school a mile away.

- At a national event, the VIPs were left standing in the rain trying to convince the doorman that they had been invited.

- Players at an All Stars match could not get into the ground because the entrance was blocked with traffic.

- The grand piano for a concert at the sports centre had been delivered to the theatre.

- At one national leisure event, catering for the conference banquet had not been arranged; the organizer in London and the hosting authority in Wales had each thought the other was organizing it.

In order to run efficient, memorable events, therefore, it is wise to consider the problems of previous events. Some major and some minor faults are listed below. Ten areas have been identified. The first mentioned is possibly the most critical, yet the most frequent omission.

- Lack of objectivity and clarity: insufficient consideration of the aims and objectives and organization structure at the outset; this invariably leads not only to poor communication and duplication of effort but also, and even more seriously, to a lack of direction, authority and controls.
- No appointment of a co-ordinator: this is the key figure; there are usually a chairman and heads of committees but often no co-ordinator with the leadership qualities, authority and responsibility for planning and operational control.
- Inadequate administration: failure to maintain accurate written records of all that transpires during the planning stages; if good records are kept, they act as reminders and checks for work to be carried out. Rarely are there flowcharts with deadlines plotted. Much is kept in one's head. This leads to misunderstandings and recriminations on the day.

- Insufficient planning time: organizations give themselves insufficient planning time. Even when they do have sufficient time too much effort is put in at the last moment. This can lead to overloading and frustration through poor planning.
- Poor organizational structure: committee and unit structures are in many cases too narrow or too unwieldy. Many are far too large. Others leave matters to one person. These individuals invariably take on far too much. They see the event as theirs. They are so keen to do the job that they will not share responsibility or delegate duties. Some very busy people take on events as social obligations and overcommit themselves. These problems are typical of an amateur approach but must not be part of the professional Leisure Manager's repertoire.
- Lack of unity and co-ordination: there are often problems arising from the expectations of organizations such as governing bodies of sport. These can stem from lack of agreement on principles, inadequate contracts and lack of consultation such as on hospitality and looking after guests. Relationships with staff then are often strained.
- Poor anticipation of potential problems: unusual problems can be encountered. The technical problems are considerable, for example, at an indoor facility: noise from other parts of a building; the import of a whole range of additional equipment; the extra floor markings or take-up of markings; the additional stage lighting, decor, the need for additional seating and many others.
- Insufficient prior adherence to licensing and safety regulations: certain events require licences. There are a range of health and safety regulations. The police must be informed about certain kinds of events and should be informed of all events attracting a crowd.
- Lack-lustre, unprofessional event: poor events often lack a professional presentation, and are therefore memorable experiences for the wrong reason.
- No evaluation or learning lessons from the past: only counting numbers and income is poor evaluation. There needs to be evaluation of the planning inputs, the processes, the event and the results, particularly the satisfactions of those attending.

Any problems that spoil an event should not be tolerated; no matter what the organization, certain problems must be ironed out for the next event. They include lack of clear objectives, weak co-ordinator and sectional heads, faulty public address, keen but ineffective announcers, insufficient staff, insufficient food and drink, failure to inform the police, no first aid, no plans for inclement weather, no press coverage, no litter containers, embarrassing pauses between activities, programmes overrunning, no hospitality for visitors, untidy and careless presentations, no colour, no glamour, nothing to make the event unique.

Some problems can be put right immediately for the next event, others need time and consideration and planning. This is the role of the Leisure Manager.

A comparison between good organization and poor organization is outlined in Table 22.1.

Table 22.1 Event management: good and poor organization

	GOOD ORGANIZATION	POOR ORGANIZATION
1 Objectives and clarity	Clear, written, agreed and all committed to	Vague aims, well intentioned hopes and dreams with no clear objectivity
2 Co-ordinator	Of calibre and authority	No one co-ordinator but many leading 'hands' overlapping
3 Administration	Skilled, organized secretarial systems, records and accounting	Unorganized and ad hoc systems
4 Planning time	Long lead-in time and built-in contingency at each stage for slippage	Short lead time and no time for slippage leading to eleventh-hour panics
5 Organization	An overall structure, with discrete units for specific tasks	Organization in the hands of too many or too few with no workable structure
6 Unity, co-ordination and communication	Team effort, positive attitudes and enthusiasm	Many work in isolation with little corporate commitment
7 Problem anticipation	Potential problems identified; alternatives and contingencies planned	No agenda for anything going wrong; 'head in the sand'
8 Licensing and regulations	Licensing authorities, police, health and first aid consulted at the outset	Licensing an afterthought
9 Professional presentation	Good start, finish and timing with some glamour, novelty and surprise	No memorable start and finish; over-running and poor presentation
10 Evaluation and lessons from the past	All are winners. Evaluation of planning the event itself and the outcome – the result	No clear evaluation, only numbers and income and no record for future events

Seven-stage event planner

Event planning can be greatly assisted by following a logical, simple process, but there is no 'one way'. Whilst the seven-stage event planner illustrated in Figure 22.3 shows a logical pattern, it must be appreciated that event management is not a linear process. Many steps need to be taken at the same time, and there are many areas of overlap which the event organizer will need to decide on with the unit team leaders. The model needs to be adapted to the particular event.

Seven–stage event planner

Stage 1 Formulate ideas or receive proposals

Stage 2: Undertake a feasibility study to make a decision Evaluate the proposal. What are assets, problems, support, cost in terms of money, effort, time? What is possible disruption to the normal programme/organization?

2A *Make and communicate the decision* If the event is to be organized by an outside contractor, establish terms, areas of responsibility in matters of staffing, equipment, accommodation, etc. and appoint representative to their committee. Sign and exchange contracts. Establish a monitoring, reporting and evaluation process.

If the organization is in-house, then undertake stages 3 – 7.

Stage 3: Agree strategy, structure and objectives

- Appoint event committee: must include people with commitment, authority and energy.
- Appoint the co-ordinator: give resources, authority and support.
- Set objectives, targets, budgets: must be measurable, timed, dated; draw up draft planning flowchart.
- Establish organization structure: fix discrete units and/or teams with unit leader: give roles, targets, responsibilities.
- Construct a marketing plan (see Chapter 20).

Stage 4: Plan methodically
Detailed planning can be assisted by use of work flowcharts, critical path networks, checklists, targets and dates. The co-ordinator will lead the planning team.

- Plan dates backwards from event day: agree planning flowchart with dates, and use it.
- Each key unit leader should have own calendar within agreed overall plan.
- Fix key meetings long in advance.
- Circulate information regularly; communicate often.
- Monitor progress; check meticulously.
- Check budgets systematically.
- Follow detailed plan: use checklists; anticipate problems, make contingency plans and emergency procedures, practise and rehearse; double-check.
- Resist afterthoughts.

Stage 5: Fine tune and rehearse
The event itself should be preceded by detailed checking and rehearsal.

Professional artists who make their performance look so easy have rehearsed until it becomes second nature. Many events however cannot be rehearsed until the day itself, though components can be and the preparation, the systems and controls can be checked and double-checked and the staff trained.

- Go over the final plan.
- Follow checklists carefully.
- Make fine-tuning adjustments.
- Prepare contingency plans and emergency procedures.
- Rehearse components and practice; some instruction and/or training may be needed for temporary or casual workforce.
- Double-check meticulously.

Stage 6: Present and manage the event An event needs 'professional' presentation. Make it memorable.

- Open with style.
- Present event with class, flair and imagination.
- Keep co-ordinator totally free for overall control and effective decisions under crisis or potentially difficult situations.
- Close event with crescendo: good impression to start and finish. End on a high note to give a lasting memory.

6A: *Immediate post-event* Clear the decks tidily and with precision: cashing up, stock checking, clearing up, making good damage.

Give thanks on the day.

Stage 7: Evaluate and account Thank officially; collect feedback from promoters, participants, staff, volunteers, spectators; report and record. Has the event fulfilled its purposes, met objectives? What lessons are there for future events? A full evaluation is needed which assesses the preparation, the organization, the event, the results and the lessons for future events – the inputs, the process and the outputs. Prepare a report including an income and expenditure account.

Events lend themselves to organization structures, work flowcharts and methods of checking action. A checklist is one of the additional methods. However, events vary so much that detailed checklists to cover all events would be inappropriate, could waste time and effort, and could run into thousands of items. It is important never to use the one checklist for all events, without situational changes and amendments. No two events are the same. Even twin events programmed at different periods or at different locations will differ in some respects. A checklist template, however, could be a valuable starting point. A detailed list or amendments could be undertaken for each event. A general checklist is at Table 22.2.

Summary

In this chapter, the wide range of events has been seen in the context of mega-events, hallmark events, major events, and local special events. Attention has been focused on local events. The Leisure Manager has to be a successful event planner and manager to provide a comprehensive leisure programme. Local special events will fall to the Leisure Manager.

Experience of running events shows that although all events differ one from another, in terms of management approaches, the similarities are greater than the differences. While policies, programme and content will differ considerably, a planning sequence similar to the one proposed in this chapter serves the requirements for many events.

No one method of organizing a special event is best and all others second best. The method will depend on the event and the circumstances surrounding it. However, some ways are more effective than others; they are more objective, they are better planned, costed and controlled.

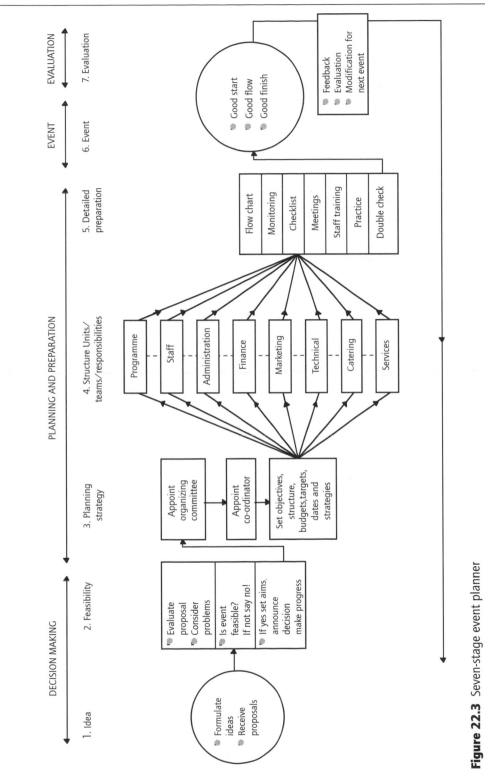

Figure 22.3 Seven-stage event planner

Table 22.2 A 'programme content' checklist

GENERAL CHECKLIST

Specific checklists will be needed for specialized events, e.g. international sports championship, concert, exhibition, fête.

FACILITIES FOR EVENTS

1 Access – check driveway, gates, paths, widths of doorways, etc. ☐
2 Alternative areas, e.g. wet weather ☐
3 Car parks – on and off site ☐
4 Changing rooms ☐
5 Control points ☐
6 Disabled access ☐
7 Exhibition areas ☐
8 Event accommodation and space layout to scale ☐
9 First aid and medical rooms ☐
10 Flooring suitability and covering ☐
11 Hospitality boxes ☐
12 Lavatories ☐
13 Loading bays ☐
14 Lost property room ☐
15 Offices ☐
16 Officials' rooms ☐
17 Performers' rooms ☐
18 Playing areas and dimensions ☐
19 Poster sites ☐
20 Press boxes ☐
21 Ramps ☐
22 Power points ☐
23 Reception areas ☐
24 Rehearsal space ☐
25 Safety – e.g. alarms, fire hoses, floor and roof loadings ☐
26 Sales points ☐
27 Seating layout ☐
28 Security rooms ☐
29 Service/delivery points ☐
30 Signposting ☐

31 Site restrictions, e.g. overhead obstructions, pillars ☐
32 Social areas, bar and catering ☐
33 Sponsors' boxes ☐
34 Storage and security of valuable goods ☐
35 VIP lounges ☐
36 Warm-up/practice areas ☐

STAFF AND PERSONNEL (FULL TIME, PART TIME, CASUAL, VOLUNTARY)

37 Administrative ☐
38 Announcers ☐
39 Attendants ☐
40 Bar staff ☐
41 Car park attendants ☐
42 Cashiers ☐
43 Caterers ☐
44 Cleaners ☐
45 Cloakroom attendants ☐
46 Doctor/medical staff ☐
47 Electricians ☐
48 Hosts ☐
49 Interpreters ☐
50 Maintenance personnel ☐
51 Master of ceremonies ☐
52 Officials ☐
53 Patrols ☐
54 Receptionists ☐
55 Safety, e.g. lifeguards ☐
56 Security guards ☐
57 Stewards ☐
58 Technicians ☐
59 Telephonists ☐
60 Traders/exhibitors ☐
61 Traffic controllers ☐
62 Ushers ☐
63 Volunteer helpers ☐

ADMINISTRATION, DOCUMENTATION
AND FINANCE

64 Accounts and auditing ☐
65 Admission ☐
66 Appeals/fundraising, grants,
   lotteries ☐
67 Arrival/departure ☐
68 Box office ☐
69 Budget and estimates ☐
70 Cashflow/security/change ☐
71 Cleaning costs ☐
72 Committees ☐
73 Contracts ☐
74 Concessions/franchise ☐
75 Copyright ☐
76 Credit card transactions ☐
77 Documentation and name tags ☐
78 Donations – to and from ☐
79 Fees ☐
80 Hire charges ☐
81 Identification/passes ☐
82 Insurance – accident, third party,
   weather, equipment, theft ☐
83 Invitations ☐
84 Legal, e.g. contract of hire ☐
85 Licensing – bar extension,
   spectators, entertainment ☐
86 Organization structure ☐
87 Postage ☐
88 Printing ☐
89 Programmes – printing and sales ☐
90 Reception ☐
91 Rentals ☐
92 Repair costs ☐
93 Sales ☐
94 Seating arrangements ☐
95 Signs and maps ☐
96 Stationery ☐
97 Stock control ☐
98 Sunday trading ☐

99 Tickets – pricing, printing, sales
   and complimentary discounts ☐

EQUIPMENT

100 Acoustics ☐
101 Audio/visual ☐
102 Chairs and tables ☐
103 Communications – bleep system,
    two-way radio ☐
104 Decoration/decor/floral ☐
105 Directional signs ☐
106 Disco ☐
107 Display boards ☐
108 Fencing/barriers ☐
109 Flags ☐
110 Heating ☐
111 Hire of equipment ☐
112 Lectern ☐
113 Lighting – stage, TV, generator,
    emergency ☐
114 Litter bins ☐
115 Marquees ☐
116 Projection equipment – film,
    slide, overhead ☐
117 Public address – records, tapes,
    national anthems, fanfares ☐
118 Rostrum/dais ☐
119 Scoreboards ☐
120 Signs, e.g. 'No Smoking' ☐
121 Spectator stands ☐
122 Staging ☐
123 Timing system equipment ☐
124 Uniforms for staff; protective
    clothing ☐

PRESENTATION AND MEDIA

125 Advertising ☐
126 Appeals ☐
127 Artwork ☐
128 Badges ☐
129 Banners ☐
130 Ceremonies ☐

131 Civic officials ☐	163 Car parking – public, special ☐
132 Commentators/announcers ☐	164 Changing accommodation ☐
133 Dress rehearsal ☐	165 Childminding/crèche ☐
134 Entertainment, including licensing ☐	166 Cleaning, before, during, after ☐
135 Films/photography ☐	167 Cloakrooms ☐
136 Interpreters ☐	168 Church services ☐
137 Logo and stationery ☐	169 Directional signs ☐
138 Marketing ☐	170 Disabled support services ☐
139 Merchandising, e.g. T-shirts ☐	171 Emergency procedures ☐
140 Newsletter ☐	172 Entertainment ☐
141 Music and music licence and performing rights ☐	173 Exhibition ☐
142 Posters, leaflets ☐	174 Health and safety ☐
143 Presentation – programme, timetable of events ☐	175 Hospitality ☐
144 Press and press releases ☐	176 Hotels ☐
145 Prizes/medals/cups and engraving ☐	177 Information services ☐
146 Protocol ☐	178 Lost property ☐
147 Publicity ☐	179 Lost children ☐
148 Public relations ☐	180 Maintenance ☐
149 Radio ☐	181 Medical ☐
150 Receptions ☐	182 Photocopier ☐
151 Souvenirs ☐	183 Police ☐
152 Sponsorship/patronage ☐	184 Post Office ☐
153 Theme/logo/image ☐	185 Red Cross/St John Ambulance ☐
154 TV/Videotaping event ☐	186 Secretarial ☐
155 VIPs ☐	187 Security – people, property, bomb scares ☐

SUPPORT SERVICES

156 Accommodation ☐	188 Shops ☐
157 Ambulance service ☐	189 Technicians ☐
158 AA/RAC ☐	190 Telephone/telex/fax/email ☐
159 Agencies ☐	191 Tourist information – guide books, maps ☐
160 Bank ☐	192 Translation services ☐
161 Bar – public, guests ☐	193 Transport ☐
162 Catering - public, performers, guests and licences ☐	194 Travel agency ☐
	195 Typewriters ☐
	196 Visits and tours ☐

What experience has shown is that there has very often been insufficient thought given to the planning and organization of the event before committees are set, decisions are made to go ahead, structures have been formulated and jobs allocated. Forward planning, organization structure, objective setting and communications are main issues integral to successful event management.

Events are important strings to the Leisure Manager's bow. Their organization is important to his or her repertoire of skills. Events lend themselves to certain styles of management such as Management by Objectives and strong, authoritative leadership and co-ordination. They need a sound, logical framework, thorough planning, imaginative marketing and promotion and excellent presentation. They need quality leisure management.

Discussion points

1 The general public often has unrealistic high expectations of local leisure events. As a professional planning and managing events, ask yourself why this is the case and how would you go about either changing perceptions or meeting expectations within the next two years.

2 Special local leisure events carry benefits for the organizations staging them and for the public attending them. Events also carry management problems. Based on an event of your choice, what fundamental principles need to apply to heighten its success and eliminate potential problems and dangers?

Useful website

Institute of Leisure and Amenity Management (ILAM): www.ilam.co.uk
The event professionals, ILAM provide information on running successful events.

23

Staffing and organizational structures

Introduction

Excellent staff are as important as excellent facilities. Therefore, senior professionals and managers in leisure services must have knowledge, experience and understanding of staff matters: selection, staff relations, staff motivation, organizational structures and something of the law as it relates to employment.

Staff – whether full-time, part-time or voluntary – are the most important resource in any leisure organization and their cost should be regarded as a highly valued investment rather than an expensive item of expenditure. The right staff need to be employed, trained, nurtured and enabled to perform well for their organizations and for themselves.

An organization structure represents the way in which the work is organized and shared out and the manner in which an enterprise is managed. Every leisure and recreation service, from the smallest to the largest, has an organization and staffing structure of some kind. Used effectively the structure provides the framework through which the work operations proceed in an orderly manner towards achieving organizational objectives.

The ways in which staff are selected, employed, organized and treated are crucial factors in the performance and level of success of management.

The need for appropriate structures

Staffing structures, the types of staff and the levels of staffing in leisure services vary considerably from authority to authority, organization to organization and from centre to centre, even where facilities are comparable and where policies appear to run parallel.

In public recreation, financed in large measure by rates and taxes and subject to local government administrative systems and standardized procedures, one might expect to find a considerable level of uniformity. While different localities have different facilities and different circumstances, it is understandable that variations exist. However, the variations in structure and personnel are so wide – from a small subsection to a comprehensive department, in towns of the same size and with similar ranges of services – that comparative studies are needed to highlight the benefits and limitations of different systems.

> At some similar, large leisure complexes, total staff numbers can vary from 50 to 80 full-time equivalents.

Staff can vary within the same organization from full-time to part-time, temporary, casual and voluntary. There are recreation executives, senior, middle and line managers, recreation officers, wardens, park-keepers, coaches, teachers, community workers, youth workers, play leaders, artists, caterers, technicians, supervisors, administrators and a wide range of technical, clerical and maintenance staff. They have variations in contracts of employment, job descriptions, training and benefits. They work different hours and different shifts and many work long, unsocial hours. With most comprehensive leisure facilities, opening hours are lengthy, as much as 100 hours a week. In these circumstances, even the most dedicated manager is in essence a part-timer.

The allocation of revenue expenditure towards staffing, particularly in public recreation facilities, takes the largest share of operating costs. In times of economic stringency, and with the regimes of competitive tendering and Best Value, reduction in staff is considered to be one method of reducing deficits or increasing net returns. It is therefore important to demonstrate clearly the appropriate – the most effective – levels of staff as a means towards achieving objectives. Organizations that fail to demonstrate value and cost effectiveness could well experience staff cuts or be subjected to 'rationalizing', 'downsizing' and 'outsourcing'.

In many public leisure and recreation organizations the staffing structure is inappropriate to the needs. Some facilities, say, an arts centre or a museum may be unhappily embedded within a local authority departmental structure with a hierarchy and status positions which have little relationship to the work of these services, the needs of staff and, possibly least of all, the needs of users. Fitting new types of facility or services into outmoded structures highlights the problem even more clearly. In one London borough, a vast community sports and recreation centre had its director, on leaving, replaced by an administrator, so that the centre's organization structure could fit into the borough's departmental structure. Many leisure centres require managers with considerable decision-making powers and senior staff to take full responsibility in unsocial hours. They need structures which are flexible enough to respond to leisure participants' unpredictable demands.

Many leisure facilities, particularly in the voluntary sector, are managed by a leader and volunteers. They take responsibility for facilities, plant, programme and personnel. Even in public leisure and recreation centres the level of part-time staff can be high. It is not unusual to find a leisure centre staffed in the evening by a super-visor or receptionist and a few part-timers: managers and senior staff having long since gone.

Staff have a variety of duties and the facilities are open for long hours. The nature of the job – that of creating satisfactory experiences for people in their leisure time – requires that staff have motivation, commitment and an understanding of customer requirements: if staff flexibility is required, then organization and employer flexibility are also required.

The principles of management which affect staffing

Some top-level managers and senior personnel are called upon to formulate policies and organizational structures. Most managers, however, are appointed to positions in existing organizations, to which they have to adapt. It is important that managers at all levels understand the organization structure, the principles on which it is based and the components which go to make it up.

According to the International City Management Association (1965), three basic principles of management must be considered in establishing an organizational struc-ture, namely:

- unity of command
- logical assignment
- span of control and
- authority and power.

Unity of command The principle states that each individual in an organization should be responsible to only one superior. Adherence to this principle establishes a precise chain of command within the organization. Situations exist in recreation organizations which do not follow such a principle. For example, at one recreation centre the head groundsman was directly answerable both to a centre manager and to an assistant technical officer at the town hall. At another authority, while the prin-ciple of unity of command exists (in that the centre manager is responsible to only one person), the Leisure Manager is answerable not to the borough director of leisure and recreation, but to the chief executive. One can easily detect problems built into the structure itself. In these examples, a key member of staff has been able to by-pass his or her senior officer. The structure could work against the best interests of the organization. It could be a cause of envy, personality clashes and the guarding of one's territory.

Logical assignment The principle states that staff doing the same work should be grouped together and that work is planned and scheduled in a logical order. Situations exist in leisure management where structures and departmentalism are put first, and the job in hand second. Without logical assignment, there will be duplication or overlap, confusion, power struggles, drawing in of responsibilities to heighten status, keeping things close to the chest, and not sharing, which all lead to poor performance. Here again, personalities are blamed but the greater responsibility rests with those responsible for the structure and its implementation.

Span of control The principle is something of a misnomer. The principle states that there are limiting factors which must be considered in deciding the number of subordinates a member of staff can effectively handle. Span of control may be more accurately defined as span of management because the limiting factors are many. They include the number of people that can be supervised, depending on the quality of staff and level of delegation, the distance over which control can be exercised, the amount of time in which to exercise control, and the number of activities that a manager can effectively manage. The span of management is, then, a statement of those limitations.

It is not possible to state the exact number of people a manager should 'control'. Much depends on the competence of subordinates and the manager's own knowledge, ability, time, energy, personality, leadership style and the environment and situation in which work must be undertaken. The type of work, in addition to the capacities of the manager, must also be considered. Organizations with narrow spans of control have the potential for good control and close supervision of staff (Figure 23.1). However, managers tend to get involved in the work of their subordinates. Narrow spans of control are often found in hierarchical organizations where the many tiers of management will incur high staff costs and the distance between the top and lower levels can make communication difficult.

Having to manage too many staff, on the other hand, will limit a manager's efficiency and effectiveness. Some public authorities put one senior manager in control of sport, arts, community, environment, parks and open spaces, children's play, youth, libraries, cemeteries, catering (including meals on wheels) and entertainment (Figure 23.2). For many the span of control is too wide and managers become overloaded, ineffective and inefficient. However, with a manager who can communicate well, delegate clearly, select and empower capable subordinates, the organization can work more effectively and at a lower cost than an organization with a hierarchy and with a smaller span of control that might be super-efficient, but far less effective. Further, the climate that comes with empowerment is more likely to encourage innovation and creative thinking with a concentration on achieving the organization's objectives and not upon the means of achieving them. Innovation needs delegated authority and the freedom of action.

Authority and power Too often these words are mistakenly treated as being synonymous. Authority is based upon a person's position within the organizational structure, incorporates the person's responsibilities, tasks, and so on. It is accepted by a person's subordinates as having 'legitimate' authority. Power on the other hand is a much broader concept and relates to the person's ability to influence or persuade others to take a particular course of action. Power can come from being a leader, even without positional authority, and power can also come from being an expert – the power of knowledge. Hence, in a more organic structure, the power within the organization can change, depending on the task or function being undertaken.

A narrow span of 'control' makes it possible to supervise work tightly but it does not give assistant staff the opportunity to make decisions or feel a sense of commitment and achievement. Leisure and Recreation need highly motivated staff and also many specialists such as coaches, community leaders, play leaders, parks and open spaces officers, and outdoor activity specialists, some literally 'paddling their own canoes', who need guidelines of principle and support, but also a level of autonomy rather than

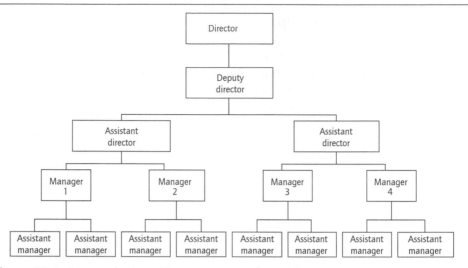

Figure 23.1 An organization with narrow spans of control

overt control and supervision. These staff develop skills peculiar to the job and special expertise. This technical know-how can be harnessed to improve motivation, job satisfaction and involvement in decision-making processes, which impinge on their area of work.

In local government, many managers have responsibility for a large geographical area. Members of staff directed by a specific manager should not be situated too closely if this results in over-supervision. However, they should not be located too far away as this can lead to under-supervision.

Time is a very limiting factor. Every manager has to allocate time to:

- routine work which is usually delegated but must be monitored
- regular work a manager must do himself or herself
- special work and assignments and creative work.

For discussion of time management refer to Torkildsen, 1993. Unfortunately, some executives and senior managers give little time to engaging with the workforce; pool supervisors, green-keepers, community art workers and play leaders might not recognize their director of leisure services. It seems logical therefore to have as broad a span as possible because fewer tiers reduce the remoteness of managers from staff; the lines of communication are shortened; broad spans tend to stretch and develop future managers; and having fewer tiers of structure should save money and time.

Organization and staffing structures

Managers will have to work within structures often not of their choosing; they will have to be negotiators, decision makers, communicators and understanders of a wide variety of professional and lay staff. An appropriate staff structure will assist the manager in the achievement of the goals of any organization, but it is no alternative to good management. Rather, it is a means to an end, and is only good if it is good for the

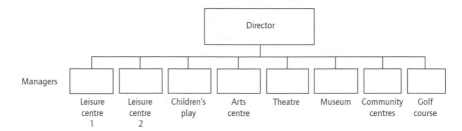

Figure 23.2 An organization with a wide span of control

organization it serves. Furthermore, organization structures provide only a framework for management and staff to work within. The type of structure will depend on several important factors:

- the nature of the controlling body (local authority; charitable trust; commercial entrepreneur; private club)
- aims and objectives of the organization (profit making; service orientation)
- the stability of the environment in which the organization operates
- distribution of facilities (localized; widespread)
- financial targets (subsidy; break-even; profit-making)
- scale and nature of the facilities and resources (sport- or art-specific; multi-leisure)
- location layout and design of facilities (compact; separated elements)
- nature of the service to be provided (community-based; sports development)
- levels of performance (top level; casual; formal; informal)
- ability of management and staff and the level of delegation possible
- the hours of operation.

Structured, well managed organizations can achieve more than a collection of individuals. Through the organization's pool of knowledge and resources, the necessary tasks can also be accomplished more quickly and efficiently.

Formal and informal organizations

There is a need to distinguish between informal and formal organizations. A formal organization has a clearly defined structure that establishes relationships and differences in status, role, rank and levels of authority, in a controlled environment where rules exist with regard to channels of communication, accepted forms of behaviour and the manner in which key tasks have to be undertaken. Additionally, such organizations have defined outcomes and in order to achieve these the overall work is divided amongst the workforce in a co-ordinated way so that they function as a unit or a department. In contrast an informal organization has a much less defined structure. It is also likely to be much smaller in size, and more likely to have a shorter life span. In certain circumstances an informal organization will be converted into a formal one, such as when an interest group forms a club or society with rules and a constitution.

It is important for leisure managers to be aware that in every formal organization there is likely to be at least one informal 'organization' that draws upon its 'membership' from different management levels and departments. It is the informal relationships which provide for lateral communication rather than 'going through the channels' and where two-way communication leads to improved understanding. While formal structures are required, managers should also encourage effective informal structures to foster the essential human dimension.

An example of good cross-communication is shown at a leisure centre in Essex. Daytime integrated sports coaching classes are run for the community and college students, within the same space and time allocation, utilizing coaches from either organization. The possibility of these classes being held would have been remote if procedures and communications had been conducted through the formal structures of the county council and the college, and the leisure facility. The informal structure and communications network enabled those with first-hand knowledge to make decisions relating to work, which they are the best to advise upon. This informal process cuts across organizational boundaries, budgets, space and time allocations, staff and administrative red tape. One of the skills of the good manager is to permit, within certain limits, a level of face-to-face work which in essence bypasses the formal chain of command.

Nancy Foy (1981) believes that it is time we 'humanized' our systems. We need not scrap them, as long as they remain human in scale. While organizations and the people in them need rituals and regular checkpoints, they also need information about their own work groups, their own outputs, and so on:

> A lot of information that can't be transmitted can normally flow informally, with complete credibility and confidentiality, once people believe they are hearing the truth and able to tell it as well.

Designing formal structures

Forming an organization structure is like creating a structure from building blocks – the work unit or the job of an individual worker is the smallest building block in the structure as a whole. Organizing is the process of dividing up the work in a structured framework. Managers have distinct tasks in setting up the staffing structure:

- dividing the work or tasks into jobs
- grouping similar tasks: usually by forming sections, units or departments
- specifying and controlling the relationships between the groups
- delegating authority for carrying out the jobs or group of jobs; this is normally done via chains of command
- specifying the authority or control over the groups which can be centralized or decentralized to varying levels
- in organizations like a large leisure centre, local authority department, theatre or park, creating line-and-staff relationships.

Dividing the work up into jobs is easier when jobs are specialized or the tasks are narrow – grass cutting, ski instruction, cleaning, accounting. Specialization is essential for many tasks but leisure managers and senior staff are increasingly generalists with specialist leanings – personnel officer-cum-duty officer. And at a grass-roots level, poolside staff may also carry out sports coaching and act as duty supervisors. Leisure jobs call for greater flexibility than industrial jobs.

In some situations staff structures have been charted even before an organization has outlined its policies and objectives. These are usually a clone of a structure elsewhere that may not even be appropriate to the new situation. The first step should not be the discussion of a structure, rather an analysis of the organization and its policies which the structure is to serve. This is not to discourage emulating a structure which has been developed successfully; standardization can lead to efficiencies. However, different situations have different priorities; each area has its own identity; each has its own budget targets; and each has its own style. Structures must be developed which meet the needs of the situation. It is true that commercial chains such as fast-food outlets provide a standardized structure, and we can learn from them, but they provide a standardized product also. Leisure services, which have a myriad of permutations, call for appropriate situational solutions.

Organization and staff structures should not however be static, determined and fixed for ever. Structures must be changed to meet changing situations. For example, a manager usually comes into a structure previously determined, and finds ways of improving performance or ways in which the staff will respond to his or her ideas. Programmes will change; staff will develop and some will move on; and financial forecasts will alter. Therefore, appraisals should be undertaken and changes implemented to meet the new situation. It is said that we can be certain of only one thing – change. Changes in structure, and changes in operational objectives, are usually necessary over a period of years, but seldom implemented in public, voluntary and institutional recreation services.

The staffing structure has an effect on the management of the organization, just as the activities themselves affect the programme and the organization. That is not to imply that the more staff one has, the better the management or more varied the programme. Rather the way staff are organized, deployed and motivated will have decided effects on the results.

Staff structures should be tailor-made to be appropriate. They also need to be altered to respond to situational changes.

Departmental structures

Historically, departmentalization by numbers was the most frequent method in the organization of tribes and armies, but with the need for specialized staff, this strictly hierarchal method is now usually confined to the lower tiers of an organization, such as the cleaning staff at a major event stadium.

To be effective, managers must divide the workload into manageable parts. The main purpose of dividing the work is to establish methods of determining section responsibilities, the distribution of authority to individuals and the processes of delegation. The most used method of dividing work is departmentalization; that is, dividing the workforce into units and departments.

There are different avenues managers can follow in creating departments, the first four suggested by Grossman (1980):

1 Function: these are departments in which staff are grouped according to function, for example, sports coaching, arts and crafts and maintenance.
2 Clientele: these departments are grouped according to the clientele they are to serve, for example, junior, youth and senior citizens.
3 Geographic: staff are grouped according to the area in which they work, for example, a large borough could have area or district departments.
4 Process: these are usually service-giving departments and grouped according to the process used in providing the particular services, for example, an information service or counselling.
5 Time or shift: staff are grouped in shifts to cover all the hours that a service or facility is open.

Functional departments Functional departments are a logical and time-proven approach and are the most common method used in the leisure industry, for example, parks department, arts and entertainment department. They encourage the use of specialization and hence make for the efficient use of staff. Also, authority is vested with the managers who are responsible for the organization's major functions.

Unfortunately, when different departments are competing for increased budgets the organization's objectives can be forgotten and greater loyalty given to the department, as distinct from the organization. All too frequently, we find that the finance department is in the driving seat, with the emphasis being given to providing an efficient service at the expense of providing an effective service, concerned with meeting the needs of the community.

Client and service departments Clientele departments encourage the staff to concentrate on clients' needs. Staff can develop an expertise within areas of specialization. They can also give confidence to the customers in that they feel they are being served by an understanding organization.

This method, however, can have its disadvantages. Some client groups may be difficult to define clearly, e.g. 'ethnic minorities', and they may feel patronized. Further, certain client groups may require specialist staff, e.g. counsellors, who may not necessarily be found among the organization's personnel. Some areas of work lend themselves to another word rather than 'department'; for example, counselling is better described as a service. Some local authorities use names which provide immediate recognition, e.g. youth service. Service-giving departments need to have personnel – in-house or external – who are both qualified and capable of giving the service.

Geographic departments The advantages of geographic departments include decentralizing the service nearer to potential clients and placing responsibility with some managers and staff at lower tiers of the organization; this gives these personnel the opportunity to take higher levels of responsibility and achieve job satisfaction. The staff involved in the decision-making process, 'at the coal face', are likely to be aware of the needs and demands of their particular area and will be more accessible to their clients and customers. Hence, the service provided is likely to be far more effective, given good staff with delegated powers.

This method of departmentalization, however, may require managers to have interdisciplinary knowledge that in the leisure field covers sports, arts, play, entertainment, and so on. It is also likely that there will be a degree of duplication of services if the area management office and the central office having their own purchasing and promotion sections. Geographic departments require very reliable and capable staff or, because of their remoteness, regular and costly monitoring will need to be put in place.

Departments based on time or shift patterns These are usually at the lower levels of an organizational structure where the service extends well beyond the normal eight-hour working day. For example, a leisure centre that is open for some 100 hours per week will usually require shifts to cover the service it provides. Problems can arise over co-ordinating of staff, with communication of information and instructions, and operationally, the hand-over by one shift to another can be problematical if tight procedures are not maintained. Running three shifts at a centre is a very expensive exercise. In the private sector, full staff shifts are used less. Work patterns, however, are changing, with core staff carrying out essential duties, using support staff for peak throughputs, events and other special programmes. The manager needs to understand the alternatives to develop the most appropriate departmental structure.

Line and line-and-staff organizations

Organizational charts normally depict 'line' organizations in which authority is passed on from the highest to the lowest levels via a chain of command. In line-and-staff organizations staff personnel are incorporated, in addition to 'line' staff. 'Staff' personnel are frequently specialists who service 'line' personnel, for example, financial, programming and personnel specialists. The financial and technical officers at one leisure centre carry out their 'staff' functions in office hours and their 'line' functions as duty

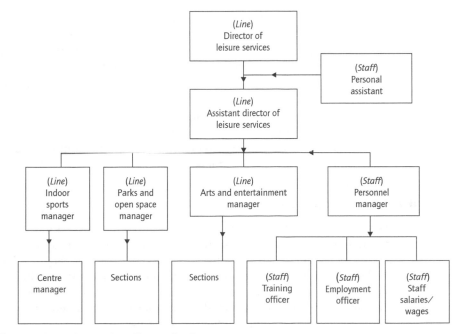

Figure 23.3 Line-and-staff organization

Table 23.1 Line functions and staff functions

LINE FUNCTIONS	STAFF FUNCTIONS
• Line directs or orders	• Staff advise
• Line has responsibility to carry out activities from beginning to end	• Staff studies, reports, recommends, but does not carry out
• Line follows chain of command	• Staff assists line but is not part of chain
• Line decides when and how to use staff for line use	• Staff always available
• Line is the doing part of the organization	• Staff is the assisting part of the organization

Source: International City Management Association (1965), *Basic Concepts of Organization*, INA, Washington, DC

managers in the evenings and at weekends. 'Line-and-staff' organizations are more flexible than 'line' organizations (Figure 23.3). They permit 'line' personnel to carry out the regular managerial and operational work, leaving certain specialist functions to 'staff' personnel. Table 23.1 shows how the International City Management Association (ICMA, 1965) differentiates the functions of line and staff.

Separate staff functions have advantages, including:

- reduction in costs (one finance officer for several sections)
- an arm's-length objectivity and
- specialist inputs into the organization.

This provides service, advisory and planning information for managers and the organization (Drucker, 1955). A potential disadvantage is that staff departments tend to grow at a faster rate than other departments, leading to greater overheads. Staff sections such as finance and planning can also gather undue power and influence. In highly technical or bureaucratic organizations, line management and staff management equate to 'workers and staff'. The nature of a leisure service organization is suited to 'line-and-staff' systems, which create greater opportunities for all 'staff' as well as 'line' personnel to provide customer service.

Different organization structures

The various organization structures used in the delivery of leisure services fall on a continuum between a mechanistic model which is rigidly structured at one extreme, to an organic model which is flexibly structured at the other (Figure 23.4). The different models are outlined below, together with the characteristics: either more 'vertical' or more 'horizontal', and more or less 'bureaucratic'. Within the compass of these various parameters are some specific 'models' and four are considered briefly: bureaucracy, the 'pyramid', matrix structure and hybrid structures.

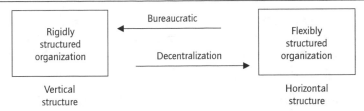

Figure 23.4 The mechanistic/organic continuum

Mechanistic organization
- Operates more effectively when the environment is stable.
- Formal structures predominate.
- Control, authority and communication usually follow hierarchical patterns.
- The work is broken down into differentiated tasks with precise instructions that become highly standardized.
- Interaction tends to follow hierarchical lines between superior and subordinate.
- There is a general assumption that those higher up the hierarchy are better equipped to make the more important decisions.
- Operational actions tend to be governed by instructions issued by superiors.

Organic organization
- Better suited to operate in an environment where change is a factor – it is adaptable to changing conditions.
- Informal structures are permitted.
- One's special knowledge and experience are looked at in terms of what they can contribute to the overall task.
- Problems are not pushed upward, downward or sideways – 'buck-passing' is discouraged.
- Control, authority and communications move through a wide network rather than a single hierarchical structure.
- Communication tends to be more lateral than vertical and content consists of information and advice rather than instructions and handed-down decisions.
- Leadership in a given situation tends to fall to the person with the most appropriate expertise and ability in that field.

Vertical and horizontal structures and decentralization
Vertical organizations tend to be highly structured and the role expectations of staff strictly controlled, leaving little room for individual discretion and initiative. In contrast, horizontal organizations tend to be more loosely structured, with fewer constraints, leaving staff with considerable discretion to define how best to achieve the overall objectives. The right balance for maximum effectiveness must be achieved.

Peter Drucker (1955) has often spoken of the need to decentralize structures:

> performance will be improved by de-centralization. It will make it possible for good men, hitherto stifled, to do a job effectively. It will make better performers out of mediocre men by raising their sights and the demands on them. It will identify the poor performers and make it possible for their replacement.

Decentralization can lead to decisions being made more quickly and nearer to the point of action. It reduces lines of communication, reduces status problems and provides greater job satisfaction (see, for example Elliott, 1989). However, decentralization is not appropriate to all situations.

Bureaucracy

Large organizations in the United Kingdom, including local authority services, exhibit the culture of organizations based on bureaucracy. The German sociologist and political economist Max Weber (see Chapter 18, Management principles and foundations) extolled the virtues of organizations based on his 'bureaucratic' model, with principles of fixed rules, office hierarchy, levels of graded authority and written documents (files) which make up the 'bureau' – the office. Once established, organizations are difficult to dismantle. The bureaucratic model is the most widely implemented form of organization. It is a vertical structure. Authority is located at the top of the hierarchy and flows downwards through the organization. The division of labour emphasizes the hierarchical structure and establishes a superior–subordinate relationship. This allows the various activities to be subdivided into a specific set of tasks with the roles of individuals clearly defined.

The pyramid

Laurence Peter, a Canadian famous for coining the term 'the Peter Principle' (whereby an individual in a hierarchy tends to rise to his or her level of incompetence) demonstrates in *The Peter Pyramid* (Peter, 1986) the ways in which proliferating bureaucracies sap human resources. He perceives that the problem with major organizations is that they are constructed upside down, with the point of the operation almost invisible underneath the baggage of top-heavy administration.

A leisure service operation, looking to prune expenditure, often cuts away at jobs at the lower, delivery levels – the customer service elements such as receptionists, grounds staff, coaching staff, cleaners, attendants – often a solution least likely to effect a cure. It cuts off the hands that actually provide the service.

There is nothing wrong with an organizational model like a pyramid but, as Kenneth Blanchard and Patricia and Drea Zigarmi (1986) point out in *Leadership and the One Minute Manager*:

> The trouble comes when you think in a pyramid ... When you think in a pyramid, the assumption is that everyone works for the person above them on the organizational ladder. As a result, managers are thought to be 'responsible' for planning, organizing, and evaluating everything that happens in the organization while their staff are supposed to be 'responsible to the directives of management' ... I prefer to turn the pyramid upside down so that top managers are at the bottom ... When that happens there is a subtle, but powerful, twist in who is responsible and who should be responsive to whom. Another problem with hierarchies is the belief that those at the top, who get paid more, are more essential to the organization than the staff below. This is mistaken, leads to poor use of human resources and is a recipe for job dissatisfaction.

The matrix structure

The matrix structure (Figure 23.5) is normally a combination of a functional departmentalization structure with an overlay of project managers, who are responsible for

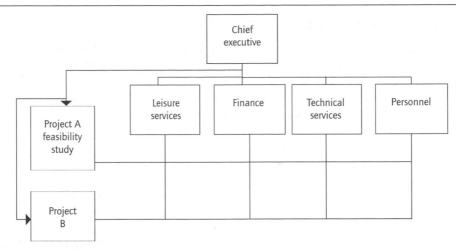

Figure 23.5 Matrix organization

completing specific topics, such as a feasibility study for a swimming pool. In this example the project manager can call upon the expertise in the different departments to assist in the production of the feasibility study: personnel services on staffing aspects; technical services on producing the designs and projections of capital costs, and so on. The advantage associated with this structure is that it concentrates on the task in hand; staffing levels are minimal and technical experts are used as and when required.

Unfortunately, problems can also be encountered when using this form of organization such as role conflict and role ambiguity – is he or she working for the department or for the project? This situation can produce tensions, work overload, or provide inadequate or too much authority to the project manager. Inadequate resources and authority can delay the project and result in time-consuming negotiation and meetings.

In order to make a matrix organization effective, there is a need for a multi-discipline team and effective teamwork (see Team building, p. 395, in Chapter 19). Objectives need to be clearly defined and known by all and delegated authority given at a senior level.

Hybrid structures

The delivery of leisure services calls for flexibility and adaptability – different forms of organizational structure will suit different situations. Trust management, partnership management or volunteer management, with different needs and resources, will require different structures. Sports, arts and outdoor leisure often call for specially created forms of looser organizational structures. In such leisure environments with outreach workers, wardens, coaches, teachers and voluntary support groups, there will be a need to cultivate a flexible management regime.

Although leisure departments in local authorities appear, on paper, as clear-cut family trees, the extent of overlap and duplication can be considerable. Leisure service delivery, therefore, sometimes calls for hybrid staffing structures, tailor-made for situations not normally found in other industries because leisure behaviour is different from work behaviour; it is far more open – people can make choices – and far less predictable.

The organization chart

The organization chart is the most common approach to portraying the organization's structure. It illustrates the hierarchy, functions and chain of command. Strict adherence to charts and family trees is not advocated, but as a general framework it helps those within and outside an organization to visualize the lines of authority and communication. Where a recreation service is geographically spread, or where there is difficulty in perceiving the roles of particular departments, the organization chart has considerable advantage. The organization chart, however, must not be given permanent status, as though it were indestructible. It portrays the organization, acts as a framework for sharing the work and indicates levels of responsibility. It should be designed to best meet the objectives of the organization and be used to further its work.

The structure, however, is not infallible; it has limitations. First, it is skeletal, tends to be inflexible and is only representative as long as the status quo remains. Second, it is not precise about amounts of authority and responsibility. Third, it does not portray the essential informal structure and relationships.

The organizational structure, however, used wisely, is one of the tools of successful management performance. Because structures emphasize hierarchies, they confer status and 'pecking orders'. Some managers therefore become over-concerned with preserving and enhancing the organization structure itself, rather than using it to help to serve the principles, aims and objectives of the organization. Organization charts serve a useful function in visualizing and reinforcing the organization and its structure. The picture-image, however, only illustrates a framework and should not become a sacred cow for bureaucracy.

Employment of staff and legislation

The employment of staff and staff relations are governed, to a considerable extent, by government legislation. In recent years, there have been fundamental changes in the law in the United Kingdom, which have far-reaching consequences for employers and employees. Legislation has set new standards in personnel policies and in employer–employee relationships and has provided statutory bodies to enforce new standards.

There are in the region of 40 Acts of Parliament which have a bearing on staff relations and employment, most of which have been introduced or have been changed in the past three decades. Most legislation has put obligations and constraints on employers and extensive rights have been given to the employees.

The new Acts have undoubtedly improved the working conditions of employees in general. Employees now have a much clearer idea of their employment rights; employers have detailed legislation to conform to and procedural guides on employment matters. In theory, if the procedures are followed, there should be less conflict. However, despite legislation, tribunals and procedural guidelines, problems of employment and staff relations seem always to exist. They are primary factors in poor public relations, poor communications, mismanagement and low morale, all leading to less successful business enterprises, whether in the private, commercial or public sectors and whether in the context of factory, school, swimming pool or opera house.

Much of the work carried out in the field of recreation and leisure is subject to a whole raft of Acts of Parliament. Unsocial hours, special duties and overtime hours of full-time staff have to be handled along with part-time staff, volunteers and temporary staff. The kinds of work involved, and the complex nature of recreation programmes often produce the pressures which cause tensions and can lead to disputes with staff, clients and customers. Managers should be aware of the laws which regulate employment and organizational issues. A thumbnail sketch of some of the relevant Acts of Parliament follows.

Equal opportunities The Equal Opportunities Commission (EOC) was established under the Sex Discrimination Act, 1975 as an independent statutory body. In October 2002, the government proposed merging the EOC, the Commission for Racial Equality and the Disability Rights Commission to form a single equality body in Great Britain responsible for the promotion of equality in relation to sex, race, disability, sexual orientation, religion and age. New regulation was to come into force shortly at the time of writing.

Sex discrimination The Sex Discrimination Act, 1975 (SDA) makes it unlawful to discriminate in employment, education and training in Britain on grounds of sex, or marriage. The SDA applies to women and men of any age, including children. The employment provisions were amended by the Sex Discrimination Act, 1986 to bring legislation in line with the European Community directives on equality. The Employment Act, 1989 amends the Sex Discrimination Act, 1975, on the implementation of the principle of the equal treatment for men and women as regards access to employment, vocational training and promotion and on working conditions.

Race relations The Home Office has responsibility for policy and legislation on racial equality. In Great Britain, the Race Relations Act, 1976 makes it unlawful for anybody to discriminate on grounds of race, colour, nationality (including citizenship), or ethnic or national origins. The Act applies to employment, training, education and the provision of goods and services. The Race Relations (Amendment) Act, 2000 extended the scope of the 1976 Act to cover the way public authorities carry out their functions. Public authorities now have a statutory general duty to work to eliminate unlawful racial discrimination and promote equal opportunities and good relations between people of different racial groups.

Health and safety The Health and Safety Commission (HSC) has overall responsibility for developing policy on health and safety at work in Great Britain and is currently working on a simpler and more effective system of regulation. The Health and Safety Executive (HSE) carries out the day-to-day functions of enforcing health and safety law. In premises, including leisure facilities, legislation is enforced by inspectors appointed by local authorities working under the guidance from the HSE.

The Health and Safety at Work Act, 1974 has the purpose of: 'securing the health, safety and welfare of people at work and to provide for the protection of the public whose health and safety might be affected by work activities'.

The general principle underlying the Act is that employers, in consultation with their employees, will draw up health and safety arrangements, within the broad obligations of the law to suit their own work areas:

- All employers with more than five employees must have a written statement covering the organization's policy on health and safety. The statement must be brought to the attention of all employees.
- The workplace must be made safe and pose no risk to the health of employees.
- Employers must give employees the information, instruction, training and supervision necessary.
- Employees must co-operate with their employer in meeting health and safety requirements and must take reasonable care of their own health and safety and that of others at the workplace.

The Management of Health and Safety at Work Regulations, 1999 set out employers' legal obligation to assess risks in the workplace. There are basic steps in conducting a risk assessment:

- look for the hazards, e.g. pieces of equipment, hazardous substances
- decide who might be harmed and how, e.g. staff, employees, public
- evaluate the risks and decide whether the existing precautions are adequate or whether more should be done
- record findings
- regularly review assessments and revise them.

Equality The Equal Pay Act, 1970 amended by the Equal Pay (Amendment) Regulations, 1988 requires men and women to be paid the same rates of pay for doing the same or broadly similar work, or work of equal value. The purpose of the Act is to eliminate discrimination in pay and other employment matters: holidays, sickness benefit, bonus, overtime, and so on. The Act applies to women and men of any age, including children. Despite being in force for over 30 years, some women are still being paid less than their male counterparts undertaking similar work.

Employment The Employment Protection Act, 1975 and the Employment Protection Consolidation Act, 1978 (as amended by the Employment Act, 1982) provide the machinery for promoting good industrial relations and give employees certain rights, including:

- maternity rights
- rights for time off work either paid or unpaid for certain reasons
- written statements of main terms and conditions of employment
- an itemized pay statement for employees and
- protection against unfair dismissal.

The 1975 Act also set up ACAS, the Advisory, Conciliation and Arbitration Service. The Employment Act, 2002 received Royal Assent on 8 July, 2002:

The Act supports the government's commitment to create highly productive, modern and successful workplaces through fairness and partnership at work. It will deliver a balanced package of support for working parents, at the same time as reducing red tape for employers by simplifying rules governing maternity, paternity and adoption leave and pay, and make it easier to settle disputes in the workplace. It marks a significant step towards the government's Election Manifesto commitment to 'help parents devote more time to their children early in life' and meets the Manifesto commitment to examine reforms which promote efficiency and fairness.

Disability In the 2001 Census, 10.9 million people in the United Kingdom described themselves as having a long-term illness, health problem or disability. The unemployment rate for disabled people was nearly twice as high as for non-disabled people. The Disability Rights Commission (DRC) was established under the Disability Rights Commission Act, 1999 as an independent body funded by the government to work towards eliminating discrimination and promoting equal opportunities for disabled people in Great Britain.

The Disability Discrimination Act, 1995 (DDA) aims to end the discrimination which many disabled people face. The Act gives disabled people rights in the areas of:

- employment
- access to goods, facilities and services
- buying or renting land or property.

The employment rights and rights of access came into force on 2 December, 1996; further rights on 1 October, 1999, and the final rights of access in October 2004. The rights of access afforded to disabled people under the Act place a duty on businesses to adjust the way they provide services to the public, changing their practices where reasonable. From 2004, they will have to take steps to remove, alter or provide means of avoiding physical barriers. A Code of Practice was issued by the Disability Rights Commission in 2002 which also provides practical guidance for employers.

The Disability Discrimination Act, 1995 defines a disabled person as someone with 'a physical or mental impairment which has a substantial and long-term adverse effect on his/her ability to carry out normal day-to-day activities'.

The European Commission made 2003 the European Year of Disabled People and funding was provided by the Commission and the UK government on projects to promote the rights and participation of disabled people.

Other Acts In addition to these general acts, is a range of other Acts of Parliament that affect the leisure industry and thus the people working in it. Legislation relating to Best Value in the delivery of local government has, like its predecessor CCT, a huge impact on leisure and its personnel (see Best Value, p. 151, Chapter 9). The Education Reform Act, 1988 introducing local management of schools and legislating on the community use of schools, and The Children Act, 1989 providing duties and powers in the way children's activities are regulated, have also had substantial effects on the employment of personnel.

The range of Acts impinging on leisure include legislation on: office premises, fair trading, consumer safety, supply of goods, public health, town and country planning, water resources, the countryside, charities, licensing and lotteries, gaming, fire precautions, football spectators and others are in many cases covered in the chapters in this book relating to these subjects.

Diversity management

The world of work, especially for employees in the leisure, tourism and hospitality sectors, has become more diverse and increasingly so with more women at senior levels, a wider ethnic mix, more flexible patterns of working and greater mobility. Further, the markets are changing. For example, older people have greater spending power than in the past; disabled people and their carers want accessible leisure facilities and accessible holidays. Diversity management recognizes that people are different:

> It includes some of the more obvious and visible differences such as gender, ethnicity, age and disability and also less visible differences such as sexual orientation, background, personality, and workstyle. Diversity management is about recognizing, valuing and celebrating these differences. It is about harnessing difference to improve creativity and innovation. It is based on the belief that groups of people who bring different perspectives together will find better solutions to problems than groups of people who are the same.
>
> HCIMA, 1999

Diversity management focuses on individuals rather than on stereotyped groups and so builds on the concepts of inclusiveness and equal opportunities.

Government legislation and regulations mean that organizations need to put in place a number of policy statements and actions to conform with the law. Key areas include:

- policy on health and safety
- policy on equal opportunities
- policy on disability
- policy on non-harassment
- policy on data protection and personal details
- policies on employee rights: terms of employment, trade union membership, grievance procedures, entitlements (including holidays, sickness, other leave such as maternity/paternity, parental, jury service, and so on).

New Equality legislation came into force in 2003: The Employment Equality (Sexual Orientation) Regulation and the Employment Equality (Religion or Belief) Regulations, 2003. It is a major step forward for unfair discrimination in the UK. The UK government played an active role in negotiating two European Directives whose impact will be significant in tackling discrimination across the European Union. The Race Directive outlaws discrimination on grounds of racial or ethnic origin in the areas of employment, vocational training, goods and services, social protection, and education.

In summary, these Acts of Parliament and other legislation illustrate the legal and contractual implications for employer and employee and these laws affect leisure organizations, leisure managers and staff. What follows – the recruitment of staff, staff appraisal and production of a staff handbook – are thus of relevance.

Staff selection and recruitment

Staff selection is one of the most important functions of employers and managers. Successful management is dependent on good staff; good staff assist an organization towards reaching its goals. They work together to achieve objectives; they overcome difficulties, they solve problems. They are flexible in both spirit and deed.

Poor staff are a millstone. They are often incompetent, lack flexibility and create blockages in the system. They become a heavy burden for the organization, resulting in redundancies at best, and ineffective organizations at worst; they expend considerable funds of energy of the organization, which could otherwise have been effectively applied to meeting objectives. It is important therefore to select staff wisely (see Further reading).

Selecting the right people for the right jobs is of crucial importance to an organization's prosperity. Selecting staff is basically about judging other people and their abilities and their appropriateness for the job. In addition to the standard letters, curricula vitae and application forms, there are many methods or combinations of methods for shortlisting or selecting staff, including:

- promotion internally
- recommendation
- head hunting
- written presentations
- verbal presentations
- discussion groups
- personality testing
- agency shortlisting or recruitment
- consultancy advice and
- interview.

Measuring the qualities of leadership potential, emotional stability, and the like, has been part and parcel of recruitment practice for many decades. However, regardless of tests of intelligence and personality, and psychometric testing, the job of selection remains inexact and subjective. The interview, in spite of its critics, remains the primary method of assessing and selecting staff. The standard format with leisure and recreation posts is that of: application form, shortlist, references and a half-hour interview by a panel. The process can be time consuming and expensive. It becomes even more expensive if the wrong person is selected. Some candidates may be impressive, but do not match the job. This may entail changing the job to meet the qualities of the candidate or living with a mismatch.

In leisure, wages, salaries, allowances, benefits, training and development, and associated costs form a significant proportion of operational costs. The efficient recruitment and utilization of human resources is an important management responsibility and can offer scope for both improved performance and cost effectiveness.

509

Job descriptions, conditions and person profiles

The 'job description', and the 'person specification' for a job are quite distinct. The job description describes the job, its functions, responsibilities and employers' expectations. Its major concerns are with the nature of the work itself and the achievements necessary to meet the goals of the organization. The job conditions set out what the employer has to offer in terms of conditions of service, pay, benefits and prospects. Job descriptions should never be so fixed and demarcated that they become a straitjacket, limiting the development of the job and the person. They should serve as parameters and guidelines encouraging initiative and enabling growth and job enrichment. Staff should have titles and job descriptions which give them a broad scope of duties and which do not limit their function.

The person specification sets out the ideal credentials required from candidates to fit the job, their personal characteristics, abilities, qualifications and experience. The specification is not a detailed description of the job. The 'person specification' and the 'job description' are often combined in one document, but selection panels ought to match personal credentials to the requirements of the job.

The leisure industry has much to learn from professional selectors of people. Leisure employers, by the nature of their function, usually lack the continuous interviewing experience and the knowledge needed to probe the job market effectively. Too often in public appointments, local authority members, for example, pride themselves on their ability to make instant decisions about people. They work on feelings and hunches. With good judges of people's character and ability that may be fine, but with biased or poor judges the results can be disastrous both for the organization and the new employee. Interviewing and selecting staff are difficult and inexact exercises, but guidelines or 'outside' or 'informed' help can reduce uncertainties and chance. For example, a good agency or consultancy service will have a selection procedure which has been rigorously tested through practical experience.

A selection process

Selecting the right person is made more effective if a logical sequence is followed, which is based on proven successful methods. Video Arts films illustrate selection techniques and the need for a methodical process. In simple terms, there are five key steps.

1   Describe and define the job. Should you fill the old one? Should you create a new one? Can you re-allocate the workload? It is wise to avoid seeking a replica of the previous job holder as no two people are alike and the job will have changed. Instead use the vacancy to bring about necessary change and improvement. The job description defines the job.
2   Specify or 'profile' the person whose qualities are likely to meet the requirements of the job. Detail the expertise, experience, skills and qualifications that are likely to fit the job. Describe the personal qualities being sought, the demands of the job and the people already working in the team.
3   Set out the conditions of the job including pay, benefits and prospects.
4   Choose methods of communicating and publicizing the job vacancy, seeking to

match the person to the job. This may require a range of internal communications, outside advertising and professional advice from specialist recruitment sources.

5 Select sensitively, carefully and methodically. Haphazard selection can be ineffective and unfair. Probe, search and enable candidates to express their capabilities, enthusiasm, weaknesses and strengths. Selection is choosing the right and best person who fulfils the needs of the job, the tasks and the relationships with others and who is well satisfied with the conditions for employment.

Selectors need to satisfy themselves on a number of matters.

- Is the candidate capable of doing the job?
- Does he or she have the right qualities and real credibility in the field?
- Will the candidate fit well into the organization and get on well with people?
- Is he or she the best of the capable candidates?
- Is it the right person for the right job?
- Does he or she have the courage to do the right things, to be effective in meeting objectives, or just the ability to be efficient – doing things right?
- Is he or she a good leader, able to make decisions and to delegate?
- Is the candidate happy with the terms and conditions?

Investment in people pays off. Staff employed will require a high level of dedication if the full potential of leisure service and facilities are to be realized. They will also need to be appraised as part of their development and for the good of the organization.

Staff appraisal

Staff need to be effective. If they are also motivated, they will experience a sense of worthwhileness, a value far beyond salaries and conditions. Being effective does not mean having certificates hanging on the office wall, it means meeting in full measure the requirements of the job. Therefore, staff need to know exactly what is required of them and how they are performing. Appraisal provides the opportunity to achieve better results.

However, a formal system is no substitute for on-the-spot action. Appraisals, used inappropriately, can become mechanical and ineffective; there is no need to wait for the appraisal day to offer counsel and feedback. Most people want to do a good job and to be valued. Sometimes, appraisals have been used for discipline, with staff being 'hauled over the coals'. Immediate problems – sloppiness and poor service – should be dealt with at the time. The appraisal system, in contrast, should be positive and constructive, measuring performance against management expectations, over time.

There are different appraisal systems. The system which is chosen should meet the objectives. Comparative systems compare one employee's performance with others; they do not allow for two-way communication. Other methods are more independent. They include:

- writing a report on the employee, which is limited by subjectivity
- appraising an individual against specified traits such as initiative

- rating an employee on a numerical or alphabetical scale and
- a range of more sophisticated techniques.

Peer group appraisal is one method which has advantages but employees tend to band together in collectives supporting each other. In this atmosphere of pulling together, it is awkward and perceived as disloyal to single out work colleagues. Results-orientated appraisals focus on performance against set objectives. They are less open to subjectivity and bias and are more amenable to performance improvement. Key determinants are the job objectives themselves. The appraisal system needs to fit into the culture of the organization. Some organizations keep results close to their chests; others have an openness which enhances mutual trust and respect.

The benefits to the appraisee are several. Employees need to know how well they are doing. On-going feedback tends to be task-specific; the appraisal, on the other hand, is concerned with the overall performance over time. Overall achievements can be formally recognized and documented. While somewhat contrived, an appraisal system is above board. It is better than conducting an unstructured appraisal behind closed doors, without the employee knowing anything about it. Staff are affected by the way in which they are managed. Employees may not be given enough attention, sufficient resources or authority or may not have had their jobs clearly explained. Some staff are unclear as to the objectives of their job; when these are clarified, accepted and owned, priorities can be set far more easily.

The appraisal system has benefits to the appraiser. It provides a structured way to feed back to each of the team; any criticisms will be in the context of the job as a whole; objectives and priorities can be clarified by two-way communication. The line manager has a means of forward planning, setting each team member individual targets.

Managers need feedback on their own styles of management and the appraisal system should enable employees to talk frankly about how a manager's style affects their work. Feedback to the manager can therefore explore opportunities, resolve problems, obtain commitment and, by tackling contentious issues, staff turnover could be reduced.

Opportunities are provided also to discuss the chances of promotion. Frank assessments as to one's prospects can be made and advice as to further career counselling can be given, though this should be outside the focus on current and improved performance.

There are also benefits to the organization. If organizations value their employees and show commitment to them, improved performance should result. The system will identify and collate training needs. It can help to measure the strengths of the staff, whether the right people are in the right jobs, whether they can fill vacancies, and who is right for promotion. Staffing strategies can be determined. Without appraisal, some key issues might be overlooked.

The appraiser needs to be someone who knows about the appraisee and the job description and must be skilled in listening and dealing with sensitive issues, and have the ability to review successes and areas for improvement, looking forward with confidence. Focusing on the past tends to be negative. The appraisal should not dwell on pay or conditions, except where these adversely affect the job. Performance related pay (PRP) is a reasonable proposition – the higher the performance, the higher the pay. However, in leisure management, with complex permutations in the measurement of outputs, it can be insensitive to single out particular performances from the overall accomplishments. Pay reviews are best left out of staff appraisals.

Appraisal reports could include:

- measurement of current duties
- professional and technical competence
- approach to work
- loyalty
- supervision of staff
- upward and downward communication
- interpersonal skills
- achievements since previous appraisal
- overall performance and
- readiness for further responsibilities.

The appraisal should end on a positive note and an unambiguous agreement between appraiser and appraiseee as to the goals and expectations between now and the next appraisal. A succinct report should be filed and it is wise to review the report with the member of staff and for both to sign it. Account will need to be taken of the Data Protection Act. The report should be used to check the employee's progress until the next appraisal interview. It is a means of motivating, improving performance, inculcating positive attitudes and planning for the future.

Staff appraisals are largely private affairs, kept to a core group: appraisee, appraiser(s) and legal/personnel manager. The system must be, and must be seen to be, fair, non-discriminatory and equal. In a climate where there is greater supply of personnel than demand, and where jobs are no longer for life, procedures are needed to deal with promotions and, regrettably, redundancy. Faced with these difficult circumstances, managers having to make painful judgements about who to keep and who to let go can be aided by sound appraisal systems. Appeals procedures must be known to all and carried out by managers operating at a level with authority to overturn previous decisions.

Staff handbook

The right staff need to be employed, trained, nurtured and enabled to perform well for the organization and themselves. A staff handbook is a useful communications document but only if it is read, understood, accepted and used, and as long as it is sufficiently flexible to meet changing circumstances. Working by the rule-book can be like 'working to rule' – the kiss of death to an organization, if ever there was one. Many organizations have wonderful personnel policies on paper; unfortunately, that is all they appear to be.

Organizations have legal responsibilities in employing staff. These need to be conveyed to staff when appointed and can be reinforced through the staff handbook.

The information-giving handbook can provide a valuable source of reference for managers and staff. It should back up and support the face-to-face, two-way communications and staff training. It should welcome, introduce, inform, explain and give new and existing staff a picture of a businesslike, friendly organization that cares about its customers, its staff, its products and services and meets its legal obligations.

The handbook's production should be clear, unambiguous and authoritative. It should be attractive and well produced, but not expensive, impracticable or glossy. It needs to be indexed for easy reference, personal and friendly in its style and suited to its readers, yet factual and concise. The handbook is basically an exercise in communication. It is essential therefore that management and staff are consulted fully as to its contents and style and its distribution, in order to achieve co-operation and acceptance. An *aide-mémoire* for producing a comprehensive handbook is set out below, drawing on the experiences and employee handbook of the Harlow and District Sports Trust and other leisure centres. The listing below is not exhaustive, but provides a basis on which readers can design their own, bespoke handbook.

Preparing a staff handbook: twenty key clauses

1 Introduction and welcome
- personal message of welcome from Chairman, Chief Executive or General Manager
- vision and mission of the organization
- aims of organization, its background and history, the current position and priorities
- products and services and their value to the clients and customers
- organization structure and committee, departmental and staffing structure

2 Policies of the organization on, for example:
- public service and customer care
- employee rights
- inclusiveness and diversity
- disability
- data protection and confidentiality
- trade union membership
- health and safety

3 Recruitment and selection
- documentation required: references, medical certificate, etc.
- personnel records and notification of changes.

4 Contract of employment Inform new employees they will receive a written statement within the legally permitted time and what that statement will cover. Inform staff of their legal rights in these matters.
- job description
- responsible to
- responsible for

5 Induction, training and assessment The sooner a new employee can be used effectively, the greater the organization's effectiveness. The job and the environment are inextricably linked.
- induction and familiarization systems
- essential training provided and additional training opportunities
- methods of appraisal and assessment
- job evaluation and review
- opportunities for promotion
- career development

6 Salaries and wages The handbook must be unambiguous.

- organization policy and statement on payment system
- precise methods of payment
- deductions, such as income tax (PAYE), national insurance contributions and any others
- additional payments, such as special payments, overtime, bonus payments
- allowances for particular duties or circumstances, e.g. unsocial hours
- expenses, e.g. travel, car, refreshment
- procedures relating to pay reviews, alterations to pay, etc.
- incentive pay or bonuses

7 Hours of work

- normal working hours
- flexitime
- timekeeping, starting and finishing times
- evening, weekend, overtime and other special hours
- meal and rest entitlements
- variation of hours
- time off in lieu

8 Time off and absence

- procedures for notification of absence, medical certificates, etc.
- time off and under what terms for public duties – e.g. political, magistrates, jury service
- maternity and paternity rights
- sick pay scheme and Statutory Sick Pay (SSP) entitlements
- medical certificates
- unauthorized absence
- requests for special unpaid leave
- hospital, dental and other personal appointments

9 Holidays and other leave

- annual holiday entitlements
- holiday increases for long service
- public holidays and 'in lieu' entitlements
- holiday pay and special pay on termination of employment
- unpaid leave
- maternity/paternity leave
- special leave, e.g. jury service

10 Fringe benefits Fringe benefits are part of the total job environment. The handbook should set out in general terms the opportunities and benefits open to the staff as a whole.

- housing scheme
- insurances
- medical scheme
- car purchase or company car

- educational and training opportunities
- social, leisure and recreation opportunities
- incentive schemes and other benefits

11 Amenities and facilities Leisure organizations will have services and amenities to offer employees. These benefits make up the job environment and can help maintain harmony and goodwill. They can also be a source of discontent if handled unfairly or perceived to be unfair. The handbook should set out:

- use of the telephone: statement of circumstances
- use of computers for authorized business only and clear guidelines on emailing and the Internet
- use of 'company' facilities and products
- personnel, welfare, medical and information services
- staff meals and refreshments
- free memberships or use of leisure facilities
- discounted services and facilities
- 'company' clubs and societies
- social amenities
- use of amenities by family members and friends.

12 Health and safety Responsibility, legally, falls on both employer and employee. Set out those responsibilities.

- policy statement, including safety officer role
- general procedures and sources of information
- safety regulations
- fire precautions and drills
- hospital, doctor, first-aid procedure
- emergency procedures

13 Property

- security of the business plant, supplies, equipment, money and property within and outside the premises
- security of personal belongings
- the right of search
- lost property procedures for public and staff

14 Code of conduct Rules and procedures are needed for safety, fairness and efficiency. However, careful and sensitive wording is needed to convey collective responsibility and good individual conduct, rather than penalties for misconduct.

15 Grievances The law sets out procedures to enable staff to seek redress of any grievance. The handbook should set out the legal procedures and the three grievance stages that must be followed.

16 Staff counselling, mentoring and personal problems Problems may stem from inside or outside the job. In the work situation counselling is needed before rules and procedures come into play. Home circumstances or personal and domestic problems can lead to low morale and poor efficiency. The organization may have established a coun-selling or mentoring system, in which case employees can be informed how they go about participating in the scheme. The handbook should inform staff where to go for help and what to do.

17 Staff involvement It is good practice to involve staff in the decision-making process. Marketing a successful organization with a good public image makes for a high staff morale and *esprit de corps*. The handbook should explain the ways in which staff can take a 'share' in shaping and keeping a successful organization:

- 'shares' in the success of the organization
- joint consultative committees
- staff representation
- meetings; suggestion schemes; in-house magazine
- 'company' events: for itself, staff families, charity, etc.

18 Retirement and pensions Organizations should prepare staff for retirement.

- retirement policy and entitlement
- voluntary early retirement and benefits
- pensions
- retirement courses and planning

19 Termination of employment

- resignation procedure and notice entitlements
- redundancy
- discharge

20 New clauses and changes

Guidelines for facility staffing and structures

Outlined below are twenty suggestions for improving leisure service staffing.

1 Understand the aims and objectives of the organization.
2 Select staff wisely and logically: match the qualities of the candidate to the job.
3 Train and deploy: the way staff are trained and deployed affects results.
4 Study legislation: the law affects both employer and employee.
5 Understand management principles: recognize the limitations of span of control and use of 'unity of command' and 'logical assignment'.
6 Create formal structures: provide clear lines of authority. People like to know where they stand.
7 Flatten hierarchies: horizontal structures empower staff to take on responsibility.
8 Permit informal structures: recognize the importance of cross-communications.
9 Construct departments and decentralize: divide the work into units and identify functions. Identify tasks and responsibilities attached to each position. Encourage decentralization.
10 Start with essential staff: when opening new facilities, start with essential staff and then build up as needs dictate. The full-time staff positions should be limited to

immediate recognizable functions. To cope with initial, additional demands, core staff should be encouraged to 'go the extra mile' led by the manager, and use trainee and part-time staff.

11 Create team management: recognize the value of team management to co-ordinate long hours and a varied programme.

12 Use 'line-and-staff' approaches: avoid rigid 'line' structures. Consider appropriate hybrids to meet particular situations.

13 Make conditions flexible: the complexity, hours and patterns of use of leisure facilities call for flexible conditions which encourage initiative and do not limit staff functions.

14 Consider alternative structures: appraise the relative value of additional, different forms of community recreation management. Train and support voluntary assistants, outreach service workers, animateurs, etc., and consider job sharing. Consult with trade unions.

15 Produce staff handbook.

16 Establish management information systems: use the organization structure to best effect in disseminating information and in communications.

17 Establish an appraisal system.

18 Use structures as means, not ends. A structure chart is a management tool. It must be used. It must be changed to meet changing situations.

19 Empower staff: many management gurus believe that tomorrow's business organizations will be non-hierarchical and a wide range of talented staff will be 'empowered' to handle resources and make managerial decisions.

20 Reward staff collectively for successes. From time to time, say twice a year, when excellent results or efforts have been made, reward the staff with a party, a gift or some novel event.

Discussion

Staff are a leisure organization's greatest asset. They should be valued as an asset not a cost. However, human resources cost money and poor staff are very costly in many ways. All employers must meet minimum levels of pay, but salaries and wages are only a starting point. Other costs include: recruitment, training and development, paid holidays, sickness pay, fringe benefits and allowances, equipment and uniforms, meals on duty and staff turnover requiring recruitment costs.

To ensure profitability or viability or to reduce costs, many organizations have cut back on staff. Hotel and service chains in the private sector and leisure departments in the public sector in some cases have shed general managers and heads of department or even the departments themselves, decentralizing functions and not filling senior jobs as they become vacant. We have seen a shift to a 'serve yourself' approach. Some budget hotels operate with no reception staff or room service and catering comes in the form of a vending machine.

These examples serve to emphasize that staff recruitment and selection of the right staff for the right jobs are critical for organizational efficiency and effectiveness.

Leisure organizations today have far more legislative hurdles to negotiate than in the past, and they are also increasingly conscious of potential litigation, particularly with activities at sport and outdoor pursuit centres.

In the past also there was often a 'psychological contract' between employer and employee: the security of a job for life (or at least for a long time) in return for skills, reliability, and loyalty to the firm. Those days are gone. Instead of one job for life, people may have several careers; Charles Handy calls them portfolio careers. What is more, it is now up to individuals themselves to forge their own careers and this is the case in the leisure profession which is so wide and constantly changing.

Corporate businesses, institutions and local authorities are large organizations and have departments and managers involved in recruitment, selection, training, performance assessment and evaluations. In many leisure organizations, however, these roles are part of the work of the Leisure Manager. Human resource management, as it is more commonly known today, asks the question: what people resources are essential to meet objectives of the organization? The well-known industrialist, Harvey-Jones, believes that staff in organizations are under-utilized. This factor has a huge effect on areas of leisure such as the hospitality sector which employs large numbers and whose service is staff-intensive. In some cases staffing costs can be as high as 90 per cent of the services budget and in some leisure centres, staffing costs can be two-thirds of the total revenue expenditure.

The leisure industry is increasingly being managed and staffed by a diverse market of people. More women and people from ethnic minorities have entered the labour force, rendering part-time employment the predominant workforce in areas such as hotels, restaurants, airports, motorway services and in other services which are available to the public in unsocial hours, for example, in leisure centres, sports facilities, theatres, entertainment venues and tourist attractions. In pubs, cinemas and large out-of-town retail outlets, again, part-time workers are employed. They include senior citizens who are chosen for their service-giving skills, time keeping, commitment and reliability, not accounting for lower levels of pay, compared to younger, full-time employees. Diversity management is now advocated to embrace the wide range of different people employed in the same organization.

Summary

This chapter has been concerned with staff and staffing structures within leisure and recreation organizations. It is clear that Leisure Managers should understand the way in which staff are recruited, selected, employed, trained and deployed in order to maximize efficiency, bring out the best in staff and lead the organization towards its goals.

The manager should understand relevant legislation relating to organizations and staff and the principles of management as they relate to staffing and the formulation of organization structures. However, managers should not be preoccupied with organizational charts, nor give them permanent status, as though they were indestructible. Jobs need to change because situations change. Structures therefore must also change or adapt.

Leisure organizations deal with people in their leisure time, who have a variety of choice. Leisure organizations therefore need to be sufficiently flexible to be appropriate to the needs and demands of their clients and customers. They have to be more organic in structure than most other industries and businesses. They have more scope to pursue greater results than purely financial bottom-line policies. Clearly, organizations such as leisure service businesses, are more than structures and systems; policies and strategies should come before structures.

This book has demonstrated that leisure and recreation management require high quality Leisure Managers and staff. Current Leisure Managers will need continuing professional development because the leisure industry is constantly changing. Potential Leisure Managers need to be recruited, trained and qualified. This is an area we now turn to in Chapter 24.

Discussion points

1 Staff are claimed to be the most valuable asset in leisure and recreation settings. Is this the case? Explain why or why not.

2 Appraisal interviewer at the start of the interview: 'I'm sure you don't like this any better than I do. But there is nothing to worry about. It's painless.' What do you think is right or wrong with this approach and what would be your approach as the interviewer?

3 Leisure and recreation management is becoming more generalist with personnel being trained in a variety of skills and therefore being able to undertake more than specialist roles. They are expected, and expect, to move around an organization and develop through 'horizontal promotions'. Discuss the implications.

4 There are no longer jobs for life. Generalist employees, particularly those with more than one specialist skill, will find it easier than single specialists in finding employment. What are the implications for organizations, managers and staff in terms personal commitment, trust, loyalty and service-giving in such a changing work environment and job market?

Further reading

The Briefcase booklets:

Davies, C. (1988), *When Can You Start?*, Video Arts, London.

Tietjen, T. (1978) *How Am I Doing?*, Video Arts, London.

Honey, P. (1987) *Can You Spare A Moment?*, Video Arts, London.

24

Leisure and recreation management education and training

Introduction

According to the *Official Yearbook of the United Kingdom 2004*, the UK labour market both full-time and part-time was 27.9 million in spring 2003; 7 million people were in part-time work and 3.3 million people were self-employed. Precise numbers of people employed in leisure-related jobs are not easy to measure because of the broad nature of the industry and also because it is hard to define. However, leisure is a growth industry of national significance both in social and economic terms and jobs in tourism and leisure are estimated at approximately 2.5 million, over 2 million in the main six sectors alone as shown in Table 24.1. Employment on this scale raises substantial questions about training and career development in the young profession of leisure and recreation management. In a time of change and growth, leisure needs to attract well-trained, excellent leaders, managers and personnel across a broad spectrum. In a relatively new industry, credible professional foundation stones are of significance in establishing a professional ethos.

Education and training are therefore of vital importance at all levels of leisure and recreation management. Without men and women of vision and standing, and without qualified and trained staff, no leisure service can hope to be efficient, let alone effective in meeting the needs and aspirations of its public. Indeed, there needs to be a committed and highly motivated flexible workforce to respond to current and future challenges. Staff are an investment. Training helps to get the

Table 24.1 Employment in the tourism and leisure industries

	JUNE 2002
Hotels and tourist accommodation	418,000
Restaurants, cafes, etc.	545,400
Bars, pubs and night clubs	535,900
Travel agents and tour operators	133,600
Libraries, museums and other cultural activities	81,400
Sport and other recreation activities	412,900
TOTAL	*2,127,200*

Source: Department for Culture, Media and Sport, *Annual Abstracts of Statistics* 2004

best out of them, for their own job satisfaction and for the organizations of which they are an integral part.

Recent history in an emerging profession

Education and training for leisure management and the continuing professional development of Leisure Managers in the United Kingdom is as advanced as almost anywhere else in the world today to the extent that there is a body of knowledge and professionalism in the field that is emerging or has emerged as a recognized 'profession'. This has come about in a relatively short time, though its roots go back over a century. The formation of the Library Association, Museums Association, and Physical Education Association go back over a century ago. The Institute of Sport and Recreation Management can be traced back to the Association of Baths Superintendents formed in 1921. The former Institute of Parks and Recreation Administration also dates back to this era. The institutions, therefore, have been in the field for a long time. However, leisure management as we know it today is of much more recent origin.

Although facilities such as theatres, swimming pools, parks, pitches, school gymnasia and entertainment and public halls had been in operation for much of the twentieth century, leisure education and training and the creation of an emerging profession of leisure management goes back only 40 years. The catalyst was the birth of the community multi-purpose indoor sport and recreation centre in the mid-1960s.

Prior to that time, the various professional bodies had been running training courses and awarding institution qualifications for many years. These qualifications generally were of an essentially specialist and technical nature and did not cover the broad spectrum of leisure and recreation management. Two institutions that have a substantial influence today upon leisure management in general, and on training and professional development in particular, are the Institute of Leisure and Amenity Management and Institute of Sport and Recreation Management. The Institute of Sport and Recreation Management (ISRM) provides a wide range of courses in the management and operation of sport and recreation facilities in addition to its own professional qualifications. The Institute of

Leisure and Amenity Management (ILAM) was created from an amalgamation of the Institute of Parks and Recreation, Institute of Municipal Entertainment and the Association of Recreation Managers. ILAM's education and training unit manage an extensive programme. Brief descriptions of ILAM and ISRM can be found in the Appendix.

There are several landmarks in the rapid development of training open to all. The need for professional management of new recreation centres prompted the Sports Council to set up a working party that reported its findings, *Professional Training for Recreation Management* (Sports Council, 1969). This led to the first postgraduate/post-experience courses and qualifications at Loughborough University that offered the first Master's degree in leisure management and at the Polytechnic of North London (now the University of North London) that offered the Diploma of Management Studies (Recreation).

The reorganization of local government in 1974 brought about new comprehensive leisure departments, a flood of new indoor leisure facilities; a greater awareness was created as to the benefits of improved management of recreation in the public sector which could be applied to a much broader field than was once appreciated. This growth led to the instigation of a government working party. The Recreation Management Training Committee (the Yates Committee) was appointed in 1977 by the Secretaries of State for Education and Science and for the Environment (DoE, 1984). The report called for a co-ordinated, strategic approach to the planning of recreation management training.

The introduction of compulsory competitive tendering (CCT) in the 1990s played a big part in the call for management efficiency and productivity. As a consequence of the demands of CCT, there was a need for an up-to-date analysis of training needs in local government.

Range of education and training courses

The leisure and tourism sector is one of the largest and fastest growth sectors of the global economy. In parallel, education and training for leisure management is also fast growing. Education and training courses, hundreds in the UK alone, show innovation and diversity, providing a wide choice for students young and older. The Quality Assurance Agency for Higher Education in preparing benchmark statements for academic standards on degree courses in Hospitality, Leisure, Sport and Tourism consulted with around 80 universities and colleges running first degree courses.

Degree titles

Hospitality sector (over 20): Hospitality Studies, Hotel Management, Hotel and Restaurant Management, Catering Management, and Hotel Business.

Leisure studies (over 20): Leisure Studies, Event Management, International Leisure Management, Countryside Leisure Management, Recreation Management, Entertainment Management, Outdoor Recreation.

Sport (over 30): Sports Science, Sports Management, European Sports Management, Sport and the Media, Football Science, Sport Tourism Management, Playwork, Exercise Physiology, and Physical Education.

Tourism (around 30): Tourism Studies, Tourism Management, Ecotourism, European Tourism, Rural and Countryside Tourism, Tourism Planning, Visitor Attractions Management.

Degree courses, however, incorporate a high level of conceptual and academic learning and, therefore, are not the total answer for Leisure Managers and operational staff. Although some managers come in at the top, complete with business and management qualifications, most leisure personnel do not. Moreover, all potential managers need training of some kind whether as managers of leisure centres, hotels, restaurants, cinemas, bingo halls, theatres, arts centres, health and fitness studios, ice rinks, swimming pools, sports halls or whether in sports development, tourism or hospitality management. Leisure management is a staff intensive business with a high level of operational employees who need vocational training and hands-on experience.

Specialist training in play, art, music, drama, libraries, sports, grounds maintenance, heritage, the countryside, tourism and many others is provided by associations, institutions and national governing bodies, some supported by national agencies. Professional training in music is provided at universities and conservatoires. There is training for dancers and choreographers provided by specialist schools and government-funded dance schools. The National Film and Television School is financed by the government and the industry and offers postgraduate and short course training. The Department for Culture, Media and Sport and the Department for Education and Skills allocate £19 million a year in grants for drama and dance students for tuition and maintenance and over 800 students a year cover their tuition fees in this way. There is a range of specialist training in most other fields of leisure and recreation, particularly in sport to the extent of specialist colleges and academies, for example in Association Football. One of the most substantial growth areas is in the training of playworkers in light of greater interest in the out-of-home care of children and the requirements of the Children Act.

The Royal National Theatre's Education Programme encourages access to drama through youth theatre projects, touring productions, workshops, work in schools, and so on.

This section of the book, however, does not deal with specific specialist training, but in the training of Leisure Managers whose work and focus is on the management of services, facilities and programmes whether in the public, voluntary or private sectors; it is not about leisure activities *per se*, which were covered in earlier parts of the book.

Added to this maze of opportunity, there exists some confusion over the use of the three terms 'training', 'development' and 'education'. At times these terms appear to be interchangeable, and sometimes one term may be all embracing, encompassing three meanings in one. Management education may be seen as a process of active learning and enquiry (including learning from one's peers), with learner input a necessary part of this process. Management training may be seen as an input process from teacher to learner, whereby the learner is equipped with the specific job-related knowledge and skills needed to carry out his or her job successfully. Management development may be seen as encompassing both management education and training, increasing the manager's adaptability and flexibility, maximizing his or her strengths, overcoming weaknesses and keeping in touch with changes in the industry.

The potential benefits of leisure, however, need to be inculcated in young people long before any thought is given to training issues. We change tack, therefore, and focus briefly on education for leisure which starts with young people.

Leisure education

> Leisure education is a function of all schools because everything in the curriculum may, at some point, become a leisure activity ... The essential function of leisure education is to promote involvement or investment of the self in positive experiences that enhance the person's feelings of self-esteem and sense of fulfilment. In whatever way this can be performed the individual's quality of life will be enhanced and the larger community as well as society in general will also benefit.
>
> American Association for Leisure and Recreation, 2003

Leisure education has had a stronger formal focus in many of the education systems in the United States and in some other parts of the world compared to the United Kingdom. More than 40 years ago Charles Brightbill wrote *Educating for Leisure-Centred Living* (Brightbill, 1966) and this was later revised by Tony Mobley (Brightbill and Mobley, 1977). These gave philosophical foundations and guidelines for educators and leisure professionals. Referring to the education community, Mundy (1998) wrote:

> Of the various influences on leisure and recreation, public education may have the greatest potential of all. The educational community remains the most critical setting for providing learning experiences that can translate into and ultimately form a young person's leisure experience for a lifetime. But whether done in school or outside of it, the goal of leisure education is to enable individuals to enhance the quality of their lives through leisure.

In the UK, however, leisure education infiltrates into the system informally and unobtrusively. Extra-curricular activities in sport, music and drama and various clubs help to educate children and young people in 'worthwhile' leisure. Children in school may have the use of gymnasia, swimming pools, playing fields, art and craft workshops, dance and drama studios, libraries, gardening projects and the like, both in school time and after school. It is true that less time is given to art, crafts, dance, drama, music and physical education in many schools since the introduction of the National Curriculum. This is exacerbated by a lessening also of after-school leisure choices. The growth area in after-school time is the emergence of homework clubs, an important and valuable asset, but not leisure.

In earlier chapters it was shown that leisure and recreation can be beneficial to individuals and the community as a whole. We need to find out, then, and understand why some children and young people experience only casual leisure (described below). Is it lack of interest because of poor motivation at school and at home, lack of time, money or transport? Some people find ways around the constraints they face; others do not. Collaboration between leisure professionals and schools could help to inculcate in children and young people the ability to recognize leisure as an avenue for fun, personal satisfaction and enrichment, to appreciate the array of pursuits on offer and how to go about making informed choices. Perhaps a policy can be adopted to ensure that children and young people have access to quality after-school leisure programmes and activities.

Leisure education as an integral part of the school can become a means of developing interests and skills for life and also help in achieving academic, social and personal goals. Outdoor education, for example, is not just about adventure activities. It offers learning about the environment, heritage interpretation, eco-tourism; it can teach life-saving skills in canoes or on mountains, and those personal qualities such as courage in the face of the elements or having to rely on and help others as a member of a team.

For many young people, the lack of leisure learning opportunities or motivations, whether at home, school or in the wider community, hinders their full development; leisure simply regarded as free time can become a time for boredom or anti-social behaviour in many forms. Young people 'at risk' can achieve self-esteem and relate socially with others through leisure activity. Leisure education has been well developed in its use in therapeutic recreation contexts with children, young people and adults with disabilities. People with disabilities can find immense satisfactions and achievements in leisure activity evidenced by the superb 'disabled' international athletes, artists and musicians; and then there are those with learning difficulties who show their abilities in the Special Olympics.

Participation in leisure activities can also have positive effects on health and fitness and in tackling obesity, though the evidence – strong as it often is – needs to be collated objectively and a robust case made to convince governments and their agencies. The report in 2003 of the American Association of Leisure and Recreation, *Leisure Education in the Schools*, lists several sources of evidence relating to leisure education.

> Research related to leisure education in the schools with students receiving special education services has reported psychosocial and leisure specific outcomes such as: increases in perceived freedom in leisure, affect, leisure awareness, activity initiation, leisure related planning and resource knowledge, and recreation participation. Additionally, there is evidence that leisure education helps prepare students for the transition from school to community and adulthood.

Serious and casual leisure

Leisure, as we know, can mean different things to different people. What kind of leisure are we to teach to the young?

> In 1993, the International Charter for Leisure Education was ratified by the World Leisure and Recreation Association. Leisure was defined as follows:
>
> 'Leisure refers to a specific area of human experience with its own benefits, including freedom of choice, creativity, satisfaction, enjoyment and increased pleasure and happiness. It embraces comprehensive forms of expression or activity whose elements are as often physical in nature as they are intellectual, social, artistic or spiritual.'

Robert Stebbins (2002), best known for his concepts of 'serious leisure' and 'casual leisure', defines his terms as follows:

Leisure is a form of human expression that varies from the very casual and informal to the highly committed and formal. The first is labeled 'casual leisure' or 'diversionary leisure', which is the immediately intrinsically rewarding, relatively short-lived pleasurable activity requiring little or no special training to enjoy it. The second labeled 'serious or substantial leisure', which is a systematic pursuit of an amateur, hobbyist or volunteer activity that participants find so substantial and interesting that, in the typical case, they launch themselves on a career centred on acquiring and expressing its special skills, knowledge and experience.

Stebbins provides examples of what he perceives as casual and serious leisure:

Most people, when they think of leisure, think of the casual variety, calling up such happy visions as conversing with friends, snoozing in the recliner, strolling in the park, and incontestably the most common leisure activity of all, watching television. Unfortunately, as this definition clearly signals, satisfaction and a full existence are most unlikely products of activity intended to produce immediate, evanescent pleasure with only minimal training needed to experience it.

Indeed, too steady and heavy a diet of casual leisure can cause a sort of psychological dyspepsia, a sense of ennui and listlessness rooted in the unsettling realization that one's life is unfolding in a way largely, if not entirely, devoid of any significant excitement. This is obviously not a problem facing most people who toil sixty hours a week, come home to still other obligations, and finally collapse late in the evening before their TV sets. As a heavily-worked friend of mine was fond of observing, 'for me, the day, what's left of it, consists of scotch and *Seinfeld*'.

Stebbins, 2001

In contrast, serious leisure has a work-like quality:

Serious leisure is the steady pursuit of an amateur, hobbyist, or career volunteer activity that captivates its participants with its complexity and many challenges. It is profound, long-lasting, and invariably based on substantial skill, knowledge, or experience, if not on a combination of these three. It also requires perseverance to a greater or lesser degree. In the course of gaining and expressing these acquisitions as well as searching for the special rewards this leisure can offer, amateurs, hobbyists, and volunteers get the sense that they are pursuing a career, not unlike the ones pursued in the more evolved, high-level occupations. But, there is no significant remuneration – in fact, there is usually no remuneration at all.

Stebbins, 2001

Stebbins sees serious leisure as contributing to community development, for populations with special needs and for youth at risk, along with all other people. He believes that young people should be encouraged to be involved in serious leisure as amateurs, hobbyists or in volunteer activity not only for personal self-fulfilment and community development, but also with a view to finding a 'leisure career' through participation in chosen activities. He sees serious leisure as 'the most worthwhile objective for leisure education' but acknowledges that serious leisure participants engage in both serious and casual leisure, while people who participate purely in casual leisure 'are not typically aware of serious leisure, or if aware only dimly so; leisure education could change this level of awareness, should educators be inclined in this way' (Stebbins, 2002, p. 8).

Although those who engage in serious leisure do so for the satisfactions and enjoyment that it brings, no less than casual leisure, the problem about serious leisure is that it tends to mirror the ideology of work and the Protestant ethic, that enjoyment and satisfaction comes as a result of effort, perseverance and commitment. However, in earlier chapters, it was suggested that a fundamental value of play is lack of obligation – a person may enter or leave an activity at will. Moreover, so many social gatherings and events in people's lives are informal or celebratory. It is claimed that informal learning is 'life long and without frontiers' and that it should be the focus of leisure education. Most informal learning happens during leisure. Open leisure situations are informal, casual ones: playing in the park, engaging in activities at fairs and festivals, visiting exhibitions, museums and tourist attractions. The 'wellness' movement advocates relaxation, meditation and stress management as important elements in the workaholic societies. From this perspective, casual leisure has much to commend it – as refreshment, escape, recuperation, relaxation, stress-relieving, casual participation. Perceived in this light, optimal leisure lifestyle should include both serious and casual leisure.

A way to deal with education for serious leisure and casual leisure is to educate for optimal leisure lifestyles in ways which complement each other.

Potential training market

Any coherent system of training must be structured around the needs of the agencies and organizations requiring leisure managers and the needs of the people who require training. If training is to be effective we need to ask 'Why is it needed?' and 'Who is it for?' before we ask 'What should it be?'.

The current and potential training market is exceptionally large and so is the range of courses required to meet the training needs of many different personnel. It can be subdivided in several ways: according to who the training is for, and the levels at which it is needed.

1 Training is needed for people employed within the leisure industry: this includes people involved in the public, voluntary and commercial sectors, covering arts and entertainment, sports, play, parks and open space, the countryside, hospitality and tourism. The industry spans a range of posts in junior, middle and top management, supervisory level staff, technical/manual staff (incorporating bar, catering staff, and so on) and administrative/reception staff and many others.

2 Training is needed for people in other industries: many related industries and professions have connections with or require knowledge and skills of leisure management; this category includes managers and staff employed in education, dual use school and community centres, industrial sports clubs, outdoor pursuit centres, community centres and youth clubs, and so on.

3 Training is needed for individuals seeking employment within the leisure industry: these include school-leavers without leisure qualifications, college students with a qualification, and those wishing to change or start a career at any age up to retirement.

This illustrates something of the range of courses required to meet the training needs of many different personnel, but at what levels? The targets are usually at the technical, operational and management levels, but rarely directed at the policy-making and executive level; yet it is these senior personnel who most influence leisure and recreation management and have the most decision-making power.

There are many kinds of training: full-time, part-time, distance learning, in-house training and a wide range of agency, institution and private training.

Full-time training Undoubtedly, full-time courses that are relevant, accessible and appropriate to the ability and skill level of the person concerned can be an effective method of acquiring new knowledge and skill. The students are more likely to be able to concentrate fully on their course work and their attention is not diverted to problems associated with their work. However, with the current emphasis of central government on producing an 'economic service' and reducing operational costs in real terms, it is unlikely that many staff in the public sector will be given secondment to attend such courses. Consequently, only students eligible for grants are able to undertake full-time courses.

Part-time training Part-time or day release courses that lead to nationally recognized qualifications or to membership of professional institutions have certain advantages. Students can benefit from mixing with students from other organizations, which can broaden their perspective. However, off-the-job training can bring difficulties in transferring skills and knowledge learnt in the classroom, unless the examples given and the problems set are provided in a simulated working environment. Other forms of off-the-job training are organized by professional institutions (such as ILAM and ISRM) and national governing bodies and associations.

Distance learning The potential of distance learning material has never been exploited sufficiently by the leisure industry, with some professional institute exceptions. The advantages of this method are that it can make courses accessible in geographical areas that do not offer such courses and gives the individual the freedom to choose the time he or she wishes to study. The disadvantages include the cost to produce and update materials, although the biggest disadvantage is the absence of the discipline associated with a formally structured course and fellow students to share problems and exploit opportunities.

Distance learning can now be provided via the Internet and this is likely to become an essential vehicle for the delivery of information and exchange, not only for distance learning but also in all aspects of the education and training programmes in leisure and recreation.

In-house training On-the-job training is preferred by commercial leisure organizations, particularly among its operational staff where skills are learned by doing, where the time-honoured method of 'tell-me-show-me-let-me-do-it-myself' applies. The public sector, particularly in the larger authorities, organizes in-service training in such areas as health and safety, customer care, promotion, first-aid and so on, but these are often one-off and lack continuity, reinforcement and monitoring of results. Better long-term results can be obtained where authorities or organizations are linked to a university, college or training agency. In some businesses and organizations, developing staff is so important that they have their own education facilities and also engage outside trainers and advisers.

The content of leisure management courses

The basis of most discussions on what to train essentially revolves around how specialist or how generalist such training should be, with the arguments tending to fall into one of three categories which, however, are not exclusive.

1 Leisure Management is composed of two separate elements: leisure and recreation and management. The management element is applicable to any management situation; businesses may be different, but management is much the same – all require management competence. There is a common business reality. This view is reinforced on many college courses, with the management and leisure elements treated independently, and taught by separate staff from separate departments. Moreover, many of the management elements are taught in a way that has limited relevance to leisure situations.

2 Leisure management is an area of knowledge in its own right, with a set of specialist skills that are applicable across the recreation sphere. This viewpoint holds that management skills are not necessarily applicable to any situation, but are specific to the context in which they are being used. Rosemary Stewart (1970) states that:

> the job of the manager is varied; the differences may be as much, if not more than, the similarities. These lists of management functions ignore the diversity of management; the job of the top manager bears little resemblance to that of the junior manager, or that of being a coke manager in a steel mill is hardly comparable with being an advertising manager to a popular shoe manufacturer. These jobs differ because they have different functions, but even more because the situation of the firm is so dissimilar.

If the argument that management training needs to be specialist in nature is accepted, then the degree to which specialization is necessary has to be determined. Pick (1978) believes that the old distinctions between heritage arts, leisure activities, community arts, sports and games do not now apply to what is actually happening in Britain:

> In a conversation between myself and two theatre administrators we listed the various events we had helped to promote in the last five years. Answers included sky diving, bingo, beagling, flower show, go-go dancing, rush weaving course, basketball tournament, kinetic sculpture, fancy dress parades, cookery demonstrations and pop concerts. Is there, I wonder, any substantial organization now which does not offer food and drink, a spread of activities, but which exists solely for one form of entertainment?

Viewed in this way, there would appear to be considerable overlap between the leisure subdivisions, particularly with regard to programming and promotional skills. Further areas of common interest may be identified by looking at an analysis of the topics most requested by arts administrators for inclusion in training schemes. These were book-keeping, fundraising/grant applications, contract characteristics (performers), law affecting venue and performance, publicity, catering management, event festival planning, box office systems analysis, print buying, inter-personal skills, wage and salary administration and communities and facilities. Nearly all these topics could be relevant equally to syllabuses for the training of leisure centre managers, community centre wardens or organizers of outdoor events in parks and the countryside and, consequently, would seem to indicate that the training requirements of a number of the subdivisions are similar in a number of ways.

3   Leisure management is composed of specialist management subdivisions (e.g. tourism, sports, parks and open spaces, countryside and arts management), with particular skills unique to that subdivision and these are broken down further, e.g. within sport, swimming pools have distinct technical qualifications, within arts there are further divisions of drama, music, painting, etc. This argument takes the viewpoint that management skills are specific to the specialist management situation: the management training requirements of a swimming pool manager are decidedly different from those of a countryside manager; those of a sports hall manager are different from those of a theatre manager. This is true to an extent since the lack of specialist technical knowledge about swimming pools, horticulture, countryside maintenance, and so on, could have a noticeably adverse effect on efficient and effective functioning. However, non-specialist managers with specialist facilities usually have a section head whose leadership is relied on for specialist functions.

One of the major problems in interpreting leisure management as a series of specialisms is that training may become supervisory or technically-orientated instead of management-orientated, and there would be vast numbers of courses and levels of duplication. Moreover, there would be lack of synergy and exchange of knowledge. The theory put forward by Kahn and Katz (1966) suggests that as one ascends the managerial ladder the amount of technical skill and knowledge required decreases, while the conceptual skills and knowledge requirement increases. This implies that the 'higher' management skills need not be specialist and these are relevant to most top management situations within the leisure industry. A further criticism of the specialist approach is that it becomes too activity-orientated.

Leisure Managers need both general management education, with core management skills, and specific management training. For example, in Chapter 23, it was suggested that managers need general understanding of legislation, but specific knowledge of the laws relating to their areas of work. For example, different regulations apply to swimming pools, arenas, theme parks, theatres and cinemas and restaurants, catering and bars. Leisure activities such as watersports, rock climbing, rides and slides, children's play areas and many others, all require high levels of safety standards and risk assessment. School trips have been severely constrained in light of the risks and potential litigation. In the tourism industry, transport operators, ferries and cruise liners, car hire firms and holiday companies, are all under legal obligations to provide safe and reliable services. Legal issues, therefore, are the concern to all branches of leisure and recreation and to all employers and employees in the public, private and voluntary sectors. Clearly, all managers will need to know about general aspects applying to all, such as equal opportunities and employment rights, but not necessarily all the specifics of areas outside their remit.

Government initiatives and standardization of qualifications

Over the past 30 years in the United Kingdom, there has been a confusing plethora of courses in leisure and recreation management. This complex picture has been streamlined of late, with the standardization of some of the occupational qualifications. However, the courses tend to be taken up more by the public sector, many commercial leisure companies preferring to run their own courses.

The National Skills Task Force reported to the government that the greatest need in the coming years will be the demand for 'higher technicians' and 'associate professionals'. Foundation Degrees have been designed in collaboration with employers, SkillsActive UK for the leisure field, and professional bodies such as ILAM and ISRM.

In terms of operational management, there are a number of changes and initiatives which have relevance for leisure:

- the creation of Sector Skill Councils
- National Vocational Qualifications
- Modern Apprenticeships
- New Deal
- Investors in People and
- the growing influence of the Internet.

Sector Skills Councils In England, the Learning Skills Council (LSC) is the planning and funding body for all post-16 education and training outside the university sector. Equivalent bodies are found in Wales, Scotland and Northern Ireland. In April 2002 the Sector Skills Development Agency was given responsibility for setting up a Sector Skills Council (SSC) to replace National Training Organizations (NTO). SSCs are independent UK-wide organizations developed by groups of employers.

The government published a skills strategy and delivery plan for England in July 2003 to develop 'a highly skilled, productive workforce', involving all government departments, the Learning and Skills Council, Sector Skills Councils, Regional Development Agencies and other agencies.

The Sector Skills Agency awards licences to the SSCs. The former NTO with responsibility for the leisure industry was SPRITO. In 2002, it was converted to the Sector Skills Council for Active Leisure and Learning, operating as SkillsActive. SkillsActive currently has five separate units: Sport, Health and Fitness, Outdoors and Adventure, Community Recreation and Play.

The government plans to provide free part-time early education for three and four year-olds, helping children learn through the Foundation Stage: the part of the National Curriculum which supports the development of children aged three up to six. At least 250,000 new childcare places are to be available by March 2006. Children's centres will be established in the most disadvantaged areas to offer families early education, childcare and health and family support, with advice on employment opportunities. Children's centres will be linked to Sure Start programmes, Neighbourhood Nurseries and Early Excellence Centres. These projects, however, call for trained, accredited staff whether paid or voluntary and qualified leaders and play and care workers.

Case study: The Playwork Unit

The National Network of Playwork Education and Training now has a Regional Centre for each area in England, with websites providing advice and support relating to the Playwork National Vocational Qualification (NVQ). The Play Unit through SkillsActive provides a Code of Practice, training and qualifications, and links with the Playwork associations including: Association of Playworkers; Children's Play Council; Fair Play; ILAM; National Assocition of Toy and Leisure Libraries; The National Playing Fields Association; Kidsactive; Kids Club Network; PLAYLINK; and the numerous early years and childcare organizations, including: Daycare Trust; The National Childminding Association; The National Day Nurseries Association; and The Pre-school Learning Allianced representing 16,000 community pre-schools in England.

Government-initiated schemes to provide training at grass-roots level include National Vocational Qualifications, Modern Apprenticeships and New Deal.

National Vocational Qualifications National Vocational Qualifications (NVQs) and the equivalent Scottish Vocational Qualifications (SVQs) are occupationally specific qualifications, based on competences, which are assessed in the workplace. The qualifications are determined from national standards developed by employer-led bodies approved by the Qualifications and Curriculum Authority. NVQs and SVQs are awarded at five levels.

Modern Apprenticeships Modern Apprenticeships provide structured learning programmes for young people that combine work-based training with off-the-job learning. Modern apprentices learn on the job, building up knowledge, gaining qualifications and earning a wage. There are two levels of Modern Apprenticeship: Foundation (FMA) and Advanced (AMA). Both levels lead to NVQs, key skills qualifications and Technical Certificates. In the leisure field, there are a number of Apprenticeships, for example: Health and Beauty, Hospitality, Recreation and Travel, Amenity Horticulture, Sport and Recreation and Cultural Heritage, which provides foundations for careers in areas such as museums, art galleries, heritage and conservation.

New Deal New Deal is the government's welfare-to-work scheme which targets funding to specific groups and job preparation: young people, the over-25 age group, over-50 age group, lone parents and disabled people. New Deal is a key part of the government's strategy to get people back to work. It gives people on benefits the support to look for work, including training and job preparation.

Quality Management Systems

There are a number of different approaches to achieving 'quality' in the management performance of organizations. Geoff Vorley and Fred Tickle, in *Quality Management Principles and Practice* (Vorley and Tickle, 2003) cover a wide range of quality management issues including quality philosophy, Total Quality Management and Quality Management Systems. They describe Quality Management as 'a dynamic subject

533

continually evolving in response to a rapidly changing world'. Quality management systems are quite distinct from Total Quality Management (TQM) which is about a shared vision among all in an organization and a continuing process of organization improvement, matters which were addressed in Chapter 8.

In the late 1970s, the British Standards Institute (BSI) developed the BS 5750 system to improve quality throughout the management process by using a structured system of standards and procedures. The European standard was EN 29000. During the 1980s, the Department of Trade and Industry (DTI) encouraged British industry to compete internationally using quality initiatives. In the late 1980s, the International Standards Organization (ISO) launched the ISO 9000 series. British industry and local government, including the fast-growing leisure sector, were faced with three similar standards, and in some settings multiple registrations were required. The Local Government Act, 1988 brought in compulsory competitive tendering (CCT) and one of the tendering requirements was for the contractor to be registered or working towards registration in a quality management system; at that time the BS 5750 was in vogue. In 1994, the three standards, BS EN and ISO, were merged and called ISO 9000. An account of the history of quality management systems, processes and techniques as they influence leisure management can be found in Christine Williams and John Buswell, *Service Quality in Leisure and Tourism* (Williams and Buswell, 2003).

There is a wide range of quality management systems which fall into two categories of accredited and non-accredited systems. Non-accredited systems tend to be in-house, self-assessment methods. They can be tailor-made to meet the needs of particular organizations, at lower cost compared to external systems. However, they are not normally recognized by external bodies and they are less likely to lead to change. Accredited systems, on the other hand, require evidence of an organization having gone through a formal process of applying quality management procedures and techniques to be awarded certification by an external body. These procedures are more likely to involve consultation with customers, critical appraisal of the organization and continuous quality management improvement. Certification can also provide competitive edge. However, they can be costly, particularly for small organizations and those in the voluntary sector.

Quality management certification is particularly useful in local government settings as it can help in meeting the government's standards, judged by the Audit Commission's Comprehensive Performance Assessment (CPA). These standards are designed to assess how well a council delivers its services such as education, social care and housing. Leisure service is now to be subject to CPA and must make its case for resources in competition with other services. Best Value is a fundamental element in service delivery (see Chapter 9). At the start of each financial year, the Office of the Deputy Prime Minister (ODPM) publishes Best Value Performance Indicators (BVPI) and annual guidance for the forthcoming year through the Audit Commission. The Commission has developed a Library of Local Performance Indicators (see Useful websites). These online indicators provide 'off-the-shelf', voluntary indicators that authorities can select according to their relevance to local circumstances.

Quality frameworks and awards schemes

In addition to different approaches to achieving quality management performance, there are different quality frameworks and award schemes that encourage and promote good practice. Awards, however, not only give recognition and status to an organization, many come as a result of training, considerable collective effort, application of quality management systems and improvement. As such, they are significantly more than certificates and trophies.

> All quality awards are made on the basis of an assessment of the applicant's performance against certain criteria. Some awards measure the result of quality activities (such as customer satisfaction), some assess the effort involved in ensuring consistency of output and others assess conformity of output to customer requirements. Most are awarded in some kind of competition among companies, but a few are not competitive – being assessments of an organization's performance with no limit to the number of winners. As well as those describing themselves as quality awards, there are other similar awards for customer satisfaction and best practice.
>
> Institute of Quality Assurance

There are international, national, regional awards and industry-specific awards. Examples of international awards include:

- European Quality Award, established in 1992 and offered by the European Foundation for Quality Management
- Asia-Pacific Area Golden Quality Award and
- Deming Prize, established in 1951 (becoming international in 1984) and offered by the Japanese Union of Scientists and Engineers.

Deming is renowned as a guru of Total Quality Management (TQM) and for his quality improvement work which revolutionized Japan's industrial productivity after the Second World War. He is also noted for the Deming cycle, or PDSA cycle, a continuous quality improvement model consisting of a logical sequence of four repetitive steps: Plan, Do, Study and Act (see Useful websites).

The Malcolm Baldrige Award is a national award, established in 1987 by the US Congress and named after the former Secretary of Commerce. It aims to provide quality awareness and is based on a weighted score of seven categories of performance criteria: leadership; strategic planning; customer and market focus; measurement, analysis, knowledge management; human resource focus; process management; and business results. The award is offered by the National Institute of Standards and Technology in the USA (see Useful websites).

In the United Kingdom, the UK Quality Award was established in 1994 and is run by the British Quality Foundation (see Useful websites) and there are quality awards in each of the home countries such as the Wales Quality Award and the Irish Quality Award. The British Quality Foundation (BQF) is the National Partner Organization of the European Foundation for Quality Management for the UK. The local and regional organizations come together as the UK Excellence Federation, providing local services throughout the UK.

There are also awards that give recognition and status to organizations that achieve certain standards of management performance, such as Charter Mark, BSI Kitemark and BSI Safety Mark. Charter Mark is the government's national standard for excellence in customer service, a registered certification mark, which is owned by the Cabinet Office. It recognizes and encourages excellence in public service and is different from most quality schemes in that it focuses specifically on the service the customer actually receives (see Useful websites). In addition, there are industry-specific awards; for example, in leisure, White Flag and Green Flag awards.

The White Flag Award is the quality award developed jointly by The Institute of Leisure and Amenity Management Ireland Ltd (ILAM Ireland) and An Taisce, with sponsorship by Evian (see Useful websites). The Award was launched in June 2001 as a pilot for Europe. The award scheme, aimed at swimming pools, sports halls, gymnasiums and other indoor leisure facilities, is based on the successful European Blue Flag for Beaches Award which is granted to beaches and marinas that pass a number of environmental and safety criteria (see Chapter 9).

In recent years there has been disquiet about the declining quality of city parks and rural green spaces. The Green Flag Award scheme, launched in 1996, is designed to recognize and encourage good quality public parks in England and Wales. It is an important means of promoting improvement in the quality of parks and green spaces. Awards are given on an annual basis; winners must apply each year to renew their Green Flag status. The Award scheme has launched a website which contains information about the Green Flag Award, together with the Green Heritage Site accreditation, and the Pennant Awards (see Useful websites).

In addition to national awards, most of the leisure, sport and recreation institutions have exemplar award schemes. For example, the Institute of Leisure and Amenity Management offers:

- Innovation in Leisure Award recognizing the achievements of managers working in the leisure industry
- Open Space Management Award presented to an organization or community group promoting the imaginative improvement of the open space environment to enhance the use of a publicly-accessible park or open space
- Dissertation Award where any university or college offering an undergraduate Leisure Management course can enter one dissertation they consider to be of exemplary standard and
- ILAM Healthy Leisure Award to reward and help improve the use of physical activity to improve the health of the local community.

Most other major institutions such as Hotel and Catering International Management Association (HCIMA) and the Institute of Sport and Recreation Management (ISRM) (see Appendix) offer award schemes for management excellence. The Hospitality Assured mark is the quality initiative of HCIMA and the British Hospitality Association to improve the level of service through self-assessment and external assessment.

The European Foundation for Quality Management Excellence Model

The European Foundation for Quality Management (EFQM) was founded in 1988 to enhance the competitive position of European organizations and their effectiveness and efficiency. Regardless of sector, size, structure or maturity, to be successful, an organization needs to establish an appropriate management system. The EFQM Excellence Model is a practical tool to help organizations do this by measuring where they are on the path to Excellence, helping them understand the gaps, and then stimulating solutions.

Introduced in 1992, the EFQM Excellence Model (see Useful websites), also known as the Business Excellence Model, is a management framework that can be used to provide continuous improvement to any organization, in any area of activity. It works on the key management discipline of self-assessment. An organization is assessed against the relevant criteria which go to make up quality performance and a score is allocated. More importantly, by matching the organization against the model criteria, strengths and weaknesses can be identified, providing a clear indication of those activities which distinguish the organization from World-Class or Best-in-Class organizations. Within this non-prescriptive approach, there are some fundamental concepts which underpin the Model:

- Results Orientation
- Customer Focus
- Leadership and Constancy of Purpose
- Management by Processes and Facts
- People Development and Involvement
- Continuous Learning, Innovation and Improvement
- Partnership Development
- Corporate Social Responsibility.

The Model is based on nine criteria. Five of these are 'Enablers' and four are 'Results'. The Enabler criteria cover what an organization does. The Results criteria cover what an organization achieves. Results are caused by Enablers and feedback from Results helps to improve Enablers.

The Model's nine boxes, shown in Figure 24.1, represent the criteria against which to assess an organization's progress towards excellence.

The European Quality Award is the most widely used organizational framework in Europe and has become the basis for the majority of national and regional Quality Awards. For example, the Excellence Model is the framework for assessing applications for The UK Business Excellence Award launched in 1994 and run by the British Quality Foundation (BQF), to recognize organizations which have excelled when measured against the excellence model. The three aims of the Awards are to:

- assist organizations to improve
- identify role models to demonstrate what can be achieved and
- recognize those who have shown exceptional ability and performance in the management of their organization.

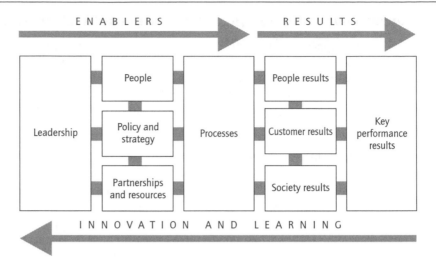

Figure 24.1 Business excellence model. ® 1999 EFQM. The model is a registered trademark of the EFQM

The BQF has piloted a new programme, Investors in Excellence (IiE), developed by Midlands Excellence in 2003 as a mark of high achievement, meeting a defined standard against each criterion of the Excellence Model. The UK Excellence Federation plans to introduce it throughout the rest of the UK as the most powerful evidence available to demonstrate an organization's capabilities and performance.

Investors in People

Investors in People UK, a public body sponsored by the Department for Education and Skills (DfES) was established in 1993 to provide national ownership of the Investors in People Standard and is responsible for its promotion and branding, quality assurance and development (see Useful websites).

The Investors in People Standard provides a framework for improving business performance and competitiveness through good practice in human resource development. The IIP Standard is delivered by a partner network:

- in England, the Learning and Skills Council (LSC) and Business Links
- in Scotland, Scottish Enterprise (SE) or Highlands and Islands Enterprise (HIE)
- in Wales, the National Council for Education and Training for Wales and the Higher Education Funding Council for Wales, jointly known as Education Learning Wales (ELWa)
- in Northern Ireland, the Department for Employment and Learning.

According to the IIP, in 2004, there were over 37,000 IIP recognized organizations in the UK employing over 27 per cent of the UK workforce, benefiting from the IIP Standard, with a 90 per cent retention rate.

In November 2004, Investors in People (IIP) unveiled a new version of the Investors in People Standard. The revised standard, launched by the Secretary of State for

Education and Skills, Charles Clarke, places new emphasis on employee involvement and on maximizing their potential and is designed to ensure it continues to offer relevant support to employers of all sectors and sizes.

> The structure of the Standard has been simplified and the changes focus on the vital role managers have in the development of employees and also encourages organizations to involve employees in decision-making. Such changes are designed to ensure the Standard remains a relevant, practical and flexible tool to support employers seeking to plan, implement and evaluate their business strategies in a highly competitive and rapidly changing environment.
>
> www.investorsinpeople.co.uk/IIP

The framework involves three basic, logical steps:

- Plan: developing strategies to improve the performance of the organization
- Do: taking action to improve the performance of the organization
- Review: evaluating the impact on the performance of the organization.

Quest

In terms of management performance in the leisure sector in the United Kingdom, Quest is the industry-specific quality management award based on the EFQM Excellence Model and is the UK's quality scheme for sport and leisure. Quest defines industry standards and good practice and encourages their development in a customer-focused management framework. Quest is recommended by the British Quality Foundation for self assessment in sport and leisure operations and is endorsed and supported by the four home country Sports Councils and a range of industry-representative organizations who have played an important role in developing the scheme:

- Local Government Association
- Chief Leisure Officers' Association
- Institute of Leisure and Amenity Management
- Institute of Sport and Recreation Management
- Leisure Management Contractors' Association and
- Scottish Association of Directors of Leisure Services.

Together with the four Sports Councils, these organizations make up Quest's Industry Policy Committee (IPC), responsible for its credibility and development (see Useful websites).

There are two categories for Quest and each has both a Self-Assessment improvement programme, and the opportunity for an independent External Assessment:

- Quest Facility Management, aimed at Sports and Leisure Facilities, in the commercial, voluntary and public sectors
- Quest Sports Development, aimed at Sports Development Units in Local Authorities, Governing Bodies and Voluntary Organizations.

There are three main stages to achieving Quest:

- Self-Assessment, in comparison to industry standards and best practice
- External Validation opportunity to receive External Assessment and
- Ongoing Maintenance with monitoring visits to maintain registration.

Quest, therefore, should be of considerable assistance to council leisure services in achieving Best Value standards through internal and external assessment and benchmarking which can lead to continuous improvement.

Towards an Excellent Service (TAES)

In Chapter 9, it was shown that the government intends to improve public services through performance management. In local government this is being driven through Best Value, performance indicators (PIs), inspection and, most recently, Comprehensive Performance Assessments (CPA). Compared to Social Services, Education, Housing and the Environment, the Leisure, Sport and Recreation service does not have a high profile in terms of allocation of resources and Best Value leisure inspections show room for improvement. However, there are some essential differences in the leisure services sector and other key services. There has been no clear guidance from central government on national priorities for the service through a performance improvement programme. Moreover, sport and recreation does not have a national framework to define excellence in terms of provision of services against which judgements and comparisons can be made, nor its own inspection service (such as Ofsted) to enhance and monitor service improvements. As a result the service is often considered less important than other key services when it is competing for resources with other local government services.

As a first step, work is taking place to implement a national 'Framework for sport in England' (see Useful websites) in line with the recommendations in *Game Plan* (DCMS and Cabinet Office, 2002) and covered in Chapter 17. Sport England in the East Midlands is co-ordinating the project to develop an excellence framework for sport and recreation services working in conjunction with representatives from a number of agencies:

- Department of Culture, Media and Sport
- Audit Commission
- Institute of Local Government Studies (Birmingham University)
- Office of the Deputy Prime Minister
- Institute of Leisure and Amenity Management
- Institute of Sport and Recreation Management
- National Association for Sports Development
- Central Council of Physical Recreation and
- various officers from local government and county sports partnerships.

The Framework identifies key 'drivers' that should be be taken into account. These include, for example, the impact of an ageing population, issues of personal well-being and obesity, levels of investment, the need to use education resources more effectively, access for different population groups and the need to develop the volunteer and professional workforce in sport more effectively.

The Framework also establishes key outcomes, such as improving levels of sporting performance, improving the health and well-being of communities, helping to raise educational standards and contributing to the overall economy. The outcomes mirror the 'shared priorities' established between central and local government through the Local Government Association described in Chapter 9.

Included in the Framework's Policy Areas for Change is 'Quality accreditation and improvement' with specific reference made to the importance of the Excellence Framework, described earlier. The Excellence Framework for Sport and Recreation Services has been developed to achieve three objectives:

1   To provide a basis for self-assessment that will enable sport and recreation providers to achieve continuous improvement for the users of the services.
2   To provide a vehicle through which the national priorities for sport and physical activity could be achieved by all the organizations involved alongside local priorities in each community.
3   To provide a basis for future inspection processes.

The Framework has been developed using existing quality management models, inspection frameworks and accreditation systems including among other consultees EFQM, Charter Mark, IIP, Quest and the CPA framework. It has been developed around eight themes, with 'equality' and 'service access' integrated into every theme:

1   Leadership
2   Policy and Strategy
3   Community Engagement
4   Partnership Working
5   Use of Resources
6   People Management
7   Standards of Service
8   Performance Measurement and Learning.

Within each theme, criteria have been developed which define key aspects of quality service. A number of 'descriptors' further define the criteria against which the service can be measured. The system, incorporating evidence schedules, enables an organization to plot its position at one of four levels: poor, fair, good and excellent. The evidence schedules identify the sorts of evidence required to demonstrate that a particular criterion has been met or not.

Initially, this is a self-assessment Framework for use by local authorities and their partners. It should help to identify the strengths and weaknesses in the management of local government leisure services and focus on improvement priorities. However, the model is designed to be applied beyond local government and the DCMS is exploring how a similar process might apply to all within the cultural services sector.

Quality management frameworks and internal and external systems are likely to lead to improvements but how robust are the systems? What measurements are there to determine whether performance actually meets expectations of customers? The Centre for Environmental and Recreational Management (CERM) at the University of South Australia developed a monitoring and evaluation system for public sector sport and leisure facility providers which has been adopted in several countries including the United Kingdom. The model enables comparison to be made between customer expectations and the actual performance of the centres, as perceived by the clients and customers – a process called 'gap analysis'. The most widely known gap analysis system is SERVQUAL, a survey instrument that identifies service gaps and prioritizes those gaps in terms of their relative impact on the service – service quality being relative, not absolute, different customers may perceive service quality differently. Service quality can be achieved by either meeting or exceeding expectations or by changing expectations. The system is based on original research undertaken by Parasuraman, Zeithami and Berry (1990).

The Internet

One of the most widely used sources for learning now and more so in future years is the world wide web. The Internet is a vast source of information, a means of providing education and training and with the potential for people to exchange knowledge and consult each other. The Internet connects millions of computers around the world and hence leisure studies have taken on a far wider, and less parochial, remit than even a few years ago. Computers in government, universities, colleges and schools, in libraries, museums, sports science laboratories, leisure centres, sports stadia and in thousands of sport, recreation, leisure and tourism organizations, provide a fertile ground for information and learning. However, this remains as information unless it is put to use in promoting and enhancing excellence in leisure and recreation management.

Ufi/learndirect has been established recently to make learning more accessible through the use of ICT. A website (see Useful websites) offers learning opportunities to people in the UK aged sixteen and over. In Scotland a similar scheme (Scottish Ufi) operates over 400 learning centres.

Professional institutes and associations

Leisure and recreation attract large numbers of representative bodies, including associations and institutes with many overlapping interests. Trained and/or qualified leisure and recreation personnel and some in training are likely to join a professional association or institute, initially for what they can get from it, including status and recognition. For a number of professional bodies, there are strict entry qualifications. The link between new national training qualifications and entry into professional organizations is very much at an exploratory stage.

An emerging or emerged profession?

Has leisure and recreation management, formerly viewed as an emerging profession, now arrived? Whether the managers in the leisure industry consider themselves to be professionals depends upon their perception of the nature of their work and its value to society, and their standing within the community. Not surprisingly, personnel within the industry perceive themselves as professionals. It is, however, questionable whether the rest of society view them in the same light. Although there is no generally accepted definition of the word 'profession', there appears to be an acceptable criterion for evaluating whether an occupation is of professional standing.

Sessoms (1975) writing about the evolution of recreation professionalism in the United States, has described a profession as implying 'a defined and distinctive body of knowledge attained through a disciplined, formal education process prior to sanction for practice. It bridges technique and immediate application with theory, sets standards and serves social needs'. Murphy (1980) claimed that while accepting the concept that recreation management encompasses a relevant body of knowledge, it is not adequately defined and lacks 'a formal education process for entry into the occupation'. But that was over twenty years ago; things have moved on since then.

Although both 'leisure and recreation' and 'management' tend to be regarded as secondary disciplines, they do however draw on other disciplines such as sociology and psychology. Entrance to some institutes is by means of a formal examination, or equivalent qualification – certificates, diplomas, degrees. In the case of ILAM, proof of practical competence is also required. All full members of the ISRM hold qualifications of the Institute. It would thus appear that the leisure and recreation management occupation has advanced significantly towards or along the professionalization continuum. However, it has some way to go and it could be argued that recreation is becoming more occupational and operational rather than professional.

The church, law and medicine are often considered as the original 'professions'. Other professions such as education and accountancy are placed somewhere on a continuum between these originals and those which are classed as 'occupations', such as advertising and coaching. Does leisure and recreation management, with a growing body of knowledge and professional workforce now constitute a profession? The service areas and job tasks have been identified, public recognition is slowly coming about, and the formalizing of structures and training is in progress. However, there is a gap between leisure management and the original professions with their adoption and enforcement of ethical codes. Indeed, the wide interpretation of what is, and what is not, acceptable leisure makes the enforcement of ethical codes difficult. In addition, leisure management involves so many other disciplines, is so diverse and complex, that it does not have the discreteness of, say, chartered accountancy, surveying or law. However, one Sector Skills Council initiative has been introduced – the creation of the Professional Development Board (PDB) co-ordinated by SkillsActive, involving a number of key organizations including: the British Olympic Association, British Sports Trust, Central Council of Physical Recreation, ILAM, Chief Cultural and Leisure Officers Association, Youth Sports Trust, UK Sport, Sports Councils and the DCMS. This body is clearly sport-related and could act for sport as a profession. Leisure, however, as this book has shown, encompasses a very much wider field and illustrates that a leisure profession is still emerging.

The profession of physical education, for example, is increasingly being challenged by the advance of professional coaches and players, sports psychologists and fitness and health experts and teachers. Similarly, in the arts and music, professional artists have an important role to play in teaching. The self-governance of schools, the involvement of parents and the heightened use of volunteers can fill gaps, normally the province of the 'professionals'.

In this book we have shown that provision for, and management of, leisure and recreation is made by all sectors: public, institutional, voluntary and commercial. The

Leisure Managers represented by the institutions and associations and the managers who emerge from the courses and training schemes represent only a small part of the world of leisure and recreation and its management, primarily those areas in the hands of public or semi-public bodies. The non-public sector, made up of thousands of voluntary organizations and commercial bodies, is barely touched by current levels of leisure management training. Even in the public sector many areas of leisure and recreation are not encompassed, for example, in the education-related leisure field.

Whether working in the public or non-public sector, Leisure Managers are concerned with creating opportunities for people to have satisfying leisure experiences. Leisure and recreation is a people-orientated business, giving a people-orientated service. Training is a means of acquiring new skills and new knowledge. No amount of training and management education, however, will guarantee making a successful manager, but with education and training, leisure personnel are more likely to become good managers.

Leisure and recreation management education, training and development, with advanced technologies and the Internet, is at the threshold of yet another giant step towards the realization of a future profession of great import in the United Kingdom and beyond.

Discussion points

1 Should leisure education be part of the schools' national curriculum? Provide a reasoned argument why it should or should not be included.

2 Many leisure leaders believe that Leisure and Recreation Management is now a bona fide profession. Make a clear case either for or against the proposition.

3 There are too many national institutions and agencies with their own agendas for the good of the fledgling or emerging 'profession' of leisure and recreation management. Discuss.

4 Continuing Professional Development (CPD) is of the utmost importance for both individuals and employers in the leisure and recreation workplace. Discuss why this is the case. To what extent do responsibilities lie with the different parties: with the individual, the employer, and the professional institute?

5 It is claimed that vocational and academic qualifications are broadly comparable at certain levels, for example, a National Vocational Qualification (NVQ) or Scottish Vocational Qualification (SVQ) level 5 is comparable to a higher degree; and NVQ or SVQ level 4 is comparable to a first degree, BTEC Higher National qualifications, or an RSA Higher Diploma. Debate the relative merits of vocational and academic qualifications for a career in leisure and recreation management.

Useful websites

Office for Standards in Education (OFSTED): www.ofsted.gov.uk

Learning and Skills Council (LSC): www.scx.gov.uk

Sector Skills Council (SSC) (Replaced National Training Organisations NTOs): www.ssda.org.uk

Ufi/learndirect: www.learndirect.co.uk

www.learndirectscotland.com

The National Council for Education and Training for Wales (ELWA): www.elwa.ac.uk

Institute of Sport and Recreation Management (see Appendix): www.isrm.co.uk

Quality Assurance Agency for Higher Education: www.qaa.ac.uk

Institute of Leisure and Amenity Management (ILAM)(see Appendix). Reports and careers information available as downloads. Useful factsheet 'Information Sources on the Internet'. www.ilam.co.uk

Institute of Quality Assurance: www.iqa.org/information

National Institute of Standards and Technology in the USA: www.quality.nist.gov

British Quality Foundation: www.quality-foundation.co.uk

Charter Mark: chartermark@cabinet-office.x.gsi.gov.uk

White Flag Award: www.ilamireland.ie/whiteflagawards

Green Flag Award: www.greenflagaward.org.uk

European Foundation for Quality Management Excellence Model: www.efqm.org

Investors in People: www.investorsinpeopleweek.co.uk

Quest: www.pmpconsult.com/quest/site/what.htm

25
Summary, discussion and conclusions

Introduction

Leisure is an ancient idea and ideal. It has survived opposition, élitism, greed, war and revolution. During its chequered history it has been thought of in ways as different as 'a quality of life reflecting the highest ideals' to 'the worst evil – the devil incarnate'. Leisure has been defined, prosaically, as 'blocks of time' and philosophically as a 'way of life'. Leisure is not time, but the use of time; the personal and social orientations of the use and the satisfactions it brings appear to be what make an activity 'leisure'.

Leisure has become the right of most people under the United Nations Declaration of Human Rights. However, time for leisure can be seen as both a blessing and a curse. Time without the means, the motivation or the opportunity, or free time forced on to people, are not regarded as leisure. To function as leisure there appears to be a need for positive approaches to life and the leisure activity itself.

The history of leisure has shown that it has been difficult to hang on to the elevated concept of the élite Ancient Greeks. Wars, religious stringencies and intellectual bias have stood in its path. Christians put the stamp of ascetic teaching on labour and leisure. Leisure (idleness) was condemned. When leisure did become accepted, it was accepted conditionally – not as value in itself, but as a means of renewing for the work ahead. The word 'recreation' epitomizes the attitude of conditional joy: work, be weary, take recreation that you may work again. Take some free time, but not too much. Too much leisure is seen as unearned time.

Leisure was thought to be totally opposite to work but increasingly leisure and work are considered to have a more fluid relationship. Effort – work – is expended both at work and in many leisure activities.

Leisure is a gift for the taking. However, our upbringing and traditional ways of life make it difficult to recognize and accept the gift. Ideally, it can become a way of living the 'good life', but only we can determine for ourselves what it will be. Yet, education and knowledge can help to open doors to opportunity and provide the skills and abilities we need in order to make the best choices for ourselves.

Discussion of findings and issues

This book is unlike others in the field of leisure management as it looks into the nature of leisure, the leisure experience, the needs of people, the range of leisure products and the practice of management in one volume. It spans twenty-five chapters but even these cannot hope to cover all areas in depth. Nonetheless they cover the broad spectrum of leisure, play and recreation and a number of the chapters delve into the subject area at some length. Indeed the chapters dealing with the main public, voluntary and commercial providers and the chapters on management between them occupy around half the volume.

In terms of management, my concern is with effectiveness rather than efficiency alone. Effectiveness is concerned with meeting the goals of an organization and the needs of people. An effective service for the greater good of the greater number of people, for example, needs to be based on sound foundations:

- principles based on equality of opportunity
- meeting the needs of different people
- planning and provision to attract the communities it is intended to serve and
- management excellence to deliver services, programmes and activities, and meet the needs of the organization.

Leisure has the potential to provide opportunities for satisfying experience and to enhance the quality of people's lives. Experiences can be of many kinds and of different intensities. Experiences which evoke 're-creation', unity, oneness, fulfilment or, in Maslow's words, 'self-actualization' are inadequately described as leisure experiences. Therefore, I invented a word and called it 'pleisure', a derivative of the words 'play', 'recreation' and 'leisure'. For such pleisure to occur, leisure managers need to provide the right conditions: levels of freedom and choice; satisfaction in the doing and positive outcomes such as well-being, achievement and self-esteem.

These innate, worthwhile experiences give satisfactions. Satisfactions lead to consuming interests. Interests help people to realize their potential. However, most people are not free agents to enjoy leisure as they might. Indeed, it is clear that leisure is linked inextricably to other elements of life, many of which are far more pressing and constraining. Therefore, leisure professionals need to know something about the needs of people in order to manage appropriately.

People have diverse needs, and different people have different needs, which change according to their circumstances and stage in life. Leisure needs, as such, may not exist, but some of the needs of people can be met through involvement in leisure pursuits. Some needs are basic to survival, some are essential to cope with living in an uncertain social world, and others concern living life to the full, seeking to find balance, harmony and self-worth.

People want to be somebody: it is therefore in this latter category that leisure opportunity can help people to meet some of their needs, to find themselves and have a favourable personal identity. However, emotional stress, financial and family worries, work obligations and crisis points in life may dominate to the extent that leisure becomes peripheral. For example, leisure for many disadvantaged people is likely to remain low, while major life constraints persist such as lack of income, poor housing, poor mobility and unrelieved pressures of parenting. These life factors support my contention that leisure cannot be divorced from other elements of life. In the context of the social significance of leisure, leisure can be perceived in a number of ways, but however we define it, leisure functions for people at three different levels:

- at an individual, personal level: where leisure is experienced
- at a group level: where individuals stand in relation to other people and
- across society: where a network of leisure services are provided.

Hence, while leisure for individuals is about personal experience, leisure in society cannot be understood only on an individual basis or on social grouping alone. In the excellent publication *Leisure in Society*, Stokowski (1994) perceives leisure as a social experience, not simply a personal or group activity; leisure is not something separate or removed from other contexts. A sociology that focuses entirely on the unique qualities of leisure experiences independent of wider social life is misleading:

> Conventional wisdom in the sociology of leisure maintains that 'leisure' is a feeling of freedom and satisfaction that people experience as a result of participation in pleasurable activities during free time. Such descriptions, however, based as they are on individual perceptions, fail to capture the social character and significance of leisure behaviour. Leisure is more than simply individual feelings or experience. It is a domain of institutionalized social relationships, structures, and meanings that persist across society and throughout time. Missing from our understanding of leisure is knowledge about how people construct leisure behaviours and meanings within the social contexts of their daily lives, how behaviours and meanings are socially structured and organized, and how the extended social structures of leisure subsequently exert influence on individual choices and experiences.

Leisure at individual and group levels

First, let us look at the individual, personal level and consider leisure in its play mould. In its purest sense, play transports the player to a world outside his or her normal world. It can be vivid, colourful, creative and innovative. Children whose play, or adults whose leisure, embraces spontaneity, manifest joy and a sense of humour are probably better able to deal with the freedom and choice that are present in leisure (see Playfulness, p. 81, Chapter 5).

But what has play to do with leisure and recreation management? Everything, because play is the cornerstone. Take the play element out of the leisure activity such as sport and the essence of the activity will be lost. The study of play teaches that it is important to invest considerable decision-making power in the hands of the participants. This is why some people like to belong to small autonomous groups, where they feel identified, where they can be masters of their own destiny, even for a short period of their routine lives. Recreation programmers would be unwise to omit autonomous groups, clubs and associations from their programmes. Another lesson of play is to resist the temptation of controlling, administering and providing for people 'on a plate'. The process of controlling the content of our behaviour ourselves is important for the play and leisure elements to flourish.

It was shown earlier in the book that many people are searching for an understanding of themselves – a search for the whole person, not a split person. This idea is exemplified in the growth of spiritual and meditative movements which emphasize a unification of the body, mind and spirit. Why have they captured the imagination of progressive, realist, affluent Westerners? Is it because of the vacuum created by our artificial splitting of the body from the mind and spirit even in our time free for leisure? As Bertrand Russell said, 'to be able to fill leisure intelligently is the best product of civilization, and at present, very few people have reached that level'.

Stebbins suggests that people's leisure is of two main types – serious and casual leisure. Serious leisure sounds like a contradiction in terms. However, although work-like, it is not work; it is not our livelihood, and it is usually unpaid, even if expenses are met. Nonetheless, it can serve as a work substitution and the choice of activities is far broader in leisure then in work. Like the workaholic who lives and breathes an occupation or profession, many people work longer and harder at leisure or turn leisure into work. Stebbins (1996) maintains in the *Ottawa Citizen* of cyclists: 'the bicycle is not to be taken lightly. Bicycling is serious business. Do not go slowly in front of a serious cyclist.' A dedicated sportsman or woman works through the pain barrier to gain peak performance. A committed gardener, biker, cook, mountain climber, surfer, dog breeder, trampolinist, theatre goer, genealogist or gambler are usually devoted to their activity as a central life interest.

Every serious leisure activity can not only offer a major lifestyle, but can also provide a personal identity – a leisure identity. 'Serious' or career volunteers also find a lively central life interest in their pursuits, whether in politics, religion, fighting poverty, human rights campaigns, or leisure. It appears that only some types of leisure – mostly the serious variety – are sufficiently profound to become central life interests. Moreover, they often need substantial support in the form of financial commitment and put pressures on families and those close to them. Serious volunteers who willingly help others are found in all walks of life. These activities have profound effects on lifestyle and personal identity.

Serious leisure comes at a cost – time, money, obligation, dedication, pressures and sometimes failure to achieve what we thought we should. But the rewards and satisfactions outweigh the difficulties and pride and ego also play a part. Indeed, serious leisure can provide a central long-lasting life interest. Often as part of a group there is the social reward of accomplishment – playing well together as a team, singing harmoniously in a choir, restoring a vintage motorbike together, playing in a band or acting in a play. There is something innately satisfying in sharing the same values, experiences and problems.

Yet casual leisure is by no means negative leisure. The word 'casual' could be seen as pejorative, demeaning or as belittling the form of leisure that most people do most of their free time. In some ways, casual leisure can be seen as akin to enjoying popular culture, including mass entertainment, watching films and television, listening to pop music, reading popular novels or visiting theme parks. Theme parks, for example, as well as providing entertainment, also offer opportunity to learn, to wonder and to experience and perceive new horizons.

Casual leisure, importantly, can also offer that time, as the poet says, to stand and stare, to relax, so important in busy lives and to recreate in body, mind and spirit. Another benefit is in social contact. People meeting up in a pub can enjoy social eating and drinking, debating sports results, talking politics, exchanging banter and bonding socially. These benefits could help to engender well-being.

As with serious leisure, casual leisure can come at a cost. People can get bored with the television. In consuming casual leisure, *ad infinitum*, we may feel we are achieving nothing. Casual popular activities, however, can become fulfilling interests such as becoming film buffs or experts in television 'soaps' thereby gaining the reputation of specialist members of the quiz night team: which can be distinctly serious leisure.

Social significance of leisure

It is clear that leisure offers opportunities for enrichment. But the time for leisure can also bring problems because freedom does not just allow us, it actually forces us to make choices. Is time for leisure a social problem? On the one hand, leisure can enhance the quality of life for the mass of people. On the other, leisure can be a twenty-first-century problem, with people incapable of coping with leisure and where for some, time hangs heavy or is consumed in self-gratification, greed, in vandalism and violence. Geoffrey Godbey (1975) refers to the creation of 'leisure potential'. The increased potential for leisure, however, has also created factors that have negated the meaning of leisure. They include: limitless materialism, increasing societal complexity and change and the carry-over of work values into leisure. He describes this backward step as 'anti-leisure', activity which is undertaken compulsively, as a means to an end, a necessity, with a high degree of externally imposed constraints, bringing anxiety, time-consciousness, minimum personal autonomy and which avoids self-actualization. Linder (1970), a Swedish economist, believes similarly that life has become so demanding in time that consumption production creates a 'leisure deficit'. The term 'time deepening' was coined to describe a person's ability to do several things simultaneously, and so crowd a greater number of activities into the same number of hours.

In the United Kingdom, there are now national strategies to use leisure such as sport to help combat health and social problems. However, the problem of using sport and leisure to solve some of the ills of the world, is that the essence of participation in these activities is that they are worthwhile in the doing, without having to justify supporting them for reasons external to their essential *raison d'être*. That the activities help society in other ways is all to the good but we should not lose sight of promoting sport, recreation and leisure as beneficial in and of themselves for the fun in the doing and the satisfaction they bring.

In times past, life used to be lived on fixed timetables, with patterns of work, shopping and leisure which provided structures to live by – a time to reap and a time to sow. These building blocks are disappearing and we are moving to flexible work patterns, round-the-clock shopping, home banking and the Internet. The pace of change has been rapid. Most of us – though not all – are enjoying higher standards of living filled with goods, services, activities and opportunities that in past years seemed unimaginable.

Stebbins (1996) notes that lifestyles and traditional ways have changed. He uses the term 'detraditionalization' to describe the rejection of certain major traditions and cultural staples of everyday life such as work, class, gender and nation. With the loss of some traditions emerges 'individualization'. A third process he describes as 'tribalization', a disintegration of mass culture, leaving a diversity of 'tribes'. These post-traditional processes are important in understanding leisure; they move us away from perceiving leisure within a single overarching definition, or as a list of activities representative of leisure.

Individualization does not necessarily remain individual, it can give birth to new serious leisure tribes, for example, skateboarders, female body builders and extreme sports enthusiasts such as snowboarders. Leisure produces tribes of all social classes and age groups. We can meet people, make new friends and widen networks and social relationships. Often as part of a group there is the social reward of accomplishment. Both casual and serious leisure tribes can engender feelings of belonging, but serious leisure tribes can make significant contributions to the community also.

Former prime minister Margaret Thatcher once said that there was no such thing as society, by which she probably meant that as individuals we all have responsibilities for ourselves and for our communities. My use of the term 'leisure in society', is in the context of the social significance of leisure, and perceives leisure not just as a matter of individuals and groups but as a social phenomenon: it is not just individually significant, it is socially significant. Leisure is an important part of the lives of people collectively. People spend a great deal of their time, energy and money on its services and products. It has infrastructures, organizational systems and delivery processes at all levels of government – parish, district, regional, national and international. It is evident in all sectors of the community – public, voluntary, institutional and commercial. It is found in nearly all societies throughout the world. Leisure is planned, marketed and managed. Leisure is regulated, governed, subject to legislation and institutionalized so that all people may have some access to leisure opportunities. Moreover, leisure participation and activities are visible representations of society and influence or are influenced by structures and meanings of leisure.

Stokowski (1994) considers leisure in its social setting:

> The process of institutionalization is facilitated by the formal and informal organization of leisure services, facilities, settings, and resources. The social significance of leisure is not only in the arrangement of relational networks of personal leisure experience but also in the instrumental relationships forming the production networks of leisure provision.

Individual behaviours are, therefore, structured in part by the system of relationships formalized by the industry and by social convention. Extending Stebbin's ideas of leisure tribes, Stokowski's concern is with the social contacts and relationships surrounding individuals and how these might encourage or prohibit leisure opportunities. The concept of 'social filters' was mentioned earlier in the book. These social structures are patterns of relationships and interactions across society.

551

The Dictionary of Social Sciences *defines an institution as: 'an aspect of social life in which distinctive value-orientations and interests, centering upon large and important social concerns, generate or are accompanied by distinctive modes of interaction.'*

The term 'institution' is, therefore, different from the term 'association'. An association is essentially composed of people, while an institution is essentially composed of interactions and interrelationships. They are social patterns that have distinctive value orientations, they direct the behaviour of human beings and characteristically tend to be permanent and to resist change. They exist because they have been reasonably successful in meeting societal needs.

Leisure and recreation in a collective social setting can thus be perceived as a social institution.

Avedon (1994) supports the social institution argument. He points out that, as in the case of other social institutions, 'recreation has form, structure, traditions, patterns of operation and association, systems of communication, and a number of other fixed aspects'. Kraus (1978) concludes that recreation has emerged as a 'significant' social institution: 'Once chiefly the responsibility of the family, the church or other local social bodies, it has now become the responsibility of a number of major agencies in our modern industrial society.'

Is there a need for leisure management?

If leisure is a freedom to choose, then personal management is of greater importance than management by someone else, particularly a faceless 'someone' like a local authority or another organization or a third party – a Leisure Manager. However, this book has shown that effective management is needed to open up opportunity, create the right environments and manage situations so that more people can be attracted to and benefit from leisure.

Effectiveness is measured by the degree to which an organization achieves its goals and objectives. This applies to all organizations, whether in commerce or leisure. In public leisure services, effective community leisure management can be measured, in part, by the degree to which a reasonable balance of market segments has been attracted. For example, if a leisure centre purports to be a centre for the community, it follows that it should attract a cross-section of the local community. Two key elements in leisure management are:

- the interaction between the organization and those who use the services, because it is a people-orientated business and
- the fact that managers are involved in the achievement of goals.

A leisure and recreation organization is a business whose functions include the creation and distribution of services, programmes and activities that are used by individuals and groups during their time for leisure. Leisure and recreation management is, therefore, the process whereby a manager works with resources – especially human – to achieve goals and objectives.

Good management is largely the result of good managers. They are individuals who are responsible and have authority for providing direction to their organization and who also have the ability to move it towards its goals. Managers are, therefore, directly responsible for much of the success or failure of an organization. Management, to be effective, needs to be flexible enough to accommodate changing circumstances and to meet the different needs of different people. Managers, therefore, have substantial influence not only in what they do, but in the way they do it. They have influence on the objectives and targets, programmes, activities and the results; their style of management can dramatically influence staff, clients and customers. Unless the goals of an organization include qualitative aspects, which are measured, then a community leisure facility cannot be said to be managed effectively. The right atmosphere and the appropriate encouragement may be all that is needed to overcome a person's anxiety in making use of a leisure facility for the first time. Sensitive, appropriate and capable management is, therefore, one of the keys to opening up leisure opportunity for each person. Such an opening door can help people towards achieving their potential.

Programming is one of the most important functions in leisure management but is an under-rated skill. It goes hand in hand with marketing. The concept of marketing is relatively simple; it is about assessing needs and demands, creating services and products to meet them and in doing so also meet the objectives of the organization. Events, too, are an important part of any comprehensive leisure programme. Well organized, they can be a boon; badly organized, they can spell disaster.

Staff are the most important resource in any leisure organization and their cost should be regarded as an investment rather than an expensive item of expenditure. The right staff need to be employed, trained, nurtured and enabled to perform well for their organization and for themselves. If not, then they are an expensive liability.

Leisure professionals must manage with excellence; they must inspire, lead, teach and instil values, so that work is done gladly, with energy and enthusiasm. Leisure has an abundance of positive selling points. People want to work for more than money; the motivation must come from the job itself, not just from salaries and fringe benefits. Work, therefore, should be satisfying in the doing. Attitudes, in delivery, can often be the ingredients that turn an average service into a great one. The profession needs to develop competent, confident people at all levels of service, able to enhance their organizations and the lives of their clients and customers. Training has been a major growth factor since the earlier editions of this book. Leisure is one of the most attractive fields for young people to study in and, hence, a plethora of courses in leisure now exist. We are also on the verge of leisure management training on the Internet. Whether there will be enough sustainable jobs in the field is a question still to be answered.

In summary, the first tenet of management is to know what we are in business for – what it is we are supposed to be managing. Leisure Managers are not only managing parks, pitches, pools, theatres and sports centres, but creating opportunities for people to experience leisure in ways satisfying to them. Therefore, there must be effective management, concerned with what is below the surface as much as what is above it. Measures of effectiveness must, therefore, include not only throughput, income and expenditure, but also the range of people, the scope of the activities and the quality of the experiences. Managers must ask themselves to what extent they have met the needs of the people they are there to serve.

Clearly, there is a need for quality Leisure Managers.

553

Towards effective community leisure and recreation management

To provide more effective community leisure management, a theoretical framework has been constructed. It consists of the three interlocking aspects of people, leisure and management, visualized as the three planes of a transparent triangular pyramid, with the base of the pyramid as a representation of the purposes of the organization. Within the pyramid are three levels of participation: the base providing for all, the middle stage providing for groups and the apex of the pyramid illustrating the importance of providing for the individual. This approach to community leisure and recreation management calls for appropriate situational balances of the needs of people, the leisure products and the management to meet objectives. I have called the model the 'leisure management pyramid'.

One of the purposes of this book has been to examine the linkages between leisure philosophy, resources and management and to build bridges between them in an attempt at improving the management of community leisure services and facilities. I have tried to link theory and practice. The value of a theory is the degree to which it explains and predicts and is of practical use. There is nothing more practical than a good theory, as long as you put it into practice; if it is no good in theory, it will be no good in practice. Three propositions are made in this book:

1 Providers and managers should be concerned with the quality of experience for the individual and not solely with quantities of numbers attending and income produced, as important as they are.
2 Leisure opportunity can lead to satisfying experiences which have positive effects on the quality of life of individual people and the community as a whole.
3 Management policy and performance can be powerful influences on both people's participation and non-participation.

Leisure and recreation management: end notes

The case for leisure and recreation investment and support is well made. Leisure opportunity can be the vehicle through which people can play and find recreation and in so doing meet some of their human needs.

If Leisure Management is to blossom into a profession with a philosophy, an ethic and professional standing, it needs to establish itself as a discipline with a basic framework of terminology and understanding. If we can understand what it is, why people play and have recreation, we shall then have a fundamental basis upon which planning should be based. If we know what motivates people to participate in leisure, then conflicts over priorities and facilities would be more readily resolved. On the other hand, if we have no basic insights into why people play and find recreation, then we cannot have any confidence either in the facilities we produce or the programmes we manage, for we will not know whether they are relevant or appropriate.

Leisure has emerged over recent history as an important sphere of life. It now has less to do with former definitions of time and specified activities and more to do with satisfying experiences. As a choice of lifestyle and a form of personal expression, it should now become less a reflection of demographic and socio-economic status and more a reflection of who we are and what leisure means to us.

Leisure consumption is one of the few growth areas in the current economic climate in the United Kingdom. Well into the foreseeable future, there will be continued demand for centres of interest to satisfy the rising expectations of people in all walks of life and all sections of the community. Rising expectations and demand for more, however, must be tempered by an appreciation of the needs of others. Hence, it is not just about money and providing facilities. It is also about changing attitudes. Fair Play for Children, an organization that exists to defend and promote the child's right to play, mentions a Mobile Play Project worker who had gathered children on a public open space only to face angry residents and hear: 'What are you attracting them here for? We've spent ten years chasing them off!' Compare that with the statement of Javier Perez de Cuellar, former UN Secretary-General, in 1987: 'The way a society treats children reflects not only its qualities of compassion and protective caring, but also its sense of justice, its commitment to the future and its urge to enhance the human condition for coming generations.' Clearly, play can shape human behaviour and help create the kind of future citizens who will be more child-friendly than we are to the present generation of children and young people. We spend huge amounts of taxpayers' money on the arts and sports, why not a fairer share for children's play and leisure education? Also, the correlation between leisure and recreation participation and variables such as social class, education and income, though far less obvious, still remain. Good management can negotiate many of the real barriers and help remove many of the artificial barriers.

All people appear to have a quest for personal identity. In a social and community context, leisure can help to give people self-worth and confidence. Moreover, resourceful people are those who can overcome obstacles and find preoccupying activities and interests. Leisure and recreation management has much to offer in the way of enabling people to develop skills, to discover themselves, make appropriate leisure choices and reach beyond their immediate grasp.

Managers must create environments in which leisure can flourish. Then they can define managerial objectives, develop skills for the job and utilize the resources at their disposal. Managers need multi-skill qualities for both general and specialist management. All providers and managers must attract people or fail.

In essence, Leisure Managers are no different from other managers; above all else, they need to be good managers. They must have skills of leadership, decision making, communication and administration. They have to choose, train and deploy staff wisely. They need objectivity, financial acumen, marketing, programming and operational ability. Management must be appropriate to different situations, and the manager must adapt his or her style of management to be appropriate to changing situations.

A Leisure Manager does not emerge fully-operational with a certificate from college. Nor is he or she someone who, through experience, can operate a facility but fails to appreciate what it means to achieve an effective service. A grasp of theory can accelerate the learning through job experience. However, the opposite is not necessarily true. Job experience may, or may not, accelerate a grasp of theory. In this book, a theory–practice orientation is advocated to produce the most effective Leisure

Managers. Yet no amount of training will guarantee to make the manager: he or she is someone with a mixture of ability, objectivity, craft and humanity.

There is much to be said for practical, common-sense approaches to management. We have somehow managed to make management something academic and difficult. While knowledge, logic and technical ability are important, there is also an important place for enthusiasm and empathy, even charisma. There is room for belief and conviction. Leisure opportunity is a tangible means of improving the lot of individuals in society. The message to policy makers is clear: make savings on capital if you must, but never on good management. A great deal can be done without major capital expenditure. 'Small things make a big difference', particularly when we are attracting clients and customers and providing opportunities for personal satisfactions and in so doing meeting the objectives of the organization.

Leisure professionals must develop a 'helicopter' view of their leisure services: the higher they go, the greater the vision. They need to view not just the array of facilities, but also the interconnections, the junctions of the various pathways, the fuels that make the processes effective, and the blockages that cause the hold-ups.

The concept of leisure management, however, provides us with a dilemma. Can leisure be managed? If leisure and recreation are concerned with personal experience, human experience defies management. It is individuals themselves who have control of their own destiny; Leisure Managers can make no guarantees of managing their leisure. However, management is the instrument by which environments can be shaped and opportunities can be provided; most people, given such opportunities, can fashion their own leisure – others can be enabled to choose and to cope. The challenge therefore is not just in facilities, programmes, costs, income or even in numbers, but in whether leisure services can provide opportunities for leisure and recreation to occur for people, at an affordable price, and at the same time, meet the organization objectives.

Emphasis has been placed in this book on effectiveness. We desperately need a method of evaluation that permits a social cost–benefit analysis. We do not want to promote the slogan 'Leisure for all – who can afford it'. Allowing the accounting mind to dictate social policy will be a tragedy for people, for leisure, for art, for sport and for the community.

At the community level, the major resource that this world has is people. Our untapped resources are in the community sector. We need to create:

- an enabling environment, encouraging leadership in the community
- a supporting environment, providing resources and
- a connecting environment, linking people to agencies, organizations and voluntary and commercial bodies.

The Leisure Manager's role as advocate and connector is important.

While leisure is personal, it is also universal. World Leisure – the World Leisure and Recreation Association – in the prologue to its *Charter for Leisure*, states:

All societies and all cultures increasingly recognize people's right to certain periods of time during which they can choose freely to occupy themselves and which experiences to select to further their quest for self-fulfilment and to improve the quality of their lives. Peace, a minimum of social stability, the opportunity to establish meaningful inter-personal contacts, and the reduction of social inequality, are some of the major prerequisites for the full implementation of that right.

Jacob Bronowski believed that leisure activity has potential for a deep sense of appreciation which can lift us to a higher plane, where we discover peace, beauty and joy in this world. This can carry over to an increased appreciation of life itself. Julian Huxley, in the *Bulletin of Atomic Scientists*, states: 'The leisure problem is fundamental. Having to decide what we shall do with our leisure is inevitably forcing us to re-examine the purpose of human existence, and to ask what human fulfilment really means.' Leisure management should be concerned with such fulfilment, with a love of life, for people and for the human expression that leisure opportunity affords.

Leisure is also a potential resource for social cohesion. After food and shelter, one of the greatest human needs is for peaceful co-existence. Leisure offers the opportunity for developing relationships. President Roosevelt said that peace in the world will only come if we cultivate the 'science of relationships'. However, today's 'science of technology' if used without wisdom, can negate human relationship. Bill Gates of Microsoft fame, the richest businessman in America, says that the new technologies with instant vision, sound and tele-conferencing will mean that in the future we will not need to meet. Communication will be the skill of transmitting information. But where will be the fellowship, the sharing, the bonds which go to make up that word 'community'?

Senator J. William Fulbright stated in 1964, long before the Internet, 'Science has radically changed the conditions of human life on earth. It has expanded our knowledge and our power, but not our capacity to use them with wisdom.' The challenge remains with even greater importance and urgency today.

A House of Lords report written over 30 years ago captured the belief and the spirit in which this book is written:

> Many people suffer from a lingering feeling that leisure is something of a luxury. As an escape from the commendable pursuits of earning a living and making a contribution to the national economy, leisure seems tainted. When carried to excess it is called idleness. But the Committee believes that it is time for the puritan view of leisure to be jettisoned. Leisure is as much a part of life as work and it plays an equally important part in man's development and the quality of his life ... In its own way it is almost as important to the well-being of the community as good housing, hospitals and schools.
>
> House of Lords, 1973

The world may change, but some things are changeless; we have been given creative, changeless gifts. It is through play, recreation and leisure that our talents for discovery, invention, music, art and sport are realized. Leisure professionals and volunteers have much to offer individuals, groups and organizations as enablers, connectors, planners, strategists and, above all, as Leisure Managers. My hope for leisure providers and managers is that they will not just concentrate on efficiency, finding more administration to satisfy less activity, but to aim for effectiveness – more people, more activities, best quality. The spirit of the world cannot be changed through money, facilities or bureaucracy, nor by government, but by imagination and ideas. Those ideas need the backing of our enthusiasm, confidence and vision – and our advocacy and management expertise.

The leisure experience described in this book stems from intrinsic, rather than extrinsic rewards: it is person-centred. Each society should respect the individuality of each of its people. Society, in turn, will benefit, for people who function at their optimal potential can help society to reach a far better level of collective well-being. As the Select Committee of the House of Lords put it: 'When life becomes meaningful for the individual, then the whole community is also enriched.'

Appendix

The Institute of Leisure and Amenity Management

Contact details

ILAM House, Lower Basildon, Reading, RG8 9NE
Tel 01491 874800
Fax 01491 874801
e-mail: infor@ilam.co.uk

Information provided by the Institution

The Institute of Leisure and Amenity Management (ILAM), a registered charity, is the professional body for leisure professionals. ILAM represents every aspect of leisure, cultural and recreation management and is committed to the improvement of management standards.

The growing importance of leisure pursuits to the quality of life demands that financial, human, physical and other resources are managed in the most effective, productive and beneficial way. ILAM plays a key role in the development of leisure management, through education, research, information, debate and discussion with government and national agencies.

The Institute operates a voluntary regional network throughout England, Ireland, Scotland and Wales.

Objectives The Institute's main objective is to extend the knowledge and efficiency of those engaged in all aspects of leisure management. This objective is achieved through the organization of conferences, seminars and training events, the dissemination of best practice information and the provision of educational schemes and programmes.

The Institute is active on three levels:

1 provision of professional information and education services
2 regional and national provision of events and opportunities for networking and
3 representation of the leisure profession at a national level.

Membership profile Members are drawn from the public, private, commercial and voluntary sectors in the UK and internationally and from all levels of the profession. Leisure resources managed by ILAM members include the natural environment of countryside, lakes and beaches, as well as built facilities, such as museums, libraries, parks, swimming pools, sports, fitness and arts centres.

559

Professional development

1 ILAM First Award
2 ILAM Certificate in Leisure Operations
3 ILAM Certificate in Leisure Management
4 ILAM Diploma in Leisure Management
5 ILAM Advanced Diploma in Leisure Management

Associated with the generic qualifications is a growing number of qualifications linked to the technical or operational aspects of leisure management. These demonstrate the under-pinning knowledge required by managers operating in a specialist discipline.

Training courses ILAM has established a comprehensive Continuing Professional Development (CPD) structure. Supporting this structure is a programme of training seminars and conferences organized as national events and staged at locations spread over the whole of the UK.

Information centre ILAM's information centre holds a unique collection of material on all aspects of leisure and is acknowledged as the most comprehensive leisure information service in the country. The Institute's collection of books and articles are indexed on a catalogue database and searches using subject keywords can be undertaken by the experienced staff who deal with a wide range of members' enquiries. The staff can offer advice on what information may be available relating to research, coursework and professional enquiries and will guide users to the most appropriate materials or refer them to alternative sources of information. The information service is free to ILAM members.

Publications *The Leisure Manager* is the Institute's professional journal. *Leisure News and Jobs* is mailed to members weekly. Books and other publications including a series of specialist titles published by ILAM are available through the bookshop.

Website The ILAM website (www.ilam.co.uk) gives access to information about events and news and provides an opportunity for professionals to communicate with each other through the Leisure Forum.

Specialist networks The Institute has in place five specialist networks, comprising respected academics and practitioners in all sectors of leisure. The networks are: arts libraries and museums; children's play; parks, places and countryside; sports services; tourism and visitor attractions.

Regional network The Institute has a network of regions covering each area of the UK and Ireland.

ILAM Services Ltd ILAM Services is a wholly owned subsidiary company of the Institute. Its core business is the management of awareness events, conferences and seminars, both for the Institute and for external clients. The annual ILAM National Conference is the flagship event of the Institute. ILAM Services also provides a consultancy service.

Institute of Sport and Recreation Management (ISRM)

Contact details

Sir John Beckwith Centre for Sport
Loughborough University, Loughborough
Leicestershire LE11 3TU
Tel 01509 226474
Fax 01509 22645
e-mail info@isrm.co.uk
URL http://www.isrm.co.uk

Information provided by the Institute

Founded in 1921 as the Association of Baths Superintendents, the institute became the Institute of Baths Management in 1961, the Institute of Baths and Recreation Management in 1979 and finally the Institute of Sport and Recreation Management (ISRM) in 1993.

The ISRM is the national professional body for sport and recreation facility management. Its mission is 'to lead, develop and promote professionalism in the management of sport and recreation'. To achieve this ISRM's aim is to improve the management and operation of recreation centres, sports faciities and swimming pools through the provision of training, advice and consultancy services. It publishes a regular magazine, *Recreation*, and technical publications. The Institute provides a range of education and development opportunities for those in the sport and recreation industry.

ISRM qualifications

1 Sport and Recreation Operations Certificate, an introductory qualification
2 Sport and Recreation Supervisory Management Certificate
3 Sport and Recreation Management Certificate, a professional recognition for facility managers
4 ISRM Diploma, the highest qualification for senior and strategic management of sport and recreation facilities.

ISRM also provides foundation vocational courses, particularly for swimming pool and spa operators.

561

Continuous Professional Development (CPD) ISRM provides continuous professional development which it defines as 'the systematic maintenance, improvement and broadening of knowledge and skills, and the development of personal qualities necessary for the execution of professional, managerial and technical duties throughout a member's career'.

References

AALR (The American Association for Leisure and Recreation) (2003), *Leisure Education in the Schools*, AALR, Reston, VA.

Adair, J. (1990), *Understanding Motivation*, Talbot Adair, Guildford.

Adair, J. and Reed, P. (1997), *Not Bosses but Leaders* 2nd edn, Kogan Page, London.

Adair, J. and Reed, P. (2003), *Not Bosses but Leaders* 3rd edn, Kogan Page, London.

Alder, H. (1993), *The Right Brain Manager*, Piatkus, London.

Allen, J., O'Toole, W., McDonnell, I., Harris, R. (2002), *Festival and Special Event Management* 2nd edn, Milton, John Wiley, Australia.

American Association for Health, Physical Education and Recreation (1972), listed in Edginton, C., Coles, R. and McClelland, M. (2003), *Leisure Basic Concepts*, AALR, Reston, VA.

Anderson, D. (1999), *A Common Wealth: Museums in the Learning Age*, TSO, London.

Arai, S. (1997), 'Volunteers within a changing society: the use of empowerment theory in understanding serious leisure', *World Leisure and Recreation*, 39 (3) 19–22.

Argyris, C. (1957), *Personality and Organization*, Harper and Row, New York.

Argyris, C. (1966), 'Interpersonal barriers to decision making', *Harvard Business Review*, 44 (2) 84–97.

Argyris, C. (1976), *Increasing Leadership Effectiveness*, Wiley, New York.

Argyris, C. and Schon, D. (1978), *Organizational Learning: A Theory of Action Perspective*, Addison Wesley, Wokingham.

Aristotle (1926), *The Politics of Aristotle* (trans. Ernest Barker), Clarendon Press, Oxford.

Arts Council (1993), *A Creative Future*, Arts Council, London.

Arts Council of England (2003), *Ambition for the Arts 2003–2006*, ACE, London.

Audit Commission (1991), *The Road to Wigan Pier? Managing Local Authority Museums and Art Galleries*, Audit Commission, London.

Avedon, E. (1974), *Therapeutic Recreation Service*, Prentice-Hall, Englewood Cliffs, NJ.

Bammel, G. and Bammel, L. (1966), *Leisure and Human Behaviour* 3rd edn, Brown and Benchmark, Dubuque, IA.

Barnard, C. (1938), *The Functions of the Executive*, Harvard University Press, Cambridge, MA.

Barnett, L. (1976), The contrast between play and other forms of learning in pre-school children's problem-solving ability. Unpublished doctoral dissertation, University of Illinois.

Barnett, L. (1979), 'Cognitive correlates of playful behaviour', *Leisure Today*, JOPERD, October.

Bass, B. (1985), *Leadership and Performance: Beyond Expectations*, Free Press, New York.

Bass, B.M. (1990), *Bass and Stogdill's Handbook of Leadership: Theory, Research and Managerial Applications*, Free Press, New York.

Belbin, M. (1981), *Management Teams: Why They Succeed or Fail*, Butterworth-Heinemann, Oxford.

Bennis, W. (1984) 'Good managers and good leaders', *Across the Board*, 21 (10) 7–11.

Bennis, W. (1989), *On Becoming a Leader*, Business Books, London.

Bennis, W. (1989), *Why Leaders Can't Lead: The Unconscious Conspiracy Continues*, Jossey-Bass, San Francisco, CA.

Bennis, W. and Nanus, B. (1985), *Leaders*, Harper and Row, New York.

Berkowitz, L.A. and Green, J.A. (1962), 'Simple view of aggression', *Journal of Abnormal and Social Psychology*, 64, 293–301.

Blake, R. and Mouton, J. (1981), *The Managerial Grid*, Gulf.

Blake, T. (1985), 'Image', *Leisure Management*, November, 5 (11) 14–15.

Blake, T. (1990), series of articles, *Baths Service and Recreation Management*.

Blanchard, C. (2000), 'First byte: the people's network and the children's library', *Youth Library Review*, 28, Spring.

Blanchard, K. and Johnson, S. (1983), *The One Minute Manager*, Willow Collins, London.

Blanchard, K., Zigarmi, P. and Zigarmi, D. (1986), *Leadership and the One Minute Manager*, Willow Collins, London.

Blanshard, C. (1998), *Managing Library Services for Children and Young People*, Library Association, London.

Blauner, R. (1964), *Alienation and Freedom: The Factory Worker and his Industry*, University of Chicago Press, Chicago, IL.

Bonel, P. (1993), *Playing for Real*, National Children's Play and Recreation Unit, London.

Bonython, E. and Burton, A. (2003), *The Great Exhibitor: The Life and Work of Henry Cole*, V & A, London.

Bowdin, G., McDonnell, I., Allen, J. and O'Toole, W. (2001), *Events Management*, Butterworth-Heinemann, Oxford.

Bradshaw, J. (1972), 'The concept of social need', *New Society*, 30 (3) 640–3.

Brandenburg, J., Greiner, W., Hamilton-Smith, H., Schotton, H., Senior, R. and Webb, J. (1982), 'A conceptual model of how people adopt recreation activities', *Leisure Studies*, 1 (3) September.

Brightbill, C. and Mobley, T.A. (1977), *Educating for Leisure-centered Living* 2nd edn, John Wiley, New York.

Brightbill, C. (1966), *Educating for Leisure-centered Living*, Stackpole, Harrisburg, PA.

Brightbill, C. (1964), Introduction, *Recreation*, 57, January, 10.

Brimacombe, P. (2003), *English Style*, Pitkin Guides, Jarrold Publishing, Norwich.

British Association of Friends of Museums (2001), submission to the Regional Museums Task Force.

Brooking, T. (undated), *Best Value Through Sport: the value of sport to the health of the nation*, Sport England, London.

Bronowski, J. (1965), *The Science of Human Values* revised edn, Harper Torchbooks, New York.

Brown, F. (1990), *Working with Children – A Playwork Training Pack*, Leeds Metropolitan University.

Butler, G.D. (1976), *Introduction to Community Recreation*, McGraw-Hill, New York.

CACE (Central Advisory Council for Education) (1967), *Children and their Primary Schools. Volume 2, Research and Surveys*, Plowden Report, Department of Education and Science, HMSO, London.

Caillois, R. (1961), *Man, Play and Games*, Free Press of Glencoe, New York.

Castells, M. (2000), *The Information Age – Economy, Society and Culture*, Blackwell, Oxford.

Chaudhuri, A. (2003), 'Is your head killing you?', *The Sunday Times*, 24 August.

Cheskin, L., quoted in Packard, V. (1965), *The Hidden Persuaders*, Penguin, Harmondsworth.

Child, E. (1985), *General Theories of Play*, Play Board, Association for Children's Play and Recreation, Birmingham.

Children's Play Council (1998), *The New Charter for Children's Play*, The Children's Society, London.

Clayton, P. (1980), *A Companion to Roman Britain*, Phaidon, Oxford.

Cnaan, R., Handy, F. and Wadsworth, M. (1996) 'Defining who is a volunteer: conceptual and empirical considerations', *Non-profit and Volunteer Sector Quarterly*, 25, 364–83.

Coleman, R. (2002), 'Characteristics of volunteering in UK Sport: lessons from cricket', *Managing Leisure*, 7, 220–38.

Collins, M. (2003) 'The trust experience – do it for service, not for money', *Recreation*, June, 24–7.

Collins, M. and Melchan, A. (1992), *Children Today, A National Overview*, National Children's Play and Recreation Unit, London.

Covey, S. (1992), *The Seven Habits of Highly Effective People*, Simon and Schuster, London.

Cowell, D. (1978), 'Marketing's application to public authority sport, recreation and leisure centres', paper presented at Marketing Education Group (MEG) Conference, Hull College of Higher Education.

Craig, S. (1989), *Marketing Leisure Services*, Leisure Futures, London.

Crandall, R. (1977), *Social Interaction, Effect and Leisure*, Institute of Behavioural Research, Texas Christian University, unpublished.

Crane, N. (2002), *Mercator: The Man who Mapped the Planet*, cited by Robert MacFarlane, *The Observer Review*, 23 June.

Cutten, G.B. (1929), *The Threat of Leisure*, Yale University Press, New Haven, CT.

DCMS (Department for Culture, Media and Sport) (1999), *Local Cultural Strategies: Draft Guidance for Local Authorities in England, June, 1999*, DCMS, London.

DCMS (Department for Culture, Media and Sport) (2000), *Creating Opportunities: Guidance for Local Authorities in England on Local Cultural Strategies*, DCMS, London.

DCMS (Department for Culture, Media and Sport) (2001), *A Sporting Future for All*, DCMS, London.

DCMS (Department for Culture, Media and Sport) (2001), *The Historic Environment: A Force for Our Future*, Architecture and Historic Environment Division, DCMS, London.

DCMS (Department for Culture, Media and Sport) (2004), *Getting Serious About Play – A Review of Children's Play*, DCMS, London.

DCMS (Department for Culture, Media and Sport) (2004), *Tomorrow's Tourism Today*, DCMS, London.

DCMS (Department for Culture, Media and Sport) (2003), *The Structure and Strategy for Supporting Tourism*, DCMS, London.

DCMS (Department for Culture, Media and Sport) (2003), *Framework for the Future: Libraries, Learning and Information in the Next Decade*, DCMS, London.

DCMS/Cabinet Office (2002), *Game Plan: A Strategy for Delivering Government's Sport and Physical Activity Objectives Report*, DCMS, London.

DCMS/DfES (Department for Culture, Media and Sport/Department for Education and Skills) (1999), *All Our Futures: Culture, Creativity and Education*, DCMS, London.

de Grazia, S. (1962), *Of Time, Work and Leisure*, Doubleday, New York.

Deming, W. (1986), *Out of Crisis*, Cambridge University Press, Cambridge.

DES (Department of Education and Science) (1965), *Support for the Arts: The First Steps*, Cmnd 2601, HMSO, London.

DES (Department of Education and Science) (1969), *Youth and Community Work in the 70s*, HMSO, London.

DES (Department of Education and Science) (1970), *The Chance to Share*, Circular 2/70, DES, London.

DES (Department of Education and Science) (1982), *Public and Private Funding of the Arts*, 8th Report from Education, Science and Arts Committee, HMSO, London.

DES/MHLG (Department of Education and Science/Ministry of Housing and Local Government) (1964), *Provision of Facilities for Sport*, Joint Circular 11/64 and 49/64:, DES, London.

DETR (Department of Transport, Local Government and the Regions) (1998), *The Common Land Policy Statement*, DETR, London.

DNH (Department of National Heritage) (1986), *Setting the Scene: The Arts and Young People*, DNH, London.

DNH (Department of National Heritage) (1995), *Sport, Raising the Game*, DNH, London.

DNH (Department of National Heritage) (1995), *Tourism: Competing With The Best*, DNH, London.

DNH (Department of National Heritage) (1996), *People Working in Tourism and Hospitality*, DNH, London.

DNH (Department of National Heritage) (1997), *Success Through Partnership*, DNH, London.

DoE (Department of the Environment) (1970), *Reform of Local Government in England*, Cmnd 4276, HMSO, London.

DoE (Department of the Environment) (1975), *Sports and Recreation*, Cmnd 6200, HMSO, London.

DoE (Department of the Environment) (1977), *Policy for the Inner Cities*, Cmnd 6845, HMSO, London.

DoE (Department of the Environment) (1978), *Recreation Management Training Committee: Interim Report*, Discussion Paper (Chair, Anne Yates), HMSO, London.

DoE (Department of the Environment) (1984), *Recreation Management Training Committee: Final Report*, HMSO, London.

DoH (1992), White Paper, *The Health of the Nation: A Strategy for Health in England*, Cmnd 1986, HMSO, London.

DoH (1998), White Paper, *Our Healthier Nation – A Contract for Health*, Cmnd 3852, TSO, London.

Dower, M. (1965), *Fourth Wave – The Challenge of Leisure*, Civic Trust.

Doyal, L. and Gough, I. (1991), *A Theory of Human Need*, Macmillan, London.

Drucker, P. (1946), *Concept of the Corporation*, John Day, New York

Drucker, P. (1955), *The Practice of Management*, Pan Books, London.

Drucker, P. (1965) Notes taken from a lecture tour.

Duke of Westminster, (1992), *The Problems in Rural Areas*, report of recommendations arising from an inquiry chaired by His Grace the Duke of Westminster, DL.

Dumazedier, J. (1960), editorial, *International Social Science Journal*, 1, Winter, 526.

Dumazedier, J. (1967), listed in Edginton, C., Coles, R. and McClelland, M. (2003), *Leisure Basic Concepts*, AALR, Reston, VA.

Dumazedier, J. (1967), *Toward a Society of Leisure*, W.W. Norton, New York.

Edelman, G.M. (1993), *Klare Lucht, Louter Vuur. Over De Stoffelijke Oorsprong Van Denken En Bewustzihn* [Bright air, brilliant fire: On the matter of the mind], Uitgeverrij Bert Bakker, Amsterdam.

Edginton, C.R., Crompton, D.M. and Hanson, C.J. (1980), *Recreation and Leisure Programming: A Guide for the Professional*, Saunders College, Philadelphia, PA.

Edginton, C., Coles, R. and McClelland, M. (2003), *Leisure Basic Concepts*, AALR, Reston, VA.

Elliott, G. (ed.) (1989), *The Manager's Guidebook*, Longman, Harlow.

Ellis, M.J. (1973), *Why People Play*, Prentice-Hall, Englewood Cliffs, NJ.

Emmet, I. (1971), 'The social filter in the leisure field', *Recreation News* Supplement, 4, 7–8.

English Sports Council (1997), *A Sporting Future for the Playing Fields of England*, ESC, London.

English Sports Council (1997), *England, the Sporting Nation: A Strategy*, ESC, London.

English Tourism Council (2001), *Time for Action: A Strategy for Sustainable Tourism in England*, ETC, London.

English Tourist Board (1978), *The Give and Take of Sponsorship*, ETB, London.

Erikson, E.G. (1950), *Childhood and Society*, Norton, New York.

Erikson, E.H. (1959), 'Identity and the life cycle', *Psychological Issues*, 1 (1).

Erikson, E. (1963), *Eight Ages of Man in Childhood and Society* 2nd edn, Norton, New York.

Estates Gazette UK (1997), *Leisure Park Report, 1997*, Estates Gazette, London.

ETB and Jones Long Wootton (1989), *Retail, Leisure and Tourism*, ETB, London.

Farrell, P. and Lundegren, H.M. (1978), *The Process of Recreation Programming*, Wiley, New York.

Fayol, H. (1930), 'Administration industrielle et générale' trans. J.A. Coubrough, *Industrial and General Administration*, International Management Institute, Geneva.

Fayol, H., trans. C. Storrs (1949), *General and Industrial Management*, Pitman, London.

Feshbach, S. (1956), 'The catharsis hypothesis and some consequences of interaction with aggressive and neutral play', *Journal of Personality*, 24, 449–62.

Fox, K. and Kotler, P., 'The marketing of social causes: the first 10 years', *Journal of Marketing*, 44 (4) 24–33.

Foy, N. (1981), 'The human side of information', *Management Review and Digest*, October.

Frean, A. (2003), 'Britons enslaved by the mobile phone', *The Times*, 10 May.

Freud, S. (1974), *The Complete Works of Sigmund Freud*, Hogarth Press, London.

Froebel, cited in Maclean, J., Peterson, J. and Martin, W. (1963), *Recreation and Leisure: The Changing Scene*, John Wiley, New York.

Gans, H.J. (1974), *Popular Culture and High Culture*, Basic Books, New York.

Getz, D. (1991), *Festivals, Special Events and Tourism*, New York, Van Nostrand Reinhold, cited in Roch, M. (2002), *Mega-Events, Global Forces and Local Responses: Reviewing the Role of 'The Local' and 'Globalisation' in Relation to the Olympics and Major Sport Events*, World Leisure Congress Proceedings, Kuala Lumpur, Malaysia.

Godbey, G. (1975), 'Anti-leisure and public recreation policy', in Parker, S. *et al.* (eds), *Sport and Leisure in Contemporary Society*, Leisure Studies Association, London.

Godbey, G. (1976), *Recreation and Park Planning: The Exercise of Values*, University of Waterloo, Ontario.

Godbey, G. (1978), *Recreation, Park and Leisure Services*, W.B. Saunders, Philadelphia, PA.

Godbey, G. (1994), *Leisure in your Life: An Exploration*, Venture, PA.

Godbey, G. and Parker, S. (1976), *Leisure Studies and Services: An Overview*, W.B. Saunders, Philadelphia, PA.

Gold, S.M. (1981), 'Meeting the new recreation planning approach', *Parks and Recreation*, 53, (6), 74–80.

Goldblatt, J.J. (1990), *Special Events: The Art and Science of Celebration*, Van Nostrand Reinhold, New York.

Goleman, D. (1995), *Emotional Intelligence*, Bantam Books, New York.

Goodale, T. and Godbey, G. (1988), *The Evolution of Leisure*, Venture Publishing, State College, PA.

Graham, P.J. and Klar, L.R. Jr (1979), *Planning and Delivering Leisure Services*, W.C. Brown, Dubuque, IA.

Gratton, C. (2003) 'The economic importance of sport', paper presented at ILAM Conference.

Gratton, C., Nichols, G., Shiblis, R. and Taylor, P. (1997), *Valuing Volunteers in UK Sport*, Sports Council, London.

Gray, D. (1980), 'What is this thing called recreation?', *Parks and Recreation*, March, 62–4, 94.

Gray, D. and Pelegrino, D. (1973), *Reflections on Recreation and Park Management*, W.C. Brown, Dubuque, IA.

Gray, D. cited in Wilder, R.L. (1977), 'EEI: a survival tool', *Parks and Recreation*, August, 23.

Gray, D.E. and Greben, S. (1974), 'Future perspectives', *Parks and Recreation*, July, 27–33 and 47–56.

Gray, D.E. and Greben, S. (1979), 'Wanted: a new word for recreation', *Parks and Recreation*, March, 23.

Green, E., Hebron, S. and Woodward, D. (1987), *Leisure and Gender – a Study of Leisure Constraints and Opportunities for Women*, Sports Council/Economic Social Research Council, London.

Griffiths, G. (1981), *Recreation Provision for Whom?* unpublished.

Groos, K. (1901), *The Play of Man*, Appleton, New York.

Grossman, A.H. (1980), *Personnel Management in Recreation and Leisure Services*, Groupwork Today, South Plainfield, NJ.

Grunfeld, F. (1982), *Games of the World*, Swiss Committee for UNICEF, Zurich.

Gulick, L.H. (1965), quoted in Nash, J.B., *Recreation: Pertinent Readings*, W.C. Brown, Dubuque, IA.

Hall, C.M. (1992), *Hallmark Tourist Events*, Bellhaven, London, cited in Roche M. (2002), *Mega-Events, Global Forces and Local Responses: Reviewing the Role of 'The Local' and 'Globalisation' in Relation to the Olympics and Major Sport Events*, World Leisure Congress Proceedings, Kuala Lumpur, Malaysia.

Handy, C. (1990), *Inside Organizations: 21 Ideas for Managers*, BBC, London.

Hart-Davis, Alice. (2003), 'These children are braver than I could ever be', *Evening Standard*, 26 August.

Hayes, R. and Walter, V. (date), *Strategic Management for Public Libraries*, Greenwood Press, Westpoint.

Haywood, L. and Henry, I. (1986) 'Policy developments in community leisure and recreation, part one', *Leisure Management*, July 6(7), 25–9.

HCIMA (1999), *Management Brief No. 1*, HCIMA.

Health and Safety Commission/Home Office/The Scottish Office (1993), *Guide to Health, Safety and Welfare at Pop Concerts and Similar Events*, HMSO, London.

Heaton, D. (1991), *Museums Among Friends*, Museums and Galleries Commission, London.

Heawood, J. (2003), 'Daydream believer', *The Observer* Escape, 6 July.

Hedges, B. (1986), *Personal Leisure Histories – Social and Community Planning Research*, Sports Council/Economic Social Research Council, London.

Heller, R. (1998), *Making Decisions*, Dorling Kindersley, London.

Heller, R. (1998), *Managing Teams*, Dorling Kindersley, London.

Heller, R. (1999), *Managing People*, Dorling Kindersley, London.

Herzberg, F., Mausner, B. and Synderman, B. (1959), *The Motivation to Work*, Wiley, New York.

Hillman, M. and Whalley, A. (1977), *Fair Play for All. A Study of Access to Sport and Informal Recreation*, 43, Broadsheet No. 571, Political and Economic Planning (PEP), London.

House of Lords (1973), *Second Report from the Select Committee of the House of Lords on Sport and Leisure*, HMSO, London.

Howard, D.R. and Crompton, J.L. (1989), *Financing, Managing and Marketing Recreation and Park Resources*, W.C. Brown, Dubuque, IA.

Hughes, B. (2002), *A Playworker's Taxonomy of Play Types*, 2nd edn, Playlink, London.

Hughes, B., and Williams, H. (1982), 'Looking at play', *Play Times*, September 1–5.

Huizinga, J. (1955), *Homo Ludens*, Beacon Press, Boston, MA.

Hutson, S. (undated), *A Review of the Role of Clubs and Voluntary Associations based on a Study of Two Areas in Swansea*, Sports Council/SSRC, London.

Hutt, C. and Hutt, J. quoted in Lindon, J. (2001) *Understanding Children's Play*, Nelson Thornes, Cheltenham.

Hutton, W. (2003), 'When do we want it? Now.', *The Observer*, 13 July.

ICMA (International City Management Association) (1965), *Basic Concepts of Organization. Bulletin 3, Effective Supervisory Practices*, ICMA, Washington, DC.

IFER/DART (Institute of Family and Environmental Research/Dartington Amenity Research Trust) (1976), *Leisure Provision and Human Need: Stage 1 Report* for DoE, IFER/DART, London.

Jacobs, M. 'Places in the experience society', paper presented at the Seventh World Leisure Congress, Kuala Lumpur, October 2002, unpublished.

Jarvis, N., and King, L. (1997), 'Volunteers in uniformed youth organizations', *World Leisure and Recreation*, 39(3), 6–10.

Jenkins, C. and Sherman, B. (1979), *The Collapse of Work*, Methuen, Fakenham.

Jenkins, C. and Sherman, B. (1981), *The Leisure Shock*, Methuen, Bungay.

Jensen, C. (1977), *Leisure and Recreation: Introduction and Overview*, Lea & Febiger, Philadelphia, PA.

Jensen, R. (1999), *The Dream Society*, McGraw Hill.

Johnson, J. (1987), series of articles, *Leisure Manager*.

Johnstone, N. (2003) 'Sharp practice', *The Observer Magazine*, 23 February.

Kahn, D. and Katz, R.L. (1966), *The Social Psychology of Organizations*, Wiley, New York.

Kando, H. (1975), *Leisure and Popular Culture in Transition*, cited in Lewis, G.H. (1978), 'Popular Culture and Leisure', *Leisure Today*, JOPER, October, 3–5.

Kanter, R.M. (1989), *When Giants Learn to Dance*, Simon and Schuster, London.

Kaplan, M. (1975), *Leisure: Theory and Policy*, John Wiley, New York.

Kato, H. (1975), cited in Lewis, G.H. (1978), 'Popular Culture and Leisure', *Leisure Today*, JOPER, October, 3–5.

Kelly, J. (1982), *Leisure*, Prentice-Hall, Englewood Cliffs, NJ.

Kelly, J. (2000), listed in Edginton, C., Coles, R. and McClelland, M. (2003), *Leisure Basic Concepts*, AALR, Reston, VA.

Kennedy, C. (1991), *Guide to the Management Gurus*, Business Books, London.

Kent, S. (1981), 'Good communications', *Parks and Recreation*, September, 27–30.

Kew, S. and Rapoport, R. (1975), 'Beyond palpable mass demand, leisure provision and human needs – the life cycle approach', paper presented to Planning and Transport Research and Computation (International) Company Ltd, Summer Annual Meeting.

Keynes, J.M. (1963), 'Economic possibilities for our grandchildren', in *Essays in Persuasion*, W.W. Norton, New York.

Kightly, C. (1986), *The Customs and Ceremonies of Britain – An Encyclopaedia of Living Traditions*, Thames and Hudson, London.

Klein, M. (1955), 'The psychoanalytic play-technique', *American Journal of Orthopsychiatry*, 25, 223–37.

Knetsch, J.L. (1969), 'Assessing the demand for outdoor recreation', *Journal of Leisure Research*, 1 (2) 85.

Koshar, R. (ed.) (2002), *Histories of Leisure*, Berg, Oxford.

Kotler, P. (1975), *Marketing for Non-Profit Organizations*, Prentice-Hall, Englewood Cliffs, NJ.

Kotler, P. and Zaltman, G. (1971), 'Social marketing: an approach to planned social change', *Journal of Marketing*, July, 35, 3–12.

Kraus, R. (1971), *Recreation and Leisure in Modern Society*, Prentice-Hall, Englewood Cliffs, NJ.

Kraus, R. (1978), *Recreation and Leisure in Modern Society* 2nd edn, Goodyear, Santa Monica, CA.

Kraus, R. (1999), listed in Edginton, C., Coles, R. and McClelland, M. (2003), *Leisure Basic Concepts*, AALR, Reston, VA.

Kraus, R. (2001), *Recreation and Leisure in Modern Society* 6th edn, Jones & Bartlett, Sudbury, MA.

Kraus, R. and Bates, B. (1975), *Recreation Leadership and Supervision*, W.B. Saunders, Philadelphia, PA.

Kraus, R.G. and Curtis, J.E. (1977), *Creative Administration in Recreation and Parks*, C.V. Mosby, Saint Louis, MO.

Kraus, R. quoted in Weiskopf (1982), *Recreation and Leisure: Improving the Quality of Life* 2nd edn, Allyn & Bacon, Boston, MA.

Laczniak, G.R. *et al.* (1979), 'Social marketing, its ethical dimension', *Journal of Marketing*, Spring, 43, 29–36.

Leigh, J. (1971), *Young People and Leisure*, Routledge and Kegan Paul, London.

Levy, J. (1978), *Play Behaviour*, John Wiley, New York.

Lewis, G.H. (1978), 'Popular Culture and Leisure', *Leisure Today*, JOPER, October, 3–5.

Library and Information Commission (1997), *New Libraries: The People's Network*, LIC, London.

Lieberman, J.N. (1977), *Playfulness: Its Relationship to Imagination and Creativity*, Academic Press, New York.

Likert, R. (1967), *The Human Organization: Its Management and Value*, McGraw-Hill, New York.

Linder, S. (1970), *The Harried Leisure Class*, Columbia University Press, New York.

Lindon, J. (2001) *Understanding Children's Play*, Nelson Thornes, Cheltenham.

Lord Redcliffe-Maud (1969), *Report of the Royal Commission on Local Government in England 1966–1969*, HMSO, London.

Lord Redcliffe-Maud (1976), *Support for the Arts in England and Wales*, Calouste Gulbenkian Foundation, London.

Lord Redcliffe-Maud (1977), *Local Authority Support for the Arts*, Calouste Gulbenkian Foundation, London.

Lord Scarman (1981), *The Brixton Disorders, 10–12th April 1981, Report of the Right Honourable Lord Scarman*, HMSO, London.

Lord Scarman (1981), *The Brixton Disorders: First Report of an Inquiry, 25 November*, for the Home Office, Cmnd 8427, HMSO, London.

MacKenzie, R. (1969), 'The management process in 3-D', *Harvard Business Review*, November–December.

Marcuse, H. (1964), *One-Dimensional Man*, Routledge, London.

Marx, K. (1952), *Manifesto of the Communist Party*, Encyclopaedia Britannica, Chicago, IL.

Maslow, A. (1954), *Motivation and Personality*, Harper and Row, New York.

Maslow, A. (1968), *Toward a Psychology of Being* 2nd edn, D. Van Nostrand, New York.

Mayo, E. (1933), *The Human Problems of an Industrial Civilisation*, Macmillan, New York.

McAvoy, L.H. (1977), 'Needs and the elderly: an overview', *Parks and Recreation*, 12 (3) 31–5.

McDougal, W. (1923), *Outline of Psychology*, Methuen, London,

McGregor, D. (1966), *The Human Side of Enterprise*, McGraw-Hill, New York.

McIver, C. (1968), *Marketing* 3rd edn, revised and edited by G.C. Wilson, Business Publications, London.

Mead, M. (1928), *Coming of Age in Samoa*, William Morrow, New York.

Mental Health Foundation (1999), *Bright Futures*, Mental Health Foundation.

Mercer, D. (1973), 'The concept of recreation need', *Journal of Leisure Research*, 5 (1) 37–41.

Meyer, H.D. (1957), 'The adult cycle', *Annals of the American Academy of Political Science and Society*, 33, 58–67.

Meyer, H.D. and Brightbill, C.K. (1964), *Community Recreation*, Prentice-Hall, Englewood Cliffs, NJ.

Millar, S. (1968), *The Psychology of Play*, Penguin Books, Baltimore, MD.

Miller, H. (1942), *Wisdom of the Heart*, New Direction, USA.

Miller, N.P. and Robinson, D.M. (1963), *Leisure Age: Its Challenge to Recreation*, Wadsworth, Belmont, CA.

Ministry of Housing and Local Government (1967), *Management of Local Government. Volume I, Report of the Committee*, HMSO, London.

Ministry of Housing and Local Government (1967), *Management of Local Government. Volume V, Local Government Administration in England and in Wales*, HMSO, London.

Mintzberg, H. (1983), *Structures in Fives: Designing Effective Organizations*, Prentice-Hall, New York.

MoE (Ministry of Education) (1960), *The Youth Service in England and Wales: Report of the Committee November 1958*, Albermarle Report, Cmnd 929, HMSO, London.

Molyneux, D.D. (1968), 'Working for recreation', *Journal of Town Planning Institute*, 54 (4) April, 149–56.

Morgan, C. and King, R. (1966), *Introduction to Psychology*, McGraw-Hill, New York.

Morton, R. cited in Stewart, D. and Shamdasani, P. (1990), *Focus Groups – Theory and Practice*, Applied Social Research Methods Series, Vol. 20, Sage, London.

Mosley, R. (2001) *Municipal Year Book*, Hemming Group, London.

Mosscrop, P. and Stores, A. (1990), in association with the Institute of Leisure and Amenity Management, *Total Quality Management in Leisure. A Guide for Directors and Managers*, Collinson Grant Consultants, Manchester.

Moynagh, M. and Worsley, R. for the Countryside Agency (2003) *A Green and Pleasant Land*, Countryside Publications, Wetherby.

MSR (1995) *An Executive Summary of The Community Value of Recreation and its Relationship to Well-Being*, Ministry of Sport and Recreation, Western Australian Government.

Mulgan, G. (1995), 'The time squeeze', *Demos*, 5.

Mundy, J. (1998), *Leisure Education: Theory and Practice* 2nd edn, Sagamore Publishing, Champaign, IL.

Murphy, J. (1975), *Recreation and Leisure Services*, W.C. Brown, Dubuque.

Murphy, J. cited in Edginton, C.R., Crompton, D.M. and Hanson, C.J. (1980), *Recreation and Leisure Programming: A Guide for the Professional*, Saunders College, Philadelphia, PA.

Murphy, W. (1980), *Professionalism and Recreation Management*, Occasional Paper, unpublished.

Murray, H. (1938), *Explorations in Personality*, Oxford University Press, New York, referred to in IFER/DART (1976), *Leisure Provision and Human Need: Stage 1 Report* for DoE, IFER/DART, London.

Museums and Galleries Commission (1991), *Local Authorities and Museums*, MGC, London

NAMMG (National Arts and Media Monitoring Group) (1992), *Towards a National Arts and Media Strategy*, National Arts and Media Monitoring Group, Arts Council, London.

Nash, J.B. (1960), *Philosophy of Recreation and Leisure*, William Brown, Dubuque, IA.

Nash, J.B. (1965), *Recreation: Pertinent Readings*, William Brown, Dubuque, IA.

National Playing Fields Association (2001), *The Six Acre Standard: Minimum Standards for Outdoor Playing Space*, NPFA, London.

National Playing Fields Association, Children's Play Council and PLAYLINK (2000), *Best Play: What Play Provision Should Do for Children*, NPFA, London.

National Statistics (2003), *UK 2004*, TSO, London.

Nelson, R. (2001), *Please Don't Do What I Tell You! Do What Needs to be Done*, Hyperion, New York.

Neulinger, J. (1974), *The Psychology of Leisure*, Charles C. Thomas, Springfield, IL.

Neulinger, J. and Crandall, R. (1976), 'The Psychology of Leisure', *Journal of Leisure Research*, 3, August, 181–4.

Neumeyer and Neumeyer (1958), *Leisure and Recreation*, Ronald Press, New York.

Nichols, G. (2003), *The Contribution of the Voluntary Sector in Sport to the Agenda of the Home Office Active Community Unit*, CCPR, London.

Nichols, G., Taylor, P., Shiblis, R., and Gratton, C. (1998) 'Can the Sports Council rely on volunteers?', *Recreation*, June, 14–16.

Norbeck, E., (1979), 'The biological and cultural significance of human play: an anthropological view', in *Leisure Today*, JOPERD, October 1979.

Nosowicz, D. (2003), article in *The Observer*, 23 February.

Oakland, J.S. (1989), *Total Quality Management*, Heinemann Professional, Oxford.

Odone, C. (2002) 'The unwork ethic', *The Observer*, 1 December.

ODPM (2002), *Living Places: Cleaner, Safer, Greener*, ODPM, London.

O'Hanlon, M. (2000), *Customs and Traditions in Britain*, Pitkin Guides, Jarrold Publishing, Norwich.

ONS (2002), *Social Trends 33*, Office for National Statistics, TSO, London.

ONS (2003), *Social Trends 34*, Office for National Statistics, TSO, London.

ONS (Office for National Statistics) (2003), *UK 2004: The Official Yearbook of the United Kingdom of Great Britain and Northern Ireland*, TSO, London.

Packard, V. (1965), *The Hidden Persuaders*, Penguin, Harmondsworth.

Palmowski, J., (2002)'Travels with Baedeker – The Guidebook and the Middle Classes in Victorian and Edwardian Britain', in Koshar, R. (ed.), *Histories of Leisure*, Berg, Oxford.

Parker, S. (1971), *The Future of Work and Leisure*, MacGibbon and Kew, London.

Parker, S. (1997), 'Volunteering – altruism, markets, causes and leisure', *World Leisure and Recreation*, 39(3), 4–5.

Parry, N. and Parry, J. (1977), 'Theories of culture and leisure', paper presented at Leisure Studies Association Conference, University of Manchester, September.

Pascale, R. and Athos, A. (1981), *The Art of Japanese Management*, Simon and Schuster, London.

Patrick, G.T.W. (1916), *The Psychology of Relaxation*, Houghton Mifflin, Boston, MA.

Peter, L. (1986), *The Peter Pyramid*, Allen & Unwin, London.

Peters, T. (1987), *Thriving on Chaos*, Macmillan, London.

Peters, T. and Austin, N. (1985), *A Passion for Excellence*, Collins, London.

Peters, T. and Waterman, R. (1982), *In Search of Excellence*, Harper and Row, London.

Piaget, J. (1962), *Play, Dreams and Imitation in Childhood* (trans. G. Gattengno and F.M. Hodgson), Norton, New York.

Pick, J. (1978), 'Training: the future', *Municipal Entertainment*, 5 (10) June.

Pickard, R. (ed.) (2001), *Management of Historic Centres*, Spon, London.

Pieper, J. (1952), *Leisure the Basis of Culture*, New American Library, New York.

Pine, J. and Gilmore, J. (1999), *The Experience Economy – Work is Theatre and Every Business a Stage*, Business School Press, Boston.

Plato (1900), *The Republic of Plato* (trans. John Davis and David Vaughan), A.L. Burt, New York.

Plato (2003) in Maclean, J., Peterson, J. and Martin, W. (1963), *Recreation and Leisure: The Changing Scene*, John Wiley, New York, cited in Edginton, C., Coles, R. and McClelland, L. (2003), *Leisure Basic Concepts*, AALR, Reston, VA.

Play Board (1985), *Make Way for Children's Play*, Association for Children's Play and Recreation, Birmingham.

Powter, G. cited in Ed Douglas (2003) 'She models, she hosts TV shows, but this summer Araceli Segarra returns to her first love with an assault on K2...', *The Observer* Sunday Magazine, July.

Poynter, D. and Turoff, M. (1998), *The Skydiver's Handbook*, Para Publishing, USA, cited in Tomlinson, J. (2001), *Extreme Sports*, Carlton, USA.

Proud, L. (2001), *Christianity in England*, Pitkin Guides, Jarrold Publishing, Norwich.

Rapoport, R., Rapoport, R.N. and Strelitz, Z. (1975), *Leisure and the Family Life Cycle*, Routledge & Kegan Paul, London.

Reid, I. (1977), *Social Class Differences in Britain: A Source Book*, Open Books, London.

Resource (2003), *Turning Vision into Action*, publisher, place.

Revill, J. (2003), 'Life makes you sick', *The Observer*, 12 October.

Ritchie (1984), cited in Allen, J., O'Toole, W., McDonnell, I. and Harris, R. (2002), *Festival and Special Event Management* 2nd edn, Milton, John Wiley, Australia.

Roberts, J. (TEST) (1979), *The Commercial Sector in Leisure*, Sports Council/SSCR, London.

Roberts, J.M. and Sutton-Smith, B. (1962), 'Child training and game involvement', *Ethnology*, 1, 166–85.

Russell, B. (1935), *In Praise of Idleness*, Allen & Unwin, London.

Schiller, F. (1965), *On The Aesthetic Education of Man*, Frederick Ungar, New York.

Scottish Executive (2002), *Tourism Framework for Action 2000–2005*, Scottish Executive, London.

2

Searle, R. and Bradley, R. (1993), *Leisure Services in Canada: An Introduction*, Venture, State College, PA.

Selwood, S. (2001), *Markets and Users*, report submitted to Resource, May 2001.

Sessoms, H.D. (1975), 'Our body of knowledge: myth or reality?', *Parks and Recreation*, November, 30 (USA).

SGLAMS (Study Group on Local Authority Management Structures) (1972), *The New Local Authorities: Management and Structure*, Bains Report, HMSO, London.

Shibli, S., Taylor, P., Nichols, G., Gratton, C. and Kokolokakis, T. (1999), 'The characteristics of volunteers in UK sports clubs', *European Journal for Sports Management*, 10–27.

Shields, A. and Wright, M. (eds) (1989), *Arenas: A Planning, Design and Management Guide*, Sports Council, London.

Shivers, J.S. (1967), *Principles and Practices of Recreational Services*, Macmillan, New York.

Shivers, J.S. (1981), *Leisure and Recreation Concepts: A Critical Analysis*, Allyn & Bacon, Boston, MA.

Shuman, B. (2001), *Issues for Libraries and Information Services in the Internet Age*, Libraries Unlimited, Englewood, Colorado.

Simmonds, B (2003), 'The Local Government Bill', *Leisure Management*, October, 40–41.

Smith, B. (2003), 'What has sports development achieved for sport?', *Recreation*, 3 May, 16.

Smith, H. (1831), *Festivals, Games and Amusements, Ancient and Modern*, Colburn and Bentley, London.

Smith, P. (1998), quoted in National Playing Fields Association, Children's Play Council and PLAYLINK (2000), *Best Play: What Play Provision Should Do for Children*, NPFA, London.

Solberg H., (2002), 'Major sporting events – the value of volunteers' work', 7th World Leisure Congress Proceedings, Kuala Lumpur, Malaysia.

Spears, L. (1994), *Inner Quest 2*, The Greenleaf Center for Servant-Leadership.

Sport England and Central Council of Physical Recreation (2003), *Towards a Level Playing Field*, Sport England, London.

Sports Council (1969), *Professional Training for Recreation Management: Report of a Working Party* (Chairman, D.D. Molyneux), Sports Council, London.

Sports Council (1998), *Facilities Planning Model, a Planning Tool for Developing Sports Facilities*, Sports Council, London.

Sports Council (1995) *What is the Sports Council?* factsheet, March, Sports Council, London.

Sports Council Study Group (1968), *The Pilkington Report*, Sports Council, London.

Sports Council/HEA (1992), *The Allied Dunbar Fitness Survey*, Sports Council, London.

Stanley-Hall, G. (1920), *Youth,* Appleton-Century, New York.

Stayte, S. and Watt, D.C. (undated), *Events from Start to Finish*, ILAM, Lower Basildon, Reading.

Stebbins, R. (1996), 'Casual and Serious Leisure: Leisure and Post-Traditional Thought in the Information Age', World Leisure and Recreation Association Fourth World Congress, Cardiff, July 1996.

Stebbins, R. (1996), 'Volunteering: a serious leisure perspective', *Non-Profit and Voluntary Sector Quarterly*, 25(2), 211–24.

Stebbins, R. (2001), 'Serious leisure', *Society* May/June, 38, 53–7.

Stebbins, R. (2002), 'Serious or Casual – An Enigma in Leisure and Leisure Education', in *World Leisure Commission on Education* (ed. Ruskin, H.), The Cosell Center, Jerusalem.

Stewart, R. (1970), *Managers and their Jobs*, Pan Books, London.

Stokowski, P.A. (1994), *Leisure in Society: A Network Structural Perspective*, Mansell, London.

Sutton-Smith, B. (1966), 'Piaget on play: a critique', *Psychological Review*, 73, 104–10.

Sutton-Smith, B. (1997), *The Ambiguity of Play*, Harvard University Press, Cambridge, Mass.

Sylva, K. (1977) 'Play and learning', in Tizard, B. and Harvey, D. (eds), (1977) *Biology of Play*, Heinemann Press, London.

Tannenbaum, R. and Schmidt, W.H. (1958), 'How to choose a leadership pattern', *Harvard Business Review*, March–April, 95–101.

Tarsus Group (2002), *Bulletin 100*, Tarsus Glrup plc, London

Taylor, F.W. (1947), *Scientific Management*, Harper and Row, New York.

Taylor, J. and Coalter, F. (2001), for Local Government Association, *Realising the Potential of Cultural Services – the Case for Urban Parks, Spaces and the Countryside*, LGA, London.

Tendrick, T. and Henderson, K. (1989), *Volunteers in Leisure*, AAHPERD, Reston, VA.

Thompson, G. (1987), *Needs*, Routledge, London, cited in Doyal, L. and Gough, I. (1991), *A Theory of Human Needs*, Macmillan, London.

Thompson, E.P. (1967), quoted in Tomlinson, A. (1979), *Leisure and the Role of Clubs and Voluntary Groups*, Sports Council/SSRC, London.

Tillman, A. (1974), *The Program Book for Recreation Professionals*, National Press Books, Palo Alto, CA.

Tolkki-Nikkonen, M. (1979), *Adult Educators in Finland*, No. 3, Department of Education, Helsinki.

Tomlinson, J., (2001), *Extreme Sports*, Carlton, USA.

Torkildsen, G. (1986), 'Managers as they see themselves and as we see them', *Leisure Management*, 6 February, (2), 26–7, 31.

Torkildsen, G. (1987), *Recreation Management: A Framework for the Effective Management of Community Recreation Facilities*, unpublished.

Torkildsen, G. (1993), *A Review of National Support for Children's Play and Recreation*, National Playing Fields Association, London.

Torkildsen, G. (1993), *Time Management*, Torkildsen's Guides to Leisure Management, Longman, Harlow.

Torkildsen, G., Carver, G., Fisher, D., Gearing, G., Warden, B., Griffiths, H. and Birch, J. (2003), *Ted Blake: An Inspiration to Leisure Managers*, ILAM, Reading.

Torkildsen, G. and Griffiths, G. (1987), *Lambourn Valley Recreation Study* commissioned by Newbury District Council, LMGT, Harlow.

Townsend, R. (1970), *Up the Organization*, Coronet Books, London.

Townsend, S. (1993) Foreword, in Bonel, P., *Playing for Real*, National Children's Play and Recreation Unit, London.

UNESCO (2003), Towards a Convention for the Safeguarding of Intangible Cultural Heritage, Press release 2003–15, Bureau of Public Information, UNESCO.

Veal, A. (2002), *Leisure and Tourism Policy* 2nd edn, CAB International, Oxford.

Veblen, T. (1953), *Theory of the Leisure Class*, Mentor, New York (originally published 1899).

Vickers, S. (2003), *Mr. Golightly's Holiday*, Fourth Estate.

Video Arts (date) *Decisions, Decisions!*, booklet to accompany the film of the same name, Video Arts, London.

VisitBritain (2003), *EnjoyEngland – the strategy: England Domestic Marketing Strategy 2003/4 to 2005/6*, VisitBritain, London.

Vorley, G. and Tickle, F. (2003), *Quality Management Principles and Practice*, 5th edn, Quality Management and Training Ltd.

Wälder, R. (1933), 'The psychoanalytic theory of play', *Psychoanalytic Quarterly*, 2, 208–24.

Wales Tourist Board (2000), *Achieving our Potential: A Tourism Strategy for Wales*, Wales Tourist Board.

Weese, W. (1996), 'Follow the leader', *Recreation*, December, 26–30.

Welsh, A.N. (1980), *The Skills of Management*, Gower, Farnborough.

Wess, R. (1989), *Leadership Secrets of Attila the Hun*, Bantam Books, London.

Westwood, J. (2000) *How to Write a Marketing Plan* 2nd edn, for *The Sunday Times*, Kogan Page, London.

Williams, B. (2003), *The Celts*, Pitkin Guides, Jarrold Publishing, Norwich.

Williams, C. and Buswell, J. (2003), *Service Quality in Leisure and Tourism*, CABI International, Wallingford, Oxon.

Wilding, R. (1989), *Supporting the Arts. A Review of the Structure of Arts Funding, 1989*, HMSO, London.

Willoughby, R. (1997), *Life in Medieval England*, Pitkin Guides, Jarrold Publishing, Norwich.

Wilson, A. and West, C. (1982), 'Effective marketing at minimum cost', *Management Today*, January, 72–8.

Wolfe, M. (1999), *The Entertainment Economy: How Mega Media-Forces Are Transforming Our Lives*, Prentice-Hall, New Jersey.

Wolfenden Committee (1960), *Sport and the Community*, CCPR, London.

Wolfenden Committee (1978), *The Future of Voluntary Organizations*, Croom Helm, London.

Wood, E. and Attfield, J. (1996), *Play, Learning and the Early Childhood Curriculum*, quoted in Lindon, J. (2001) *Understanding Children's Play*, Nelson Thornes, Cheltenham.

Wren, D. (1972), *The Evolution of Management Thought*, Ronald Press, New York.

Young, P.T. (1961), *Motivation and Emotion*, Wiley, New York.

Yuen, F.C. and Shaw, S.M. (2003), 'Play: the reproduction and resistance of dominant gender ideologies', *World Leisure Journal*, 2, 45, 14.

Zeithami, V., Parasuraman, A. and Berry, L. (1990), *Delivering Quality Service: Balancing Customer Perceptions and Expectations*, Free Press, New York.

Index